Business Sustainability in Asia

Compliance, Performance, and Integrated Reporting and Assurance

ZABIHOLLAH REZAEE

JUDY TSUI

PETER CHENG

GAOGUANG ZHOU

WILEY

For general information on our other products and services or for technical support, please contact our Customer Care Department within the United States at (800) 762–2974, outside the United States at (317) 572–3993, or fax (317) 572–4002.

Wiley publishes in a variety of print and electronic formats and by print-on-demand. Some material included with standard print versions of this book may not be included in e-books or in print-on-demand. If this book refers to media such as a CD or DVD that is not included in the version you purchased, you may download this material at http://booksupport.wiley.com. For more information about Wiley products, visit www.wiley.com.

Library of Congress Cataloging-in-Publication Data is Available:

ISBN 978-1-119-50231-9 (Hardcover)
ISBN 978-1-119-50220-3 (ePDF)
ISBN 978-1-119-50225-8 (ePub)

Cover Design: Wiley
Cover Image: © Nikada/iStock.com

Printed in the United States of America.

V10007524_011119

To my parents Rudolfah and Fatemeh, sister Mariyah, wife Sabella, and children Nik? and Rose – ZR

To my husband Andrew, my son Timothy, daughter-in-law Catherine and my granddaughter Chloe, my daughter Jackie and son in law Daniel, my son Benjamin and daughter-in-law Jessica – LJ

To Alex and my children Nicholas Cy?tal, and Stephanie – PC

To my parents – CZ

Contents

CHAPTER 3
Institutional Settings in Asia Relevant to Business Sustainability

CHAPTER 4
Drivers and Sources of Business Sustainability Initiatives in the World Including Asia

CHAPTER 5

CHAPTER 7
Social Dimension of Sustainability   **233**

CHAPTER 8

Ethical Dimension of Sustainability   **263**

Foreword

BY DR KELVIN WONG

The book entitled *Business Sustainability in Asia*, coauthored by Professors Rezaee, Tsui, Cheng, and Zhou, is an excellent reference for the emergence of business sustainability worldwide and particularly in Asia. Business sustainability has gained significant attention from global investors, regulators, the business community, public companies, and academicians in the past decade. This book focuses on five dimensions of sustainability performance:economic, governance, social, ethical, and environmental (EGSEE). It addresses the increasing focus on business sustainability and its factors of performance, disclosure, and risk and their implications for business practice, education, and research worldwide. Proper measurement of sustainability performance, as well as accurate and reliable disclosure of sustainability performance, and effective assessment of sustainability risks remain major challenges for organizations of different types and sizes, particularly in Asia. The book focuses on business sustainability in 12 jurisdictions in Asia from the Mainland China to Hong Kong, among others,and Vietnam. The sustainability theme in Asia is important for many reasons including the significant growth in sustainability efforts and activities in Asia in the past decades. Moreover, Asia has stepped up in forging an alliance with Europe to take a leading role on environmental initiatives by tackling climate change.

Given the continuing growth in business sustainability in Asia, this is a comprehensive book that introduces the emergence of business sustainability, followed by in-depth discussions of the three important business sustainability factors of performance, disclosure, and risk. The book offers guidance to organizations worldwide to properly integrate all five EGSEE dimensions of sustainability into their business models, strategic plans, and practices. It also provides guidelines for complete and accurate measurement, recognition, and disclosure of all five EGSEE dimensions of sustainability performance in an integrated reporting model.I highly recommend this book as a valuable resource in advancing business sustainability worldwide and, particularly in Asia. I believe anyone who is involved with business sustainability from the corporate board of directors to executives, investors, policymakers, regulators, and standard-setters should buy and read this book.

Dr. Kelvin Wong
Executive Director and Deputy Managing Director
of COSCO SHIPPING Ports Limited
Chairman of the Financial Reporting Council, Hong Kong
Immediate Past Chairman of the Hong Kong Institute of Directors

Business sustainability has advanced from branding and greenwashing to strategic imperative and impact investing in sustainable finance in the past decade. It is defined in this book as a process of focusing on the achievement of all five dimensions of sustainability performance namely economic, governance, social, ethical and environmental (EGSEE) in creating shared value for all stakeholders. Integrated reporting on both financial elements of economic sustainability performance (ESP) and non-financial elements encompassing governance, social, ethical, and environmental (GSEE) dimensions of sustainability performance has been demanded by investors, required and/or encouraged by regulators and performed by business organizations worldwide. Global business organizations report their integrated financial ESP and non-financial (GSEE) sustainability performance in creating shared value for all stakeholders from shareholders to customers, employees, suppliers, creditors, environmental agencies and organizations, government and society.

This book specifically focuses on business sustainability in Asia, for several reasons. First, sustainability activities in Asia have significantly grown in the past decade as business organizations in the region have faced greater pressure from regulators to engage in sustainability and corporate social responsibility (CSR) programs. Second, this trend is expected to continue as Asian countries in general and Mainland China in particular step up alliances with European countries to take a leading role in CSR and environmental initiatives through addressing product quality and safety, and tackling climate change. Third, the recent decision of the United States to exit the 2015 Paris Agreement is expected to encourage other countries (e.g., Mainland China, India, Singapore) to accelerate the pace by providing leadership in sustainability initiatives. Finally, the achievement of sustainable economic growth, prosperity and performance has been observed in Asia and is expected to continue in the foreseeable future.

A number of professional organizations, including the Global Reporting Initiative (GRI), the International Integrated Reporting Council (IIRC), the Sustainability Accounting Standards Board (SASB), and the Corporate Reporting Dialogue (CRD), have issued numerous sustainability reporting and assurance guidelines to assist business organizations in disclosing their economic and GSEE sustainability performance to all stakeholders. Sustainability performance information can be disclosed on a voluntary basis or on a mandatory basis. In Hong Kong, there are listing standards that require listed companies to comply with ESG requirements in annual reports commencing in the 2016 fiscal year. Large European companies (more than 6,000 employees) are now required to disclose their environmental, social and diversity activities for the 2017 financial year and onwards. The Delaware Certification of Adoption of Transparency and Sustainability Standards Act was signed into law on June 27, 2018; this represents Delaware's initiative to support sustainability practices by enabling Delaware-governed entities to disclose their commitment to CSR and sustainability.

Global business organizations have issued integrated sustainability reports on all or some of the five EGSEE dimensions of sustainability performance in the past decade. Theoretically, companies that effectively manage their business sustainability by improving EGSEE performance conduct their business more effectively and ethically, enhance their reputation, fulfill their social responsibility and environmental commitments, and thus contribute to their bottom-line financial economic sustainability performance. However, ESP and GSEE sustainability performance disclosures supplement each other and are not mutually exclusive. The relative importance of EGSEE sustainability performance with respect to each other and their integrated contribution to the overall firm value maximization is affected by whether EGSEE are viewed as complementary or conflicting factors in the context of sustainability theories. Sustainability performance dimensions (EGSEE) can be seen as complementary because firms must be financially sustainable in the long term to be able to perform well in the other areas of governance, social, ethical and environmental activities. This book offers guidance to organizations for proper measurement, recognition and reporting of all five EGSEE dimensions of sustainability performance. Sustainability integrated reporting refers to the continuous process of promoting, measuring, recognizing, reporting and auditing sustainability performance in the five areas of EGSEE. Traditionally, organizations have reported their financial performance on economic transactions. Given the growing global attention to corporate sustainability and the major economies in developing nations, this book examines the emergence of corporate sustainability in Asia, particularly in Hong Kong and Mainland China.

In this book, five primary themes will present a framework for the five dimensions (EGSEE) of business sustainability performance. First, business sustainability is driven by and built on the stakeholder theory, which is the theoretical basis for creating shared value for all stakeholders. Second, the main goal and objective for business organizations is to maximize firm value by improving financial and non-financial dimensions (EGSEE) of sustainability performance. The third theme focuses on the time horizon of balancing short-, medium-, and long-term performance, with a keen emphasis on long-term sustainable performance. The fourth theme is the multi-dimensional nature of sustainability performance in all EGSEE areas, which are interrelated. The final theme of the book is its focus on and relevance to Asia because sustainability initiatives and activities in Asia have significantly grown in the past decade and are expected to continue to grow in the future. The relative importance of the dimensions with respect to each other and their contribution to the firm's overall long-term value maximization is affected by whether these EGSEE dimensions are viewed as competing, conflicting or complementing.

We hope you will find this book a valuable resource in understanding and promoting business sustainability worldwide and particularly in Asia. This book will be of interest to anyone who is involved with business sustainability, CSR and corporate governance, the financial reporting process, investment decisions, legal and financial advising, audit functions and business sustainability education. Specifically, corporations, business executives, board members, internal and external auditors, accountants, lawmakers, regulators, standard-setters, users of financial statements (investors, creditors, and pensioners), investor activists, business academics and other professionals (attorneys, financial analysts and bankers) will benefit from this book. Business sustainability performance dimensions, principles, mechanisms and functions as well as sustainability compliance, integrated reporting and assurance presented in this book are applicable to organizations of all types and sizes. Profit-oriented enterprises, non-governmental organizations, state-owned enterprises and not-for-profit and governmental entities can benefit from our discussions. We hope you will find this book useful and valuable in achieving your personal and professional goals.

Zabihollah Rezaee
Judy Tsui
Peter Cheng
Gaoguang Zhou
3/06/2019

Acknowledgments

We acknowledge the quality reporting that is cited throughout the book including publications of professional organizations such as the Global Reporting Initiative, the International Integrated Reporting Council, and the Sustainability Accounting Standards Board.

The encouragement and support of our colleagues at the University of Memphis and Hong Kong Baptist University are also acknowledged. The assistance of our graduate students Charles Bell, Matthew Cantin, Chinenye Egbuna, Yueming Li, Kai Wang, and Xuemei Zheng is also appreciated. We thank the members of the John Wiley & Sons, Inc., team for their hard work and dedication, including Koushika Ramesh for managing the book through the production process, Jean-Karl Martin for their marketing efforts and Sheck Cho, Executive Editor for editorial guidance.

Our special thanks are due to our families: the Rezaee family, the Rezaee family, the Tsui family, the Cheng family, and the Zhou family Without their love, enthusiasm, and support, this book would not have come to fruition when it did.

Zabihollah Rezaee
Judy Tsui
Peter Cheng
Gaoguang Zhou
March 06, 2019

List of Abbreviations

Accounting Standards Council	ASC
Accounting Standards for Business Enterprises	ASBE
American Accounting Association	AAA
American Certified Fraud Examiners	ACFE
American Institute of Certified Public Accountants	AICPA
Asian Corporate Governance Association	ACGA
Association of Advanced Collegiate School of Business	AACSB
Association of Chartered Certified Accountants	ACCA
Board of Directors	BOD
Carbon Reduction Commitment	CRC
Certified Public Accountants	CPAs
Certified Sustainability Reporting Assurer	CSRA
Chartered Global Management Accountants	CGMA
Chartered Institute of Management Accountants	CIMA
Chief Sustainability Officer	CSO
Chinese Communist Party	CCP
Climate Disclosure Standards Board	CDSB
Coalition for Environmentally Responsible Economies	CERES
Corporate Disclosure and Governance Committee	CCDG
Corporate Governance Committee	CGC
Corporate Governance Report	CGR
Corporate Social Responsibility	CSR
Department of Environment and Natural Resources	DENR
Economic Sustainability Performance	ESP
Economic, Social and Governance	ESG
Economic, Governance, Social, Ethical and Environmental	EGSEE
Environmental Management Systems	EMS
Environmental Protection Agency	EPA
Environmental Protection Bureau	EPB
Earnings Per Share	EPS
Extensible Business Reporting Language	XBRL
Financial Reporting Standards Council	FRSC
Foreign Corrupt Practices Act	FCPA
Foreign Direct Investment	FDI

General Agreement on Trade in Services	GATS
Global Impact Investing Network	GIIN
Governance, Social, Ethical and Environmental	GSEE
Greenhouse Gas	GHG
Gross Domestic Product	GDP
Hong Kong Institute of Certified Public Accountants	HKICPA
Hong Kong Stock Exchange	HKSE
Impact Investment Exchange	IIX
Information Technology	IT
Initial Public Offerings	IPOs
Institute of Internal Auditors	IIA
Institute of Management Accountants	IMA
Internal Control Over Financial Reporting	ICFR
International Accounting Standards Committee	IASC
International Accounting Standards	IAS
International Auditing & Assurance Standards Board	IAASB
International Corporate Governance Network	ICGN
International Federation of Accountants	IFAC
International Financial Reporting Standards	IFRS
International Integrated Reporting Council	IIRC
International Monetary Fund	IMF
International Organization of Securities Commissions	IOSCO
International Standardization Organization	ISO
International Standards on Assurance Engagements	ISAE
Investor Responsibility Research Center Institute	IRRCI
Key Performance Indicators	KPIs
Lead Director Network	LDN
Management Discussion and Analysis	MD&A
Multi-national Companies	MNCs
Multiple Bottom Line	MBL
National Bureau of Statistics	NBS
National Committee on Corporate Governance	NCCG
National Greening Program	NGP
National Human Rights Institution	NHRI
National Stock Exchange	NSE
Net Present Value	NPV
Non-Governmental Organizations	NGOs
Organization for Economic Co-Operation and Development	OECD
People's Republic of China	PRC
Principles for Responsible Investment	PRI
Public Company Accounting Oversight Board	PCAOB
Return on Assets	ROA
Return on Equity	ROE
Sarbanes-Oxley	SOX
Securities and Exchange Commission	SEC
Small and Medium-Sized Enterprises	SMEs

Social Investment Forum	SIF
Socially Responsible Investment	SRI
Statement of Financial Accounting Standards	SFAS
Superfund Amendment and Reauthorization Act	SARA
Sustainability Accounting Standards Board	SASB
Sustainable Development Goals	SDGs
Sustainable Management and Investment Guideline	SMILE
Sustainable Supply Chain Management	SSCM
Tokyo Stock Exchange	TSE
Toronto Stock Exchange	TSX
Triple Bottom Line	TBL
United Nations Conference on Trade and Development	UNCTAD
United Nations Educational, Scientific and Cultural Organization	UNESCO
United Nations Environment Programme	UNEP
United Nations Global Compact	UNGC
United Nations Sustainability Development Goals	UNSDGs
United Nations	UN
World Business Council for Sustainable Development	WBCSD
World Economic Forum	WEF
World Federation of Exchanges	WFE
World Trade Organization	WTO

CHAPTER 1

Introduction to Business Sustainability

1. EXECUTIVE SUMMARY

Business sustainability is gaining considerable attention from investors, regulators and businesses worldwide and particularly those in Asia. In today's business environment, global businesses face increasing scrutiny and profound pressure from lawmakers, regulators, the investment community and their various stakeholders to focus on their multiple-bottom-line (MBL) of economic, governance, social, ethical and environmental (EGSEE) performance. Global organizations recognize the importance of sustainability performance in creating shared value for all their stakeholders from shareholders to creditors, customers, suppliers, employees, government, society and the environment. A growing number of public companies worldwide and listed companies in Asia in particular are now issuing sustainability reports on some or all five EGSEE dimensions of sustainability performance. This trend is expected to continue well into the future. This chapter presents an introduction to business sustainability performance, reporting and assurance in the context of the Asian business environment.

2. INTRODUCTION

Business organizations worldwide and public companies in Asia in particular are now facing the challenges of adopting proper management strategies and practices to effectively respond to social, ethical, environmental and governance issues while creating sustainable financial performance. Traditionally, business organizations have reported their performance on economic transactions. Their sole focus on financial results has become less relevant. In recent years, stakeholders, investors, regulators, global institutions and organizations, and the public at large have increasingly demanded information on both financial and non-financial key performance indicators (KPIs) in this platform of MBL accountability and sustainability reporting.[1] This chapter introduces the definition and concept of business sustainability and offers guidance to organizations for properly integrating sustainability into their business models, strategic plans and practices. It also provides guidelines for complete and accurate measurement, recognition and disclosure of all five EGSEE dimensions of sustainability performance in an integrated reporting model.

3. DEFINITION

Business sustainability has evolved from a focus on corporate social responsibility (CSR), corporate governance, and internal operational efficiencies to integration into organizations' strategies, culture and practices toward long-term and multi-dimensional sustainability performance. Sustainability can have different meanings as perceived by different stakeholders. From the academic and practical aspect, business sustainability can be defined as environmental preservation to create a better environment for future generations. It can be viewed as fulfilling the company's CSR responsibility for society above and beyond mandatory obligations. From a financial perspective, sustainability is considered as focusing on short-, medium- and long-term financial performance to generate value for shareholders. It can be also viewed as conducting business activities ethically with effective corporate governance to ensure going concern and continuity of the business.

Business sustainability is also a multi-disciplinary function of accounting, economics, ethics, finance, management, marketing, law and supply chain management, among others, with a keen focus on improving economic vitality, ethical behavior, ecological health, governance measures and social justice. It can "bring benefits in terms of risk management, cost savings, access to capital, customer relationships, human resource management and innovation capacity."[2] It also facilitates engagement with stakeholders regarding sustainable growth and risks in building trust in the company and with shareholders by enhancing effective capital allocation and achieving long-term investment goals. The 2013 *Global Corporate Sustainability Report* encourages companies to engage their management and suppliers in the establishment of more sustainable practices and integration of sustainability into their supply chain processes.[3]

Business sustainability has evolved in the past three decades, with an initial focus on sustainable development in leaving a better environment for future generations, to CSR, corporate governance, and now with the main goal of creating shared value for all stakeholders including shareholders. Business sustainability is not a single event; it is a journey to improve both financial economic sustainability performance (ESP) and non-financial governance, social, ethical and environmental (GSEE) performance to create shared value for all stakeholders. In this context, sustainability focuses on activities that generate financial (long-term earnings, growth and return on investment) and non-financial (environmental, social, ethical and governance) sustainability performance that concerns all stakeholders. The terms business sustainability, CSR and triple bottom line (focusing on environmental, social and governance (ESG)) have been used interchangeably in the literature and authoritative reports. Business sustainability can also be defined as a social objective with a keen focus on achieving the triple bottom line performance of profit, planet and people.[4] However, business sustainability is regarded as much broader than CSR and even ESG and has recently gained more acceptance.[5] It has advanced from a main focus on CSR to integration into corporate culture, mission, strategy, business model and management processes.[6]

Business sustainability for organizations refers to not only providing products and services that satisfy customers, but also operating in a socially responsible manner, protecting the environment and presenting reliable and transparent sustainability reports. The focus on business sustainability can benefit business organizations in many ways, including higher market and accounting performance, improved business reputation, enhanced product innovation and earnings growth, customer and employee satisfactions and creation of more stakeholder value. Yet, sustainability can be viewed as a box-ticking compliance and risk-mitigation exercise. It is defined in this book by encompassing all the above definitions in creating synergy for business strategies, activities and performance from ethical, environmental, social, compliance, legal, governance and economic dimensions in creating shared value for all stakeholders. A report released by the International Federation of Accountants (IFAC, 2015: 3) indicates that global business organizations are expected to "take responsibility for a broader range of sustainability issues, such as social and environmental aspects that will ultimately affect financial performance and an organization's ability to create value over time."[7] In summary, business sustainability is defined as a process of focusing on the achievement of all five: economic, governance, social, ethical and environmental (EGSEE) dimensions of sustainability performance in creating shared value for all stakeholders.

4. THEMES OF THIS BOOK

Business sustainability has advanced from the branding and greenwashing of focusing on CSR to the strategic imperative of achieving both financial economic sustainability performance (ESP) and non-financial GSEE sustainability performance in the past decade. There are five primary themes in this book, which present a framework for the five dimensions of business sustainability performance (EGSEE) and 10 sustainability principles.[8] These five themes are also applicable in all 12 Asian jurisdictions and their economies. First, the business sustainability framework is driven by and built on the stakeholder theory, which is the process of protecting the interests of all stakeholders, with a keen focus on achieving long-term and enduring financial and non-financial performance for all corporate constituencies from shareholders to creditors, employees, customers, suppliers, society and the environment. The stakeholder theory implies that business organizations are responsible to many of constituencies and thus add value for all stakeholders, as listed above.[9] This stakeholder view of business organizations and business sustainability is supported by researchers, regulators and the business and investment community.

Second, the main goal and the objective function for business organizations is to maximize firm value. The goal of firm value maximization under the business sustainability framework can be achieved when the interests of all stakeholders are considered. The main focus is on long-term shareholder value creation and maximization while considering tradeoffs among the other apparently competing and often conflicting interests of society, creditors, employees and the environment. Theoretically, management's engagement in non-financial GSEE sustainability activities, performance and disclosure can be viewed as value increasing or value decreasing for investors. On the one hand, companies should effectively manage and improve GSEE performance, enhance their reputation, fulfill their social responsibility, and promote a corporate culture of integrity and competency. On the other hand, companies can survive and generate sustainable performance only when they continue to be financially profitable and are able to create shareholder value. Nonetheless, financial ESP, and non-financial GSEE sustainability performance and reporting complement each other and are not mutually exclusive. Companies that are governed effectively, are socially and environmentally responsible, and conduct themselves ethically, are expected to produce sustainable performance, create shareholder value and gain investor confidence and public trust.

The third theme is the time horizon of balancing short-, medium- and long-term performance with a keen focus on long-term performance. Business sustainability focuses on the achievement of long-term and enduring performance and enables corporations to focus on maximizing long-term performance instead of meeting periodic financial targets. Businesses can no longer focus only on short-term earnings performance in beating analysts' forecasts to generate positive stock movements.

The fourth theme is the multi-dimensional nature of sustainability performance in all EGSEE areas. The multi-dimensional EGSEE sustainability performance is interrelated and integrated. The relative importance of the dimensions, with respect to each other and their contribution to the firm's overall long-term value maximization, is affected by whether these EGSEE dimensions are viewed as competing, conflicting or complementary. One view is that these EGSEE dimensions are complementary because a firm that is governed effectively adheres to ethical principles and commits to CSR and environmental obligations, enabling sustainable generation of long-term financial performance. Another view is that corporations must do well financially in the long term to be able to do well in terms of CSR and environmental activities. On the one hand, corporations that are managed ethically, governed effectively and are socially and environmentally responsible are expected to produce sustainable performance, create shareholder value and gain public trust and investor confidence. On the other hand, more economically profitable and viable corporations have more resources to create jobs and wealth and are in a better position to fulfill their social and environmental responsibilities.

The final theme of the book is its focus on and relevance to Asia, for several reasons. First, sustainability activities in Asia have grown significantly in the past decade as business organizations in Asia face greater pressure either through voluntary or mandatory requirements from regulators to engage in sustainability and CSR programs. Second, this trend is expected to continue as Asian countries in general and Mainland China in particular step up to forge alliances with European countries to take a leading role in CSR and environmental initiatives by addressing product quality and safety and tackling climate change. Third, the United States' recent decision to exit the 2015 Paris Agreement is expected to encourage other countries (e.g., Mainland China, India and Singapore) to step up by providing leadership in sustainability initiatives. Fourth, the growth in Asian economies in the recent decade, in particular Mainland China, allows companies to focus more on non-financial sustainability programs. Finally, the achievement of sustainable economic growth, prosperity, and performance has been observed in Asia and is expected to continue in the near future.

Business sustainability in general and CSR in particular as a concept has evolved over time, with different interpretation of its practices across different sectors, cultures and countries in Asia. Corporate accountability, citizenship, ethics, responsible entrepreneurship, corporate sustainability, responsible competitiveness and other terms have been used to describe CSR in Asia. But it can generally be explained as the responsibility of corporations toward the society within which they operate.

This responsibility usually spans three areas, which include: economic, social and environmental responsibility. CSR started as a form of realization that corporations have responsibilities to society beyond profit maximization, which triggered the motivation behind philanthropy.[10] Currently, the motivation for CSR has advanced from mere philanthropy toward awareness of the environmental implications of industrialization and of the social well-being of both internal and external stakeholders in Asia. Instead of pure and simple philanthropy, CSR has recently assumed the form of what is called 'social investment,' with the establishment of more social enterprises.[11]

5. ATTRIBUTES

Two attributes of business sustainability are sustainability performance and sustainability disclosures. Both attributes are important to all stakeholders. The sustainability performance attribute underscores that firms which focus on their non-financial performance including social and environmental performance are managed more effectively with good corporate governance and are more financially sustainable. The voluntary or mandatory disclosure attribute of sustainability performance posits that "good type" firms that focus on non-financial (governance, social, ethical and environmental (GSEE)) and sustainable financial performance have more incentive to disclose information to differentiate themselves from "bad type" firms that do not focus on GSEE and financial sustainability, in order to avoid getting a bad reputation. Disclosure of GSEE sustainability may signal management commitment to greater transparency of both financial and non-financial performance, thereby reducing information asymmetry and increasing firm value.

Companies should strive to maintain good business sustainability in their everyday practices to create shared value for stakeholders and to minimize information asymmetry to all stakeholders. If a company withholds information about its practices, whether intentionally in efforts to minimize the effect on the bottom line or unintentionally as a result of not performing due diligence on its processes, this may result in increased perceived riskiness of the venture, decreased share price, concerns regarding management's ability to lead the organization along the path toward sustainability in generating sustainable performance and growth. Thus, good sustainability is important for a company in the short run to ensure viability in the ever-changing marketplace. However, to build a strong company in the long run, business sustainability must be put into practice to prepare for the future and to mitigate unforeseen or inescapable events. One of the key features of putting business sustainability into practice is that when faced with problems from multiple stakeholders, a company with good sustainability practices can pivot its position to answer the problems in the best manner possible.

6. PRINCIPLES

Business sustainability has been promoted in response to demands from investors, necessary compliance with requirements of regulators, and voluntary initiatives by corporations considering interdependencies between global financial markets, the business community and investors in advancing sustainable performance. More than 8,000 companies in 140 countries have adopted the 10 sustainability principles established by the United Nations Global Compact and integrated these principles into their strategic planning and operations.[12] These 10 sustainability principles are classified into the four general categories of human rights, labor, environment and anti-corruption. They are, in turn, related to the three dimensions (social, environmental and ethical) of sustainability performance, as explained in the previous section. The 2013 *Sustainability Report* of the United Nations (UN) Global Compact suggests two ways for companies to achieve business sustainability: (1) by integrating the 10 principles into their strategies and operations and (2) by taking actions that support continuous improvement in sustainability performance.[13] The UN Global Compact report also provides the Global Compact Management Model as a practical tool for companies to improve their sustainability performance.[14] The suggested model consists of six managerial processes of committing to, assessing, defining, implementing, measuring and communicating sustainability strategies, operations and performance in ensuring alignment with the 10 principles and compliance with applicable laws, rules and regulations.[15]

7. DIMENSIONS OF SUSTAINABILITY PERFORMANCE

Business sustainability performance can be beneficial to both internal and external stakeholders. Stakeholders are those who have vested interests in a firm through their investment in the form of financial capital (shareholders), human capital (employees), physical capital (customers and suppliers), social capital (society), environmental capital (environment) and regulatory capital (government). Stakeholders have reciprocal relation and interaction with a firm in the sense that they contribute to the firm's value creation and their wellbeing is affected by the firm. In essence, sustainability performance can affect and be affected by stakeholders.

Sustainability performance is typically classified into financial and non-financial performance and grouped into the five dimensions of Economic (E), Governance (G), Social (S), Ethical (E) and Environmental (E), abbreviated as EGSEE.[16] Although business sustainability continues to evolve, several dimensions of sustainability performance pertaining to social and environmental initiatives have gained widespread global acceptance. These initiatives include an ethical workplace, customer satisfaction, just and safe working conditions, non-discriminatory fair wages, workplace diversity, environmental preservation, clear air and water, minimum age for child labor, safe and quality products, concern for the environment and fair and transparent business practices. Each industry has its own applicable set of sustainability financial and non-financial KPIs. Each business organization must carefully identify its own social and environmental responsibilities given the context of the business culture in which it operates. The list of financial and non-financial sustainability KPIs depends on a variety of factors: industry, legal regimes, cultural background, corporate mission and strategy, corporate culture, political infrastructure and managerial philosophy. Despite these disparate sustainability performance dimensions and their KPIs, sustainability has become an integral component of business. This section describes each of the EGSEE sustainability performance dimensions and their related KPIs.[17]

7.1 Economic Sustainability Performance

The most important and commonly accepted dimension of sustainability is "economic performance." The primary goal of any business organization is to create shareholder value through generating sustainable economic performance. Business organizations should focus on activities that generate long-term corporate profitability rather than short-term performance. The economic dimension of sustainability performance can be achieved when business organizations focus on long-term sustainability performance and improved effectiveness and efficiency of production. Long-term economic sustainability performance should be communicated to shareholders through the preparation of high-quality financial reports in compliance with global accounting standards as well as the Global Reporting Initiative (GRI) Guidelines.[18]

The economic dimension of sustainability should reflect the financial strengths and concerns of an organization as well as the economic impacts on its stakeholders and society.[19] Economic sustainability performance can be measured directly through financial activities between an organization and its stakeholders or indirectly through non-financial costs and benefits of economic relations and their effects on stakeholders. The financial economic dimension of sustainability is further presented in chapter 5.

7.2 Governance Sustainability Performance

The corporate governance landscape has changed significantly in the aftermath of the global 2007–2009 Financial Crisis. The lack of effective corporate governance has been perceived as an overriding contributing factor in the global Financial Crisis. Internal and external corporate governance measures have since been established by policymakers, regulators and corporations to improve the quality of corporate governance and thus stakeholder trust and investor confidence in corporate sustainable performance and reporting. Regulatory reforms in the United States such as the Sarbanes-Oxley Act of 2002[20] and the Dodd-Frank Act of 2010[21] are designed to improve the quality and effectiveness of corporate governance. Effective corporate governance promotes accountability of the board of directors and executives; enhances sustainable operational and financial performance; improves the reliability and quality of financial information; and strengthens the integrity and efficiency of the capital market, which results in economic growth and prosperity for the nation. Effective corporate governance sustainability requires setting an appropriate tone at the top defining roles and responsibilities of all corporate gatekeepers, from the board of directors and executives to internal and external auditors and legal counsel, and promoting accountability for them. The effectiveness of corporate governance is also affected by legal, regulatory, internal and external mechanisms and best practices to create shared value for all stakeholders, as further explored in chapter 6.

7.3 Social Sustainability Performance

The social dimension of sustainability performance reflects the transformation of social goals into practices that benefit an organization's stakeholders. Social performance measures an organization's social mission and its alignment with the interests of society. The social dimension of sustainability performance ranges from ensuring high quality of products and services, better customer satisfaction and improved employee health and wellbeing, to making a positive contribution to the sustainability of the planet and quality of life for future generations.

Socially responsible investment (SRI) is becoming nowadays an increasingly important part of business. Though the mantra of business has long been to increase shareholders' profits, the advent of benefit corporations (or B-corporations) has brought with it a chance for shareholders to affect businesses' methods of doing business to increase their own desire for social change instead of personal enrichment. The United Nations Principles of Responsible Investing (PRI) were initiated in 2005 to encourage global investors to integrate ESG into their investment decisions.[22] Recently, under sustainable and socially responsible investing (SRI) principles, investors consider various sustainability issues in their investment analyses and SRI have increased by more than 22 percent to $3.74 trillion in managed assets during the 2010–2012 period.[23] The social dimension of sustainability performance is typically viewed as CSR and is further explained in chapter 7.

7.4   Ethical Sustainability Performance

The ethical dimension of sustainability performance and particularly corporate ethical culture plays an important role in ensuring the achievement of corporate goals and financial sustainability. The effectiveness of ethical sustainability performance depends on a corporate culture of integrity and competency and an appropriate tone at the top. Characteristics of an ethical organization culture are codes of conduct for directors, officers and employees; a system of responsibility and accountability; and a workplace that promotes honesty, mutual respect and freedom to raise concerns. The persistence and existence of corporate scandals and financial crises have shown that companies which conduct their business ethically are more sustainable in the long term and can generate high quality and quantity of earnings, economic growth and development. The ethical dimension of sustainability performance is often integrated into business environment and corporate culture in achieving financial economic sustainability performance, as further discussed in chapter 8.

7.5   Environmental Sustainability Performance

Stakeholders are demanding clearer and more transparent information about the impacts of an organization's activities and operations on the environment beyond what is legislated for by law. The environmental dimension of sustainability performance includes creating a better work environment, reducing the carbon footprint, improving air and water quality and maximizing the positive effects of an organization on natural resources and the environment. The Coalition for Environmentally Responsible Economies (CERES) and the UN Environment Program, in collaboration with the UN Global Compact, promote environmental initiatives.[24]

Governments throughout the world are instituting measures to ensure that the environment is better protected, at the behest of society at large. Effective achievement of environmental sustainability performance requires businesses to create the right balance in maximizing their economic profit, protecting the environment and ensuring a better environment for the next generations. Climate change and greenhouse gas emissions affect organizations of all types and sizes worldwide and thus should be integrated into sustainability initiatives, decisions, actions and performance. The environmental dimension of sustainability performance will be discussed in detail in chapter 9.

8. VALUE RELEVANCE OF SUSTAINABILITY PERFORMANCE

Integration of the five EGSEE dimensions of sustainability performance into managerial strategies and practices enables companies to conserve scarce resources, optimize production processes, identify product innovations, achieve cost efficiency and effectiveness, increase productivity and promote corporate reputation. The 2013 *Global Corporate Sustainability Report* released by the United Nations Global Compact addresses the state of corporate sustainability and presents the actions taken by companies worldwide in integrating sustainability into their strategies, operations and culture.[25] The report encourages companies to engage their suppliers in the establishment of more sustainable practices and the integration of sustainability into their supply chain processes. In the context of shareholder wealth maximization and stakeholder welfare maximization, sustainability activities and performance enhance the long-term value of the firm by fulfilling firms' social responsibilities, meeting their environmental obligations and improving their reputation.

The 2013 United Nations study suggests that the non-financial GSEE dimensions of sustainability performance are value relevant to investors by presenting new risks and opportunities that are fundamental in performance analyses and portfolio investment valuation.[26] The study argues that GSEE performance information facilitates investors to conduct economic and industry analyses of GSEE non-financial information. This includes trends, externalities and industry competitiveness effects of GSEE that may affect shareholder value creation as well as assessment of the company's sustainability strategies and practices. These assessments may change the traditional investment valuation parameters and assumptions.[27] Proper understanding of sustainability theories, standards, risk assessment, and performance has been a major challenge for companies in measuring, recognizing and disclosing the five EGSEE dimensions of sustainability performance and for corporate stakeholders (including shareholders) in evaluating their investment portfolios.

Several theories (including agency/shareholder, stakeholder, signaling/disclosure, institutional, legitimacy and stewardship), which will be discussed in subsequent chapters, can explain the interrelated dimensions of sustainability performance and their integrated links to corporate culture, business model, and managerial strategies, processes and practices and their implications for international businesses. These theories are interrelated and compatible. Hence, they can individually and collectively address the different EGSEE dimensions of sustainability performance in creating stakeholder value. The International Standardization Organization (ISO) has issued several ISO standards relevant to business sustainability.[28] The ISO standards establish practical foundations that serve as the buildup based on the sustainability theoretical framework. Sustainability reports reflecting all five EGSEE dimensions of sustainability performance are deemed to be useful when they are complete and accurate, and when their reliability, objectivity and credibility are affirmed by ISO certifications. Thus, high-profile international firms can demand their trading partners to comply with ISO 9000 quality control, ISO 14000 environmental and ISO 26000 CSR standards. These ISO certifications of sustainability performance reports provide external assurance about the credibility and legitimacy of management processes and effective communication of sustainability performance to all stakeholders through integrated sustainability reporting. In recent years, risk-taking by firms and investment banks has become contagious when company executives are incentivized to take excessive risk (as evidenced by outrageous risk at Enron, WorldCom and banks issuing subprime mortgages). Global business changes constantly and becomes more volatile, unpredictable and complex. Six sustainability-related risks including strategic, operations, compliance, financial, security and reputation are relevant to sustainability performance.[29] Proper consideration, assessment and management of these six risks become increasingly important and play an essential role in achieving EGSEE sustainability performance.

A 2014 survey of investors conducted by PricewaterhouseCoopers (PwC) found that about 80 percent of responding investors said they considered non-financial GSEE sustainability issues in their investment decisions, when acting as voting proxies and in creating investment portfolios in the past year. Among the top sustainability issues considered by investors are climate changes, resource scarcity, CSR and good citizenship. Investors' primary drivers for considering sustainability issues, in order of performance, are risk reduction (73 percent), avoiding firms with unethical conduct (55 percent), performance enhancement (52 percent), cost reduction (36 percent), attracting new capital (30 percent), improving capability to create value (30 percent) and being responsive to interest groups (21 percent).[30]

Business sustainability enables management to focus on long-term and enduring financial and non-financial performance and to disclose high-value and forward-looking information to all stakeholders. With GSEE sustainability information, management has the opportunity to gather and use relevant financial and non-financial information for planning and forecasting with the related relevant metrics that drive the business. Management can better focus on sustainable value-deriving activities and use relevant information to effectively communicate the company's sustainability performance, which creates value for stakeholders. Business sustainability promotes better business strategy, planning and decision-making, supply chain and financial and non-financial management. It is important to communicate sustainability performance information regarding business profits, processes, people and planet (the environment) to all stakeholders in an integrated sustainability report.

9. EMERGENCE OF BUSINESS SUSTAINABILITY IN ASIA

The International Monetary Fund reports the World Economic Outlook in April 2018.[31] Three of the 10 largest world economies are in Asia. With Mainland China's emergence as the second largest economy, together with Japan (third) and India (seventh), they report a combined GDP (Gross Domestic Product) of US$22.1 trillion, which rivals that of their North American counterparts: US (first) and Canada (tenth) with a total of US$22.2 trillion, as well as the combined US$12.3 trillion GDP for the European countries of Germany (fourth), United Kingdom (fifth), France (sixth) and Italy (eighth). Despite demanding economic performance, Asian sustainability reporting performance lags behind Europe and North America and is ranked third among the continents.

The Asian economies together have distinct characteristics from those of Europe and North America. While the Asian countries share many similarities, each country has its own unique culture, political and economic system, which are vastly different from one another. Mainland China and India are the oldest ancient civilizations and Chinese and Indian cultures impose significant influence on countries in the region. The religious and philosophical influence of Mainland China (Confucianism) and India (Buddhism) on respected traditions cut deep in every Asian country. Central to Asian cultural heritage is the command of respect for the head or patriarch of the family, whose decisions cannot be challenged. Family hierarchy runs deep into business enterprises. This in turn greatly impacts the governance system in Asian companies. Most of the Asian countries evolved from the autocratic rule of monarchies to pluralistic socialist systems and democracies. The political process for modern democratization empowers different governments which exert influence and regulation on the operation of companies. The varying powers of governments to legislate for and implement sustainability policies further affect the development of sustainability strategies and disclosures.

One can note that there is no specific Asian model of CSR sustainability practice because of the vast, diverse histories and cultures which span the countries and jurisdictions of Asia. CSR activities in Asia are linked to the nature of the respective value systems of each country. This book presents and evaluates 12 Asian economies, including Mainland China, Hong Kong, India, Indonesia, Japan, South Korea, Malaysia, the Philippines, Singapore, Taiwan, Thailand and Vietnam. Various aspects of the business sustainability performance dimensions; sustainability reporting and assurance; and sustainability education, practices and research will be discussed throughout the subsequent chapters. Drivers of sustainability including political, cultural, governmental and legal drivers and regulation, globalization and civil society will be analyzed.

The emergence of sustainability in Asia is closely aligned with the economic development of the region. In their efforts to increase the GDP of their respective countries, Asian companies are adopting policies toward globalization and partnering with Western multi-national companies (MNCs). These MNCs are usually from countries with leading CSR practices and CSR-based standards such as labor rights and environmental performance. They screen and choose their Asian partners in accordance with these practices and standards. In response to the demands of MNCs, many Asian companies attempted to improve their CSR performance and tighten their CSR standards in managing their supply chains. Consequently, these MNCs provide learning opportunities for their Asian counterparts. In the process of their CSR development, Asian countries realize the economic incentives in improving their sustainability performance. Globalization and the export of products to foreign countries provide further incentives for Asian companies to promote CSR and sustainability initiatives. Across Asia, sustainability initiative and performance vary greatly. Nonetheless, the region has made substantial improvement and achieved milestones in sustainability performance in all five EGSEE dimensions.

10. SUSTAINABILITY REPORTING AND ASSURANCE

The role of corporations in our society has evolved from profit maximization to creation of shareholder value and in recent years protection of the interests of all stakeholders. In today's business environment, global businesses are under scrutiny and profound pressure from lawmakers, regulators, the investment community and stakeholders on their sustainability performance. Corporate disclosure, both mandatory and voluntary, is the backbone of financial markets worldwide. Public companies are required to disclose a set of financial information as long as their securities are held by the public. The primary purpose of corporate disclosure is to provide economic agents (e.g., shareholders, creditors) with adequate information to make appropriate decisions. Mandatory corporate reporting, including financial reports disseminated to investors and filed with regulators, is designed to provide investors with relevant, useful and reliable information in making sound investment and lending decisions. Voluntary sustainability reports are usually considered as any disclosures outside of financial statements that are not required by regulators and standard-setters.

Until the late 1990s, sustainability reports had been largely voluntary as part of a firm's supplementary disclosures. In recent years, many jurisdictions including Australia, Austria, Canada, Denmark, France, Germany, Malaysia, Netherlands, Sweden, Hong Kong and the United Kingdom have adopted sustainability reporting. Regulators in other countries are expected to follow suit. Many global regulators, standard-setters and other organizations, including the Sustainability Accounting Standards Board (SASB), the GRI and the International Integrated Reporting Council (IIRC) are now promoting and suggesting guidelines for integrated/sustainability reporting and assurance. Business sustainability requires organizations to focus on achieving all five EGSEE dimensions of sustainability performance by taking initiatives to advance some social good beyond their own interests, compliance with applicable regulations and enhancement of shareholder wealth. Simply stated, business sustainability means enhancing corporations' positive impacts and minimizing their negative effects on society and the environment while creating value for stakeholders.

Over recent years, companies have begun to stray from the mindset of "profit only" to the recognition that building and maintaining sustainable business practices is a good strategy for their companies. In April 2013, the IIRC released a draft of its consultation on a framework of integrated reporting intended to provide guidelines on communication with stakeholders.[32] The IIRC's proposed framework addresses the fundamental concepts of integrated reporting and its guiding principles in relation to an organization's strategy, governance, performance and prospects. The 2013 *Global Corporate Sustainability Report* released by the United Nations Global Compact reviews the actions taken by companies worldwide in advancing their business sustainability.[33] The report uses the 10 principles of sustainability and proposes a model to be adopted as a benchmark in assessing corporate sustainability actions and performance. The report presents the responses of 2,000 companies in 113 countries regarding their sustainability progress and challenges. The key findings of the 2013 *Sustainability Report* are (1) companies are taking proper actions to achieve sustainability performance as evidenced by 65 percent of signatories committing to sustainability at CEO level, and about 35 percent having trained their managers to integrate sustainability into their strategies and operations (2) large companies are leading the way toward sustainability performance and integrated reporting while small and medium-sized enterprises (SMEs) still face challenges to achieve sustainability (3) supply chains are a roadblock to the achievement of improved sustainability performance (4) companies are moving forward with a focus on the achievement of all dimensions of sustainability performance from education to poverty eradication, employment growth and climate change.[34]

An accountability assurance principle means conducting business in an ethical and socially responsible manner. A proper assurance process requires timely and deliberate planning, aggressive actions, effective implementation, enforceable accountability, continuous monitoring and independent third-party assurance on the sustainability reports. Assurance on sustainability reports lends incremental credibility and objectivity to sustainability performance information provided by business organizations. Sustainability assurance can be provided by third-party assurance providers, public accounting firms and internal auditors, as discussed in chapter 5.

In addition to a few mandatory sustainability guidance established in Asia and Europe, there are several voluntary guidelines for sustainability reporting, including the reporting frameworks released by the GRI, the Connected Reporting Framework and the reporting publications of AccountAbility. Currently, sustainability reports are voluntary and (generally) not audited by external auditors. Existing sustainability reports bear different names (green reporting, CSR reporting); serve different stakeholders in achieving a variety of purposes; and vary in terms of content, structure, format, accuracy and assurance. A more standardized, integrated and audited process is required to make sustainability reports on EGSEE performance comparable, commonly acceptable and relevant to all corporate stakeholders. Recently, the provided a comprehensive Sustainability Reporting Framework to enable greater organizational transparency.[35] In 2013, the International Integrated Reporting Council developed the International Integrated Reporting Framework, which provides guidelines for companies to integrate financial and non-financial performance information to benefit all stakeholders.[36] On May 15, 2014, the European Parliament issued a new directive that requires listed companies to disclose information on their environmental, social and diversity initiatives in addition to financial information on economic performance.[37] It is expected that companies in other countries will follow suit and, in the near future, sustainability reports will reflect both financial and non-financial information relevant to all five EGSEE dimensions of sustainability performance and assurance will be provided on these reports to enhance their credibility and reliability.

The value relevance of sustainability reports measured in terms of objectivity, transparency, reliability, usefulness and credibility are important to both internal and external users of reports. Assurance providers play an important role in enhancing the roles of sustainability reports. Sustainability assurance can be provided internally by internal auditors or by external assurance providers. While internal auditors are well qualified to assist management in the preparation and assurance of sustainability reports, external users of sustainability reports may demand more independent and objective assurance on the reports. This type of assurance can be provided by certified public accountants (CPAs), professional assurance providers or equivalent accredited individuals, groups or bodies. Existing auditing standards are intended to provide reasonable assurance on financial and internal control reports prepared by management. However, the degree of reliance placed on non-financial information such as sustainability reporting has not been well established. Assurance standards on different dimensions of sustainability performance reports vary in terms of rigor and general acceptability. Assurance standards on other dimensions of sustainability including governance, ethics and social and environmental standards are yet to be fully developed and globally accepted.

In the United States, the Delaware Certification of Adoption of Transparency and Sustainability Standards Act ("the Act") was signed into law on June 27, 2018.[38] The Act becomes effective on October 1, 2018 and represents Delaware's initiative to support sustainability practices by enabling Delaware-governed entities to disclose their commitment to CSR and sustainability. It reflects Delaware's recognition that sustainability is a business imperative rather than a greenwashing and should be integrated into the business environment and corporate culture in promoting innovation and long-term financial growth, societal benefits and environmental protection. The Act is intended to demonstrate a firm commitment to sustainability and a proper response to the increasing calls from investors, customers and clients for greater transparency in sustainability practices. The Act is voluntary and applies only to those Delaware-law governed entities that seek to become certified as reporting entities, and gives much flexibility to entities to develop their own sustainability strategies and practices in meeting their sustainability goals and needs. However, there are several mandatory features of the Act that require the entity's governing body to approve its standards and assessment measures, and those standards and measures to be made publicly available. The Act also recommends that sustainability practices be addressed at the highest levels of the organization. The 2018 Delaware Act is a voluntary disclosure regime requiring adopting entities to provide reports on their sustainability and related standards and metrics.

Around the world, there is an increasing trend toward issuing sustainability reports. Europe has led sustainability reporting practices, starting in 2011. However, Asian countries started to catch up from 2013, reaching their peak in 2015.[39] The improvement of sustainability reporting in Asia is attributable to the efforts of various regulators such as those from stock exchanges, industry and financial sectors.

11.   PROFESSIONAL ORGANIZATIONS INFLUENCING SUSTAINABILITY

Sustainability promotes long-term profitability and competitive advantage; helps maintain the wellbeing of society, the planet and people; and creates value for all stakeholders. Global authoritative standard-setters, including the IFAC, the GRI, the International Integrated Reporting Council (IIRC), the Sustainability Accounting Standards Board (SASB) and the Corporate Reporting Dialogue (CRD) now promote integrated/sustainability reporting. Sustainability reporting measures, recognizes and discloses the five EGSEE dimensions of sustainability performance. The goal of long-term firm value maximization under business sustainability can be achieved when the interests of all stakeholders including shareholders are considered. Regulators, investors and companies throughout the world continue to value a firm's sustainability performance.

It is expected that integrated reporting will play an important role in future corporate reporting and in rebuilding investor trust and confidence in public financial information. Trust in public company financial reporting has been eroded in recent years. Conventional corporate reporting, based on historical financial information, predominantly focuses on the economic dimension of sustainability performance and short-term value drivers. Integrated reporting provides an opportunity to go beyond this short-term focus on financial performance and enables companies to incorporate both financial and non-financial KPIs in demonstrating their stewardship and social utility, environmental initiatives and simultaneously, economic value. Integrated reporting is a vehicle by which public companies communicate their value creation strategies, decisions, and actions through short-, medium- and long-term performance in all five EGSEE sustainability performance metrics to all stakeholders. It enables business organizations to integrate EGSEE sustainability performance reporting into the mainstream corporate reporting process.

The GRI was launched in 1997 to bring consistency and global standardization to sustainability reporting. GRI initially focused on incorporating environmental performance into corporate reporting with its *Sustainability Reporting Guidelines*, which were published in 2000, 2002, 2006, 2011 and 2013. GRI is now considered the sole global standard-setter in sustainability reporting. The current version, the "G4 Guidelines," was issued in May 2013. In addition to extra disclosure requirements from the previous version, Version 3.1, G4 expands the scope of disclosures to include the "Ethics and Integrity" element and substantially strengthens "Corporate Governance" measures.[40] The GRI, in its G3 (initially) and G4 *Guidelines*, promotes sustainability reporting as a standard practice of disclosing sustainability-related issues relevant to businesses and stakeholders.[41] The goal of long-term value maximization is achieved when all stakeholders' interests are considered. The main focus is on long-term shareholder value creation and maximization while considering tradeoffs among other apparently competing and often conflicting interests of society, creditors, employees and the environment. The various dimensions of sustainability performance are related. The economic and other sustainability performance dimensions are complementary because a firm that is effectively governed, that behaves ethically and that commits to social and environmental initiatives is also sustainable while generating long-term financial performance. Although the primary goal of many corporations will continue to be enhancing shareholder value by producing sustainable economic performance, they must also effectively deal with ESG issues to ensure value is added for their shareholders and other stakeholders.

Important principles of integrated reporting being developed by IIRC are: (1) ensuring that corporate strategy is articulated well as a core part of the report, (2) connecting all parts of the business as a whole, (3) making information concise and easily readable, (4) being future oriented and inclusive of multiple stakeholders and (5) taking care to provide materiality, value and assurance to the audience of the report.[42] These principles help companies understand the importance of integrated reporting and its effect on their businesses. More can and will be added in due time as the IIRC works with companies to further develop best practices. The fourth generation (G4) of the GRI *Guidelines* covers economic, governance, social and environmental performance.[43] The GRI reporting process enables organizations to disclose self-declared sustainability information based on one of three application levels (A, B or C) depending on the extent of information provided. The GRI initially focused on a triple bottom line of economic, social and environmental performance with Version 3.1 (G3) of its sustainability framework. In its *G4 Guidelines*, the GRI promotes sustainability reporting as a standard practice of disclosing sustainability-related issues relevant to companies' businesses and their stakeholders.[44] The *G4 Guidelines* present Reporting Principles, Standard Disclosures and an Implementation Manual for sustainability reporting on economic, governance, social, ethical and environmental performance (EGSEE) by all organizations regardless of their type, size, sector or location.[45]

The Sustainability Accounting Standards Board (SASB) establishes and creates sustainability accounting standards suitable for developing measures to disclose material sustainability issues for 88 industries in 10 sectors. The SASB suggests the process for mandatory filings to the US Securities and Exchange Commission (SEC), such as Forms 10-K and 20-F, through the first quarter of 2015. The SASB's primary concern is to establish standards that enable peer-to-peer comparison between companies which can be useful for investment decisions and allocation of capital.[46] In June 2011, the Global Initiative for Sustainability Ratings (GISR) developed environmental, social and governance (ESG) ratings standards with an eye toward maximum harmonization with leading complementary standard-setters, most notably the GRI, the IIRC,[47] the Carbon Disclosure Project (CDP) and SASB.[48] Harmonizing SASB standards with existing disclosure standards avoids additional reporting costs for companies and aligns the SASB's work with global corporate transparency efforts. In April 2013, the IIRC released the draft of its consultation on a framework of integrated reporting intended to provide guidelines on communication with stakeholders.[49] The IIRC's proposed framework addresses the fundamental concepts of integrated reporting and its guiding principles for an organization's strategy, governance, performance and prospects. The products of the SASB, GRI and IIRC can be used in complementary ways for the development of a sustainability report for investors and all stakeholders. The SASB provides standards for mandatory filings, whereas GRI and IIRC provide frameworks for voluntary reporting.

12. BEST PRACTICES OF SUSTAINABILITY PERFORMANCE, REPORTING AND ASSURANCE

Sustainability performance, reporting and assurance evolves as investors demand more relevant sustainability disclosures, regulators require more extensive sustainability reports and business organizations integrate sustainability into their strategic decisions, actions and performance. Along with the evolving process, best practices of sustainability performance, reporting and assurance are being developed. According to greenbiz.com and UPS, there are five ways to convey the vital importance of sustainability to senior executives:[50]

1. Sustainability enables cost reduction and efficiency improvement.
2. Sustainability incentivizes organizations to focus on risk assessment, management and mitigation (financial, operational, compliance, strategic and reputational risks).

3. Sustainability creates new competitive and revenue-generating opportunities.
4. Sustainability encourages innovation.
5. Sustainability promotes talented employee recruitment, development and retention.

A recent report by the Conference Board presents many cases in which non-financial GSEE sustainability actions and performance have had a positive impact on financial performance.[51] The report also highlights the importance of establishing the links between financial and non-financial GSEE sustainability by adopting relevant KPIs. Sustainability information on GSEE is typically considered an externality, beyond the disclosure of economic performance, which may have positive or negative consequences as viewed by market participants. Examples of positive externalities are board independence and diversity, majority voting, environmental initiatives regarding climate change, customer satisfaction, job creation and fair employment.[52] Examples of negative externalities are CEO duality, natural resource depletion, pollution and human rights abuses.[53] In disclosing their externalities in terms of strengths and concerns, firms tend to over-emphasize positive externalities and under-emphasize concerns as incorporated into the ESG scores.

13. MANAGERIAL IMPLICATIONS OF SUSTAINABILITY PROGRAMS AND ACTIVITIES

Business organizations worldwide are now recognizing the importance of quality as it relates to sustainability performance and the link between profitability and sustainability. Justifications for a focus on sustainability strategies and performance are moral obligation, maintaining a good reputation, ensuring sustainability, license to operate and creating shared value. In a shared value approach, corporations identify potential social issues of concern and integrate them into their strategic planning. There are many sustainability factors that a company should consider, for example, pressure from the labor movement, development of moral values and social standards, development of business education, change in public opinion about the role of business and corporate responsibility to society and the environment. Companies which are, or aspire to be, leaders in sustainability are challenged by rising public expectations, increasing innovation, continuous quality improvement and heightened social and environmental problems. Businesses should fulfill their social and environmental responsibilities for reasons such as public image, consumer movements, government requirements, investor education, tax benefits, better relations with stakeholders, employee satisfaction, a sense of pride and an appropriate way to improve quality.

Asian firms have been seen to juggle economic prosperity, social responsibility and environmental management, as well as to incorporate them with their businesses, stakeholders and society at large. It is seen that the integration process is a rather systematic and yet complex task for managers to handle. This poses a problem for Asian companies as it is seen that their CSR initiatives lack coherent sustainability strategies that align with the firms' objectives. Currently, CSR initiatives are more compliance-oriented. Sustainability initiatives with complete data-based technologies will be able to measure the expectation and performance of CSR initiatives.

This will emerge endogenously, becoming more relevant within firms in the future as the region grows and expands. The challenge of a unified system and controlled environment still lingers in sustainability reporting as firms still collate data using Excel spreadsheets. This does not make the figures or the process wrong, but it is not the same as using a screened system to compile and analyze data. A screened system is a system that shows which sustainability data is reported and where the data is stored. Such a system will do a better job of comparing performance for specific periods and make analysis seamless.[54]

14. CONCLUSIONS

Business sustainability requires organizations to focus on achieving all five EGSEE dimensions of sustainability performance by taking initiatives to advance social good beyond their own interests and compliance with applicable regulations and enhancement of shareholder wealth. Simply put, business sustainability means enhancing corporations' positive impacts and minimizing their negative effects on society and the environment while creating positive impacts on shareholders, the community, the environment, employees, customers and suppliers. The true measure of success for corporations should be determined not only by their reported earnings, but also by their governance, social responsibility, ethical behavior and environmental performance. Business sustainability has received considerable attention from policymakers, regulators and the business and investment community over the past decade and it is expected to be the main theme for decades to come.

In conclusion, the sustainability performance dimensions and related risk, theoretical sustainability frameworks and practical sustainability standards presented in this book should be useful to companies and their management, policymakers and regulators, investors and educators. All theories, including agency/shareholder, stakeholder, signaling, institutional and legitimacy, focus on key measures of sustainable performance such as operational efficiency, customer satisfaction, talent management and innovation, which should all be derived from internal factors of strategy, risk profile, strengths and weaknesses, and corporate culture as well as external factors of reputation, technology, completion, globalization and utilization of natural resources. These theories and standards help in explaining companies' objectives as reflected in management strategies and practices of creating sustainable value for shareholders while protecting the interests of other stakeholders such as creditors, employees, customers, suppliers, government and society.

15. CHAPTER TAKEAWAY

1. Integration of business sustainability to the corporate culture and strategic planning requires identification of all stakeholders, development of strategies and KPIs to create shared value for all identified stakeholders and proper disclosure of sustainability performance.
2. Integrating the five EGSEE dimensions of sustainability performance to management processes enables companies to conserve scarce resources, optimize production processes, identify product innovations, achieve cost efficiency and

effectiveness, increase productivity, promote corporate reputation and create stakeholder value.

3. Effective implementation of all five EGSEE dimensions of sustainability performance is essential in creating sustainability value for all stakeholders.
4. Sustainability managers should understand that shareholder value can be improved by enhancing value creation for other stakeholders.

ENDNOTES

1. Much of discussion presented in this and other chapters of this book come from two books on sustainability recently published by one of the authors. A. Brockett and Z. Rezaee, *Corporate Sustainability: Integrating Performance and Reporting* (New York: John Wiley & Sons, Inc., 2012), and Z. Rezaee, *Business Sustainability: Performance, Compliance, Accountability and Integrated Reporting* (London and New York: Greenleaf Publishing Limited, 2015).
2. European Commission, Communication from the Commission to the European Parliament, the Council, the European Economic and Social Committee and the Committee of the Regions (Brussels, 25.10.2011, COM(2011) 681 final), http://www .europarl.europa.eu/meetdocs/2009_2014/documents/com/com_com(2011)0681_/com_ com(2011)0681_en.pdf.
3. United Nations Global Compact (UN Global Compact), *Global Corporate Sustainability Report 2013*, https://www.unglobalcompact.org/docs/about_the_gc/Global_Corporate_ Sustainability_Report2013.pdf.
4. N. Cruz and R. Marques, "Scorecards for sustainable local governments," *Cities* 39 (2014): 165–170.
5. United Nations Global Compact (UN Global Compact), *Global Corporate Sustainability Report 2013*, https://www.unglobalcompact.org/docs/about_the_gc/Global_Corporate_ Sustainability_Report2013.pdf.
6. Global Reporting Initiative (GRI), *G4 Sustainability Reporting Guidelines*, May 2013, www.globalreporting.org.
7. International Federation of Accountants (IFAC), *Accounting for Sustainability: From Sustainability to Business Resilience*, July 2015, https://www.ifac.org/publications-resources/ accounting-sustainability.pdf.
8. Z. Rezaee, *Business Sustainability: Performance, Compliance, Accountability and Integrated Reporting* (London and New York: Greenleaf Publishing Limited, 2015).
9. Michael C. Jensen, "Value Maximization, Stakeholder theory, and the Corporate Objective Function," *Journal of Applied Corporate Finance* 14, no. 3 (2001): 8–21.
10. World Business Council for Sustainable Development, *Corporate Social Responsibility: Meeting Changing Expectations* (WBCSD Publications, 1999) ISBN No. 2-94-0240-03-5, http://umemphis.worldcat.org/title/corporate-social-responsibility-meeting-changing-expectations/oclc/42053359.
11. F. A. Uriarte Jr, *The ASEAN Foundation and the Emerging CSR Issues and Challenges* (Jakarta: ASEAN Foundation, 2008), 38.
12. UN Global Compact, *Global Corporate Sustainability Report*.
13. Ibid.
14. Ibid.
15. Ibid.
16. Brockett and Rezaee, *Corporate Sustainability*.
17. Much of discussion on EGSEE dimensions of sustainability performance and their related KPIs throughout the book comes from Z. Rezaee, *Business Sustainability: Performance, Compliance, Accountability and Integrated Reporting* (London and New York: Greenleaf Publishing Limited, 2015).

18. Global Reporting Initiative (GRI), G4 Exposure Draft: Frequently asked questions about the G4 Exposure Draft and the second G4 Public Comment Period), 2013, https://www.globalreporting.org/SiteCollectionDocuments/G4-Exposure-Draft.pdf.

19. Ibid.

20. Sarbanes-Oxley Act of 2002, Pub. L. 107–204, enacted July 30, 2002, adding 15 U.S.C. § 7201 *et seq.* provisions of the United States Code, as explained in the notes accompanying 15 U.S.C. § 7201, hereinafter the "Sarbanes-Oxley Act" or "SOX."

21. Dodd-Frank Wall Street Reform and Consumer Protection Act of 2010, Pub. L. 111–203.

22. United Nations Principles of Responsible Investing (UN PRI). 2005. The Fresh fields Report, www.unepfi.org/fileadmin/documents/freshfields_legal_resp_20051123.pdf/.

23. Social Investment Forum (SIF), *Report on Sustainable and Responsible Investing Trends in the United States* (US SIF, November 2012).

24. CERES and the Environmental Defense Fund.

25. UN Global Compact, *Global Corporate Sustainability Report.*

26. United Nations, "How Investors Are Addressing Environmental, Social and Governance Factors in Fundamental Equity Valuation," United Nations-Supported Principles for Responsible Investment (PRI), February 2013, https://www.unpri.org/download?ac=312.

27. Ibid.

28. International Organization for Standardization (ISO), various ISO standards, www.iso.org.

29. Z. Rezaee, *Business Sustainability.*

30. PricewaterhouseCoopers (PwC), *Sustainability Goes Mainstream: Insights into Investor Views* (May 2014), http://www.pwc.com/us/en/pwc-investor-resource-institute/index.jhtml.

31. International Monetary Fund (IMF), *World Economic Outlook*, April 2018, https://www.imf.org/external/pubs/ft/weo/2018/01/weodata/index.aspx.

32. International Integrated Reporting Council, *Consultation Draft of the International Integrated Reporting Framework*, April 2013, http://integratedreporting.org/wp-content/uploads/2013/03/Consultation-Draft-of-the-InternationalIRFramework.pdf.

33. Ibid.

34. Ibid.

35. GRI, *G4 Sustainability Reporting Guidelines.*

36. International Integrated Reporting Committee, *IIRC Consultative Draft*, 2013, section 3.12, p. 19, http://integratedreporting.org/wp-content/uploads/2013/03/Consultation-Draft-of-the-InternationalIRFramework.pdf.

37. European Commission, *Non-Financial Reporting*, 2014, https://ec.europa.eu/info/business-economy-euro/company-reporting-and-auditing/company-reporting/non-financial-reporting_en.

38. Delaware General Assembly, House Bill 310: An Act to Amend Title 6 of the Delaware Code Relating to the Certification of Adoption of Sustainability and Transparency Standards by Delaware Entities, June 27, 2018, https://legis.delaware.gov/BillDetail/26304.

39. The 2016 KPMG report defines the Asian-Pacific countries as follows: Australia, Bangladesh, Mainland China, Hong Kong, India, Indonesia, Japan, Malaysia, Maldives, Pakistan, Philippines, Singapore, South Korea, Taiwan, Thailand, Vietnam, https://assets.kpmg.com/content/dam/kpmg/pdf/2016/05/aspac-indirect-tax-guide-2016.pdf.

40. GRI, *G4 Sustainability Reporting Guidelines.*

41. Global Reporting Initiative (GRI), G4 Exposure Draft: Frequently asked questions about the G4 Exposure Draft and the second G4 Public Comment Period), 2013, https://www.globalreporting.org/SiteCollectionDocuments/G4-Exposure-Draft.pdf.

42. International Integrated Reporting Committee (IIRC), *Towards Integrated Reporting: Communicating Value in the 21ˢᵗ Century*, 2011, http://theiirc.org/wp-content/uploads/2011/09/IR-Discussion-Paper-2011_spreads.pdf.
43. GRI, *G4 Sustainability Reporting Guidelines*, https://www.globalcompact.de/wAssets/docs/Reporting/G4_FAQ.pdf.
44. Ibid.
45. Ibid.
46. Sustainability Accounting Standards Board (SASB), *Conceptual Framework of the Sustainability Accounting Standards Board*, October 2013, https://www.sasb.org/wp-content/uploads/2013/10/SASB-Conceptual-Framework-Final-Formatted-10-22-13 .pdf.
47. International Integrated Reporting Committee, *IIRC Consultative Draft*, 2013, section 3.12, p. 19, http://integratedreporting.org/wp-content/uploads/2013/03/Consultation-Draft-of-the-InternationalIRFramework.pdf.
48. Climate Change Reporting Taxonomy (CCRT), *Climate Change Reporting Taxonomy Due Process*, 2013, https://www.globalcompact.de/wAssets/docs/Reporting/G4_FAQ.pdf.
49. International Integrated Reporting Council, *IIRC Consultative Draft*.
50. K. Kuehn, "Five Ways to Convince Your CFO that Sustainability Pays," 2010, www.greenbiz.com.
51. M. Bertoneche & C. V. Lungt, "Director Notes, The Sustainability Business Case: A Model for Incorporating Financial Value Drivers," *The Conference Board*, June 2013, www.conference board.org.
52. Z. Rezaee, "Business Sustainability Research: A Theoretical and Integrated Perspective." *Journal of Accounting Literature* 36 (2016): 48–64.
53. Ibid.
54. Brendan O'Dwyer, "The Case of Sustainability Assurance: Constructing a New Assurance Service," *Contemporary Accounting Research* 28, no. 4 (May 2011).

CHAPTER 2

Sustainability Principles, Theories, Research and Education

1. EXECUTIVE SUMMARY

Companies today face the challenges of adopting proper sustainability strategies and practices to effectively respond to social, ethical, environmental and governance issues while creating sustainable financial performance and value for their shareholders. The goal of firm value maximization under business sustainability can be achieved when the interests of all stakeholders are considered. The main focus is on long-term shareholder value creation while considering trade-offs among other apparently competing and often conflicting interests of all stakeholders including society, creditors, employees, suppliers, customers and the environment. The relative importance of the five dimensions—economic, governance, social, ethical and environmental (EGSEE)—of sustainability performance with respect to each other and their contribution to overall firm value creation is affected by whether these sustainability performance dimensions are viewed as competing with, conflicting with or complementing each other and what sustainability theory or theories are applied to define tensions among EGSEE sustainability performance dimensions. This chapter examines several principles, theories and standards relevant to all five EGSEE dimensions of sustainability performance in explaining the tensions between them as well as the associated risk. This chapter also presents sustainability research and education.

2. INTRODUCTION

Business sustainability has been debated in the literature and has changed business organizations' strategies and practices in focusing on long-term and multi-dimensional sustainability performance. Corporations' primary goals have refocused from maximizing profit to increasing shareholder wealth. Now, in light of the moves toward business sustainability worldwide, those goals are shifting toward creating shared value for all stakeholders including shareholders. Companies today face the challenges of adopting proper business models and sustainable supply chain management strategies and practices to effectively respond to social, ethical, environmental and governance issues while creating sustainable financial performance and value for their shareholders. Scholars also attempt to adopt appropriate sustainability theories to explain the relationship between financial economic sustainability performance and non-financial governance, social, ethical and environmental sustainability performance.

This chapter addresses the agency/shareholder, stakeholder, legitimacy, signaling, institutional and stewardship theories and applies various quality control, environmental, social and governance standards to explain the integrated and interrelated dimensions of sustainability performance and their relevance to shared value creation.[1] These theories and standards suggest that companies should focus on the key measures of sustainable performance such as operational efficiency, supply chain management, customer satisfaction, talent management and innovation. These measures are derived from the internal factors of strategy, risk profile, strengths and weaknesses and corporate culture as well as the external factors of reputation, technology, competition, globalization and utilization of natural resources. Companies should use a principles-based approach in integrating financial and non-financial sustainability information into their business model, from purchasing and inbound logistics, production design and manufacturing process, to distribution and outbound logistics.

3.   INSTITUTIONAL BACKGROUND

Conceptually, there are two distinct views on why a firm should focus on both financial economic sustainability performance (ESP) and non-financial governance, social, ethical and environmental (GSEE) sustainability performance. Practically, the ethics component can be integrated into other financial and non-financial dimensions of sustainability performance. One view is that a firm exists solely to maximize profits and create value for its shareholders within the realm of law and morality. In this context, a firm's objective is to improve ESP sustainability performance and to engage in GSEE sustainability initiatives merely to benefit its public image, prevent government intervention and/or gain government favor, improve its corporate governance effectiveness, obtain industry leadership, improve reputation with customers and society or improve market share. Under this view, any investment in non-financial GSEE is considered an expense that reduces a firm's bottom line and thus negatively affects shareholder wealth.

Another view is that a firm is the property of its owners and not stakeholders. As such, the owners have the right to decide how their property will be handled; as either for profit (ESP-focused), for social good (GSEE-focused) or for both, if desired. In this context, any engagement in non-financial GSEE sustainability performance is intended to improve the bottom line earnings based on the perception that a firm with more effective corporate governance measures, that conducts its business ethically and that takes corporate social responsibility (CSR) and environmental initiatives, is better off financially in the long term. Under this view, any expenditures pertaining to non-financial GSEE are considered as an investment that can provide potential returns on investment and ultimately increase long-term financial earnings.

In recent years, however, there has been a move toward a middle ground view of "doing well by doing good" by focusing on both financial ESP and non-financial GSEE sustainability performance. This view is gaining momentum worldwide and is promoted throughout this book. Investors now seek investments that are aligned with their social values (value alignment), for example, by owning stocks only in companies whose activities are consistent with the investor's moral and/or social values. Other investors may want to invest in portfolio companies that can create more social value (social value creation). Recently there is a trend toward impact investing, which started in North America and Europe. Impact investing is defined as accepting a lower return on investment in companies that "do well and do good" by focusing on GSEE performance.[2] This trend is currently being advocated in Hong Kong and Asia. Many private wealth arms of global banks such as Bank of America's Private Wealth Management and BNP are developing products focusing on impact investors. With impact investing, securing the financial return is not the sole objective of investors, as they consider social and environmental impacts as well.[3] Thus, impact investing is defined as an investment with financial return as well as non-financial impacts on society and environment.

Theoretically, management engagement in GSEE activities, performance and disclosure can be viewed as value increasing or value decreasing by investors. On the one hand, companies that effectively manage their business sustainability, improve GSEE performance, enhance their reputation, fulfill their social responsibility and promote a corporate culture of integrity and competency can be financially sustainable in the long term. On the other hand, companies can only survive and generate sustainable performance when they generate profits and cash which in turn are used to invest in social and environmental initiatives. An intensive and yet inconclusive debate has taken place about whether GSEE programs constitute a legitimate activity for corporations to engage in.[4] The costs of these programs are immediate and tangible but the related benefits may not be realized in the short to medium term and outcomes are often not easily quantifiable (e.g. CSR initiatives). Sustainability disclosures on GSEE are typically considered as externalities beyond the disclosures of ESP and can be viewed positively or negatively by investors and other market participants. Examples of positive externalities are diversity and independence of the board of directors, majority voting by shareholders, executive compensation that is linked to performance, pay for performance, environmental initiatives regarding climate change and greenhouse gas emissions, high-quality and safe products, customer satisfaction, ethical workplaces, job creation and fair employment. Examples of negative externalities are chief executive officer (CEO) duality where the position of the CEO and the chair of the board of directors is the same, excessive risk-taking by executives, natural resource depletion, pollution, aggressive management and human rights abuses. These positive (negative) externalities have been documented to have favorable (unfavorable) effects on the firm's cost of capital and thus its market value.[5] Sustainability theories discussed in the next section are intended to explain the possible tension among the five EGSEE dimensions of sustainability performance, in particular the tension between financial ESP and non-financial GSEE dimensions.

4. SUSTAINABILITY PRINCIPLES

As business sustainability is gaining increasing attention and recognition as a strategic imperative and being integrated into corporate culture and business environment, its principles are being defined by several professional organizations.

The five principles of sustainability, developed based on the definition of sustainability as "a dynamic equilibrium in the process of interaction between a population and the caring capacity of its environment...," provide guidelines for public companies to effectively manage the social, environmental and financial aspects of their business.[6] The five sustainability principles as defined by the Brundtland Commission are the material, economic, life, social and spiritual domains.[7]

1. The Material Domain: This principle suggests continuous flow of resources through and within the economy as permitted by physical laws and provides justifications for regulating the flow of materials and energy. Policy and operational implications of this principle are concerned with the promotion of highest resource productivity, recycling of non-regenerative resources and regenerating energy resources that underlie existence.

2. The Economic Domain: This principle posits that there exist economic and accounting guiding frameworks for managing wealth and aligning economic performance with the planet's ecological processes. Policy and operational implications of this principle are concerned with the effective management of all capitals, including natural, financial, manufacturing, human and social, with a focus on the wellbeing of all stakeholders. It also relies on market mechanisms and smart regulation for the proper allocation of resources and capital assets.

3. The Domain of Life: This principle promotes diversity of all forms of life as the basis for appropriate behavior in the biosphere. Policy and operational implications of this principle are concerned with accountability and stewardship, responsibility for the planet and conservative use of scarce resources.

4. The Social Domain: This principle suggests the basis for providing the maximum degree of freedom and self-realization for all humans and their social interactions. Policy and operational implications of this principle are concerned with the promotion of tolerance as a foundation for social interactions, good citizenship, democratic governance, equitable and fair access to resources, sustainability literacy and sustainability enhancing concepts.

5. The Spiritual Domain: This principle advocates the recognition of the necessary attitudinal orientation as a need for a universal code of ethics. Policy and operational implications of this principle are concerned with the understanding of humanity's unique function in the universe, the creation of synergy in human endeavors and linking the inner transformation of individuals to transformation in society.

The United Nations Global Compact has established 10 sustainability principles and more than 8,000 companies worldwide have adopted and integrated these principles into their strategic planning, decisions and operations.[8] These 10 sustainability principles are classified into four general categories of human rights, labor, environment and anti-corruption as summarized in Exhibit 2.1, and are relevant to all five EGSEE dimensions of sustainability performance. The ultimate success of business organizations should be measured in terms of their ability and willingness to achieve all five EGSEE dimensions of sustainability performance by adopting

EXHIBIT 2.1 United Nations Global Compact Ten Principles of Sustainability Performance[9]

Principle	Description	Categories	Sustainability Performance
1	The protection of international human rights should be respected and supported.	Human Rights	
2	Businesses shall not take part in the abuse of human rights.		
3	Freedom of association and the right to collective bargaining should be supported.		Social
4	Forced and compulsory labor should be eliminated.	Labor	
5	Child labor should be effectively eradicated.		
6	Discrimination in employment and occupation should be abolished.		
7	Businesses should take safety measures against environmental challenges.		
8	Greater environmental responsibility should be promoted.	Environment	Environmental
9	The advance and distribution of environmentally friendly technology should be encouraged by business.		
10	Businesses should combat extortion, bribery and all forms of corruption.	Anti-Corruption	Ethical

these principles of sustainability. These sustainability principles should assist business organizations to:

- Focus on creating sustainable performance that benefits humans, society and the environment.
- Adopt sustainability as an integrated component of their mission and recognize that sustainability integrates social, economic, governance, ethical, environmental and cultural interactions.
- Encourage the discussion of sustainability concepts throughout the company.
- Commit to ongoing assessments of the company's progress toward sustainability.
- Commit to the development and implementation of policies and operating procedures that promote the fulfillment of these principles.

These principles collectively suggest that sustainability enables businesses to meet the needs of the current generation without compromising the needs of future generations. A combination of these sustainability principles should be used as the foundation and guidelines for business organizations in transforming business sustainability from a greenwashing exercise into a strategic imperative of integrating business environment and corporate culture. Specifically, these principles should be viewed as foundations for the development of the sustainability theories explained in the following section.

5. SUSTAINABILITY THEORIES

The concept of sustainability performance suggests that a firm must extend its focus beyond maximizing short-term shareholder profit by considering the impact of its operations on all stakeholders including the community, society and the environment.[10] Several theories including shareholder/agency, stakeholder, legitimacy, signaling/disclosure, institutional and stewardship help to explain the interrelated EGSEE dimensions of sustainability performance and their integrated link to business models and corporate culture in creating shared value for all stakeholders.[11] This section presents these theories and their implications for business sustainability practice, education, research and standards.

5.1   Shareholder/Agency Theory

Shareholder/agency theory defines the relationship between shareowners (principal) and management (agent) and addresses the potential conflicts of interest between management and shareholders. There may be conflicts of interest between owners (shareholders) and agents (management) in a corporate setting when agents are charged with the responsibility of managing the business affairs in the best interest of owners. Shareholder/agency theory addresses how corporations are managed and suggests that the interests of owners and agents are often not aligned. Shareholder/agency theory explains the economic function and valuation implications of sustainability performance in maximizing positive externalities and minimizing negative externalities of sustainability activities that are intended to create shareholder value. This theory suggests that management maximizes the interests of shareholders by engaging in positive net present value (NPV) projects that create shareholder value. This shareholder wealth maximization theory specifies that shareholders are the owners of the firm and that management has a fiduciary duty to act in the best interest of owners to maximize their wealth.[12]

Shareholder/agency theory focuses on risk sharing and the agency problems between principal (owner) and agent (management). In the presence of information asymmetry where the agent (management) acts on behalf of the principal (shareholders) and knows more about their actions and/or intentions than the principal, the agent has incentives not to act in the best interest of owners and/or to withhold important information from them. With proper monitoring, the principal incurs agency costs of monitoring, bonding and residual claims to align their interests with those of the agent.[13] Agency theory (viewing management as accountable only to shareholders for creating shareholder value and where their interests may diverge from those of the shareholders) has traditionally been the dominant theory of corporate finance, management and governance research. While agency theory has been useful to explain the principal–agent relationship and interest divergence for individualistic utility maximization and motivation, this theory may not adequately address the emerging complex organizational structure that is oriented toward business sustainability in protecting the interests of all stakeholders.

The implications of shareholder/agency theory for sustainability performance is that management incentives and activities may be focused around meeting short-term earnings targets and away from achieving sustainable and long-term performance for all stakeholders including shareholders. Under this theory, non-financial GSEE sustainability activities, particularly CSR expenditures, are typically viewed as the allocation of firm resources in pursuit of activities that are not in the best financial interests of shareholders even though they may create value for other stakeholders. Firms thus focus only on creating shareholder value and leave decisions about social responsibility to individual investors. Shareholder/agency theory suggests that there is an information asymmetry among stakeholders as only the senior management typically know the true representation of financial and non-financial reports. Thus, to mitigate the perceived information asymmetry, management may choose to voluntarily disclose non-financial GSEE performance information. Agency theory postulates that GSEE activities can create shareholder value when they increase future cash flows by increasing revenue (better customer satisfaction), reducing costs (reducing waste, better quality and cost-effective products and services, retaining talented and loyal employees) and reducing risks (complying with regulations, avoiding taxes and fines).

5.2 Stakeholder Theory

Stakeholder theory and the "enlightened value maximization" concept recognize the maximization of sustainable performance and the long-term value of the firm as the criterion for balancing the interests of all stakeholders.[14] In the context of shareholder wealth maximization and stakeholder welfare maximization, GSEE sustainability efforts may create both synergies and conflicts. The stakeholder theory suggests that sustainability activities and performance enhancement of the long-term value of the firm fulfill the firm's social responsibilities, meet their environmental obligations and improve their reputation.[15] However, these sustainability efforts may require considerable resource allocation that can conflict with the shareholder wealth maximization objectives and thus management may not invest in sustainability initiatives (social and environmental) that result in long-term financial sustainability.

Under the stakeholder theory, all stakeholders have a reciprocal relation with a company. The stakeholder theory is applicable to business sustainability in the sense that synergy and integration among all elements of the supply chain and financial processes are essential in achieving overall sustainable performance objectives. Stakeholders not only value the firm's sustainability performance but also become aware of such activities and take action in holding the firm responsible. The application of the stakeholder theory to business sustainability suggests that a company should be viewed as a nexus of all constituencies in creating shared value for all stakeholders. This theory suggests the integration of all business activities including the supply chain; inbound and outbound logistics, processes and operations; finished products; customer interface; distribution channels; services; and financial reporting processes to achieve sustainability performance in all five EGSEE dimensions. According to this theory, sustainability performance dimensions (ESP and GSEE) are viewed by stakeholders as value-added activities that create shared value for all stakeholders.

Stakeholder theory has been and will continue to be the prevailing theory of corporate sustainability since 1984 when Freeman published his book, *Strategic Management: A Stakeholder Approach*.[16] Mitchell, Agle and Wood (1997)[17] discuss a normative theory of stakeholder identification in explaining why management may consider certain groups (e.g., owners, non-owners) as the firm's stakeholders and a descriptive theory of stakeholder salience in describing the conditions under which management may recognize certain groups as stakeholders. One of the most prevailing and broad definitions of a stakeholder is provided by Freeman (1984: 46) as "any group or individual who can affect or is affected by the achievement of the organization's objectives." In the context of business sustainability, stakeholders can be classified as internal stakeholders who have direct interest (stake) and bear risks associated with business activities and external stakeholders. Stakeholders are those who have vested interests in a firm through their investments in the form of financial capital (shareholders), human capital (employees), physical capital (customers and suppliers), social capital (society), environmental capital (environment) and regulatory capital (government). Stakeholders have reciprocal relations and interactions with a firm in the sense that they contribute to the firm value creation (stake) and their wellbeing is also affected by the firm's activities (risk). The legitimacy and institutional theories discussed below are closely related to the stakeholder theory in the sense that only those with legitimacy claims and institutional identification can be considered as stakeholders. Stakeholders are those who have property/legal claims (shareholders), contractual agreements (creditors, employees, management, suppliers), moral responsibilities (society, customers) and presumed/legal claims (the environment, government, competitors).

5.3 Legitimacy Theory

Legitimacy theory is built on a socio-political view and suggests that firms are facing social and political pressure to preserve their legitimacy by fulfilling their social contract. This theory justifies the importance of the social and environmental dimensions of sustainability performance. Firms engage in voluntary disclosure activities to obtain legitimacy and thereby fulfil the "social contract," thus gaining the support of society.[18] The legitimacy theory suggests that social and environmental sustainability performance is desirable for all stakeholders including customers and non-compliance with social norms and environmental requirements threatens organizational legitimacy and financial sustainability.[19]

The legitimacy theory is important in improving the reputation of a company's products and services as desirable, proper, of a quality that is acceptable within the social norms and values and beneficial rather than detrimental to the environment and society. For example, tobacco companies may increase shareholder wealth, under the shareholder theory, by selling their products at the risk of those products being detrimental to the health of customers. Business sustainability should be an integral component of corporate culture, business environment and strategic decisions and actions, including supply chain management, particularly when there is a conflict between the corporate goals of maximizing profits and social goals. The existence and persistence of such a conflict requires corporations to establish and maintain sustainability strategies including supply chain policies, programs and practices to ensure their board of directors and senior executives set an "appropriate tone at the top" and take sustainability and the social interest seriously.

5.4 Signaling/Disclosure Theory

The signaling/disclosure theory helps in explaining management incentives for achieving all five EGSEE dimensions of sustainability performance and reporting ESP and GSEE sustainability performance, as well as investors' reaction to the disclosure of sustainability performance information.[20] This theory suggests that firms tend to signal "good news" using various corporate finance mechanisms including voluntary reporting of non-financial GSEE sustainability performance. However, the expected link between a firm's voluntary GSEE sustainability performance reporting and the use of these signals is ambiguous. Firm voluntary reporting may act as a complement to signal information about expected future performance. Alternatively, these signaling mechanisms could be a substitute suggesting a negative relationship between the probability of voluntary disclosure and the use of these signals.[21]

The signaling/disclosure theory suggests that firms with good sustainability performance differentiate themselves from firms with poor sustainability performance and thus, by sustainability reporting, firms signal their good sustainability performance, which cannot easily be mimicked by non-sustainable firms. This theory relates to the ability to communicate credibly with all stakeholders and supply chain partners regarding synergy, integration and the resource dependency of different components of supply chain management and the sending of a uniform signal regarding achievement of all five EGSEE dimensions of sustainability performance.[22]

5.5 Institutional Theory

Institutional theory focuses on the role of normative influences in the decision-making processes that affect organization structure and offers a structural framework that can be useful in addressing various issues, conditions and challenges that enable the structure to become institutionalized.[23] The focus is on the social aspects of decision-making, such as the decision to invest in CSR expenditures and the conditions under which the investment decisions on CSR or environmental initiatives are made and their possible impacts on the environment and society. The institution theory views a firm as an institutional form of diverse individuals and groups with unified interests, transactions governance, values, rules and practices that can become institutionalized. Institution theory primarily focuses on rationalization, legitimacy, and practicality and aspects of social structure and related processes in establishing guidelines and best practices in compliance with applicable laws, rules, standards and norms. Institutional theory posits that the institutional environment and corporate culture can be more effective than external forces (laws, regulations) in impacting organizations' structures and innovation that would result in technical efficiencies and effectiveness. A more pragmatic institutional theory promotes corporate sustainability by viewing a firm as an institution to serve human needs and protect the interests of all stakeholders from shareholders to creditors, employees, customers, suppliers, society and the environment. A company as an institution is sustainable as long as it is creating shared value for all stakeholders including shareholders. Thus, the implication of the institutional theory for promoting business sustainability is that social/environmental initiatives, corporate measures and ethical practices will ultimately reach a level of legitimization and best practice whereby failure to adopt them is considered irresponsible and irrational.

5.6 Stewardship Theory

Stewardship theory is derived from sociology and psychology and views management as custodians of the long-term interests of a variety of stakeholders rather than as exhibiting self-serving and short-term opportunistic behavior, as under agency theory. Stewardship is "the extent to which an individual [manager] willingly subjugates his or her personal interests to act in protection of others' [stakeholders] long-term welfare" and thus it is very applicable to the emerging concept of corporate sustainability.[24] Two aspects of this definition, long-term orientation and protection of interests of all stakeholders, are the main drivers of corporate sustainability. Stewardship theory is applicable to corporate sustainability because it considers management strategic decisions and actions as stewardship behaviors that "serve a shared valued end, which provides social benefits to collective interests over the long term."[25] Under the stewardship theory, management is the steward of all capitals from the financial capital provided by shareholders to the human capital offered by employees to the social capital extended by society and the environmental capital enabled by the environment.

The concept of sustainability performance and the sustainability theories discussed above suggest that a firm must extend its focus beyond maximizing short-term shareholder profit under the shareholder/agency theory by considering the impact of its operation and entire value chain on all stakeholders including the community, society and the environment. Disclosure of the EGSEE dimensions of sustainability performance, while signaling the company's sustainability performance and establishing legitimacy with all supply chain partners, poses a cost-benefit trade-off that has implications for investors and business organizations. For example, any environmental initiatives pertaining to reducing pollution levels or saving energy costs may require huge upfront capital expenditures but in the long run will also reduce contingent and actual environmental liabilities. Sustainability information on EGSEE is typically considered as a set of externalities beyond disclosure of financial performance which can be viewed positively (e.g., social and environmental initiatives, board diversity and independence) or negatively (e.g., natural resource depletion, pollution and human rights abuses) by market participants and supply chain partners. These factors are important determinants of firms' future performance, operational risks and supply chain management beyond the factors that are typically included in the basic financial statements.

Taken together, the six theories are not exclusive and there are other sustainability theories that have implications for business sustainability. Firms will realize that their main objective function is to create shareholder value in compliance with agency/shareholder theory while protecting the interests of other stakeholders under the stakeholder theory, contributing to society and human needs in accordance with the institutional theory, securing their legitimacy under the legitimacy theory, differentiating themselves from low ESG/CSR firms through the disclosure/signaling theory and pursuing the long-term interests of a variety of stakeholders as suggested by stewardship theory. According to the stakeholder theory, sustainability performance dimensions (ESP and GSEE) are viewed by stakeholders as value-added activities that create stakeholder value. In compliance with the signaling/disclosure and legitimacy/institutional theories, good firms (high sustainability performance) differentiate themselves from poor firms (low sustainability performance) by signaling their legitimacy as a good corporate citizen and by corporate transparency and reputation as well corporate culture. In accordance with the impression management and reputation risk management theories, voluntary disclosure of GSEE sustainability performance can be viewed by stakeholders in general and shareholders in particular as good corporate citizenship and as a socially and environmentally responsible image which enables the firm to create a good impression and manage its reputational risks. Thus, achieving legitimacy under the institutional/legitimacy theory is crucial in ensuring management makes a good impression and properly assesses its reputational risks.

The concept and theory of emerging business sustainability requires management to simultaneously consider divergent economic, governance, social, ethical and environmental issues. Stewardship theory enables management to effectively exercise stewardship over a broader range of financial and non-financial assets and capitals including financial, physical, human, social and environmental capitals. Stewardship, among other theories, enables firms and their management to translate GSEE sustainability performance to financial performance leading to value creation. The relationships between business, society and the environment are complex and often tense and management must realize ways to address the potential tension and maximize both ESP and GSEE sustainability performance. However, a single, cohesive and integrated theory of business sustainability is apparently lacking in explaining the multi-dimensional and apparently conflicting aspects of sustainability performance. Management is generally responsible for stewarding corporate resources including assets and capitals with an ethical vision toward how to benefit the broader range of stakeholders including society and the environment. Thus, management should not impose its vision of doing good on society but instead seek compliance with regulatory measures and best practices of sustainability in creating shared value for all stakeholders.

These theories, while explaining the possible tensions and constraints imposed on the main business objective of creating shareholder value, have often ignored the integration among various dimensions of sustainability performance. They have used a narrow aspect of sustainability performance that emphasizes either ESP under the shareholder theory or GSEE sustainability performance under the stakeholder, signaling, legitimacy and institutional theories. Nonetheless, under stewardship theory, management acts as the steward of strategic, financial, human, social and environmental capital, and as the active and long-term-oriented steward of all stakeholders including shareholders. Thus, stewardship theory is more relevant to business sustainability and can provide a means by which management can engage with all stakeholders and focus on the achievement of both financial ESP and non-financial GSEE sustainability performance. A combination of stakeholder and stewardship theories can be more suitable in explaining sustainability education, practice and research.

Regardless of which theory is more relevant to a particular firm, with perhaps an integrated theory being more effective, there should be a set of globally accepted sustainability-related standards to guide business organizations in advancing their sustainability initiatives.

6. SUSTAINABILITY STANDARDS

Sustainable business for organizations means not only providing products and services that satisfy the customer and doing so without jeopardizing the environment, but also operating in a socially responsible manner. The business literature suggests the use of sustainability standards developed by the International Organization for Standardization (ISO) in measuring both financial ESP and non-financial GSEE sustainability performance along with preparation of integrated sustainability reporting and obtaining assurance on sustainability performance reports.[26] The ISO standards and certifications can promote compliance with environmental regulations and social standards. Therefore, the ISO enables a consensus to be reached on solutions that meet both the requirements of businesses and the broader needs of society. Pressure to do so comes from customers, consumers, governments, associations and the public at large. At the same time, far-sighted organizational leaders recognize that lasting success must be built on credible business practices and the prevention of activities such as fraudulent accounting and labor exploitation. A comprehensive set of ISO standards is needed to explain the link between sustainability theories and all five dimensions of sustainability performance. Several standards of the ISO are relevant to the five EGSEE dimensions of sustainability performance.[27] Specifically, ISO 9000 on quality control, ISO 14000 on environmental programs, ISO 20120 on sustainability events, ISO 26000 on CSR, ISO 27001 on information security and ISO 31000 on risk assessment are relevant.[28]

6.1 ISO 9000

ISO 9000 is the standard that provides a set of standardized requirements for a quality management system regardless of what the user organization does, its size or whether it is in the private or the public sector. It is the only standard in the family against which organizations can be certified—although certification is not a compulsory requirement of the standard. The other standards in the family cover specific aspects such as fundamentals and vocabulary, performance improvements, documentation, training and financial and economic aspects. The ISO 9000 standards are intended to improve the quality of products and services and thus are directly related to enhancing financial economic sustainability performance (ESP). ISO 9000 can also be linked to non-financial GSEE dimensions of sustainability performance in the sense that it improves the quality of services and products provided by business organizations.

6.2 ISO 14000

The ISO 14000 family addresses various aspects of environmental management, risk assessment, reporting, and auditing. The very first two standards, ISO 14001:2004 and ISO 14004:2004 deal with environmental management systems (EMS). ISO 14001:2004 provides requirements for an EMS and ISO 14004:2004 gives general EMS guidelines. The other standards and guidelines in the family address specific environmental aspects including labeling, performance evaluation, life cycle analysis, communication and auditing. Guidelines provided in ISO 14000 regarding environmental performance, reporting and auditing are relevant to the environmental dimension of sustainability performance.

6.3   ISO 20121

ISO 20121 entitled "Sustainability Events" addresses resources, society and the environment. This standard offers guidelines and best practices to help manage sustainability efforts and events and control their social, economic and environmental impacts. ISO 20121 offers benefits for integrating its guidelines in all stages of management processes including corporate infrastructure and supply chain management that promote best business practices and reputational advantages.

6.4   ISO 26000

ISO 26000 covers a broad range of an organization's activity from economic to social, governance, ethics and environmental issues. It is a globally accepted guidance document for social responsibility that assists organizations worldwide in fulfilling their CSR goals. Social responsibility performance promoted in ISO 26000 is conceptually and practically associated with the development of achieving sustainable performance because the fulfillment of social responsibility necessitates and ensures sustainability development. ISO 26000 goes beyond profit maximization by presenting a framework for organizations to contribute to sustainable development and the welfare of society. The core subject areas of ISO 26000 take into account all aspects of the triple bottom line's (TBL) key financial and non-financial performance relevant to people, planet and profit.

- **People:** ISO 26000 encourages companies to recognize human rights as a critical aspect of social responsibility by ensuring the countries in which they operate respect political, civil, social and cultural rights of citizens.
- **Planet:** ISO 26000 promotes sustainable resource management to ensure that business organizations are not exploiting the environment in which they are operating.
- **Profit:** The primary goal of business organizations has been and will continue to be to earn profits in a socially responsible way to ensure shareholder value creation and the achievement of the desired rate of return on investment.

6.5   ISO 27001

The purpose of ISO 27001 is to offer organizations guidance on keeping information assets secure by providing guidelines and suggesting requirements for an information security management system (ISMS). The ISMS is a systematic approach to managing sensitive information and protecting its integrity, and helps identify the risks associated with important information and the control activities designed and implemented to manage those risks.

6.6 ISO 31000

The ISO 31000 standards set out principles, framework and process for the management of risks that are applicable to any type of organization in the public or the private sector. It does not mandate a "one size fits all" approach, but rather emphasizes the fact that the management of risk must be tailored to the specific needs and structure of the particular organization. Guidelines provided in ISO 31000 are applicable in the assessment and management of risks associated with all five EGSEE dimensions of sustainability performance. These risks include strategic, financial, compliance, operational, supply chain, cyberattack and reputational risks.

Implementation of these ISO standards in various dimensions of sustainability performance and certifications of compliance with the standards promote improvements in the quality of products and services that directly affect earnings, ensure compliance with environmental regulations and social standards, strengthen governance measures and ethical value and thus improve the effectiveness of sustainability performance. These standards also establish practical foundations that can be developed based on the sustainability theoretical framework. Sustainability reports reflecting all five EGSEE dimensions of sustainability performance are deemed to be useful when they are complete and accurate, and their reliability, objectivity and credibility are ascertained by ISO certification. These ISO certifications of sustainability performance provide external assurance about the credibility and legitimacy of the integrated sustainability reports disseminated to stakeholders.

7. GLOBAL IMPLICATIONS OF SUSTAINABILITY PRINCIPLES, THEORIES AND STANDARDS

Business organizations worldwide are now recognizing the importance of sustainability performance and the link between the financial ESP and the non-financial GSEE dimensions of sustainability performance. Justifications for business sustainability are moral obligation, social responsibility, maintaining a good reputation, ensuring sustainability, environmental conscientious, license to operate and creating stakeholder value. Social performance can be viewed by management as non-value adding and non-essential activities that may not necessarily increase shareholder value, but should improve the image and reputation of the company as a socially responsible citizen. Sustainability performance which can be driven by the signaling and legitimacy incentives measures how well a company translates its social goals into practice. Sustainability performance can be achieved from many activities focusing on producing and delivering high-quality products and services that are not detrimental to society. The goal is to become a positive contributor to the sustainability of the planet and to improve employee health and wellbeing beyond compliance with applicable laws, regulations, standards and common practices.

In creating shared value for all stakeholders, corporations identify the potential social, environmental, governance and ethical issues of concern and integrate them into their strategic planning and supply chain management practices. There are many reasons why a company should integrate sustainability performance to its corporate culture, business environment and supply chain management. These factors include pressure from the labor movement, the development of moral values and social standards, the development of business education and change in public opinion about the role of business, environmental matters, governance and ethical scandals. Companies which are, or aspire to be, leaders in sustainability are challenged by rising public expectations, increasing innovation, continuous quality improvement, effective governance measures, high standards of ethics and integrity, and heightened social and environmental problems.

Globalization created incentives and opportunities for business organizations and their stakeholders and executives to influence their business sustainability initiatives and strategies. Corporations can choose from a variety of sustainability initiatives with regard to the scope, extent and type of sustainability strategies, focusing on different issues, functions and areas. The sustainability program can be designed to minimize conflicts between corporations and society caused by differences between private and social costs and benefits, and to align corporate goals with those of society. Examples of conflicts between corporations and society are related to environmental issues such as pollution, acid rain and global warming, and issues such as wages paid by multi-national corporations in poor countries and child labor in developing countries. Corporate governance measures which include the rules, regulations and best practices of sustainability programs can raise companies' awareness of the social costs and benefits of their business activities. The benefits of a sustainability program include addressing environmental matters, reducing waste, reducing risk, improving relations with society and discouraging regulatory actions. Sustainability programs enable corporations to take proper actions to promote social good and advance social goals above and beyond creating shareholder value or complying with applicable laws and regulations (e.g., anti-pollution). Sustainability programs should also promote a set of voluntary actions that advance the social good and go beyond the company's obligation to its various stakeholders. Non-financial sustainability activities should be measured and disclosed in the same way that financial activities are.

Four implications of sustainability theories and standards are presented in this chapter for businesses to try to integrate the EGSEE dimensions of sustainability performance into their strategic decisions and actions. First, the business sustainability framework and its five EGSEE sustainability performance dimensions are driven by and built on the stakeholder theory, which is the process of creating shared value for all stakeholders. Second, the main goal and objective for business organizations is to maximize firm value. The goal of firm value maximization can be achieved under business sustainability by protecting the interests of all stakeholders including investors, creditors, suppliers, customers, employees, the environment and society. Business sustainability promotes the achievement of long-term financial performance that generates enduring future cash flows for investors to maximize long-term share value and thus overall firm value. Focusing on GSEE sustainability performance enables the achievement of long-term firm value maximization by creating value for shareholders while meeting the claims of other stakeholders. The third theme is the time horizon of balancing short-term and long-term performance in all five EGSEE dimensions of sustainability performance. The final theme is the multi-dimensional nature of sustainability performance in all EGSEE areas. Multi-dimensional EGSEE sustainability performance is interrelated and should be integrated to supply chain management.

The International Business Council of the World Economic Forum (WEF, 2018) developed a new paradigm for business sustainability which suggests a roadmap for corporate governance partnership between corporations and their boards of directors and investors, particularly shareholders, to achieve business sustainability performance of long-term investment and growth.[29] The new paradigm focuses on best practices of business sustainability and corporate governance in forging a meaningful, impactful and successful private sector solution in advancing business sustainability. The new paradigm suggests focusing on the achievement of long-term performance that generates shared value for all stakeholders. It is expected that the new paradigm will encourage:[30]

1. Public companies and their stakeholders, particularly investors, to support tax policies that enable and promote long-term investment.
2. Public companies and their stakeholders, particularly investors, to work toward creating long-term sustainable performance.
3. Close working relationships between government and corporations to obviate the need for regulation and legislation to enforce a longer-term approach.

8. SUSTAINABILITY RESEARCH

Much anecdotal evidence and many empirical findings suggest a positive relationship between financial ESP and non-financial GSEE sustainability performance for companies with strong commitment to governance, social and environmental efforts.[31] All five EGSEE dimensions of sustainability performance are important to stakeholders. However, ESP is regarded as the main objective for business organizations primarily because companies have to do well financially in order to do good for society.[32] A 2013 KPMG report suggests the key measures of ESP as being financial cash flows, earnings and return on investment, non-financial operational efficiency, customer satisfaction, talent management, innovation reputation, technology, competition, globalization and utilization of natural resources.[33] Prior research identifies the six measures of ESP as (1) average return on equity for the current year (2) sales scaled by total assets (3) sales growth scaled by total assets (4) ratio of market to book value of equity (5) research and development expenses scaled by total assets and (6) advertising expenses scaled by total assets.[34]

   Early sustainability-related research with a primary focus on CSR addressed the rationale for CSR expenditures and the relationship between CSR activities and firm performance.[35] In compliance with stakeholder theory, CSR/GSEE activities are viewed as an integral component of a firm's mission of protecting the interests of all stakeholders including society and the environment and as such GSEE expenditures are regarded as investments.[36] Much of the academic literature has focused on CSR with its drivers, performance and impacts on financial operations, earnings and market performance. The extant CSR literature, as reviewed below, suggests that CSR performance is associated with financial performance, how it affects the cost of capital, improves firms' valuation, impacts stock price crash risk, discloses private information, reduces exposure to risk of conflicts with stakeholders, reduces earnings management and discourages stock short selling and tax avoidance. Sustainability performance and reporting has been a topic of great interest in the supply chain management literature.

Five streams of related research address the various aspects of sustainability. The first stream of research consists of several papers[37] documenting the relevance of green and social initiatives to business by investigating whether it pays to be green and socially responsible and how business organizations should deal with environmental and social issues. This stream of research focuses on the relevance of social and environmental issues to firms' entire value chains from inbound and outbound logistics to processes and operations, finished products, customer interface, distribution channels and customer services.

The second stream of research discusses the benefits of sustainability and whether sustainability investments in environmental and social issues pay off in terms of customers' perception of products and services. This stream of research[38] often uses the term "sustainable supply chain management" (SSCM) to highlight managerial decisions and actions in achieving financial performance (management of materials, capital flows, production process and information) and other activities in dealing with environmental and social issues and their comparison with best practices in supply chain management.

The third stream of research discusses the theoretical framework for business sustainability and its implications for sustainability performance, reporting and assurance. These studies[39] suggest the use of multiple theories in relating sustainability performance to supply chain management and other managerial strategies.

The fourth stream of research pertains to the role and use of ISO standards and certifications in improving the quantity and quality of sustainability reporting and assurance. By focusing on the implementation of certification under ISO 14000 environmental standards, these studies suggest that such certification can promote compliance with environmental regulations and social standards.[40]

These four streams of related research use both conventional financial key performance indicators (KPIs) such as earnings and return on investment and conceptualization KPIs such as social and environmental performance in linking sustainability performance to financial performance and supply chain management.[41] Prior research, while examining several aspects of sustainability performance and reporting assurance, has not sufficiently addressed a holistic approach to integrate all five EGSEE dimensions of sustainability performance into firms' entire value chains from strategic planning by top-level management to purchasing and inbound logistics, production design and manufacturing process, distribution outbound logistics and marketing and customer services.

The final stream of research deals with the link between financial and non-financial GSEE dimensions of sustainability performance and the impact on firms' financial and market performance. Several studies find that corporations that initiate CSR disclosure programs typically exhibit better financial and market performance as evidenced by reductions in their costs of equity and increases in analyst coverage in the following year.[42] Other studies find that sustainability may result in improved firm performance as proxied by the associations between environmental supply chain practices and both accounting- and market-based financial and operational performance. Overall, these studies report a U-shaped relationship between financial and non-financial (CSR) dimensions of sustainability performance where very small and very large firms are more likely to engage in CSR activities and performance.

Taken together, these five streams of research primarily focus on environmental, social and governance (ESG) sustainability issues in an isolated fashion. These studies, while indirectly examining several aspects of business sustainability, have not sufficiently addressed a holistic approach of integrating all five EGSEE dimensions of sustainability performance into corporate culture, business model, management processes and value chains from the strategic planning of top-level management to purchasing and marketing and customer services.

Exhibit 2.2 provides a summary of a selected small sample of published articles on business sustainability and CSR-related research. Academic research reviewed in this section suggests some of the challenging key GSEE issues. They are: competition issues (the use of advertising and the arrival of new types of GSEE risk with new technology), environmental issues (climate change and regulatory changes for hazardous substances and waste), human rights (labor rights), product responsibility (access, safety, risk, disclosure labeling and packaging), bribery and corruption (financial reporting fraud, financial scandals, money laundering), respect for privacy, ensuring transparency and accountability, institutionalization of GSEE, stakeholder engagement, battle for talent, community investment, supply chain and product safety, social enterprises and poverty alleviation.

Mandatory and voluntary corporate disclosures provide vital information to the financial markets. The type and extent of voluntary disclosures have recently received considerable attention as more than 14,000 firms worldwide disclose sustainability information on various environmental, social and governance dimensions of their sustainability performance. Public companies are required to disclose a set of financial statements under the corporate mandatory disclosures regime and they also disclose other information through corporate voluntary disclosures. Looking from a macroscopic perspective at the issue of effecting widespread business sustainability practices through mandatory or voluntary schemes may give insights into how best to generate clear, concise and valuable sustainability reporting for different environments. A recent paper by Ioannou and Serafeim (2011)[43] seeks to ascertain how these interactions among, in this case, various countries' overall outlooks and contexts influence their leaning toward one dimension of sustainability or another. For example, the researchers found that firms in countries that encourage them to compete tend to focus less on environmental and social concerns while the same detriments are found in those countries with a majority/plurality of leftist governance. The reasons for the similarity between those two groups, disparate as the two groups may seem to be, lie in the conflicting motivations of the stakeholders in question. The paper suggests that, in the first case, the lower performance in environmental and social matters is due in large part to the increase in competitive efficiencies while the latter group's actions may be explained by higher corporate taxes and the subsequent fiscal inability to take on more CSR matters. There is a need for an active balancing of the various issues surrounding CSR by a dynamic set of regulations, guidelines, initiatives and best practices. To that end, there is a great demand for research in this area from the various perspectives of accounting, finance, economics, psychology, sociology, political science and other disciplines.

EXHIBIT 2.2 Synopsis of selected sustainability-related publications

Author(s)	Data Source(s)	Purpose	Dependent Variables	Explanatory Variables	Findings
Cho, Lee, and Pfeiffer	*Journal of Accounting and Public Policy* 2012	Examine whether CSR performance affects information asymmetry.	Information asymmetry	CSR performance scores from KLD STAT	That both positive and negative CSR performance reduce information asymmetry whereas the influence of negative CSR performance is much stronger than that of positive CSR performance
Davis, Guenther, Krull, and Williams	*Accounting Review* 2016, KLD database	Examine the association between corporate tax payments and CSR.	Cash taxes paid/ lobbying expenditures for tax purposes	CSR/ESG variables (environmental, social and governance)	CSR is negatively associated with five-year cash effective tax rates and positively linked to tax lobbying expenditures, suggesting that, on average, CSR and tax payments act as substitutes
Hoi, Wu, and Zhang,	*Accounting Review* 2013, KLD database, Compustat	Investigate the association between corporate social responsibility and tax avoidance.	Aggressive tax avoidance	Irresponsible CSR activities	Firms with excessive irresponsible CSR activities are more aggressive in avoiding taxes, suggesting that corporate culture affects tax avoidance
Huang, and Watson	*Journal of Accounting Literature* 2015	Review research on published in 13 top account-ing journals over the last decade.	CSR variables	Financial and market variables	Present information on (1) determinants of CSR; (2) the relation between CSR and financial perfor-mance; (3) consequences of CSR; and (4) the roles of CSR disclosure and assurance

(continued)

EXHIBIT 2.2 *(Continued)*

Author(s)	Data Source(s)	Purpose	Dependent Variables	Explanatory Variables	Findings
Hummel and Schlick	*Journal of Accounting and Public Policy 2016,* KLD database, Bloomberg	Examine the relation between sustainability performance and sustainability disclosure using voluntary disclosure and legitimacy theories.	Sustainability disclosure	Sustainability performance	Consistent with voluntary disclosure theory, superior sustainability performers choose high-quality sustainability disclosure to signal their superior performance whereas poor sustainability performers prefer low-quality sustainability disclosure to disguise their true performance and to simultaneously protect their legitimacy based on legitimacy theory
Jain, Jain, and Rezaee	*Journal of Management Accounting Research 2016,* KLD and Bloomberg databases	Investigate whether short sellers take into consideration CSR/ESG sustainability performance in making investment decisions.	Financial and market performance, Short interest	CSR/ESG sustainability variables	That firms' market value and future financial performance are lower, whereas operating risk is higher for firms with low composite ESG scores. Also, a negative association between ESG scores and short selling, indicating that short sellers avoid firms with high ESG scores and tend to target firms with low ESG scores

Khan, Serafeim, and Yoon	*Accounting Review*, 2016, KLD database, Sustainability Accounting Standards (SASB) database	Develop a novel data set to measure firm investments on material sustainability issues by hand-mapping recently available industry-specific guidance on sustainability materiality.	CSR performance classified as ESG strengths and concerns	Materiality Index	Firms with good ratings on *material* sustainability issues outperform firms with poor ratings on these issues whereas firms with good ratings on *immaterial* sustainability issues do not outperform firms with poor ratings on the same issues
Landrum and Ohsowski	*International Journal of Sustainability in Higher Education* 2017, Sustainability courses in the USA	Identify the content in introductory business sustainability courses in the USA to determine the most frequently assigned reading material and its sustainability orientation.	Sustainability management	Sustainability education, content analysis	In total, 55% of the top readings (courses) assigned in the sample advocate a weak sustainability paradigm, and 29% of the top readings (courses) advocate a strong sustainability paradigm

(continued)

EXHIBIT 2.2 (*Continued*)

Author(s)	Data Source(s)	Purpose	Dependent Variables	Explanatory Variables	Findings
Ng and Rezaee	*Journal of Corporate Finance* 2015, KLD database	Examine the association between economic sustainability performance and ESG sustainability performance and cost of capital.	Cost of capital	Economic and ESG sustainability variables	That economic and ESG sustainability performance is negatively associated with cost of equity, and that economic and ESG sustainability performance interactively affect cost of equity
Rezaee	*Descriptive Journal of Accounting Literature*, 2016	Present a synthesis of research in business sustainability in the past decade.	Business sustainability	Economic, governance, social, ethical, and environmental	The goal of firm value creation can be achieved when management create shared value for all stakeholders
Richter and Arndf	*Journal of Business Ethics* 2018	Investigate the CSR character of British American Tobacco (BAT) Switzerland.	Cognitive processes underlying the CSR decision-making process	An in-depth exploratory case study	That BAT Switzerland does not follow traditional patterns of building CSR and thus can be classified as a "legitimacy seeker," characterized by a relational identity orientation and legitimation strategies

8.1 Some Selected Recent Studies

A recent survey sponsored by the Investor Responsibility Research Center (IRRC) Institute in conjunction with the National Association for Environmental Management (NAEM) finds the following: (1) investors, companies and regulators are increasingly interested in the various dimensions of sustainability performance and their potential impacts on firm value (2) investors often complain about difficulties in obtaining meaningful sustainability information on non-financial GSEE performance and (3) companies are concerned about "survey fatigue" and the potential cost of providing sustainability information.[44] The survey also documents that (1) there is lack consistency among companies in capturing, storing, and disclosing sustainability information, which is tracked at different levels and details (2) there is an urgent need for improvements in communicating sustainability information to all stakeholders and (3) sustainability reporting and assurance guidelines and practices should be advanced and promoted to create consistency in reporting of sustainability information.[45]

The 2012 survey conducted by the MIT Sloan Management Review–Boston Consulting Group indicates that 31 percent of surveyed companies report that sustainability is contributing to their profits while 70 percent have considered sustainability permanently on their management agenda.[46]

According to greenbiz.com and sustainability development at UPS, there are five ways to convince senior executive about the vital importance of sustainability:[47]

1. Sustainability enables reduction of costs and improvement of efficiency.
2. Sustainability incentivizes organizations to focus on risk assessment, management and mitigations (in terms of financial, operational, compliance, strategic and reputational risks).
3. Sustainability creates new competitive and revenue opportunities.
4. Sustainability encourages innovation.
5. Sustainability promotes talented employee recruitment, development and retention.

Recent studies also find a positive association between the disclosure of CSR, one dimension of business sustainability, and both the costs of equity and debt capital.[48] Other studies, using sustainability data in 58 countries, find that the mandatory adoption of sustainability reporting was associated with increased social responsibility of business leaders; improved sustainable development, employee training and corporate governance; enhanced managerial credibility and ethical practices; and reduced bribery and corruption.[49] Another study investigates whether firms that disclose CSR information also produce more transparent and reliable financial information and find that socially responsible firms are less likely to engage in either accrual based (AEM) or real earnings (REM) management and to be the subject of SEC (SEC, 2010) investigations.[50] It appears that prior research in business sustainability is fragmented, with an integrated approach covering all EGSEE dimensions lacking. Different studies have addressed one or more components of business sustainability without a comprehensive framework for interdisciplinary integration.

The studies on CSR disclosure in Mainland China are built on the theories that developed in Western countries. Shen (2007) is among the earliest studies to examine the determinants of CSR reporting in Mainland China. Using Shanghai and Shenzhen

Stock Exchange-listed firms as samples, she finds that large and profitable firms are more likely to issue CSR reports.[51] Using 2008–2009 non-ST (Special Treatment) firms as samples, Fang and Jin (2012) find that large, profitable, and better-governed firms are more likely to provide CSR reports in Mainland China and that there is a significantly positive relationship between CSR disclosure and stock price, suggesting that investors favor CSR reporting.[52] As CSR disclosure provides more information to investors, it is predicted that firms with CSR are likely to be more transparent. Using 2008 A share firms listed in the Shanghai Stock Exchange as samples, Yang and Wang (2011) show that the earnings in firms with CSR reports are more informative than those without CSR reports.[53] Li and Xiao (2012) report that CSR disclosure is negative related to bid-ask spread, suggesting that CSR reporting reduces asymmetry of information between investors and firms.[54] They also find that firms with CSR disclosure are significantly positively associated with stock liquidity, confirming their hypothesis that investors favor firms with CSR disclosure. Ye and Zhang (2011) show significantly positive association between the deviation from optimal CSR performance and cost of debt.[55]

9. BUSINESS SUSTAINABILITY EDUCATION

The global investment community is holding public companies responsible and accountable for their business activities and their financial reporting process. As business schools are the main providers of professional accountants, they play important roles in preparing ethical and competent future business leaders who understand business sustainability. The public, policymakers, regulators, businesses the accounting profession and the academic community are now scrutinizing colleges and universities to explore ways by which to hold these institutions more accountable for achieving their mission in providing higher education with a relevant curriculum. Therefore, business sustainability education and research has recently been addressed by the global community and accreditation bodies. For example, the Association of Advanced Collegiate Schools of Business (AACSB) International has established an Ethics/Sustainability Resource Center which poses questions like "Do you think business schools should conduct more research on sustainability and how business can contribute to it?" on its website. All respondents as of July 17, 2012 have responded "Yes" to this question, suggesting there is an urgent need for research on sustainability.[56] The AACSB in its accrediting standards (Standard 9) identifies sustainability as a knowledge area by stating that "society is increasingly demanding that companies become more accountable for their actions, exhibit a greater sense of social responsibility and embrace more sustainable practices."[57]

The proposed integrated framework for defining the post-2015 UN development agenda suggests a vision built based on the core values of human rights, equality and sustainability for the entire world's present and future generations. Four key dimensions of the UN integrated framework are social development, economic development, environmental sustainability, and peace and security.[58] Despite progress in business sustainability education, it appears that research and education in business sustainability are fragmented, with an integrated approach covering all EGSEE dimensions lacking in many universities.

Business sustainability has been one of the top five emerging education majors in the past decade, as suggested by the *Chronicle of Higher Education*.[59] Sustainability is also considered one of the "hottest" and most demanding majors that lead to jobs.[60] Realizing the importance of incorporating sustainability into curriculums, academics are trying to integrate sustainability in higher education. Business sustainability practices require an integrated approach to sustainability reporting and assurance, and sustainability education demands a knowledge base in both financial ESP and non-financial GSEE sustainability performance and reporting. Despite the importance of sustainability disclosures to corporations and investors and the move toward integrated sustainability reporting and assurance, there is limited research on the integration of sustainability education into the business curriculum. Academics examine the coverage of sustainability education and find that as demand for and interest in sustainability education has increased in recent years, more business schools are planning to provide such education.[61]

A study was conducted in 2010 to provide a matrix of options for integrating sustainability into management and business education. It illustrates how the matrix can be used with the example of a business school in the Northeastern United States.[62] The matrix provides a framework for discussion and a framework for action by presenting faculty, staff and administrators with options for integrating sustainability into the business curriculum. Another recent study found that as demand for and interest in sustainability education has increased, more business schools are planning to provide such education.[63] Business schools can provide business sustainability education with a keen focus on providing cutting-edge sustainability education in all aspects of sustainability from theories to standards and risks as well as knowledge and practices on sustainability performance, reporting and assurance. The achievement of the sustainability education goal is constrained by many factors including the availability of teaching resources, cost and benefit feasibility, quality accreditation, technology and innovation, regulatory compliance and commitment from administrators and faculty.

10. CONCLUSIONS

Business sustainability requires business organizations to focus on achieving all five EGSEE dimensions of sustainability performance by taking initiatives to advance social good beyond their own interests and compliance with applicable regulations and enhancement of shareholder wealth. Simply put, business sustainability means enhancing corporations' positive impacts and minimizing their negative effects on society as well as minimizing harm to society and the environment, and creating positive impacts on shareholders, the community, the environment, employees, customers and suppliers.

The true measure of success for corporations should be determined not only by their reported earnings but also by their governance, social responsibility, ethical behavior and environmental performance. Business sustainability has received considerable attention from policymakers, regulators and the business and investment community over the past decade and it is expected to remain the main theme for decades to come. The sustainability theories, standards, policies, programs, activities and best practices presented in this chapter should assist business organizations worldwide to integrate the five EGSEE dimensions of sustainability performance into their corporate culture, business environment, strategic decisions and supply chain management, to improve their KPIs as well as the quality of financial and non-financial sustainability information disseminated to their stakeholders.

In conclusion, sustainability principles, the theoretical framework, the practical sustainability standards, research and education suggest that:

1. Sustainability strategies should be integrated into corporate decision-making processes including strategic decisions on supply chain management in promoting the achievement of all five EGSEE dimensions of sustainability performance.
2. Companies should use a principles-based approach in integrating both financial ESP and non-financial GSEE sustainability performance information into their corporate reporting.
3. All theories including agency/shareholder, stakeholder, signaling, legitimacy, institutional and stewardship focus on key measures of sustainable performance such as operational efficiency, customer satisfaction, talent management, and innovation derived from internal factors of strategy, risk profile, strengths and weaknesses, and corporate culture as well as external factors of reputation, technology, competition, globalization and utilization of natural resources.
4. These theories help in explaining companies' objectives of creating sustainable value for shareholders while protecting the interests of other stakeholders such as creditors, employees, customers, suppliers, government and society.
5. Cutting-edge business sustainability education should stem from relevant theories and standards to promote its integration into the relevant components of business curriculums in colleges and universities.

11.   CHAPTER TAKEAWAY

1. Integration of sustainability performance into business and investment analysis, supply chain management, and decision-making processes.
2. Incorporation of all five EGSEE dimensions of sustainability performance into business culture, corporate environment and business policies and practices.
3. Integration of sustainability principles into business sustainability practices in advancing the promotion of appropriate disclosure of sustainability performance.
4. Collaboration among all stakeholders to enhance the effectiveness of implementing sustainability theories and programs, and their development.
5. Periodic disclosure of both financial and non-financial KPIs relevant to sustainability performance to all stakeholders.
6. Faculty and administrators in colleges and universities should continue to add business sustainability education as a subject or topic to be integrated into relevant curriculums.
7. There are tremendous opportunities for playmakers, regulators, standard-setters, researchers, and academics to establish more effective sustainability guidelines, provide sustainability education and conduct sustainability research.

ENDNOTES

1. Z. Rezaee, "Business Sustainability Research: A Theoretical and Integrated Perspective," *Journal of Accounting Literature* 36 (2016): 48–64.
2. Global Impact Investment Network (GIIN), *What You Need to Know about Impact Investing*, 2018, https://thegiin.org/impact-investing/need-to-know/.
3. Global Impact Investing Network, *About Impact Investing*, 2013, http://www.thegiin.org/cgi-bin/iowa/resources/about/index.html.
4. Rezaee, "Business Sustainability Research."
5. A. C. Ng and Z. Rezaee, "Business Sustainability Performance and Cost of Equity Capital," *Journal of Corporate Finance* 34 (2015): 128–149.
6. The Sustainability Laboratory, *Sustainability: Definition and Five Core Principles*, 2015, http://www.sustainabilitylabs.org/assets/img/SL5CorePrinciples.pdf.
7. Ibid.
8. United Nations Global Compact, *Global Corporate Sustainability Report*, 2013, https://www.unglobalcompact.org/AboutTheGC/global_corporate_sustainability_report.html.
9. United Nations Global Compact, *Global Corporate Sustainability Report*.
10. A. Brockett and Z. Rezaee, *Corporate Sustainability: Integrating Performance and Reporting* (Hoboken, NJ: John Wiley & Sons, Inc., 2012).
11. Rezaee, "Business Sustainability Research."
12. A. Shleifer and R. Vishny, "A Survey of Corporate Governance," *Journal of Finance* 52 (1997): 737–783.
13. M. Jensen, "Value Maximization, Stakeholder Theory, and the Corporate Objective Function," *European Financial Management* 7 (2001): 297–317.
14. Ibid.
15. P. M. Clarkson, Y. Li, G. D. Richardson, and F. P. Vasari, "Does It Really Pay to Be Green? Determinants and Consequences of Proactive Environmental Strategies," *Journal of Accounting and Public Policy* 30 (2011): 122–144.
16. R. E. Freeman, *Strategic Management: A Stakeholder Approach* (Boston: Pitman, 1984).
17. R. K. Mitchell, B. R. Agle, and D. J. Wood, "Toward a Theory of Stakeholder Identification and Salience: Defining the Principle of Who and What Really Counts," *Academy of Management Review* 22, no. 4 (Oct. 1997): 853–886.
18. J. Guthriea and L.D. Parkerb, "Corporate Social Reporting: A Rebuttal of Legitimacy Theory," *Accounting and Business Research* 19, no. 76 (1989): 343–352.
19. Ibid.
20. M. Grinblatt and C. Hwang, "Signaling and the Pricing of New Issues," *Journal of Finance* (June 1989): 393–420.
21. Ibid.
22. B. L. Connelly, D. J. Ketchen, and S. F. Slater, "Toward a 'Theoretical Toolbox' for Sustainability Research in Marketing," *Journal of the Academy of Marketing Science* 39, no. 1 (2011):86–100.
23. J. Meyer and B. Rowan, "Institutionalized Organizations: Formal Structure as Myth and Ceremony," *American Journal of Sociology* 83 (1977): 340–363.
24. M. Hernandez, "Promoting Stewardship Behavior in Organizations: A Leadership Model," *Journal of Business Ethics* 80 (2008): 121–128.
25. M. Hernandez, "Toward an Understanding of the Psychology of Stewardship," *Academy of Management Review* 37, no. 2 (2012): 172–193.
26. P. Bansal and T. Hunter, "Strategic Explanations for the Early Adoption of ISO 14001," *Journal of Business Ethics* 46 (2003): 289–299.
27. International Organization for Standardization (ISO), *ISO 26000, Social Responsibility*, 2010, https://www.iso.org/standard/42546.html.
28. Rezaee, "Business Sustainability Research."

29. International Business Council of the World Economic Forum, *The New Paradigm* (WEF, 2018), http://www.wlrk.com/docs/thenewparadigm.pdf.

30. Ibid.

31. Rezaee, "Business Sustainability Research."

32. Rezaee, "Business Sustainability Research."

33. KPMG, *Beyond Quarterly Earnings: Is the Company on Track for long-term success?* Audit Committee Roundtable Report, Spring 2013, auditcommittee@kpmg.com.

34. Ng and Rezaee, "Business Sustainability Performance."

35. R. M. Roman, S. Hayibor, and B. R. Agle, "The Relationship between Social and Financial Performance," *Business and Society* 38, no. 1 (1999): 109–125.

36. R. E. Freeman, *Strategic Management: A Stakeholder Perspective* (New Jersey: Prentice-Hall, 1984).

37. C. J. Corbett and R. D. Klassen, "Extending the Horizons: Environmental Excellence as Key to Improving Operations," *Manufacturing and Service Operations Management* 8, no.1 (2006): 5–22.

38. P. Rao and D. Holt, "Do Green Supply Chains Lead to Economic Performance?" *International Journal of Operations and Production Management* 25, no. 9 (2005): 898–916.

39. C. R., Carter and P. L. Easton, "Sustainable Supply Chain Management: Evolution and Future Directions," *International Journal of Physical Distribution & Logistics Management* 41, no. 1 (2011): 46–62.

40. P. M. Clarkson, Y. Li, G.D. Richardson and F. P. Vasari, "Revisiting the Relation Between Environmental Performance and Environmental Disclosure: An Empirical Analysis," *Accounting, Organizations and Society* 33, nos. 4–5 (2008): 303–327.

41. P. R. Kleindorfer, K. Singhal and L. N. Van Wassenhove, "Sustainable Operations Management," *Production and Operations Management* 14, no. 4 (2005): 482–492.

42. D. Dhaliwal, O. Li, A. Tsang and Y. Yang, "Voluntary Nonfinancial Disclosure and Cost of Equity Capital: The Initiation of Corporate Social Responsibility Reporting," *Accounting Review* 86 (2011): 59–100.

43. I. Ioannou and G. Serafeim, "What Drives Corporate Social Performance? International Evidence from Social, Environmental and Governance Scores." Working Paper No. 11-016, Harvard Business School, 2010, http://www.hbs.edu/faculty/Publication%20Files/11-016.pdf.

44. P. A. Soyka and M. E. Bateman, "Finding Common Ground on the Metrics that Matter." Investor Responsibility Research Center (IRRC) Institute, 2012, https://irrcinstitute.org/wp-content/uploads/2012/02/FINAL_Metrics_that-Matter.pdf.

45. Ibid.

46. Boston Consulting Group (BCG), Press Release: Business Sustainability Survey, January 24, 2012, www.bcg.com.

47. K. Kuehn, "Five Ways to Convince Your CFO that Sustainability Pays," 2010, www.greenbiz.com.

48. D. Dhaliwal, O. Li, A. Tsang and Y. Yang, "Voluntary Nonfinancial Disclosure and Cost of Equity Capital: The Initiation of Corporate Social Responsibility Reporting," *Accounting Review* 86 (2011): 59–100.

49. I. Ioannou and G. Serafeim, "The Consequences of Mandatory Corporate Sustainability Reporting." Working Paper No. 11-100, Harvard Business School, 2011, http://ssrn.com/abstract=1799589.

50. Y. Kim, M. S. Park, and B. Wier, "Is Earnings Quality Associated With Corporate Social Responsibility?" *Accounting Review* 87, no. 3 (2012): 761–796.

51. Shen Hongtao, "Corporate Characteristics and Social Disclosure: Evidence from Listed Companies in China 公司特征与公司社会责任信息披露——来自我国上市公司的经验证据," *Accounting Research* (in Chinese) 会计研究 3 (2007): 9–16.

52. F. Hongxin and J. Yunyun, "Listed Companies' Contribution to Non-Shareholder Stake: Determinants and Value Relevance of Voluntary Disclosure 上市公司对非股东利益相关者的贡献—自愿披露的决定因素与价值相关性," *Research on Financial and Economic Issues* 财经问题研究 339, no. 2 (2012): 40–49.

53. Y. Hao and W. Jinzhi, 上市公司社会责任信息的价值相关性分析 *Finance and Accounting Communication* 财会通讯 11 (2011): 86–88.

54. L. Zhu and X. Qiupin, "Corporate Social Responsibility, Investor Behaviors and Stock Liquidity 企业社会责任、投资者行为与股票流动性," *Research on Financial and Economic Issues* 财经问题研究 340, no. 3 (2012): 24–31.

55. K. Ye and R. Zhang, "Do Lenders Value Corporate Social Responsibility? Evidence from China," *Journal of Business Ethics* 104, no. 2 (2011): 197.

56. AACSB International, Ethics/Sustainability Resource Center, 2012, http://www.aacsb.edu/resources/ethics-sustainability/.

57. AACSB International, "Eligibility Procedures and Accreditation Standards for Business Accreditation," 2015, www.aacsb.edu/_/media/AACSB/Docs/Accreditation/Standards/2013-bus-standards-update-jan2015.ashx.

58. United Nations Global Compact, *Guide to Corporate Sustainability*, 2014 https://www.unglobalcompact.org/docs/publications/UN_Global_Compact_Guide_to_Corporate_Sustainability.pdf.

59. K. Fischer and D. Glenn, "Five College Majors On the Rise," *Chronicle of Higher Education*, 2009, http://chronicle.com/article/5-College-Majors-On-the-Rise/48207/.

60. C. Gandel, "Discover 11 Hot College Majors that Lead to Jobs," *US News and World Report*, 2013, https://www.usnews.com/education/best-colleges/articles/2013/09/10/discover-11-hot-college-majors-that-lead-to-jobs.

61. Z. Rezaee and S. Homayoun, "Integrating Corporate Sustainability Education into the Business Curriculum: A Survey of Academics," *Journal of the Academy of Business Education* 15 (Spring 2014): 11–28.

62. C. A. Rusinko, "Integrating Sustainability in Management and Business Education: A Matrix Approach," *Academy of Management Learning & Education* 9, no. 3 (2010): 507–519.

63. Z. Rezaee and S. Homayoun, "Integrating Business Sustainability Education into the Business Curriculum: A Survey of Academics," *Journal of the Academy of Business Education* 15 (Spring 2014): 11–28.

CHAPTER 3

Institutional Settings in Asia Relevant to Business Sustainability

1. EXECUTIVE SUMMARY

Business organizations play important roles in society by interacting with a variety of constituencies in serving and creating values for all stakeholders. Public companies are increasingly focusing on business sustainability, as highlighted in chapter 1, and making progress on setting expectations for their suppliers to integrate sustainability into their strategies and practices. Proper communication of sustainability performance is important in disclosing commitments to create stakeholder value. Business organizations worldwide and in Asia produce financial and non-financial information to satisfy the needs and demands of all their stakeholders including investors, creditors, customers, employees, suppliers, government and society. This chapter presents Asian institutional settings relevant to business sustainability.

2. INTRODUCTION

The past decade has witnessed widening attention to accountability and social responsibilities of corporations caused by a wave of global financial scandals at the turn of the twenty-first century. This has led to the growing demand for corporate accountability on issues ranging from economic to social responsibilities. The demand for more transparent corporate reporting reflecting economic, governance, social, ethical and environmental (EGSEE) sustainable performance is increasing in the context of sustainability reporting. Corporate sustainability reporting originally focused on environmental and corporate social responsibility (CSR) matters and gradually emerged as presenting all multiple-bottom-line (MBL) issues. Sustainability reporting, CSR or MBL reporting reflects the role of corporations in society. Sustainability reporting focuses on both financial economic sustainability performance (ESP) and non-financial governance, social, ethical and environmental (GSEE) sustainability key performance indicators (KPIs) to ensure corporations are held accountable to all stakeholders.

3. GLOBAL MOVE TOWARD SUSTAINABILITY PERFORMANCE, REPORTING AND ASSURANCE

Business sustainability has been promoted for several decades as an integrated and holistic business model for senior management to focus strategically on the achievement of all five EGSEE dimensions of sustainability performance in creating shared value for all stakeholders. Sustainability factors of performance, disclosure and risk affect the company's financial performance, risk assessment, supply chain management and investment portfolios and thus should be considered in assessing operating and investment decisions. Business sustainability has gained more attention in recent years as institutional investors focus on the long-term ESP and integration of non-financial GSEE sustainability performance into their investment portfolio analyses. For example, Laurence Fink, the chairman and CEO of BlackRock, whose firm has US$4.6 trillion under management including US$200 billion in sustainable investment strategies, sent a memo to S&P 500 companies as well as European companies that his investment firm is now focusing more on long-term financial ESP and non-financial GSEE sustainability performance in investment analysis.[1]

Sustainability performance information can be disclosed on a voluntary or mandatory basis. Finland was the first country to adopt a mandatory sustainability reporting law in 1997, and other countries adopting similar laws include Australia, Austria, Canada, Denmark, France, Germany, Malaysia, Netherlands, Sweden and the United Kingdom.[2] Since 2015, Hong Kong listing rules made sustainability reporting mandatory for listed companies. In September 2015, the United Nations (UN) proposed a holistic framework of the Sustainable Development Goals (SDGs) to design indicators and an integrated monitoring framework in addressing the three dimensions of economic development, social inclusion and environmental sustainability.[3] The European Commission has long promoted CSR sustainability and its integration into corporate strategic decisions and has recently endorsed the adoption by the Council of the Directive on disclosure of environmental, social and diversity information for more than 6,000 companies for their 2017 financial year.[4] The 2018 Delaware Act in the United States is a voluntary disclosure regime requiring adopting reporting entities to provide reports on their sustainability and related standards and metrics starting on October 1, 2018.[5] The remainder of this chapter focuses on business sustainability in Asia.

4. INSTITUTIONAL SETTINGS IN ASIA

Each country has its own corporate governance measures, CSR programs, and sustainability initiatives that are shaped by its economic, cultural, political, social and legal requirements, circumstances and infrastructure. Corporate governance measures, CSR programs and sustainability initiatives can be established at corporate level or at national level, often with the integration of both levels. The business sustainability model and corporate governance system of a country with its internal and external mechanisms are determined by a number of interrelated factors including political infrastructure, cultural norms, legal system, ownership structures, market environments, level of economic development, sustainability initiatives, CSR activities and ethical standards.[6] In this chapter, institutional settings comprising the above elements will be examined to shed more light on each economy's development of business sustainability.

4.1 Institutional Settings in Mainland China

With the establishment of the People's Republic of China (PRC) in 1949, Mainland China introduced the socialist planning (command) economy following the

Soviet Union. Mainland China began to transform its planning system to a more market-oriented economy beginning in 1978. In the early 1990s, Mainland China implemented substantial economic reforms with the main focus on expanding the role of the private sector in its economy. Since then, most of the state-owned companies, except large monopolies, had been privatized or liquidated.[7] Many Mainland Chinese firms have been transformed from government entities to publicly traded state-owned enterprises (SOEs). The transition of the country's economic system from a centrally planned to a market-based economy fueled strong economic growth. The annual gross domestic product (GDP) growth was around 8.0 percent from 1978 to 1995. In 2013, Mainland China became the second-largest economy in the world after the United States. But Mainland China's GDP per capita of US$3,800 was much less than that of the United States. Mainland China's GDP increased to 6.9 percent year on year in the first half of 2017 and achieved 6.8 percent in the third quarter.[8] According to the forecast of the International Monetary Fund (IMF), real GDP in Mainland China is projected to be around 6.4 percent in 2018. As it enters the 13th Five-Year Plan period (2016–2020), the Mainland Chinese economy continues to grow at a fast pace but is gradually moderating as the population ages and the economy rebalances from investment to consumption, from external to internal demand, and from manufacturing to services.[9] The trend of GDP in Mainland China in the past two decades shows continuous and steady growth with moderating growth in recent years at about 6.4 percent. The remarkable economic growth achievement in Mainland China enables the country to have large amounts of environmental and social expenditure.

The Mainland Chinese concept of responsible business is largely influenced by Confucianism. Zi Gong (250–475 BC), Confucius' student, applied Confucianism in business and can be regarded as the first "Confucian Trader."[10] In ancient Mainland China, many Confucian traders followed and embraced Confucianism, creating the so called "traditional Chinese" CSR values. From 1949 to 1983, Confucianism gradually lost its eminence due to the prevalent political ideology. Especially during the Cultural Revolution, Confucianism was widely criticized as having dated values which were contradictory with communistic values. During this period, enterprises' main social responsibilities were to contribute to the community and the country. The economic reform in the 1900s generated a large number of private firms. Many of these private firms passively followed Western CSR requirements in order to qualify as suppliers of Western multi-national corporations (MNCs). Starting from 2000, several stakeholders including academics, governments, NGOs, and international organizations promoted CSR in Mainland China. The concepts of Harmonious Society, Outlook on Scientific Development and Ecological Civilization promoted by President Hu in the 2000s signified that the Mainland Chinese government had realized the importance of CSR.

Corporate environment including corporate governance and CSR activities in Mainland China has evolved in the past several decades through the transformation of the socialist system into a market economy system. To promote market-based corporate governance and corporate financing, stock exchanges in Shanghai and Shenzhen were established in the early 1990s.[11] Establishment of stock markets in Mainland China have enabled the equity and shareholding system to be integrated into corporate governance and CSR and become an important criterion for stock listing in the two exchanges. The Mainland China Securities Regulatory Commission (CSRC) was established by the Mainland Chinese government to monitor and regulate the capital markets. In January 2011, the Organization for Economic Co-operation and Development (OECD) released its report indicating that corporate governance in Mainland China had emerged and that Mainland China had shifted from a planned economy to a market economy with a focus on CSR.[12] It should be noted that CSR is a concept that is inherently consistent with the communist ideology. Until 1978, most Mainland Chinese enterprises were state-owned with administration-driven, unified and collective governance.

The Company Law and the Securities Law, both introduced in the 1990s, provide the foundation for developing a corporate governance framework in Mainland China.[13] The CSRC is responsible for developing regulations, policies and guidelines for listed companies and monitoring effective implementation and enforcement of related regulations and achievement of CSR objectives. In 2002, the CSRC issued a Code of Corporate Governance that promotes governance principles and mechanisms for protecting shareholder rights and monitoring directors and executives of listed companies.[14] Other corporate governance regulatory bodies including the National People's Congress, the State Council, the Ministry of Finance, the People's Bank of China, the Shanghai Stock Exchange and the Shenzhen Stock Exchange also participate in establishing listing standards and corporate governance and CSR guidelines.[15] A survey conducted by CSR-Asia and the Embassy of Sweden in Beijing in 2015 reports that the key driver of CSR development in Mainland China is government (76 percent) and the major incentive for implementing CSR sustainability is compliance with central government policy (55 percent).[16]

4.2   Institutional Settings in Hong Kong

Hong Kong is a Special Administrative Region (SAR) of the People's Republic of China. Its status is defined by the Basic Law (adopted in 1990 by the National People's Assembly of China), which serves as the "Constitution" of the Territory. The Basic Law encompasses the "One Country, Two Systems" principle and leaves the legal system (common law) largely unchanged. The institutional settings in Hong Kong are shaped by the executive power and the legislative power of the Hong Kong government Administration and the Legislative Council.

The territory is governed by a Chief Executive, elected by 1,200 voters including National People's Congress deputies representing Hong Kong legislators, eminent tycoons and personalities and representatives of the different functional constituencies including professional sectors such as legal, accounting, surveying and other industry representatives.[17] The government answers to the Chief Executive and is composed of 13 Bureaus and three Departments, which are assisted by 18 senior functionaries who hold the title of "Permanent Secretaries." The unicameral legislative power is conferred to the Legislative Council. The Council votes for and amends laws and is also empowered to introduce new legislation. It examines and approves the budget, tax policies and public expenditure; appoints judges to the Court of Final Appeal; and appoints the President of the High Court. It is also responsible for monitoring the conduct of the Chief Executive and ensuring the government appropriately applies its laws and policies.[18]

The four pillar economic sectors of Hong Kong are trading and logistics (21.6 percent), tourism (4.7 percent), financial services (17.7 percent), professional services and other services (12.5 percent). The percentages are in terms of value added to GDP in 2016.[19] On the other hand, the six industries which in Hong Kong have clear prospects of further development are cultural and creative, medical services, education services, innovation and technology, testing and certification services and environmental industries, which together accounted for 8.9 percent of GDP in terms of value added in 2015. Hong Kong is a highly attractive market for foreign direct investment (FDI) as it is the financial hub of Asia with a large presence of international and MNCs. According to the UNCTAD World Investment Report 2017, global FDI inflows to Hong Kong amounted to US$108 billion in 2016, ranked fourth globally and behind Mainland China (US$134 billion) in Asia. In terms of outflows, Hong Kong ranked third with US$62 billion in Asia, after Mainland China (US$183 billion) and Japan (US$145 billion).[20]

Hong Kong is popular cosmopolitan city for regional headquarters or representative offices of MNCs to manage their businesses in the Asia-Pacific region, particularly Mainland China. Hong Kong society, which is strongly influenced by Confucianism, is characterized by strong power distance (hierarchy in relationships), high collectivism, lower uncertainty avoidance, moderate masculinity and long-term orientation (Hofstede, 2003).[21] Because Hong Kong is a high collectivism society, local people who are in a group tend to get more privileges than people outside the group. Moreover, people from Hong Kong are more likely to respect their family and kinship group, because a child learns to respect the group to which it belongs, usually the family, and this would differentiate between group members and those outside the group. It is also common for Hong Kong people to seek help from relatives on various occasions particularly in a family-owned business.[22]

Hong Kong had been colonized by the British for over 100 years. During the colonial period, there existed cultural mismatches between the culture and orientation of the newly settled colonizer and the citizens of the city. This created a sociocultural plurality in Hong Kong although such plurality did not affect the corporate culture of Chinese family companies. Even with a dominant position in the international financial market and with significant investments by multi-national and international organizations in Hong Kong, Chinese family-owned businesses still play a significant role in Hong Kong's economy.

The cultural dimensions as defined by Hofstede (2003) are manifested in the corporate governance structure and CSR practices in family-owned firms in Hong Kong. In an effort to build investor confidence in corporate governance and CSR practices in Hong Kong companies, the government has made efforts to limit these cultural patterns especially for Hong Kong listed family-owned firms. In 1993 and 1994, to improve transparency and accountability, the Stock Exchange of Hong Kong (HKEX) and the Hong Kong Society of Accountants (HKSA) set up a Corporate Governance Working Group, which prescribed a number of recommended corporate governance practices and disclosures.[23] These included separation of the CEO and board chairman roles, a requirement of at least two (independent) non-executive directors, limitation of family members on the board to no more than 50 percent, and a requirement for two board committees to be composed mainly of non-executive directors. Disclosure requirements have been updated and the corporate governance code recommends that there should be a clear division of the responsibilities of board members to ensure a balance of power and authority such that power is not concentrated in any one individual.[24] It also included the mandatory disclosure of the relationship (including financial, business, family or other material/relevant relationships) among board members and between the chairman and the chief executive officer.

4.3 Institutional Settings in India

The institutional settings in India are influenced by its political system, economy and culture. Since its independence in 1947, India has become a democratic country, governed by the Bharatiya Janata Party (BJP)-led National Democratic Alliance (NDA), with a vibrant economy. Elected by an electoral college on July 25, 2017, Ram Nath Kovind is the fourteenth President of India representing the NDA.[25] India's president is not directly elected by residents but by an electoral college, similar to that of the United States.[26] In a recent budget session of the Parliament, the President stated that 2018 is the year for releasing the dream of "New India." The government of India is committed to pay more attention to the welfare of workers and women.

The economy of India has been transformed from an agricultural and trading base to a diverse economy of manufacturing and services. The agricultural sector retains its vital role in the Indian economy. India's mixed economy includes farming, agriculture, manufacturing, information technology (IT), e-commerce, automobile and services. Services are the main drivers of the Indian economy, contributing to more than 50 percent of India's output for less than one-third of its labor force.[27] The growing economy of the past 20 years has shifted India from a weak developing country into the one of the five major emerging national economies, namely Brazil, Russia, India, Mainland China and South Africa (BRICS). According to the Inclusive Development Index 2018, India was ranked at sixty-second out of 74 emerging economies with an improving trend.[28] Two recent reforms in India concerned the 2016 demonetization (cancellation of high-value banknotes) and the Goods and Services Tax (GST) reform in July 2017.[29] Based on the IMF's statistics, India's average GDP was 6.7 percent in 2017, and is estimated to be 7.4 percent in 2018 with the economy bouncing back from the two major recent policy reforms.

The total population of India is around 1.3 billion. According to the US *International Religious Freedom Report*, Hindus represent 79.8 percent of the population, Muslims 14.2 percent, Christians 2.3 percent and Sikhs 1.7 percent. Other religions include Buddhists, Jains, Zoroastrians (Parsis), Jews and Bahais.[30] Despite the existence of vastly diverse religions in India, people from different religions and cultures live together in harmony. Hindu philosophy has a strong influence on Indian CSR. According to the Merriam-Webster dictionary, *Vedanta* is "a conventional system of Hindu philosophy developing in a qualified monism the conjectures of the Upanishads on final reality and the release of the spirit."[31] The *Vedanta* principle is applied to individual goals (liberation) and business society. In the *Vedanta* philosophy, the goal of business is to maximize wealth for society through ethical behaviors. *Puruṣārtha* in the *Vedanta* philosophy represents the goals of human pursuit. An individual can realize himself or herself by balancing and fulfilling the four objectives of *Puruṣārtha*, namely *Dharma* (duty), *Artha* (wealth), *Kama* (desire) and *Moksha* (liberation), which ensure the wellbeing and progress of humanity and society.[32] From the CSR perspective, the role of business in sustainability development and environmental issues is well identified and encouraged in the *Vedantic* principles. For example, good *karma* is expected to be addressed for long-term goals. In the business setting, firms should not only focus on their own interests but also on the welfare of their stakeholders. The Hindu philosophy of *karma* has set a good organizational behavior (OB) framework by promoting CSR.[33]

4.4   Institutional Settings in Indonesia

After a long period of Dutch colonial rule and Japanese wartime occupation, the Republic of Indonesia was formally established in 1945. In the early days of its existence, Indonesia was a nation of diverse ethnic, religious and cultural backgrounds distributed across thousands of islands under a central government. Five years after its independence, Indonesia existed as a "United Republic of Indonesia" under the federal government for seven months but then changed back to the "Unitary State of the Republic of Indonesia" designation according to the 1945 Constitution. Indonesia's highest political body is the People's Consultative Assembly (Indonesian: *Majelis Permusyawaratan Rakyat Republik Indonesia*, MPR), which is elected by citizens and headed by the President of Indonesia. The MPR meets every five years to discuss and finalize national policy. Since the end of the New Order era, provincial governments have been demanding that the form of centralization be removed. Indonesia started legislating for regional autonomous governments as a means of decentralization in 1999, and this was implemented in 2001.

Since 1968, Indonesia has made some achievements in its economic development after adjusting its economic structure and product markets. In the first 25-year long-term construction plan, Indonesian GDP grew at an average annual rate of 6 percent and inflation was kept within 10 percent. In April 1994, Indonesia officially entered the second 25-year long-term construction plan, that is, the phase of economic take-off. The government has relaxed investment restrictions to attract foreign investment and has taken measures to vigorously support small and medium-sized enterprises (SMEs), develop tourism and increase exports. In 1997, the Financial Crisis broke out in Southeast Asia and Indonesia's economy declined sharply. The Indonesian government immediately launched a four-year national development plan to help restore Indonesia's economy to pre-crisis levels. By 2003, the country's economy had gradually returned to stability. In recent years, the Indonesian government has been strongly supporting efforts to curb Indonesia's traditional dependence on exports of raw materials while at the same time trying to enhance the manufacturing sector in the economy. Infrastructure development is also a key goal of the government, which is expected to have a great impact on the Indonesian economy.[34] After a slowdown in 2011–2015, Indonesia's economic growth accelerated again in 2016. According to the World Bank, Indonesia's GDP grew by 5 percent to US$93 million in 2016, which was 0.1 percent more than in 2015.[35]

While Indonesia is a market economy, SOEs and large private conglomerates dominate. Moreover, wealth is concentrated at the highest levels of society (and there is often a close link between the country's corporate and political elite). However, Indonesia's micro, SMEs, which accounted for 99 percent of the total number of Indonesian enterprises, are the backbone of the Indonesian economy. Indonesian business culture is deeply influenced by that of the Chinese, among whom Confucianism is representative. As most of Indonesia's large enterprises are controlled by Chinese,[36] Chinese culture has penetrated into the development of

Indonesian enterprises for a long time. Chinese corporate culture, derived from Confucian tradition, attaches great importance to family and friendship, so the relationship between family and business is substantial.[37] Many large businesses are controlled and owned by a single family. Besides the Chinese, Indonesia is also deeply influenced by Islamic culture. Islamic culture permeated the government and Muslim-owned enterprises very early had a profound cultural, social and moral impact on Indonesian society. For example, the Islamic Sharia provides that private persons shall not control public facilities (roads, oil, mining, etc.) that are essential to public society and that the results of private productivity shall benefit the community and the Muslim population.[38]

4.5   Institutional Settings in Japan

Japan began to build an economic power state at the end of World War II. From 1945 to 1952, the United States' occupation of Japan resulted in the rebuilding of the country and the creation of a democratic nation. In the late 1980s, domestic demand propelled the Japanese economy. This development involved fundamental economic restructuring, moving from dependence on exports to reliance on domestic consumption. However, during the same period, rising stock and real estate prices contributed to the buildup of an economic bubble in the Japanese economy. The economic bubble came to an abrupt end as the Tokyo Stock Exchange crashed in 1990–1992 as real estate prices peaked in 1991. Growth in Japan throughout the 1990s at 1.5 percent was slower than that in other major developed economies, giving rise to the term "Lost Decade." During this period, the Japanese government undertook "structural reform" intended to wring speculative excesses from the stock and real estate markets. Unfortunately, these policies led Japan into numerous deflation periods between 1999 and 2004. Meanwhile, Japan adopted another technique called "quantitative easing." The Bank of Japan expanded the money supply internally to induce expectations of inflation. By 2005, the economy finally began a seemingly sustained recovery. In July 2006, the government ended its zero-rate policy. In 2008, the Japanese Central Bank continued to have the lowest interest rates among developed economies. Deflation still persisted[39] and the Nikkei 225 Index had fallen over 50 percent. In yet another effort, on April 5, 2013, the Bank of Japan announced that it would be purchasing 60–70 trillion yen in bonds and securities to attempt to eliminate deflation by doubling the money supply in Japan over the next two years. Markets around the world responded positively to the government's proactive policies, with the Nikkei 225 adding more than 42 percent since November 2012. In 2017, strong global demand and the Bank of Japan's ultra-accommodative monetary policy continued to shore up Japan economic activities.

The CSR practice in Japan is largely influenced by Confucian culture. According to the survey of Boardman and Kato (2003),[40] in the Tokugawa period from 1603 to 1868, Japanese merchants set up merchant house codes (*kakun*) rooted mostly in Confucian philosophy, which was a common practice among merchant families. However, during the Meiji period (1868–1912), some individual entrepreneurs started to suspect the compatibility between high moral standards and predominant business operations.[41] From 1960, Japan also sought to change the application of CSR activities from the legal perspective. In 1991, following the crash of the Tokyo Stock Exchange, the Charter for Good Corporate Behavior, a prototype for today's

CSR, was created by the Nippon Keidanren in compliance with Western CSR practices. Starting from the 2000s, the Japanese government and other institutions issued several guidance documents and standards to further promote CSR in Japan. The Japanese government also enhanced cooperation among different sectors by using "round-table conferences on social responsibility." Japan has voiced opinions in the drawing up of international rules such as ISO 26000, the OECD *Guidelines for Multi-national Enterprises* and GRI and IIRC guidelines over the past years.[42]

4.6   Institutional Settings in South Korea

The Republic of Korea (South Korea) was founded on August 15, 1948. Syngman Rhee was the first President of the Republic of Korea. After the establishment of Rhee's administration, de jure sovereignty passed to the new government. In the 1960s, General Park Chung-hee came into power under the military. The government in the 1980s was committed to economic growth by focusing on computer technology development. South Korea joined the UN and the OECD in 1991 and 1996 respectively. Moon Jae-in won the presidential election in May 2017 and replaced the former president, Park Geun-hye, who was sentenced to a 24-year jail term due to a corruption scandal.

South Korea is a developed country with a mature financial market. It is a member of the G20 as well as the N11. With a mixed economy, South Korea is dominated by family-owned enterprises (*Chaebols*). The economic miracle (the Miracle of Han River) reflected the fast economic growth following the Korean War in the 1950s. According to data from the World Bank, real GDP in South Korea grew by about 2.8 percent in 2016 compared to the previous year. South Korean President Moon Jae-in's economic policy is well known as "*J-nomics*" with the slogan "from *Chaebol* to people."

The information and communication technology (ICT) sector plays an important role in the economic development of South Korea. According to the OECD Economic Outlook, South Korea is one of the world's top 10 exporters of ICT goods, which account for 10.4 percent of total value added.[43] Confucianism, Christianity and Buddhism are the major religions in South Korea. Confucian culture spread from Mainland China through the Korean peninsula during the Joseon Dynasty. Since then, Confucianism has influenced the country's political and social development through legislation and education. In South Korea, Confucian culture is a core element of classical morality and a source of wisdom for everyday living and affects the South Korean view of CSR.[44]

4.7   Institutional Settings in Malaysia

Malaysia is a Southeast Asian country occupying parts of the Malay Peninsula and the island of Borneo. It is known for its beaches, rainforests, and mix of Malay, Chinese, Indian and European cultural influences.[45] Malaysia declared its independence from the United Kingdom in 1957. Since then, it has continued to enjoy relative prosperity, initially as a commodity exporter (rubber, tin, then palm oil and petroleum), with total income rising at 6–7 percent each year from 1970 until 2000. Real GDP grew by an average of 6.5 percent per year from 1957 to 2005. The peak of its economic performance was between the early 1980s through the mid 1990s, as the economy experienced sustained rapid growth averaging almost 8 percent annually. High levels of foreign and domestic private investment played significant roles as the economy diversified and modernized. Once heavily dependent on primary products such as rubber and tin, Malaysia today is an upper-middle-income country with a multi-sector economy based on services and manufacturing. Malaysia is one of the world's largest exporters of semiconductor components and devices, electrical goods, solar panels and information and communication technology (ICT) products.

Malaysia is a parliamentary democracy with a federal constitutional monarchy. The Paramount Ruler, commonly referred to as the *Yang di-Pertuan Agong*, is the head of state as well as the leader of the Islamic faith in Malaysia. Legislative power is divided between federal and state legislatures. Executive power lies in the "cabinet" led by the Prime Minister who must be a member of the lower house and commands a majority. Malaysia has two constituencies of law with the first being applied to the entire nation, passed by parliament, and requiring a two-thirds majority to amend. The second is Sharia or Islamic law, which applies to Muslims. The states normally determine Sharia Law.

The culture of Malaysia is diverse and derives from the varied cultures of the people of Malaysia. The first people to live in the area were the *Orang Asal*, who are the indigenous people of Malaysia. They were followed by the Malays, who immigrated there from mainland Asia in ancient times. Chinese and Indian cultural influences increased over time during trade with these countries alongside immigration to Malaysia. Other cultures which influenced that of Malaysia include Persian, Arabic and British.

The role of religion in charity in Malaysia has unique characteristics. Malaysia is a Muslim-majority country, with their faith as Muslims requiring them to contribute 25 percent of their income to charitable causes. This institution of giving (*Zakat*) is well established in Malaysia. Corporate philanthropy is motivated by tax incentives. The majority of Malaysian companies engage in CSR activities to maximize performance opportunities.[46]

4.8   Institutional Settings in the Philippines

For more than three centuries, the Philippines was a colony of Spain; it was named after a sixteenth-century King of Spain. The Philippines was taken over by the United States in the early twentieth century after the success of the revolt against Madrid's rule. After the Philippines' declaration of autonomy in 1935, Spain and the United States continued to have significant influence on this country, especially in terms of language, religion and government. It was not until 1946 that the Philippines achieved full independence, with an American-style constitution.[47]

The Philippines has a well-organized and well-structured political system composed of the democratic republic, representatives and the President. In this political system, the President is both the head of state and the head of government. The state has a multi-party system. The political hierarchy in the Philippines is not a traditional vertical hierarchy. On the contrary, the country has a horizontal hierarchy which consists of three levels, namely the executive, the legislature and the judiciary. From each of these levels there are further subdivisions in the form of vertical levels. The political hierarchy begins with the national politicians and officials. It is divided into different departments to facilitate effectiveness of administrative work. Then there are the provincial, municipal and town levels. In 2016, Rodrigo Duterte took over as President of the Philippines.

Since the 1960s, the Philippines has adopted an open economic policy and actively attracted foreign investment with remarkable results. However, the economic development of the Philippines declined due to external factors such as the recession in the West. In the early 1990s, through a series of measures to revitalize the economy, the Philippines economy recovered. Since the beginning of the twenty-first century, the Philippines has taken the development of the economy and the elimination of poverty as the core policies of its administration. It has increased investment in agriculture and infrastructure construction, focused on the development of the tertiary industry and tourism, and implemented an export-oriented economic model, such that the economy continues to grow steadily. As of 2013, the main sources of foreign capital in the Philippines were from Japan, the United States, the United Kingdom, Germany, South Korea, Malaysia, Hong Kong and Mainland China, with investment in manufacturing services, real estate, financial intermediation, mining and the construction industries.

Bayanihan is a Filipino custom that derives from the Filipino word *Bayan*, which means a country, town or community. The word *Bayanihan* itself literally means "being in a bayan." It refers to the community spirit in which people work together to achieve a common goal. When people around them are urgently in need of help, Filipinos always reach out without asking anything in return. Such is the spirit that embodies the Filipinos' idea of helping each other.

The development of business responsibility in the Philippines is very much influenced by *Bayanihan*. *Bayanihan* is also defined as a pioneer of corporate philanthropy and CSR. Philanthropy has always been a tradition in the Philippines where personal donations and voluntary services are considered "hidden forces" in the social and economic life of the Philippines, among families and groups of relatives. It is particularly common in organizations or social welfare institutions associated with religious churches. The spirit of *Bayanihan* is also embodied in mutual aid lending.[48] While many Filipinos may not be financially well off enough to donate to charities, the country has many volunteers. Volunteerism is also a strong testament to the *Bayanihan* character and the spirit of CSR in the Philippines.[49]

However, it is also in this cultural context that the Philippines may be negatively affected in the development of CSR by amicable personal relationships. According to Lydia Sarmiento, former head of human resources of integrated poultry producer Vitarich Corp and current president of the family foundation, CSR in the Philippines stems from Filipinos' values of religious beliefs and a culture of caring for the family (including employees).[50] Because Filipinos' empathy leads them to help each other, when an employee makes an error in business, their colleagues are likely to cover up the problem for them even to the detriment of the company and shareholders. Managers may provide economic privileges to their family members as assistance, which has a negative impact on fair competition.

4.9 Institutional Settings in Singapore

Singapore was founded in the nineteenth century, when the British Empire established the city as a trading post. After years of development, the city has grown rapidly into a transit trade center, attracting immigrants from Mainland China, India, the Malay Islands and other regions. Singapore became a British colony in 1946. With the development of nationalism and promotion of autonomy, Singapore held its first general election in 1959. With a majority of 43 votes, the leader of the People's Action Party (PAP) became Singapore's first Prime Minister. On August 9, 1965, Singapore officially became an independent democracy.[51]

The Constitution of Singapore provides that executive power is vested in the President. However, the Constitution also gives the Cabinet the power of providing "general direction and control of the government." In most cases, the President acts on the advice of the Cabinet or departments under the Cabinet. In practice, the Prime Minister of the Republic of Singapore, appointed by the President, is the head of the government of the Republic. The Prime Minister is, by default, the most powerful person in the national regime. Lee Hsien Loong is Singapore's third Prime Minister, a position he held since 2004.

Singapore's economy has been growing rapidly since its independence in 1965. Its strong economic performance is the result of an open and outward-looking development strategy. During the past decades, the composition of Singapore's exports has evolved from labor-intensive products to high-value-added products dominated by electronics, chemicals and biomedicine. With the rapid growth of the financial and commercial sectors in the Singapore economy, the impact of the service industry on the Singapore economy has become eminent over the years. In 2017, services generated nearly 70 percent of nominal value added while the other 25 percent was generated by the commodity production sector.[52]

In response to changing challenges and opportunities, Singapore has been reassessing and formulating its long-term economic strategies and corresponding policies. To achieve its objective of becoming an international financial center, Singapore has taken various targeted measures. The Monetary Authority of Singapore has adopted a more enlightened and liberated approach to shift its focus from regulation to risk supervision. Besides this, the Monetary Authority of Singapore has implemented other measures such as actively developing the debt market, revolutionizing corporate governance, and making domestic funds more accessible to fund managers. Singapore's ability to develop into an Asian business and financial center was the result of its stable political and economic performance, excellent infrastructure, geographical location and a well-educated labor force.[53]

On January 15, 1991, the Singaporean government formally established the "Shared Values," which are the embodiment of Singaporean culture. The main content of the Shared Values includes specifically: "(1) Nation before community and society above self (2) Family as the basic unit of society (3) Community support and respect for the individual (4) Consensus not conflict and (5) Racial and religious harmony."[54] The CSR of Singapore is closely related to the culture of this country. The importance and influence of Shared Values on the successful implementation of CSR in Singapore cannot be underestimated.

Shared Values can be compared to an axiom of national faith or a national ideology. For CSR, "consensus not conflict," described by the fourth Shared Value, is particularly prominent and important because it is conducive to the harmony of the whole society. It also emphasizes the first Shared Value of communitarian interests and the legal concepts and legal system of the Singaporean elite, which are based on a cultural relativism and community-based understanding of the rights and obligations of individuals in society. The communitarian concepts of rights and responsibilities shape the approach to CSR in Singapore. In general, priority is given to the promotion of the rights and interests of the community rather than the interests of the individual. It should be noted that the concept of the rights of any stakeholder is not an important component of CSR disclosure in Singapore. Given the range of issues that could arise and the sensitive nature of CSR, a consensual approach was fully justified as it is consistent with Singapore's overall philosophy of governance.[55]

4.10 Institutional Settings in Taiwan

According to ancient Chinese records, Taiwan has been under Chinese jurisdiction since ancient times. In 1894, with the defeat of the Qing Dynasty in the Sino-Japanese War, Taiwan surrendered to Japan under the Treaty of Shimonoseki. At the end of World War II, Japan announced its acceptance of the provisions of the Potsdam Proclamation on August 15, 1945 and returned Taiwan to Mainland China. In 1949, when the Kuomintang was defeated in the civil war, its leader Chiang Kai-shek fled to Taiwan with the Kuomintang military and political personnel. Taiwan was once again separated from Mainland China. In 1979, the Standing Committee of the National People's Congress of Mainland China issued a letter to the Taiwan compatriot declaring a policy of peaceful reunification of Taiwan with the motherland, aiming to realize a genuine ceasefire between the two sides of the Taiwan Strait. In 1990, Taiwan established a non-governmental organization, the Straits Exchange Foundation (SEF), to deal with matters arising from cross-strait exchanges. In 1991, the Association for Relations (ARATS) was founded by Mainland China on Taiwan Strait issues. In 1992, the ARATS and the SEF reached a consensus (the "1992 consensus") stating that the two sides across the Straits would adhere to the One-China principle. So far, Taiwan and Mainland China have officially launched cultural and close relationship exchanges.

The Kuomintang government adopted the policy of planned economy and moderate intervention in the early period of its migration to Taiwan. With economic aid from the United States, Taiwan's economy was rebuilt through those difficult times. Since the 1960s, Taiwan has developed an export-oriented capitalist economic system in which the electronic and information industry accounts as the main export. The electronic and information industry in Taiwan occupies an important position in the global industrial chain. Most of the computer electronic components in the world are produced in Taiwan. International trade is the lifeblood of Taiwan's economy. Mainland China is Taiwan's largest trading partner both in imports and exports, followed by the United States and Japan. Unlike its neighbors South Korea and Japan, Taiwan's economy is dominated by SMEs rather than large conglomerates and MNCs. At present, the Taiwan authorities are actively promoting industrial transformation and enhancement as well as planning to focus on the development of cultural creativity, biotechnology, medical care, tourism, green energy and refined agriculture in six major emerging industries, along with ten major service industries.

Taiwan and Mainland China are culturally alike. Mainland China is typically recognized as a country with a Confucian culture and Taiwan is no exception. According to Ip (2008), Confucian family doctrine and nepotism in Taiwan are the two main factors that influence business ethics and CSR of Taiwanese enterprises.[56] Confucian family doctrine is the mainstream culture of Chinese-community countries and regions such as Mainland China, Taiwan, Hong Kong and Singapore.[57] Confucian family doctrine believes that the interests of the family are higher than those of the individual and the interests of family members are higher than the interests of non-family members. In the business context, the interests of the family are given priority in terms of power, values and wealth, while public interest is likely to be undermined by the notion of the primacy of family interest.[58] As a result of this cultural atmosphere, cronyism is popular and widespread. Cronyism in Asia places great emphasis on the concept of *guanxi*, which means relationship will matter and relations will provide help and support. *Guanxi* usually refers to connections among people who are close, particularly family members and friends. Once infiltrated into the government and corporate sectors, this cultural identity can lead to corporate scandals, government corruption and other misconduct. Therefore, family centered *guanxi* is a major cultural barrier to the implementation of CSR in Taiwan.[59]

4.11 Institutional Settings in Thailand

The Kingdom of Thailand is located in Southeast Asia. Known historically as Siam, the country was renamed Thailand in 1939 with Bangkok as its capital. Thailand's major language is Thai and the currency is the baht (THB). The military has ruled the country since 1947 and continues to have substantial influence on various government policies. A new military-drafted constitution was signed by King Vajiralongkorn in April 2017, which indicates that democratic regulation and rule may follow a general election expected to be held during 2018.[60]

In the 1960s, Thailand had made economic reforms in opening its market and attracting foreign investments. The export sector had diversified from agriculture to the electronic and textile sectors.[61] By the mid 1970s, Thailand had transformed from a socio-agricultural economy to an industrialized economy.[62] Since 1970, Thailand has made progress in its socio-economic development[63] with an average of 4.2 percent GDP growth per capita annually in purchasing power parity (PPP) terms. The development of tourism has provided more job opportunities for the residents of Thailand. The Thai tourism industry contributed around 9.4 percent of the GDP in 2017.[64]

Thailand experienced a difficult time during the 1997 Financial Crisis. At that time, His Majesty King Bhumiphol Adulyadej introduced the "Sufficiency Economy," which was intended to help recover the economy by achieving the sustainable development goals (SDGs) launched by the UN.[65] In the 2000s, Thailand's economy was transformed to a manufacturing and services-driven economy. Today, Thailand plays an important role in the electronic sector and the automobile's global value chains (GVCs). The electronic and automobile sectors represent 20 percent and 30 percent of the total manufacturing output respectively in Thailand.[66]

As the second-largest economy in the Association of Southeast Asian Nations (ASEAN), after Indonesia, Thailand is an upper-middle-income country with an open economy and a GDP of US$404 billion with 3.2 percent annual growth in 2016.[67] Over the past decade, Thailand has experienced slow economic growth, declining foreign direct investment and political instability.[68] With a view to catching up with the high-income countries by 2036, the government of Thailand introduced a *Thailand 4.0* vision that drives a productivity- and technology-oriented economy. Before *Thailand 4.0*, *Thailand 1.0* emphasized agricultural sector development, *Thailand 2.0* focused on the power sector while *Thailand 3.0* addressed heavy industry.[69] *Thailand 4.0* introduces structural reforms such as attracting FDI, enhancing policy framework, promoting innovation and improving human capital.

Buddhism is the primary religion in Thailand with around 95 percent of the population being Buddhist. Muslims account for about 4 percent and Catholics and Christians for less than 1 percent,[70] with the remaining population representing the Hindu, Sikh and Jewish religions. The Buddhist culture in Thailand is partially influenced by Chinese Taoism beliefs such as ancestor worship. Buddhism plays an important role in Thailand's cultural and social development. For example, Thai temples are characterized by tall domes, golden statues, unique architecture and amazing detail.[71] In the context of Thai business culture, relationship building plays an important role in both business and social engagements. The development of CSR is likewise influenced by Thai culture and traditional religious beliefs. "Doing good deeds for others and making merit" is an important value that guides Thai people to behave ethically, which is primarily practiced through philanthropy and charitable donations.[72] Hierarchy and seniority (age, authority, etc.) are important within the business organization. For instance, it is not appropriate for senior managers to meet junior representatives. Senior staff meet and negotiate only with those with comparable positions.

4.12   Institutional Settings in Vietnam

Before the 1945 August Revolution, Vietnam was a feudal colonial country under French colonialism.[73] The Socialist Republic of Vietnam (Vietnam) is located on the Indochinese peninsula with an estimated 94.58 million inhabitants in 2018.[74] The capital city has been Hanoi since Vietnam was reunified as the Socialist Republic of Vietnam. The main language is Vietnamese and the major religion is Buddhism.[75] Vietnam is a one-party socialist state. Established in 1930, the Communist Party of Vietnam (CPV) represents the interests of the working class and the state. The CPV adopts Marxism-Leninism and Hồ Chí Minh ideas as its firm ideological foundations, with supervision by its people. According to the World Report (2017), the CPV has a monopoly power that controls most of the nation's renovation, modernization and industrialization.[76] Under French colonial rule, the banking and credit system was governed by the Indo China Bank, which was the central bank in the Indochinese region (Vietnam, Cambodia and Laos) as well as a bank with commercial banking operations and investments. After the August Revolution, the economic and financial activities in Vietnam improved and there was a need for an independent and autonomous monetary, banking and credit system. In 1951, the Second Congress of the Vietnam Workers' Party established new economic and financial policies. President Ho Chí Minh announced that the Vietnam National Bank was to become the first people's democratic state bank in Southeast Asia. In 1961, the Vietnam National Bank was renamed the State Bank of Vietnam (SBV). The Vietnam economy experienced a recovery stage during the post-war period (1975–1985).[77] Since 1987, Vietnam's economy has been transformed from a "command market economy" to a "market-oriented economy."[78] In the 1990s, the operational mechanism of the banking system of Vietnam was transformed from a one-tier to a two-tier system.[79]

Export-oriented manufacturing and the agricultural sector contribute greatly to Vietnam's GDP, which is estimated at a 6.8 percent growth rate for 2017. The nation's increasing demand and foreign investment are also key drivers of the Vietnamese economy.[80] Compared to the same period in 2017, Vietnam's GDP was estimated to grow at 7.38 percent at national level for the first quarter of 2018 while final consumption increased by 7.13 percent, accumulated assets rose by 6.46 percent and the trade balance of goods and services increased 1.19 percent with a trade surplus compared to the same period in 2017.[81] The consumer price index increased by 0.73 percent while average core inflation rose by 1.32 percent in the first quarter of 2018 as compared to 2017.[82]

The major religions are Buddhism, Christianity, Islam, Caodaism and the Hoa Hao sect. Buddhism was the first introduced to Vietnam among the other main religions. However, Buddhism has deep influences on the nation's social and cultural development, in fine arts such as literature, architecture and painting. For example, many traditional pagodas and temples were built in the eleventh century, when Buddhism was the dominant Vietnamese religion.[83] The values of Vietnamese lifestyle were widely influenced by Confucian ethics, which can be traced from ancient Chinese culture. Confucianism has existed for more than 2,000 years of Vietnamese history.[84]

In Vietnam's business culture, seniority is very important in government agencies and SOEs. For example, it is expected that colleagues be addressed by a designation of their position in the firm, especially senior colleagues. Ranking is another important concept in Vietnam's business environment. Juniors are expected to show great respect to senior managers, such as display of an appropriate seating position or giving gifts to the seniors.[85]

5. INSTITUTIONAL SETTINGS IN ASIA RELEVANT FOR BUSINESS SUSTAINABILITY

Institutional settings in different Asian jurisdictions have been examined individually with respect to interrelated factors: political, cultural, legal, ownership, market environment, and level of economic development. Common factors together with differing factors will be analyzed by grouping jurisdictions which are similar and those which are different.

Firstly, Mainland China and Vietnam share a common ideology, communism, which they have shared throughout their respective histories. Both countries have one political party ruling the country though the levels of economic development are vastly different in terms of size, type, maturity and growth. Both have which form a significant part of their economic development. In recent years, both have been known as socialist countries which have adopted market economies at various stages of development. Mainland China started its economic reform in the 1970s with Vietnam being opened only in the early 1990s. This has significant influence on business sustainability as the Western influence of CSR arrived at different times.

Secondly, both countries share the same cultural philosophy, Confucianism, which has a great impact on CSR and business sustainability. In addition, Confucian philosophy is also a significant element of morality and ethics for Japan, South Korea and Indonesia as well as Taiwan, and it underlies the concept of CSR in these countries. On the other hand, Hindu philosophy has a strong influence on Indian CSR whereas Muslim philosophy impacts CSR in Malaysia. The unique *Bayanihan* culture influences CSR in the Philippines by focusing on a culture of caring for the family, including employees. Buddhism as the primary religion in Thailand has influenced CSR in this country by emphasizing "doing good deeds for others and making merits."

Thirdly, another two factors that have affected business sustainability are the level of economic development and market environments. Hong Kong and Singapore have been the two dragons in Asia in the last few decades, prior to the emergence of Mainland China, having been influenced by Western MNCs and Western CSR principles and practices. Hence, these two cosmopolitan cities stand out as having implemented and enforced CSR in their businesses to a much larger extent than other nations in Asia.

Finally, one common factor that can be identified as a significant influencer in Asia is *guanxi* or relationships. Most Asian countries have deep roots in "strong power distance," whereby relationships are characterized by hierarchy, i.e. seniors are higher in rank than juniors, parents are respected as seniors and children are regarded as juniors. Confucian philosophy forms the basis of relationships in Asian countries with many citizens being Chinese or having had close relationships and geographical proximity with Mainland China in ancient times. The strong influence of *guanxi* may have focused on family relationships in family-owned firms rather than pursuing public interests as advocated by CSR. The extreme protection of relationships may have led to corruption and cronyism, as documented and evidenced in Mainland China, India, Indonesia, Japan, South Korea, Malaysia, the Philippines, Taiwan, and Vietnam. Mainland China under the leadership of President Xi Jinping has come down hard on corruption and cronyism since shortly after he was elected General Secretary of the Communist Party of China (CPC) in the 18th CPC National Congress on November 14, 2012. The anti-corruption campaign covers all party members regardless of rank ("tigers and flies"). The Central Commission for Discipline Inspection (CCDI), an internal control institution of the CPC, is responsible for supervising party members in the anti-corruption campaign by inspecting and eliminating those who engage in corrupt activities and go against the CPC party line. In 2017, the CPC punished a total of 527,000 officials, including 58 officials at provincial/ministerial level or higher.[86]

6. CONCLUSIONS

Conventional corporate reports do not effectively reflect corporate accountability to all stakeholders. Future corporate reporting should disseminate high-quality financial and non-financial information regarding all five EGSEE dimensions of sustainability performance to enable all corporate stakeholders to make sound decisions. Sustainability performance information can be reported on a voluntary basis (United States) or on a mandatory basis (Europe and Hong Kong). Institutional settings in Asia have been examined, since these form the basis for voluntary or mandatory sustainability reporting. Several jurisdictions in Asia have adopted mandatory sustainability reporting (e.g., Hong Kong, Indonesia, Malaysia, Singapore and Thailand) in recent years (2016 and onwards) or are considering adopting mandatory sustainability reporting (Mainland China). Furthermore, many Asian countries are regarded as emerging markets and economies and thus their sustainability initiatives can provide incentives and guidelines for other developing economies.

Every country in Asia has its own CSR programs and sustainability initiatives that are shaped by its economic, cultural, political, social and legal requirements. Sustainability initiatives can be established at a corporate level or at a national level, often with the integration of both levels. The business sustainability model in Asian countries is determined by a number of interrelated factors including political infrastructure, cultural norms, legal system, sustainability initiatives, CSR activities, ethical standards, ownership structures, market environments and level of economic development. Business sustainability in Asia has made steady progress in the past decade. Development in Asia can be used as a benchmark for standard-setters (GRI, IIRC and SASB), business organizations and researchers in other countries in promoting sustainability performance, reporting and assurance.

7. CHAPTER TAKEAWAY

1. Business sustainability factors of performance, disclosure and risk are shaped by a number of interrelated factors including political infrastructure, cultural norms, and legal system.
2. State ownership structures, market environments and level of economic development have influenced the development of sustainability programs in Asia.
3. Business sustainability in Asia has grown significantly in the past decade.
4. Asian corporate governance measures and corporate culture including business sustainability initiatives are different from those of Western countries, due to the presence of state ownership, political influences, and internal control structure.
5. Business sustainability development in Asia has implications for the global advancement of business sustainability.

ENDNOTES

1. M. Levine, "Larry Fink Wants Companies to Talk More About the Future," February 2, 2016, https://www.bloomberg.com/view/articles/2016-02-02/larry-fink-wants-companies-to-talk-about-the-future.
2. Z. Rezaee, "Business Sustainability Research: A Theoretical and Integrated Perspective," *Journal of Accounting Literature* 36 (2016): 48–64.
3. Leadership Council of the Sustainable Development Solutions Network, *Indicators and a Monitoring Framework for the Sustainable Development Goals: Launching a Data Revolution for the SDGs*, 2015, http://unsdsn.org/wp-content/uploads/2015/03/150320-SDSN-Indicator-Report.pdf.
4. European Commission, Disclosure of Non-Financial Information: Europe Information: Europe Council, The European Economic and Socio-Environmental Issues, September 29, 2014, http://europa.eu/rapid/press-release_STATEMENT-14-291_en.htm.

5. Delaware General Assembly, House Bill 310: An Act to Amend Title 6 of the Delaware Code Relating to the Certification of Adoption of Sustainability and Transparency Standards by Delaware Entities, June 27, 2018, https://legis.delaware.gov/BillDetail/26304.
6. Z. Rezaee, *Corporate Governance Post-Sarbanes-Oxley: Regulations, Requirements, and Integrated Processes* (Hoboken, NJ: John Wiley and Sons, Inc., 2007).
7. Focus Economics, *China Economic Outlook*, 2017, December 18, https://www.focus-economics.com/countries/china.
8. World Bank, *China Economy Update*, 2017.
9. Organization for Economic Co-operation and Development (OECD), *OECD Economic Surveys: China*, 2017.
10. L. Wang and H. Juslin, "The Impact of Chinese Culture On Corporate Social Responsibility: The Harmony Approach," *Journal of Business Ethics* 88, no. 3 (2009): 433–451.
11. C. J. Lee, "Financial Restructuring of State-Owned Enterprises in China: The Case of Shanghai Sunve Pharmaceutical Corporation," *Accounting, Organization and Society* (2001): 263–280.
12. OECD (2011), Corporate Governance of Listed Companies in China: Self-Assessment by the China Securities Regulatory Commission, OECD Publishing, https://www.oecd.org/corporate/ca/corporategovernanceprinciples/48444985.pdf.
13. Ibid.
14. M. Gao and H. Zhang, *Report On Finance Governance Index of China's Listed Companies* (Economic Science Press, 2013).
15. Z. Rezaee, D. Lo, A. Suen, and J. Cheung, "Regulatory Reforms in the Aftermath of the 2007–2009 Global Financial Crisis and their Implication in Hong Kong," *US-China Education Review* 3, no. 5 (2013): 345–354.
16. CSR-Asia, *A Study on Corporate Social Responsibility Development and Trends in China*, 2015, http://www.csr-asia.com/report/CSR-development-and-trends-in-China-FINAL-hires.pdf.
17. "Hong Kong Economic and Political Overview," https://www.nordeatrade.com/se/explore-new-market/hong-kong/political-context?accepter_cookies=oui&.
18. Ibid.
19. Census and Statistics Department, Hong Kong SAR, *Hong Kong Monthly Digest of Statistics*, May 2018, https://www.statistics.gov.hk/pub/B71805FB2018XXXXB0100.pdf.
20. Economic and Trade Information on Hong Kong, 2017, http://Hong-Kong-Economy-Research.Hktdc.Com/Business-News/Article/Market-Environment/Economic-And-Trade-Information-On-Hong-Kong/Etihk/En/1/1X000000/1X09OVUL.Htm.
21. G. Hofstede, *Culture's Consequences: Comparing Values, Behaviors, Institutions and Organizations Across Nations* (Sage Publications, 2003).
22. Y. Tim and E. Wong, "The Chinese at Work, Collectivism or Individualism?" (unpublished working paper, 2001).
23. Hong Kong Society of Accountants, *First Report of the Working Group on Corporate Governance*, 1995.
24. Code on Corporate Governance Practices (HKEX), Appendix 14, p. 7, http://www.hkex.com.hk/-/media/hkex-market/listing/rules-and-guidance/listing-rules-contingency/main-board-listing-rules/appendices/appendix_14.
25. BBC News, "India Country Profile," 2018, http://www.bbc.com/news/world-south-asia-12557384.
26. BBC News, "Voting Under Way to Elect New Indian President," 2017, http://www.bbc.com/news/world-asia-india-40628027.
27. R. Kumar and D. Siddy, *Sustainable Investment in India* (Washington, DC: International Finance Corporation, 2009).

28. World Economic Forum, *The Inclusive Development Index 2018 Summary and Data Highlights* (Cologne/Geneva: World Economic Forum, 2018).

29. Focus Economics, *India Economic Outlook*, 2018, https://www.focus-economics.com/countries/india.

30. US Department of State, *International Religious Freedom Report for 2016*, 2016, https://www.state.gov/documents/organization/269174.pdf.

31. Merriam-Webster, "Vedanta," n.d., https://www.merriam-webster.com/dictionary/Vedanta.

32. B. Muniapan, "The Roots of Indian Corporate Social Responsibility: Practice from a Vedantic Perspective," in *Corporate Social Responsibility in Asia: Practice and Experience*, ed. K. C. P. Low, S. O. Idowu and S. L. Ang, s. l. (Springer, 2014).

33. Ibid.

34. Indonesia Investments, *Economy of Indonesia*, https://www.indonesia-investments.com/culture/economy/item177.

35. World Bank, GDP (Current US$), 2016, http://data.trendeconomy.com/dataviewer/wb/wbd/wdi?ref_area=EST&series=NY_GDP_MKTP_CD.

36. M. Kemp, "Corporate Social Responsibility in Indonesia: Quixotic Dream or Confident Expectation?" Technology, Business, and Society Programme Paper Number 6, United Nations Research Institute for Social Development, 2001.

37. G. Whelan, *Corporate Social Responsibility in Asia—A Confucian Context. The Debate over Corporate Social Responsibility* (New York: Oxford University Press, 2007) 105–118.

38. A. E. Widjaja, *Corporate Social Responsibility (CSR) and Its Current Practices in Indonesia*, Institute International Management, National Cheng Kung University, July 2011.

39. OECD, *Economic Survey of Japan 2008: Bringing an End to Deflation Under The New Monetary Policy Framework*, 7 April 2008.

40. C. M. Boardman, and H. K. Kato, "The Confucian Roots of Business Kyosei," *Journal of Business Ethics* 48, no. 4 (2003): 317–333.

41. B. Sharma, *Contextualizing CSR in Asia: Corporate Social Responsibility in Asian Economies* (Singapore: Lien Centre for Social Innovation, 2013).

42. Ministry of Economy, Trade and Industry, *Japan's Policy for CSR*, April 2012.

43. OECD, *OECD Digital Economy Outlook 2017: Spotlight on Korea*, 2017, https://www.oecd.org/korea/digital-economy-outlook-2017-korea.pdf.

44. W. Min, "Differing Attitudes to Confucianism across East Asia," 2012, https://www.nippon.com/en/column/g00072/.

45. Z. A. Yusof, D. Bhattasali, "Economic Growth and Development in Malaysia: Policy Making and Leadership" (Commission on Growth and Development Working Paper No. 27, Washington, DC: World Bank, 2008), http://documents.worldbank.org/curated/en/183111468050085348/Economic-growth-and-development-in-Malaysia-policy-making-and-leadership.

46. UBS-INSEAD, *UBS-INSEAD Study on Family Philanthropy in Asia*, 2011, https://Sites.Insead.Edu/Social_Entrepreneurship/Documents/Insead_Study_Family_Philantropy_Asia.Pdf.

47. BBC News, "Philippines Country Profile," January 2018, http://www.bbc.com/news/world-asia-15521300.

48. Asian Institute of Management RVR Center for Corporate Responsibility, *Corporate Social Responsibility in the APEC Region—Current Status and Implications*, Asia-Pacific Economic Cooperation, 2005.

49. B. Calica, "Bayanihan: The Spirit of CSR in the Philippines," TELUS International Philippines, March 12, 2012.

50. L. Rimando, "How CSR Is Evolving in the Philippines," Newsbreak, April 06, 2012.

51. "About Singapore," Singapore Tourism Board, 2018, http://www.visitsingapore.com.
52. Department of Statistics Singapore, *Share of GDP by Industry*, February 2018, https://www.singstat.gov.sg.
53. Monetary Authority of Singapore, *The Singapore Economy*, 2018, http://www.sgs.gov.sg/.
54. National Library Board Singapore, *Shared Values*, Singapore Government, July 2015.
55. E. K. B. Tan, *The State of Play of CSR in Singapore*, Social Insight Research Series, Lien Centre for Social Innovation Reports, 2011.
56. P.-K. Ip, "Corporate Social Responsibility and Crony Capitalism in Taiwan," *Journal of Business Ethics* 79, no. 1–2 (2008): 167–177.
57. Ibid.
58. G. Eweje, *Corporate Social Responsibility and Sustainability: Emerging Trends in Developing Economies* (Emerald Group Publishing Limited, September 2014), ISBN 978-1-78441-152-7.
59. B. Sharma, *Contextualizing CSR in Asia: Corporate Social Responsibility in Asian Economies* (Singapore: Lien Centre for Social Innovation, 2013).
60. PWC, *Thailand Overview*, 2018, http://taxsummaries.pwc.com/ID/Thailand-Overview.
61. OECD, *Multi-Dimensional Review of Thailand: Volume 1: Initial Assessment* (Paris: OECD Publishing, 2018).
62. APEC, *Corporate Social Responsibility in the APEC Region—Current Status and Implications: Economy Paper: Thailand*, s. l., Asia-Pacific Economic Cooperation, n.d.
63. H. Asada, *Thailand 4.0: Boosting Productivity*, 2018, https://oecdecoscope.wordpress.com/2018/04/12/productivity-and-thailand/.
64. https://www.wttc.org/-/media/files/reports/economic-impact-research/countries-2018/thailand2018.pdf.
65. APEC, *Corporate Social Responsibility in the APEC Region—Current Status and Implications: Economy Paper: Thailand*, s. l., Asia-Pacific Economic Cooperation, n.d.
66. OECD, *Multi-Dimensional Review of Thailand: Volume 1: Initial Assessment* (Paris: OECD Publishing, 2018).
67. "Thailand—Market Overview," 2017, https://www.export.gov/article?id=Thailand-market-overview.
68. Asia Foundation, *Thailand*, https://asiafoundation.org/where-we-work/thailand/.
69. H. Asada, *Thailand 4.0: Boosting Productivity*, 2018, https://oecdecoscope.wordpress.com/2018/04/12/productivity-and-thailand/.
70. International Student Volunteers, *Religion in Thailand*, 2013, http://www.isvolunteers.org/blog/religion-in-thailand/.
71. "Thailand Religion," https://www.travelonline.com/thailand/information/thailand-religion.html.
72. APEC, *Corporate Social Responsibility in the APEC Region—Current Status and Implications: Economy Paper: Thailand*, s. l., Asia-Pacific Economic Cooperation, n.d.
73. State Bank of Vietnam, "About SBV: The History," https://www.sbv.gov.vn/webcenter/portal/en/home/sbv/aboutsbv/history?_afrLoop=761215684780000#%40%3F_afrLoop%3D761215684780000%26centerWidth%3D80%2525%26leftWidth%3D20%2525%26rightWidth%3D0%2525%26showFooter%3Dfalse%26showHeader%3Dfalse%26_adf.ctrl-state%.
74. Statista, "Vietnam: Total Population from 2010 to 2022 (in million inhabitants)," https://www.statista.com/statistics/444597/total-population-of-vietnam/.
75. BBC News, "Vietnam country profile," 2017, http://www.bbc.com/news/world-asia-pacific-16567315.
76. Socialist Republic of Vietnam Government Portal, "Political System," http://www.chinhphu.vn/portal/page/portal/English/TheSocialistRepublicOfVietnam/AboutVietnam/AboutVietnamDetail?categoryId=10000103&articleId=10001578.
77. State Bank of Vietnam, "About SBV: The History."

78. International Finance Corporation, *Corporate Governance Manual* (Hanoi: World Bank Group, 2010).
79. State Bank of Vietnam, "About SBV: The History."
80. World Bank, "Vietnam Overview," World Bank Group, 2018, http://www.worldbank .org/en/country/vietnam/overview.
81. General Statistics Office of Vietnam, "Monthly Statistical Information: Social and Economic Situation in The First Quarter of 2018," 2018, https://www.gso.gov.vn/default_ en.aspx?tabid=622&ItemID=18799.
82. L. Hang, "Vietnam's CPI Increases by 0.73 Percent in February 2018," https://www.sbv .gov.vn/webcenter/portal/en/home/sbv/news/news_chitiet?leftWidth=20%25&show Footer=false&showHeader=false&dDocName=SBV329972&rightWidth=0%25& centerWidth=80%25&_afrLoop=2942741636561406#%40%3F_afrLoop%3D29427 41636561406%26centerWidth%3D80%2525%26dDocName%3DSBV329972%26 leftWidth%3D20%2525%26rightWidth%3D0%2525%26showFooter%3Dfalse%26 showHeader%3Dfalse%26_adf.ctrl-state%3D1c0fykf5xq_51.
83. Vietnam National Administration of Tourism, "Religon and Belief," http://www .vietnamtourism.com/en/index.php/about/items/2154.
84. Vietnam Culture, "Understanding Vietnamese Business Culture," http://www.vietnam-culture.com/articles-116-17/Understanding-Vietnamese-business-culture-and-etiquette .aspx.
85. Ibid.
86. C. Gao, "China's Anti-Graft Campaign: 527,000 People Punished in 2017," *The Diplomat*, 12 January 2018, https://thediplomat.com/2018/01/chinas-anti-graft-campaign-527000-people-punished-in-2017/.

CHAPTER 4

Drivers and Sources of Business Sustainability Initiatives in the World Including Asia

1. EXECUTIVE SUMMARY

In the aftermath of the global 2007–2009 Financial Crisis, business organizations have improved their performance in all five economic, governance, social, ethics and environmental (EGSEE) dimensions. Corporations have also begun to effectively communicate their EGSEE sustainability performance to their stakeholders through sustainability reporting. This chapter discusses initiatives and drivers of recent moves toward business sustainability performance and integrated sustainability reporting and assurance with a keen focus on Asia. Integrated EGSEE sustainability performance reporting can be promoted through market forces, mandatory sustainability reporting by listing standards of stock exchanges or a combination of mandatory and voluntary initiatives.

2. INTRODUCTION

Many public companies now voluntarily manage, measure, recognize, and disclose their commitments, events and transactions relevant to all five EGSEE dimensions of sustainability performance. More than 12,000 organizations worldwide are currently disclosing various EGSEE dimensions of their sustainability performance. According to the Global Reporting Initiative (GRI), in 2000, fewer than 50 global companies disclosed sustainability information on a voluntary basis. By 2005 this number had increased to 300 organizations, 1,500 companies in 2009, over 2,000 in 2010, over 5,000 in 2014, over 12,600 in 2017 with over 48,500 sustainability reports and the number keeps growing.[1] Although there is no mandatory guidance for sustainability performance reporting at this time, there are several guidelines on sustainability reporting for reference, including the reporting frameworks released by GRI, the integrated reporting guidelines promoted by the International Integrated Reporting Council (IIRC) and the guidelines established by the Sustainability Accounting Standards Board (SASB). An alternative to mandatory sustainability reports is to standardize sustainability performance reporting and assurance by considering (1) standardizing the inconsistent sustainability reports that are currently issued (2) establishing a globally accepted reporting framework for sustainability information that creates uniformity in objectively reporting all five dimensions of EGSEE performance (3) obtain assurance on sustainability reports and (4) ensuring that a wide range of users including investors have access to uniform and comparable sustainability reports accompanied by uniform sustainability assurance statements. These and other suggestions for developing a set of globally accepted best practices for sustainability performance, reporting and assurance are presented in this chapter, with the focus on drivers of sustainability performance reporting and assurance in Asia.

3.   GLOBAL MANDATORY BUSINESS SUSTAINABILITY INITIATIVES

Global and national stock exchanges have promoted sustainability performance reporting by adopting laws, regulations and listing standards that specifically mandate sustainability reporting. In recent years, many countries including Australia, Austria, Canada, Denmark, France, Germany, Hong Kong, Malaysia, Netherlands, Sweden and the United Kingdom have adopted mandatory reporting on financial economic sustainability performance (ESP) and non-financial GSEE sustainability performance.[2] It is expected that regulators in other countries will follow suit, moving toward mandatory sustainability performance reporting and assurance. Stock exchanges worldwide either require or recommend that their listed companies report sustainability information (e.g. Singapore Stock Exchange in 2011; Toronto Stock Exchange in 2014; Hong Kong Stock Exchange in 2016) and more than 6,000 European companies are required to disclose their non-financial GSEE sustainability performance and diversity information for their financial year 2017 and onwards.[3] The 2018 Delaware Act is a voluntary disclosure regime requiring adopting reporting entities to provide reports on their sustainability and related standards and metrics.[4]

In the past several decades, growing concerns regarding financial scandals (e.g. Enron, WorldCom, Palmarat and Satyam), environmental impact, corporate social responsibility (CSR), governance and ethical behavior of corporations have encouraged policymakers and regulators to address these concerns by establishing laws and regulations to mitigate their negative impacts. One example in the United States is the passage of the Sarbanes-Oxley Act (SOX) of 2002 to combat financial statement fraud and prevent further occurrences of financial scandals by improving corporate governance and financial reporting and audit processes.[5] SOX and the related Securities and Exchange Commission (SEC) regulations also require public companies in the United States to establish and maintain effective internal control over financial reporting to combat fraud and irregularities in reporting related to government laws and SEC regulations. The SEC in the past several decades has issued numerous regulations for disclosure of environmental liabilities including Releases Number 5170 in 1971, Number 5386 in 1973, the climate change interpretive guidance in 2010, and conflict minerals rules in 2012.[6] Other examples include the revision of the Danish Financial Statements Act to require sustainability reporting; the guidelines for external reporting of environmental, social and governance sustainability performance by state-owned companies in Sweden; and mandatory integrated reporting under the Grenelle II Act in France and the King Code III in South Africa.[7]

The European Commission has also been promoting CSR and its integration into corporate strategic decisions by defining CSR as "a concept whereby companies integrate social and environmental concerns in their business."[8] This definition of CSR suggests that companies should take actions beyond their mandatory requirements toward promotion of social and environmental benefits. Business sustainability with a keen focus on CSR can "benefit in terms of risk management, cost savings, access to capital, customer relationships, human resource management and innovation capacity."[9] Disclosure of this information promotes interaction with stakeholders that are related to non-financial GSEE sustainability performance. Disclosure of non-financial GSEE sustainability performance demonstrates companies' commitment and move toward achieving the European Union's treaty objectives of "the Europe 2020 strategy for smart, sustainable and inclusive growth including the 75 percent employment target."[10] At the same time, it facilitates stakeholders' engagement regarding sustainable growth and understanding of risks. It also helps stakeholders to build trust in a company by understanding how capitals are allocated and long-term investment goals are achieved.

On September 29, 2014, the European Commission endorsed the adoption by the Council of the Directive on disclosure of non-financial sustainability information for more than 6,000 large public companies for their financial year 2017.[11] The primary objectives of the Directive are to (1) increase transparency in sustainability reporting (2) increase sustainability performance on social and environmental matters and (3) contribute effectively to long-term economic growth and employment. In addition to reporting on their own operations, covered organizations will need to include information about their supply chain. Affected companies should report their environmental performance, social and employee-related information, human rights policies, anti-corruption and bribery issues and diversity on the board of directors.

4.   GLOBAL VOLUNTARY BUSINESS SUSTAINABILITY INITIATIVES

Several organizations worldwide including the GRI, the IIRC, the SASB, and the United Nations Global Compact have issued guidelines regarding voluntary disclosure of sustainability performance information (see Exhibit 4.1). These guidelines have been used by over 15,000 public companies worldwide in disclosing their sustainability performance information. This section summarizes these sustainability-related guidelines and their issuing organizations.

4.1   Global Reporting Initiative (GRI)

The GRI was launched in 1997 to bring consistency, complete and global standardization to sustainability reporting. The evolution of GRI guidelines began with the initial focus on incorporating environmental performance into corporate reporting with its first publication, *Sustainability Reporting Guidelines*, in 2000. The GRI *Sustainability Reporting Guidelines* are updated periodically to reflect new developments in sustainability reporting. The *G4 Guidelines* were released in May 2013 following *Guidelines* G1, G2 and G3. The *G4 Guidelines* present Reporting Principles, Standard Disclosures and an Implementation Manual for sustainability reporting on economic, governance, social and environmental sustainability performance metrics with ethics being integrated in the other four metrics. The *Guidelines* are to be used

EXHIBIT 4.1   Organizations engaged in sustainability

Guidelines/ Framework	Intent/Purpose	Description/Coverage
European Commission	European Directive requiring public companies to disclose their social, environmental, governance, and diversity performance activities	About 6,000 large European companies, starting 2017
Global Reporting Initiative (GRI)	Guidelines, G4 of which provides framework for disclosure of economic, governance, environmental and social performance	Global; all corporations, any type and size
Sustainability Accounting Standards Board (SASB)	Provides guidelines for reporting non-financial information on material and related appropriate KPI metrics on EGSEE performance that can be reported in Form 10-Ks	Publicly listed US corporations; foreign companies that are traded on a US exchange. Guidance by industry
United Nations Global Compact (UNGC)	A platform for business and non-business entities to develop a sustainable and inclusive global economy and report on non-financial performance in areas of human rights, labor, environment and anti-corruption	Business and non-business entities worldwide
Accountability AA1000 standards	Principles-based standards to assist organizations worldwide to become more sustainable, socially responsible and economically accountable	Global corporations, not-for-profit organizations and government entities
ISO 26000	Guidelines on the triple bottom line of focusing on planet, people and profit to assist organizations in effectively fulfilling their social responsibilities	All business and non-business organizations worldwide regardless of type and size
Stock Exchanges	Guidelines requiring stock exchanges to report their environmental, social and governance performance	Listed companies on the stock exchanges
International Integrated Reporting Council (IIRC)	Promotes integrated reporting by providing the International IR Framework for organizations to communicate ESG performance with their stakeholders	All business and non-business organizations worldwide regardless of type and size

by all organizations regardless of type, size, sector or location.[12] They focus more heavily on materiality considerations in the reporting process and the final report. The intention is to make sustainability reports "more relevant, more credible and more user-friendly" by encouraging companies to center their reports on the organization's goals and the impacts they may have on society and other stakeholders.[13] In these *Guidelines*, the GRI promotes sustainability reporting as a standard practice of disclosing sustainability-related issues that are relevant to companies' business and their stakeholders.

The *G4 Guidelines* have two parts. "Reporting Principles and Standard Disclosures" contains the criteria necessary for an organization to prepare its sustainability report "in accordance" with the Guidelines, and the "Implementation Manual" instructs practitioners how to apply the Reporting Principles, how to prepare disclosure information and how to interpret various concepts in the *Guidelines*. The *G4 Guidelines* also provide a set of steps to follow for preparing a sustainability report; organizations must: (1) obtain an overview and understanding of the *Guidelines* (2) choose their preferred option for compliance ("in accordance") from Core or Comprehensive based on the needs of the organization and its stakeholders (3) prepare to disclose the General Standard Disclosures, then the Specific Standard Disclosures (both based on the compliance option selected in step two) and finally (4) prepare the sustainability report and decide how to disseminate it.[14]

The two "in accordance" options, Core and Comprehensive, focus on the process of identifying materiality to be disclosed under the concept "Aspects," which refer to those issues that have the most influential economic, environmental and social impacts or have a marked effect on the decisions and perceptions of stakeholders. The "Core" information should be disclosed in all cases and is meant to serve as a background for disclosing the impacts of performance in the economic, governance, social and environmental sustainability dimensions. The Comprehensive option requires additional Standard Disclosures on strategy and analysis, governance and ethics and integrity along with more extensive reporting on all "indicators" related to the material aspects identified earlier in the process, beyond the minimum information in accordance with the Core requirements.[15] When preparing the report, a company may make reference to other documents where it has already made the required disclosure as long as the reference is "specific... and the information is publicly available and readily accessible." Electronic or paper-based reports are both acceptable and organizations may choose to file one or the other or both, depending on the information needs of the stakeholders and the organization's internal strategies and goals.[16] In compliance with the GRI *Guidelines* to date (G1 to G4), the types of sustainability report based on the GRI categories determine how disclosing firms apply GRI Frameworks in preparing their sustainability reports. GRI classifies sustainability reports by their level of application of the GRI Frameworks into 11 ranks or scores: "Undeclared," "Reference Only," "In Accordance" or "In accordance—Core," "Content Index Only," "C," "C+," "B," "B+", "A" and "A+". Higher ranks indicate a better application of the GRI Framework.

G4 introduces 27 new disclosures with a new structure for the guidance documents. G4 provides guidance on how to select material topics and illustrates the boundaries of where these occur. In G4, there are two options, core and comprehensive, which concentrate on the process for defining material aspects and boundaries. The revised guidelines emphasize materiality in sustainability reporting and include new and updated disclosures in various areas including governance (G4-34-55), ethics and integrity (G4-56-58), supply chain (G4-12 and G4-EC9), anti-corruption (G4-SO3-SO6), energy (G4-EN3-EN7) and greenhouse gas (GHG) emissions (G4-EN15-21).

An Implementation Manual was created in order to apply the reporting principles and prepare the standard disclosures.[17] There are five key changes for G4 as compared to G3.1:[18]

1. Materiality takes center stage: The *G4 Guidelines* require explanation of the process that companies use to identify their Material Aspects.
2. Reporting boundaries are redefined: According to the *G4 Guidelines*, companies need to report on the process they use to define the boundary of impact for each Material Aspect.
3. "In Accordance" levels replace A, B, C levels: Organizations need to meet more criteria to achieve the Core and Comprehensive "In Accordance" levels, and to use the *G4 Guidelines* more as a broad guide to reporting than they did to achieve the previous A, B or C application levels.
4. New governance disclosure requirements: The *G4 Guidelines* contain 10 new standard disclosures on governance. In order to achieve the "Comprehensive" level of reporting, organizations will need to disclose more complex governance indicators.
5. New supply chain requirements: Compared with G3, G4 requires companies to disclose significantly more information on supply chain impacts including details of supply chain assessments, risks identified, the organization's performance in managing these risks and the management processes put into place.

4.2 International Integrated Reporting Council (IIRC)

In April 2013, the International Integrated Reporting Council (IIRC) released the draft of its framework consultation on integrated reporting, which provides guidelines on communication with stakeholders.[19] The IIRC's proposed framework addresses fundamental concepts of integrated reporting and its guiding principles on an organization's strategy, governance, performance and prospects. In its December 2013 Integrated Reporting Framework, the IIRC promotes a more integrated approach to corporate reporting by improving the quality and quantity of information disseminated to providers of financial capital including shareholders and other stakeholders.[20]

In late September 2015, the IIRC appointed a new board of directors which was "reflective of the global reach and influence of integrated reporting across a broad range of areas including Africa, North and South America, Asia, Europe and Oceania." The board consists of experts from the areas of banking, finance, government and retail. According to Paul Druckman, IIRC Chief Executive, there are over 1,000 businesses worldwide using Integrated Reporting in 27 countries.[21] The IIRC suggests six capitals, including financial, manufactured, intellectual, human, social and relationship that organizations can utilize in creating shared value for all stakeholders.[22] In compliance with stewardship theory, management is responsible for stewarding corporate resources with an ethical vision toward how to benefit broader society. Management should not impose its vision of "good" on society but instead seek compliance with regulatory measures and the best practices of sustainability. However, a stewardship mindset requires that management strategies and actions be focused on the continuous improvement of both financial ESP and non-financial GSEE components of sustainability performance in compliance with the integrated sustainability framework of the IIRC.

The IIRC also published a framework known as the Integrated Reporting (IR) Framework expressing therein how companies should communicate with their shareholders. An "Integrated Report" is to promote transparency and address how an organization's performance will benefit both shareholders and stakeholders. The purpose of the report is to be a further extension of a company's external financial reports and is aimed at a specialist audience such as regulators and lawyers. The IIRC also released a prototype to aid compilation of non-financial information with financial information.

4.3　Sustainability Accounting Standards Board (SASB)

In October 2013, the Sustainability Accounting Standards Board (SASB) released its Sustainability Conceptual Framework consisting of objectives, key definitions and characteristics of sustainability accounting and disclosures, methodology for assessing the materiality of sustainability issues and structure, and harmonization of sustainability accounting standards.[23] The SASB has developed sustainability accounting standards relevant to disclosing material sustainability issues for 88 industries in 10 sectors. The SASB also establishes and creates sustainability accounting standards suitable for developing measures to disclose material sustainability issues. The standards launch the process for mandatory filings to the Securities and Exchange Commission, such as Forms 10-K and 20-F, through the first quarter of 2015. The SASB's objective is to create standards that enable peer-to-peer comparison between companies which can be useful for investment decisions and allocation of capital.[24] Harmonizing the SASB standards with existing disclosure standards avoids additional costs for companies and aligns the SASB's work with global corporate transparency efforts.

4.4　United Nations Global Compact

The 2013 *Global Corporate (GC) Sustainability Report* released by the United Nations Global Compact (UNGC) addresses the state of corporate sustainability today and presents the actions taken by companies worldwide in integrating sustainability to their strategies, operations and culture. The report encourages companies to engage their suppliers in the establishment of more sustainable practices and integration of sustainability into their supply chain processes.[25] The report finds that companies are increasingly focusing on business sustainability and making progress on setting expectations for their suppliers to integrate sustainability into their strategies and practices. Other benefits of sustainability reporting are improved reputation, increased employee loyalty and customer satisfactions. However, there are several sustainability challenges that could threaten business value if not addressed properly, but these challenges can also be turned into business opportunities.

According to the recent update of Global Sustainability by the UNGC, over 12,000 organizations in over 160 countries are currently members of the Global Compact with the majority coming from Europe and Latin America.[26] The new guide presents performance of member organizations worldwide with respect to the 10 principles of the UNGC that are related to human rights, labor, environment and anti-corruption. The report indicates that investors continue to demand that companies act upon and report sustainability, while companies have found that it is beneficial to integrate corporate responsibility into their business operations. These new initiatives enhance stakeholder relations, improve commitment by the CEO, promote internal information sharing and provide information for investors.[27]

4.5 United Nations Sustainable Development Goals (UNSDGs)

In September 2015, the United Nations (UN) proposed the holistic framework of the Sustainable Development Goals (SDGs) to design indicators and an integrated monitoring framework in addressing the three dimensions of economic development, social inclusion and environmental sustainability.[28] The 17 sustainable development goals (SDGs) build on the United Nations Millennium Development Goals of 2000–2015 and involve new areas such as climate change, economic inequality, innovation, sustainable production and consumption, and peace and justice.[29] These SDGs are relevant to three dimensions of sustainability development—economic, social and environmental development—and thus can be linked to all EGSEE dimensions of sustainability performance. The SDGs are supported by 169 targets and 232 indicators and are aligned with GRI G4 performance indicators.[30] Corporations frequently use these goals and link them to sustainability performance from the sourcing of raw materials and inputs for production to product innovations that lead to positive environmental, health or societal impacts; employee safety, training and diversity; compliance with ethical principles and human rights standards; and community initiatives in the areas of health and wellbeing, education, employment and economic empowerment. Exhibit 4.2 presents all 17 SDGs, indicating their relevance and link to the five EGSEE dimensions of sustainability performance. For example, SDG 6 is a proxy for clean water and sanitation; a combination of SDGs 5, 10 and 16 focuses on human rights and equalities; SDG 13 is related to climate action; and SDGs 14 and 15 are applicable to the nature of life below water and life on land.

The 17 United Nations sustainable development goals are related to sustainability reporting and assurance as they address economic, social, ethics, governance and ecological sustainability performance. In November 2016, the International Federation of Accounting (IFAC) published a policy document that considers many of the 17 SDGs relevant to the accounting profession including some addressing quality education, gender equality, economic growth, innovation, production, climate action and societal issues.[31] The 2017 report of PricewaterhouseCoopers (PwC) suggests that the majority of global firms (over 62%) referred to the SDGs in their reporting.[32]

4.6 Social Investment Forum (SIF)

In 2009, the Social Investment Forum (SIF) requested that the Obama Administration take the initiative to restore investor confidence by strengthening mandatory reporting on corporate environmental, social and governance.[33] To provide more

EXHIBIT 4.2   United Nations Sustainability Development Goals (UNSDGs)

SDG 1   **NO POVERTY:** a measure of Social dimension based on:
  (a) By 2030, ensure all make more than $1.25/day
  (b) Equal access to economic resources
  (c) Increase mobilization of economic resources
  (d) Economic and social protection measures by 2030

SDG 2   **ZERO HUNGER:** a measure of Social dimension based on:
  (a) End hunger by 2030 via universal nutrition (Zero Hunger Challenge)
  (b) End malnutrition by 2030
  (c) Increase investment in farming and agricultural endeavors
  (d) Adopt food commodity markets

SDG 3   **GOOD HEALTH AND WELLBEING:** a measure of Social dimension based on:
  (a) Maternal Mortality Rate ratio
  (b) Reduce infant mortality in all countries
  (c) End AIDS and other serious disease epidemics by 2030 (World Bank)
  (d) Universal reproductive care
  (e) Universal health coverage

SDG 4   **QUALITY EDUCATION:** a measure of Social dimension based on:
  (a) Expected years of schooling UNESCO (2016)
  (b) Literacy rate of 15–24-year-olds, both sexes (%) 2001–2013 UNESCO (2016)
  (c) Net primary school enrolment rate (%) 1997–2014 UNESCO (2016)
  (d) Population aged 25–64 with tertiary education (%) (a) – 2011 OECD (2016)
  (e) PISA score (0–600) 2012 OECD (2016)
  (f) Population aged 25–64 with upper secondary and postsecondary
  (g) Non-tertiary educational attainment (%) 2011–2013 OECD (2016)

SDG 5   **GENDER EQUALITY:** a measure of Social dimension based on:
  (a) Proportion of seats held by women in national parliaments (%) 2012–2014 IPU (2015)
  (b) Female years of schooling of population aged 25 and above (% male) – 2014 UNDP (2015)
  (c) Female labor force participation rate (% male) – 2010–2014 ILO (2016)
  (d) Estimated demand for contraception that is unmet (% of women married or in union, ages 15–49) 2015 WHO (2016)
  (e) Gender wage gap (% of male median wage) – 2012 OECD (2016)

(continued)

EXHIBIT 4.2   (*Continued*)

SDG 6   **CLEAN WATER AND SANITATION:** a measure of Social dimension based on:
  (a) Universal water access by 2030
  (b) Adopt universal sanitation rules by 2030
  (c) Universal management, ecosystems and sanitation of water by 2030

SDG 7   **AFFORDABLE AND CLEAN ENERGY:** a measure of Social dimension based on:
  (a) Universal, modern energy by 2030
  (b) 2x energy efficiency by 2030
  (c) Infrastructure upgrades

SDG 8   **DECENT WORK AND ECONOMIC GROWTH:** a measure of Social dimension based on:
  (a) Full employment for all by 2030
  (b) Increase youth employment
  (c) Create policies and technologies to increase economic growth and promote diversity
  (d) Promote protection of international labor rights
  (e) Eliminate forced labor

SDG 9   **INDUSTRY, INNOVATION AND PRODUCTION:** a measure of Social dimension based on:
  (a) Create an international infrastructure that promotes diversity and inclusion
  (b) Increase global accessibility to the internet
  (c) Encourage education in technology or research-related fields
  (d) Promote financial funding for development of infrastructure

SDG 10   **REDUCED INEQUALITY:** a measure of Social dimension based on:
  (a) Increase income growth of the bottom 40%
  (b) Include all races and sexes in economic, political, and social systems by 2030
  (c) Reduce cost of immigration
  (d) Improve regulation of the global marketplace
  (e) Work with World Trade Organization to increase wellbeing of developing nations

SDG 11   **SUSTAINABLE CITIES AND COMMUNITIES:** a measure of Social dimension based on:
  (a) Housing for all by 2030
  (b) Reduce death due to poverty or economic status
  (c) Improvement settlement management globally by 2030
  (d) Transportation for all by 2030

EXHIBIT 4.2 *(Continued)*

SDG 12 **RESPONSIBLE CONSUMPTION AND PRODUCTION:** a measure of the Environmental dimension based on:

(a) Percentage of anthropogenic wastewater that receives treatment (%) 2012 OECD (2016)

(b) Municipal solid waste (kg/year/capita) – 2012 World Bank (2016)

(c) Non-recycled municipal solid waste (kg/person/year) (a) – 2009–2013 OECD (2016)

SDG 13 **CLIMATE CHANGE:** a measure of the Environmental dimension based on:

(a) Energy-related CO_2 emissions per capita (CO_2/capita) – 2011 World Bank (2016)

(b) Climate Change Vulnerability Monitor (0–1) – 2014 HCSS (2014)

SDG 14 **LIFE BELOW WATER:** a measure of the Environmental dimension based on:

(a) Conserve and sustainably use the oceans, seas and marine resources for sustainable development

(b) Manage this resource which is vital to humanity and affects climate change

(c) Manage and protect marine and coastal ecosystems from pollution

SDG 15 **LIFE ON LAND:** a measure of the Social dimension based on:

(a) Red List Index of species survival (0–1) 2016

(b) IUCN and BirdLife International (2016)

(c) Annual change in forest area (%) 2012 YCELP & CIESIN (2014)

(d) Terrestrial sites of biodiversity importance that are completely protected

(e) (%) 2013

(f) BirdLife International, IUCN & UNEP-WCMC (2016)

SDG 16 **PEACE AND JUSTICE:** a measure of the Social dimension based on:

(a) Homicides (per 100,000 people) 2008–2012 UNODC (2016)

(b) Prison population (per 100,000 people) – 2002–2013 ICPR (2014)

(c) Proportion of the population who feel safe walking alone at night in the city or area where they live (%) 2006–2015 Gallup (2015)

(d) Corruption Perception Index (0–100) – 2014

(e) Transparency International (2015)

(f) Proportion of children under 5 years of age whose births have been registered with a civil authority, by age (%) 2014 UNICEF (2013)

(g) government efficiency (1–7) – 2015/2016 WEF (2015)

(h) Property rights (1–7) – 2014/2015 WEF (2015)

(continued)

EXHIBIT 4.2 *(Continued)*

SDG 17 **PARTNERSHIPS FOR THE GOALS:** a measure of the Social
         dimension based on high-income and all OECD DAC countries:

   (a) International concessional public finance, including official development assistance (% of GNI) 2013 OECD (2016)
   (b) For all other countries: Tax revenue (% of GDP) 2013 World Bank (2016)
   (c) Health, education and R&D spending (% of GDP) – 2005–2014 UNDP (2015)

accountability, the SIF proposed that the SEC require public companies to (1) report annually their sustainability information in compliance with the GRI *Guidelines* and (2) disclose their short-term and long-term sustainability risks in the Management Discussion and Analysis (MD&A) section of their 10-K forms.[34] Furthermore, in March 2013, the United States Sustainability Accounting Standards Board (SASB) released its proposed sustainability accounting standards for the health care sector (SASB, 2013).[35] A 2013 Joint Study by the Investor Responsibility Research Center Institute (IRRCI) and the Sustainable Investments Institute (Si2) reports that only 1.4 percent of S&P 500 companies (seven firms) issued a standalone sustainability report by mentioning sustainability reporting in their regulatory filing of 10-K reports whereas almost all S&P 500 companies disclosed at least one piece of sustainability information, 74% placed monetary value on their sustainability-related disclosures and about 44% of the companies linked their executive compensation to some type of sustainability criteria.[36]

4.7 Carbon Disclosure Project (CDP)

The Carbon Disclosure Project (CDP) is an international, not-for-profit organization that includes 655 institutional investors and collects information from companies on their greenhouse gas emissions and assessment of climate change and water risk and opportunity. The CDP website hosts many functions for the exploration of climate data. The CDP open data portal allows a user to search for relevant scores, emissions and other necessary data related to carbon indices and various other climate conditions. Through data sharing and outreach, the CDP's goal is to ensure that resources are used reliably and efficiently to reduce the overall carbon footprint. The Climate Disclosure Standards Board is an organization that hosts multiple nongovernmental organizations (NGOs) from around the globe. Similar to the CDP, the board intends to improve the dissemination of information regarding the environment through a framework which was released in 2010. On November 6, 2012, the CDP and the Climate Disclosure Standards Board (CDSB) released the XBRL climate change reporting taxonomy.[37] This taxonomy streamlines the process for reporting climate change information so that the information can be more easily promulgated into financial reports and disseminated to interested parties.

    In summary, in June 2011, the Global Initiative for Sustainability Ratings (GISR) developed environmental, social and governance (ESG) ratings standards with an eye toward maximum harmonization with leading complementary standard-setters, most notably the GRI, the International Integrated Reporting Committee,[38] the Carbon Disclosure Project and SASB.[39] Harmonizing SASB standards with existing disclosure standards avoids additional costs for companies and aligns the SASB's work with global corporate transparency efforts. In April 2013, the IIRC released the draft of its framework consultation on integrated reporting intended to provide guidelines on communication with stakeholders.[40] The IIRC's proposed framework addresses fundamental concepts of integrated reporting and its guiding principles on an organization's strategy, governance, performance and prospects. The products of the SASB, GRI and IIRC can be used in complementary ways for the development of a sustainability report for investors and all stakeholders. The SASB provides standards for mandatory filings whereas GRI and IIRC provide frameworks for voluntary reporting.

4.8 Delaware Act of 2018

The Delaware Certification of Adoption of Transparency and Sustainability Standards Act ("the Act") was signed into law on June 27, 2018. The Act becomes effective on October 1, 2018 and represents Delaware's initiative to support sustainability practices by enabling Delaware-governed entities to disclose their commitment to CSR and sustainability. It reflects Delaware's recognition that sustainability is a business imperative rather than a greenwashing and should be integrated into business environment and corporate culture in promoting innovation and long-term financial growth, societal benefits, and environmental protection. The Act is intended to demonstrate a firm commitment to sustainability and a proper response to the increasing calls from investors, customers and clients for greater transparency in sustainability practices. The Act is voluntary and applies only to those Delaware law governed entities that seek to become certified as reporting entities and gives much flexibility to entities to develop their own sustainability strategies and practices in meeting their sustainability goals and needs. However, there are several mandatory features of the Act that require the entity's governing body to approve its standards and assessment measures for those standards, and that measures be made publicly available. The Act also recommends that sustainability practices be addressed at the highest levels of the organization.

To meet this requirement, the board of directors must adopt resolutions creating "standards" including principles and guidelines for assessing and reporting the impact of the firm's activities on society and the environment. Top executives must establish proper measures and assess their effectiveness in evaluating sustainability performance to meet the requirements of sustainability standards approved by the board. The Act provides much flexibility for reporting entities to select their own standards and tailor them to the specific needs of their industry or business. Entities and their governing body (the board of directors) may seek insight from investors, clients and customers and obtain advice from third party experts and advisors in establishing their sustainability standards and assessment measures. Participating entities can obtain a certification of adoption of transparency and sustainability standards from the Delaware Secretary of State by: (1) establishing and preparing a standards statement including the standards and assessment measures (2) payment of relatively nominal fees to the Delaware Secretary of State (3) agreeing to the entity's becoming and remaining a reporting entity and (4) filing a renewal statement annually to continue as a reporting entity. The certification allows the reporting entity to disclose its participation in Delaware's sustainability reporting regime. The renewal certification statement requires disclosure relevant to changes to the entity's standards and assessment measures, an acknowledgment that its most recent sustainability reports are publicly available on its website and the related link to that site.

The 2018 Delaware Act is a voluntary disclosure regime requiring adopting reporting entities to provide reports on their sustainability and related standards and metrics. Reporting entities are provided with flexibility to report on their financial as well as non-financial sustainability performance while retaining privileged information, trade secrets or competitively sensitive information. Thus, Delaware entities that decide to disclose sustainability performance information can obtain certification from the Delaware Secretary of State under the Act as to their transparency in sustainability reporting. This certification demonstrates the entity's commitment to sustainability efforts and compliance with related sustainability standards and measures and serves as a signal to investors, clients and customers that the entity is taking its sustainability efforts seriously.

5. DRIVERS AND SOURCES OF BUSINESS SUSTAINABILITY INITIATIVES IN ASIA

An academic study has shown that CSR performance is better in developed economies than in developing economies and that Japan tops CSR performance ratings in Asia, followed by South Korea, India and Thailand.[41] Hong Kong lagged behind other Asian in the report. Another Country Sustainability Ranking Update on environmental, social and governance (ESG) profiles of 65 countries around the globe reveals that major Asian emerging economies showed the biggest gains in reporting and ranking. Countries such as South Korea, Indonesia, India, and Mainland China have all been able to increase their overall ESG scores.[42] The following subsections present sources and drivers of sustainability in 12 Asian jurisdictions.

5.1 Mainland China

Many sustainability initiatives have been undertaken in the past two decades in Mainland China. One of the reasons is due to the recognition by the government that environmental conditions have been deteriorating and that local governments, in particular, are sacrificing environmental concerns for GDP growth. These initiatives include enacting related laws, initiating policies and mandating CSR disclosures. The 13th Five-Year Plan (2016–2020) has directed the Communist Party and the government to mitigate these issues by setting pollution deduction targets, increasing energy efficiency, improving access to education and medical services, and expanding social care coverage.[43] Exhibit 4.3 presents the timeline, laws, regulations and guidelines on sustainability-related issues in Mainland China.

5.1.1 Legal Drivers
Along with economic development, several laws were enacted to deal with emerging social and environmental issues. The first version of the Company Law enacted in 1994 specifies labor rights in Articles 15 and 16. Subsequent

EXHIBIT 4.3   Timeline of CSR-related laws and events in Mainland China

Timeline	Historical Events
1988	Enterprise Law

Introduction Stage (1990s)

1990s	CSR began in Mainland China due to the requirements of Western multinational corporations as part of their supply chain management, as Mainland China became the "factory and shop floor" for the multinational world. During this period, CSR requirements from MNCs mainly focused on labor conditions and supply chain management
Dec 1989	Enactment of Environmental Protection Law
1992	Trade Union Law (passed in 1992)
1993	Consumer Protection Law (passed in 1993)
1994	Labor Law (passed in 1994) explicitly addressed issues of labor rights and employee rights
1998	The domestic private sector in Mainland China started to seriously engage CSR after the All-China Federation of Industry and Commerce (ACFIC) called on industry to contribute to disaster relief projects

Observation Stage (2000–2006)

Oct 28, 2001	Mainland Chinese government revised the Trade Union Law (TUL)
2003	The China Business Council for Sustainable Development (CBCSD) was established in 2003 as a joint initiative between the China Enterprise Confederation (CEC) and the World Business Council for Sustainable Development (WBCSD)
2004	State-Owned Assets Supervision and Administration Commission of the State Council (SASAC) has research team on sustainability reporting
	Tsinghua University's Department of Construction Management has research team on sustainability reporting
2005	Mainland Chinese President Hu Jintao introduced a socio-economic goal "building a harmonious society" to emphasize CSR development
	China National Textile and Apparel Council developed a Social Responsibility Management System—the China Social Compliance 9000 for the Textile and Apparel Industry
	Ministry of Civil Affairs is responsible for China Charity Awards
Oct 27, 2005	The term "corporate social responsibility" first appeared in the third version of the Company Law of China

Development Stage (since 2006)

2006	President Hu Jintao at the Central government Economic Working Conference stated that the government should encourage corporations to establish modern business values and to assume social responsibility. Company Law gives explicit recognition to CSR; it requires companies to adhere to social and business ethics as well as fulfill social responsibilities.

(continued)

EXHIBIT 4.3   *(Continued)*

Timeline	Historical Events
	Sixty-six members of the Executive Committee of Foreign Investment Companies (ECFIC), a self-regulated organization for MNCs in Mainland China, issued a document entitled *Beijing Declaration on CSR*, in which they agreed to promote MNCs' CSR in Mainland China and commit to the harmonious development of business and society through self-regulation on 12 issues, including law, taxes, intellectual property, employment, employee rights, environmental stewardship, social welfare, corporate information disclosure and corporate citizenship
May 2006	The Bank of China launched the first Social Responsibility Investment (SRI) fund in Mainland China, the Sustainable Growth Equity Fund
Sep 2006	Shenzhen Stock Exchange released a set of *Social Responsibility Guidelines for Listed Companies*
2007	More than 1,400 MNCs in Mainland China published a Written Proposal for Fulfilling Social Responsibilities, advocating compliance with regulations and laws, high product and service quality, employee protection, harmonious employment relationships, biological environment protection and energy conservation
	The Mainland China Banking Regulatory Commission required the State Environmental Protection Administration to pass on details of corporate environmental law violators to Mainland China's central bank, which blocked or withdrew loans to a dozen such companies
July 2007	Mainland China officially launched the first of its green finance policies
Oct 2007	Shanghai Pudong New Area government published index evaluation of CSR; 60 criteria referring to ISO 26000
Oct 15, 2007	President Hu Jintao's report at 17th Party Congress addressed social development by focusing on improving people's livelihoods
Nov 2007	The China Banking Regulatory Commission released *Recommendations on Strengthening Large Commercial Banks' Social Responsibilities*, which require large banks to comply with the 10 basic principles of the UN Global Compact
2008	The State-Owned Asset Supervision and Administration Commission issued *Guiding Advice on Fulfilling Social Responsibility by Central Enterprises*
	The World Bank awarded Mainland China a US$441 million loan to help promote clean energy technologies and reduce emissions from Mainland China power plants
Feb 2008	"Green Insurance" policy regulating insurance companies and "Green Securities" policy regulating Mainland China's capital markets implemented
Apr 2008	Eleven industrial associations jointly presented the *Social Responsibility Guide of the China Industrial Companies and Industrial Associations*

EXHIBIT 4.3   (*Continued*)

Timeline	Historical Events
May 2008	The Shanghai Stock Exchange issued two official documents, the *Shanghai CSR Notice* and the *Shanghai Environmental Disclosure Guidelines*
Dec 2008	The Shanghai Stock Exchange further accelerated CSR disclosure by mandating three types of companies to issue annual CSR reports—companies listed in the Shanghai Stock Exchange Corporate Governance Index, companies that list shares overseas and companies in the financial sector
Apr 2009	Global Compact Local Network China was formally launched
Aug 2009	Shanghai Stock Exchange published the "Social Responsibility Index," selecting the top 100 socially responsible companies listed on the stock exchange
Feb 2010	The Asian Development Bank approved a US$135 million loan to Mainland China for developing low-carbon coal-fired power plants
Apr 24, 2014	Mainland Chinese government revised the Environmental Protection Law for the first time
Jan 1, 2015	The new Environmental Protection Law entered into effect
May 24, 2015	The Shanghai Stock Exchange (SHSE) released *Notice on Information Disclosure Period Matters for Listed Companies*
May 30, 2016	SHSE released *Guidelines for Suspension and Exemption of Information Disclosure of Listed Companies*
Aug 26, 2016	The first eco-friendly asset-backed securities—the Green Asset-backed Securities of ABC Huiying-Goldwind Sci & Tech Wind Power Tolling Right and Income Right—were listed on the SHSE
Dec 2016	Environmental Protection Tax Law

legislation clarifies the responsibilities of firms in environmental protection, labor protection, and philanthropy. In 2006, Mainland China amended the Company Law and incorporated the concept of CSR into the law. More specifically, Article 5 of the law requires "a company should comply with the laws and administrative regulations, social morality, and business morality. It shall act in good faith, accept the supervision of the government and the public, and bear social responsibility." To give enterprises incentives to engage in CSR, the Corporate Income Tax Law (2007) was introduced to allow the tax-deductible donations from 3 percent to 12 percent of annual profits.

5.1.2 Political Drivers   The Communist Party of China (CPC) plays an important role in leading Mainland China's government to promote CSR. In 2003, Outlook on Scientific Development was proposed at the Third Plenary Session of the 16th Central Committee, emphasizing the goal of socio-economic development as "putting people first and aiming at comprehensive, coordinated and sustainable development" (CPC Central Committee, 2003). In 2006, the concept of corporate involvement in promoting greater social responsibility was officially put forward by the Central Party Committee with the issuance of the Decision on Building a Harmonious Society.[44] The government then released the *Guidelines for Corporate Responsibility Reporting in China*.

At the suggestion of the State Council in October 2011, Mainland China's Corporate Social Responsibility Monitoring and Evaluation System released the document *Strengthening Major Activities of Environmental Protection* suggesting that Mainland China has put environmental protection in an important strategic position and continuously made progress in resolving environmental problems over past years.[45] In November 2013, social responsibility was announced as one of the eight focus areas for further reform for Mainland Chinese State-Owned Enterprise (SOEs) at the Third Plenary Session of the 18th Central Party Committee on comprehensive reform. In late 2013, the Third Plenary Session of the 18th Central Committee of the Communist Party of China (CPC) decided to focus on changes designed to "improve the development outcomes evaluation system; correct the tendency of evaluating social performance simply based on the economic growth rate; pay more attention to employment, income, social security, people's health status, environmental damage, ecological benefits, excess capacity..." On July 15, 2014, President Xi Jinping gave a speech at the Sixth BRICS Summit titled "New Start, New Prospect and New Impetus," which called for the "unswerving promotion" of "sustainable economic growth."[46]

5.1.3   State-Owned Enterprises (SOEs)   Mainland China's SOEs are major players in the economy. Since the mid 1980s, many Mainland Chinese firms have been transformed from government entities to publicly traded SOEs. Mainland China's SOEs are under political pressure to comply with the official guidelines and are more likely to report their CSR performance. As the majority shareholder, the government controls and manages the SOEs through the State-Owned Assets Supervision and Administration Commission of the State Council (SASAC). In 2008, the SASAC issued the policy directive *Guidelines to the State-Owned Enterprises Directly Managed under the Central government on Fulfilling Corporate Social Responsibilities*. It also announced its *Corporate Social Responsibility Guidelines for the Central Level State-Owned Enterprises* to encourage them to participate in CSR reporting.[47] In 2009, during a meeting with the leaders of SOEs, the SASAC mandated all SOEs under their management to set up CSR mechanisms within their governance structures. By the end of 2012, the SASAC further mandated all SOEs under its supervision to publish their first CSR report if they had not already done so. This policy initiated the subsequent momentum that led to the release of more than 1,600 Mainland Chinese sustainability reports. Half of these reports were from SOEs or listed companies and they represented a significant jump from the 22 CSR reports issued in Mainland China between 1999 and 2005.[48]

5.1.4   Multinational Corporations (MNCs)   MNCs have significant influence on CSR sustainability in Mainland China. Mainland China began to attract MNCs to invest in 1978. The Western CSR concepts that the MNCs brought into Mainland China have made significant contributions to Mainland China's CSR practices. MNCs included CSR requirements in screening and selecting their local partners and they launched the campaign for factory audits which generated wide attention. After Mainland China joined the World Trade Organization (WTO) in 2001, the impact of MNCs in influencing local firms' CSR performance accelerated with the increased number of MNCs operating in Mainland China.

Furthermore, MNCs influence the CSR practices of local Mainland Chinese partners through supply chain management. In 2006, 66 members of the Executive Committee of Foreign Investment Companies (ECFIC), a self-regulated organization for MNCs in Mainland China, issued a document entitled *Beijing Declaration on CSR*. Members of the ECFIC agreed to promote the MNCs' requirements for CSR in Mainland China and commit to the harmonious development of business and society through self-regulation on 12 issues including law, taxes, intellectual property, employment, employee rights, environmental stewardship, social welfare, corporate information disclosures and corporate citizenship. This initiative fostered the beginning among MNCs in Mainland China of the broadening of CSR practice beyond supply chain management. In 2007, more than 1,400 MNCs in Mainland China published a Written Proposal for Fulfilling Social Responsibilities which advocates compliance with regulations and laws, high product and service quality, employee protection, harmonious employment relationships, biological environment protection and energy conservation. Many fora, seminars and promotions focusing on CSR were held in Mainland China during this period. With numerous CSR awards being established, the general public's attitude toward CSR has gradually become more positive. Companies were enthusiastic about using CSR as a public relations tool to promote their images and brands. In September 2008, the Ministry of Commerce issued the draft *CSR Guideline for Foreign Investment Companies*, which set the foundation for MNCs' CSR practice in Mainland China.

5.1.5 CSR-Related Financial Institutions   Several CSR-related financial institutions and policies provide Mainland Chinese firms with incentive to engage in CSR by affecting their access to finance and financing costs. The Social Responsibility Investment (SRI) fund is a financial institution that enables access of a large amount of equity capital to qualified firms. In May 2006, the Bank of China started the first SRI fund in Mainland China, the Sustainable Growth Equity Fund. In March 2008, the Industrial Management Company offered the first SRI IPO, the Xingye SRI Fund, to Mainland China's investors. At the beginning of 2008, the Shenzhen Securities Information Company and the Tianjin TEDA Company created Mainland China's first SRI index, the TEDA Environmental Protection Index, which comprises the top 40 environmentally responsible firms listed on the Shanghai Stock Exchange (SHSE) and the Shenzhen Stock Exchange (SZSE). In August 2009, the SHSE also launched the "Responsibility Index," which includes the top 100 socially responsible firms on the stock exchange. Sustainability-themed assets have attracted interest in Mainland China. These assets have grown 157 percent annually since 2014, from $450.9 million to $2.9 billion, with most of them related to clean energy.

Mainland China has been at the forefront of SRI business leadership and innovation with its environmental disclosure requirements for IPOs. In 2008, the Chinese Ministry of Environmental Protection (MEP) launched the "Green Securities" and "Green IPO" policies in partnership with the Mainland China Securities Regulatory Commission. These policies impose restrictions on companies in raising capital by requiring environmental record disclosures if they intend to be listed on the two stock exchanges. The regulations require enterprises in 14 polluting industries to go through an environmental assessment by the MEP before initiating an IPO or obtaining refinancing from banks. Within the first year of enacting the new rules, 20 out of 38 companies had their IPOs rejected or were subject to further assessment by the MEP.[49] With the issuance of its first corporate green bond in 2015, Mainland China has since become the world's largest issuer of climate-aligned bonds, according to the Climate Bonds Initiative (CBI), with US$36.2 billion in issuances in 2016.[50] The bulk of its unlabeled climate-aligned bonds are for the railway and transport sector. It is developing a green bond market and has turned to certification firms such as Deloitte, EY and Trucost for assistance.[51] On August 26, 2016, the first eco-friendly asset-backed securities—the Green Asset-backed Securities of ABC Huiying-Goldwind Sci & Tech Wind Power Tolling Right and Income Right—were listed on the SHSE.[52]

5.1.6 Active Stakeholders and NGOs   Two events prompted Mainland China's stakeholders to engage consumers and the public in actively monitoring firms' CSR activities. The Sanlu Milk scandal in 2008 made Mainland Chinese consumers more aware of their role in monitoring the quality of products and protecting their rights through litigation, petition and social media. Partially in response to public concern on food safety, the Mainland Chinese government undertook measures to improve food safety to restore the consumer confidence in public governance and Mainland Chinese food companies. In the same year, an 8.0-magnitude earthquake hit Sichuan and caused landslides and power failures. This natural disaster triggered rapid expansion and public awareness of CSR in Mainland China. Firms were rewarded for responding to the earthquake by giving donations quickly and generously.

NGOs also play an increasingly important role in Mainland China's CSR practice. Broadly speaking, there are two types of NGOs that foster CSR practices in Mainland China, namely, Mainland Chinese branches of international CSR NGOs and domestic CSR NGOs. A notable NGO is the Global Compact Network Mainland China, which was launched in 2009. By December 2017, there were 283 company participants. The organization commits to encourage Mainland Chinese enterprises to follow the Global Compact's 10 principles and promote sustainable development of Mainland Chinese companies. Other NGOs include the China Business Council for Sustainable Development and the Chinese Federation for CSR.

5.1.7 Stock Exchanges   The two stock exchanges in Mainland China promote CSR through setting and enforcing CSR disclosure standards for their listed companies. The Shenzhen Stock Exchange (SZSE) released the *Guide on Listed Companies' Social Responsibility* in 2006. In May 2008, the Shanghai Stock Exchange (SHSE) issued *Guidelines of Shanghai Stock Exchange for Environmental Information Disclosure of Listed Companies* and *Notice on Strengthening Social Responsibility of Listed Companies*, which require certain listed companies to disclose environmental information in a timely manner and encourage all companies to provide CSR reports along with their annual financial reports. The two stock exchanges mandated certain listed companies including the SHSE Corporate Governance Index firms, overseas-listed firms listed on the SHSE, financial firms listed on the SHSE and the Shenzhen 100 Index firms, to report ESG in December 2008.

5.1.8 Industry Initiatives   Some industries take initiatives to promote CSR in Mainland China. In 2007, the China Banking Regulatory Commission (CBRC) promulgated *Recommendations on Strengthening Large Commercial Banks' Social Responsibilities*,[53] which mandate Mainland China's large banks to comply with the principles under the UN Global Compact. CBRC also urged banks to consider a firm's CSR performance when making credit decisions by considering, for example, the *Guidelines on Credit Underwriting for Energy Saving and Emissions Reduction* issued in 2007.[54] The China National Textile and Apparel Council (CNTAC), a countrywide federation of textile-related industries, developed its first CSR management code, a Social Responsibility Management System—the China Social Compliance 9000121 (CSC 9000T), for Mainland China's textile industry. The standard facilitates textile firms to implement a CSR management system that complies with the related laws and regulations in Mainland China as well as with international standards. In April 2008, the *Social Responsibility Guide of the China Industrial Companies and Industrial Associations* was jointly released by 11 industrial associations (including coal, mechanics, steel, petroleum and chemicals, light industry, textiles, building materials, non-ferrous metals, electricity and mining industries) to guide the firms to comply with CSR standards.

5.2 Hong Kong

5.2.1 Government Initiatives

The Hong Kong government commits to promoting various dimensions of business sustainability. In March 2003, the Council for Sustainable Development was established by the Chief Executive to enhance sustainable development by providing advice to the government on sustainability policies. In recent years, with increasing awareness of the importance of sustainability, the government has paid more attention to business sustainability, as evidenced by the 2017–2018 budget speech. For Green finance policy, the Financial Services Development Council's report issued in 2016 indicated that Hong Kong will dedicate itself to become a regional green finance hub.[55] This goal was reiterated by the present Chief Executive Carrie Lam in her 2017 policy address.

Several sustainability-related policies have been introduced by the government. For example, the Environmental Protection Bureau (EPB) introduced the Cleaner Production Partnership Programme in April 2008 to encourage and help Hong Kong-owned factories that have operations in Guangdong Province to employ cleaner-production management and practices. The program has organized around 390 cleaner-production technology advancement activities and approved more than 2,400 funding applications as of March 31, 2015. The program will provide an additional HK$150 million in a five-year plan that ends on March 31, 2020.[56] Another EPB-initiated environmental project, the Carbon Footprint Repository, was launched by the government to facilitate Hong Kong listed companies to report their carbon footprint and share their good carbon management practices in 2014.[57]

5.2.2 NGO and Business Association Initiatives

Non-governmental organizations (NGOs) and business associations collaborate to promote the development of ESG in Hong Kong. Many organizations survey, rank and award companies according to their ESG performance and disclosure practices. These surveys and awards provide publicity and motivate companies to achieve international standards. NGOs and business associations have also been lobbying governments for legislative change.

Business associations such as the Hong Kong General Chamber of Commerce promote ESG activities and reporting by, for example, forming the Environmental and Sustainability Committee to study and advise the Chamber on issues relating to sustainability and their integration with ESG developments in Hong Kong.

The Sustainability and Integrated Reporting Advisory Group of the Hong Kong Institute of Certified Public Accountants (HKICPA) takes forward the integrated reporting concept. HKICPA also promoted the corporate governance dimension of sustainability by launching the "Best Corporate Governance Awards" in 2000, and the Awards have since become one of the most well-established corporate governance awards in Hong Kong. The primary objective of the contest is to encourage corporate governance practices and disclosures and to exemplify the best corporate governance practices in Hong Kong. To promote CSR disclosure in Hong Kong, HKICPA introduced the Sustainability and Social Responsibility Reporting ("SSR") Awards to recognize and exemplify those firms with excellent performance in ESG reporting practices in 2011. The Best Corporate Governance Awards added a category of H-share companies in 2006 and extended the category to include other giant Mainland Chinese companies in 2012. So far, the Awards have six main categories and 20 possible awards pertaining to corporate governance.

Oxfam Hong Kong leverages Oxfam's worldwide capacity and local expertise to mobilize the power of people against poverty. Since 2004, Oxfam Hong Kong has been promoting the integration of ESG into corporate policies and business operations in Hong Kong. Oxfam Hong Kong conducted three pioneering studies in 2008, 2009 and 2016, respectively to evaluate the CSR performance of the Hang Seng Index (HSI) constituents by analyzing the implementation of CSR initiatives in their respective companies. These companies constitute the top-90th percentile of the total market capitalization and the top-90th percentile of the total turnover on the Hong Kong stock market. The HSI constituents provide a solid role model for the other listed companies to follow.

CarbonCare InnoLab (CCIL) is a Hong Kong-based independent NGO committed to responding to the climate change and sustainability challenges by nurturing and promoting innovative solutions, policies and practices. In 2011, CCIL launched two carbon-related awards for listed and private companies and public organizations with excellent performance in carbon management (CarbonCare® Label) and pioneering carbon reduction actions (CarbonCare® Action Label). In 2016, in response to tighter ESG reporting requirements, CCIL added the CarbonCare® ESG Label series to recognize those organizations with high performance in ESG reporting.

The Caring Company Scheme was initiated by the Hong Kong Council of Social Service (HKCSS) in 2002 with the aim of promoting corporate citizenship and a more inclusive society. From the first year of its establishment, the scheme awarded 259 companies with the Caring Company logo. In 2017–2018, the scheme awarded around 3,700 organizations. In addition to promoting organizations' social responsibility by awarding the Caring Company logo, HKCSS also established the HKCSS CSR Institute in December 2010 to provide a platform for promoting knowledge and practice of CSR through a series of training and sharing activities. The Institute attempted to incorporate innovative CSR practices such as ISO 26000 and the GRI *G3 Guidelines* into their training programs.

Other local non-governmental and governmental initiatives have been established to promote ESG practices in Hong Kong. Such organizations are the Hong Kong CSR Charter established by Community Business, the Corporate Citizenship Programme launched by the Hong Kong Productivity Council and the Carbon Reduction Charter of the Hong Kong Environmental Protection Department.

Independent thinktanks such as Civic Exchange also promote ESG by publishing research papers, engaging stakeholders and educating the public.[58]

5.2.3 ESG Funds and Green Finance The availability of ESG funds is limited in Hong Kong. According to the Securities and Futures Commission, as of 2017 there are only four ESG funds out of more than 2,000 listed funds in Hong Kong.[59] Three of the funds are international (BNP Paribas' Parvest Sustainable Equity High Dividend Europe Classic-Capitalization; Allianz Global Sustainability A EUR; UBS (Lux) Equity SICAV – Emerging Markets Sustainable (USD) P-acc), with one local fund (Hang Seng Corporate Sustainability Index A HKD). The latter primarily invests in Hang Seng Corporate Sustainability Index constituent firms. Several institutions started to consider allocating funds to ESG-related investment. For example, the *South China Morning Post* reported that the Hong Kong Monetary Authority, managing the around HK$3.99 trillion (equivalent to US$0.52 trillion) Exchange Fund, considered ESG to be an important factor for its investment analysis processes.[60] According to the same report, the Hospital Authority Provident Fund Scheme estimated that more than 90 percent of its assets of more than HK$58 billion (equivalent to US$7.54 billion) were managed by funds that are signatories of the Principles of Responsive Investment. In 2018, the Hong Kong Special Administrative Region (HKSAR) government announced its plan of issuing HK$2.5 million (equivalent to US$319,428) green bond, indicating the government's desire to promote green finance in the future.[61] The increasing amount of money allocated to ESG funds will provide incentives for Hong Kong firms to engage in CSR activities to have better access to financing.

5.2.4 Stock Exchange The Stock Exchange of Hong Kong (HKEX) has long recognized the trend of CSR/ESG practices and reporting. In 2003, Prof. Judy Tsui and Prof. Ferdinand Gul conducted three consultancy reports as part of company law reform for the Treasury and Financial Services Bureau of the Hong Kong government titled *Survey on International Institutional Investors' Attitudes toward Corporate Governance Standards in Hong Kong, Roles and Functions of Audit, Nomination and Remuneration Committees* and *Survey on the Corporate Governance Regimes in Other Jurisdictions*, which formed the basis for corporate governance reform including CSR in the Hong Kong listing rules. To promote awareness of ESG, the HKEX sponsored several free seminars and workshops on ESG disclosures for listed companies in 2011. 823 delegates from 498 HKEX listed companies and 518 representatives from 348 HKEX listed companies attended the seminars and workshops. The HKEX then drafted the *ESG Reporting Guide*,[62] provided a reporting toolkit and made other ESG reporting-related information public to facilitate issuers in preparing ESG reports. In 2015, the HKEX issued a consultation paper on the review of the environmental, social and governance reporting guide to the public to solicit opinions on the report. After completing the consultation, the HKEX issued the ESG guide in its listing rules and mandated issuers to provide ESG reports based on a "comply-or-explain" approach, commencing 1 January 2016.

5.3 India

5.3.1 Legal Driver The 2013 Companies Act ("the Act") governs CSR in India. The Act and the CSR (policy) Rules came into effect on April 1, 2014. The Ministry of Corporate Affairs (MCA) is responsible for the enforcement of the Act and its regulation.[63] The Act requires that Indian companies with an annual turnover of more than 1,000 Crore INR (equivalent to US$150,000,000), a net worth of more than 500 Crore INR (equivalent to US$75,000,000) or a net profit of more than five Crore INR (equivalent to US$750,000) in a financial year should spend 2 percent of their net profits on CSR programs. The Act also requires Indian companies to form CSR committees consisting of corporate board members with at least one independent director to deal with CSR affairs.[64]

5.3.2 Civil Society   Civic engagement in India played an important role in the political struggle for independence in 1947 while Indian women first came out into the public to fight against British colonial power. Beginning in the 1960s, civil society organizations (CSOs) began to be recognized as service providers with financial support from the government in the form of grants. During the post-independence period (from 1947), India emerged with a mixed economy, with a very wealthy sector alongside serious poverty issues. The State Governments of India had to deliver development services to the poor through CSOs. During the 1980s and 1990s, the public expected business and industry associations to contribute more toward social welfare and narrow down the wage gap.[65]

In today's India, over 3 million CSOs and social movements are facilitating socio-economic, political and cultural development and playing a vital role in promoting, protecting and strengthening CSR issues such as human rights and environmental protection.[66] However, the civic space is constrained by government interference with freedom of association and speech.[67] Although many CSOs can provide CSR services, the protection of human rights, the prevention of sexual harassment and the freedom to express of diverse views are shrinking.[68]

5.3.3 Standards and Codes of Conduct   Established in 1987, the Bureau of Indian Standards (BIS) is the national standard setter of India, committing to standardization, certification and testing activities with the aims of ensuring the supply of safe and quality goods, reducing public health hazards, promoting exports and import substitutes, etc. In 2017, BIS' Management and Systems Department organized a National Seminar on *Good Governance in CSR* to formulate CSR standards. It was the first step toward framing and implementing a good Guidance Standard for integrated and sustainable socio-economic and environmental growth in India.[69]

5.3.4 Socially Responsible Investment   India has a limited domestic SRI market in the listed equity domain. The first SRI fund (ABN AMRO Sustainable Development Fund) in India was launched by ABN AMRO in March 2007 and raised the equivalent of approximately US$12 million. After the break-up of ABN AMRO in 2008, the fund is now managed by Fortis Bank. Launched in January 2008 by Standard & Poor's and other research teams, the S&P ESG India Index is the first investable index of companies which produces a score for environmental, social and governance (ESG) disclosure practices in the public domain.[70] The Indian SRI market includes both domestic and global SRIs although the global SRIs have a dominant market share.

According to a 2017 Oxfam report, 95 global socially responsible funds have invested in India with an average 18.5 percent of their funds allocated to Indian companies (total fund size is around US$78 billion). There are 41 Global Environmental & Social (E&S) seeking funds (total funds of around US$67 billion), which are global funds based on integrating ESG criteria that have invested an average of 25 percent of their funds in Indian equities. However, the Indian ethical funds underperformed when compared to the other two SRI funds (Global E&S seeking funds and global socially responsible funds).[71] On May 30, 2017, the Securities Exchange Board of India (SEBI) released the *Disclosure Requirements for Issuance and Listing of Green Bonds*, which helps to attract investments from capital markets for funds in the renewable energy area.[72]

5.3.5 The Scheduled Castes and Scheduled Tribes (SC/ST) Communities
The SC/ST communities in India are the historically disadvantaged socio-economic groups. The SCs have been at the bottom of the Hindu social hierarchy with limited opportunities for social mobility and growth. The STs live in and around forest areas with severe challenges of socio-economic mobility. The SCs/STs, even after years of government initiatives and subsidies, remain the two most backward communities in India.[73] The government of India has made progress to improve the situation of the SCs/STs by enacting legislation and regulations related to education, financial support and skills training, and established special courts aimed at preventing atrocities and violence.[74]

5.4 Indonesia

5.4.1 Legal Driver
Several laws stipulate firms' social and environmental obligations in Indonesia.[75] The State-Owned Enterprises Law (Law No. 19/2003) mandates SOEs to be active in helping small and medium-sized enterprises (SMEs), cooperatives and the people, and these spend 2 percent of their profits on CSR. The Investment Law (Law No. 25/2007) defines CSR and specifies investors' responsibility with respect to CSR. The Limited Liability Companies Law (Law No. 40/2007) is the first law imposing a CSR obligation on limited liability companies in the natural resources industry and/or related industries. This law also requires firms to allocate funds to implement CSR and allows firms to account for the expenditure in their financial statements.

5.4.2 SRI and Sustainability Lending
In 2009, the Yayasan Keanekaragaman Hayati Indonesia (KEHATI), known as the Indonesian Biodiversity Foundation, collaborated with the Indonesian Stock Exchange (ISE) to launch the KEHATI SRI Index, the first in Indonesia. The KEHATI SRI Index selects 25 companies based on their performance in six categories including social, environmental and corporate governance. In addition to the SRI index, other SRIs also contribute to the development of green finance in Indonesia. According to the United Nations Environment Programme (UNEP), the assets managed by sustainable investment funds in 2014 are double those of 2011 and reached US$1.14 billion.[76]

The Bank Indonesia Act (10/1998) mandates banks to assess environmental impact in making decisions to grant large or high-risk loans. The Bank Indonesia Act promulgates Regulation No. 7/2/PBI/2005, requiring banks to assess the "measure[s] taken by the debtor to conserve the environment" in their credit-granting decision. In addition to legislation and regulation effort, Bank Indonesia takes initiatives to develop green credits by organizing workshops for bank officials, developing green-lending guidelines and conducting studies. Despite these effort, banks' green financing made up around 1.37 percent of total bank financing in 2013. In recognition of this, the Indonesian government began to take measures to develop sustainability financing. In 2014, the Financial Services Authority of Indonesia (Indonesian: *Otoritas Jasa Keuangan* or OJK) initiated a *Roadmap for Sustainable Finance in Indonesia*, outlining a development plan for sustainability financing for 2015–2019.

5.4.3   Private Initiatives

5.4.3.1   Millennium Challenge Account-Indonesia (MCA-Indonesia)   The Millennium Challenge Account-Indonesia (MCA-Indonesia) is a government institution and is governed by the Minister of National Development Planning/Head of the National Development Planning.[77] The MCA-Indonesia launched a Compact Program with the objective of reducing poverty, gas emissions and energy cost; raising household income; and promoting public services. There are three projects in the Compact Program, namely the Green Prosperity Project, the Community-Based Health and Nutrition to Reduce Stunting Project and the Procurement Modernization Project.[78]

5.4.3.2   The Yayasan Keanekaragaman Hayati Indonesia (KEHATI)   The Yayasan Keanekaragaman Hayati Indonesia (KEHATI), known as the Indonesian Biodiversity Foundation, is a non-profit grant-making foundation. The values of the KEHATI are sustainability, accountability, independence, trust, diversity, fairness and sense of concern. The KEHATI provides funding, shares expertise and offers support programs to non-governmental organizations (NGOs), community organizations, and research and educational institutions as well as independent community organizations.[79] The KEHATI has established two green investments, namely the KEHATI Mutual Fund and the KEHATI Sustainable and Responsible Investment Index (KEHATI SRI Index).[80]

5.4.3.3   Indonesia Business Links (IBL)   Indonesia Business Links (IBL) is a not-for-profit foundation that promotes business ethics, youth empowerment and responsible waste management. The IBL is actively hosting training programs and workshops regarding CSR and ethical practices in cooperation with SMEs, NGOs and the government.[81] Since 2006, the IBL has hosted CSR conferences every two years at both domestic and global level. On average, there are approximately 500 participants, mostly from SOEs and MNCs, who discuss the development and future challenges of CSR with local CSR professionals.[82] The IBL also organizes CEO network meetings focusing on CSR every three months. The workshops and seminars held by the IBL aim to share CSR information and knowledge to promote sustainable development in the business community.[83]

5.4.3.4   The National Center for Sustainability Reporting (NCSR)   The National Center for Sustainability Reporting (NCSR) was established to help the implementation of Sustainable Development in Indonesia.[84] Since 2007, the NCSR has provided professional certification training on Sustainability Reporting. GRI's Standards Certified Training is one of the programs offered by the NCSR, which is the first

GRI Certified Training Partner in Indonesia, Malaysia and Thailand since 2011.[85] Certified Sustainability Reporting Assurer (CSRA) is another program offered by NCSR. People who obtain the CSRA are qualified to provide sustainable reporting assurance services for companies that are in line with the AA1000AS standards set by AccountAbility, one of the most influential CSR reporting assurance standard-setters globally.

5.5 Japan

5.5.1 Exports Japan is the fourth largest export economy in the world. With a large middle-class consumption base, Japan is a major consumer and producer of goods and services and has an important commercial presence in global markets. Japan's technology and manufacturing-related industries play leading roles in the global economy and global supply chains.[86] In 2016, Japan exported US$605 billion and imported US$583 billion, resulting in a positive trade balance of US$21.6 billion.[87] Because of its international trade status, companies in Japan are willing to engage in socially responsible activities because they anticipate benefits from these actions, such as improved global reputation leading to higher prospects and ability to charge a premium price. These benefits would have the potential to offset the additional costs associated with CSR compliance. Indirectly, it is widely accepted in Japan that CSR is positively related to export performance.[88]

5.5.2 Influence from Western Countries The basic form of CSR has been influenced by principles of liberal and democratic rights, justice and social structures in the United States and Europe.[89] In Japan, the impact of Western influence on CSR can be summarized as follows.

5.5.2.1 Triple bottom line Triple bottom line is a concept that is widely used by managers in making decisions related to CSR policies and activities. In 2009, a survey of 13 MNCs in Japan (Fukukawa and Teramoto, 2009) suggested that the managers of these companies referred to sustainability as a long-term pursuit and a way to ensure continuity of their businesses. These companies comply with sustainability reporting partly because of the potential impact on the valuation of their companies in the capital market.

5.5.2.2 Globalization As part of the globalization process, Japanese companies with overseas partners and subsidiaries experience Western practices of CSR. They and their overseas affiliates are generally required to respond to CSR-related issues. All managers of the 13 MNCs surveyed by Fukukawa and Teramoto (2009) referred to "globalization" as one of the reasons for their company adopting CSR management. The increased interest at home and abroad undoubtedly influenced Japanese companies' approach in adopting CSR practices.

5.5.3 Socially Responsible Investment In recent years, the relationship between CSR and corporate financial performance especially in the field of social responsibility investment (SRI) has received considerable research and attention.[90,91] The UK Investment Forum specifically defines SRI as "investments enabling investors to combine financial objectives with their social values."[92]

The origin of SRI in Japan can be traced back to 1999. At that time, Japan set up many "eco-funds" to enable investors to invest in environment friendly enterprises and investors responded enthusiastically. By December 2007, the value of these funds' equity investments had reached 1.12 trillion yen (around US$0.01 trillion). As a result, the Social Investment Forum (SIF), a non-profit organization whose mission is to promote the development of SRI in Japan, was founded in 2003. In the same year, many large companies began to establish special departments dedicated to promoting activities related to CSR, overseeing the preparation of environmental sustainability reports and promoting stakeholder participation. Morningstar Japan launched its first Japan-specific SRI index, named MS-SRI. In August 2009, the Japanese Ministry of the Environment announced a plan to develop guidelines specifically for environmental finance with the aim of increasing eco-conscious investment and the practice of environmental finance.[93]

Four key actors can be identified in the Japanese SRI field, namely SRI research organizations, SIF Japan, financial institutions and stock listed companies. SRI organizations and Japanese companies have worked together in developing SRI in Japan despite both groups having different motives for their actions. Japanese companies tried to regain trust by adopting socially responsible practices while the SRI organizations use the Japanese companies to evaluate the role and importance of SRI development in Japan through mobilizing CSR debate and enhancing CSR disclosure. Japanese companies were also driven to adopt sustainable practices by the media and coverage and promotion of these activities increased drastically in 2003; by 2005 media attention became the prime driver of CSR reporting.[94,95]

5.5.4 Legal Drivers In late 1993, the Japanese government passed the Basic Environment Law. This law set forth the responsibility of the central and local governments, corporations and the public to preserve the environment. The issuance of the Environmental Reporting Guidelines in 2000 and the Environmental Accounting Guidelines in 2005 by the Ministry of Environment urged businesses to implement environment awareness practices and invest in environmental protection.

In the past two decades, multiple government departments such as the Ministries of the Environment, Economy, Trade, Industry, Health, Labor and Welfare issued a series of laws and regulations on CSR and environmental responsibility and guidelines for voluntary compliance. Because Japanese society is not the same as Western societies, the Japanese government has opted for the use of voluntary guidelines and recommendations to regulate CSR activities to ensure a cooperative relationship between the company and the government.[96]

5.5.5 Political Drivers For a long time, the Japanese government has been keen to promote the development of CSR. In recent years, the government of Japan has taken various comprehensive measures to build a society with sustainable development through the improvement of environmental, economic and social conditions. The government was working to build an inclusive and participatory society that would enable every citizen to realize his or her full potential.

On May 20, 2016, the Japanese government established a new cabinet body entitled "SDGs Promotion Headquarters," headed by the Prime Minister and composed of all sectoral ministers. The SDGs Promotion Headquarters promotes close cooperation between relevant ministries and government agencies and serves as a control center for the full and effective implementation of measures related to the sustainable development goals. In December 2016, the agency adopted a set of guiding principles for the implementation of the sustainable development goals. Under the guiding principles, Japan established the vision to "become a leader toward a future where economic, social and environmental improvements are attained in an integrated, sustainable and resilient manner while leaving no one behind." The Japanese government's goals were to serve as a model for the world in building sustainable development and to continue to work with other countries to build sustainable societies around the world.[97]

5.5.6 Stock Exchange The Japan Exchange Group, Inc. (JPX) was established by the merging of the Tokyo Stock Exchange Group and the Osaka Securities Exchange on January 1, 2013.[98] JPX has been involved in the formation of Japan's Corporate Governance Code, the launch of several innovative fund markets, the building of sustainability structures such as the ESG and exchange-traded funds (ETF)-related indices and the recognition of outstanding companies that have promoted employee health, productivity and women's empowerment. JPX seeks to work with other exchanges globally on sustainable stock exchange initiatives as well as to promote Japan's development.[99]

5.6 South Korea

5.6.1 Public Initiatives The function of Korea Smart Grid Institute (KSGI) is to implement the government's Smart Grid Roadmap. The Institute establishes the technological test-bed[100] and complies with the policy for smart grid-related issues[101] to implement the vision of *Green Growth, Low Carbon*[102] initiated by former President Lee Myung-Bak. From 2015 to 2016, the International Smart Grid Action Network (ISGAN) sponsored a series of functions to promote smart grid in line with international sustainable energy policy. In 2016, ISGAN and the Global Smart Grid Federation (GSGF) jointly hosted the ISGAN Award of Excellence annual competition, which focuses on the topic of "Excellence in Smart Grids for Renewable Energy Integration."[103]

The Korean Agency for Technology and Standards (KATS) is a government agency as well as an active member of the International Organization for Standardization (ISO), the International Electrotechnical Commission (IEC) and the Portable Application Standards Committee (PASC) of the Institute of Electrical and Electronics Engineers (IEEE). KATS contributes to South Korean companies' technological infrastructure development and product safety.[104] KATS established the *Good Recycled* program with the objective to transform recycled goods into high-quality green products.[105] In 2016, KATS monitored more than 4,500 electrical and children's products in South Korea. KATS cooperates with the Korea Product Safety Association (KPSA) and NGOs to jointly monitor and strengthen the recall policies for unqualified products.[106] The IEC-IEEE-KATS (International Electrotechnical Commission-Institute of Electrical and Electronics Engineers-Korean Agency for Technology and Standards) launched a project called Future Challenges in Standardization in 2018, focusing on the future challenges of technologies, environment and standardization.[107]

5.6.2 Private Initiatives The Federation of Korean Industry (FKI) is committed to globalization, development of CSR, and maintaining an improved socio-economic climate domestically and globally. In 2014, FKI established the Committee on Corporate Philanthropy with the theme "Effective Communications in Corporate Philanthropy." FKI also operated the CSR Academy in 2014. In 2015, FKI held a CSR conference at the FKI Tower Conference Centre.[108] FKI also conducted a study to investigate the CSR activities of major South Korean businesses. This study revealed that South Korean corporates had focused their philanthropic activities only on art and culture until the 1990s. Today, South Korean businesses are investing in CSR activities which are concerned with public interest and popular culture.[109]

5.6.3 Non-Government Organizations The Korean Federation of Environment Movement (KFEM) launched the Sustainable Management and Investment Guideline (SMILE) to promote CSR practices at the level of the firm. The Global Compact Korea Network (GCKN) engages with companies' CSR performance in areas such as human rights, labor standards, environmental protection, and anti-corruption. GCKN contributes to organizing the Global Compact China-Japan-Korea Roundtable Conference (2009), which promotes CSR issues in South Korea.[110]

5.6.4 Socially Responsible Investments The National Pension Service (NPS) established SRI-friendly investment infrastructure in South Korea. SRI trustee investment is around 5.13 trillion won (around US$4.57 billion), which accounts for more than 70 percent of total SRI in South Korea. SRI public offering funds have a total net asset of 1.63 trillion won (around US$1.44 billion). SRI exchange-traded funds (ETF) maintain a total value of 13.9 trillion won (around US$12.37 billion) in South Korea.[111] The value of South Korean SRI was estimated at US$8 billion in 2013, which was lower than Hong Kong and Malaysia but higher than Indonesia, Mainland China and Singapore among Asian jurisdictions.[112]

5.7 Malaysia

In the 1950s, the primary focus was on businesses' responsibilities to society and philanthropy. In the 1960s, key events, people, and ideas were instrumental in characterizing the social changes ushered in during this decade.[113] Over time, there has been a significant increase in CSR and local companies in Malaysia are gradually embracing this trend. This growth in CSR awareness can be attributed to increasing government and regulatory involvement, and awareness of sustainability concerns among local media, while the civil and private sectors are becoming more engaged with corporate responsibility.[114] Among the Association of Southeast Asian Nations (ASEAN) countries, Malaysia has shown remarkable progress in sustainability reporting as a result of increased government and regulatory requirements (Lopez, 2010).[115] Environmentally friendly technologies are being developed and local companies are gradually embracing sustainable business practices in efforts to gain competitive advantage over competitors or qualify for government incentives or as a result of pressure from stakeholders and foreign parent companies.

5.7.1 CSR Disclosure for Companies The Malaysian government is one of the few in Asia to enact CSR reporting requirements for PLCs (Public Limited Companies). Since the inception of the GRI in 1999, 16 different Malaysian companies have published GRI reports (by July 2012).[116] Although the continuous effort by the Malaysian government to protect the natural environment started in the 1980s, social and environmental reporting was made mandatory only in 2006. With this legislation, effective for annual reports for the year ending 2007 onwards, companies listed on Bursa Malaysia (BM) (Malaysian Stock Exchange) must include information on four focal areas of CSR, namely community, workplace, employees and environment.[117] In 2012, a PwC survey covering over 700 companies from Malaysia, the Philippines, Indonesia, Thailand and Vietnam showed that nearly 80 percent of Malaysian companies report some form of sustainability, mostly due to the regulations set by Bursa Malaysia for all public listed companies to disclose their sustainability activities in their annual reports. It also highlighted that Malaysian companies scored high in terms of compliance with regulations and meeting customer demands.[118]

While making CSR disclosure mandatory is indeed a step in the right direction, enforcement is important so that CSR disclosure is not undertaken merely to comply with legal requirements.[119] The concept of accounting "substance over form" is particularly relevant here. CSR Asia conducted an analysis of media reporting and concluded that CSR is still seen largely as philanthropy rather than as a necessary social obligation (CSR Asia, 2009). In addition, the Malaysian Association of Chartered Certified Accountants (ACCA) in conjunction with their 2007 Malaysia Environmental and Social Reporting Awards (ACCA, 2007) revealed that companies are overly focused on philanthropic activities (UNICEF Malaysia, 2012).[120] Although there are different annual award programs in Malaysia to recognize the CSR contribution of local businesses, the practice of CSR still has room for growth beyond philanthropy.

Malaysia is lagging behind in terms of environmental disclosure practices when compared to other Asia-Pacific countries. There are insufficient campaigns and promotions to raise awareness among local companies of activities regarding the environment. Lack of a recognized disclosure framework and the high cost of disclosure are other reasons to account for low levels of environmental disclosure.[121] The Malaysia Accounting Standard Board (MASB) does not provide a precise standard and guidelines on environmental disclosure. According to Paragraph 10 of FRS 101, the Presentation of Financial Statements, companies are encouraged to prepare environmental reports in addition to their financial statements (Buniamin, 2010).[122] There is also a requirement under the Malaysian Environmental Quality Act 1974 that provides guidelines for Malaysian companies in managing their disclosure on environmental sustainability. Section 33A of that Act, on environmental audit, and Section 34A on impact on the environment, are the only guiding principles for companies on disclosure on environmental sustainability (Bursa Malaysia, 2012). However, what information to disclose is to be decided by the company.

5.7.2 CSR Initiatives As a result of several environmental challenges and corporate misconduct cases in Malaysia, the importance of extending firms' accountability to all stakeholders and acting in a socially responsible way in all areas of business activity has increased. Several initiatives have been taken by the government to enhance the development of CSR reporting in Malaysia.

5.7.3 Government Initiatives In Malaysia, the government has been the main driver in pushing the CSR agenda since the 1997 Asian Financial Crisis. Corporate Governance (CG) reform, followed by financial sector reform and a National Integrity Plan, are all measures that sought to encourage the business sector to embrace CSR. Most recently, the government published the *Silver Book*, a guide for government-linked companies on how to articulate and manage a company's social obligations.

To continuously promote CSR, policymakers converged in 2004 to create a new Ministry of Energy, Green Technology and Water to further buttress their support of environmental sustainability protection. The Ministry's primary function is to facilitate and regulate the growth of industries in these sectors to ensure the availability of high-quality, efficient and safe services at a reasonable price to consumers throughout the country.[123]

5.7.4 Companies Commission The Companies Commission of Malaysia also known as Suruhanjaya Syarikat Malaysia (SSM) under the purview of the Ministry of Domestic Trade, Co-operatives & Consumerism is a statutory body that regulates companies and businesses in Malaysia. The SSM launched its Corporate Responsibility Agenda (CR Agenda) on June 30, 2009; this aims to instill corporate responsibility into the corporate culture of Malaysian businesses and to promote good corporate governance through national agendas such as:

- The Ninth Malaysia Plan, which includes the promotion of ethical business practices and CR programs toward improving the state of national corporate governance.
- The National Integrity Plan, whose strategic objective is to improve corporate governance and business ethics, which are all linked to CR.
- Increase of the tax ceiling for tax deductions from 5 percent to 7 percent of aggregate income on contributions made by the private sector to charitable organizations and imposition of the requirement for publicly listed companies to report their CR initiatives in their annual financial reports.[124]

5.7.5 Socially Responsible Investing The establishment of "Dana Al-Aiman" by ASM Investment Services is regarded as the first ethical fund in Malaysia.[125] In 2003, Maybank Management Bhd launched the first SRI fund, "The Mayban Ethical Trust Fund," in Malaysia. In 2006, Prime Minister Abdullah Badawi announced in his Budget speech that all listed companies in Malaysia are required to disclose CSR, and that government-linked fund companies, including the Employee Provident Fund, are required to take CSR performance into account in their investment decisions. To further provide finance for SRIs, the Securities Commission Malaysia (SC) introduced the Sustainable and Responsible Investment (SRI) Sukuk framework. The introduction of an ESG index by Bursa Malaysia Bhd in 2014 further enhanced the SRI framework in Malaysia. Malaysian SRIs are among the key players in the Asian SRI market. According to the Global Sustainable Investment Review 2016, Malaysia has the largest SRI share (30 percent share) in Asia (excluding Japan).[126]

5.7.6 CSR Awards Awards are given for exceptionally good practices in the area of CSR to encourage businesses to practice and report CSR activities, including the impact of their business operations on the environment and the society they operate in, and to raise awareness of corporate transparency issues. These awards include:

1. Association of Chartered Certified Accountants (ACCA) Malaysia Sustainability Reporting Awards (MaSRA). The MaSRA award has been in existence since 2002. Its primary objective is to encourage both private and public businesses in Malaysia to embrace sustainable practices and reporting to enhance business performance.
2. Prime Minister's CSR Award for the recognition of companies that have contributed positively to their communities through CSR programs.[127]
3. StarBiz-ICR Malaysia Corporate Responsibility Award, which encourages and promotes the importance of responsible business practices in Malaysian companies.

The Prime Minister in his 2007 Budget Speech announced that private sector contributions to the community would be recognized and awarded through the Prime Minister's CSR Awards Sponsorship. CSR awards given at top government level is a significant recognition of the impact that the business sector can have on the community.[128]

5.8 The Philippines

5.8.1 Political Drivers The Philippine government has been making unremitting efforts to promote the development of CSR in the Philippines, where volunteerism is the most important element of CSR. In 1964, the Philippine government established the Philippine National Service Committee through Executive Order No. 134. After years of business and civic support, the committee developed into the Philippine National Volunteer Service and Coordinating Agency in 1980.

"Encouraging businesses to create their own CSR projects" is part of the Corporate Citizenship Program of the National Development Governance Project in the Philippines. The project aims to enhance Filipino citizens' understanding of globalization and CSR issues, and the ability of corporate citizens to better implement CSR in enterprises in a globalized environment. The project was integrated into other projects from 2002 to 2004 (elections, justice, anti-corruption, economic management and civil service, the right to development, globalization, decentralization and local governance reform and governance reviews).[129]

To further promote the development of CSR in the Philippines, the Philippine government recently issued a tax code to provide incentives related to CSR. These incentives include:

A limited or full deduction of income tax on contributions (Section 29)

Abolition of inheritance tax (Section 80d)

Abolition of donor's tax (Section 94a(3))

5.8.1.1 Non-Governmental Organizations (NGOs) NGOs are intermediary bodies composed of and operated by full-time staff in a variety of industries. NGOs in the Philippines serve major organizations and business enterprises as well as performing the functions of advocacy and lobbying. The Philippines has adopted one of the freest and most open laws and policies in Asia. Since 1986, it has had an open policy environment and lobbying is allowed in different arms of government (national and local governments) as well as in the executive and legislative branches. For CSR, the Philippines has also established several associations to promote corporate citizenship in the business community.[130]

5.8.1.2 Philippine Business for Social Progress (PBSP) Founded in 1970, PBSP is a business-led foundation designed to contribute to sustainable development and poverty eradication. For different CSR issues, sustainable solutions have been issued in the core areas of health, education, environment, livelihoods and enterprise development. In response to changes in CSR's development, PBSP also continues to engage strategically with companies through social investment, responsible business practices and philanthropy. Throughout its history, the organization has mobilized and invested more than 5 billion Philippine pesos (around US$95 million) in social development programs from the operating funds of its members and the Office of Development Assistance (ODA), which is a grant aimed at promoting sustainable development as defined in Republic Act 8182—ODA Act of 1996.

5.8.1.3 League of Corporate Foundations (LCF) The League of Corporate Foundations is a network of more than 90 corporate foundations and a variety of other enterprises that have contributed over the past 90 years to promoting and strengthening the implementation of the CSR strategy for sustainable national development. LCF was officially registered in the Philippine Securities and Exchange Commission on August 26, 1996. It has developed many social activities related to CSR over the past two decades. In 2001, with the President's declaration of the first week of July as National CSR week, LCF was designated as the overall coordinating body for monitoring specific practices of the CSR. The Association of Southeast Asian Nations CSR Network was founded in 2010 with LCF as one of its founding members. The ASEAN CSR Network is a group of organizations which promotes and advocates for the advancement of CSR in Southeast Asia. Over the years, private enterprises have been encouraged to participate in CSR activities organized by LCF. In this process, public sector partnerships and multi-sectoral cooperation has also strengthened private enterprise participation in CSR activities in various fields including arts and culture, education, environment, health, enterprise development, CSR research and training.[131]

5.8.2 Stock Exchange The activities of the Philippine Stock Exchange (PSE) have had a great impact on the social and economic development of the country as well as on the promotion and practice of CSR in the Philippines. Since 1995, the PSE has been committed to participating in and developing a variety of public welfare activities and community services. The PSE joined the Philippine Business for Social Progress (PBSP) and became an active member. The PSE has been supporting projects for various social welfare activities in cooperation with the PBSP. In order to popularize and deepen the significance of CSR in the Philippines, the PSE Foundation, Inc. (PSEFI) was founded on November 10, 1995. Since then, PSEFI, PSE's right hand in CSR, has been designed to help the more vulnerable members of society and to provide them with a variety of basic services. PSEFI's accession to the League of Corporate Foundations in April 1997 further strengthened its commitment to social service.[132]

In recent years, PSE has developed laws and guidelines related to CSR to assist enterprises in practice and application of CSR. In 2007, PSE published the *Interpretation of the Suitability Rule of the Exchange*. In this guidance, the PSE provides recommendations for the sustainability of enterprises.[133] In 2017, the PSE also issued the *Corporate Governance Guidelines for Listed Companies*. The PSE requires enterprises to respect and protect the rights and interests of employees, communities, the environment and other stakeholders and to formulate plans related to the community and environment.[134]

5.8.3 Socially Responsible Investment Compared with other countries, the SRI market in the Philippines is still in its infancy, and there is not much information on the development of SRI in this country. Therefore, it is difficult to identify active SRI investors and ESG-related personnel in the market. To promote SRI in the Philippines, the government and other relevant organizations have taken a number of initiatives to meet the sustainable development needs of the country. Measures have focused on investing in infrastructure sensitive to climate change and local community as well as on improving the financing channels for SMEs.

Despite the above, the Philippines Investment Alliance for Infrastructure (PINAI) Fund was set up in 2013 and managed by Macquarie Infrastructure and Real Assets. This was the first dedicated infrastructure fund jointly financed by the government Service Insurance System, the Asian Development Bank, Algemen Pensionen Groep of the Netherlands and Macquarie Group. PINAI aims to fund businesses and projects linked to equity to promote sustainable growth in the country. An integrated Environmental Social Management System will safeguard the environment, prevent involuntary resettlement and protect local people.

In addition, two of the largest financial institutions in the Philippines, an integrated Environmental Social Management System (ESMS), and the Land Bank of the Philippines have launched several green industry financing programs for SMEs and local government units. The Bank of the Philippine Islands works with the International Finance Corporation to provide low-carbon investment programs for SMEs. This initiative is important in building a sustainable growth model for the Philippines.[135]

5.9 Singapore

5.9.1 Economic Drivers As Singapore becomes the region's economic powerhouse, it has increasingly recognized the importance of CSR to enhance its export competitiveness, economic dynamism and productivity through innovation, enterprise, competition, skills and investment. Singapore is an industrialized economy which is dependent on trade with continuing expansion in the international markets. It is natural to promote CSR that is closely related to Singapore's export-oriented economy and the direction of its future development. CSR can be seen as a good marketing strategy to enhance its international image and a means to avoid excessive economic costs. Consequently, Singapore companies are under pressure from international partners and exposed to regulatory risk, and must avoid reputational damage caused by socially irresponsible activities. In this context, Singapore makes great efforts to promote CSR to maintain its export competitiveness and to adhere to global standards such as ISO 26000 and to be compatible with Western companies' requirements.[136]

5.8.2 Political Drivers

The government of Singapore see itself as a catalyst and practitioner of CSR. On the environmental front, the government of Singapore made a strategic choice to build the country in the form of a Garden City when it became independent in 1965. In order to protect the natural environment, the Singapore government has envisioned a green environment by building abundant parks and gardens and cleaning up rivers and waterways. In addition to these, it has been encouraging its citizens to conserve water and energy as scarce resources. The strategy is reflected in a carbon tax that the government recently announced in its 2017 budget, which will become effective in 2019.[137]

At the corporate level, the government of Singapore allows autonomy for local enterprises to develop their own CSR initiatives. The government considers carefully the recommendations and views expressed by various sectors of the community on any implementation of CSR. The intention of the Singapore government is to identify the latest corporate standards of conduct, the legal effects of which are based on voluntary compliance with a minimum level of government intervention. In Singapore, corporate self-regulation is achieved through complementary mechanisms including domestic and international social and market forces, industry norms and, to a lesser extent, legal liability.[138]

5.8.3 Financial Institutions and Stock Exchange

Sustainability has become a key factor for companies to ensure successful long-term value creation and investors have increasingly called for greater transparency in the environmental, social, governance and CSR practices of listed companies.[139] In this context, the Singapore Exchange (SGX) has committed to improving corporate governance and promoting environmental and social initiatives in Singapore. In June 2011, SGX launched the *Sustainability Reporting Guide* with a view to promoting greater disclosure of environmental, social and corporate governance issues by listed companies on the SGX.[140] In 2017, SGX introduced a "compliance or interpretation" system for sustainable development reports, requiring listed companies to disclose and explain their sustainability practices, which became effective in 2018. In addition, SGX has shown great interest in Singapore's green bond market, including the introduction of the Green Bond Grants Scheme, which was launched in March 2017 by the Monetary Authority of Singapore (MAS).[141]

Local banks in Singapore have been playing an important role in promoting CSR and ESG. In 2015, the Singapore Banking Association issued guidelines for responsible financing. Over the next few years, Singaporean banks are expected to assess customer ESG risks as part of the credit evaluation process. The Monetary Authority of Singapore (MAS) contacts senior management and the board of directors of local banks to promote the full adoption of industry standards and enhanced ESG disclosure by enterprises. Specific measures include completing the ESG assessment of all its corporate customers and enhancing ESG disclosure through peer reviews and industry best practices.[142]

With increasing attention to climate and environmental risks, Singapore's insurance industry began to attempt to quantify and model such risks. Research and analysis are conducted by the Institute of Disaster Risk Management (ICRM), Nanyang Technological University, Singapore (NTU) and the Singapore Observatory, as well as insurance brokers and risk model firms at the National Disaster Research Centre (NDRC). The research and development projects include finding solutions for disaster risk financing. ICRM, for example, is leading a project to establish a database for the analysis and exchange of data on natural disasters with the aim of creating a comprehensive and interactive database on the economic losses of natural disasters. In the coming years, participants in the Singapore insurance industry will be expected to consider environmental risks in their own risk and solvency assessments. Key players are breaking down ESG into investment and underwriting processes and supporting climate risk recovery solutions from Singapore.[143]

5.9.4 Socially Responsible Investment Socially Responsible Investment (SRI) funds in the United States and Europe are growing steadily with more than US$4 trillion under management in 2005–2006. In order to diversify the portfolio, interest in the sub-fund in the Asian region has been increasing annually. The FTSE4Good index, one of the global sustainability indicators, was first registered in Singapore in 2007. In 2008, a large European bank arranged for an SRI analyst to analyze for the first time the environmental, social and governance performance of Asian companies in Singapore. In recent years, the SGX has become aware of the potential impact of SRI funds and has carried out preliminary research in this field.[144] A common form of SRI in Asia is community investment which supports specific activities through finance, investment or loans. The expansion of this form of investment is conducted through direct investment in public enterprises. For example, the Singapore-based Impact Investment Exchange (IIX) aims to provide a regulated trading platform for securities issued by sustainable and non-profit social enterprises in Asia. The platform provides a mobile and transparent market for enterprise investment, enabling enterprises to raise funds and expand their social and environmental impact while at the same time providing investors with good financial, social and environmental returns.[145]

With the rise of SRI, Singapore strengthened the guidelines for investing in sustainable SRI development. MAS and SGX are stepping up their push in this area. To move the overall environment toward more sustainable investment and to focus on CSR, the central bank announced in a statement on October 5, 2015 that it supports the provision of guidance programs to investors, especially institutional investors, on sustainability, social and environmental issues.[146] In addition, the Singapore Banking Association has issued a set of criteria for responsible financing in Singapore in 2015.[147]

5.10 Taiwan

5.10.1 Cultural Impact The business culture, with its Taiwanese characteristics, has great influence on CSR in Taiwan. The two pillars of business culture that support the development of enterprises are Confucian patriarchy and nepotism in Taiwan. Crony capitalism is interpreted as a capitalist political and economic system in which opportunities, interests and resources are allocated mainly on the basis of intimate relationships between people, or *guanxi* in Chinese culture. In the concept of *guanxi*, family relationships are key factors. These self-oriented relationships are extremely vulnerable to corruption and pose a serious threat to integrity and fairness in economic and political development. Confucian familyism (Ip, 1996) is the mainstream culture of Taiwanese society, and enabled the formation of Taiwan-style crony capitalism.[148] Confucian familyism puts the interests of the family at the top of the morality agenda. When there is a conflict of interest between family members and non-family members, this doctrine advocates that the priority should be given to protecting the interests of family members over those of non-family members. Therefore, the Confucian family doctrine and cronyism are intertwined.

Former Taiwan President Chen Shuibian, his immediate family members and close associates have become typical symbols of runaway crony capitalism. They were alleged to have engaged in unethical acts and colluded in serious crimes with a number of companies. There is a long list of charges against them including improper political interference in the activities of private enterprises, conflicts of interest, insider dealing, neglect of duty, corruption, falsification of documents, misappropriation of public funds, money-laundering, etc. Business people flocked to the then first lady, Lady Wu Shuzhen, to gain favor and benefits for their companies. This is clear evidence of cronyism at the top and it is a manifestation of abuse of power. The improper relationships between these companies and the former President and his family were typical CSR issues, including corruption. Whether CSR can thrive in Taiwan depends on how enterprises can effectively control cronyism and yet remain true to Confucian familyism. All walks of life in Taiwan are making efforts to this end.[149]

5.10.2 Export Economy   In 2017, Taiwan's GDP stood at US$5.71 billion, ranking 22nd in the world.[150] International institutions such as the International Institute for Management Development, the Business Environment Risk Intelligence and the World Economic Forum have rated Taiwan highly on its overall economic performance and competitiveness. Taiwan's exports rose in January from a year earlier on the back of strong global demand in 2018, marking a 16-month year-on-year increase in Taiwan's export sales according to its Ministry of Finance.[151]

Taiwan's strong export orientation and high global foreign direct investment contribute to promoting CSR activities in the region. To maintain the stability of exports, enhance the confidence of international enterprises in Taiwan's products and further expand the influence of Taiwan enterprises in the international market, Taiwan enterprises need to meet international standards and abide by global norms on CSR. In addition, with Mainland China being one of Taiwan's largest trading partners, its transformation to a sustainable mode of operation under the concept of the "harmonious society" in recent years has had a great impact on the application of CSR in Taiwan. Since Mainland China is the largest export destination and manufacturing base for Taiwanese enterprises, Taiwan's economic development has benefited from the rapid expansion of the Mainland. It should be noted that the path of CSR transformation in the Mainland has directly affected Taiwanese businessmen with manufacturing bases in Mainland China. The current trend in the environment is toward more standardized and socially responsible enterprises. So Taiwanese companies need to change their traditional practices and take more responsibility for their own business practices both in Mainland China and Taiwan.[152]

5.10.3 Political Drivers   The Taiwan government has played a leading role in promoting and standardizing CSR. The government actively promotes the OECD

Guidelines for Multinational Enterprises and monitors the application of relevant CSR norms such as the United Nation's Global Compact and the Global Sullivan Principles among others. On the issue of labor, the Taiwan government set up the Taiwan Council of Labor Affair to encourage enterprises to pay attention to labor rights and autonomy. In addition, it has pushed the Legislative Yuan to pass the "Labor Three Law Amendment Draft," which provides the regulatory basis for resolving labor issues.

On environmental issues, the Industrial Development Authority of the Ministry of Economy has established databases for promoting and monitoring progress in sustainable development. The Development Council has led the domestic environmental protection industry to provide companies with support and enabled Taiwanese companies to become models of environmental protection recognized by APEC members.[153] On May 3, 2017, the government approved the amendment of the Company Law to create the legal basis to support the advancement of CSR in Taiwan. Vice President Chen Chien-jen believes that companies should be responsible for the health of their employees, communities and the environment to achieve sustainable development of the environment, society and the economy.[154]

5.10.4　Financial Institutions　The government of Taiwan seeks to promote the practice of CSR among domestic and international firms. The Financial Supervisory Commission (FSC) revises the scope of CSR disclosure for Taiwan firms. The government published the *Corporate Social Responsibility Best Practice Principles for the Taiwan Stock Exchange* (TWSE/TPEx), which launched the *Ethical Corporate Management Best Practice Principles* for listed companies. These steps were taken to ensure that listed companies fulfill CSR and implement integrity management measures.[155] In addition, FSC published the *Corporate Governance Roadmap 2013* to provide guidance for Taiwanese enterprises on CSR policies. TWSE also introduced the "TWSE RA Taiwan Employment Creation 99 Index" and "TWSE High Salary 100 Index" indicators. By designing and promoting these indicators, TWSE hopes that businesses will increase employment opportunities and wages for employees. Since 2011, the FSC has been guiding TWSE and TPEx to organize the Business Integrity and Corporate Social Responsibility for Listed Companies Forum, through which model enterprises share their practical experience of corporate integrity and CSR. TWSE joined the World Federation of Exchanges Working Group on Sustainable Development in 2014 to bring Taiwan's capital market norms in line with international standards in environmental, social and corporate governance. This creates a platform to learn and share new information and allows Taiwanese enterprises to keep pace with the development of global CSR.[156] In addition, TWSE announced in 2015 that designated listed companies must disclose CSR reports in accordance with the GRI *G4 Guidelines*.

5.10.5　Socially Responsible Investment　According to a 2014 Association for Sustainable & Responsible Investment in Asia (ASrIA) survey, Taiwan has maintained a stable level of socially responsible investment. Between 2011 and 2013, its sustainable investment remained at around US$700 million, reaching a moderate level in the Asian region.[157] The FTSE4Good TIP Taiwan ESG Index was established in 2017. This index promotes social responsibility investment (SRI) and improves the management mechanism of corporate management tools. The FTSE4Good TIP Taiwan ESG

Index is part of the FTSE Russell's extensive investment index and reflects the performance of Taiwanese companies in environmental, social and corporate governance, marking a new milestone in sustainable investment in Taiwan.[158]

5.11 Thailand

5.11.1 Legal and Political Drivers   The Ministry of Labor established the *Thai Labor Standard: Thai Cooperate Social Responsibility* (TLS 8001—2003) in 2004. The Pollution Control Department (PCD) was established in 1992 under the Royal Decree on the Organizational Division of Pollution Control Department and the Ministry of Science, Technology and Environment. The PCD prepares environmental quality management plans; monitors, controls, prevents and mitigates pollution; as well as developing appropriate methods for the management of solid waste.[159] In 1950, Prime Minister Field Marshal Plaek Pibulsongkram established the National Economic Council (NEC), which provided advice to the government on national economic issues. In 1959, Prime Minister Field Marshal Sarit Dhanarajata restructured the NEC, and renamed it the Office of the National Economic Development Board (NEDB). Social development was officially emphasized in the agenda of the National Plan in 1972, which restructured the NEDB as the National Economic and Social Development Board (NESDB) under the Office of the Prime Minister. The functions of the NESDB are to provide suggestions on national economy and social development and to establish the coordination mechanism between the NESDB, concerned agencies and state enterprises.[160] CSR legislation also supports CSR activities in Thailand. One notable legislative activity is the enactment of the Product Responsibility Law in 2009, which concerns potential injuries due to manufacture, import and sale of goods.

5.11.2 Multinational Corporations   Foreign Direct Investment (FDI) to Thailand reached US$7.1 billion in 2017.[161] As one of the large FDI destinations in Asia, Thailand has attracted a large number of MNCs. MNCs influenced many aspects of CSR. In order to meet the CSR standards set by MNCs, local supply chain manufacturers are pressured to implement various standards including ISO quality (ISO 9000), safety (ISO 18000) and environment standards (ISO 14000). MNCs also actively implement CSR activities which directly contribute to the improvement of social and environmental conditions in Thailand. For example, Nike initiated the Nike Village Development project, which involves people from Nike, the government and the community in facilitating development in some districts in Thailand.

5.11.3 Non-Governmental Organizations (NGOs)   The Thailand Business Council for Sustainable Development (TBCSD) was established by former Prime Minster Mr. Anand Panyarachun in 1993. The 36-member council constitutes individuals from 36 highly profitable local companies and MNCs. The TBCSD aims to promote the sustainable development goals (SDGs) by increasing environmental awareness at firm level.[162] The Carbon Reduction Certification for Buildings is one TBCSD project, which honors low-energy-consumption buildings. The buildings which qualify under this certification are environmentally friendly and can reduce greenhouse gas (GHG) emissions to a certain acceptable level.[163]

The Thailand Environment Institute (TEI) was established in 1993 to deal with environmental issues. The TEI has strong connections with the government, local communities, civil society organizations (CSOs) and multinational organizations to promote global environmental standards and policies in Thailand.[164] Since 2005, the TEI has held a series of training programs with emphasis on environmental knowledge, natural resources management, and sustainable and efficient use of energy. The TEI also provides courses on laws and regulations. Up to 2013, more than 16,000 people had attended TEI training, workshops and seminars.[165]

5.11.4 Stock Exchange　The Stock Exchange of Thailand (SET)'s objective is to establish a solid SDG foundation for the capital market. The SET promotes sustainable development by increasing stakeholders' awareness of long-term sustainable strategies in business processes and investments. In 2007, SET established the Social Responsibility Center (SR Center) under its original name, the Corporate Social Responsibility Institute. This SR Center offers sustainability opinions and recommendations for stakeholders in the capital market including the SET itself.[166]

5.12　Vietnam

5.12.1 Legal and Political Drivers　Vietnam has been a socialist-oriented market economy ruled by the Communist Party of Vietnam (CPV). In the mid 1980s, Vietnam introduced a major economic reform called *Doi Moi* (renovation). Since then, the country has removed several trading barriers, attracted more FDI, and been well integrated into the global economy. Despite that, the ideology of Vietnam is the basis for the government to take social issues seriously. Nevertheless, the ideology is not consistent with the prevailing CSR standards, which largely originate from Western countries. In response to increasing globalization, the Vietnam government gradually reformed its policies and embraced the Western concept of CSR. For example, the EU–Vietnam Free Trade Agreement include CSR clauses which drive Vietnamese companies to engage in CSR activities more actively.[167] In Vietnam, the Ministry of Labour, Invalids and Social Affairs coordinates CSR initiatives. The Vietnam government also exerts influence on the economy through SOEs. Due to Vietnamese ideology, SOEs shoulder more social responsibilities than private companies.[168]

5.12.2 Multinational Corporations　Following *Doi Moi*, Vietnam passed the FDI law in 1987 and has amended this law several times subsequently. Since the passage of the law, foreign direct investment in Vietnam has experienced a significant increase. The accession to the WTO in 2007 further fueled FDI growth in Vietnam, leaping from US$2.5 billion during 2000–2005 to US$8.4 billion in 2008–2014. In 2005, the contribution of FDI to the GDP reached 201 percent, signifying the significant impact of FDI on the economy.[169] Several world-class MNCs started operations in Vietnam and brought CSR practices to the country. Like other countries in Asia, many local companies that seek to become suppliers of MNCs have to follow the CSR requirements set by the MNCs. The MNCs also provide benchmarks for CSRs that allows local firms to improve their CSR practices.

5.12.3 Non-Governmental Organizations　The 1992 Constitution of the Socialist Republic of Vietnam states that its residents have freedom of assembly and association.

Since then, the government has established legal channels for the development of NGOs. However, there is no specific law for associations in Vietnam. As a result, most NGOs seek legal recognition and work under the state's regulations.[170] A 2013 survey reported that NGOs in Vietnam are engaging in promoting philanthropic programs, with only 11 percent of the NGOs interviewed benefiting from charity. Technical cooperation is the main type of interaction (35 percent) between NGOs (especially Vietnamese NGOs) and the private sector. Many Vietnamese NGOs are serving to reduce poverty in the rural areas. CSR issues like environmental protection is only a long-term strategic objective. In this regard, only 13 percent of NGOs have strategic cooperation relations with the private sector, which implies that Vietnamese NGOs lack professionalism and credibility in their management.

Established in 2007, the Global Compact Network Vietnam (GCNV) was created jointly with the United Nations in Vietnam and the Vietnam Chamber of Commerce and Industry (VCCI). The GCNV is the Vietnamese network for the United Nations Global Compact (UNGC). The GCNV represents 70 members including domestic and international firms, non-governmental organizations (NGOs), schools or institutions and UN and other government agencies.

In November 2015, the GCNV held the CSR Calendar Forum—Special Edition on AEC (ASEAN Economic Community)[171] in order to improve the technical standards and customer satisfaction of SMEs in the AEC. Members who attended the CSR forum shared their ideas on social-environmental-technical-ethical issues through "The Blackbox of technical and ethical expectations."[172] In September 2016, the GCNV held the CSR Calendar Forum on Food Safety, which had close connections with other CSR issues like transparency and environmental concerns. A series of fora were held to promote the importance of food safety, address standards and technology in food production and build up trust within retailers' value chains.[173]

The American Chamber of Commerce in Hanoi (AmCham Hanoi) provides services for American businesses in Vietnam. AmCham Hanoi's objective is to improve Vietnam–America business.[174] AmCham's CSR Recognition Award honors the member companies with the best CSR projects in four areas, namely (1) business goals and societal needs (2) long-term strategic management (3) communication and sharing and (4) sustainability.[175] In 2017, Dow Vietnam won this CSR Award for the firm's long-term contributions to Vietnam's economy.

5.12.4 Socially Responsible Investment   Established in 2006, Vietnam Holding (VNH) is an investment fund promoting equity in Vietnam. VNH acts as a sustainable investment in line with the environmental, social and governance (ESG) practices of the United Nations *Principles for Responsible Investing*.[176] The majority of investments in VNH are from Ho Chi Minh City Stock Exchange (HOSE) and Hanoi Stock Exchange (HNX) listed firms which have long-term investment strategies. VNH holds the VNH Forum annually to discuss ESG themes and issues. VNH also provides ESG workshops at industry level. The VNH Foundation helps children with health problems.[177] In 2016, VNH conducted a case study on Engagements Affecting Portfolio Construction which was included in PRI's "A Practical Guide to ESG Integration for Equity Investing."[178]

6. ANALYSIS OF DRIVERS AND SOURCES OF BUSINESS SUSTAINABILITY IN ASIA

In summary, countries in Asia have their own sustainability programs and initiatives that are shaped by their unique individual economic, cultural, political and legal infrastructures. The key driver for business sustainability in Mainland China is the Central government, which is run by the Communist Party of China (CPC). The high level of government initiatives and interventions is intended to align the nationwide CSR sustainability programs with the country's development policy. The CPC plays the most significant role in CSR, especially for SOEs and publicly listed companies in both the Shanghai and Shenzhen Stock Exchanges.

The key driver for business sustainability in Hong Kong is the Stock Exchange, which commenced with the introduction of ESG disclosure as early as 2005. In 2015, it also issued the *Environmental, Social and Governance (ESG) Reporting Guide*, which requires listed companies to disclose CSR on a comply-or-explain basis, effective for financial years ending on or after December 31, 2015. Apart from the HKSE, other business associations such as the Hong Kong General Chamber of Commerce and professional institutes such as the Hong Kong Institute of Certified Public Accountants (HKICPA) also enhanced the promotion of ESG and business sustainability.

India started with a history of philanthropy, with religion as the fundamental basis for early business sustainability. With this basis, the government became the key driver of business sustainability, with CSR as the main element for business enterprises.

ESG in Indonesia is mainly driven by the government through legal enactment for SOEs and listed companies in the natural resource and related industries. Other private organizations and foundations have been influenced by MNCs in Western countries to enhance the promotion of CSR in Indonesia.

In Japan, the main drivers for business sustainability are similar to those of other countries, that is, the government enacting laws, together with the stock exchange. One significant influence on the government is the importance placed on the export economy. MNCs from the West consider CSR important, hence they act through the government to drive CSR in Japan.

Unlike Japan, the government and private agencies and organizations are considered to be the main drivers for South Korea's business sustainability.

The key driver for Malaysia's business sustainability is the government in enacting CSR reporting requirements for its publicly listed companies. Making CSR disclosure a mandatory legal requirement is a unique feature of Malaysia as compared with many Asian countries. Private and public organizations also organize CSR awards to encourage good practices.

The key driver for business sustainability in the Philippines is similar to those of Indonesia, namely the government and the stock exchange. Recently, the government enacted revisions to the tax codes to provide incentives for CSR activities.

The Singaporean government is the main driver for business sustainability alongside non-profit organizations such as the Singapore Global Compact Network, which has made significant progress in advocating for CSR in Singapore.

Taiwan's business culture based on relationships accounts for the main driver of the development of business sustainability. Similar to Japan, as an export economy, Taiwan and its government are influenced by Western MNCs to adopt CSR norms.

The main driver of business sustainability for Thailand is the stock exchange, which has established a solid foundation for the sustainable development goals. In addition, Western MNCs also influenced the development of CSR practices in Thailand.

Vietnam's Sustainable Development Strategy for 2011–2020, approved by its government, is the key driver of business sustainability. Similar to Mainland China, Vietnam's ideology of communism forms the basis for its CSR activities and programs. It follows from this that CSR has also been widely promoted by its labor and union laws as well as by professional organizations such as its Chamber of Commerce.

In most Asian economies, such as Hong Kong, Singapore and Thailand, SRI is just beginning to be developed and its recognition by stakeholders including investors is limited.

7. CONCLUSIONS

Business sustainability is an important corporate decision and its economic consequences are of considerable interest to all stakeholders including investors and regulators. Recent developments on mandatory and voluntary sustainability disclosure enable management to exercise judgement in disclosing sustainability information. Anecdotal and academic evidence suggest that more mandatory or voluntary disclosures of sustainability performance information are good practice. There are many drivers of sustainability in Asia including political, economic, cultural and the capital market. These drivers may affect the implementation of business sustainability activities and programs in various countries.

8. CHAPTER TAKEAWAY

1. Business organizations should increase the quality and quantity of all stakeholder engagements with sustainability development.
2. Global mandatory and voluntary business sustainability initiatives have been explored as bases for influencing business sustainability in Asia.
3. Countries in Asia have their own sustainability programs and initiatives that are shaped by their individual economic, cultural, political, and legal infrastructures.
4. There are many unique features of sustainability in Asia; of these, the two sociopolitical factors which affect the implementation of sustainability are the influence of the government and regional differences.

ENDNOTES

1. Global Reporting Initiative (GRI), 2017, http://database.globalreporting.org/search/.
2. Z. Rezaee, *Business Sustainability: Performance, Compliance, Accountability and Integrated Reporting* (London and New York: Greenleaf Publishing Limited, 2015).

3. European Commission, *Disclosure of Non-Financial Information*, Europe Information: European Council, the European Economic and Social, Environmental Issues, 2014, https://ec.europa.eu/info/business-economy-euro/company-reporting-and-auditing/company-reporting/non-financial-reporting_en.
4. Delaware General Assembly, House Bill 310: An Act to Amend Title 6 of the Delaware Code Relating to the Certification of Adoption of Sustainability and Transparency Standards by Delaware Entities, June 27, 2018, https://legis.delaware.gov/BillDetail/26304.
5. Sarbanes-Oxley Act (SOX), 2002.
6. Rezaee, *Business Sustainability*.
7. Investor Responsibility Research Center Institute (IRRCI), *How Investors Integrate ESG: A Typology of Approaches*, April 2017, https://irrcinstitute.org/wp-content/uploads/2017/04/FinalIRRCiReport_HowInvestorsIntegrateESG.ATypologyofApproaches.pdf.
8. European Commission, *Corporate Social Responsibility (CSR)*, 2011, http://ec.europa.eu/growth/industry/corporate-social-responsibility_en.
9. Ibid.
10. Ibid.
11. European Commission, *Disclosure of Non-Financial Information*, Europe Information: European Council, the European Economic and Social, Environmental Issues, 2014, https://ec.europa.eu/info/business-economy-euro/company-reporting-and-auditing/company-reporting/non-financial-reporting_en.
12. Global Reporting Initiative (GRI), *G4 Sustainability Reporting Guidelines*, 2013, https://www.globalreporting.org/resourcelibrary/GRIG4-Part1-Reporting-Principles-and-Standard-Disclosures.pdf.
13. Ibid.
14. Ibid., 7–8.
15. Ibid., 11–12.
16. Ibid., 13.
17. KPMG, *GRI's G4 Guidelines: The Impact on Reporting*, 2013, http://www.kpmg.com/Global/en/IssuesAndInsights/ArticlesPublications/Documents/g4-the-impact-on-reporting-v2.pdf.
18. Ibid.
19. International Integrated Reporting Committee (IIRC), *IIRC Consultative Draft*, 2013, section 3.12, p. 19, http://www.theiirc.org/consultationdraft2013/.
20. Ibid.
21. Ibid.
22. IIRC, *IIRC Consultative Draft*.
23. Sustainability Accounting Standards Board (SASB), "US SASB Publishes Exposure Drafts on Health Care Sector Sustainability Reporting," 2013, http://www.iasplus.com/en/othernews/united-states/2013/sasb-health-care-ed.
24. Ibid.
25. United Nations (UN), *How Investors Are Addressing Environmental, Social and Governance Factors in Fundamental Equity Valuation, United Nations-Supported Principles for Responsible Investment (PRI)*, February 2013, http://www.unpri.org/viewer/?file=wp-content/uploads/Integrated_Analysis_2013.pdf.
26. United Nations Global Compact (UNGC), *Guide to Corporate Sustainability*, 2015, https://www.unglobalcompact.org/docs/publications/UN_Global_Compact_Guide_to_Corporate_Sustainability.pdf.
27. Ibid.
28. Sustainable Development Solutions Network, "Indicators and a Monitoring Framework for the Sustainable Development Goals: Launching a Data Revolution for the SDGs," 2015, http://unsdsn.org/wp-content/uploads/2015/03/150320-SDSN-Indicator-Report.pdf.
29. Ibid.

30. Global Reporting Initiative (GRI), *Linking the GRI Standards and the European Directive on Non-Financial and Diversity Disclosure*, 2017, https://www.globalreporting.org/standards/resource-download-center/linking-gri-standards-and-european-directive-on-non-financial-and-diversity-disclosure/.

31. International Federation of Accountants, *The 2030 Agenda for Sustainable Development: A Snapshot of the Accountancy Profession's Contribution* (New York: International Federation of Accountants, 2016), https://www.ifac.org/publications-resources/2030-agenda-sustainable-development.

32. PwC, *SDG Reporting Challenge 2017, Exploring Business Communication on the Global Goals*, 2017, https://www.pwc.com/gx/en/sustainability/SDG/pwc-sdg-reporting-challenge-2017-final.pdf.

33. Ibid.

34. Ibid.

35. Sustainability Accounting Standards Board (SASB), "US SASB Publishes Exposure Drafts on Health Care Sector Sustainability Reporting," 2013, http://www.iasplus.com/en/othernews/united-states/2013/sasb-health-care-ed.

36. IIRC, *IIRC Consultative Draft*.

37. Climate Change Reporting Taxonomy (CCRT), *Climate Change Reporting Taxonomy, Taxonomy Architecture and Style Guide*, 2012, https://www.cdproject.net/Documents/xbrl/CCRT-taxonomy-architecture-and-style-guide-v1-0.pdf.

38. IIRC, *IIRC Consultative Draft*.

39. Climate Change Reporting Taxonomy (CCRT), "Climate Change Reporting Taxonomy (CCRT) Due Process," 2013, https://www.cdproject.net/en-us/news/pages/xbrl-due-process.aspx.

40. International Integrated Reporting Council (IIRC), *Consultation Draft of the International Integrated Reporting Framework*, April 2013, www.theiirc.org/consultationdraft2013.

41. Y. Cai, C.H. Pan, and M. Statman, Why Do Countries Matter So Much in Corporate Social Performance? *Journal of Corporate Finance* 41 (2016): 591–609.

42. Country Sustainability Ranking Update—November 2017, http://www.robecosam.com/images/Country_Ranking_Update_October_2017.pdf.

43. World Bank, *The World Bank in China*, March 28, 2017, http://www.worldbank.org/en/country/china/overview.

44. CSR Asia, *A Study on Corporate Social Responsibility Development and Trends in China*, Embassy of Sweden in Beijing, 2015.

45. State Council of China, *Suggestions of the State Council on Strengthening Major Activities of Environmental Protection*, October 17, 2011.

46. P. Duan and R. G. Eccles, "The State of Sustainability in China," *Journal of Applied Corporate Finance* 26, no. 3 (2014): 76–84.

47. L. Bu, M. Bloomfield, and J. An, *CSR Guide for Multinational Corporations in China*, Harmony Foundation of Canada, 2013.

48. M. Liu, "Is Corporate Social Responsibility China's Secret Weapon?" World Economic Forum, March 17, 2015, https://www.weforum.org/agenda/2015/03/is-corporate-social-responsibility-chinas-secret-weapon/.

49. S. Dan, *Exchanges and Sustainable Investment* (Paris: World Federation of Exchanges, 2009).

50. CBI and the China Central Depository & Clearing Company, *China Green Bond Market 2016*, https://www.climatebonds.net/files/files/SotM-2016-Final-WEB-A4.pdf.

51. Ibid.

52. Shanghai Stock Exchange, "Historical Events," 2016, http://english.sse.com.cn/aboutsse/sseoverview/historical/.

53. China Banking Regulatory Commission official website: www.cbrc.gov.cn/english/home/jsp/index.jsp.

54. Guidelines on Credit Underwriting for Energy Conservation and Emission Reduction, http://www.cbrc.gov.cn/EngdocView.do?docID=200908050CE9DC53F577564BFF554A F1CDE5E600.
55. http://app1.hkicpa.org.hk/APLUS/2018/01/pdf/10_Business.pdf.
56. https://www.gov.hk/en/residents/environment/business/cppp.htm.
57. http://www.info.gov.hk/gia/general/201412/15/P201412150407.htm.
58. Consultation Paper Environmental, Social and Governance Reporting Guide, December 2011, HKEX.
59. N. Leung, "Limited HK ESG Funds Force Investors to Look Further Afield," 2017, https://www.asiaasset.com/news/ESG_funds_nl_nim_final_DM.aspx.
60. "Why Is Asia Lukewarm to Sustainable Investing?" *South Morning Post*, October 14, 2017, https://www.scmp.com/business/companies/article/2115233/why-asia-lukewarm-sustainable-investing.
61. "Hong Kong Outlines Grant for First-Time Corporate Bond Issuers and Plans for Green Bonds in Budget," *South China Morning Post*, March 01, 2018, https://www.scmp.com/business/article/2135161/hong-kong-outlines-grant-first-time-corporate-bond-issuers-and-plans-green
62. HKEX, *Consultation Paper on Review of the Environmental, Social and Governance Reporting*, 2015, http://www.hkex.com.hk/-/media/HKEX-Market/News/Market-Consultations/2011-to-2015/July-2015-Consultation-Pape/Consultation-paper/cp201507.pdf.
63. KPMG, *India's CSR Reporting Survey 2017*, 2018, s. l.
64. PwC, *Handbook on Corporate Social Responsibility in India* (Haryana: Pricewaterhouse-Coopers Private Limited, 2013).
65. B. Sharma, *Contextualising CSR in Asia: Corporate Social Responsibility in Asian Economies* (Singapore: Lien Centre for Social Innovation, 2013).
66. D. Kode and M. Jacob, *India: Democracy Threatened by Growing Attacks on Civil Society*, CIVICUS World Alliance for Citizen Participation, 2017, s. l.
67. Human Rights Watch, *World Report 2017*, https://www.hrw.org/world-report/2017/country-chapters/india.
68. CIVICUS, *State of Civil Society Report 2018*, https://www.civicus.org/index.php/state-of-civil-society-report-2018.
69. Bureau of Indian Standards, *Good Governance in Corporate Social Responsibility*, Management Systems Department (BIS), 2017, s. l.
70. R. Kumar and D. Siddy, *Sustainable Investment in India* (Washington, DC: International Finance Corporation, 2009).
71. Oxfam India, *Drops Before The Rain?* (New Delhi: Oxfam India, 2017).
72. Press Trust of India, "SEBI Finalises Norms for Listing of Green Bonds," 2017, https://economictimes.indiatimes.com/markets/stocks/news/sebi-finalises-norms-for-listing-of-green-bonds/articleshow/58444005.cms.
73. Corporate Responsibility Watch, *Status of Corporate Responsibility in India, 2017*, Praxis, 2017, s. l.
74. UN India, "Scheduled Castes and Scheduled Tribes," http://in.one.un.org/task-teams/scheduled-castes-and-scheduled-tribes/.
75. CSR Netherlands, "Country Scan: CSR in Indonesia," 2016, https://mvonederland.nl/sites/default/files/media/Country%20Scan%20Indonesia%2C%20v2.2.pdf
76. UNEP, "Towards a Sustainable Financial System in Indonesia," 2015 http://web.worldbank.org/archive/website01585/WEB/IMAGES/INDONESI.PDF?MOD=AJPERES
77. Millennium Challenge Account-Indonesia (MCA-Indonesia), "About Us | MCA-Indonesia," http://www.mca-indonesia.go.id/en/about_us/trustee_institution.
78. Millennium Challenge Account-Indonesia (MCA-Indonesia), "About Us | Vision & Mission," http://www.mca-indonesia.go.id/en/about_us/vision_and_mission.

79. KEHATI. 2013. History of KEHATI foundation. Available at http://kehati.or.id/about-us-2/

80. Layungasri, G. R. 2010. Challenges for Sustainability Index: Is Being 'Green' Economically Viable for Indonesian Mining Companies? Available at http://dx.doi.org/10.2139/ssrn.1589120

81. Indonesia Business Links (IBL), "About Us," http://www.ibl.or.id/en/profile/about-us.

82. Indonesia Business Links (IBL), "Events | IBL Conferences on CSR," http://www.ibl.or.id/en/events.

83. Indonesia Business Links (IBL), "Events | Non-Conferences Events," http://www.ibl.or.id/en/events.

84. National Center for Sustainability Reporting (NCSR), "About NCSR," http://www.ncsr-id.org/about-ncsr/.

85. National Center for Sustainability Reporting (NCSR), "GRI Standards Certified Training," http://www.ncsr-id.org/gri-certified-training/.

86. "Japan—Market Overview," June 12, 2017, https://www.export.gov/article?id=Japan-Market-Overview.

87. Observatory of Economic Complexity, "Japan," 2016, https://atlas.media.mit.edu/en/profile/country/jpn/.

88. D. M. Boehe and L. B. Cruz, "How Does Corporate Social Responsibility Influence Export Performance," EnANPAD, XXX IIIEncontro da ANPAD, Sao Paulo/SP—19 a 23 de setembro de 2009.

89. K. Fukukawa and Y. Teramoto, "Understanding Japanese CSR: The Reflections of Managers in the Field of Global Operations," *Journal of Business Ethics* 85 (2009): 133–146, DOI: 10.1007/s10551-008-9933-7.

90. J. D. Margolis and J. P. Walsh, *People and Profits: The Search for a Link between a Company's Sodal and Financial Performance* (Mahwah, N.J.: Erlbaum, 2001).

91. M. Orlitzky, F. L. Schmidt and S. L. Rynes, "Corporate Social and Financial Performance: A Meta-Analysis," *Organization Studies* 24, no. 3 (2003): 403–441.

92. M. J. Munoz-Torres, M. A. Fernandez-Izquierdo and M. R. Balaguer-Franch, "The Social Responsibility Performance of Ethical and Solidarity Funds: An Approach to the Case of Spain," *Business Ethics* 13 (2004): 200.

93. B. Sharma, *Contextualising CSR in Asia.*

94. C. Louche and K, Sakuma, "Socially Responsible Investment in Japan: Its Mechanism and Drivers," *Business and Professional Ethics Journal*, Philosophy Documentation Center, 82, no. 2 (2008): 425–448.

95. Daiwa Investor Relations, *The year of IR—Livedoor, Enron, Continued Disclosure and Scandals, Increasing Interest in CSR* (in Japanese), 2006.

96. K. KokubuTh, H. Kitada and B. M. Haider, *Corporate Sustainability Barometer in Japan*, Kobe University, 2013.

97. Division for Sustainable Development, *Japan's Efforts Toward Achieving the SDGs Through PPAP, Public, Private Action for Partnership*, 2017.

98. Japan Exchange Group "About JPX," May 2015.

99. Japan Exchange Group, "Japan Exchange Group Joins the Sustainable Stock Exchanges Initiative," December 2017, https://www.jpx.co.jp/english/corporate/news-releases/0070/20171206-01.html.

100. S.-Y. Kim and J. A. Mathews, "Korea's Greening Strategy: The Role of Smart Microgrids," *Asia-Pacific Journal: Japan Focus* 14, no. 24 (2016).

101. Bloomberg, "Company Overview of Korea Smart Grid Institute," https://www.bloomberg.com/research/stocks/private/snapshot.asp?privcapId=109930653.

102. B. Sharma, *Contextualising CSR in Asia.*

103. International Smart Grid Action Network, *ISGAN Annual Report Year 5*, Korea Smart Grid Institute, 2016, s. l.

104. International Organization for Standardization, "KATS (Korea, Republic of)," https://www.iso.org/member/1663.html.

105. B. Sharma, *Contextualising CSR in Asia*.

106. Korean Agency for Technology and Standards, *Standards Build Trust: KATS Annual Report 2016*, Korean Agency for Technology and Standards, 2017, s. 1.

107. IEC-IEEE-KATS, "Future Challenges in Standardization," 2018, https://www.iecieeekats.com.

108. Federation of Korean Industries, "Introduction," http://www.fki.or.kr/en/about/Intro.aspx.

109. Federation of Korean Industries, "CSR activities Lead Up to Culturally Advanced Country," 2014, http://www.fki.or.kr/en/research/View.aspx?content_id=90d0c066-511f-4d38-ae82-61084dc72d99&cPage=1&search_type=0&search_keyword=.

110. B. Sharma, *Contextualising CSR in Asia*.

111. D. Oh and S. A. Ahn, "Improving South Korean Corporate Govenance," 2015, http://www.iflr.com/Article/3429769/Improving-South-Korean-corporate-governance.html.

112. Yonhap, "S. Korea's Socially Responsible Investment Estimated At US$8 bln," 2015, http://english.yonhapnews.co.kr/business/2015/02/03/0501000000AEN201502030026003 20.html?6088ccb0.

113. R. C. Moura-Leite and R. C. Padgett, "Historical Background of Corporate Social Responsibility," *Social Responsibility Journal* 7, no. 4 (2011): 528–539.

114. J. Lopez, "Malaysia Leads in Sustainability Reporting," *Accountants Today* (2010): 10–13.

115. Ibid.

116. Global Reporting Initiative, Sustainability Disclosure Database, http://database.globalreporting.org/search.

117. M. Sulaiman, N. Abdullah and A. H. Fatima, "Determinants of Environmental Reporting Quality," *Malaysia International Journal of Economics, Management and Accounting* 22, no. 1 (2014): 63–90.

118. PwC, "going beyond philanthropy? Pulse-check on sustainability," 2012, https://www.pwc.com/my/en/assets/publications/pulse-check-on-sustainability.pdf

119. Ibid.

120. UNICEF, *CSR Policies in Malaysia "Enhancing Child Focus"* 2013, www.Unicef.Www.Unicef.Org/Malaysiaorg/Malaysia

121. M. Norhasimah, A. S. B. Norhabibi, A. A. Nor, M.Q.A.S. K. Sheh and M. A. Inaliah, "The Effect of Environmental Disclosure on Financial Performance in Malaysia," *7th International Economics & Business Management Conference*, 5th and 6th October 2015.

122. S. Buniamin, "The Quantity and Quality of Environmental Reporting in Annual Report of Public Listed Companies in Malaysia," Issues in Social and Environmental Accounting, 4, no. 2 (2010): 115–135.

123. Ministry of Energy, Green Technology and Water, www.Kettha.Gov.My/En/Content/Aboutministry.

124. S. Syarikat, "Malaysia: Corporate Responsibility Agenda 'Driving Business beyond Profitability'," 2009 http://www.ssm.com.my/docs/SSMCRAgenda.pdf.

125. A.A. Adam and E.R. Shauki, "Socially Responsible Investment in Malaysia: Behavioral Framework in Evaluating Investors' Decision-Making Process," *Journal of Cleaner Production* 80 (2014): 224–240.

126. Global Sustainable Investment Alliance, *The Global Sustainable Investment Review 2016*, 2016, http://www.gsi-alliance.org/wp-content/uploads/2017/03/GSIR_Review2016.F.pdf.

127. Prime Minister's CSR Awards, Starbiz-ICR Malaysia CR Awards: https://www.najibrazak.com/en/speeches/presentation-ceremony-of-prime-ministers-csr-awards-2009/; https://www.pressreader.com/malaysia/the-star-malaysia/20110402/285490772402111.

128. Ibid.

129. APEC, *Corporate Social Responsibility in the APEC Region*, 2005.
130. Asian Institute of Management RVR Center for Corporate Responsibility, *Corporate Social Responsibility in the APEC Region—Current Status and Implications*, Asia-Pacific Economic Cooperation, 2005.
131. League of Corporate Foundations, "About the LCF," 2010, http://www.lcf.org.ph/.
132. PSE Foundation Inc, "History," 2018, http://www.pseacademy.com.ph/LS/staticpages/id-1308744966964/PSE_Foundation_Inc.html.
133. PSE, *Interpretation of the Suitability Rule of the Exchange*, November 27, 2007.
134. PSE Corporate, *Governance Guidelines for Listed Companies*, March 31, 2017.
135. Association for Sustainable & Responsible Investment in Asia (ASrIA), *Asia Sustainable Investment Review*, 2014.
136. E. K. B. Tan, *The State of Play of CSR in Singapore*. Social Insight Research Series, Lien Centre for Social Innovation Reports, 2011.
137. Ministry of Finance, "Singapore's Role in Deepening Regional Green Finance," Singapore government, November 2017.
138. E. K. B. Tan, *The State of Play of CSR in Singapore*.
139. Singapore Exchange Ltd, *Sustainability*, 2017, http://investorrelations.sgx.com/sustainability.cfm.
140. Singapore Exchange Ltd, *Corporate Social Responsibility (CSR) Report*, 2011.
141. Ministry of Finance, "Singapore's Role in Deepening Regional Green Finance."
142. Ibid.
143. Ibid.
144. M. Ong, *Contextualizing Corporate Social Responsibility in Singapore*. Centre on Asia and Globalization, National University of Singapore, September 2008, ISSN 1793-835X.
145. G. Williams, *Socially Responsible Investment in Asia* (Lien Centre for Social Innovation, Singapore Management University, 2010).
146. Association for Sustainable & Responsible Investment in Asia, *2014 Asia Sustainable Investment Review*, 2014.
147. "ABS Releases Guidelines for Responsible Lending," *Straits Times*, October 8, 2015, https://www.straitstimes.com/business/banking/abs-releases-guidelines-for-responsible-lending.
148. P.-K. Ip, "Confucian Familial Collectivism and the Underdevelopment of the Civic Person" in *Research and Endeavors in Moral and Civic Education*, ed. L. N. K. Lo and S. W. Man (Hong Kong: The Chinese University Press, 1996), 39–58.
149. P.-K. Ip, "Corporate Social Responsibility and Crony Capitalism in Taiwan," *Journal of Business Ethics* 79 (2008): 167–177, DOI: 10.1007/s10551-007-9385-5.
150. International Monetary Fund, World Economic Outlook Database, October 2017.
151. CNA, "Taiwan Reports Export Growth for 16th Straight Month in January," Feb. 2, 2018.
152. B. Sharma, *Contextualising CSR in Asia*.
153. H.-T. Chang, *Corporate Social Responsibility in the APEC Region*, Asia-Pacific Economic Cooperation, 2005.
154. B. Chiu, H. Ya-chuan and S. C. Chang, "Taiwan to Legislate on Corporate Social Responsibility: Vice President," Central News Agency, May 3, 2017.
155. World Investment Forum and United Nations UNCTAD, *Sustainable Stock Exchanges: Real Obstacles, Real Opportunities*, 2010.
156. Taiwan Stock Exchange, "Corporation Corporate Social Responsibility Overview," 2014 http://cgc.twse.com.tw/frontEN/responsibility.
157. Association for Sustainable & Responsible Investment in Asia (ASrIA), *Asia Sustainable Investment Review*, 2014.
158. FTSE Russell, "FTSE Russell Introduces FTSE4Good TIP Taiwan ESG Index, December 18, 2017, http://www.ftserussell.com/files/press-releases/ftse-russell-introduces-ftse4good-tip-taiwan-esg-index.

159. PCD, "About," http://www.pcd.go.th/en_ab_about.cfm.

160. NESDB, "History and Role of NESDB," http://www.nesdb.go.th/nesdb_en/ewt_news .php?nid=4258.

161. https://data.worldbank.org/indicator/BX.KLT.DINV.CD.WD?locations=TH&name_ desc=true.

162. TBCSD, "About: History," http://www.tei.or.th/tbcsd/about_tbcsd/index.html.

163. TBCSD, "What is Carbon Reduction Certification for Building?" http://www.tei.or.th/ carbonreductionbuilding/about/what-e.html.

164. TEI, "Background of Thailand Environment Institute (TEI)," http://www.tei.or.th/en/ about.php.

165. TEI, "Capacity Building for Environmental management Personnel Training Program Thailand Environment Institute Foundation," http://www.tei.or.th/en/courses_training .php.

166. Stock Exchange of Thailand, "About Social Responsibility Center (SR Center)," https:// www.set.or.th/sustainable_dev/en/sr/about/about_p1.html.

167. R. Peels, E. M. Echeverria, J. Aissi, and A. Schneider, *Corporate Social Responsibility in International Trade and Investment Agreements: Implications for States, Business, and Workers* (Hanoi: International Labour Office, 2016), http://www.ilo.org/wcmsp5/ groups/public/-%2D-dgreports/-%2D-inst/documents/publication/wcms_476193.pdf.

168. M. Nguyen, J. Bensemann, and S. Kelly, "Corporate Social Responsibility (CSR) in Vietnam: A Conceptual Framework," *International Journal of Corporate Social Responsibility* 3, no. 1 (2018): 9.

169. https://oxfordbusinessgroup.com/overview/bucking-trend-foreign-direct-investment-and-trade-continue-climb.

170. Batik International, *Civil Society and Corporate Social Responsibility in Vietnam* (Hanoi: Center for Development and Integration, 2013.

171. ASEAN Economic Community (AEC).

172. Global Compact Network Vietnam, *CSR Calendar Forum—Special Edition on AEC in HCMC, November 26th 2015*, http://www.globalcompactvietnam.org/detail.asp? id=220.

173. Global Compact Network Vietnam, *CSR Calendar Forum on Food Safety*, 2016, http:// www.globalcompactvietnam.org/detail.asp?id=247.

174. American Chamber of Commerce in Hanoi, "About Us," http://www.amchamhanoi.com/ about-us/.

175. American Chamber of Commerce in Hanoi, "CSR Award 2017," 2017, http://www .amchamhanoi.com/csraward2017/.

176. Vietnam Holding Limited, "Sustainability," http://www.vietnamholding.com/ sustainability.

177. Vietnam Holding Limited, "About VNH," http://www.vietnamholding.com/about.

178. Vietnam Holding Limited, "Sustainability," http://www.vietnamholding.com/ sustainability.

CHAPTER 5

Financial Economic Dimension of Sustainability

1. EXECUTIVE SUMMARY

Previous chapters briefly discussed the five economic, governance, social, ethical and environmental (EGSEE) dimensions of sustainability performance. The fast-growing move toward business sustainability has created unprecedented challenges for business organizations worldwide to present reliable and useful financial and non-financial information on their key performance indicators (KPIs) pertaining to all five EGSEE dimensions of sustainability performance. The primary function of business entities is to create shareholder value through continuous sustainable economic performance. This chapter discusses the importance of economic sustainability performance; (ESP) and related KPIs, measurement, recognition and reporting in the form of financial statements; and performance assurance in the framework of audit reports on financial statements and internal control over financial reporting (ICFR). This chapter also describes in detail the financial ESP dimension, its importance and relevance in ensuring a sustainable organization, and its value relevant disclosures, reporting and assurance worldwide and in Asia. Non-financial governance, social, ethical and environmental (GSEE) dimensions of sustainability performance and reporting are discussed in detail in the next several chapters.

2. INTRODUCTION

Investor confidence in financial markets is the key driver of economic growth, prosperity and financial stability for nations and this confidence can be significantly improved by focusing on long-term sustainable economic performance. Economic sustainability performance with a keen focus on long-term financial performance is gaining more attention from investors. In the context of the agency theory, where information asymmetry is assumed to be present, financial short-termism could occur. The agent (management) acting on behalf of the principal (shareholders) has incentives to achieve self-interested short-term financial performance due to lack of proper monitoring of the agent. When the interests of the agent are not aligned with those of the principal, the agent has incentives not to act in the best interest of long-term financial sustainability performance and/or to withhold important sustainability financial information from the principal and the investors. Short-termism is referred to as an excessive focus on a company's quarterly reported financial results rather than on sustainable, enduring and long-term economic performance. This short-termist practice undermines the sustainable economic performance of many companies by encouraging management to emphasize short-term performance by meeting analysts' quarterly earnings forecasts. This chapter examines the achievement of long-term sustainable economic performance in obtaining shareholder value creation.

3.   SHARED VALUE CREATION

Business organizations worldwide are being criticized for primarily focusing on short-term profit maximization and shareholder value enhancement with minimal attention paid to the impacts of their operations on society and the environment.[1] As business sustainability is gaining attention and being integrated into the corporate culture and business model, there has been a shift from the creation of shareholder value to the development of "sustainable shared value creation" to protect the interests of all stakeholders.[2] The concept of shared value is defined as "policies and practices that enhance the competitiveness of a company while simultaneously advancing the economic and social conditions in the communities in which it operates."[3] Under the shared value creation concept, management focuses on continuous performance improvement of business operations in generating long-term value while maximizing the positive impacts of operations on society and the environment by measuring sustainable performance in terms of both ESP and GSEE sustainability performance. Thus, corporate objectives have advanced from profit maximization to increasing shareholder wealth and now to creating shared value for all stakeholders.

Sustainable shared value creation, being the primary objective for many business organizations, can be achieved by focusing on the economic dimension of sustainability performance. Corporate management, asset managers, equity analysts and even shareholders are motivated toward, and thus their behaviors are biased toward, short-term performance for a variety of reasons.[4] The focus on short-term considerations may have an adverse impact on long-term and sustainable shareholder value creation, and reduce the expected value of future returns, consequently reducing current share prices. Stocks can be priced lower than their potential value through overemphasizing short-term considerations, encouraging asset managers to trade more frequently and forcing short-changing of long-term investors. This fixation on short-term considerations contributed to the financial scandals of Enron, WorldCom and other similar companies. Long-term and sustainable shareholder value creation is promoted through developing strategic plans and investments with sound, long-term objectives and linking executive compensation to long-term performance.

The short-termist behavior of many corporate managers is in sharp contrast to the long-term view of sustainable economic performance. The main objective of any business organizations is to create shareholder value and thus maximize firm value by establishing proper balance between economic sustainability performance and other non-financial dimensions of sustainability performance. The enlightened value-maximization concept of sustainability performance is supported by recent anecdotal evidence which suggests that companies that "see sustainability as both a necessity and opportunity, and change their business models in response, are finding success."[5] Furthermore, sustainability information can lead to a better understanding of the link between management actions and sustainable performance and thus could reduce noise in the corporate reporting process as well as short-termist attributes.

4.   FINANCIAL ECONOMIC SUSTAINABILITY PERFORMANCE

Transparency in financial and non-financial reports has always been part of the conceptual reporting framework regardless of investors' attitude toward risk (e.g., risk averse, tolerant of risks or embraces risk).[6] The financial economic sustainability performance (ESP) dimension is the most important component of sustainability in creating shareholder value. The ESP is disclosed to shareholders in a set of financial statements prepared by management. These financial statements are typically prepared in compliance with national accounting standards and/or the International Financial Reporting Standards (IFRS). The traditional corporate reporting model reflects financial information disseminated to shareholders whereas business sustainability covers a broad range of stakeholders and reflects a broader range of multiple-bottom-line EGSEE performance. The ESP dimension is the cornerstone of business sustainability and its disclosure is the release of information pertaining to the profitability of the company. The ESP dimension of sustainability performance presents long-term financial sustainability as reflected in the audited financial statements, which could contain following:

1. Management certification of financial statements.
2. Management certification of the assessment of the effectiveness of internal control over financial reporting.
3. Independent auditor's report on financial statements.
4. Independent auditor's report on internal control over financial reporting (ICFR).
5. Audited financial statements, including their notes.
6. Management's discussion and analysis (MD&A) of financial condition and results of operations.
7. Five-year summary of selected financial data.
8. Summary of selected quarterly financial data for the past two years.

Audited financial statements which typically provide information concerning an entity's financial condition and results of operations as a proxy for future business performance may not provide relevant information to investors and other stakeholders. Investors demand forward-looking financial and non-financial information on KPIs concerning the entity's EGSEE activities. High-quality financial information reflecting the ESP dimension of performance enables investors to assess the risks and return associated with their investments. In the post Sarbanes-Oxley (SOX) era, public companies in the US present their audited financial statements and audited internal control over financial reporting (ICFR). Section 404(a) of SOX 2002 requires that management certify the effectiveness of ICFR. This ICFR certification states the management's responsibility for designing and maintaining effective ICFR, and documenting the effectiveness of internal controls through testing related control activities. Executive certification of the effectiveness of ICFR indicates that there is only a remote possibility that material misstatements may not be prevented, detected or corrected on a timely basis. Any detected material weaknesses in internal control must be disclosed in management's report along with actions taken to correct those material weaknesses.

Section 404(b) of SOX requires that the independent auditor opine on the effectiveness of ICFR. The Public Company Accounting Oversight Board (PCAOB) in the US has issued auditing standards for independent auditors to audit and opine on ICFR. PCAOB Auditing Standard (AS) No. 2, *An Audit of Internal Control over Financial Reporting Performed in Conjunction with an Audit of Financial Statements*[7] is superseded by AS No. 5, which makes the audit of ICFR more effective and efficient. PCAOB AS No. 5 requires auditors to use a risk-based approach in the audit of ICFR. The independent auditor's report on ICFR can be either issued separately or combined with an opinion on the financial statements. The auditor should also render an opinion on the effectiveness of ICFR. Reporting and auditing of financial statements and ICFR is vital to assist shareholders in making appropriate investment and voting decisions. Public companies in the US are required to publish audited annual financial statements and audited ICFR. Section 404 SOX is intended to improve the effectiveness of the design and operation of internal control over financial reporting.[8] PCAOB AS No. 5 is intended to improve the audit by (1) focusing the audit on the matters most important to internal control (2) eliminating unnecessary audit procedures (3) simplifying the auditor requirements and (4) scaling the integrated audit for smaller companies.

Preparation of reliable, useful and relevant financial information on the ESP dimension of sustainability performance is a key responsibility of management. Executive certifications of financial and ICFR reports have global reach in providing accurate and complete information on ESP. However, management may have incentives to mislead investors and when opportunities are provided, they may attempt to manipulate financial information. The effective and vigilant overseeing of management reporting activities by the board of directors can reduce managerial opportunistic behavior. As the agent of investors, management has more information about ESP and may act inappropriately in withholding such information from investors if the principal (investors) fails to monitor the agent or if the interests of the agent are not aligned with those of the principal.

5. FORWARD-LOOKING FINANCIAL REPORTS

Corporate reports are intended to provide investors with relevant, transparent, timely and reliable information in making sound investment decisions, which improves the efficiency of the financial markets. Public companies are required to report a set of financial statements to their shareholders under the corporate mandatory disclosures regime, and a set of voluntary disclosures on their product innovations, research and development and growth and earnings forecasts, which are often viewed as forward-looking information. Regulators and standard-setters worldwide have shown interest in improving the financial reporting process by focusing on both financial and non-financial KPIs.[9]

Investors demand forward-looking financial and non-financial information and companies provide such information to all their stakeholders. PricewaterhouseCoopers (PwC) has presented guidelines for public companies to meet investors demands for forward-looking financial and non-financial information.[10] The PwC guide is based on the following several pillars of corporate effective communication with stakeholders: (1) commitment of adequate resources for proper disclosures and how they are managed (2) identification of material risks and uncertainties that may affect the company's sustainable performance (3) development of significant relationships with principal stakeholders to ensure sustainable performance (4) presentation of data pertaining to trends and factors that are likely to affect the company's future prospects and (5) identification of any material uncertainties threatening the achievement of the company's objectives, goals and strategic activities.[11]

6. VALUE RELEVANCE OF FINANCIAL ECONOMIC SUSTAINABILITY

As the number of public companies reporting their sustainability performance is growing worldwide, the value relevance of sustainability performance reports has been addressed by regulators, investors and the business community. In recent years, there has been an increased focus on integrated sustainability performance reports. Theoretically, management's engagement in sustainability activities, performance and reports can be viewed as value increasing or value decreasing for investors depending on the costs and benefits of disclosing sustainability performance information. Obviously, companies that effectively manage their business sustainability, improve CSR performance, strengthen their reputation, fulfill their social responsibility and promote a corporate culture of integrity and competency are sustainable in creating shareholder value. Thus, business sustainability focuses on activities that generate long-term financial performance in firm value maximization as well as voluntary activities that result in the achievement of non-financial sustainability performance that concerns all stakeholders.

The value relevance of voluntary sustainability information is measured by the firm-specific costs and benefits of providing such information. The firm value is expected to increase where the firm-specific benefits of sustainability performance information exceed the costs of providing such information. Market-wide effects of firm sustainability information are important if the net benefit at firm level affects the entire market or the net benefit is ignored or not fully internalized by firms. Market-wide effects of voluntary sustainability disclosures can be measured in terms of the impacts on firm valuation. This suggests that investors are willing to pay a premium for firms that engage in sustainability activities by assigning higher valuation to these firms in the financial markets. There are three costs associated with sustainability performance reporting. First, the direct cost of producing sustainability reports and obtaining assurance on the reports. The second cost is the opportunity cost of managerial time and effort spent on the preparation of sustainability reports. Finally, there are the *proprietary costs* of voluntary disclosures if the firm reveals valuable information such as information about profitable customers and markets or trade secrets, or exposes operating, organizing, or reporting weakness to regulators, unions, investors, customers, suppliers or competitors.[12] There is also the possibility that the likelihood of litigation is higher when firms voluntarily disclose sustainability information. Thus, the cost-benefit trade-offs in voluntary disclosure of sustainability performance information should be assessed to determine their value relevance.

7. FINANCIAL ECONOMIC SUSTAINABILITY REPORTING IN ASIA

7.1 Mainland China

7.1.1 Accounting Regulation and Enforcement To converge with International Accounting Standards, Mainland China's accounting system has experienced at least four major progressive reforms starting from 1990s. The first milestone reform was the issuing of the *Enterprise Basic Accounting Standards* (EBAS) in 1992, which provides the first conceptual framework of accounting standards in Mainland China.[13] The *Accounting System for Joint Stock Limited Enterprise* (ASJSLE) replaced EBAS in 1998 to reduce the discrepancies between Mainland Chinese Accounting Standards and International Accounting Standards. In 2001, the Ministry of Finance (MOF) issued the *Accounting System for Business Enterprises* (2001 Accounting System) to further align Mainland Chinese Accounting Standards with International Accounting Standards. Despite these efforts, "these standards are highly prescriptive and largely rules based."[14] The most significant initiative to converge with IFRS was the introduction of the Accounting Standards for Business Enterprises (ASBE) (also referred to as the new Mainland Chinese Accounting Standards (CAS)) in 2006. All listed companies are required to adopt the ASBE effective from January 1, 2007. The ASBE consists of one basic standard, 38 specific standards, and adoption guidance. Like IFRS, fair value is adopted in the ASBE. To facilitate the implementation of the ASBE, several interpretations of standards were issued in 2007 and 2008. To improve the financial reporting quality, the Chinese Securities and Regulatory Commission (CSRC) issued a new set of auditing standards that are largely based on the International Auditing & Assurance Standards Board (IAASB), effective from January 1, 2007.

In Mainland China, the Accounting Law outlines the general principles of accounting and defines the role of government and matters relating to accounting principles, standards, and practices. The Ministry of Finance (MOF), supervised by the State Council, formulates accounting and auditing standards and regulates the accounting profession in Mainland China.

7.1.2 Factors that Influence Financial Reporting Quality in Mainland China The effectiveness of the legal system in Mainland China is an important factor that affects the financial reporting quality of Mainland Chinese firms. Wong (2016) points out that Mainland China has promulgated sound laws but was unable to implement and enforce this legislation mainly because of its court system.[15] There is no independent judiciary in Mainland China as the courts are controlled by either the central or the local government, which may directly or indirectly hold stock ownership of state-owned firms. This organizational structure leads to court proceedings that may be improperly influenced.[16] The underdeveloped legal system and firms' dependence on connections with the government for protection and rent seeking render this relationship-based system of doing business a necessity in Mainland China.[17]

The role of the state in the financial market is also ambiguous. On the one hand, the state controls many firms (such as state-owned enterprises (SOEs)) in various ways. On the other hand, the state regulates the stock markets by setting accounting regulations and enforcing them. Such ambiguity results in conflicts of interest and impedes the objective enforcement of accounting regulations. The concentrated ownership in private firms also renders insiders less incentivized to provide high-quality financial reporting. The controlling shareholders have a strong incentive to mask their exploitation of the minority shareholders by reporting opaquely.

7.1.3 Differences Between Chinese GAAP and IFRS Mainland China retained its domestic rules on accounting for related-party transactions, government subsidies, and reversal of impairments of depreciable assets. These are areas that have domestic political and economic significance in Mainland China. Especially for SOEs, the differences between the Mainland Chinese Generally Accepted Accounting Principles (GAAP) and IFRS treatments have substantial impacts on the financial statements.

7.1.3.1 Related-Party Transaction Related-party transactions are considerably more common in Mainland China than in most Western countries. The reported numbers are rendered more malleable due to the identity of the related parties and the terms on which they transact. Some Mainland Chinese entities take advantage of the standards to manage accounting numbers. For example, SOEs are exempted from the "related-party" disclosure provisions because of the dominance of government ownership in these enterprises. Enforcing related-party transactions based on the definition in IFRS results in the situation that around 95 percent of transactions involve related parties.[18]

7.1.3.2 Impairment of Assets Provisions Mainland China's rules also differ from those of the IFRS in the "impairment of assets" provisions. Mainland China's accounting standard allows companies to write down the value of businesses, physical assets and goodwill as well as to revalue assets upward if conditions change. The Mainland Chinese companies are disinclined to revalue firm assets and recognize impairment of assets, which may be perceived as an attempt to manipulate company financials.[19]

7.1.3.3 Fair Value Measurement Implementation is another problem area. The Accounting Standards for Business Enterprises (ASBE) 4 and 6 do not allow firms to choose fair value measurement while IFRS allows that.[20] The fair value provision is not easy to implement in Mainland China mainly because the government controls the price of certain assets such as unlisted securities and it is difficult to find independent parties to assess the assets.[21]

7.1.4 Drivers of Convergence with IFRS IFRS is established on the basis of accounting principles in developed countries and is now being adopted or is soon to be adopted in most countries around the world. To Mainland China, the adoption of IFRS enhances the transparency of its financial reporting, lowers the level of information asymmetry and improves the quality of accounting information.[22] To the extent that IFRS adoption by a country leads to an increase in the transparency of financial reports, IFRS adoption provides incentives for businesses and individuals globally to invest in Mainland China.[23]

7.1.5 Internal Control Report Required for Listed Companies Similar to the rules of the internal control system in the US, Mainland China issued the *Basic Standard for Enterprise Internal Controls* (BSEIC) in 2008, mandating all listed firms (both on the Shanghai and Shenzhen Exchanges) to assess the effectiveness of their internal control systems and to publish auditors' opinions on the effectiveness of internal control along with the annual financial reports. With these efforts, the transparency of Mainland Chinese companies' reporting has improved significantly.

7.2 Hong Kong

7.2.1 Accounting Regulation and Enforcement Having been a British colony for around 100 years, the accounting standards and practices adopted in Hong Kong were heavily influenced by those of the UK. The accounting professional body, the Hong Kong Society of Accountants (HKSA), was incorporated by the Professional Accountants Ordinance (Chapter 50, Laws of Hong Kong) on January 1, 1973. The HKSA evolved to become the current Hong Kong Institute of Certified Public Accountants (HKICPA) on September 8, 2004. Prior to the adoption of International Accounting Standards (IAS)-based accounting standards in 1992, Hong Kong's accounting standards were very similar to those in the UK.

The Hong Kong Financial Reporting Standards (HKFRS) have fully converged with the International Financial Reporting Standards (IFRS), with annual reporting periods commencing from January 1, 2005.[24] The convergence results in a substantial increase in disclosure transparency, reporting quality and comparability. Although Hong Kong-based listed companies are required to provide financial statements based on HKFRS, companies that are domiciled in Hong Kong but incorporated outside Hong Kong are permitted to use either HKFRS or IFRS as their basis to prepare financial statements.

7.2.2 Drivers of Successful Implementation of IFRS

7.2.2.1 Family Ownership Hong Kong has the third-highest percentage of listed companies with dominant family ownership in the region after Indonesia and Malaysia[25] (*SCMP*, 2002).The controlling families finance their capital through controlling financial institutions or establishing close economic/social ties with banks. Because the financiers have access to client firms' financial information through private channels, this family ownership structure lowers the demand for public financial information in Hong Kong.[26] The concentrated family ownership structure creates strong incentives for the controlling families to tunnel valuable assets from the company. To avoid challenges from external parties and mask self-dealing activities, the controlling shareholders very often withhold private information. This may negatively affect financial reporting quality.[27]

7.2.3 Internal Control Report Required for Listed Companies In December 2014, HKEX published its corporate governance requirements—the *Consultation Conclusions on Risk Management and Internal Control: Review of the Corporate Governance Code and Corporate Governance Report* ("the Consultation Conclusions"). These requirements have affected all Hong Kong listed companies and come into effect for accounting periods beginning on or after January 1, 2016[28] (KPMG, 2016). That is, the listed companies have to prepare Risk Management and Internal Control report effective from 2016.

7.3 India

7.3.1 Accounting Regulation and Enforcement India's accounting system has evolved over time tracing back to the early sixteenth century when the Silk Road became the key route to prosperity by connecting India and southern Europe. The subsequent entry of the East India Company had widespread influence on Indian commerce and soon the economy was virtually taken over by the company's owners. With the great potential of the East India Company in terms of business opportunities, natural resources and human resources, the British government decided to colonize India and took control of the company. The British rules serve to explain the almost identical pattern of accounting and financial reporting practices between India and England.[29] However, India attained independence in 1947 after a long struggle, with changes made to accounting practices to meet the needs of the Indian economy.[30]

In India, there are 18 official languages and dozens of dialects which are distributed in 28 states and seven federal territories. The accounting practices of unorganized rural/agricultural sectors and small-scale urban industrial sectors vary greatly from one region to the other. It is difficult to establish a degree of uniformity in accounting and trade practices in these industries and sectors. In addition, many Indian companies are controlled by conservative families and are reluctant to disclose publicly financial information because of privacy and fear of competition.[31]

With the objective of simplifying accounting practice, in 1949 the Indian government established the Institute of Chartered Accountants of India (ICAI), passing the ICAI Act in the same year. The Accounting Standards Board was established by the ICAI in 1977 to coordinate accounting policies and practices in India. In 2006, a special working group was set up by ICAI with the goal of developing a roadmap for India's convergence with IFRS.[32] Although this date was postponed because of pending resolution of several issues involving taxation laws, the co-existence of multiple regulatory frameworks, the lack of sufficient resources, insufficient awareness of IFRS and the incremental costs of the adoption of the Indian Accounting Standards (Ind-AS),[33] the adoption of the Ind-AS was announced on January 6, 2015 by the Ministry of Corporate Affairs (MCA) to be effective from the financial year 2016–2017.[34] For the first phase, the Ministry planned to start implementing IFRS for enterprises with a net worth of more than 100 billion rupees (around US$1.5 billion) from April 1, 2015. In the second phase, both listed and unlisted companies whose net worth is more than 50 billion rupees (around US$0.75 billion) and less than 100 billion rupees (around US$1.5 billion) have to merge with IFRS commencing from the financial year starting on April 1, 2016. In the third and fourth stages, small companies are required to prepare financial reports based on IFRS beginning April 1, 2017. Banks are exempted from complying with the IFRS.[35]

7.3.2 Factors that Influence Successful Implementation of IFRS

7.3.2.1 Central government Intervention and government Ownership Although India is a capitalist country, the Central government intervenes in the economy by holding ownership of firms in key industries. From 1947 to the end of 1970, the characteristics of India's economy were heavy involvement of the Central government in its socialistic planning and import substitution industrialization (ISI). Economic production has shifted from mainly agriculture, forestry, fishery and textile manufacturing to various heavy industries and transportation industries. However, the lack of competition results in poor quality and low production efficiency. Faced with the economic crisis, the government began to open up the economy in 1991. Market-oriented economic reform includes privatization of some state-owned industries. However, a large part of the heavy industry is still state-owned with high tariffs and restrictions on foreign direct investments.[36]

7.3.2.2 Lack of IFRS Knowledge In a 2012 survey, Patro and Gupta (2012) found that about 99 percent of respondents in India did not have IFRS training and 92 percent did not have access to electronic or written reading materials related to IFRS. In addition, the survey showed that 56 percent of respondents said that India lacked accountants with sufficient IFRS knowledge. India's multinational companies (MNCs) and accounting firms that provide professional services to and companies have been recruiting accounting professionals who are knowledgeable about IFRS.[37]

To ensure the timely adoption of IFRS in India, ICAI has been organizing IFRS training programs for its members and other interested parties. However, there is a huge gap between the supply of well-trained professionals and the demand for such professionals.[38]

7.3.3 Requirement for Internal Control According to the Companies Act of 2013 (the 2013 Act), a company's auditor is required to state in its audit report whether the company has a sound internal financial control (IFC) system in place.[39] In addition, the 2013 Act requires listed companies to provide management discussions and analyses (MD&A) covering industry structure and development, opportunities and threats faced by the company, and internal control and risks affecting the performance of the business sector or products.[40] The directors of listed companies have to disclose whether they have a complete IFC system and whether such IFC is sufficient and effective.

7.4 Indonesia

7.4.1 Accounting Regulations and Enforcement For more than 300 years, Indonesia was a Dutch colony. During this period, the first accounting legislation, Indische Compatibles Wet (ICW) (1864), was released, establishing a cash-based budget and trade reporting system. Indonesia has a diverse and isolated political system, which is the very first institution in Indonesian society. Therefore, accounting plays a crucial role in maintaining the colonial government.[41] After World War II (1949), the Dutch, under international pressure, formally recognized Indonesia's independence. Driven by economic and political reforms in 1967, new accounting standards began to be implemented. The Indonesian Accounting Standards (PAI), the first US-based codified accounting system, was launched in 1973. Following the launch of the PAI, the Dewan Standar Akuntansi Keuangan (DSAK) (Indonesian Institute of Accountants (or Ikatan Akuntan Indonesia, IAI)), the national accounting profession body that oversees the setting of accounting standards in Indonesia, established a permanent standard-setting body within its organizational structure—the Indonesian Accounting Principles Committee (KPAI).[42]

With significant developments in the Indonesian capital market, the government began to demand a higher level of accounting standards from the early 1990s. The IAI changed the basis for the establishment of accounting standards in 1994 from US GAAP to International Accounting Standards (IAS) and formally decided to support the coordination scheme initiated by the International Accounting Standards Committee (IASC).[43] In 1999, for the first time in its history, Indonesia introduced democratic principles, public elections, racial tolerance policies and civic pluralism.[44] As part of the greater democratic reforms, the Indonesian Central government also introduced public sector financial reporting reforms including accrual accounting and public reporting.[45,46] These systems were practiced until the adoption of Law No. 17 (2003) when the government adopted new accounting standards.[47] After the 1997 Financial Crisis, Indonesia began accepting financial support from the International Monetary Fund (IMF). The IMF required reform of the banking and financial systems, which has led to changes in accountability.[48,49] The legislation was passed in the late 1990s to meet the World Bank's expectations of "good governance," to include public accountability and transparency, respect for the rule of law, anti-corruption measures, democratization, decentralization and local government reforms.[50] Between 1994 and 2007, the IAI published six revisions of the Indonesian Accounting Standards with codified pronouncements. These revisions were largely made to accommodate amendments to existing standards and to add new accounting standards to deal with changes in the business environment.[51]

7.4.2 Convergence to IFRS Unlike the "big bang" approach adopted by the European Union member countries and developing economies, Indonesia adopted IFRS in a gradual manner. Indonesia incorporated IFRS into its local accounting standards with minor changes while taking local laws and the business environment into account. In 2008, the IAI officially announced full convergence toward IFRS. The IAI proposed to complete full convergence through three stages and expected to achieve the goal by 2012.[52] The Indonesian Accounting Standards published on September 1, 2007 the beginning of this convergence plan, in which many Indonesian Financial Accounting Standards (PSAKs) were pronounced, and signified full adoption of IFRS. However, among a total of 33 standards, only 10 were adopted from IFRS by 2008. Due to the slow progress, IAI delayed the full convergence process until 2012.[53]

The publishing of the Indonesian Accounting Standards on June 1, 2012 marked the completion of the first stage of the IFRS convergence process. Not all IFRS were adopted in this phase but there is progress toward Indonesia's accounting standards moving close to IFRS.[54] DSAK initiated the second stage of the IFRS convergence program in 2012 with the completion of the second stage on January 1, 2015, marked by 42 accounting standards, of which 38 were adopted from IFRS and four were developed by DSAK itself. This progress means that the gap between Indonesian Accounting Standards and IFRS has been reduced. As a result, the full convergence process is still pending.

7.4.2.1 Factors that Influence Successful Implementation of IFRS
7.4.2.1.1 Complexity of Certain Accounting Standards Prior to the application of IFRS, Indonesian Accounting Standards were mainly based on historical cost accounting while IFRS encouraged the use of fair value accounting. The new standards adopted by Indonesia can be complex and require substantial judgement for their implementation. For example, due to the complexity of the valuation of financial instruments and derivatives, the Indonesian Association of Commercial Banks applied for postponement of implementation of these standards as Indonesian banks were not equipped with the necessary resources. In response to this call, IAI postponed the effective date of these standards to January 1, 2010 and further extended this to January 1, 2012.[55]

7.4.2.1.2 Professional Judgement Required by IFRS   In addition to the challenges in understanding these new standards, the application of judgement and interpretation became a big concern. Accounting for land is an example where accountants' judgement is required in implementing IFRS in the Indonesian context. Buyers of land in Indonesia may not have ownership but may acquire only the right to build on, cultivate and use the land. The adoption of IFRS for land purchase has led to different interpretations of the appropriate accounting treatment. Whether land rights are treated as fixed assets without being depreciated, or fixed assets that should be amortized, or intangible assets that are not to be amortized, is controversial. The DSAK issued an explanation of the accounting standards stating that land rights should be reported under property, plant and equipment. Therefore, the value of land rights should not be amortized unless holders of land rights are unable to exercise their rights.[56]

7.4.2.1.3 Inadequate Training and Education   Education programs regarding accounting, auditing, preparation of financial statements and the new accounting standards are necessary to train accountants on IFRS and its implementation in the Indonesian environment. The professional accounting agencies such as IAI and the Indonesian Institute of Certified Public Accountants (IAPI) recognize the need for accounting education. Continuing professional education programs, workshops and seminars are being offered to enhance the ability of accountants to implement Indonesian IFRS. Despite the efforts of the accounting profession and academics, Indonesia still lags behind in introducing new IFRS-based concepts into the accounting curriculum. Therefore, one of the challenges faced by the IFRS education program in Indonesia is to promote the development of accounting education, making the implementation of IFRS possible.[57]

7.4.2.1.4 Fast Pace of IFRS Developments   The continued revision of the IFRS and the promulgation of the new accounting standards led to the fact that Indonesia's IFRS did not reflect subsequent amendments to IFRS in a timely manner. As the 2015 Indonesian Accounting Standards adopted IFRS in 2014, issues in the IFRS revised after 2014 are not resolved in this version. The time lag for the Indonesian IFRS adoption program is related to the standard-setting process, which requires the DSAK to follow certain stages in the formulation and implementation of the new standards.[58]

7.4.2.1.5 Translation Issues   A common problem in the convergence of IFRS is translation issues. The original IFRS was published in English so the integration of IFRS in Indonesia involved translating the standards into Indonesian. Studies have shown that when IFRS is adopted in non-English-speaking countries, the translation of IFRS from English to local languages can delay the integration process.[59] In addition, the integration of IFRS in Indonesia is made more difficult arising from the difficulty in translating word for word. Instead, the Indonesian Accounting Standards Board prefers to adopt selective IFRS practices and make minor modifications in order to bring the standards in line with Indonesia's commercial and legal environment.[60]

7.4.3 Challenges and Drivers of Convergence with IFRS Most of the economic incentives come from the globalization of the Indonesian economy. Foreign investors in the capital market owned about 64 percent of shares on the Indonesian stock exchange as at the end of 2015. The Indonesian capital market regulations allow foreign investors to hold 100 percent of its listed companies. Between 2005 and 2015, the amount of foreign direct investment (FDI) inflows into the country increased by nearly 100 percent (World Bank, 2016). Indonesia needs foreign investment to support its national economic growth. The adoption of IFRS and transparent financial reporting is crucial in supporting FDI growth.[61]

The political pressure for IFRS convergence may come from supranational institutions. For example, the IAI is a full member of the International Federation of Accountants (IFAC), and thus has the obligation to adopt IFRS as the national accounting standards. In addition, the status of Indonesia as a G20 member promoted the full integration of IFRS in the country. The adoption of IFRS is a commitment of G20 member states. Hence Indonesia is obligated to ensure that its national standards are consistent with IFRS. The IAI reports that the current Indonesian IFRS integration program is a response to agreements between G20 members.

7.4.4 Internal Control System The National Committee on Corporate Governance (NCCG), established in 1999 by the Decree of the Coordinating Minister for Economy, Finance and Industry, is responsible for codifying corporate governance principles and implementing the code by developing an institutional framework in Indonesia.[62] The NCCG published its first *Code of Good Corporate Governance* in the year of its establishment. In 2006, the NCCG revised the 2001 *Code of Good Corporate Governance* to incorporate new clauses. Indonesia's *Code of Good Corporate Governance* (2006) stipulates that a firm must have an effective internal control system in place.[63] The *Code* further specifies that the board of directors has responsibility to establish and maintain a sound internal control system within a company. To help the board of directors to achieve this goal, the *Code* requires the audit committee to assist the Board of Commissioners to ensure the effectiveness and adequateness of the internal control system.

7.5 Japan

7.5.1 Accounting Regulation and Enforcement Accounting regulation in Japan is based on the Company Law, the Securities and Exchange Law (SEL), and the Corporate Income Tax Law. These three pieces of legislation are linked and apply in a connected way in regulating financial reporting in Japan. The Company Law is administered by the Ministry of Justice (MOJ) and its fundamental principle is creditor and shareholder protection. Disclosures on creditworthiness and the availability of earnings for dividend distribution are of primary importance. Publicly owned companies must meet the requirements of the SEL, which are administrated by the Financial Services Agency (FSA). The main objective of the SEL is to mandate listed companies to provide information for investor decision-making.[64] Finally, the Tax Law has significant influence on financial reporting as it stipulates accounting recognitions and treatments to determine taxable income.

7.5.1.1 Convergence to IFRS Japan has committed to improving its accounting standards since the late 1990s when it started to reform its accounting standards to align with the US Generally Accepted Accounting Principles (GAAP) and/or International Accounting Standards (IAS).[65] The Accounting Standards Board of Japan (ASBJ) is the private sector Japanese accounting standard-setting body, which is directly responsible for the development and promulgation of accounting standards.[66] In 2005, the ASBJ and International Accounting Standards Board (IASB) agreed to a plan to achieve closer convergence between Japanese GAAP and IFRS. They reached the "Tokyo Agreement" in 2007 under which 26 major differences between Japanese GAAP and IFRS would be eliminated by the end of 2008, with the remaining differences being removed by 2011.[67]

7.5.1.2 Business Accounting Council Requirements On June 30, 2009, the Business Accounting Council (BAC) of Japan announced its decision to allow the optional adoption of IFRS starting from March 2010 fiscal year end for consolidated financial statements of listed companies. This is the starting point of Japan's convergence to IFRS.[68] The voluntary adoption of IFRS was allowed only for listed companies that established an appropriate internal system to prepare IFRS-based reporting and whose financial and business activities were conducted globally.[69] After five meetings from June 30, 2011 to December 22, 2011, the BAC issued a discussion paper on the application of IFRS in Japan (hereinafter "the 2012 Report"; BAC, 2012). The voluntary adoption of IFRS for consolidated financial statements of well-organized, global listed companies was recommended repeatedly while the mandatory adoption of IFRS was not suggested.[70]

7.5.1.3 The 2013 Report by BAC After the 2012 Report, the BAC held another five meetings from March 26, 2013 to June 19, 2013, to further discuss the adoption of IFRS in Japan. The outcome of these meetings was the issuance of the *Present Policy on the Application of IFRS* by the BAC (hereinafter "the 2013 Report"; BAC, 2013). The BAC's policies have been largely influenced by the US Securities Exchange Commission (SEC) decisions which postponed the adoption of IFRS in the US; the IFRS Foundation has pressured Japan to make a clear commitment to accelerating the adoption of IFRS in Japan.[71] To facilitate voluntary adoption, the 2013 Report allowed the use of IFRS for companies that have established an appropriate internal system to prepare IFRS-based reporting. The requirement to adopt IFRS voluntarily was relaxed and the terms "global" and "listed" were removed to encourage more Japanese companies to adopt voluntary adoption of IFRS.[72]

The Tokyo Stock Exchange (TSE) has announced that as of June 30, 2017, 171 companies (accounting for 30 percent of the TSE market capitalization) have adopted or plan to adopt IFRS. The 171 companies include 152 companies that have already adopted or are in the process of adopting IFRS and another 19 companies that have publicly stated that they plan to adopt IFRS. The TSE has also announced that an additional 214 companies (22 percent of the TSE market capitalization) have stated in their most recent financial statements that they are considering the move to IFRS.[73]

7.5.2 Factors that Influence Successful Implementation of IFRS

7.5.2.1 Code Law Country Japan has a code law system which was derived from the German legal and French accounting systems during the Meiji Era (1868–1910). In a typical code law country, governments or quasi-governmental bodies establish code law-based accounting standards, prescribing regulations ranging from abstract principles to detailed procedures. The code law-based accounting standards may impair the successful implementation of IFRS as IFRS is a principle-based standard and requires accountants to exercise their professional judgement.

7.5.2.2 Influence of government Central government also exerts tight control on accounting and financial reporting in Japan.[74] Thus, the accounting profession in Japan is relatively small and has less influence compared to the UK and US. In addition, Japanese accountants have less discretion in making accounting judgements.[75]

7.5.2.3 Cross-holding The way in which businesses are financed influences financial reporting and attitudes of interested parties toward accounting information. In Japan, banks own a significant proportion of their clients' shares and may even be the largest shareholder through cross-holding (or *keiretsu*). In general, shares in Japanese companies are held on a long-term basis. The heavy involvement of the banks and the long-term share ownership mean that there is less focus on short-term earnings information in Japan than in the UK or US.[76] For these credit-based companies, disclosure is not necessarily important as firms can get access to such information from banks directly. This also explains why the specific accounting rules in Japan place greater emphasis on prudent asset valuation.[77]

7.5.3 Internal Control The Financial Instruments and Exchange Act (2006) requires all listed companies to submit an annual assessment of the company's internal controls with an internal control assurance report by an auditor, beginning in 2008.[78]

7.6 South Korea

7.6.1 Accounting Regulations and Enforcement After the 1997 Asian Financial Crisis, the Korea Accounting Institute (KAI) developed the K-GAAP based on the International Accounting Standards. Despite that, K-GAAP is quite different from IFRS. To further converge with IFRS, the South Korea IFRS Adoption Task Force was inaugurated in 2006. In 2007, the Task Force announced the IFRS adoption roadmap, specifying the scope of application, starting period, and implementation plans. According to the roadmap, non-financial listed companies are required to adopt IFRS from 2009 and financial firms would start adopting IFRS from 2011. In 2009, the IFRS Implementation Support Task Force was established to cope with the emerging practical issues for early-adopting firms. To minimize compliance costs, the roadmap required the South Korean IFRS (hereinafter, K-IFRS) to be ready before the end of 2007 and to translate the IFRS into Korean word by word. Organizations that had 2 trillion Korean Won (around US$1.78 billion) worth of assets were given an extra grace period for the adoption of IFRS in 2013 and were expected to publish quarterly and semi-annual financial reports.[79]

7.6.2 Factors that Influence Successful Implementation of IFRS
7.6.2.1 Standard-Setting Bodies Unlike other Asian jurisdictions such as Hong Kong, Indonesia, Malaysia, the Philippines, and Thailand which have standard-setting bodies that are independent from the government, South Korea's standard-setting board is largely controlled by the government. Hence, most of the accounting standards follow closely the local tax laws, leading to low relevance of accounting reports.[80]

7.6.2.2 Ownership A majority of companies in South Korea are owned and controlled by family groups, the *chaebol*. A chaebol is a financial group consisting of a number of companies which are engaged in various businesses and are usually owned and controlled by one or two interrelated family clans. South Korea's chaebols are very similar to Japan's *keiretsu*. They both maintain close ties with other affiliates of the group with a significant amount of equity holdings. Unlike the keiretsu, which are controlled by finance companies, the chaebol is controlled by the family and maintains a centralized operation in the group headquarters. Such organizational structure enables individual owners to control all group affiliates. This kind of ownership structure is inherently characterized by less transparency and lowers the demand for high-quality financial reporting.

7.6.2.3 Institutional Investors Banks have a large impact on South Korean companies. Traditionally, the main source of financing for South Korean companies is bank loans. In recent years, they began to finance their projects by equity financing. The close financial relationships between banks and South Korean companies put banks in the position of having a significant impact on companies' operations. Because banks can access firms' financial information directly in South Korea, the demand for high-quality financial reporting is weak.

7.6.2.4 Tax Code The uniqueness of the South Korean accounting standards lies in the influence that accounting has on the tax code. Like the tax laws of other countries, the South Korean tax laws emphasize the realization of cash. They are influenced strongly by office-holding politicians. This in turn diminishes the quality of accounting information.[81] Tax laws also affect specific accounting treatments. For example, the South Korean tax law does not allow capitalization of goodwill and amortization of revalued assets to equity. It is the only country in the world that does not use equity methods for affiliates.

7.6.3 Drivers of Convergence with IFRS To mitigate the negative impacts of the Asian Financial Crisis in 1997, South Korea strategizes to attract more foreign direct investment through the promotion of transparency of South Korean companies' financial reporting. One initiative is to set up a private sector accounting standards board similar to the Financial Accounting Standards Board (FASB) in the US. The Korea Accounting Institute (KAI) was established to enhance the South Korean GAAP in meeting international standards. Regardless, the international community's assessment of the transparency of South Korean financial statements remains less than satisfactory. The government adopted IFRS (South Korea Accounting) in an effort to improve the quality of accounting standards and enhance the credibility of accounting information. Meanwhile, there was the global convergence of accounting standards toward IFRS as many countries at that time had either passed or started to adopt the IFRS.[82]

7.6.4 Internal Control System According to the South Korean Securities and Exchange Act in 2003, all security companies must establish basic internal control procedures and standards. Managers need to "observe statutes or subordinate statutes, operate the company's assets in a sound manner and protect its customers" in performing their duties. And at least one person (or "compliance officer") is assigned to check if the internal control standards are in place and to investigate whether there are violations of the internal control standards. The designated person must report internal control assessment results to the auditor or the inspection committee if deviations are detected.[83]

7.7 Malaysia

7.7.1 Accounting Regulation and Enforcement

Before its independence in 1957, Malaysia was under British rule for over 80 years, thus its accounting standards and reporting practices also originated from the UK. After early announcements about IAS were made in the 1970s, IAS took over as the major force shaping Malaysian formal accounting standards.[84] With Malaysia's early adoption of some IAS[85] standards during the period from 1978 until 1997, the Malaysia Accounting Standards Board (MASB) standards were already in line with those issued by IASB. However, the IASB standards were modified to adapt to the local environment and became national standards. The issuances made by the Malaysian Association of Certified Public Accountants (MACPA) together with the Malaysian Institute of Accountants (MIA) were not enforceable for companies in the early days. In 1997, a Parliamentary Act established MASB and conferred the MASB standards with legal standing for all firms. The standards issued by MASB became enforceable under the Companies Act 1965 as well as under other relevant Acts for specialized industries like insurance.[86]

In 2005, MASB renamed the MASB standards to the Financial Reporting Standards (FRS), intending to align them with standards issued by the IASB except for some minor modifications. In January 2006, all Malaysian firms were required to converge the local reporting standards with IFRS by preparing financial statements according to IFRS. Instead of mandating the following of the whole set of accounting standards in the preparation of financial statements, Malaysia introduced a two-tier financial reporting framework whereby the IFRS framework is made mandatory for public entities while private entities can continue to use the old MASB standards (known as the PERS (Private Entity Reporting Standards) framework).

7.7.2 Factors that Influence Successful Implementation of IFRS

Although the Malaysian accounting system is influenced by the UK, the reporting environment shares features with other code law countries, such as the importance of banks as capital providers (Ball et al., 2003), high ownership concentration, insider governance, weak investor protection and enforcement and strong government intervention in the economy (Suto, 2003; Tam & Tan, 2007).[87,88] Malaysian financial reporting has therefore been criticized as being of low quality (Ball et al., 2003). Audit quality may also be compromised as there are fewer incentives for auditors to maintain independence.[89]

The political economy in Malaysia is highly influenced by family ownership and political connection.[90] This type of political economy has enabled corporate entities in Malaysia to seek capital funds from "insiders" rather than from the capital market. Therefore, there is less demand for informative financial statements by the public. Being politically connected facilitates firms in getting private information. Hence any information asymmetry between shareholders and managers is settled through "insider communication" rather than through "public disclosure." Abdullah et al. (2015) found a negative relationship between family control and IFRS disclosure levels in Malaysia. They also pointed out that the situation where family members in management positions hold board seats can lead to ineffective monitoring and poor governance, which is associated with low-quality financial reporting.[91]

7.7.3 Drivers of Convergence with IFRS   The Asian Financial Crisis in 1997 was an alarm bell for corporate governance reform in Asian countries including Malaysia. One such effort at reform was to effectively converge with IFRS to enhance reporting quality and facilitate effective monitoring. Another important driver of convergence is foreign direct investment, for which enhanced IFRS in financial reporting is essential. In 2007, total foreign direct investment in Malaysia was US$8,403 million while the total market capitalization of the Malaysian stock exchange was US$326 million. The average annual growth of market capitalization in Malaysia is 40 percent (Liew, 2007).[92] In 2007, there were 1,036 companies listed on the Kuala Lumpur Stock Exchange (KLSE), which ranks 27th in terms of market capitalization (US$325,663) in the world (Standard & Poor's, 2008).[93] Malaysia is ranked 24th in the world for foreign direct investment (FDI). The growth in the market capitalization and inflow of capital have generated a need for the country to have sound financial reporting and disclosure of information.[94] Malaysia officially adopted IFRS in 2012, which is viewed as a step in the right direction toward improving the quality of the financial reporting process.

7.7.4 Internal Control Systems   In December 2000, Bursa Malaysia first issued its *Statement on Internal Control: Guidance for Directors of Public Listed Companies*.[95] The guidance is aimed at assisting Malaysian listed companies to disclose their internal control system in their annual reports and comply with the listing rules of the KLSE. In 2001, the Malaysian Securities Commission appointed the Institute of Internal Auditors Malaysia (IIAM) to form a taskforce to formulate guidelines to help the boards of directors of listed companies to effectively discharge their responsibilities pertaining to the establishment of internal audit. The guidelines highlight internal control as an important characteristic. In 2012, the taskforce revised the guidelines by referring to the Malaysian Code on Corporate Governance issued in March 2012.[96] The guidelines require boards to be responsible for establishing an effective internal control system, and the CEO and CFO to assure the board with respect to the adequateness and effectiveness of the internal control system within a company.

7.8   The Philippines

7.8.1 Accounting Regulation and Enforcement   From 1565 to 1571 the Spanish took over the Philippines islands, which they would hold for more than 300 years. However, the Philippines' long accounting history was formed from the need to trade with neighboring countries, long before it became a Spanish colony. The Philippines became an American colony in 1898 after the Philippine–American War. The enactment of the Accountancy Law in 1923 is a milestone in accounting history. It granted qualifications to professional accountants who had completed and passed the CPA exam, and established the Board of Accountancy (BOA) to regulate the accounting industry. In 1929, the Philippines Institute of Certified Public Accountants (PICPA), a private non-joint-stock company and one of the longest surviving professional accounting organizations in Asia, was founded.

The PICPA has contributed immensely to the development of accounting standards in the Philippines.[97] Because Philippine foreign trade was conducted primarily with the United States between the 1920s and early 1970s, Philippine accounting standards were adapted from the US GAAP.[98]

Even before the 1997 Asian Financial Crisis, the International Monetary Fund (IMF) forecast that the growth of the Philippine economy would be 6 percent in 1998, higher than most Asian countries with similar characteristics and stage of development. One important reason, as identified by Noland (2000), is that it has a sound financial system including accounting system, as compared with other Asian countries.[99]

7.8.2 Move Toward IFRS With increasing trade with European countries, Philippine accounting standard-setters announced in 1997 a gradual shift toward the International Financial Reporting Standards (IFRS). Soon after the 1997 Asian Financial Crisis, the Philippines introduced structural reforms on globalization and corporate governance to further improve its accounting system, including relating to financial disclosure.[100] The Accounting Standards Council (ASC) was founded in November 1981 by the PICPA, which oversees the formulation of general accounting principles in the Philippines.[101] The official transition began in 2001 and was completed in 2005 (IASPlus, The Philippines, January and November 2005 updates).

In 2004, the Professional Regulatory Commission set up the Financial Reporting Standards Council (FRSC) under the Rules and Regulations of the Philippines Accountancy Act of 2004. The FRSC replaced the original ACS and aims to assist the BOA in carrying out functions such as enforcement and implementation of accounting standards in the Philippines. In November 2004, FRSC approved the Philippines Accounting Standard (PAS) and the new Philippines Financial Reporting Standard (PFRS) (equivalent to IAS and IFRS for IASB).[102]

The Philippines Security Exchange Commission (SEC) together with other members of the International Securities and Commission Organization (IOSCO) agreed to adopt IFRS to maintain international standards in order to improve the reliability and integrity of the country's capital market.[103] However, listed companies and limited liability companies implement different accounting frameworks authorized by the SEC.[104] Being regulated by BOA, the Professional Regulation Commission (PRC) supports the adoption of IFRS because its duty is also to implement the General Agreement on Trade in Services (GATS).

Since 2005, listed and limited liability companies that exceed the financial limit set by the Philippines SEC were expected to adopt the Philippines Financial Reporting Standards (PFRS), which have converged fully with IFRS.[105] The Philippines Interpretations Committee (PIC) was later established by FRSC, in 2006, to further improve financial reporting standards in the Philippines.[106]

7.8.3 Factors that Influence Successful Implementation of IFRS The Philippines was rated one the highest in relative explanatory power of residual earnings among six other Asian countries. According to Graham & King (2000), this impressive performance may be due to the independence of its accounting standard-setting organization.[107] The organization in charge of standard-setting comprises both private and government members including representatives from various government and preparer groups. Given the colonial and economic ties of the Philippines with the US, it is not surprising that the Philippines' accounting practices are influenced by US GAAP.[108]

Limitations faced by implementation bodies in the Philippines according to UNCTAD (2005) include (1) difficulty in adapting some international standards to the local business environment (2) late issuance guidance from regulatory bodies (3) high compliance cost and (4) inadequate training and education. The IASB intends to promote a "stable platform" of IFRS for 2005 and is expected to continue issuing new IFRS or amendments thereto.[109]

SMEs in the Philippines account for 99 percent of businesses and the threshold for submitting audited financial statements was established many years ago. The audited financial statements submitted are fairly below standard. This suggests that the system indirectly promotes low audit standards. The main reason for this is lack of training and lack of qualified personnel to review these statements from the SEC and Bureau of Internal Revenue Unit. A high variance of audit quality in large and small audit firms exists in the industry. Some suggest that audit firms should be divided into different layers and that each layer would comply with different levels of quality control procedures.[110]

7.8.4 Internal Control System

The installation, implementation, and strengthening of internal control systems in Philippine bureaucracy has been mandated under the 1987 Philippine Constitution, existing laws and administrative rules and regulations. In 2002, the Philippines SEC stipulated that boards of directors should oversee firms' internal control systems and that CEOs are ultimately responsible for firms' internal controls.[111] The *National Guidelines on Internal Control Systems* (NGICS) is an initiative taken by the national government to affirm its commitment to the citizenry regarding accountability, effective operations, prudence in finances, and quality service. It unifies in one document existing Philippine laws, rules and regulations on internal controls to serve as a benchmark for designing, installing, implementing and monitoring internal controls in the public service.[112]

7.9 Singapore

7.9.1 Accounting Regulation and Enforcement

The establishment of accounting standards in Singapore was highly related to its colonial history. In 1819, Singapore was colonized as a trading station of the British East India Company on the island. During World War II, Singapore was occupied by Japan between 1942 and 1945. After the war, Singapore gained independence from Britain by federating with other former British territories to form Malaysia. It separated from Malaysia two years later and became a sovereign nation in 1965.[113] Lacking a formal accounting standard-setting agency before 1987, Singapore adopted British standards directly and customized them for its own economic environment. The Singapore Institute of Certified Public Accountants (SICPA), the national professional body for accountants in Singapore, was established in 1987 with IASC as the main reference in setting local accounting standards. All IAS standards were converted into accounting standards adapted to Singapore and most of them were adopted by the end of 1995 as the Singapore Financial Reporting Standards (SFRS).[114]

Singapore-incorporated companies that were listed on other stock exchanges requiring IFRS, foreign-owned companies listed in Singapore, or companies authorized by the Accounting and Corporate Regulatory Authority of Singapore (ACRA, a statutory board under the Ministry of Finance of the Singapore government) were allowed to use IFRS.[115] In Singapore, convergence with IFRS began in 2002 while full convergence of SFRS with IFRS Standards for Singapore listed companies on the Singapore Exchange (SGX) was the strategic direction set by the 2009 Accounting Standards Board (ASC).[116] The financial reporting standards issued by the ASC are largely consistent with the IFRS standards. The ASC is responsible for ensuring the reliability and comparability of financial statements so as to increase the credibility and transparency of Singapore's financial reports.[117]

On May 29, 2014, ASC announced that Singapore listed companies would adopt the new financial reporting framework, which is the same as the IFRS standards, starting from January 1, 2018. Unlisted companies can voluntarily apply for the new framework at the same time. Companies that have transitioned to the new financial reporting framework will adopt IFRS1 *First-time Adoption of International Financial Reporting Standards*. Because the new framework will be the same as the IFRS standards, companies will have the option of complying with IFRS standards or with the new Singapore financial reporting framework.[118]

7.9.2 Internal Control System The Stock Exchange of Singapore (SES) was established in 1973 as a result of the disruption of currency exchange between Singapore and Malaysia. Companies on the main board of SES are divided into five categories, namely industrial and commercial, finance, real estate, hotels and plantations. In 1999, the SES and the Singapore International Currency Exchange merged into the SGX, the first comprehensive securities and derivatives exchange in Asia.[119] To promote listed companies' corporate governance, SGX codified several corporate governance principles by including the requirement of internal control systems. SGX listing rule 719(1) requires that an issuer should establish a robust and effective internal control system within a company and the audit committee may commission an internal audit on internal control matters. In September 2011, SGX amended listing rules 1207(10) and 1204(10) and required the boards of listed firms to opine on the adequacy of internal controls within a company.[120]

The Corporate Governance Committee (CGC) of Monetary Authority of Singapore (MAS) first issued the *Code of Corporate Governance* on March 21, 2001, mandating that boards maintain effective internal control systems and that audit committees review internal control systems.[121] The 2012 revised version of the *Code of Corporate Governance* further stipulates the responsibilities of the board and management with respect to internal controls.[122]

7.10 Taiwan

7.10.1 Accounting Regulation and Enforcement In 1949, the Kuomintang government led by Chiang Kai-shek moved to Taiwan after the civil war in Mainland China.[123] After the war, Taiwan experienced rapid industrialization and economic growth and became one of the "Four Little Dragons of Asia." From 1982 to 1998, Taiwan's accounting principles were characterized primarily by the US GAAP. In 1971, the

Taiwan Accounting Review Committee passed the first accounting principles: the Generally Accepted Accounting Principles.[124]

In the early 1980s, the Taiwan economy experienced a new turning point. Many foreign banks, such as Chase Bank of the United States, began to set up branches in Taiwan. However, these branch offices of foreign banks suffered bad debts arising from loans defaults due to unqualified opinions issued by local accounting firms. The foreign investors raised concerns about the quality of Taiwan's accountants. The poor development of accounting has constrained the development of the economy. The Minister of Finance held several meetings with the chairs of the National Federation of Certified Public Accountants Associations, the Taiwan Institute of Certified Public Accountants and the Taipei City Institute of Certified Public Accountants, and they collectively decided to set up the Accounting Research and Development Foundation (ARDF). The objective of the Foundation is to develop accounting and auditing standards through fair and independent institutions for financial accounting and auditing standards and to actively promote accounting education and training.[125]

7.10.1.1 IFRS Convergence
Beginning in 1999, ARDF decided to converge with IFRS gradually in order to cope with the trend of economic globalization. From 1990 to 2009, a number of important accounting standards bulletins were updated with reference to IFRS. On July 1, 2004, the Financial Supervisory Commission (FSC), a government agency, was established to take charge of the development, supervision, regulation and review of Taiwan's financial market and financial services enterprises.[126] ARDF is an accredited institution for the establishment of standards in Taiwan. All standards (including IFRS and IAS) and related interpretations are translated into traditional Chinese by ARDF and approved by the FSC.[127]

In October 2008, the FSC announced that it would set up a task force to ensure the adoption of IFRS in Taiwan. In May 2009, the FSC developed measures to implement IFRS in two stages. In the first phase, starting from 2013, listed companies and financial institutions (with the exception of credit unions, credit card companies, and insurance intermediaries) were required to prepare financial reports using IFRS standards. Companies approved by FSC could adopt the IFRS guidelines in advance as early as 2012.[128] In the second phase, the FSC required non-listed companies, credit unions, credit card companies and insurance intermediaries to start preparing financial reports using IFRS standards in 2015. If these companies wanted to use IFRSs in advance, they could start to do so from 2013.[129]

7.10.2 Drivers of Convergence with IFRS
7.10.2.1 **Trade Between Mainland China and Taiwan** Since Mainland China proposed the "three direct links" initiative in early 1979, the Cross-Strait economy and trade have experienced rapid development. In 1979, the Cross-Strait trade volume was only US$77 million. By 2007, the Cross-Strait trade volume had reached US$124.5 billion. At the same time, Mainland China had also become the preferred overseas investment location for Taiwanese business people. As much as 40 percent of total overseas investment by Taiwanese business people is in the Mainland China market and 70 percent of manufacturers have invested in Mainland China. The development of economic and trade relations between the two sides of the strait generates keen demand for uniformity of accounting language. As Mainland China required all

Mainland Chinese listed firms to adopt IFRS (ASBE) effective from January 1, 2007, Taiwan needed to converge to IFRS as quickly as possible.[130]

7.10.2.2 Need for Enterprises to Invest Overseas By the mid 1980s, due to the substantial increase in the cost of production in Taiwan, its overseas investment had started to increase substantially and it has become one of the largest investors in Asia. In 2008, the total of Taiwan's foreign investment had reached as high as 40 percent of GDP, not only 24 percent greater than the world average, but also ahead of 30 percent of industrialized countries, equivalent to EU countries. Foreign investment is an important driver of Taiwan's economic growth. The adoption of IFRS can improve the transparency, comparability, and reliability of financial reporting. It can also reduce the costs for overseas businesses to invest in the island.[131]

7.10.3 Factors that Influence Successful Implementation of IFRS

7.10.3.1 Family Ownership Like other Asian economies, Taiwan has a high proportion of family-owned companies. There is close relationship between the board of directors and supervisors among the majority of Taiwanese companies. Thus, setting effective governance mechanisms for these family-owned companies has been a difficulty for regulators. *Wealth Magazine* (2002) reported that five leading manufacturing companies including the largest listed on the TSE had a husband and wife serving as chair of the board and supervisor respectively. Such examples completely undermine the supervision system. There is a need for further examination of the overall corporate governance structure. As in the case of family ownership, the weak supervision system weakens the internal control system and affects financial reporting quality.[132] In addition, concentrated family ownership coupled with weak investor protection in Taiwan allows controlling families to conceal financial information from the public.

7.10.4 Internal Control Report
According to the *Corporate Governance Best Practice Principles for TWSE/TPEx Listed Companies*, TWSE/TPEx listed companies should take into account overall business activities in designing and implementing a comprehensive control system.[133] According to the *Regulations Governing Establishment of Internal Control Systems by Public Companies*,[134] listed companies must submit an internal control system statement, CPA audit report on the internal control system, and CPA checklist on the audit and review of the internal control system. The TWSE determines whether the company has complied in accordance with the *Public Company Internal Control System Establishment Guidelines* (the *Guidelines*, effective January 1, 2014, issued by TWSE).[135]

7.11 Thailand

7.11.1 Accounting Regulation and Enforcement
To promote the development of the accounting industry, Thai accountants proposed to establish an accounting professional organization in 1948. After being approved by the National Culture Council, the Accountant Association of Thailand (AAT) was founded on October 13, 1948.[136] The AAT developed the first version of the Accountant Act in 1953. After almost 10 years, a revised Act, the Public Accountant Act 2505 BE (1962) was promulgated and it took effect on November 2, 1962.[137] In 1975, the AAT was officially renamed to the Institute of Certified Accountants and Auditors of Thailand

(ICAAT), expanding its scope to include more accounting professions among its members.[138] However, only ICAAT's members are bound by these standards.[139] While accounting standards in many Asian countries were heavily influenced by British accounting due to colonization, accounting standards in Thailand were affected by both British and American standards.[140] In 1972, the Recommended Accounting Concepts and Principles (1972) were issued, which established the US GAAP as an original basis for financial statements, apart from some concepts derived from the UK and Germany. Although Thailand continues to draw upon the US standards, it has gradually been adopting the International Accounting Standards (IAS) issued by the International Accounting Standards Committee (IASC).[141]

With the high interest rates in Thailand, the country has attracted a flood of foreign capital investors. From 1990 to 1996, Thailand enjoyed a decade of rapid growth and became widely known as the "fifth tiger" in Asia. The excellent performance of the global economy led investors to take an optimistic view of the Stock Exchange of Thailand (SET), whose index hit record levels in 1993. To improve Thailand's capital markets, the Securities Exchange Commission (SEC) was established in 1992 to take up supervisory responsibility in the Thailand security market.[142]

The 1997 Asian Financial Crisis broke out and changed Thailand in a number of ways. As a result of liquidity problems, many financial institutions went bankrupt and were closed by the Bank of Thailand (BOT). With foreign money withdrawn from banks, the currency was under pressure and with an inadequate foreign currency reserve, the government had to abandon the peg dollar mechanism. The Thai currency crisis further spread to neighboring Asian countries.[143] After a series of rescue measures like reduction of tax and tariffs and capital refinancing and restructuring of small to medium enterprises, Thailand began recovering from the recession in 1999. The crisis of 1997 compelled the government to establish a healthy and stable market environment as the basis of economic development. In this period, it reformed monetary and financial policies, improved the quality of disclosure and restored trust and reputation in order to revive the domestic economy. The structure of Thailand's financial market has also changed radically since its collapse in 1997. The BOT has shut down 56 banks and financial institutions. Research on the impact of the economic crisis on Thailand shows that the financing source for companies in Thailand has shifted from banks to money markets.[144]

Believing in the benefits of transparent disclosure, ICAAT and SET took steps to improve the disclosure quality of corporations in Thailand.[145] The ICAAT announced in 1998 that the Thai Accounting Standards (TAS) would be based on the International Accounting Standards (IAS). The changes in accounting standards, including the adoption of new accounting issues, had the potential to change the recognition criteria, the measurement criteria and the ways to disclose accounting information in Thailand.[146] With the development of the financial system and the openness of enterprises, a number of laws and regulations have been implemented to improve financial reporting practices in order to cope with potential economic crisis.[147] In 2000, the King issued the Accounting Act BE 2543 (2000), which was based on the advice and consent of the National Assembly. After the release of the new Act, all Thai companies were required to comply with the Thai Accounting Standards (TAS), and penalties were imposed for violations.[148] Subsequently, the Accounting Professions Act BE 2547 (2004) took effect in 2004, strengthening the role of the industry and clarifying the regulatory role of the Ministry of Commerce.[149] Under the new Act, the Federation of Accounting Professions (FAP) was named as the only professional accounting organization in Thailand, responsible for regulating the accountancy profession under oversight from the Accounting Professions Regulatory Commission.[150] Thailand has made great efforts to improve the quality of its financial reporting over the past decade. Considerable progress is evident in strengthening all aspects of the accounting and auditing framework and it is moving toward full convergence of Thai national accounting and auditing standards with international benchmarks.[151]

7.11.2 Convergence to IFRS In 1998, the ICAAT announced that Thailand's Accounting Standards (TAS) would be based on International Accounting Standards (IAS). The changes in accounting standards including the adoption of new accounting issues that would change the recognition criteria, measurement criteria, and ways of disclosing accounting information in Thailand.[152] The current Thai Financial Reporting Standards (TFRS) are prepared and promulgated by the Accounting Standards Committee (ASC), a subsidiary of FAP. Over the years, TFRS has been converging with IFRS. As of January 1, 2014, the TFRS has become a standard with word-for-word compliance with IFRS.[153] TFRS also revised standards to better adapt to the local environment, beyond the scope of the International Accounting Standards Board (IASB).[154] With respect to the continuing convergence with IFRS, FAP made a clear commitment to apply newly released IFRS into TFRS no later than one year from the effective date with the exception of the standards discussed below.

The "fair value" measurement of financial instruments is highly dependent on professional judgement. The relevant standards of financial instruments are not adopted by TFRS. The translation from IFRS into the Thai language needs to go through the FAP's due process. Thailand has been in the process of establishing a translation licensing agreement with IASB. A quick turnaround in translation will shorten the adoption lag time and may eliminate the one-year delay in adoption.[155]

A timeline for convergence to IFRS in Thailand has been scheduled and announced by the FAP, with the first target in 2011. The FAP urged the top 50 companies in terms of market capitalization and liquidity on the Stock Exchange of Thailand (SET 50) to participate in the first stage of convergence to the IFRS scheme, followed by the SET 100. Subsequently, the IFRS were to be fully adopted in 2013. The remaining listed companies should adopt IFRS by 2015.[156] Due to numerous challenges arising during the transition process, the plan was not executed as scheduled.

7.11.3 Factors that Influence Successful Implementation of IFRS

7.11.3.1 Family Ownership Large family-owned businesses are common in Thailand. Claessens et al.[157] (2000) show that 61.6 percent of listed companies in Thailand were under family control in 1996. Many of these families are of Chinese origin, influenced by the importance of family in traditional Chinese ideology.[158] Thailand has no active long-term debt market. Thai companies normally use short-term debt to finance their operating activities and even for acquisition of long-term assets. Prior to the Asian Financial Crisis, foreign companies had high outstanding short-term debts, rendering them vulnerable to currency fluctuations.[159]

With the prevalence of family-owned companies, there is no incentive to disclose more financial information to stakeholders.

Ball et al. (2003) contend that a wide family network reduces the need for accounting transparency and timely public disclosure in Asia. They argue that family-controlled companies prefer internal capital and bank loans rather than equity financing to maintain control of their businesses. In addition, banks in South East Asian countries are mostly controlled by families and they became the main finance source for enterprises.[160] After the Asian Financial Crisis, regulators in Thailand paid attention to the prevalence of short-term foreign debt and the regulatory measures that were taken to improve accounting practices. The SEC of Thailand revised the accounting practices of listed companies to conform to international best practices. More stringent requirements have been made to improve disclosure, including of external liabilities and off-balance-sheet liabilities. In addition, all listed companies shall have an audit committee composed of independent directors.[161]

7.11.3.2 Links Between Tax and Financial Reporting In Thailand, tax and financial reporting are closely linked. There are characteristics of the tax regulations in Thailand that reduce the quality of financial reporting. The Thailand Tax Law requires consistent financial and tax reporting if the company intends to claim expense exemption for tax purposes. This has prompted companies to manipulate financial reporting to reduce taxes such as depreciation and goodwill and to smooth earnings. In this regard, Ball et al. (2003) argue that Thailand's financial reporting is strongly influenced by tax incentives and therefore has lower quality.[162]

7.11.4 Challenges and Drivers of Convergence with IFRS In the wake of the 1997 Financial Crisis, there have been changes in the Thai economic environment. Before the crisis, Thailand's banks and companies had a very close relationship particularly in the authorization of loans. After the crisis, however, bankers and businesses developed some distance between them. Banks needed to recapitalize and allow more foreign equity investment, which resulted in an increase in the number of external shareholders. With the changes in the financial system and in enterprise operations, Thailand had to apply "high-quality" standards such as the IFRS to improve the comparability, reliability and decision-making usefulness of accounting information disclosed by business entities. More importantly, foreign direct investment (FDI) has been an essential driver of Thailand's economic development. However, FDI inflows have been falling since the peak of US$15.5 billion in 2013. In December 2014, the "Seven-Year Investment Promotion Strategy" (2015–2021) was approved by the Thailand Board of Investment (BOI) to attract more foreign investors. According to the estimation of the Bank of Thailand UNCTAD World Investment Report[163] in 2017, FDI fell sharply to US$3 billion in 2016, but bounced back to US$8 billion in 2017.[164]

7.11.5 Internal Control System for Listed Companies Assessing a company's internal control is an essential procedure in the SEC approving an IPO application. In an amendment to the Organic Act on Counter Corruption BE 2542[165] (1999), companies operating in Thailand are now required to have "appropriate internal control measures" in place to ensure compliance with the law and to limit their potential liability from acts of bribery carried out by connected persons for their benefit (including the potential liability of company directors).[166] According to the *Best Practice Guidelines for Audit Committees* required by SET,[167] an effective internal control system is required to ensure the effective operation of the company, which includes the provision of accurate and reliable financial reports.

7.12 Vietnam

7.12.1 Accounting Regulation and Enforcement
Vietnam is located in Southeast Asia and is bordered by Mainland China to the north. After the Vietnam War, Vietnam rebuilt its infrastructure, and established socialism from 1954. During this time, the Vietnamese economy operated as a centrally planned economy.[168] From 1960 to 1969, the accounting system in Vietnam was strongly influenced by Mainland China as a result of its similar planned economy regime. From 1969 to 1989, Vietnam changed to the Soviet Union's government-centralized system and the former Soviet Union began to influence the development of accounting in Vietnam.[169] With the opening of foreign trade in 1995 and commercial freedom in 1999, Vietnam opened its economy, and allowed private enterprises to engage in import and export activities. The Vietnamese accounting system was adjusted to serve a market economy instead of a planned economy.[170]

From 1995 to 1998, the European project (EUROTAPVIET) provided Vietnamese accounting students with knowledge of the IAS. This project suggested to the Vietnamese government the benefits of convergence to IFRS. The EU was instrumental in assisting Vietnam to join the IFAC and it became a member of the international accounting professional associations.[171] In 2003, the National Assembly passed the Accounting Law, which came into effect on January 1, 2004. Issuing the Accounting Law was a milestone in Vietnamese accounting history as it provided a legal basis for professional accounting activities for the public and private sectors, which became a solid foundation for later convergence to IFRS.

Vietnamese accounting activities are heavily regulated by the government and state authorities. The Vietnamese accounting system is rule based and has strict rules and low flexibility compared with principle-based IFRS. Related accounting standards in Vietnam clearly mandate the chart of accounts in the balance sheet and income statement while IFRS has no strict guidance, allowing different treatment methods to meet different needs.[172] In converging toward IFRS, Vietnam's accounting has been continuously improved. Although there are no mandatory IFRS guidelines in Vietnam currently, many Vietnamese companies can selectively apply IFRS. In fact, Vietnamese publicly listed companies, especially cross listing companies in overseas stock markets, provide two separate financial statements, one based on the current Vietnamese Accounting Standards (VAS) and another based on IFRS.[173]

7.12.2 Factors that Influence Successful Implementation of IFRS
7.12.2.1 The Role of government By legislating for VAS, the state has maintained a monopoly position on accounting and auditing verification, practice, and supervision procedures.[174] The government's control over financial institutions suggests that the State-Owned Commercial Banks (SOCBs) have a close relationship with SOEs even after Vietnam's Doi Moi reforms aimed to shift the central planned economy to a market economy.[175] There are more than 5,000

companies that are either owned by SOEs or managed by a related government department in Vietnam. The government also manages auditing firms in Vietnam. As such, the role of government in the economy creates a conflict of interests. For example, the government may pressure audit firms to issue favorable audit opinions to SOEs.

7.12.2.2 Transparency Issues The government-controlled financial reports lack transparency. This is normal for countries with a centralized controlled economy system when compared to an open free market. Government officials are reluctant to disclose information as they were not required to do so in the past. But now, the accounting system provides information not only to the state but also to stakeholders and external investors. Business transactions have become increasingly complex and officials are reluctant to disclose information due to its poor quality.[176]

7.12.3 Drivers of Convergence with IFRS   With the Doi Moi reform and opening (initiated in 1986), foreign direct investment in Vietnam experienced a sharp increase, driving the economy of Vietnam and contributing to the development of the domestic private sector. Through narrowing the differences between VAS and IFRS, Vietnamese companies can attract potential investors and compete with foreign competitors by adopting mandatory VAS for financial statements. This improves the quality of accounting reports and strengthens investor confidence. By incorporating IFRS, Vietnam's international reputation is enhanced by compliance with international rules and becomes a credible global trading partner. The shift from VAS to IFRS benefits Vietnam's accounting and academic communities.[177]

7.12.4 Internal Control System   In 2000, the Ministry of Finance of Vietnam announced the second phase of the Vietnamese Audit Standards and stipulated that listed companies should establish and operate an appropriate and efficient internal control system. Auditors performing financial reporting auditing should not only gather auditing evidence from the accounting system but also ensure the effectiveness of the design and implementation of the internal control system.[178]

8.   CONCLUSIONS

Financial economic sustainability performance is the most important dimension of sustainability performance. Business organizations must be economically and financially sustainable in creating shareholder value to survive and be able to achieve other dimensions of sustainability performance. Financial and internal control reporting systems must be robust, effective and reliable in producing and disseminating high-quality financial information to properly reflect economic sustainability performance. The effectiveness of financial ESP and internal control systems ICFR requires management to identify significant risks that may cause material misstatements and to design control activities to minimize negative impacts. Management is primarily responsible for the achievement of sustainable economic performance with effective reporting of such performance to all stakeholders, particularly investors. This chapter presents financial economic sustainability in 12 Asian economies. All 12 jurisdictions in Asia have adopted accounting information systems in compliance with IFRS guidelines in producing reliable, comparable and relevant financial information on the economic dimension of sustainability performance. ICFR is also practiced in the majority of jurisdictions ensuring effective and efficient internal controls relevant to the economic dimension of sustainability performance.

9. CHAPTER TAKEAWAY

1. Economic sustainability performance (ESP) has and will continue to be the integral component of business sustainability performance as business organizations have to be financially stable and to perform well financially before contributing to the environment and society.
2. Improving financial ESP starts from tone at the top with commitment by the board of directors and top executives to effective economic sustainability performance, reporting and assurance.
3. Companies should integrate financial sustainability development into decision-making, planning, implementation and evaluation processes.
4. Companies should establish and maintain sound corporate financial reporting for sustainability and accountability with a keen focus on supporting the information needs of long-term investors regarding sustainable economic performance.
5. Companies should ensure that audit strategies and audit quality on ICFR are effective, efficient, adequate and in compliance with applicable accounting and auditing guidelines and standards.

ENDNOTES

1. M. E. Porter, and Kramer, M. R. "Creating Shared Value," *Harvard Business Review*, January–February, (2011): 62–77.
2. Ibid.
3. Ibid, p. 65.
4. Committee for Economic Development, *Built to Last: Focusing Corporations on Long-Term Performance*, 2007, www.ced.org/docs/report/report_corpgov2007.pdf.
5. D. Kiron, N. Kruschwitz, K. Haanaes, M. Reeves, and E. Goh. "The Innovation Bottom Line: How Companies that See Sustainability as Both a Necessity and an Opportunity, and Change Their Business Models in Response, Are Finding Success," MIT Slogan: Management Review, 2013, http://csbf.org.nz/wp-content/uploads/the-innovation-bottom-line.pdf.
6. Much of discussion of financial ESP comes from A. Brockett, and Z. Rezaee. 2012. Corporate Sustainability: Integrating Performance and Reporting, *November 2012*, John Wiley & Sons, Inc.
7. Public Company Accounting Oversight Board (PCAOB), *Auditing Standard No. 2: An Audit of Internal Control over Financial Reporting Performed in Conjunction with an Audit of Financial Statements*, 2004, www.pcaobus.org/Standards/Standards_and_Related_Rules/Auditing_Standard_No.2.aspx.
8. Sarbanes-Oxley Act (SOX), July 30, 2002, www.law.uc.edu/CCL/SOact/soact.pdf.
9. D. Reilly, "Profit as We Know It Could Be Lost with New Accounting Statements," *Wall Street Journal* May 12, 2007, A1, wsj.com/public/article/SB117893520139500814-m5r4gJLCTET50No6lq_tuIrvFug_20070522.html?mod=blogs.

10. PricewaterhouseCoopers (PwC), *Guide to Forward-Looking Information: Don't Fear the Future—Communicating with Confidence*, January 2006, www.pwc.com/Extweb/pwcpublications.nsf/docid/E97847126DD93E13802570FA004100D7.

11. Ibid

12. C. Leuz, "Proprietary Versus Non-Proprietary Disclosures: Evidence from Germany," in *The Economics and Politics of Accounting*, ed. C. Leuz, D. Pfaff, and A. Hopwood (Oxford: Oxford University Press, 2004), 164–197.

13. R. A. Davidson, A.M. Gelardi, and F. Li, "Analysis of the Conceptual Framework of China's New Accounting System," *Accounting Horizons* 10, no. 1 (1996): 58.

14. L. C. J. Ho, Q. Liao, and M. Taylor, "Real and Accrual-Based Earnings Management in the Pre-and Post-IFRS Periods: Evidence from China." *Journal of International Financial Management & Accounting*, 26, no. 3, 2015. 294–335.

15. T. J. Wong, "Corporate Governance Research on Listed Firms in China: Institutions, Governance and Accountability," *Foundations and Trends® in Accounting* 9, no. 4 (2016): 259–326, DOI: http://dx.doi.org/10.1561/1400000039.

16. M. Layton, "Is Private Securities Litigation Essential for the Development of China's Stock Markets?" *New York University Law Review* 83, no. 6 (2008): 1948–1978.

17. T. J. Wong, "Corporate Governance Research on Listed Firms in China."

18. S. Taub, Today in Finance: China to adopt IFRS.2/16/2006, 2006.

19. Ibid.

20. D. Kiron, N. Kruschwitz, K. Haanaes, M. Reeves, and E. Goh. "The Innovation Bottom Line: How Companies that See Sustainability as Both a Necessity and an Opportunity, and Change Their Business Models in Response, Are Finding Success," MIT Slogan: Management Review, 2013, http://csbf.org.nz/wp-content/uploads/theinnovation-bottom-line.pdf.

21. Ibid.

22. T. Hui-Sung Kao, "The Effect of IFRS, Information Asymmetry and Corporate Governance on the Quality of Accounting Information," *Asian Economic and Financial Review* 4, no. 2 (2014): 226–256.

23. L. A. Gordon, M. P. Loeb, and W. Zhu, "The Impact of IFRS Adoption on Foreign Direct Investment," *Journal of Accounting and Public Policy* 31, no. 4 (2012): 374–398.

24. IFRS Jurisdiction Profile, updated on January 12, 2018, http://www.ifrs.org/-/media/feature/around-the-world/jurisdiction-profiles/hong-kong-sar-ifrs-profile.pdf.

25. *South China Morning Post (SCMP)*, August 28, 2002, p. 2 (ProQuest ID: 155923101).

26. J. P. Fan and T. J. Wong, "Corporate Ownership Structure and the Informativeness of Accounting Earnings in East Asia," *Journal of Accounting and Economics* 33, no. 3 (2002): 401–425.

27. B. Jaggi, S. Leung, and F. Gul, "Family Control, Board Independence and Earnings Management: Evidence Based on Hong Kong Firms," *Journal of Accounting and Public Policy* 28, no. 4 (2009): 281–300.

28. KPMG, *New HKEX Requirements on Risk Management and Internal Control: How Companies Are Responding to the Code Requirements*, 2016, https://assets.kpmg.com/content/dam/kpmg/cn/pdf/en/2016/08/companies-responding-code-requirements-v1.pdf.

29. C. Marston, *Financial Reporting in India* (London: Croom Helm, 1986).

30. S. E. Perumpral, M. Evans, S. Agarwal, and F. Amenkhienan, "The Evolution of Indian Accounting Standards: Its History and Current Status with Regard to International Financial Reporting Standards," *Advances in Accounting, Incorporating Advances in International Accounting* 25, no. 1 (2009): 106–111.

31. Ibid.

32. P. Jain, "IFRS Implementation in India: Opportunities and Challenges," 2011, https://www.researchgate.net/publication/228435057_IFRS_Implementation_in_India_Opportunities_and_Challenges, accessed Jan 11, 2018

33. R. S. Dhankar and A. Gupta "Transition to International Financial Reporting Standards (IFRS) or Ind-AS in India," *Global Journal of Finance & Management* 6, no. 7 (2014): 609–614.

34. S. Sharma, M. Joshi, M. Kansal, "IFRS Adoption Challenges in Developing Economies: An Indian Perspective," *Managerial Auditing Journal* 32, no. 4/5 (2017): 406–426, DOI: https://doi.org/10.1108/MAJ-05-2016-1374.

35. A. K. Chakrabarty, "Convergence of IAS with IFRS: Theoretical Aspects and Present Status in India," *Journal of Commerce* 6, no. 1 (2014): 1–12.

36. F. Choi and G. Meek, *International Accounting: Pearson New International Edition*, 7th ed (Harlow: Pearson Education Ltd, 2013), 96–110.

37. A. Patro and V. K. Gupta, "Adoption of International Financial Reporting Standards (IFRS) in Accounting Curriculum in India-An Empirical Study," *Procedia Economics and Finance* 2 (2012): 227–236.

38. Jain, "IFRS Implementation in India."

39. KPMG, *ICAI Releases Revised Guidance on Internal Financial Controls Over Financial Reporting*, 2015.

40. Choi and Meek, *International Accounting: Pearson New International Edition*.

41. A. S. Sapiie, "Sejarah akuntansi di Indonesia (The History of Accounting in Indonesia)" (unpublished master's thesis, University of Indonesia, Jakarta, 1980).

42. A. F. Maradona and P. Chand, "The Pathway of Transition to International Financial Reporting Standards (IFRS) in Developing Countries: Evidence from Indonesia," *Journal of International Accounting, Auditing and Taxation* 30 (2018): 57–68.

43. Ibid.

44. S. Effendi and T. Hopper, "Management Control, Culture and Ethnicity in a Chinese Indonesian Company," *Accounting, Organizations and Society* 32 (2007): 223–262.

45. Y. Wanandi, "Indonesia: A Failed State?" *Washington Quarterly* 25, no. 3 (2002): 135–146.

46. R. McLeod, "The Struggle to Regain Effective government Under Democracy in Indonesia," *Bulletin of Indonesian Economic Studies* 41, no. 3 (2005): 367–386.

47. H. Harun, K. Van-Peursem, and I. Eggleton, "Indonesian Public Sector Accounting Reforms: Dialogic Aspirations a Step Too Far?" *Accounting, Auditing & Accountability Journal* 28, no. 5 (2015): 706–738.

48. "International Economy: Asia," Second Quarter, *Barclays Economic Review* (1998): 23.

49. H. Harun, "Obstacles to Indonesian Public Sector Accounting Reforms," *Bulletin of Indonesian Economic Studies* 43, no. 3 (2007): 365–375.

50. Harun, Van-Peursem, and Eggleton, "Indonesian Public Sector Accounting Reforms."

51. Maradona and Chand, "The Pathway of Transition to International Financial Reporting Standards (IFRS) in Developing Countries."

52. Ibid.

53. M. Mukhtaruddin and Z. Sulong, "International Financial Reporting Standards Convergence and Quality of Accounting Information: Evidence from Indonesia," *International Journal of Economics and Financial Issues* 7, no. 4 (2017): 433–447.

54. Maradona and Chand, "The Pathway of Transition to International Financial Reporting Standards (IFRS) in Developing Countries."

55. Ibid.

56. Ibid.

57. Ibid.

58. World Bank, *Report on the Observance of Standards and Codes (ROSC) Indonesia: Accounting and Auditing*, 2011, https://www.worldbank.org/ifa/rosc_aa.html.

59. R. K. Larson and D. L. Street, "Convergence with IFRS in an Expanding Europe: Progress and Obstacles Identified by Large Accounting Firms' Survey," *Journal of International Accounting, Auditing and Taxation* 13, no. 2 (2004): 89–119.

60. Maradona and Chand, "The Pathway of Transition to International Financial Reporting Standards (IFRS) in Developing Countries."
61. Maradona and Chand, "The Pathway of Transition to International Financial Reporting Standards (IFRS) in Developing Countries."
62. W. E. Daniel, "Corporate Governance in Indonesian Listed Companies—A Problem of Legal Transplant," *Bond L. Rev.* 15 (2003): i.
63. Indonesia's Code of Good Corporate Governance 2006, http://www.ecgi.org/codes/docu ments/indonesia_cg_2006_en.pdf.
64. Choi and Meek, *International Accounting: Pearson New International Edition.*
65. K. Yorihiro, "Update: IFRS developments in Japan," *Financial Executive* 27, no. 8 (2011): 14–15.
66. http://www.ifrs.org/-/media/feature/around-the-world/jurisdiction-profiles/japan-ifrs-profile.pdf.
67. Yorihiro, "Update: IFRS developments in Japan."
68. N. Tsunogaya, A. Hellmann, and S. Scagnelli, "Adoption of IFRS in Japan: Challenges and Consequences," *Pacific Accounting Review* 27, no. 1 (2015): 3–27.
69. N. Tsunogaya, "Issues Affecting Decisions on Mandatory Adoption of International Financial Reporting Standards (IFRS) in Japan," *Accounting, Auditing & Accountability Journal* 29, no. 5 (2016): 828–860.
70. Ibid.
71. Ibid.
72. Ibid.
73. http://www.ifrs.org/-/media/feature/around-the-world/jurisdiction-profiles/japan-ifrs-profile.pdf, updated on 12 January 2018.
74. Choi and Meek, *International Accounting: Pearson New International Edition.*
75. Ibid.
76. C. Nobes and R. Parker, *Comparative International Accounting*, 12th ed. (Harlow, England; New York: Pearson, 2012).
77. Ibid.
78. Choi and Meek, *International Accounting: Pearson New International Edition.*
79. J. I. Jang, K. J. Lee, Y. Seo, and J. Cheung, "Economic Consequences of IFRS Adoption in Korea: A Literature Review," *Journal of Applied Business Research* 32, no. 6 (2016): 1649–1662.
80. R. C. Graham, and R. D. King, "Accounting Practices and the Market Valuation of Accounting Numbers: Evidence from Indonesia, Korea, Malaysia, the Philippines, Taiwan, and Thailand," *International Journal of Accounting* 35 (2000): 445–470.
81. Ibid.
82. Jang, Lee, Seo, and Cheung, "Economic Consequences of IFRS Adoption in Korea."
83. http://unpan1.un.org/intradoc/groups/public/documents/apcity/unpan011491.pdf.
84. R. Ball, A. Robin, and J. S. Wu, "Incentives Versus Standards: Properties of Accounting Income in Four East Asian Countries," *Journal of Accounting and Economics* 36, no. 1–3 (2003): 235–270.
85. Before IFRS was issued by IASB, the standards used were International Accounting Standards (IAS) issued by the International Accounting Standards Committee (IASC) from 1973 to 2001.
86. M. M. Marzuki and E. A. Wahab, "Institutional Factors and Conditional Conservatism in Malaysia: Does International Financial Reporting Standards Convergence Matter?" *Journal of Contemporary Accounting & Economics* 12, no. 3 (2016): 191–209.
87. M. Suto, "Capital Structure and Investment Behaviour of Malaysian Firms in the 1990s: A Study of Corporate Governance Before the Crisis," *Corporate Governance: An International Review* 11, no. 1 (2003): 25–39.
88. O. K. Tam and M. Guo-Sze Tan, "Ownership, Governance and Firm Performance in Malaysia," *Corporate Governance: An International Review* 15, no. 2 (2007): 208–222.

89. M. Favere-Marchesi, "Audit quality in ASEAN," *International Journal of Accounting* 35, no. 1 (2000): 121–149.
90. Jaggi, Leung, and Gul, "Family Control, Board Independence and Earnings Management."
91. M. Abdullah, L. Evans, I. Fraser, and I. Tsalavoutas, "IFRS Mandatory disclosures in Malaysia: The Influence of Family Control and the Value (Ir) Relevance of Compliance Levels," *Accounting Forum* 39, no. 4 (2015, December): 328–348.
92. P. K. Liew, "Corporate Governance Reforms in Malaysia: The Key Leading Players Perspectives," *Corporate Governance: An International Review* 15, no. 5 (September 2007): 724–740.
93. Standard & Poor's, S&P Global Ratings, 2008, https://www.standardandpoors.com/en_US/web/guest/home.
94. B. Muniandy and M. J. Ali, "Development of Financial Reporting Environment in Malaysia," *Research in Accounting Regulation* 24, no. 2 (2012): 115–125.
95. F. H. Fadzil, H. Haron, and M. Jantan, "Internal Auditing Practices and Internal Control System," *Managerial Auditing Journal* 20, no. 8 (2005): 844–866.
96. Statement on Risk Management & Internal Control—Guidelines for Directors of Listed Issuers, http://www.iiam.com.my/wp-content/uploads/2015/12/guideline-risk-management-new1.pdf.
97. L. Dumlao, V. Ibarra, and C. Lopez, "Corporate Governance and Developments in the Philippines Accounting Profession," Allied Academies International Conference. *Academy of Accounting and Financial Studies. Proceedings* 13, no. 2 (2008): 8–13.
98. Y. Nagano, "National Accounts in Philippines Economic History: A Preliminary Report on Data Gathering and Research Trends." IDEAS Working Paper Series from RePEc, 2007.
99. M. Noland, "The Philippines in the Asian Financial Crisis: How the Sick Man Avoided Pneumonia." IDEAS Working Paper Series from RePEc, 2000.
100. Dumlao, Ibarra, and Lopez, "Corporate Governance and Developments in the Philippines Accounting Profession."
101. http://www.picpa.com.ph/frsc.html?article=About%20FRSC%20and%20PIC&page=FRSC.
102. https://www.aseanbriefing.com/news/2015/11/02/an-overview-of-ifrs-adoption-in-asean-part-three.html.
103. C. L. Fajardo, "The Evolution of Financial Accounting Standards in the Philippines," (working paper, National University, California, 2008).
104. https://www.aseanbriefing.com/news/2015/11/02/an-overview-of-ifrs-adoption-in-asean-part-three.html.
105. http://www.sgv.ph/adopting-international-standards/.
106. Fajardo, "The Evolution of Financial Accounting Standards in the Philippines."
107. Graham and King, "Accounting Practices and the Market Valuation of Accounting Numbers."
108. S. M. Saudagaran and J. G. Diga. "The Institutional Environment of Financial Reporting Regulation in ASEAN," *International Journal of Accounting* 35, no. 1 (2000): 1–26.
109. Fajardo, "The Evolution of Financial Accounting Standards in the Philippines."
110. Dumlao, Ibarra, and Lopez, "Corporate Governance and Developments in the Philippines Accounting Profession."
111. http://www.ecgi.org/codes/documents/phillipines_sec_memo_2002_en.pdf.
112. National Guidelines on Internal Control Systems, https://www.dbm.gov.ph/wp-content/uploads/2012/03/NGICS-body.pdf.
113. L. Smith, A. Limaye, Y. Huang, and C. Okafor, "Accounting, IFRS, and Capital Markets in India, Singapore, and South Africa," *Internal Auditing* 26, no. 4 (2011): 32–37.
114. Ball, Robin, and Wu, "Incentives Versus Standards."

115. Smith, Limaye, Huang, and Okafor, "Accounting, IFRS, and Capital Markets in India, Singapore, and South Africa."
116. http://www.ifrs.org/-/media/feature/around-the-world/jurisdiction-profiles/singapore-ifrs-profile.pdf.
117. P. Yapa, D. Kraal, and M. Joshi, "The adoption of 'International Accounting Standard (IAS) 12 Income Taxes': Convergence or Divergence with Local Accounting Standards in Selected ASEAN Countries?" *Australasian Accounting Business & Finance Journal* 9, no. 1 (2015): 3–24.
118. http://www.ifrs.org/-/media/feature/around-the-world/jurisdiction-profiles/singapore-ifrs-profile.pdf.
119. Smith, Limaye, Huang, and Okafor, "Accounting, IFRS, and Capital Markets in India, Singapore, and South Africa."
120. https://www.ey.com/sg/en/services/assurance/board-matters-quarterly---issue-12---june-2012---sgx-listing-rules.
121. http://www.mas.gov.sg/~/media/resource/fin_development/corporate_governance/CG%20Code%202001%20Code.pdf.
122. http://www.mas.gov.sg/~/media/resource/fin_development/corporate_governance/CGCRevisedCodeofCorporateGovernance3May2012.pdf.
123. R. S. Chen, "Development of the Accounting Profession in Taiwan," California State University Northridge, Northridge, CA, http://www.jaabc.com/jaabcv2n2preview.html.
124. Translated from 郭红彩.台湾财务会计准则演变解读与启示——从U.S.GAAP 到 IFRS. 财会通讯: 综合 (上 04 (2013): 111–113.
125. http://www.ardf.org.tw/english/aboutus2.html.
126. https://www.fsc.gov.tw/en/home.jsp?id=9&parentpath=0,1.
127. http://www.ifrs.org/-/media/feature/around-the-world/jurisdiction-profiles/chinese-taipei-ifrs-profile.pdf.
128. Ibid.
129. Ibid.
130. Translated from Cai Qiuyu, "Reflections on the Internationalization of Accounting Standards in Taiwan and Its Enlightenment," *Journal of Fujian Commercial College*, 2010.
131. Ibid.
132. I. Filatotchev, Y. Lien, and J. Piesse, "Corporate Governance and Performance in Publicly Listed, Family-Controlled Firms: Evidence from Taiwan," *Asia Pacific Journal of Management* 22, no. 3 (2005): 257–283.
133. http://twse-regulation.twse.com.tw/ENG/EN/law/DAT0201.aspx?FLCODE=FL020553 and http://law.fsc.gov.tw/law/EngLawContent.aspx?Type=E&id=1347.
134. Taiwan Stock Exchange Corporation ("TWSE"), *Procedures for the Review of Internal Control System Reports Issued by Certified Public Accountants*, http://twse-regulation.twse.com.tw/ENG/EN/law/DAT0201.aspx?FLCODE=FL007273.
135. http://twse-regulation.twse.com.tw/TW/law/DAT0201.aspx?FLCODE=FL021141.
136. http://www.fap.or.th/en/Article/Detail/66271.
137. Ibid.
138. Ibid.
139. Saudagaran and Diga, "The Institutional Environment of Financial Reporting Regulation in ASEAN."
140. Ball, Robin, and Wu, "Incentives Versus Standards."
141. Saudagaran and Diga, "The Institutional Environment of Financial Reporting Regulation in ASEAN."
142. A. Jaikengkit, "The Development of Financial Reporting, the Stock Exchange and Corporate Disclosure in Thailand," *Research in Accounting Regulation* 15 (2002).
143. Ibid.
144. Ibid.
145. Ibid.

146. http://www.jap.tbs.tu.ac.th/files/Article/Jap05/JAP05Sinlapaporn.pdf.

147. S. Sutthachai and T. Cooke, "An Analysis of Thai Financial Reporting Practices and the Impact of the 1997 Economic Crisis," *Abacus* 45, no. 4 (2009): 493–517.

148. Ibid.

149. http://www.fap.or.th/en/Article/Detail/66271.

150. https://www.ifac.org/about-ifac/membership/members/federation-accounting-professions.

151. World Bank, *Kingdom of Thailand: Accounting and Auditing* (Washington, DC: World Bank, 2008), https://openknowledge.worldbank.org/handle/10986/8052 License: CC BY 3.0 IGO.

152. http://www.jap.tbs.tu.ac.th/files/Article/Jap05/JAP05Sinlapaporn.pdf.

153. https://www.aseanbriefing.com/news/2015/10/26/an-overview-of-ifrs-adoption-in-asean-part-two.html.

154. Ibid.

155. Ibid.

156. M. Klose and P. Sabangban, "Thailand's Convergence to IFRS," *Controlling & Management* (2011), https://slideheaven.com/thailands-convergence-to-ifrs.html.

157. S. Claessens, S. Djankov and L. Lang, "The Separation of Ownership and Control in East Asia Corporations," *Journal of Financial Economics* 58, no. 1–2 (2000): 81–112.

158. Ball, Robin, and Wu, "Incentives Versus Standards."

159. A. Rahman, J. Yammeesri and H. Perera, "Financial Reporting Quality in International Settings: A Comparative Study of the USA, Japan, Thailand, France and Germany," *International Journal of Accounting* 45, no. 1 (2010): 1–34.

160. Ball, Robin, and Wu, "Incentives Versus Standards."

161. Rahman, Yammeesri and Perera, "Financial Reporting Quality in International Settings."

162. Ball, Robin, and Wu, "Incentives Versus Standards."

163. World Investment Report 2017, UNCTAD, http://unctad.org/en/PublicationsLibrary/wir2017_en.pdf?lien_externe_oui=Continue.

164. https://en.portal.santandertrade.com/establish-overseas/thailand/foreign-investment.

165. https://www.bakermckenzie.com/-/media/files/insight/publications/2015/07/al_bangkok_amendmentanticorruptionlaws_jul15.pdf?la=en.

166. http://www.conventuslaw.com/report/thailand-official-guidelines-on-internal-control/.

167. https://www.set.or.th/en/regulations/rules/individual_files/BorJorRor2500_EN.pdf.

168. D. Ngoc Phi Anh and D. Nguyen, "Accounting in a Developing Transitional Economy: The Case of Vietnam," *Asian Review of Accounting* 21, no. 1 (2013): 74–95.

169. F. B. Narayan and T. Godden, "Financial Management and Governance Issues in Viet Nam," ADB Diagnostic Study, 2000: 1.

170. Ngoc Phi Anh and Nguyen, "Accounting in a Developing Transitional Economy."

171. Narayan and Godden, "Financial Management and Governance Issues in Viet Nam."

172. D. H. T. Phan, B. Mascitelli, and M. Barut, "Perceptions Towards International Financial Reporting Standards (IFRS): The Case of Vietnam," *Global Review of Accounting and Finance* 5, no. 1 (2014): 132–152.

173. D. Phan and B. Mascitelli, "Optimal Approach and Timeline for IFRS Adoption in Vietnam: Perceptions from Accounting Professionals," *Research in Accounting Regulation* 26, no. 2 (2014): 222–229.

174. T. M. V. Bui, "A Study of the Development of Accounting in Vietnam," (PhD thesis, RMIT University, RMIT, Melbourne, 2011), 462.

175. J. Kovsted, J. Rand, F. Tarp, D. Nguyen, V. Nguyen, and T. Thao, "Financial Sector Reforms in Vietnam: Selected Issues and Problems." IDEAS Working Paper Series from RePEc, 2003.

176. Narayan and Godden, "Financial Management and Governance Issues in Viet Nam."

177. Phan, Mascitelli, and Barut, "Perceptions Towards International Financial Reporting Standards (IFRS): The Case of Vietnam."

178. http://moj.gov.vn/vbpq/en/lists/vn%20bn%20php%20lut/view_detail.aspx?itemid=7.

CHAPTER 6

Governance Dimension of Sustainability

1. EXECUTIVE SUMMARY

The financial economic dimension of sustainability performance, reporting and assurance was discussed in chapter 5. Non-financial dimensions of sustainability performance and reporting including governance, social, ethical and environmental (GSEE) are presented in chapters 6–9. Regulators, investors and business organizations worldwide are now interested in more information about GSEE. Effective corporate governance can improve business sustainability, corporate culture, corporate strategic decisions, sustainable performance, reliable financial reports future prospects and growth. The existence and persistence of differences in global economic structure, financial systems and corporate environment causes countries to adopt their own corporate governance reforms and measures. However, globalization, cross-border trade and capital formation necessitate a convergence in corporate governance measures and regulatory reforms. The emerging global corporate governance reforms are shaping capital markets' structure worldwide and altering their competitiveness and the protection provided to investors. This chapter presents the governance dimension of sustainability performance, reporting and assurance worldwide and in Asia.

2. INTRODUCTION

A dynamic financial system, reliable financial information and effective corporate governance are essential for global economic development and growth. In the aftermath of the 2007–2009 Global Financial Crisis, companies worldwide have improved their corporate governance measures to strengthen their regulatory reforms to promote public trust and investor confidence in their financial reporting. The globalization of capital markets and the demand for investor protection in response to financial scandals worldwide, such as Enron, WorldCom, Parmalat, Ahold and Satyam, also require consistency and uniformity in regulatory reforms and corporate governance practices.

Consideration of non-financial GSEE sustainability activities can create both synergies and conflicts. These non-financial GSEE sustainability activities and performance can enhance the long-term value of the firm by fulfilling its social responsibilities, meeting its environmental obligations, creating ethical workplaces and improving its reputation. However, these sustainability activities may require considerable resource allocation that may conflict with shareholder wealth maximization objectives and discourage management from investing solely in initiatives that would result in long-term financial sustainability. This chapter describes in detail the non-financial governance dimension of sustainability performance with a focus on Asia, although a synopsis of this dimension has been presented in chapter 1.

3. GOVERNANCE DIMENSION OF SUSTAINABILITY PERFORMANCE

Corporate governance has evolved as a central issue with regulators and public companies in the wake of the 2007–2009 Global Financial Crisis. Corporate governance is defined from a legal perspective as measures that enable and ensure compliance with all applicable laws, rules, regulations and standards. From the agency theory perspective, corporate governance is defined as a monitoring process to align management interests with those of shareholders in creating shareholder value.[1] Companies normally undergo a series of corporate governance reforms aimed at improving the effectiveness of their governance, internal controls and financial reports. Effective corporate governance promotes accountability, improves the reliability and quality of financial information and prevents management fraudulent behavior. Poor corporate governance adversely affects the company's potential, performance, financial reports and accountability and can pave the way for business failure and financial statement fraud. Corporate governance including the oversight function assumed by the board of directors, the managerial function delegated to management, the internal audit function conducted by internal auditors, the external audit function performed by external auditors and the compliance function enforced by policymakers, regulators and standard-setters are vital to the quality of financial information. Corporate reputation, customer satisfaction, ethical workplaces, CSR and environmental initiatives are non-financial drivers of sustainable economic performance and long-term growth that are addressed in this chapter and the following chapters under the non-financial dimensions of sustainability performance. Business sustainability requires that the company be managed effectively through robust corporate governance mechanisms.

Globalization and technological advances have promoted global convergence in corporate governance. The move toward convergence in corporate governance has become substantially more prevalent in the aftermath of the 2007–2009 Global Financial Crisis. Corporate governance participants including the board of directors, top executives, internal and external auditors and other corporate gatekeepers, should establish the process to ensure the goals of both shareholder value creation and stakeholder value protection for public companies are achieved. The corporate governance structure is shaped by corporate governance principles, internal and external governance mechanisms and corporate governance functions as well as policy interventions through regulations. Corporate governance mechanisms are viewed as a nexus of formal and informal contracts that are designed to align the interests of management with those of the shareholders. The effectiveness of both internal and external corporate governance mechanisms depends on the cost-benefit trade-offs among these mechanisms and is related to their availability, the extent to which they are being used, whether their marginal benefits justify their marginal costs and the company's corporate governance structure. Several corporate governance reforms (e.g., Sarbanes-Oxley Act of 2002, Dodd-Frank Act of 2010) have changed the relationship between shareholders, management, and boards of directors and other corporate gatekeepers in the United States by creating an appropriate "balance of authority" exercised by boards, management and share-holders in the corporate decision-making process and governance. Directors are now accountable to a wide range of stakeholders including shareholders, creditors, employees, customers, suppliers, government and the communities in which the corporation operates.

4. NEW PARADIGM FOR CORPORATE GOVERNANCE

Investors have always been concerned about the effectiveness of corporate governance in protecting their interests. Many suggestions and recommendations are made by concerned investors regarding how to improve corporate governance. These recommendations have led to the development of a new paradigm for corporate governance which emphasizes tone at the top promoting long-term strategies in achieving sustainable financial and non-financial performance.[2] The new paradigm for corporate governance recognizes the importance of sustainable value over short termism, integrates long-term corporate strategy with substantive corporate governance, requires transparency as to director involvement and promotes the following best practices of corporate governance:[3]

1. **Lead with the Strategy.** The main driver of effective corporate governance is the strategy set by the board of directors to create shared value for all stakeholders. The strategy defines the company's mission and its vision, explains key drivers of strategy and business outcomes that are built into the business model and corporate environment. This strategy should be dynamic and remain viable as the business environment, competitive landscape and regulatory regime change.

2. **Confirm Board Involvement in the Strategy.** The board of directors should set a tone at the top in the development and implementation of corporate strategies and in guiding, debating and overseeing strategic choices. The company should also explicitly communicate how the board has actively overseen long-term plans along with its commitment to support corporate strategies. Communication of corporate strategies and strategic planning with investors is essential in the new paradigm for corporate governance.

3. **Make the Case for Long-Term Investments, Reinvesting in the Business for Growth and Pursuing R&D and Innovation.** The company should have a proper balance between short-term and long-term investments and clearly disclose to investors how such investments are reviewed and contribute to long-term growth and value creation.

4. **Describe Capital Allocation Priorities.** Priorities for capital allocation should be set by the board of directors based on recommendations by executives. The board of directors should also review and approve management's capital allocation policies.

5. **Explain Why the Mix of Directors Is Right in the Boardroom.** Board diversity in terms of skills, expertise, ethnicity and gender can significantly improve corporate governance effectiveness. Communicate the diverse skills, expertise and attributes of the board as a whole and of individual members to investors. Be transparent about director recruitment processes that address the future company and board needs as well as procedures for increasing the diversity of the board and its orientation, tutorials and retreats for an in-depth review of key issues.

6. **Address Sustainability, Citizenship and Environmental, Social and Governance (ESG)/Corporate Social Responsibility (CSR).** The company should integrate relevant financial economic sustainability performance and non-financial

environmental, social and governance (ESG) sustainability performance into corporate culture and the business model with a full commitment by the board of directors. Disclosure of sustainability performance information through integrated sustainability reporting and assurance to investors is crucial in the new paradigm.

7. **Articulate the Link Between Compensation Design and Corporate Strategy.** Create a proper link between executive compensation and firm performance and effectively disclose to investors how compensation practices encourage and reward long-term growth, promote implementation of the strategy and achievement of business goals and protect shareholder value.

8. **Discuss How Board Practices and Board Culture Support Independent Oversight.** Investors are concerned about the independence of the board of directors in the presence of chief executive officer (CEO) duality. Clearly articulate CEO duality and the actual practices and responsibilities of the lead director or non-executive chair, independent directors and committee chairs.

4.1   Commonsense Governance Principles

The effectiveness of corporate governance depends on the governance principles that guide corporate governance participants in fulfilling their responsibilities. The Conference Board, in October 2016,[4] issued a publication of common sense governance principles that consist of the following:

- Every board should meet regularly without the CEO present and every board should have active and direct engagement with executives below CEO level.
- Directors should be elected by a majority of either "for" or "against/withhold" votes (with abstentions and non-votes not counted).
- Board refreshment should always be considered in order that the board's skillset and perspectives remain current.
- Every board should have members with complementary and diverse skills, backgrounds and experiences.
- If the board decides on a combined CEO/chair role, it is essential that the board have a strong independent director.
- Institutional investors that make decisions on proxy issues that are important to long-term value creation should have access to the company, its management and, in some circumstances, the board.
- Companies should provide earnings guidance only to the extent they believe it is beneficial to shareholders.

5.   DRIVERS OF CORPORATE GOVERNANCE

5.1   Drivers of Corporate Governance in the United States

The primary drivers and sources of standards for corporate governance in the United States are corporate law, securities law, listing standards and best practices.[5] These sources and divers of corporate governance in the United States are extensively discussed in the literature and Rezaee (2018) provides a synopsis of these sources as presented in this section.[6]

5.1.1 State Corporate Laws In the US, corporations are established and are subject to the regulations of the state in which they were created and about 50% of public companies in the United States are incorporated in the State of Delaware. State corporate law impacts corporate governance by defining the fiduciary duties, authorities and responsibilities of shareholders, directors and officers; and by empowering shareholders to elect directors, to inspect the company's ledgers, books, records and financial reports, to receive proxy materials and approve major business transactions such as mergers and acquisitions. State corporate laws enable shareholders to monitor directors and officers in working for the best benefit of shareholders.

5.1.2 The Federal Securities Laws Federal Securities Laws are either developed through the judicial processes or passed by Congress and are intended to protect investors in public companies from receiving misleading information such as materially misstated financial statements and to improve investor confidence in the integrity and efficiency of the capital markets. The Federal Securities Laws are the primary disclosure-based statutes that require public companies to file a periodic report with the Securities and Exchange Commission (SEC) and to disclose certain information to their shareholders to enable them to make investment and voting decisions. Congress responded to the wave of financial scandals during at the turn of the 21st century by passing the Sarbanes-Oxley Act of 2002 (SOX),[7] which expanded the role of federal statutes in corporate governance by providing measures to improve corporate governance, financial reports and audit activities. The aftermath of the 2007–2009 Global Financial Crisis prompted Congress to pass the Dodd-Frank Wall Street Reform and Consumer Protection Act of 2010[8] to minimize the likelihood of a future financial crisis and systemic distress by empowering regulators to require higher capital requirements and by establishing a new regulatory regime and corporate governance measures for large financial services firms. These regulatory reforms and their impacts on corporate governance are discussed in the next section.

5.1.3 Listing Standards National Stock Exchanges play an important role in shaping and reshaping corporate governance of the listed public companies by establishing mandatory listing standards. Listing standards often go beyond government reforms by addressing the uniform voting rights to majority voting practice for the election of directors, shareholder approval of executive compensation, mandatory internal audit function and risk assessment.

Investor are now often invest globally and to address the the importance of global exchanges, in November 2009, the United Nations (UN) invited the world's stock exchanges to open dialogue with investors, regulators, policymakers, researchers and companies to find creative ways to improve corporate environmental, social and governance disclosure and performance with the goal of encouraging responsible long-term approaches to investment. It was a call to recognize the momentum achieved by responsible investment as part of the solution to the Global Financial Crisis. All listing authorities and stock exchanges are encouraged to make it a listing requirement that companies should (1) consider how responsible and sustainable their business model is and (2) provide non-financial GSEE information and (3) disclose a forward-looking sustainability strategy to the vote at their annual general meetings (AGM).[9] At the same time, the PRI signatories are called upon to support the initiative by showing a commitment to trade on stock exchanges that maintain this listing provision. This last element is critical in making it clear to stock exchanges that there is a business case for their making changes.[10] As a result, there is nascent movement by exchanges to require new listings to be more transparent in their governance of and management of their sustainability performance and disclosure. The Johannesburg Stock Exchange and the Singapore Exchange (SGX) require their listed companies to report on sustainability considerations and Mainland China's state-owned Assets Supervision and Administration Commission now expects the largest state-owned companies to report as well.

5.1.4 Best Practices One effective way to improve corporate governance is to look up to leaders in the industry and follow their best practices. Best practices are typically non-binding corporate governance guidelines intended to improve corporate governance practices of organizations above and beyond state and federal statutes and listing standards. Examples of some of these best practices include the "say-on-pay" system of shareholders approving executive compensation, the majority voting system and separating the CEO and the chairperson of the board of directors, the latter practice being intended to improve the effectiveness and objectivity of corporate governance.

The primary role of corporate governance is to ensure that managers act in the best interest of the company and its stakeholders, not for self-interest or the interests of the majority shareholders. Good corporate governance ensures accountability of the board and management to stakeholders including shareholders. Strengthened accountability promotes transparency, which should lead to an increase in capital inflows from domestic and foreign investors and thus the potential for lower cost of capital. Governance performance mechanisms establish policies and practices that address the conflict of interests between shareholders and managers. The strength of governance mechanisms includes (1) executive compensation linked to performance (2) ownership strength and (3) transparency. Concerns of governance are (1) high compensation (2) ownership concentration and (3) CEO duality.

5.2 Drivers of Corporate Governance in Asia

The world economies can be classified into two categories, namely market-based and relation-based systems.[11] Market-based systems which rely mostly on formal contracts that are agreed by two parties are more likely to be observed in Western countries such as the US, the UK and Australia, whereas relation-based systems that rely on trust among individuals to ensure formal and, more likely, informal contract formation and enforcement are prevalent in Asia. In Asia, many economies are relation-based and therefore subject to the cost of misallocation of scarce capital. Since the 1997 Asian Financial Crisis, a considerable number of corporate governance reforms have been conducted to address the issues rooted in the relation-based systems in Asian countries. There are two features of corporate governance reforms in Asia.[12] On the one hand, Asian countries follow closely Western corporate governance standards and practices. Consequently, Western theories and concepts of corporate governance have significant influence on Asian corporate governance reforms. One the other hand, indigenous culture and social norms affect the process of adopting international corporate governance rules and ultimately affect the effectiveness of these standards. In other words, culture and legacy are the driving forces impacting Asian corporate governance performance.

5.2.1 Legal System Many Asian countries (jurisdictions) were colonized by the UK, France, the Netherlands and Spain and therefore their legal systems are largely affected by these countries. For example, Hong Kong, Singapore and Malaysia adopt common law as they are former British colonies. Although Hong Kong returned to Mainland China in 1997, the "one country, two systems" policy allows its legal system (common law) to remain largely unchanged for 50 years. Other Asian countries (jurisdictions) including Mainland China, Japan, South Korea, Thailand, Indonesia and Taiwan can be broadly classified as code law jurisdictions, although the legal systems in some countries, such as Japan, are also influenced by common law. The prevailing view in the legal and corporate governance literature contends that common law provides better investor protection, which enhances the effectiveness of corporate governance, than does code law.[13]

Corporate governance codes or principles are enforced differently throughout Asia, with alternatives for the extent of compliance, namely binding, voluntary and/or comply-or-explain approaches.[14] In general, India and Vietnam follow the binding approach. Mainland China, South Korea, the Philippines and Indonesia follow the voluntary approach. As with other common law jurisdictions in the rest of the world, Hong Kong, Malaysia, and Singapore employ the comply-or-explain approach. Some code law jurisdictions such as Mainland China, Taiwan, Indonesia and Thailand also use the comply-or-explain approach. Interestingly, some countries such as Mainland China and Indonesia employ both the voluntary and the comply-or-explain approaches, reflecting the fact that there are different expected benefits from these two approaches in different areas of corporate governance.

5.2.2 Cultural Influence Culture is one of the most important implicit institutions that affect corporate governance around the world. Recent studies show that two of Hofstede's cultural dimensions, namely individualism and uncertainty avoidance, have stronger explanatory power compared to other country-level variables used in prior literature.[15] More specifically, these studies show that Hofstede's individualism (uncertainty avoidance) is significantly positively (negatively) associated with corporate governance measures which capture the proximity to corporate governance practices based on the Anglo-Saxon approach (such as transparent disclosure, equity-based compensation and independent boards). Although cultural backgrounds in Asia are diverse, these cultures have the common feature of a high level of collectivism. In Asia, Confucianism, a form of family-centered collectivism, has a strong impact on Chinese values and the individual's value in countries such as Mainland China (including Hong Kong and Taiwan), South Korea, Japan and Singapore and has significant impact on Asian corporate governance practices. Confucianism values encourage both social and business network relationships (*guanxi*) and they tend to be based on personal friendship and trust (*xinyong*) rather than on a formal relationship. As a result, relation-based systems prevail in societies that are strongly affected by the Confucianist ideology.[16] Such relation-based systems result in several corporate governance issues in Asia. For example, independent directors cannot monitor corporate insiders effectively because of the restrictions exposed by the social network. Such a system is more likely to result in questionable related-party transactions that are suspected to exploit minority shareholders. In family-controlled firms, a dominant corporate form in Asia, trust is restricted to family (or expanded family) and therefore precludes the benefits of hiring competent professional managers from the external labor market.

5.2.3 Corporate Ownership and Controls The ownership structure in Asia is very different from that in the US and the UK where shares are held diffusely. In Asia, ownership is concentrated in one or several controlling shareholders. Family-controlled firms are the most prevalent form of ownership in almost all Asian jurisdictions, such as Japan, Hong Kong, South Korea, Malaysia and Singapore. This can be attributed to weak investor protection regimes in Asia. Although ownership is generally concentrated across Asian countries, the majority shareholders and the form of ownership concentration differ in each country. For example, in some countries where the state has strong influence on the economy, state-controlled firms hold most of the shares. Mainland China is one of the largest Asian economies where state-owned enterprises (SOEs) are the dominant players in the economy. In India, Singapore and Vietnam, the state also controls a considerable number of listed companies. In Japan, families control companies through *keiretsu*, a form of mutual shareholding structure through which many companies are interconnected in a network where each of them holds shares in the other companies. In South Korea, many giant family-owned firms are *Chaebol*, from a combination of "Chae" (wealth or rich) and "bol" (clan or family). In the 1990s, the World Trade Organization (WTO) reported that *Chaebol* owned around two-thirds of the market share in South Korean manufacturing.[17] In other Asian economies, many families control firms through pyramid structures.

The concentrated ownership structure gives rise to different governance problems as the majority shareholders have both the ability and incentives to extract benefits at the expense of the minority shareholders. For example, the government in Mainland China enforces the country's laws and therefore may command the SOEs to pursue social policies such as lowering the unemployment rate and reducing the government's deficit budget which are not consistent with shareholder value maximization. The government could also intervene in the market to protect the SOEs and put private companies in a disadvantageous position. In the East Asian economies, family-controlled firms are likely to exploit the minority shareholders by self-dealing.[18] The concentrated ownership incentivizes the controlling shareholders to make their financial reporting opaque in order to reduce the leakage of proprietary information about the firms' rent-seeking activities and to make self-dealing easier by preventing potential disciplinary measures by the board of directors and the market.[19]

5.2.4 Board Structure The 1997 Asian Financial Crisis (AFC) triggered Asian countries to improve corporate governance by reforming their board structure. Many regulators in Asia realized that increased board independence could help to curb the controlling shareholders' tendency to exploit minority shareholders. South Korea responded to the AFC by quickly reforming its board structuring code. The 2003 amendment of Listing Act in South Korea stipulates that large listed companies must have at least three outside directors, with half of the outside directors being appointed directors of the board. The Japanese Corporate Governance Code took effect in June 2015 requiring that "The board should be well-balanced in knowledge, experience and skills in order to fulfill its roles and responsibilities and it should be constituted in a manner to achieve both diversity and appropriate size." The code also states "Independent directors should fulfill their roles and responsibilities with the aim of contributing to sustainable growth of companies and increasing corporate value over the mid to long term. Companies should, therefore, appoint at least two independent directors who sufficiently have such qualities." To improve the effectiveness of supervisory boards in Mainland China, the China Securities Regulatory Commission (CSRC) made two major amendments in the Company Law in October 2005. First, the law mandated that at least one-third of the supervisory board's membership must consist of elected labor representatives. Second, the supervisory board has the authority to dismiss senior executives and the right to file legal complaints against senior executives. Despite such efforts, commentators still doubt whether independent directors can monitor companies effectively because of the collectivist culture and the influence of the majority shareholders in Asia.

6. CORPORATE GOVERNANCE FUNCTIONS

Well-balanced corporate governance functions can produce effective corporate governance, investor protection, reliable financial reports, credible audit and assurance services and sustainable business. The seven corporate governance functions presented in this section are the oversight, managerial, compliance, internal audit, legal services and financial advisory, external audit and monitoring functions.[20] The viability and efficacy of corporate governance depends on the effectiveness of its functions. Corporate governance mechanisms are effective when all participants fulfill their responsibilities and their roles.[21]

6.1 Oversight Function

The oversight function of corporate governance is entrusted in the board of directors who are elected by shareholders to represent and protect their interests. As the representative of shareholders, the board of directors has a fiduciary duty to oversee managerial strategies, decisions and actions. The board is responsible for hiring, compensating, overseeing and firing executives who are appointed to manage the business organization for the benefit of shareholders. It should act in the best interest of the company and its stakeholders in good faith and with due diligence and care. The board usually fulfills its responsibility through the effective work of board committees.

The effectiveness of the oversight function is influenced by directors' independence, expertise, authority, resources, composition, qualifications and accountability and is ultimately determined by the strategic decisions made by the board of directors. Sound and effective board strategy is becoming more important in the post 2007 Global Financial Crisis era by monitoring executives' risk appetite, particularly as related to international operations. The board of directors should have a complete understanding and knowledge of corporate culture and its operation and how that affects the company's risk profile. The board should challenge management strategic decisions and seek information about risk management and compensation. The board should communicate efficiently and effectively with a wide range of stakeholders to boost their confidence and encourage them to share their concerns with the board. The board of directors should[22]:

1. Engage in strategic decisions to ensure business success.
2. Appoint the most competent and ethical CEO and approve hiring of other senior executives.
3. Design executive compensation schemes that are linked to sustainable performance by rewarding high-quality performance and reduce opportunism and excessive risk-taking by executives.

4. Remove executives when they become incompetent and/or unethical.
5. Understand the business of the company and be familiar with and actively engage in corporate strategic decisions.
6. Focus on the achievement of short, medium and log-term goals.
7. Keep informed about major corporate activities and related performance.
8. Oversee corporate affairs and compliance with all applicable laws, rules, regulations, standards and best practices.
9. Understand corporate reporting in all five (EGSEE) dimensions of business sustainability.
10. Set a tone at the top in promoting and committing to sustainability success.
11. Oversee the reliability and usefulness of financial reports.
12. Oversee business risk assessment and management.
13. Oversee cybersecurity and IT control assessment and management.
14. Oversee the establishment of anti-fraud and anti-money laundering policies and procedures.
15. Pay attention to succession planning.
16. Ensure diversity of directors and top executives.
17. Oversee the effectiveness of internal controls.
18. Understand shareholders' perspectives on the company.
19. Work with management to ensure alignment of management interests with those of shareholders and to protect the interests of other stakeholders (employees, creditors, customers, suppliers, government, environment and society).

Directors are normally classified as executive directors (inside directors), non-executive directors (outside directors) and independent non-executive directors (independent directors). One important issue relevant to the structure, leadership and effectiveness of the board of directors has been whether the position of the board chairperson should be separated from that of the CEO. Corporate governance best practices in Europe support the separation of the chairperson and CEO roles (CEO duality).[23] The Dodd-Frank Act of 2010 and related SEC rules require listed companies to disclose their board leadership structure and explain why they have determined that such a leadership structure is appropriate given their specific circumstances or characteristics.[24] The board of directors should meet regularly, at least on a quarterly basis, to fulfill its oversight responsibilities Directors should devote adequate time and effort to board meeting attendance and preparation.

6.1.1 Board Committees The entire board of directors are responsible for the oversight function. However, to fully utilize directors' expertise, the board is classified to several committees. Board committees normally function independently of each other. They are provided with sufficient resources and authority and evaluated by the board of directors. Board committees bring more focus to the board's oversight function by giving proper authority and responsibilities and demanding accountability for the discharge of members' responsibilities. Listing standards of national stock exchanges in the US (e.g., NYSE, AMEX, and Nasdaq) require that listed companies form at least three board committees, which must include audit, compensation and nominating committees. In addition to these three mandatory committees, public companies often have governance and other committees such as finance, IT and disclosure. The next three sub-sections discuss the three mandatory board sub-committees for listed companies and various other committees that the board may create.

6.1.1.1 Audit Committee The audit committee is responsible for overseeing internal controls, financial statements, risk assessment and external and internal auditor activities. The effectiveness of the audit committee depends on its independence, financial expertise, qualifications and resources. The audit committee should be composed of at least three independent directors with at least one financial expert member, and have adequate resources for funding the independent auditor and any outside advisors engaged by the audit committee. The extended oversight responsibilities for the audit committee are:

1. Appointment, compensation and retention of registered public accounting firms;
2. Preapproval of audit services and permissible non-audit services;
3. Review of the independent auditor's plan for an integrated audit of both internal control over financial reporting (ICFR) and the annual financial statements;
4. Review of audited annual financial statements and quarterly financial reports by the independent auditor;
5. Monitoring of the auditor's independence;
6. Ensuring the auditor rotation requirement;
7. Ensuring that audit committee members are independent;
8. Ensuring that audit committee members select and oversee the issuer's independent account;
9. Overseeing the effectiveness of IT security, anti-fraud policies and program and money laundering.
10. Overseeing the procedural process for handling complaints regarding the issuer's accounting practice; and
11. Exercising the authority of the audit committee to engage advisors.

6.1.1.2 Compensation Committee The compensation committee has the responsibility of evaluating executive and director performance and establishing top management compensation and benefit programs. The purposes of the compensation committee[25] are to (a) determine and approve the compensation of the company's Chief Executive Officer and other executive officers (b) approve or recommend to the board that it approve the company's incentive compensation and equity-based plans (c) assist the board in its oversight of the development, implementation and effectiveness of the company's policies and strategies relating to its human capital management function, including but not limited to those policies and strategies regarding recruitment, retention, career development and progression, management succession (other than that within the purview of the corporate governance and nominating committee), diversity and employment practices and (d) prepare any report on executive compensation required by the rules and regulations of the Securities and Exchange Commission (SEC). The committee should be composed of all independent directors and they should rotate periodically. The committee is directly responsible for ensuring that all aspects of executive compensation are fully and fairly disclosed in the annual proxy statement.

Section 953(b) of the Dodd-Frank Wall Street Reform and Consumer Protection Act of 2010 mandates the reporting of the CEO-to-Employee Pay Ratio for publicly traded companies and the disclosing of the median of the annual total compensation of all employees (except the CEO) and the ratio of CEO compensation to median employee compensation.[26] This reporting requirement is intended to assist investors to better understand the link between CEO compensation and the company's performance as well as the compensation of other employees.

A transparent CEO-to-Employee Pay Ratio enables the board of directors, particularly the compensation committee, to be better informed in overseeing and approving an effective CEO compensation scheme that discourages excessive risk-taking behavior by the CEO.

6.1.1.3 Nominating Committee The primary responsibility of the nominating committee is to nominate directors who fit well in the boardroom, can fairly represent shareholders and are able to work effectively with management. The nominating committee is usually responsible for identifying, evaluating and nominating new directors to the board, re-nominating existing directors and facilitating the election of new directors by shareholders. Ever-increasing corporate governance reforms and related SEC rules and listing standards require the nominating committee to be composed of at least three independent directors. The independence of the nominating committee has reshaped the balance of power between the board and management, in particular the CEO, who traditionally had driven the nominating process at many public companies. The recent move toward the practice of the majority voting system in the election of directors enables the nominating committee to give more credence to shareholders.

In the post 2007 Global Financial Crisis era, the accountability and responsibility of the board of directors has become center stage in corporate governance. An important issue relevant to board accountability is the method of electing the most competent and ethical directors. The prevailing and accepted regulatory method of director election in the United States has been the "plurality method." Under a plurality voting standard, the nominated director with the most votes "for" is elected, which means that a candidate can be elected as long as she/he receives one vote "for," irrespective of the number of votes "withheld." Shareholders cannot vote "against" a director nominee; they can only vote "for" or "withhold" support. Best practices of corporate governance in Europe advocate the "majority" voting standard in which a director would not be elected unless the majority of votes (above 50 percent) were cast in her/his favor. The use of the majority voting standard in bringing more democracy and accountability to the board has been considered and addressed by policymakers, regulators and the business community in the United States. However, the Dodd-Frank Act of 2010 did not require the majority voting standard for director elections, which is inconsistent with the best practices of corporate governance adopted in European countries.

6.1.1.4 Other Board Standing Committees The board of directors may establish special committees beyond the three mandatory committees of audit, compensation and nominating to assist the full board with special matters and issues. Special committees are often established to ensure due diligence and effectiveness and to assist the board to discharge its fiduciary duties. Public companies may form standing or special committees to deal with issues requiring expertise such as risk assuagement and mergers and acquisitions. The board can also establish special committees to deal with emerging issues such as compliance and ethics, environmental issues, sustainability initiatives, investigation of alleged wrongdoing and non-compliance with applicable laws, rules and regulations by directors and officers. The most common special committees are governance/strategic, compliance/ethics, litigation, cybersecurity/risk assessment and special investigation committees.

6.1.2 Board Oversight Strategy on Sustainability The board primarily oversight strategy should focus in creating shared value for all stakeholders. As sustainability is gaining attention from investors, regulators and bushiness, the board of directors should set a tone at the top in promoting and achieving sustainability performance. This includes proper strategies to create shared value for all stakeholders by achieving continuous improvements in all five EGSEE dimensions of sustainability performance. The best board strategy is one that effectively represents and protects the interests of all stakeholders from investors to employees, customers and society. On July 13, 2011, the Lead Director Network (LDN) invited a select group of independent directors from Fortune 500 companies to discuss ways to improve board governance. Participants discussed the four important aspects of board strategy set out below:[27]

- **The board's role in corporate strategy**—Participating directors were in common agreement that the board oversight strategy is the most important fiduciary duty of the board of directors. The board's involvement in strategic oversight ensure corporate success should be promoted.
- **International opportunities and risks**—A large majority of participating directors believe that companies should capitalize on globalization, expand their operation and customer base internationally and participate in the global capital markets while considering global market risks, political instability, bribery and corruption, money laundering, cybersecurity, cyberattacks, human rights, threats to intellectual property rights and scarce resources.
- **Improving strategic oversight of international opportunities and risks**—The board of directors should broaden their knowledge, expertise and experience in the international aspects of their businesses and/or hire advisors who possess adequate knowledge of globalization, corporate governance measures and expertise in different geographies.
- **The lead director's unique role in strategy**—Lead directors play an important role in setting the agenda and direction for the board and managing the board particularly when there is CEO duality. They should focus their attention on corporate strategy including strategic opportunities and risks.

A study conducted by the Conference Board in 2010 indicates that boards of directors do not focus on and do not adequately address business sustainability. Many companies do not have an effective structural framework to properly facilitate director oversight of their sustainability program.[28] Directors do not have credible and timely information on the KPIs and measures of EGSEE sustainability performance. Findings of the 2010 Conference Board survey regarding sustainability in the boardroom are highlighted below:

1. Many current sustainability initiatives and motivational drivers that widen the interest and influence of stakeholders in corporate sustainability performance (EGSEE) and more demand by regulatory bodies, enforcement agencies and activist investors for sustainability disclosures have encouraged boards of directors to pay more attention to corporate sustainability.
2. The majority of corporate boards do not have adequate information or do not utilize such information on many dimensions of EGSEE sustainability performance.

3. The majority of companies do not use the available business sustainability standards, policies, procedures and practices in developing uniform and consistent sustainability disclosures.

4. The majority of companies do not evaluate the impacts of sustainability activities (e.g. social, environmental) in their financial performance. There should be more focus on not only financial impacts but also social and environmental impacts of business operations.

5. Some of the emerging sustainability issues (climate change, pollution, green house gas emission CSR, ethical workplace, human rights political spending and board diversity) are gaining the attention of investors and thus boards of directors.

6.2 Managerial Function

Management is mainly responsible for running and managing the organization for the benefit of its stakeholders and particularly shareholders. The managerial function of corporate governance is assumed by the management team appointed by the board of directors, led by the chief executive officer (CEO) and supported by the chief financial officer (CFO), the controller, the treasurer and other senior executives to manage the company for the benefit of its stakeholders. The effectiveness of the managerial function is determined by the alignment of interests of management with those of shareholders and other stakeholders. Management's primary responsibilities are to achieve all five EGSEE dimensions of sustainability performance. Many companies have established the position of the Chief Sustainability Officer (CSO) to ensure effective achievement of EGSEE sustainability performance. The effectiveness of the managerial function depends on the independence of the board of directors from management (CEO duality), proper executive compensation which can be linked to sustainable performance and the soundness of whistle-blowing policies and programs.

6.2.1 Executive Compensation   Executive compensation comprises of salary, bonuses, the value of stock options, restricted stock, long-term incentive pay and other compensation paid to CEOs and other top executives. Senior executives are typically paid a salary, an annual bonus and long-term incentive compensation. Financial scandals and crises have raised concerns regarding the reasonableness and effectiveness of executive compensation in motivating management to create sustainable performance. Executives should be compensated to align their interests with those of investors and to provide incentives for them to create shareholder value while refraining from excessive risk activities.

The Dodd-Frank Act is intended to improve corporate governance effectiveness and disclosure in many areas, including non-binding or advisory shareholder votes on "say-on-pay" and "say-on-golden-parachutes" regarding payments to executives associated with mergers and acquisitions and major asset transactions. The Dodd-Frank Act requires that at least once every three years, shareholders vote on executive compensation, and that at least once every six years a proxy form or shareholders meeting discuss whether shareholder voting should occur every one, two or three years. According to the provisions of the Dodd-Frank Act, "say-on-pay" means a non-binding vote by shareholders of a publicly traded company for approval or disapproval of the company's executive compensation program. Nonetheless, any negative say-on-pay vote should not be automatically interpreted as evidence of failure by the company directors and officers to fulfill their fiduciary duties. Companies are required to disclose (1) the relationship between senior executives' compensation and the company's financial performance in terms of graphs and charts (2) the ratio of CEO compensation and the median total compensation to employees excluding CEO compensation and (3) whether employees or directors are allowed to hedge against a decrease in value of options included in their compensation scheme.[29]

Several suggestions are provided for improving the effectiveness of executive compensation including the following:[30]

1. The dual problems of moral hazard and collective action should be curbed by creating new disclosure and compensation regimes.
2. The true losers in the Financial Crisis had little control over the incentives of risk managers on Wall Street and elsewhere so policymakers need to address the basic human problems inherent in the trading firm on more than just economic grounds.
3. Public policy should not incentivize the better-informed financial elite to make decisions at the expense of the everyday investor.
4. The provisions in Dodd-Frank that affect the executive pay process will have the broadest and most significant impact on the pay process.
5. The proxy statement continues many of the trends noted in prior years, namely enhanced attention to the risk profile of compensation strategies; more companies adopting claw-back policies; increased acceptance of shareholder say-on-pay votes and increased use of independent compensation consultants.
6. To prevent the situation that executives' personal interests can tumble a corporation and send ripples of pain elsewhere, independent compensation committees have been charged with creating appropriate incentives for executives.
7. There should be effective board compensation committee oversight of executive compensation policies and practices.
8. A direct linkage should be provided between executive compensation and overall long-term sustainable performance.
9. Executive compensation schemes should be designed to be aligned with the company risk appetite and tolerance.
10. Public disclosure of executive compensation schemes and their components should be improved.
11. Non-performance-based pay should be minimized.
12. Management interests should be aligned with those of shareholders by linking executive compensation to sustainable performance.

Companies should tailor one or a combination of the above measures into executive compensation schemes that reward sustainable performance. The best executive pay for performance measure is the one that rewards good sustainable performance, provides incentives for executives to achieve the highest possible sustainable performance while taking justifiable prudent risk, minimizes the compensation cost to shareholders, attracts and retains key talent and promotes the culture of integrity and competency.

6.3 Compliance Function

Organizations are required to comply with a set of applicable laws, rules, regulations and standards. The compliance function of corporate governance is composed of a set of laws, regulations, rules, standards and best practices established with intent to create a compliance framework for public companies to operate by in order to achieve their goals of sustainable performance. Policymakers, regulators and standard-setters are being criticized for their reactive rather than proactive approach in establishing and enforcing cost-effective, efficient and scalable rules and regulations.[31] Regulations should set an environment and framework within which public companies can achieve sustainable performance while following such regulations and exercising a culture of honesty, integrity and accountability. An effective compliance function requires regulations be cost-effective, proactive and scalable to enable companies to create sustainable performance while are in compliance with applicable regulations.

6.4   Internal Audit Function

The internal audit function of corporate governance is assumed by internal auditors who provide both assurance and consulting services to the company its board of directors and executives in the areas of operational efficiency, risk management, internal controls, financial reporting and governance processes. Assurance reports provided by internal auditors are currently intended for internal use by the board of directors management. Internal auditors are well trained and are positioned to provide numerous assurance services but may require additional exposure to and training in the concepts of all five EGSEE dimensions of sustainability performance to fulfill an effective control function.

Internal auditors assist management in complying with the Section 302 and 404 requirements of SOX by reviewing management's certifications on financial statements and internal control over financial reporting and providing some type of assurance on the accuracy of those certifications. Internal auditors can also provide opinions on their organization's risk management process, internal control systems and governance measures for internal as well as regulatory purposes.

6.5   Legal and Financial Advisory Function

The legal and financial advisory function of corporate governance is assumed by professional advisors, internal legal counsel, financial analysts and investment bankers who normally assist companies in evaluating the legal and financial consequences of business transactions. Legal counsel provide legal advice and assist the company in complying with applicable laws, regulations, rules and other legal requirements. SOX makes legal counsel an integral component of the internal processes of the corporate governance structure to monitor corporate misconduct. Financial advisors including financial analysts and investment bankers provide financial advice, financial strategic planning and investor relation advice to the company, the directors, the officers and other key personnel.

6.6   External Audit Function

The external audit function of corporate governance is conducted by external auditors in expressing an opinion on the presentation of the company's financial statements in conformity with generally accepted accounting principles. In the US, external auditors lend credibility to the company's financial statements, and thus add value to its corporate governance through their integrated audit of both internal control over financial reporting and audit of financial statements as required by SOX. In the aftermath of financing scandals (Enron), the Public Company Accounting Oversight Board (PCAOB) was established to regulate the accounting profession in the United States to improve audit quality. External auditors are well qualified to provide assurance on all five EGSEE dimensions of sustainability performance.

6.7 Monitoring Function

Investors should be attentive and look after their investment in public companies. The monitoring function of corporate governance is the direct responsibility of shareholders and other stakeholders and it is achieved through direct engagement of investors in the business and financial affairs of corporations. Shareholders play an important role in monitoring public companies to ensure the effectiveness of their corporate governance and in strengthening shareholder rights by (1) demanding timely access to information (2) empowering shareholders thorough proxy statements and the majority voting system (3) enhancing shareholders' rights and (4) promoting shareholder democracy. The monitoring function of corporate governance requires that participate in the election of the directors and engaging in the proxy process. Institutional investors play an important role in corporate governance through monitoring investee corporations' governance and financial reporting. This is most likely to occur in the case of institutional investors, who generally hold substantial investments for decades and whose interest is aligned with the long-term economic and other sustainability of the company.

Institutional investors consist of pension funds, hedge funds, mutual funds, insurance companies and endowments of not-for-profit entities like foundations and universities. Institutional investors are often market makers due to the size of their holdings and they play an even larger role as they often communicate with other investors in tracking indicators on company performance. As major shareholders, institutional investors are more often engaged in the election of directors who focus more on strategic initiatives sustainability issues, oversight of the governance function and assurance of the achievement of long-term sustainable performance. To effectively monitor corporations, institutional investors **promote the goals of the individual investors, focus on long-term sustainable performance by minimizing the tendency to short termism and act as stewards of publicly held corporations.** Institutional investors also play an important role in reducing information asymmetry between management and shareholders by forcing management to be transparent in financial reporting and obtaining private information from management and conveying that to shareholders and hence to the capital markets. Institutional investors influence the governance of public companies in which they invest by putting forth proposals intended to improve corporate governance effectiveness.

7. EMERGING ISSUES IN GLOBAL CORPORATE GOVERNANCE

Corporate governance has played and will continue to play an important role in the quality of financial reports, the efficiency of financial markets and the way organizations manage their business affairs and activities. Each country has developed its own corporate governance reforms, which are shaped by its economic, cultural and legal circumstances. The worldwide responses to corporate scandals and the 2007–2009 Global Financial Crisis promote convergence in corporate governance across borders. Convergence is particularly vital in the areas of investor rights and protections, board responsibilities and financial disclosure. While complete convergence in corporate governance reform may not be feasible, global corporate governance practices should be promoted to improve efficiency and liquidity in the global capital markets. In addition, the following are emerging issues in global corporate governance:

- Corporate governance reforms should create an environment in which public companies can operate in creating shareholder value, protecting the interests of other stakeholders and rebuilding investor trust through effective enforcement of these reforms.

- Regulations must be cost effective, efficient, proactive and scalable.
- New corporate governance reforms should
  a. Address the systematic risk of all business transactions and particularly the risk of business failures and potential insolvency,
  b. Protect the interests of all stakeholders (investors, government, customers, creditors, suppliers, employees, society),
  c. Promote accountability for businesses and their directors and officers,
  d. Encourage convergence and global cooperation and coordination.
- Persisting challenges in corporate governance are:
  a. Compliance: Effective compliance with the implementation rules of both the Sarbanes-Oxley Act of 2002 and the Dodd-Frank Act of 2010 (DOF) as related to whistle-blowing and the Foreign Corrupt Practices Act (FCPA) (anti-bribery, anti-money laundering) is a major challenge for public companies.
  b. Board Leadership: CEO duality and the efficacy of separating the roles of chair of the board and CEO in differentiating between leadership of management oversight and management function is gaining new attention.
  c. CEO Succession Planning: CEO succession planning is one of the most important challenges among the responsibilities of the board of directors.
  d. Risk Assessment and Management: Effective risk assessment and management continue to be an important issue facing public companies in the aftermath of financial scandals and crises.
  e. IT Governance: Recent cyberattack incidents forces public companies to establish an IT governance in assessing and managing cybersecurity risks and establishing proper internal controls to prevent and detect their occurrences.
  f. Executive Compensation: Executive compensation has been and will be an important agenda for boards of directors, particularly for the compensation committee, especially where the compensation of executives is perceived to be excessive and corporations fail to implement "say-on-pay" non-binding votes by shareholders in approving executive pay.

8. GLOBAL CONVERGENCE IN CORPORATE GOVERNANCE

There are no globally accepted corporate governance reforms and best practices. Differences are mainly driven by a country's statutes, corporate structures, political infrastructure and culture. Country statutes could pose challenges for regulators in adopting corporate governance reforms and financial reporting disclosure for both domestic companies and multinational corporations. Globalization, technological advances, move toward business sustainability, and the ever-growing regulatory reforms worldwide have promoted advances in global convergence in corporate governance. Recently, there have been influential attempts to improve corporate governance mechanisms and establish a set of globally accepted corporate governance measures, worldwide. This prevalence combined with globalization and increases in technology have resulted in a trend toward a global corporate governance model. What has not been established, though, is whether global corporate governance convergence will actually occur anytime in the near future. Some corporate governance measure such as the establishment of the audit committee, public oversight function of the accounting profession, mandatory internal control reporting can be easily reconciled where as other corporate governance measures influenced by political and cultural differences are not easy to be converged. While there are numerous countries, organizations and regulators and policymakers working toward a consistent global governance model, there seems to be a greater number of forces (political and cultural differences) acting as barriers to the goal at this point in time.

Nonetheless, there is a global move toward the adoption of a more long-term orientation on sustainability performance. This movement requires boards of directors to actively engage in guiding and overseeing a company's strategy for long-term sustainable value creation. However, the achievement of long-term sustainable value creation is affected by differences in global corporate governance measures. Primary determinations of differences in corporate governance in the United States and other countries focus on (1) corporate ownership and control (2) capital markets (3) culture and (4) the legal system.[32]

8.1 Corporate Ownership and Control

Corporate ownership in countries other than the United States is much more highly concentrated through large banking institutions, government or family ownership. The concentration of corporate ownership and control can significantly influence corporate governance in those countries. Ownership structure is an important aspect of corporate governance, which determines the nature and extent of both internal (for example, composition of the board) and external (for example, rules and regulations) mechanisms needed to protect investors and minimize agency costs (for example, information asymmetry and self-dealing by management). Ownership structure can be (1) highly dispersed with substantial ownership by institutional investors (e.g. pension funds, mutual funds and insurance companies), such as in the United States and the United Kingdom, and usually open to cross-border portfolio holdings or (2) concentrated, with ownership primarily in the hands of families, such as in Europe and Japan, with potential agency costs arising between controlling owners and minority shareholders.

8.2 Public Ownership and Control

Public companies in the United States raise both equity and debt directly from the public through capital and debt markets whereas in Europe and Asia banks are the primary source of capital for companies. Public companies' lending arrangements with banks and banks' ownership of large blocks of shares empower banks to monitor and control the companies' affairs and influence their corporate governance. Efficient capital markets provide the means to alleviate scarce financial resources, which in turn facilitates access to global investments and also provides the forum for global exchanges to list public companies. Capital markets also facilitate scrutiny of management and mitigation of financial constraints.

8.3 Culture

Under the US market-based corporate governance structure, shareholder value creation is the primary objective of public companies. In many other countries, corporations are responsible for protecting the interests of various stakeholders including shareholders, employees, customers, suppliers, government and the public. Thus, the need to balance the interests of all stakeholders drives such corporate governance structure. Compared with the open social culture of the US, the close familial culture prevalent in many countries also affects the corporate decision-making process.

8.4 Legal System

A country's legal system is a key factor that influences corporate responsibility and authority as well as the composition and fiduciary duties of its directors and officers. The extant literature in accounting and finance examines the relationship between legal protection of investors and the development of financial markets and corporate governance. This literature concludes that the legal system is an integral component of corporate governance. Thus, better legal systems contribute to market liquidity and efficiency. The legal system contributes to the nature and the degree of investor protection across legal regimes. The global political uncertainty triggered by the surprise results of the November 2016 US Presidential election and the summer "Brexit" vote in the UK have created more challenges for corporate governance which may require that boards take a more proactive role in planning for potential political uncertainties and the related costly risks.

The differences in legal system are considered as the most impediment to the convergence in corporate governance. However, a move toward convergence in corporate governance has been promoted since 1999 by the Organization for Economic Co-operation and Development (OECD). The OECD has established a set of corporate governance principles which were later adopted by the International Corporate Governance Network (ICGN) designed to protect all global investors. The ICGN is a voluntary global membership organization of over 500 leaders in corporate governance including institutional investors who collectively represent funds under management of around US$18 trillion based in 50 countries.[33] The ICGN's mission is to strengthen and promote convergence in corporate governance standards worldwide.

9. CORPORATE GOVERNANCE IN ASIA

Countries have their own corporate governance reforms, measures and best practices which are reflective of the economic, political, cultural and legal circumstances. The global regulatory responses to corporate scandals and financial crises demand convergence in corporate governance worldwide. This convergence is particularly relevant in the areas of investor rights and protections, board structure, independence and responsibilities along with uniform and standardized financial and non-financial disclosures. While complete convergence in corporate governance may not be possible, global corporate governance measures and cross-border standards enforcement should be promoted to improve efficiency, soundness and liquidity in the global capital markets. Each country in Asia has its own corporate governance reforms, which are influenced by its economic, cultural and legal circumstances. The following discusses each country's corporate governance regime.

9.1 Mainland China

The Mainland Chinese government has recently initiated several corporate governance measures to support economic and financial market growth. In this respect, several state-run regulators and agencies were established to promote comprehensive and effective governance for listed companies in Mainland China.[34] The China Securities and Regulatory Commission (CSRC) issued a *Code of Corporate Governance* in 2002 that promotes governance principles and mechanisms to protect shareholder rights and to monitor directors and executives of listed companies. The CSRC is responsible for developing regulations, policies and guidelines for listed companies and monitoring the effective implementation and enforcement of regulations.

Other corporate governance regulatory bodies, including the National People's Congress, the State Council, the Ministry of Finance, the People's Bank of China, the Shanghai Stock Exchange and the Shenzhen Stock Exchange, also promulgate listing standards and corporate governance guidelines.

In January 2011, the Organization for Economic Co-operation and Development (OECD) released its report indicating that corporate governance in Mainland China has emerged and developed as it has shifted from a planned economy to a market economy.[35] The Company Law and the Securities Law, both introduced in the 1990s, provide the legal framework for Mainland China's corporate governance, which comprises of four levels, namely basic laws, administrative regulations, regulatory provisions and rules for self-regulation.

Prevailing shareholder rights in Mainland China include securing methods of conveying or transferring shares; ownership registration; getting relevant, reliable and timely material information on the corporation; participating and voting in general shareholders' meetings; electing and removing members of the board; and sharing the profits of the corporation. Information disclosures of Mainland Chinese corporate governance include company objectives, major share ownership and voting rights, companies' financial and operating results and the remuneration policy for directors and officers. The directives relating to the election of directors address directors' qualifications, the selection process, governance structures and policies. The contents of corporate governance code or policy and the process by which it is implemented must be communicated to shareholders. The Mainland Chinese board system requires strengthening of the board's fiduciary duties, including loyalty, due diligence and protection of the benefits of the company and the shareholders; the establishment of the independent director system (at least one-third of the board) and special committees of the board; and the development of mechanisms for board supervision and restraint of management.

9.1.1 Social Norms Mainland China is a society based on relationships. Business transactions are typically carried out between parties with close private social ties—*guanxi*—which serves as a catalyst to enforce contracts privately. Previous study suggested that an individual's behavior is governed not by universal law but by social norms in the form of rituals and informal rules. The most fundamental unit in a person's network is the family. For example, the eldest son typically inherits the family wealth and takes the helm of the family business. The advantage of *guanxi* society is that in the absence of a stable government to enforce universal laws, individuals can use their own social ties to build trust, exchange private information and regulate contracts, with reward and punishment mechanisms within the social structures. Through the *guanxi* relational system, individuals' interests are protected within a close-knit network. However, these self-interests may be in conflict with those outside the network and society in general. The rituals and informal rules within a private network are not necessarily the universal rules that govern Chinese society. Deep trust established within a small network of friends could result in mistrust and even conflict between other private networks in a society.[36] As a result, *guanxi* has important implications for corporate governance in Mainland China, e.g. enhancing corporate finance performance and avoiding regulatory punishment by building up political connections.

9.1.2 Legal and Regulatory Framework Mainland China is a code law country. Courts are controlled by the government and the judiciary is not independent. The courts may not be able to make unbiased judgments when SOEs or the government are involved. With an under-developed legal system, Mainland China counts on regulators to regulate and enforce investor protection. The China Securities Regulatory Commission (CSRC) is analogous to the United States SEC. The Commission was established in 1992. Led by Mainland China's State Council, the CSRC sets rules for issuance and listing of shares, regulates various activities in financial markets, and investigates and penalizes violations of relevant laws and regulations. However, due to manpower and budget constraints, the CSRC has difficulty in effectively monitoring the substantive implementation of corporate governance.

9.1.3 Highly Concentrated Ownership

Ownership in Mainland China's listed firms is highly concentrated. Owners tend to exercise more control over Mainland Chinese companies than do their Western counterparts.[37] Another feature of Mainland China's stock market is that government agencies have a high level of ownership and a strong influence over many of the country's publicly listed firms. According to Wong (2016), SOEs account for around a third of Mainland China's Gross Domestic Product (GDP) and almost 40 percent of investment with a rate of return of less than half that of the private sector. There is room to enhance growth by reallocating more capital to the private sector.[38] Members of the Communist Party are often appointed to company boards and Mainland Chinese regulations require publicly listed companies to provide "necessary support" for the functioning of the Communist Party within their firms.[39]

In private firms, there is high ownership concentration by the largest shareholder. Wong (2016) shows that the controlling shareholders own more than 30 percent of private firms. The majority shareholders' ownership allows them to effectively control firms' major decisions. Such ownership structure provides both incentive and opportunity for majority shareholders to exploit minority shareholders in Mainland China.

9.1.4 Two-Tier Board Structure

Mainland China's company law specifies that firms must have a two-tier board structure, which is similar to the German convention of having a supervisory board overseeing a board of directors. The revised Company Law of December 1999 required that all SOEs must set up a supervisory board.[40] The supervisory board must have at least three members. The membership of a supervisory board consists of shareholders and elected labor representatives and the members of the supervisory board cannot be the directors of the board or senior executives of the firm.[41]

To improve the effectiveness of supervisory boards, the CSRC made two amendments to the Company Law in October 2005. First, the CSRC mandated that at least one-third of the supervisory board's membership consist of elected labor representatives. Second, the supervisory board now has the authority to dismiss senior executives and the right to file legal complaints against senior executives.[42]

In principle, the supervisory board has the responsibility to monitor the directors and management, especially financial control systems and financial statements. However, many members are from within the firm and the board largely rubber stamps the decisions of directors and management in practice.[43] Dahya et al.[44] (2002) conducted interviews with supervisors in Mainland China and concluded that, unlike those in other countries, Mainland Chinese supervisory boards are ineffective. Mainland Chinese supervisory boards play only an advisory role in the corporate governance process; they lack the power to discipline poorly performing executives and supervisors have no incentive, financial or otherwise, to serve as monitors.

9.1.5 Shareholder Rights   In 2006, Mainland China's Company Law was revised to mandate greater disclosure of information to stockholders. Shareholders elect directors and vote at shareholders' meetings but they also have access rights to company charters, shareholder lists and the minutes of meetings of both the supervisory board and the board of directors.[45]

Mainland Chinese company law divides the rights of shareholders into "self-benefit rights" and "co-benefit rights" according to the purposes of the relevant right. Self-benefit rights (beneficiary rights) refers to shareholders' rights to acquire economic benefits including the right to request the distribution of a dividend, the right to request the distribution of residual assets, the right to transfer shares and the right to request share purchases. Co-benefit rights are shareholders' rights to govern or participate in the relevant company's governance including rights to participate in the company's decision-making, operations, management, supervision and control.[46]

9.1.6 Disclosure and Transparency   In the process of capital market development and corporate governance reform, the Mainland Chinese legislative bodies and the relevant government agencies, regulatory institutions and self-regulatory organizations have attached great importance to the development of corporate information disclosure and actively promoted its improvement in terms of quality and transparency. In 2007, the CSRC imposed stricter requirements for disclosure of company information. Disclosure of material information must be made simultaneously to all parties and companies are required to have an internal process to ensure that the CSRC disclosure standard is met. To improve financial reporting quality, Mainland China's government committed to converge with international accounting standards from the 1990s. The most significant initiative was the introduction of the new Mainland Chinese Accounting Standards (CAS) in 2006. All listed companies are required to adopt the CAS effective from January 1, 2007. Overall, information disclosure by listed companies has improved with constant progress in terms of the accuracy, scope and depth of disclosed information as well as its use by investors and intermediaries.[47]

9.1.7 Executive Compensation   Conyon and He (2016) report that executives in Mainland China are typically remunerated by cash salaries and bonuses.[48] Stock options and equity compensations were uncommon before 2006.[49] Conyon and He (2011) also found that CEOs of about 50 percent of public firms in Mainland China own shares.[50] According to a survey by Deloitte, the average salary paid to executives at A-share companies was 856,500RMB (around US$129,000), with a steady increase of approximately 5.6 percent between 2014 and 2015. About 50 percent of these are chairs of their companies, about 30 percent CEOs and about 20 percent other executives.[51] The *Nikkei Asian Review* reported that the average compensation of the highest paid executives was one million RMB (US$147,000) in 2016. Executives in the financial industry continued to lead the pack with an average annual wage of 3.59 million RMB (around US$0.54 million), followed by those in real estate who made 1.86 million RMB (around US$0.28 million).[52] As for the equity incentive, Deloitte found that restricted shares were more popular than stock options. A-share companies started to launch employee stock ownership plans in June 2014.

Previously, the compensation packages of SOE officers had no significant differences from those of employees. Bonuses and other incentive payments were reintroduced in 1979 and the payments had to be paid out of the entity's retained profits. The differential gap in payments to managers and employees was widened by a series of reforms in 1986 and 1988 from three to five times. The Shenzhen experiments in 1994 and 1996 resulted in a more standardized compensation system. The annual salary consists of a fixed base salary and performance salary. Furthermore, Mainland China's two-tier board structure requires compensation packages to be approved by the supervisory board (whose membership includes members of the Communist Party of China (CPC)), as well as explained to shareholders and publicized.[53]

The reform of executive pay of SOEs gradually resulted in large pay gap between executives and ordinary employees, which is quite inconsistent with the ideology in Mainland China and tainted the public image of CPC. After President Xi took office in 2008, the CPC started capping the executive pay at SOEs to reinforce the President's policy of cracking down on lavishness. In 2014, the President directed executives at the country's large SOEs, including the Big 4 state-owned banks, to cut their pay.[54] From 2015, the CPC imposed a pay limit of 8,000 RMB (around US$1,288) per month on executive pay at SOEs, representing a pay cut of around 50 percent compared to previous years.[55]

9.2   Hong Kong

The Hong Kong code on corporate governance reporting, issued as Appendix 14 of the Main Board Listing Rules, came into effect in 2005: "This establishes the principles of good corporate governance and two levels of recommendations of code provisions and recommended best practices." The New Companies Ordinance, which was enacted in Hong Kong in March 2014 provides the legal framework for the formation and operation of companies and contains extensive provisions to safeguard the interests of stakeholders including shareholders and creditors. The New Companies Ordinance addresses many aspects of corporate governance including the appointment of directors; the fiduciary duties of directors; the requirement to exercise the proper level of care, skills and diligence that would be exercised by a reasonably diligent person; the preparation and disclosure of a comprehensive directors' report and rules to address possible conflicts of interest by directors. In April 2014, the Hong Kong Institute of Certified Public Accountants issued *A Guide on Better Governance Disclosure*.[56] The *Guide* focuses on significant areas of the revised code including board, internal controls, audit committee and communication with shareholders. The Hong Kong Stock Exchange has effectively integrated its 2005 code requirements on corporate governance with ESG reporting. The Hong Kong Stock Exchange code provisions for sustainability reporting are detailed in Appendix 24: Environmental, Social and Governance (ESG) Reporting Guide of the Hong Kong Stock Exchange Listing Rules for the Main Board. The Guide identifies general disclosure and key performance indicators (KPIs) on four ESG areas namely Workplace Quality, Environment Protection, Operating Practices and Community Involvement, in addition to Corporate Governance.

9.2.1   The Stock Exchange of Hong Kong Limited (HKSE)   The HKSE has a market capitalization of $3.37 trillion adjusted US dollars as of March 2017 although the primary trading currency is the Hong Kong Dollar. It is the sixth-largest exchange in the world before Euronext. As of October 31, 2016, the HKSE had 1,955 listed companies, 989 of which are from Mainland China (Red chip, H share and P chip), 856 from Hong Kong and 110 from other countries and regions (e.g. Macau, Taiwan, Malaysia, United States, Singapore, etc.). Hong Kong Exchanges and Clearing Limited owns the HKSE and is itself listed on the HKSE.

In its annual IPO review and outlook for 2018, Ernst & Young laid out the prediction based on the number of IPOs and proceeds raised for the year: 436 companies mopped up 230.4 billion Yuan (US$35.1 billion) from the A-share market. According to the *South China Morning Post*, the New York Stock Exchange ranked top in 2017 with US$39.5 billion in terms of proceeds raised, followed by Shanghai at US$20.9 billion and Hong Kong ranked third at US$16.5 billion with a total of 160 IPOs. The bullish performance of the Hang Seng Index (HSI), which gained 34 percent in 2017, was ranked first among global major indices including Nasdaq and the Dow Jones Industrial Average. Such performance benefited the IPO market and 28 overseas companies were attracted to listing in Hong Kong, the highest in six years, raising a total of HK$10.02 billion (around US$1.3 billion).[57]

Hong Kong's business community has continuously been urged to seek improvements in corporate governance and to uphold the highest professional ethics and integrity. A number of important corporate governance initiatives have been carried out or are under way. The Hong Kong government and other corporate regulatory bodies such as the HKSE and the Securities and Futures Commission (SFC) are making progress in bringing good corporate governance standards into effect. Other non-profit institutions that promote better corporate governance practices include:[58]

- The Hong Kong Institute of Directors (HKIOD)
- The Asian Corporate Governance Association (ACGA)
- The Hong Kong Institute of Certified Public Accountants (HKICPA)
- The Hong Kong Institute of Chartered Secretaries (HKICS)
- The Hong Kong Law Reform Commission (HKLRC).

9.2.2 OECD–Asian Round Table on Corporate Governance The OECD–Asian Roundtable on Corporate Governance was established in 1991, with Hong Kong being the only Roundtable economy with a corporate governance code, i.e. the voluntary 1993 Code of Best Practice. It served as a regional forum for exchanging experiences and advancing reform of corporate governance while promoting awareness and the use of OECD Principles of Corporate Governance.[59]

Today, most Asian Roundtable jurisdictions have developed codes and other guidance based largely on the OECD Principles. In recent years, there have been reviews of the existing codes with the addition of more specific and demanding expectations with regard to corporate behavior and enhanced monitoring. With recent updates, Hong Kong has moved on to the third generation of its Corporate Governance Code.[60]

9.2.3 Hong Kong Institute of Directors (HKIOD) The Hong Kong Institute of Directors (HKIOD) is a group of long-serving practicing and potential directors charged with responsibility as culture builders to promote corporate governance in Hong Kong. The goal of the Institute is to have good governance practice embraced by all types of businesses regardless of firm size and whether they are private companies or non-profit organizations.[61]

9.2.4 2016 HKIOD Corporate Governance Score-Card Project The Score-Card project by the HKIOD was set up to evaluate corporate governance of Hong Kong companies on a regular basis as well as to encourage the adoption of best practices of corporate governance through a systematic evaluation of current practices.[48] According to the CEO of HKIOD, Dr. Carlye Tsui, there has been promising testimony reflecting the Hong Kong market's increasing awareness of and emphasis on corporate governance.

The HKIOD organizes over 100 professional education and training courses for company directors every year. The scope of these professional courses covers rules and regulations, strategic direction, board culture and practice, and director competency, with special emphasis on issues such as the role of the independent non-executive director, board-level risk management and ESG reporting. The Score-Card monitors the Hong Kong market with enhanced assessment criteria. Moreover, it helps Hong Kong to design bespoke education and training programs to meet the specific challenges faced by company directors in the market.[62]

9.2.5 Current Status and Challenges of Corporate Governance Hong Kong has become the financial hub of Asia with a significant reliance on financial services although it faces increased competition from stock markets in Shanghai and Shenzhen. The financial regulatory framework of Hong Kong listed companies is guided by the Company Ordinance of 2014, the Securities Law from the Securities and Futures Ordinance (Cap. 571) and the Main Board Listing Rules of 2016. The HKSE has a total of 1,955 listed companies, with a total market capitalization of US$3.37 trillion (World Federation of Exchanges (WFE), 2016). The board structure of Hong Kong listed companies requires at least three independent non-executive directors and they must represent at least one-third of the board.

The board structure is mainly unitary but firms are free to choose their own board structure within the guidance of the HKSE. According to an OECD report on corporate governance in Asia, in 2012, 75 percent of Hong Kong listed companies had a dominant shareholder on their board (for example, an individual/family or state-owned entity) who owned 30 percent or more of the issued shares (OECD, 2015).[63]

Companies showing improvement in their corporate governance standards tend to have better opportunity to secure investors in the financial market. Among 84 listed companies that were surveyed in both 2012 and 2016 by the HKIOD, 75 percent report that they have enhanced their corporate governance performance. The Hong Kong government is making an effort to maintain its position in the international financial market by promoting corporate governance through relevant authorities to attract local and overseas investors.

The Chief Regulatory Officer and Head of Listing HKEX, Mr. David Graham, remarked during the launch of the HKIOD Corporate Governance Score-Card in 2016 that most companies had shown improvements in their corporate governance standards. Promoting good corporate governance among Hong Kong listed companies would continue to be one of HKEX's top priorities. However, according to the HKIOD Score-Card of 2016, recently listed companies and those newly added to the major Hong Kong indices had yet to meet the prevailing standards and their practices dragged other companies down.

Oxfam also ranked the 50 HSI companies based on their performance in corporate governance activities in 2016. Their performance reflects the strict governance framework for Hong Kong listed companies. According to the survey, corporate reporting indicates a compliance-based approach to corporate governance regionally with mandatory reporting in place for key issues such as ownership, audit and compliance and director conduct.

9.2.6 Influence of Culture in Corporate Governance and Family-Controlled Firms in Hong Kong
The principles of corporate governance are generic in nature but its practice continues to be subject to cultural influences. The PwC *2016 Global Family-Controlled Businesses Report* involved interviews with 100 senior corporate executives of family-controlled enterprises (48 from Mainland China and 52 from Hong Kong).

The report concluded that family business contributed much to the increase in the employment rate as well as to Gross Domestic Product (GDP) growth in Hong Kong. It also stated that more than 60 percent of the private sector in Hong Kong was accounted for by family businesses and that the city's top 15 families controlled assets amounting to 84 percent of GDP.

Corporate governance in Hong Kong had naturally been influenced by the British during the colonial period. However, it had not been successfully integrated with Chinese family companies. There was a gap between what the law intended to regulate and the conduct of typical Chinese companies. The regulation of corporate governance was not fully implemented as the existing laws did not reflect Chinese values and the social norms of the Hong Kong people. Despite the reported preference among Asian family firms for family-management succession, Asian family firms have increasingly recognized that, to meet the demands of global markets, they need to professionalize their entities (for example, by the appointment of professional non-family managers rather than family members, among others). The *PwC Family Business Survey* (PricewaterhouseCoopers, 2014) reported that nearly 40 percent of Asian family firms expressed the view that professionalizing the entity during the next five years (i.e., from 2015 to 2020) was a major challenge facing the entity.[64]

A typical problem for family businesses across Asia is that they are reluctant to open up to outside professional management. Family owners felt challenged if external management and succession are considered better corporate governance for their firms. Eric Landolt, Head of Family Advisory for Asia-Pacific at UBS, draws the link explicitly between governance and recruiting external talent. He stated: "If you have a family-controlled business where the structures and the governance are vague, and it is not clear how the decisions are taken at the ownership level, that will probably not be attractive to external management. It will be challenging for those companies to attract key professional talent."[65]

9.2.7 Future Opportunity for Corporate Governance in Hong Kong The Hong Kong Corporate Governance Code is a non-statutory document issued under the Rules Governing the Listing of Securities which applies only to companies listed on the HKSE. The corporate governance code states that the code provisions and the recommended best practices are not mandatory rules. Issuers have a high degree of flexibility on the manner of adopting these practices. It is recommended that legislation be promulgated to provide the corporate governance code with full statutory backing in order to create a uniform standard which ensures good quality of corporate governance.

The reports *Investor Opinion Survey on Corporate Governance* and the *Investor Perspectives on Corporate Governance—A Rapidly Evolving Story* published by McKinsey & Company, Inc. in 2000 and 2004 respectively have consistently reported that 70 to 80 percent of investors are willing to pay a premium for well-governed companies. According to McKinsey, the real challenge is to ensure that these corporate governance principles are embedded in sufficient detail in local legislation and subsequently implemented and enforced.[66]

Thomas Mok, Principal of Mok & Cast, opined that for Hong Kong to maintain the status of an international financial center, it should gage and refer to the existing international standards adopted by the OECD. The OECD's concern is that if a corporate governance code lacks full statutory backing and is not consistent with the rule of law, this diminishes its fundamental requirements of certainty, transparency and enforceability, clear articulation of regulatory responsibilities, independence and accountability.

9.3 India

India won independence in August 1947. In the early twentieth century, India's main stock exchanges were in Bombay, Calcutta, Madras and Ahmedabad, with clearly defined governing, listing and trading guidelines.[67] Early corporate governance was dominated by the "managing agency system" for which management could attain "control rights" that were not in proportion to their stock ownership.[68] Modern industrial growth was structured with corporate law. The 1956 Companies Act built on such foundations to govern public and private limited companies as well as to protect investors' rights.

Moving toward socialism, SOEs in India dominated the economy. The 1951 Industries (Development and Regulation) Act, which was abolished in 1991, required industrial units to obtain licenses from the central government. The 1956 Industrial Policy Resolution resulted in the creation of more state-owned industries accompanied by the rise of corporate sector problems. Corruption and inefficiency in India's corporate sector were two major problems in the following decades. As a result, India failed to develop liquid and efficient equity markets and corporate governance had to take a back seat.

Under these circumstances, the majority of long-term credit was issued by three development finance institutions (DFIs) in India namely Industrial Finance Corporation of India, the Industrial Development Bank of India and the Industrial Credit and Investment Corporation of India. Due to inefficient monitoring, the DFIs did not adequately protect minority shareholders and creditors, which caused high agency costs associated with debt and equity.[69] The situation was improved after the economic and liberalization reforms introduced by the Indian government at the beginning of 1990s.[70]

Before the economic reform, the Bombay Stock Exchange (BSE) was a monopoly stock exchange in India. The economic reforms in 1990s developed four new institutions, namely the National Stock Exchange of India (NSE), the Securities and Exchange Board of India (SEBI), the National Securities Clearing Corporation (NSCC) and the National Securities Depository.

9.3.1 Legal Framework and Codes   A common law system operates in India.[71] The corporate sector in India is governed by the Companies Act. The 1956 Companies Act, which has been amended several times, covers various corporate governance issues such as shareholder rights, directorships and disclosures. The Companies Act 2013 superseded that of 1956 to become effective on April 1, 2014. The Companies (Amendment) Act 2017 was a significant legal reform in India, aligning Indian company law with global standards. The Act introduced significant changes in accountability, disclosures, investor protection and corporate governance.

India's largest industry and business association, the Confederation of Indian Industry (CII), took the first institutional initiative to develop and promote a codified system for corporate governance in 1998 with the publication of the Desirable Corporate Governance: A Code.[72] The second major corporate governance initiative is India's prime regulatory authority, the SEBI, which regulates the securities market and stock exchanges. The SEBI (Listing Obligations and Disclosure Requirements) Regulations of 2015 was a transformation from contractual (listing agreement between the stock exchange and the listed company) to legal obligations,[73] stipulating the obligations of listed entities. The regulations also require companies to announce publicly any substantial changes in shareholding and changes of control or ownership.

Corporate governance is also driven by the two biggest and most liquid stock exchanges in India, the Bombay Stock Exchange (BSE) and the National Stock Exchange of India (NSE). Established in 1875, the BSE is Asia's first and the fastest-growing stock exchange. The BSE is older than the Tokyo Stock Exchange and ranks twelfth, with a 2.2 percent share of market capitalization of the 20 largest stock exchanges and groups in the world (2013–2016).[74] The NSE is the leading stock exchange in India, with the fourth-largest equity trading volume in 2015 according to the World Federation of Exchanges (WFE).

9.3.2 Ownership Structure and Board Structure Concentrated ownership is the main feature of Indian companies since independence. Most large corporations are SOEs and family-owned companies. During the 1990s, India's highly centrally planned and regulated economy transformed into a market-oriented economy. These open market reforms enabled private institutional investors to invest in the large market capitalized firms of India. Economic reforms and globalization further attracted more retail investors and foreign investors. Non-institutional shareholders including corporate bodies, qualified foreign investors, individual shareholders and non-resident Indians are part of the ownership pattern of corporations.[75]

The board structure in India is one-tier and the 1956 Companies Act requires that the minimum number of directors in a company is three.[76] The maximum number of directors is 15 but an exception can be made by a special vote of all the shareholders at a general shareholders' meeting.

9.3.3 Shareholder Rights Shareholders' meetings are classified as annual general meetings (AGMs), extraordinary general meetings (EGMs) and meetings convened by the NCLT in India. AGMs are required to be held every year on issues such as financial performance and the appointment of new boards of directors (BODs). The 1956 Companies Act stipulates various shareholder rights including the following:[77]

- To elect or remove directors and engage in management
- To attend and vote on resolutions at meetings
- To enjoy the profits of the company in the form of dividends
- To apply to the court in the case of oppression or mismanagement
- To monitor documents and registers to be kept by the company under the regulations and to ask for extracts therefrom.

9.3.4 Disclosure and Transparency Under the 1956 and 2013 Companies Acts, the annual balance sheet, profit and loss account, and reports by the board and the auditors of Indian companies are submitted to the board for approval and for adoption by shareholders at the AGM.[78] Listed companies have three additional requirements, namely to submit annual accounts to the stock exchange where the company is listed, and to submit a cash flow statement and the abridged unaudited financial summaries every quarter.[79]

SOEs are required by the 2013 Companies Act to disclose financial reporting standards on their company websites. Listed SOEs are required to follow SEBI's disclosure requirements including disclosure of financial statements and information on business operations, audit committee composition, compliance with accounting standards, compensation of directors and compliance with the company code of conduct. Regarding accounting and audit requirements, SOEs must prepare their accounts in accordance with the Indian Accounting Standards, which are reportedly based on the International Financial Reporting Standards (IFRS).[80]

Clause 49 of the Listing Agreements of SEBI requires companies to provide specific corporate disclosures of the following:[81]

1. Related-party transactions
2. Accounting treatment
3. Risk management procedures
4. Proceeds from various kinds of share issues
5. Remuneration of directors
6. Management Discussion and Analysis section in the annual report discussing general business conditions and outlook
7. Background and committee memberships of new directors as well as presentations to analysts.

9.3.5 Executive Compensation The 1956 and 2013 Companies Acts provide for limits on executive compensation, evaluation methods and requirements for shareholder approval. The remuneration packages of individual directors generally are salary, benefits, bonuses, stock options and pensions.[82] According to Bloomberg, CEOs of companies listed in India's Sensex Index earn 229 times more than the average worker, the second-biggest gap worldwide in 2017.[83]

9.3.6 Kotak Committee Reform The SEBI Panel under the chairmanship of Uday Kotak proposed recommendations on Indian corporate governance in 2017. The "Kotak Committee" reviewed the corporate governance principles and made recommendations to make governance more transparent as well as to improve the governance standard of listed companies. The recommendations suggested changes that relate to board diversity, board and committee independence, related-party transactions and director remuneration, among other factors.[84] The Ministry of Finance and SEBI would finalize the proposed changes in board monitoring and implementation of the Companies Act 2013 and the existing SEBI regulations in line with international practices. It was proposed that the boards of listed companies have at least six directors, with half of the board consisting of independent members rather than one-third as is the current requirement. Independent disclosures are expected to help boost investor confidence. In compliance with the 2013 Companies Act requirement that there be at least one woman on the board, the Kotak Committee recommends that at least one of the independent directors should be a woman.[85]

The effective implementation of the 2013 Companies Act in India has been challenging for the boards of directors of many Indian public companies as the Act requires changes to their corporate governance practices. Some of the implementation challenges of the 2013 Companies Act relate to an increase in directors' fiduciary duties, accountability and perhaps liabilities:

1. The increased scope of responsibilities for the Nomination and Compensation/Remuneration Committee which require directors to have the right set of skills to serve on boards;
2. Board oversight of CEO succession planning and evaluations of executives;

3. A mandatory minimum of at least one female independent director for most listed companies;
4. Board oversight and proactive role in risk management particularly as regards cybersecurity risks;
5. The requirement of the establishment of a corporate social responsibility (CSR) committee and that the company spend 2 percent of net profits on CSR-related activities such as environmental, social and governance initiatives.

9.4 Indonesia

9.4.1 Development of Corporate Governance The Financial Crisis of 1997 to 1998 had a great impact on Indonesia's society, economy and politics. The incident sent the number of Indonesians living in poverty skyrocketing at the time. Some experts believe that institutional deficiencies were the main factors contributing to Indonesia's economic recession including imperfect central bank regulation, irregular practices within banks and lack of financial regulation.[86] Since then, Indonesia has recognized the importance of corporate governance and has made a number of improvement efforts. The government and other private institutions have taken measures including the establishment of corporate governance institutions, the development and revision of relevant laws, and improvement of corporate governance standards. In 1999, under the coordination of the Coordinating Minister for Economic Affairs, a national corporate governance committee was established, followed by the promulgation of Indonesia's first Code of Good Corporate Governance in 2001. The code was revised in 2006. In the following years, the Capital Market and Financial Institutions Supervisory Body made a series of changes and oversaw their implementation to improve the protection of investors. In 2006, corporate governance regulations for banks were published, monitored and enforced by Bank Indonesia. In addition, Indonesia has enacted a series of legislative reforms on governance. Examples include the Law on Foreign Investment adopted in 1967 and amended in 2007, the International Environmental Law adopted in 1995 and amended in 2007, the Law on Insurance Business adopted in 1992 and the Competition Law adopted in 1999.[87]

9.4.2 Regulatory Framework Indonesia is a civil law country. The main law on corporate governance is Law No. 40 of 2007 on Limited Liability Companies (the Company Law). The Company Law covers matters relating to company building, capital issues, corporate governance, shareholder rights and meetings, significant corporate actions, and dissolution and liquidation of companies. In addition to the Company Law, listed companies are also bound by Law No. 8 of 1995 on the Capital Markets (the Capital Market Law). Under the Capital Market Law, listed companies are required to have at least 300 shareholders, who own their shares and have limits on capital set by government regulations. In addition to specific governance of listed companies, the Capital Market Law also covers issues such as minority shareholder protection, insider trading, market manipulation, fraud and conflict of interest trading.

Although the Company Law covers a wide range of corporate governance regulations (mainly on the duties of the board of directors), it does not provide guidance on specific corporate governance processes when there are no government regulations to supplement and support it. Consequently, a company's articles of association (AOA) is usually the key document that determines the general governance requirements of the company. Listed companies must also comply with the regulations and rules issued by the Financial Services Authority or Otoritas Jasa Keuangan. In 2006, the National Committee on Governance also published the Code on Good Corporate Governance, which provides further guidance for good corporate governance practices in Indonesia.

9.4.3 Ownership and Board Structure

Indonesia has a two-tier board structure which consists of an independent board of supervisors and a management committee. The board of supervisors is composed of non-executive members and independent members. It is responsible for supervising and advising the management committee. The management committee is composed mainly of executive directors and is responsible for the management of the company and the operation of its business. The Corporate Governance Code requires limited liability companies to have at least one director and listed companies must have at least two directors and at least one independent director.[88]

As for ownership structures, Indonesia has concentrated ownership with many private companies owned by a single controlling shareholder, family members or a small number of shareholders. The number of controlling shareholders generally does not change despite the dramatic expansion of the company. This concentrated ownership structure often lacks corresponding regulation and supervision, which leads to the underdevelopment of Indonesia's capital markets. In addition, some major business groups are established in the form of subsidiaries controlled by the parent company. The resulting cross-shareholdings and lack of transparency tend to result in opaque ownership structures. Such a structure could be detrimental to the interests of individual shareholders.[89]

9.4.4 Shareholder Rights

According to the Company Law, the board of directors (BOD) is generally responsible for the operation and management of the company, under the supervision of the Board of Commissioners (BOC). However, the BOD may not make decisions on certain matters without the approval of shareholders. These matters are regulated by the Company Law and they include:

- Revising the company's articles of association including increasing or reducing certified capital, reducing subscription and paid-up capital or repurchasing the company's capital.
- Making acquisitions, mergers or spin-offs or plunging the company into bankruptcy or liquidation (which requires 75 percent voting rights of shareholders).
- Transfer or guarantee of all or most of the assets of the company (which also requires 75 percent voting rights of shareholders).

In addition, other rights of shareholders include:

- To approve the fees to be paid to the members of the BOD and the BOC at the AGM.
- To approve the annual work plan and budget before the beginning of the financial year.
- To approve the payment of dividends into the statutory reserve fund in addition to the provisional dividend.

- To approve the annual financial statements and the management of acquittals (generally carried out annually).
- To appoint members to the BOC and BOD (including filling vacancies).

Shareholders in private companies can add additional restrictions on the board in the Articles of Association (whether or not approval from the BOC or other shareholders is required). For listed companies, the BOD must comply with the Indonesian Financial Services Authority (Otoritas Jasa Keuanganm, OJK) rules when it requires shareholders to approve certain transactions (including conflict of interest transactions and major transactions).[90]

9.4.5 Disclosure and Transparency In Indonesia, the BOD is responsible for corporate disclosure and transparency. On November 10, 1995, Law No. 8 of 1995, the Capital Market Law, came into effect; it describes the main disclosure rules in Indonesia. According to the Capital Market Law, actions to disclose and make information available to the public are largely determined by the Indonesian Capital Market and Financial Institution Supervisory Agency. From January 1, 2013, this function was performed by the Indonesian Financial Services Authority (Otoritas Jasa Keuangan, OJK) as the new capital markets regulator.[91]

Under the OJK regulations, all material information about a listed company must be disclosed within two working days. In addition, there are other reporting and disclosure requirements (including general or financial information, etc.) that require enterprises to disclose specific corporate matters which include:

- Annual and semi-annual operating results of the enterprise.
- Certain important transactions that do not conform to the scope of shareholder approval.
- Certain related-party transactions.
- General management support agenda and results of general management support.
- Any private placement by the company (permission is granted only in limited circumstances).
- Conversion of convertible securities into shares, declaration of dividends, alteration of the capital of the company.
- Any material information that may affect the value of listed securities of a listed company or may affect an investor's investment decisions.[92]

9.4.6 Executive Pay and Performance In 2006, the Indonesia Code of Good Corporate Governance required the disclosure of executive compensation policies and the total compensation of boards. The code stipulates that detailed individual directors' compensation policies should be disclosed in the company's annual financial statements. In addition, an item on the AGM should be included to provide shareholders with an opportunity to discuss remuneration matters. According to the code, directors' remuneration may consist of fixed and variable components. The fixed component is usually the base salary and the company is required to provide comparison of the executive salary with that of another in a similar company. The variable component is based on the contribution of executives to the company's short- and long-term financial performance, and consists of annual bonuses based on KPIs.[93]

9.5 Japan

9.5.1 Legal Aspect   In Japan, the corporate governance rules are developed from three legal sources. The first is the Companies Act. The Companies Act along with its subordinate regulations sets forth the basic principles that a company needs to abide by regarding the rights and obligations of management, the organizational structure, the disclosure of information, etc. The Companies Act applies whether companies are listed or not. The second law is the Financial Instruments and Exchange Act. This Act, along with its subordinate regulations, requires listed companies to disclose issues relating to corporate governance by way of filing annual securities reports or quarterly reports, disclosing material information in a timely manner by way of extraordinary reports and submitting internal control reports to the authorities. The third is the securities listing regulations published by the Tokyo Stock Exchange (TSE). The main corporate governance requirements for listed companies are to submit corporate governance reports and to elect and disclose the names of at least one "Independent Officer." The Independent Officer is an outside director or outside statutory auditor who does not have a conflict of interest with shareholders.[94]

9.5.2 Cultural Impact   Japanese corporate culture is often described as a family system which is based on the principles of a traditional family. The seeds of this family concept of companies are deeply rooted in the Japanese culture of obedience, hierarchy and loyalty.[95] The Confucian ethic of traditional lifetime relationships in a family was extended to the company. According to cultural theories, the *kaisha* (company) symbolizes the organization in which people are not only united by contractual relationships but includes an element of association resembling that of a family.[96] "The company is the people" is a common saying in Japan.[97] By characterizing itself as a family unit, the company has achieved a greater level of loyalty between management and employees. There is a solidarity among employees to protect each other as they believe that whatever they do is done for the company.[98] Such a cultural feature significantly influences corporate governance in Japan. It improves the cohesion of the enterprise and motivates the staff. Because staff have a sense of ownership in the company, they will set personal interests aside for the greater good of the company, which may indirectly decrease the agency problem. However, such cultural features also enhance managerial power. Staff will follow their leader's advice absolutely, losing the opportunity for personal development.

9.5.3 Cross-Shareholding   The structure of a large publicly traded company in Japan is traditionally characterized by cross-shareholding (*keiretsu*), referring to mutual shareholding through a network of companies that are interconnected whereby each company holds shares in the other companies. *Keiretsu* literally means "economic line-ups" and includes more than what is covered by the concept of cross-shareholding. *Keiretsu* is a structural arrangement of Japanese firms characterized by close business relationships intertwined with long-term commitments among members. There are various types of *keiretsu* but the main type is the *keiretsu* corporate group with the primary bank at the center.[99] Normally, the shares held under these ongoing stable shareholding arrangements constitute the controlling portion of the firm's shares.[100] There is a mutual understanding among the companies that these shares are not to be traded but to be kept as a safety mechanism. Member companies within a *keiretsu* offer each other preferential treatment in commercial and financial transactions. They exchange information through the primary bank and in times of crisis, they are expected to help each other. Generally, *keiretsu* contributed to the relatively stable and concentrated ownership structure of Japanese companies.[101]

9.5.4 Long-Term Employment Long-term employment is a typical feature of the Japanese corporate governance model. This system is not regulated under the legal system but is based on informal norms and practice. An employee is recruited directly upon graduation and is expected to remain in service with the company for his or her entire career. He or she can expect not to be fired or discharged except under some extraordinary circumstances.[102] The basis of this agreement is the commitment of employers to provide secure employment to their employees in return for loyalty and "lifetime" service. The modern Japanese long-term employment system was allegedly designed as a compromise entered into between management and unions aimed at overcoming existing labor problems. It is a mutually beneficial bargain rather than a solution imposed by social norms.[103] Long-term employment in its present form developed as a result of mutual economic benefits. It contributed to higher productivity, which benefited both shareholders and management through increased profits, as well as employees through greater employment security. The Japanese government supports lifetime employment because it contributes to reducing tensions between employers and employees. There are several elements of the long-term employment system that are typical for Japan such as recruitment of graduates, seniority-based wages, internal transfers based on a rotation system, and on-the-job training in firm-specific skills, making it extremely difficult for employees to take employment with other firms.[104]

9.5.5 Board Structure Since the 1990s, many Japanese corporations have improved their information disclosure and auditing functions to ensure the effectiveness of their governance by bringing in outside directors and outside auditors, separating their decision-making mechanisms from their business operation mechanisms, introducing a system of operating officers and carrying out other reforms as well.[105] But changes are afoot in Japan's overall approach to corporate governance in recent years.

The amended Companies Act in Japan was enacted in June 2014 and came into effect in April 2015.[106] The amendment introduces a new corporate governance structure for large public companies in Japan through an audit/supervisory committee, and new rules for outside directors. The audit/supervisory committee governance structure is intended to facilitate the appointment of outside directors and to provide a corporate governance system that is more familiar to foreign investors. Japan's Corporate Governance Code, which was reformulated in 2015, is intended to make Japanese corporate governance measures more consistent with those of Western governance systems. The code requires that boards have at least one outside director. There are currently two governance structures for listed companies in Japan. These structures are the Statutory Auditor System and the Full Committee System. The Statutory Auditor System is the traditional two-tier board system whereas the Full Committee System is an alternative structure introduced in 2003. Companies can adopt their own governance structures with voluntary boards such as management advisory boards. Statutory auditors are different from independent outside auditors as they are company board members in charge of monitoring the directors and managers from both an accounting and operational standpoint. The full governance committee system in Japan consists of the audit, nomination and remuneration committees. Each committee is composed of at least three directors and a majority of members in each committee must be outside directors. The 2015 amended Companies Act contains a new "comply-or-explain" rule whereas listed companies that do not have any outside directors on the board must disclose in their annual business reports "why the company believes that having outside directors is not appropriate."

The Japanese Corporate Governance Code took effect in June 2015 and sets rules regarding whistle-blowing, disclosure, stakeholders' rights and many more. One focus of the Corporate Governance Code is the board of directors, including its composition and responsibilities. According to the code, "The board should be well-balanced in knowledge, experience and skills to fulfill its roles and responsibilities, and it should be constituted in a manner to achieve both diversity and appropriate size." It also states, "Independent directors should fulfill their roles and responsibilities with the aim of contributing to the sustainable growth of companies and increasing corporate value over the mid- to long-term. Companies should, therefore, appoint at least two independent directors who sufficiently have such qualities." This implies that it is critical to appoint qualified persons and make the best use of them. Japanese companies have responded well to this call. In July 2014, approximately 65 percent of TSE listed companies had outside directors and by July 2015, nearly 90 percent did. And as of December 2015, all Nikkei 225-listed companies had at least one outside director.[107]

The Japanese corporate governance challenges are:

1. Board gender diversity: a very small portion (3 percent) of directorships are held by women.
2. Former executives and chairs remaining in "advisor" roles beyond the end of their formal tenure.

9.5.6 Shareholder Rights and Powers   Under the Companies Act, the operation of a company is handled by the directors except that material issues (as defined below) have to be approved by a shareholders' meeting. Some issues require a greater proportion of voting right than others (e.g. amendments to the articles of incorporation, mergers, etc.).

The rights and powers of the shareholders' meetings include the following items:

- Amendments to the articles of incorporation;
- Appointment and dismissal of directors and auditors;
- Approval of financial statements (except for companies which satisfy certain requirements);
- Approval of mergers, demergers, share exchanges/transfers or business transfers (with *de minimis* exceptions);
- Payment of dividends (unless otherwise provided for in the articles of incorporation);
- Issuance of shares or stock options at especially favorable prices; and
- Determination of directors' remuneration and discharge of directors' liabilities.[108]

9.5.7 Disclosure and Transparency Establishment and disclosure of internal control has become increasingly relevant with respect to ensuring the reliability of financial reporting. To ensure that the information disclosed in the securities market is reliable, the Japanese version of the Sarbanes-Oxley Act (the Financial Instruments and Exchange Law) was enacted, which requires the following:[109]

- To ensure the appropriateness of the information released in financial reports, directors must establish and operate an effective system of internal controls within their companies.
- Companies must evaluate the effectiveness of their internal controls as they relate to financial reporting and disclose this information to investors in the form of "internal control reports."
- Companies must be audited to ensure that their evaluation methods and results are appropriate.

9.5.8 Executive Pay and Performance Executive compensation is mainly regulated by the Companies Act. All companies must disclose to shareholders the annual total amount of compensation paid or agreed to be paid to executives in their annual financial reports. These amounts can be considered with respect to the total number of officers and directors respectively. Listed companies must disclose information in great detail to the public with regard to the company's policy on executive pay, the names of the executives paid at or above ¥100M (around US$900,000), and the amount of personal compensation each executive receives. Such companies are required to disclose this information in their annual securities reports in the manner prescribed by the Financial Instruments and Exchange Act (FIEA). In addition, listed companies must provide a similar level of disclosure in their corporate governance reports in accordance with the format prescribed by the relevant stock exchange rules.[110]

9.6 South Korea

9.6.1 Development of *Chaebol* The word *Chaebol* is constituted of *Chae* (wealth or rich) and *bol* (clan or family), and *Chaebol*s are family-owned enterprises in South Korea.[111] The Confucian cultural influence promoted hierarchical business (in particular the wealthy family) tradition in the South Korean corporate structure, which led to strong dominant leadership within the *Chaebol*.[112] The *Chaebol* was largely controlled by family ownership and management that performed in a self-interested manner, disregarding the rights of the minority shareholders.[113] This unique business group in South Korea is known for its abuse of power and operates with limited transparency.[114]

The *Chaebol* in the late 1950s operated with the support of the government and has always been heavily influenced by the government's corporate agenda.[115] For example, the Samsung Group, the former Leogki Geumseong (Lucky-Goldstar) now the LG Group, and the Hyundai Motor Company all received favors and concessions from the government. During the 1960s, *Chaebol*s opened up to the foreign market. Companies attracted foreign investment, including SsangYong Group, Hyosung Corporation, Hanwha Group (formerly Korea Explosives Co.) and Hanjin Group. South Korea experienced high economic growth in the 1970s. Current large *Chaebol*s in

South Korea include Lotte Group, Doosan Group, Kolon Industries, former Sunky-ong Group (now SK Group or SK Holding) and Daewoo Group.[116] South Korea was transformed to a democracy in the 1980s. During this period, the *Chaebol* influenced political elections by providing huge financial support to politicians.[117]

Before the 1997 Asian Financial Crisis, the *Chaebol* aimed at pursuing economic growth and increasing market capitalization at the expense of shareholders' value.[118] According to Gul and Kealey (1999), *Chaebol* firms have a higher level of debt than non-*Chaebol* firms. The unique characteristics of *Chaebol* are the concentrated relationships of family members and the diluted role of the board of directors, which leads to problematic agency problems. The owners are family members, who control the resource allocations and make self-serving non-value-maximization decisions that often impair minority shareholders' interests.[119] In the 1990s, the World Trade Organization (WTO) reported that *Chaebol*s owned around two-thirds of the total market share in South Korean manufacturing[120] and a held a dominant position in the South Korean economy.

9.6.2 Drivers of Corporate Governance

9.6.2.1 Non-Governmental Organizations (NGOs)
The 1997 Asian Financial Crisis led to the collapse of many *Chaebol*s in the late 1990s. During the post-crisis period, South Korean NGOs played a positive and significant role in the development of corporate governance in South Korea. Since then, South Korean companies have realized the importance of sustainable long-term goals. The NGOs also contributed to corporate transparency and accountability, particularly in the *Chaebol*.[121] The two most famous NGOs are Solidarity for Economic Reform (SER) and People's Solidarity for Participatory Democracy (PSPD). They filed a large number of derivative suits against *Chaebol*-affiliated companies for wrongdoing and promoted reforms related to the protection of shareholder rights and against white collar crimes.[122]

The SER is committed to improving corporate governance through minority shareholder campaigns and shareholder activism. In 2001, the SER established an affiliated research center titled Centre for Good Corporate Governance (CGCC).[123] SER also launched the South Korea Corporate Governance Fund (KCGF), which provides corporate governance consultation services for small and medium-sized companies (SMEs) that are listed on the South Korea Stock Exchange. The fund also aims at enhancing corporate governance and protecting shareholder rights in South Korea.[124]

The PSPD is an NGO dedicated to enhancing transparency and accountability of the state and corporations. The PSPD contributes to the protection of minority shareholders' rights by monitoring both the South Korean government and companies' abuse of power.[125] For example, PSPD partnered with minority shareholders and brought lawsuits against the South Korea First Bank for illegal loans and bribery. As a plaintiff, the PSPD also targeted large *Chaebol*s such as Samsung, Hyundai and Daewoo. The PSPD asked Hyundai to repay its customers for the illegal transfer of a huge amount of bad securities from its investment funds to customers' trust funds.[126]

9.6.2.2 Korea Corporate Governance Index (KCGI)
In 2005, Bernard S. Black, Woochan Kim, Hasung Jang and Kyung-Suh Park developed and introduced the Korea Corporate Governance Index (KCGI), which is based on the five elements

of corporate governance, namely shareholder rights, board structure, board procedures, disclosure and ownership parity. Like other corporate governance indices in other economies, KCGI helps to improve South Korean corporate governance by supplementing the existing corporate governance regulations and by providing motives to follow good practices.

9.6.2.3 Korea Corporate Governance Service (KCGS) Korea Corporate Governance Service (KCGS) is a foundation for enhancing corporate governance in South Korea. KCGS evaluates all listed South Korean firms' corporate governance performance regarding their corporate disclosure, CSR and environmental protection activities. KCGS also provides CSR research and consulting services on sustainability reporting.[127] KCGS released its South Korean listed firms' Governance Rating in 2014, which facilitated investors in making their investment decisions.

9.6.2.4 The Korea Fair Trade Commission (KFTC) The KFTC is "a government administrative organization under the authority of the Prime Minister and operated as a quasi-judicial body." The KFTC provides services in the areas of fair competition, protecting consumer rights, creating a competitive environment for small and medium enterprises (SMEs) and limiting the concentration of economic power.[128] In 2004, the KFTC began to disclose the *Chaebol* ownership structures and operated a website for ownership disclosure in 2007.[129]

9.6.3 Legal Framework and Corporate Litigation

9.6.3.1 Legal Framework The Korean Commercial Code (KCC) provides the primary legal basis for all commercial transactions in South Korea. The National Assembly of the Republic of Korea passed a bill to amend the KCC in 2015 which allowed certain mergers and acquisitions (M&As), structures and activities[130] that were not permitted in the past. The Securities Exchange Act regulated all listed South Korean firms with the aim if protecting shareholders through fairness in the issuance and trading of securities. The Korea Securities Exchange Listed Company Regulations (LCR) specifically regulates firms listed on the Korea Stock Exchange.

9.6.3.2 Corporate Litigation The South Korean derivative suit system is a virtual image of US corporate law.[131] After the Asian Financial Crisis in the late 1990s, the minimum shareholding for listed firms to file a derivative lawsuit was downgraded from 5 percent to 0.01 percent. The South Korean Securities and Exchange Act requires a six-month holding period before a lawsuit can be brought. This is a drawback for shareholders of South Korean firms, compared to the US and Japanese derivative suit systems. As for the legal costs allocation system, South Korea follows the British rule: "a losing plaintiff must pay the litigation costs—including attorney fees—reasonably incurred by the defendant."[132] The special features of the South Korean derivative suit system are that plaintiff shareholders do not have to be contemporaneous shareholders, the possibility of the board blocking the lawsuit is limited, and the court may decide on the approval of the plaintiff with regard to the security deposit.[133] According to a 2007 SER study, 17 of the 40 lawsuits filed and adjudicated during the 1997–2006 period were decided for the plaintiffs. The lawsuit objecting to Samsung Electronics was a warning for the boards of directors of *Chaebol*-affiliated firms.[134]

The National Assembly of South Korea passed the Securities Class Action Act in 2005. The Act applies to South Korean listed firms which have irregularities in their financial reporting disclosures and to firms which are charged with insider trading, market manipulation or failing in the duty of external audit.[135] Securities class action suits in opposition to firms with book values of assets less than 2 trillion won (around US$1.8 million) were not authorized before 2007.[136]

9.6.4 Primary Areas of Corporate Governance

9.6.4.1 Ownership Structure and Shareholder Rights There are 1,991 companies listed in the South Korea Exchange with shareholding ownership largely controlled by *Chaebol*s. South Korea has a total market capitalization of US$1.259 trillion as of 2016.[137] Before the 1997 Asian Financial Crisis, the legal institutions and the *Chaebol* ownership structure were possible causes of poor corporate governance particularly in the efficacy of the disclosures of both financial and non-financial information of companies' performance. In 1996, the major shareholders of the large *Chaebol*s controlled around 23 percent of the outstanding shares as well as over half of the voting rights in the appointment of the board of directors and top management teams within *Chaebol*-affiliated companies.[138] Based on the *Chaebol* ownership data disclosed by KFTC, Han and Woochan (2008) highlighted that during the period from the late 1990s to the early 2000s, there was a slight decrease in the average family-controlled ownership with an offsetting increase in voting rights compared to 1996.[139]

The increase in foreign ownership and the change of ownership structures in South Korean companies are two key reasons for better corporate governance of such companies. During the late 1990s, the share of US mergers and acquisitions (M&As) was around 27 to 30 percent but the trend declined in the early 2000s. By the end of 2004, foreign ownership of publicly traded firms in South Korea was more than 40 percent with a decrease to around 30 percent in the 2000s.[140] In 2006, foreign ownership of South Korean listed firms was up again to around 37 percent, a jump from 13 percent in 1996.[141]

9.6.4.2 Board Structure The 2003 amendment of the Listing Act in South Korea stipulated that large listed companies (with total assets greater than 2 trillion won, around US$1.8 million), including the Korean Securities Dealers Automated Quotations (KOSDAQ), were required to establish an audit committee and an appointments committee with board members and outside directors. Large listed South Korean firms must have at least three outside directors, of which half should be appointed to the board of directors.[142]

9.6.4.3 Stakeholder Rights The annual general meeting (AGM) reform improved South Korean shareholders' rights.[143] In 2000, 224 out of 406 South Korean companies held their AGMs on the same day. The PSPD recommended that listed firms are to allow more shareholders to participate in AGMs, with extensive shareholder discussions.[144]

9.6.4.4 Transparency and Disclosure South Korean listed firms are required to report detailed financial and non-financial information through the ALIO system, an information system which discloses the information of publicly listed institutions.

The Ministry of Strategy and Finance imposes penalties on publicly listed institutions which fail to comply with the disclosure regulations of the Act on the Management of Public Institutions. In 2013, the Financial Services and Capital Markets Act was amended for listed companies to include the disclosure of the compensation of management and board members who earned more than 500 million won (around US$0.45 million). In 2014, the Financial Services Commission (FSC) established the Financial Company Governance Improvement Taskforce, which requires listed South Korean firms to disclose detailed corporate governance performance in their annual reports.[145]

9.6.4.5 Executive Compensation The average salary of executives in South Korean firms is 22 times higher than that of employees. The compensation gap between top executives and workers is even larger in the major *Chaebols* in South Korea. For example, Samsung Electronics' CEO Kwon Oh Hyun earned 6.69 billion won (around US$6.02 million) a year, which was 62 times more than the average staff member at the company's average annual wage of 107 million won (around US$96,300). Samsung Biologics' CEO Kim Tae Han earned more than 50 times the wage of the average worker. LG Household & Health Care's CEO also made around 50 times the average worker's salary.[146] As regards executives who are family members within companies, Hyundai Motor Group's Chung Mong-koo made 9.8 billion won (around US$8.82 million) in 2015, followed by Hanjin Group's Chairman Cho Yang-ho, LG Group's Chairman Koo Bon-moo and Hyosung Group's Chairman Cho Suck-rae.[147]

9.7 Malaysia

Before the Asian Financial Crisis, Malaysia experienced a number of business scandals. Prominent cases of poor corporate governance involved both privately-owned and government-owned institutions such as:

- The Bank Rakyat Scandal in 1977: its then chairman, the late Harun Idris, was sentenced to jail along with the bank's managing director Datuk Abu Mansor-Basir and general manager Ismail Din for corruption. They were accused of forgery and abetment of criminal breach of trust.[148]
- The government-owned Bank of Bumiputra and the bank's Hong Kong subsidiary Bumiputra Malaysia Finance Ltd. (also known as BMF) were involved in a scandal concerning bad loans with real estate developer Carrian Nominee Ltd. It was reported that BMF continued to lend to Carrian after the latter announced in October 1982 that it could not repay its debts.[149]
- The Pan-Electric Industries Ltd/Multipurpose Holdings scandal in 1981: the then president of a leading political party (Tan koon swan) abused their authority and position by channeling funds to save ailing Singapore-based firm Pan EL.[150]
- The Perwaja Steel Scandal: Perwaja Steel lost RM10 billion (around US$2.4 billion) as a result of possible misappropriation of funds and mismanagement by the former chair of the company, Eric Chia Eng Hock.[151]

Each of these scandals were associated with entities that had poor governance structures that allowed top executives and government to carry out unethical practices. Contributing poor governance factors include low-quality directors, weak internal controls, poor audits and inadequate disclosure. These are the common weak corporate governance characteristics in Malaysia and some other Southeast Asian countries.

The initiative for a standard and reliable corporate governance system began with the establishment of the Finance Committee on Corporate Governance in 1998, which consisted of both government and industry representatives. Furthermore, the implementation of the Committee's recommendations resulted in significant amendments to the Listing Requirements of the Kuala Lumpur Stock Exchange (KLSE).

9.7.1 Malaysian Code of Corporate Governance (MCCG)

The Malaysian Code of Corporate Governance (MCCG) has been a significant tool for corporate governance reform in Malaysia. It has positively influenced the corporate governance practices of companies, especially listed companies, through the "comply-or-explain" approach to listing requirements such as disclosure of application of principles, disclosure of the extent of application of best practices and the requirement for explanation of any deviations. MCCG focuses on four major areas, which include the board of directors, directors' remuneration, shareholders, and accountability and audit. The code is hybrid in nature, similar to the Combined Code on Corporate Governance in the United Kingdom.[152]

MCCG was reviewed in 2007 and 2012 to ensure that it remains relevant and is aligned with globally recognized best practices and standards. It introduced quality criteria for directors such as appropriate continuous education, skills, knowledge, expertise and experience, professionalism, integrity, and in the case of independent directors, ability to act independently. In 2017, MCCG was revised and the new version superseded earlier editions by taking on a new approach to promote greater internalization of corporate governance culture. The proposals ("apply or explain") seek an alternative to provide clear and meaningful explanations of how firms have adopted the core practices and achieved the intended outcome of each practice.[153] Bursa Malaysia has also launched an Environmental, Social and Governance (ESG) Index for publicly listed companies (PLCs). This ESG Index is expected to increase the number of listed companies which conform to good corporate practices. This in turn will attract Socially Responsible Investment (SRI) funds. Bursa Malaysia believes that markets can thrive if investor protection is maintained. As a result, Malaysia was ranked fourth among 142 countries for its commitment to investor protection by the World Economic Forum (2011).[154]

9.7.2 Ownership Structure

Concentration of ownership and control in Malaysian companies and conglomerates varies between the government, families and other institutions. In 1969, there was an emergence of companies owned by ethnic Malaysians (*Bumiputera*) and the government, which initially had 1.5 percent ownership, in order to overcome the dominance of the Malaysian corporate sector by foreigners, who owned 62.1 percent, and by the Chinese, who owned 22.8 percent. The continued quest to dissolve foreign/Chinese ownership of Malaysian corporate equity lingered over time until the United Malays National Organization (UMNO) formed a multi-party coalition (Barisan Nasional) which reduced the influence of the Malaysian Chinese Associations (MCA) in their government. Ten years after the

New Economic policy program, they managed to increase the *Bumiputeras* share of corporate holdings by 12.5 percent. In 1981, Mahathir Mohamad was appointed prime minister and the quest continued to strengthen the *Bumiputeras'* presence in Malay ethnically owned corporations.

With the help of Daim Zainuddin, the prime minister was able to incorporate large companies led by Malay capitalists with international standards after one decade. By the mid 1990s, there were many PLCs controlled by ethnic Malays with high political connections who received government concessions and patronage from the government. This resulted in a significant increase in corruption and transfer of wealth between top politicians and business people in Malaysia. During the Asian Financial Crisis, many of these "well-connected companies" did not survive. After the crisis, the concentration of the elite business class in Malaysia was dissolved, especially as regards the top 100 firms at that time in KLSE.[155] Currently in Malaysia there are two predominant types of ownership structure. They are pyramidal ownership and golden share ownership.

9.7.3 Pyramidal Ownership Pyramidal structure is defined as "a situation in which the same entrepreneur, through a chain of control relations, controls many firms." This means that the ultimate owner owns the majority of one firm that in turn owns the majority of another firm. This type of ownership structure is most common with family-owned firms, which represent a significant number of active firms in Malaysia.

9.7.4 Golden Share Ownership The Malaysian government holds a single unit "golden share" which it uses to exercise control over essential decisions which are of national interest. It is used by the government to influence decision-making in some strategic industries. These Malaysian Government Linked Companies (GLCs) control the selection of the board of directors, the right to speak at general assembly meetings and the right to oppose any decision made by the board of directors that would potentially conflict with government policies.

A paper by A. B. Che-Ahmad and A. S. Mustafa (2017) shows that the ownership-control structure of the top 100 firms listed in BM use pyramid structure and golden shares. Most listed firms are family-owned firms which control their affiliated firms using the pyramidal ownership structure while golden shares allow the government to direct firms' strategic decisions and to nominate the board of directors.[156]

9.7.5 Board Structure The board of directors is charged with ensuring the alignment of the firm's activities and its specified objectives. The 2017 update of the MCCG stated that the positions of chair and CEO should be held by different individuals. Separation of the positions of chair and CEO promotes accountability and facilitates division of responsibilities between them. In this regard, no one individual can influence the board's discussions and decision-making. The responsibilities of the chair should include leading the board in its collective strategic oversight of management while the CEO focuses on the business and day-to-day management of the company. This division should be clearly defined in the board charter.

9.7.6 Independent Directors Board composition influences the ability of the board to fulfill its oversight responsibilities. An effective board should include the right group of people with an appropriate mix of skills, knowledge, experience and independence that fit the company's objectives and strategic goals. The 2017 MCCG mandates that at least half of the board must be comprised of independent directors. For large companies, a majority of the board must be comprised of independent directors. In prior publications, the MCCG stated a limit of nine years on the tenure of independent directors. This has been relaxed, now stating that if the board intends to retain an independent director beyond nine years, it should justify this and seek shareholder approval at the annual shareholders' meeting. If the board continues to retain the independent director after the twelfth year, the board should seek annual shareholder approval through a two-tier voting process.

8.7.7 Remuneration The MCCG 2017 pointed out that director remuneration policies which do not appropriately align directors' remuneration with company strategy and performance can diminish shareholders' returns, weaken corporate governance and reduce public confidence in business. Companies are encouraged to fully disclose the detailed remuneration of each member of senior management on a named basis.[157]

8.7.8 Current Status of Corporate Governance According to the third edition of the Corporate Governance Guide issued by Bursa Malaysia in 2017, a range of reform measures have been implemented over the years to strengthen the corporate governance ecosystem.

- The introduction of the new Companies Act in 2016.
- The release of the Malaysian Code on Corporate Governance in April 2017 ("MCCG") Bursa Corporate Governance Guide 2017 (third edition).
- This latest incarnation of the Guide has been developed to reflect the new modes of thinking as well as the "CARE" (Comprehend, Apply and Report) concept that underpins the MCCG. The CARE concept urges companies to effect the spirit behind the practices while appreciating the significance of the principles in supporting long-term value creation.[158]
- Enhancements to the corporate governance disclosure framework under Bursa Malaysia Securities Berhad Listing Requirements ("Bursa Securities Listing Requirements").

These generate practical efforts to ensure and promote more transparent and meaningful application of good governance practices which stakeholders can rely on for their investment decision-making and for keeping up to date with the activities of the company.[159]

An international survey conducted by ROSC (Report on the Observance of Standards and Codes) on corporate governance assessment showed Malaysia in fourth place among the 10 Asian countries that were evaluated. Malaysia received a corporate governance enforcement score of 4.9, an increase from a previous score of 3.5, and an institutional mechanism and corporate governance culture score of 3.8 (Chantanayingyong, 2006).[160] Improvement in corporate governance practices in Malaysia could be observed from the scores. This could be due to the positive influence of the government on corporate governance in Malaysia and the consistent updates of the MCCG to ensure best practices of corporate governance in Malaysia.[161]

9.8 The Philippines

9.8.1 Development of Corporate Governance in the Philippines
In 1999, there was a shocking corporate scandal in the Philippines. BW Resources Corporation's share price hit an all-time high in 1999 and then collapsed in the same year. The scandal has tarnished the image of the stock market and undermined the confidence of private investors. The scandal was the result of manipulation of its financial performance by BW Resources' management to achieve the goal of boosting the value of the company in a highly competitive global market. In addition, the Asian Financial Crisis of 1997–1999, the collapse of the Nasdaq index, and the abuse of power by some corporate giants have highlighted the need for proper disclosure and transparency in conducting business. Recognizing this need, the Securities and Exchange Commission of the Philippines (SEC) began efforts to promote good corporate governance. On April 5, 2002, the SEC released the Code of Corporate Governance through SEC Memorandum Circular No. 2, Series of 2002.[162]

9.8.2 Regulatory Framework
The Securities and Exchange Commission (SEC) of the Philippines and the Philippines Stock Exchange (PSE) are primarily responsible for developing corporate governance guidelines, monitoring corporate compliance and regulating the domestic stock market. To improve corporate governance in the Philippines, the Philippines Stock Exchange has issued the Consolidated Listing and Disclosure Rules, the Philippines Mineral Reporting Code and other corporate governance guidelines and regulations.[163]

Due to the increasing complexity of business transactions, the SEC Philippines established a set of board-level and discretionary compliance guidelines based on the Code of Corporate Governance in 2009 which includes the expansion of non-executive outsiders on the board of directors, the definition of ownership, the risk management system and the enhancement of the independence of the board of directors. The code also takes into account the OECD's "transparency" principles of corporate governance by detailing corporate disclosure regimes including periodic financial statements, information and proxy statements required by listed companies as well as other significant disclosure regulatory documents.[164]

9.8.3 Ownership and Board Structure
In the Philippines, concentrated ownership structures of listed companies dominate business or extended family groups. According to the Claro survey in 2016, the average public ownership of listed companies accounts for 36 percent of the total outstanding shares. However, some older companies actually have higher public ownership.

The average number of independent directors in a company is only 2.45, which is slightly higher than the requirement of two directors in the Corporate Governance Code and the average number of non-executive directors is 4.12. With an average board size of 9.32, the proportion of independent and non-executive directors suggests that outsiders are in the minority. Coupled with the equity concentration system, listed companies are effectively under the control of the holding group. In addition, the average number of independent directors in the audit committee and the nominating committee was less than two. In fact, these two functions are essential to shareholder supervision and monitoring of the board of directors. In developed countries, of directors appointed to audit committees, independent directors form the majority.[165]

9.8.4 Shareholder Rights The main shareholder rights in the Philippines are described in the following sub-sections.[166]

9.8.4.1 Right to Participate in Annual Shareholders' Meeting The Corporation Code of the Philippines (Corporation Code) provides only for the essential elements of information on shareholders' general meetings including written notice of the annual shareholders' meeting to be sent to all shareholders on record at least two weeks prior to the meeting indicating the time and place of the meeting. Publicly listed companies are also required to disclose their operations at least 21 working days in advance in the Annual Corporate Governance Report in order to make announcements at the annual general meeting and present agenda items that require shareholder approval. There are no requirements in the Corporation Code that a company has to specify the agenda of a general meeting of shareholders in the written notice of the meeting. In order for shareholders to make an informed decision on a matter for consideration and approval, the enterprise should explain to the shareholders the issue or matter on the agenda and the rationale for the proposed items.

9.8.4.2 Right to Nominate Candidates to the Board A publicly listed company should give non-controlling shareholders or shareholders who own above an estimated number of shares the power to select candidates for the board of directors. Through amendments to the Companies Act, these shareholders have the right to nominate all directors who are eligible to stand for election under the law or the rules of the Securities and Exchange Commission. In addition, after an amendment has been approved, the Securities and Exchange Commission shall establish by notice or enforceable rules and regulations certain thresholds for the exercise of this right.

9.8.4.3 Right to Seek Redress for Violation of Rights Violation of shareholders' rights that take place outside the scope of the company are still considered to be intra-company disputes. However, the quasi-judicial role of the Securities and Exchange Commission in intra-company disputes was abolished as the Securities Regulatory Act of 2000 was passed. These cases were taken over by the ordinary courts. Unfortunately, this approach did not help to mitigate the problem as the violations of shareholders' rights persisted. Recognizing the ineffectiveness of the system, a specific provision of "alternative dispute resolution" was now included in the revision of the Companies Act. As a result, all disputes that go beyond the scope of corporate governance are referred to arbitration at the first level.

9.8.5 Disclosure and Transparency The level and quality of disclosure in a particular country greatly influences the inflow of capital and strengthens investor confidence in corporations and local businesses, especially with regard to foreign investors. Both disclosure and transparency help to ensure ethical and professional conduct. As a result, the country can raise more capital, make access to development finance more equitable for enterprises and enable enterprises to obtain a more efficient allocation of resources in the market.[167] In general, disclosure and transparency build confidence among stakeholders by strengthening the capacity of capital markets to operate and expand business participation thereby contributing to the creation of sustainable wealth.

The Philippine SEC released a new Code of Corporate Governance for Publicly-Listed Companies on November 22, 2016. The main feature of the Code is the application of the "comply-or-explain" approach, which combines voluntary compliance with mandatory disclosure. While companies are not required to enforce compliance with the code, they are required to disclose in their annual corporate governance reports whether their business practices comply with the code, to identify any irregularities and to explain the reasons for the irregularities. The new code has 16 principles and is divided into five parts. The second part deals with disclosure and transparency. Principle 2 defines the roles and responsibilities of the board of directors, which should be clearly understood by all directors as well as by shareholders and other stakeholders. Principle 8 focuses on enhancing corporate disclosure and requires companies to develop disclosure policies that are realistic and in line with best practices and regulatory expectations.[168] The Philippine Stock Exchange's Consolidated Listing and Disclosure Rules, published on October 1, 2013, compiles all existing Philippines Stock Exchange (PSE) rules governing the registration of securities on the exchange as well as the continuing listing and disclosure requirements of listed companies. These rules are consistent with the PSE's status as a self-regulating body and with the relevant provisions of the Securities Regulation Code.[169]

9.8.6 Executive Pay and Performance   Under the guidelines for listed companies published in 2016, boards should link the pay of key executives and board members to the long-term interests of the company. In order to establish a limited compensation management system, enterprises should develop policies that specify the relationship between remuneration and performance including specific financial and non-financial indicators to measure performance, and develop specific regulations for employees who have a significant impact on the overall risk profile of the company. In addition, directors are prohibited from being involved in discussions or deliberations on the terms of their own remuneration. If compensation is well-managed and aligned with the business and risk strategies, and objectives and values, companies can effectively prevent conflicts of interest, and attract and retain competent talent. Efficient compensation management can promote a risk culture in which risk-taking behavior is discouraged.[170]

9.9   Singapore

9.9.1 Development of Corporate Governance in Singapore   Corporate governance was officially recognized in Singapore with the enactment of the Company Act (CA) in 1967. In the same period, the Stock Exchange of Malaysia and Singapore were separated to form individual stock exchanges, Kuala Lumpur Stock Exchange for Malaysia and Singapore Stock Exchange for Singapore. In the late 1990s, the Monetary Authority of Singapore (MAS) decided to undertake a massive restructuring of the financial sector as they embarked on the journey to become one of the top financial centers. Unfortunately, the Asian Financial Crisis (AFC) occurred shortly afterwards, which took them a few steps backward in their restructuring plan. In between the review of Singapore's financial sector and the Financial Crisis, committees led by the private sector were inducted to continue the restructuring process. Their suggestions and recommendations resulted in the enactment of the first Code of Corporate Governance in Singapore (2001). The Singapore Institute of Directors (SID) was established to promote a high standard of corporate governance and ethical conduct of directors. SID has remained relevant even after the AFC by creating awareness through recognition through awards of companies which complied with corporate governance practices. SID published papers which were intended to guide boards of directors, committees and management in following corporate governance standards. Other tools were used to promote corporate governance including the ASEAN Corporate Governance Scorecard and the Singapore Governance and Transparency Index.

The development of corporate governance in Singapore has improved over the years. In 2017, the MAS announced the formation of the corporate governance Council to review the Code of Corporate Governance in the country. According to the Asian Corporate Governance Association and CLSA, Singapore and Hong Kong were among the top in corporate governance rankings in fulfilling the basic tenets of corporate governance rules and practices, enforcement, political and regulatory environment and accounting and auditing. Singapore also ranked top in the Asia-Pacific area according to the study organized by KPMG and ACCA which reviewed corporate governance requirements across countries. Regardless, Singapore continues to enhance its corporate governance mechanisms.[171]

8.9.2 Regulatory Framework

9.9.2.1 **Legal and Quasi-Legislative Regulation** Singapore is a common law country. Company law and securities law form the regulatory framework for corporate governance in Singapore. These are reflected in common law rules and statutory laws such as the Companies Act (Cap. 50) and the Securities and Futures Act (Cap. 289). In addition to these laws, there are quasi-legislative provisions such as the SGX-STX Listing Manual (the SGX listing rules), which applies only to companies listed on the SGX-STX of the Singapore Stock Exchange Limited. It is mandatory to comply with these and other listing rules of the Singapore Stock Exchange. Any company that fails to comply faces civil or criminal sanctions or administrative penalties such as condemnation, suspension of stock trading or delisting.[172]

9.9.2.2 **Codes and Best Practices** Codes and best practices are important to ensure the role of and compliance with corporate governance standards. They are not mandatory rules but they serve as guidance for encouraging best practices to enhance stakeholder confidence in corporate governance standards. One such code of best practice is Singapore's Code of Corporate Governance 2005 (the code). Adherence to the code may not be mandatory but listed companies on the Singapore Stock Exchange are required to identify their corporate governance practices in their annual report as well as to disclose any digression from the code with comprehensive explanation in the annual report for deviation (section 710 of the Listing Manual of the Singapore Stock Exchange). The code aims to encourage companies to embrace and adopt practices aimed at providing accountability while creating value for shareholders/stakeholders to enable them to act in an informed manner.[173]

9.9.3 Board Structure and Ownership Structure According to the 2014 *Singapore Directorship Report*, companies had on average six board members. The largest board had 20 directors and the smallest had three. In terms of board structure and composition, 34.1 percent of board seats were occupied by executive directors, 18.4 percent by non-executive directors and 47.5 percent by independent directors. Fifty-seven percent of companies were chaired by executive directors of which 30.8 percent were also chief executives while the remaining 26.2 percent served as executive chairs rather than company chief executives. Independent directors accounted for less than half of board seats. In 97 percent of companies, at least one-third of the board of directors were independent directors. In 54.5 percent of companies, more than half of the board of directors were independent directors.[174]

While the average board size of six directors remained relatively stable, by 2016 there appeared to be a shift toward smaller boards. The size of the board is positively related to the size of the market value. Large companies tend to have larger boards. There is an increasing trend for boards to have more independent directors. This can be seen from the increase in the proportion of independent board seats since the 2014 report, with 49 percent of independent board seats and 51 percent of non-independent board seats, a fall from 53 percent, identified in the 2016 *Singapore Directorship Report*. A total of 62 percent of companies have independent directors making up at least half of the board, which is a significant increase from 55 percent in 2014.[175] As for Singapore's ownership structure, it is similar to most parts of the world (with the exception of the United States and the United Kingdom). But big companies are usually concentrated in their holdings and either family-owned or state-controlled.

9.9.4 Shareholder Rights Shareholder rights and engagement in Singapore are regulated by a combination of statutory and non-statutory instruments under common law. The Companies Act (CA) and the Securities and Futures Act (SFA) make up the relevant core statutory framework, which is supplemented by non-statutory instruments such as the Listing Manual of the Singapore Stock Exchange (Listing Manual), the Singapore Code of Corporate Governance (Governance Code) and the Singapore Code on Takeovers and Mergers (Takeover Code).

There are a number of instruments used in the regulation of shareholder rights in Singapore, which include both statutory and non-statutory rules for shareholder engagement. The main points are as follows:[176]

Summoning a general gathering of shareholders: If the shareholders comprise greater than 10 percent of the total number of shares issued by the company, they have the right to schedule a general meeting directly.

Shareholder transparency: Active shareholders of a listed company should be informed of the voting rights of the major shareholder or any shareholder, director, or CEO of a company with a share interest above 5 percent of total voting shares. This information must be publicly disclosed as stated under the Capital Control Act and the Standard Financial Agreement.

Dismissal of a member of the board: A director of a listed company may be removed from office at any time by ordinary resolution of the shareholders, even if something to the contrary is stated in the articles of association or any agreement between the company and the director.

Derivative action: In order to ensure accountability, the Anti-Corruption Act provides a statutory derivative action that enables shareholders to bring proceedings on behalf of the company against the misdeeds of a director/third party for the director's conduct, which requires court leave depending on the company's right to claim.

9.9.5 Disclosure and Transparency   According to the Singapore Academy of Corporate Management, the corporate governance framework ensures that all important issues that involve the company are disclosed correctly and in a timely fashion including financial and non-financial reports on the company's position, performance, ownership and governance.[177] This led to the inauguration of the Corporate Disclosure and Governance Committee (CCDG) in August 2002, which is supervised by the Singapore Stock Exchange. The Committee's responsibilities include the formulation of financial reporting standards for companies, strengthening compliance with reporting standards and disclosure framework reporting standards, and updating them in a timely manner to ensure that they conform to international best practices. The Corporate Disclosure and Governance Board tracks activities in business activities and corporate governance and responds to the demands of Singapore's business and investment community.[178]

In recent years, the SGX has been focusing on the corporate governance disclosure of listed companies on the main board and has commissioned relevant institutions to investigate. In 2016, KPMG conducted an independent review of 545 companies on the disclosure of corporate governance guidelines. The study examined the information disclosed in the companies' annual reports for the financial years 2014 and 2015. The results reported that disclosure under the Corporate Governance Code by the main board listed companies was good, with room for improvement. In the study, the highest score was 90 percent and the lowest 28 percent. The study found that the average score was about 60 percent.[179]

9.9.6 Executive Pay and Performance   Principle 7 of the Code of Corporate Governance requires a formal and transparent process to develop policies on executive remuneration and to determine the remuneration program of individual directors. No director shall participate in the negotiation of their own remuneration. To that end, Singaporean companies are expected to establish a remuneration committee whose main terms of reference are to review and determine remuneration packages for individual directors and key administrative staff in accordance with agreed and established criteria. The remuneration committee shall also review the specific remuneration of each manager and make recommendations to the board. It shall cover all aspects of remuneration including but not limited to directors' fees, salaries, allowances, bonuses, choices, share-based awards and other awards and benefits in kind.[180]

9.10 Taiwan

9.10.1 Development of Corporate Governance in Taiwan   Taiwan was not left out during the Asian Financial Crisis as there were still cases of corporate fraud and bad debts years after the crisis of 1997. Subsequent to the crisis, the Organization for Economic Co-operation and Development (OECD) Council of Ministers reiterated the importance of improving corporate governance in both privately owned and state-owned corporations. Following the OECD's initiative, Taiwan intensified its awareness of the corporate governance standards by implementing the system of independent directors, the audit committee system and codes of corporate governance practices. It went further by amending the relevant laws (Company Law and Securities and Exchange Act) in 2006, which supports its quest to maintain high corporate governance practices in the jurisdiction.

9.10.2 Regulatory Framework All companies incorporated in Taiwan are subject to the jurisdiction of the Company Act. As the legal basis of corporate governance, the Company Act supervises the operation of the shareholders' general meeting, the board of directors and supervisors. To comply with international trends and standards, the law issued rules on restricted stock, split voting rights and electronic voting to create an attractive environment for international investors. In addition, the Act requires a company's board of directors to adopt a cumulative voting procedure in elections that aims at fulfilling all corporate governance responsibilities.[181]

Listed companies in Taiwan are also bound by Securities and Exchange Act (SEA) and its subsidiary regulations as well as the rules issued by the Taiwan Stock Exchange (TWSE) and the Taipei Stock Exchange (TPEx). These rules establish and promote specific requirements for corporate disclosure to ensure transparency of listed companies. SEA was promulgated on April 30, 1968 and last amended on December 7, 2016 providing a comprehensive legal framework for securities regulation in Taiwan.[182] On January 11, 2006, the SEA amendment was released. The amendment introduced the system of independent directors and audit committees as well as strengthening and improving the functions, structure and operation of the company's board of directors.

The TWSE and TPEx exchanges have made efforts to improve compliance with corporate governance standards by stipulating the requirements for listing firms on both exchanges. They went further by developing principles to guide domestic firms, with the issuing of the Governance Best Practice Principles, the Code of Practice for Corporate Social Responsibility and the Code of Practice for Integrity Management to establish a general understanding of building a corporate governance culture and enhancement of social responsibility.[183]

9.10.3 Ownership and Control Small and medium-sized enterprises (SMEs) are the most important form of enterprise in Taiwan, accounting for more than 90 percent of the total number of enterprises. The board members of SMEs tend to be family members, which means that external shareholders comprise only a very small number of non-family members or business partners. Important decisions in the company are actually made by "family committees." Even as the company grows and goes public, family control remains a major feature of large companies. In most cases, the shares of listed companies are controlled by the family. This form of family business has both advantages and disadvantages. The advantage is that a management team of family members will have strong leadership and cohesion. The drawback is that companies controlled by a family often abuse their management rights for self-interested benefits, thereby harming the interests of minority shareholders.

Since the 1980s, with the transformation of traditional labor-intensive industry to high-technology industry, the trend for separation of ownership and control has increased in Taiwan. An explanation for this phenomenon is that in order to remain competitive, high-technology companies are expected to share ownership with scientists, engineers and managers.[184]

9.10.4 Board Structure According to the Company Act, a limited company must establish a board of directors to supervise its business activities. The one-tier board structure is widely used in Taiwan. The board of directors shall consist of not less than three directors. According to Article 26-3, the board of directors of a listed company should be composed of at least five directors.

In general, the chair represents the company while the other directors represent the company only if authorized by the board of directors. The shareholders' meeting, the board meeting and the managing directors' meeting are presided over by the chair of the board of directors. The board was given a wide range of powers through a series of meetings. Except for matters which shall be carried out in accordance with the resolution of shareholders according to the laws or articles of association, the specific business plan of the company shall be decided by resolution of and adopted by the board of directors. The board may also establish internal rules for the enterprise to regulate procedures for specific types of transactions such as the granting of loans and the provision of endorsements or guarantees.[185]

9.10.5 Shareholder Rights Generally, the main shareholder rights are as follows:[186]

9.10.5.1 Voting Rights Shareholders have the income rights of a company and the right to vote on the matters stipulated in the Company Act. Generally, subject to the provisions of the Company Act, every issued share is entitled to one vote (for example, the holder of a special share or a company legally holding its own shares).

9.10.5.2 Inspection and Pre-emptive Rights The Company Act stipulates that the board shall prepare business reports, financial statements and recommendations on the distribution of loss or surplus income for audit by the directors before submitting them to the shareholders' general meeting for approval. The shareholders' meeting may select and appoint inspectors to carry out inspections.

When the company intends to issue new shares, in addition to the shares reserved for employees by the Company Act, it shall notify its existing shareholders to subscribe for new shares and enjoy the pre-emptive voting right.

9.10.5.3 Rights of Dissenting Shareholders When the company considers a specific type of transaction such as the sale or acquisition of all of the company's business or assets or a break-up or merger, the board of directors shall submit the proposal to the shareholders' general meeting. Any shareholder who disagrees in writing or orally before or during the meeting may waive the right to vote. When a dissenting shareholder requires the company to buy back its shares at a reasonable price, it shall repurchase the shares in writing within 20 days after the adoption of the resolution.

9.10.6 Disclosure and Transparency As information disclosure is an important part of corporate governance, strengthening disclosure also promotes the improvement of national policies and enables enterprises to effectively improve the transparency and accessibility of relevant information. The goal of information disclosure is to provide relevant information, improve the value of enterprises, reduce financing costs and protect the interests of investors. This will promote healthy development of the market while achieving the goal to "open information, expand participation." Following this trend in July 2002 the Executive Yuan established the Financial Reform Committee. In response to the emphasis on corporate governance and transparency of corporate information in other countries and regions of the world, the Financial Reform Committee has made the promulgation of information disclosure and evaluation systems a priority. In 2003, the Taiwan Stock Exchange Corporation and the Taipei Exchange commissioned the Securities and Futures Institute to carry out the development of an information disclosure system and carried out the first annual disclosure and evaluation review of enterprises.[187] To promote good disclosure, TWSE and TPEx announced the Public Company Material Information Disclosure Process in 2008 to help a company's internal staff better understand the relevant laws and regulations.[188] In 2013, the Supervisory Commission listed "Disclosure of Material Corporate Governance Information" as one of the five goals of 2013 Corporate Governance Roadmap. It can be predicted that the disclosure of non-financial information will become more common in the future.

9.10.7 Executive Pay and Performance According to the Company Act, if the company's articles of association do not provide for the remuneration of directors, directors' remuneration shall be determined by the shareholders' general meeting. The SEA requires all listed companies to set up a remuneration committee with at least three members and to regularly review projects such as corporate performance and directors' compensation. For details on the membership of and the exercise of the functions and powers of the committee, reference is made to the Regulations Governing the Appointment and Exercise of Powers issued by the remuneration committee of a limited company listed on a stock exchange.[189]

9.11 Thailand

Thailand's stock market fell sharply during the 2008 Financial Crisis, losing almost half of its market capitalization. Nevertheless, the capital market has rebounded sharply with the market capitalization to GDP ratio (87.1) being higher than that of many higher income countries in Asia in 2010. The Stock Exchange of Thailand (SET) index reached 1,391.93 points in 2012 compared to 2008 when it fell below the 400 point.[190] The SET has over 500 listed companies with listings on two boards namely the SET and the Market for Alternative Investment (MAI). The majority of listed companies in MAI are smaller and fast-growing companies. At the end of 2012, the SET listed 558 companies. The MAI's market capitalization was 133 billion THB (around US$3.99 billion). In the same year, there were 18 IPOs, which raised 15 billion THB (around US$450 million).

9.11.1 Legal Framework Thailand is a civil law country with common law influence on its corporate governance legal framework. In Thailand, listed and public companies are governed by the 1992 Public Limited Companies Act (PLCA). Other companies are governed by the Civil and Commercial Code. The Department of Business Development (DBD) in the Ministry of Commerce is responsible for company registration and implementation of the Act. The 1992 Securities and Exchange Act (SEA) regulates the capital market and authorizes the SEC in monitoring listed companies. The SEA was amended in 2008, including clearer responsibilities for board members, improvement of shareholder rights, enhancement of the whistle-blowing system and provisions to increase the independence and professionalism of the SEC.[191]

9.11.1.1 The Securities and Exchange Commission (SEC) Founded in 1992, the SEC is an independent regulatory body under the 1992 SEA B.E. 2535.[192] The main goal of the SEC is to monitor and develop the capital market and create an efficient, fair and transparent investment environment in Thailand. The SEC also increases the oversight of insider trading and actively monitors auditors of listed companies.[193] At the SEC Conference of 2018, the SEC released the Strategic Plan 2018–2020, which focuses on equal market access for innovation-driven sustainable growth.[194]

9.11.1.2 State-Owned Enterprises (SOEs) and The State Enterprise Policy Office (SEPO) According to a 2013 report from the World Bank, Thailand owns 58 listed SOEs (companies in which the state has over 50 percent ownership) with more than 250,000 employees, 6 trillion THB (around US$180 million) total assets and 2.7 trillion THB (around US$81 million) of revenues.[195] Corporate governance in Thailand has the characteristic of predominantly centralized state ownership. The State Enterprise Policy Office (SEPO) is in charge of two committees, namely the State Enterprise Policy Committee (SEPC or Super Board) and the Performance Assessment Committee. The SEPC establishes policies for SOEs at the national level. The SEPC has SOE board appointment rights. The Performance Assessment Committee is responsible for evaluating the performance of board members and executives of SOEs.[196]

9.11.2   Thai Institute of Directors (Thai IoD) Established in 1999 as a not-for-profit membership organization, the Thai Institute of Directors Association (Thai IoD) is responsible for the enhancement of directorship and corporate governance to align with global standards.[197] Since 2000, the Thai IoD has released its *Corporate Governance Report of Thai Listed Companies* (CGR), which serves as a corporate governance model for Indonesia, Malaysia and the Philippines.[198]

9.11.3   Primary Areas of Corporate Governance
9.11.3.1 Board Structure Board members consist of executive, non-executive and independent directors. The Thai IoD *Corporate Governance Report* reported that 72 percent of boards have at least two-thirds non-executive directors, 89 percent of boards have 30–50 percent independent directors, and a few firms have more than one-half independent directors.[199] The SET released guidance stating that the board shall have around five to twelve directors depending on the nature of the business.[200] Within the board of directors, independent directors have the responsibility and right to express their opinion of the work of management freely.[201]

9.11.3.2 Disclosure and Transparency In Thailand, the disclosure requirements for the annual reports of listed firms are primarily in line with international standards. For example, information which is monitored by the SEC and SET can be accessed through the firm's official websites and the Department of Business Development.[202] Disclosure requirements for listed SOEs in Thailand are subject to the SEC and those for non-listed SOEs are subject to the SEPO. In December 2011, the Cabinet of Thailand announced that all SOEs and listed firms are required to follow the same standards on information disclosure and must disclose their annual reports online. Firms that have more than 500 million baht (around US$15 million) of assets are required to disclose information regarding their shareholding structure, corporate governance standards, executive compensation and partnerships.[203]

9.11.3.3 Shareholder Rights In Thailand, shareholders have the right to trade their shares freely, attend the shareholders' meetings and access company information such as the financial statements, documents or list of shareholders, under the 1992 PLCA. Shareholders also have the right to appoint board members, and approve dividends, new shares and related-party transactions (RPTs).[204]

9.11.3.4 Executive Compensation In Thailand, the SET's 2006 and 2012 Principles of Good Governance guide listed firms in determining and disclosing their directors' remuneration. The board is required to disclose the form of remuneration, the payments to each director and the remuneration policies. Director remuneration should be paid according to experience, obligations, scope of work, accountability, and responsibilities and contributions. Inlakorn, et al. (n.d.) found that average board and executive remuneration is about 561,978 Baht (around US$16,859) while non-executive director remuneration is around 708,293 Baht (around US$21,249). The cash remuneration includes retainer fee, attendance fee and incentive payment. The determination of retainer fee is based on current practice in the industry, firm performance, and size, and directors' responsibilities, knowledge, abilities and experience. Incentive payments are linked to the creation of value for shareholders like net profits and dividends. The level of attendance fees should be determined appropriately such that the directors are encouraged to attend board meetings regularly.[205]

9.12 Vietnam

Prior to the 1980s, SOEs dominated the Vietnam economy under the "command market economy." The adoption of the Foreign Investment Law in 1987 attracted foreign invested enterprises (FIEs), which have been growing rapidly since the 1990s. At that time, FIEs were not allowed to change into joint stock firms or to offer new shares. The National Assembly of Vietnam adopted the Law on Enterprises (LOE) in 1999, which introduced the legislative framework for domestic corporate governance. As a result, employment opportunities increased with the growing private sector. Since the 2000s, Vietnam has become more competitive globally with the development of diverse domestic production and increasing private enterprise. The legal framework of Vietnam's corporate governance has also improved although the actual practice by local firms is yet to become mature. Moreover, the rapid economic development is impeded by a number of corporate scandals in Vietnam.[206]

Vietnam has made efforts to improve the legal and regulatory framework in order to become a member of the WTO. For instance, the National Assembly adopted around 90 new laws and established committees to introduce global standards of corporate governance and protection of shareholder rights from 2004 to 2009.[207] Due to these serious efforts and 12 years of negotiation, Vietnam joined the WTO in 2007 as its 150th member.[208] In the same year, the Ministry of Finance (MoF) introduced the Corporate Governance Regulations, which are in line with OECD Principles.[209]

9.12.1 Players in Promoting Corporate Governance

9.12.1.1 Capital Markets Vietnam's two stock exchanges are the Ho Chi Minh Stock Exchange (HOSE) and the Hanoi Stock Exchange (HNX). HOSE's market capitalization was around US$53.8 billion and HNX's around US$6.9 billion in May 2016. There are approximately 7,000 listed firms in these two stock exchanges with most being SOEs.[210] Vietnam had a total of 26,785 enterprises registered for new establishment with 278.5 trillion dongs (around US$11.98 million) of capital in the first quarter of 2018. Compared to 2017, the number of enterprises grew by 1.2 percent while the registered capital rose by 2.7 percent.[211]

9.12.1.2 State Securities Commission (SSC) The SSC primarily serves non-bank listed firms, and has enforcement powers of suspension or removal of licenses. The SSC was established as a governmental agency in charge of organizing and regulating the operations of the securities market with the objectives of maintaining an orderly, safe, transparent, equitable and efficient securities market and protecting shareholder rights.[212] In 2013, the SSC had 350 employees including 37 in securities issuance, 30 in the inspectorate and 30 in surveillance.[213] The SSC held the *ASEAN Green Bond Standards Roundtable Meeting* jointly with the International Finance Corporation (IFC) in March 2018 aimed at promoting sustainable and green capital market.[214] On March 19, 2018, the SSC held the *28th ASEAN Capital Markets Forum* (ACMF) meeting with capital market regulators from 10 ASEAN jurisdictions in Asia.[215]

9.12.1.3 State Bank of Vietnam (SBV) The SBV (the central bank) is a government agency serving banks and other financial institutions in Vietnam in accordance with the Law on the State Bank of Vietnam and the Law on Credit Institutions since the 1990s. The function of the SBV includes managing the monetary and foreign exchange at state level, stabilizing the value of Vietnamese currency and providing public services under the socialist orientation.[216] Under the SBV, the Capital Market Development Board was established to research and design securities projects and prepare requirements for the securities market. Collaborating with the MoF, the SBV provides investigations of the issuance of securities and proposes the model for Vietnam's securities market.[217]

9.12.1.4 SOEs and SCIC In Vietnam, SOEs have a dominant position in the nation's economy. Over the past two decades, many SOEs have been transformed into joint stock firms in which the state holds the majority interest.[218] SOEs in Vietnam have the function of exercising ownership rights and regulations. They enjoy easy access to finance and favorable government conditions with limited pressure to develop competitiveness and enhance transparency.[219] The state owns 51 percent of the interest in the majority of SOEs and appoints boards of directors (BOD) at the general meeting of shareholders (GMS).[220]

The State Capital Investment Corporation (SCIC) was founded under the Prime Minister on June 20, 2005 with the purpose of assessing governance, promoting SOE restructures and increasing the utilization of state capital.[221] By the end of 2017, the SCIC's portfolio consisted of 133 companies with state capital valued at VND 19,107 billion (around US$0.82 billion) out of the charter capital of VND

90,656 billion (around US$3.9 billion). As a state shareholder, SCIC serves to assess SOEs' financial management capability and propose SOE reforms. Recently, the SCIC held the *2017 Business and Communist Party Review* and the *2018 Plan Expansion Workshop* emphasizing that the SCIC is committed to protecting ownership representation rights, enhancing the efficiency of corporate governance and ensuring that management practices at SOEs are in line with the State Ownership Representatives Regulation and global standards.[222]

9.12.2 Primary Areas of Corporate Governance

9.12.2.1 Shareholder Rights Shareholders in Vietnam have difficulty in exercising their rights in company affairs due to inadequate information being provided before the General Meeting of Shareholders (GMS). For example, reports presented at the meeting are not always translated into English. In addition, most investors are retail investors who are focused on short-term investments. The Law on Enterprises (LOE) requires that notice be given to shareholders at least 10 days in advance of the GMS, which is shorter than in many OECD countries with an average of 21 days' notice. The LOE also introduces proxy voting and e-voting at GMS in order to protect shareholder rights.[223]

9.12.2.2 Ownership Structure Many small private firms in Vietnam have the characteristics of concentrated ownership. These firms are owned by a small number of family members, a few shareholders, or even a single controlling shareholder. Generally, concentrated ownership creates limited transparency and monitoring ability and weak protection of external shareholders/investors. Many joint stock firms' controlling shareholders have positions on the board, which may result in the failure of the aim of separate ownership and control. For example, as members of the board of directors (BOD), controlling shareholders may have the power to monitor themselves, and access to internal information. Therefore, failure of separate ownership and control may create accountability issues and poor information disclosure.[224]

9.12.3 Board Structure

The 1990 Company Law and the 1995 Law on SOEs introduced concepts related to the BOD, Supervisory Board and General Director in Vietnam. However, the laws are not widely adopted and implemented by companies in Vietnam. For example, board members who lack experience in corporate governance may not be aware of their responsibilities in the day-to-day company operations. Joint stock firms in Vietnam follow the LOE to elect members of the BOD and the Supervisory Board in GMS. The GMS or the BOD directly elects the chair of the BOD.[225] In joint stock commercial banks, the appointment and dismissal of board members follow the regulations of SBV (the central bank).[226] Insurance companies in Vietnam follow the insurance regulations in that the board members are approved by the MoF.[227]

9.12.4 Transparency and Disclosure

SOEs play a dominant role in Vietnam's economy. SOEs are required to provide relevant information to state-owned agencies and disclose the approved information on the companies' official websites. The information shall be sent to the state-owned agencies and the Ministry of Planning and Investment (MPI). The state-owned agencies will publish the information on the official website and the MPI will provide information on the government website www.business.gov.vn. There are several laws and regulations governing SOE transparency and disclosure including the Law for State Capital Invested

Management (2014), Decree 99 (2012), PM's Decision 929 (2012), Decree 81 (2015) and Decree 87 (2015).[228]

9.12.5 Executive Compensation   The 2005 LOE requires that compensation of board members must be disclosed in their annual financial statements as separate items.[229] The LOE also requires that the remuneration, wage and bonus of board members and executives be disclosed with their working hours and the company's business performance. The compensation of the board members is approved at the shareholders' meeting while the executive compensation is decided and approved by the board. The chief executive officer has the right to decide the remuneration of the managers and officers.[230]

10. CORPORATE GOVERNANCE REPORTING AND ASSURANCE

Corporate governance reports identify key corporate governance participants (corporate gatekeepers), the role that play in corporate governance and how effectively they fulfill their responsibilities. In the past two decades, several corporate governance reforms in the United States have been established (SOX 2002, Dodd-Frank 2010) to restore investor confidence. Corporate governance reporting is intended to present reliable, useful, timely, relevant and transparent information regarding the way organizations are managed and operated from the independence and effectiveness of the board of directors to executive performance compensation, risk management and investor democratic election. Effective corporate governance reporting should disclose all corporate governance KPIs in a systematic and standardized format. The content and format of such reports should be tailored to the company's organizational culture, business environment applicable regulatory measures, corporate governance structure consisting of principles, mechanisms and functions, as well as the roles and responsibilities of all corporate gatekeepers.

    Corporate governance determines the way in which an organization is operated and managed to create shareholder value while protecting the interests of all other stakeholders including employees, customers, suppliers, environment, society and government. Effective corporate governance facilitates achievement of sustainable performance and compliance. Thus, corporate governance reporting should provide information about an organization's performance in enhancing investor value as well as compliance with applicable laws, regulations, standards and best practices to protect interest of stakeholders. Credibility of corporate governance reports can be enhanced by assurance reports issued by external auditors, internal auditors or other third-party assurance providers. A group of professional organizations and accounting firms consisting of the Chartered Institute of Management Accountants (CIMA), PricewaterhouseCoopers (PwC) LLP and Randley Yeldar has developed a corporate governance report structure that is flexible enough to be adopted gradually and aligned with best practices of many high-profile companies and can be adapted to future changes and reforms. The proposed corporate governance reporting structure consists of:[231]

1. Telling a governance story which makes common sense is reliable, useful and relevant to investors.
2. Demonstrating compliance with all applicable laws, rules and regulations to show how effectively governance measures, reforms and best practices are complied with.

Elements of the proposed corporate governance report are:[232]

1. Chair's message—personal reporting on governance including the chair's views on good governance and the culture of the board.
2. Narrative governance report—detailed reporting on governance activities in key areas including characteristics of effective governance (skills, experience, knowledge and personality traits).
3. Compliance report—details of key activities of the board and its committees (audit, compensation, nominating) as well as compliance reports from each board committee.
4. Accountability report—detailed report on the effectiveness of the board and its committees, their performance evaluations and accountability.
5. Communication report with shareholders—reflecting how the information needs of investors are met.

The Council of Institution of Investors (CII) believes that public companies should have written and documented corporate governance policies and procedures as well as a code of ethics that applies to their directors, officers and employees.[233] The disclosed structure, policies and procedures should provide adequate protection to investors and hold corporations accountable to their stakeholders. The guiding principles and best practices adopted by many national stock exchanges require expanded corporate governance practice disclosures, leading many public companies to re-examine their practices and provide disclosures of such practices. The Deloitte & Touche 2003 survey reveals that while only about 23 percent of surveyed companies disclose their corporate governance practices on their websites, an additional 14 percent are planning to expand their practice disclosures above and beyond what is required by the SEC.[234]

The Commission of the European Communities requires listed companies to include in their annual report a comprehensive statement reflecting the major elements of their corporate governance structure and practices including:

- The operation of the shareholders' meetings,
- A description of shareholder rights and how they can be exercised,
- The composition of the board of directors and its committees (e.g., audit, compensation, nomination/corporate governance),
- The shareholders with major holdings, their voting and control rights and related major agreements,
- Any direct or indirect relationships between major shareholders and the company,
- Any material transactions with related parties,
- The existence and nature of a risk management system, and
- A reference to the company's code on corporate governance.[235]

11.　CONCLUSION

The role of corporate governance is to manage corporate affairs and activities for the benefit of shareholder by aligning management incentives with investor interests. Good corporate governance is committed to transparency, which leads to an increase in capital inflows from domestic and foreign investors. Good corporate governance also implies the need for a network of monitoring and incentives set up by the company to ensure accountability of the board and management to shareholders and other stakeholders. The strongest form of defense against governance failure is derived from an organization's culture and behaviors. Effectiveness depends on employees' integrity and begins with the tone that management sets at the top. Boards should routinely oversee their own actions set against acceptable governance principles. Organizations should ensure their boards have the qualifications and experience to approve an organization's strategy and to evaluate how it is executed and reported. Beyond the organization, the corporate governance system of a country and its standards are determined by factors such as political beliefs, culture, legal system, accounting system, transparency, ownership structures, market environments, level of economic development and ethical standards.

Corporate governance participants must structure the process to ensure the goals of both shareholder value creation and stakeholder value protection for public companies are aligned effectively. The corporate governance structure consists of principles, functions and mechanisms and is influenced by internal and external governance mechanisms as well as policy interventions through regulations. Corporate governance mechanisms are viewed as a nexus of contracts that are designed to align the interests of management with those of major and controlling as well as minority shareholders. The effectiveness of internal and external corporate governance mechanisms depends on the trade-offs among these mechanisms and is related to their availability, the extent to which they are being used, whether their marginal benefits exceed their marginal costs and the company's corporate governance structure. Cost-effective and efficient corporate governance rules and guidelines presented in this chapter can align the interests of directors, management and shareholders in achieving sustainable performance which in turn promotes market efficiency and economic prosperity.

Corporate governance in Asia is shaped by various factors pertaining to Asia such as the legal system, culture and politics. Overall, the Asian model of corporate governance is known as either the *family-controlled* or *government-owned* model. This Asian model of corporate governance is characterized by (1) concentration of ownership in a family, families, or states (2) the existence and enforcement of internal corporate governance mechanisms by family members or government and (3) a main focus on effective protection of the interests of majority owners (insider shareholders) and relatively less protection for minority investors. As the economies of Asian nations develop with foreign investors, be they institutional or otherwise, corporate governance mechanisms must improve with more demands for transparency and disclosures.

12. CHAPTER TAKEAWAY

1. Employ common sense and practical corporate governance principles. Make sure that corporate governance is on the agenda for the board of directors and top-level management team.
2. Increase commitments to business sustainability in terms of board and management attention and sound investment.
3. Reconsider and re-evaluate the role and responsibilities of all corporate governance participants including the board of directors, management, internal and external auditors and legal counsel to ensure that they comply with regulatory reforms.

4. Link executive compensation to long-term, enduring and sustainable performance.
5. Ensure vigilant oversight by the board of directors on internal control over financial reporting financial reports and audit processes.
6. Improve board oversight of management in achieving sustainable corporate governance by strengthening board independence .
7. Encourage and enable all stakeholders, particularly shareholders, to take a more proactive role in monitoring corporate governance.
8. Establish effective and enforceable global corporate governance rules and guidelines.
9. Hold companies worldwide accountable to their shareholders and other stakeholders including creditors, employees, customers, suppliers, society and the environment.

ENDNOTES

1. Z. Rezaee, *Corporate Governance Post Sarbanes-Oxley, Regulations, Requirements, and Integrated Processes* (Hoboken, NJ: John Wiley & Sons, Inc., 2007).
2. M. Lipton, "The New Paradigm for Corporate Governance," February 2016, http://www.wlrk.com/webdocs/wlrknew/WLRKMemos/WLRK/WLRK.25111.16.pdf
3. Ibid.
4. Conference Board. *Commonsense Principles of Corporate Governance*, 2016, http://www.governanceprinciples.org/wp-content/uploads/2016/07/GovernancePrinciples_Principles.pdf.
5. Rezaee, *Corporate Governance Post Sarbanes-Oxley.*
6. Z. Rezaee. 2018. Corporate Governance in the Aftermath of the Global Financial Crisis, in four volumes, published by Business Expert Press in March 2018.
7. Sarbanes-Oxley Act (SOX), July 30, 2002. Available at: www.law.uc.edu/CCL/SOact/soact.pdf.
8. Dodd-Frank Wall Street Reform and Consumer Protection Act of 2010, Pub. L. 111-203 (2010).
9. Experts in Responsible Investment Solutions (EIRiS), Sustainable Stock Exchanges: Improving ESG Standards among Listed Companies, 2010, http://www.eiris.org/files/research%20publications/SustainableStockExchanges2010.pdf
10. Ibid.
11. R. Rajan, G. Raghuram, and L. Zingales, "Which Capitalism? Lessons from the East Asian Crisis." *Journal of Applied Corporate Finance* 11, no. 3 (1998): 40–48.
12. J. Allen, "The State of Asian Corporate Governance: A Presentation by Jamie Allen," CARE Conferencel Hong Kong Polytechnic University, June 9, 2014, *Journal of Applied Corporate Finance* 26, no. 3 (2014): 67–70.
13. T. Beck, A. Demirgüç-Kunt, and R. Levine. "Law and Finance: Why Does Legal Origin Matter?" *Journal of Comparative Economics* 31, no. 4 (2003): 653–675.
14. OECD, *OECD Survey of Corporate Governance Frameworks in Asia*, 2017.
15. D. Griffin, O. Guedhami, C. C. Y. Kwok, K. Li, and L. Shao, "National Culture: The Missing Country-Level Determinant of Corporate Governance," *Journal of International Business Studies* 48, no. 6 (2017): 740–762.
16. Rajan, Raghuram, and Zingales, "Which Capitalism?"
17. C. Tejada, "Money, Power, Family: Inside South Korea's Chaebol," 2017, https://www.nytimes.com/2017/02/17/business/south-korea-chaebol-samsung.html?action=click&contentCollection=DealBook&module=RelatedCoverage&region=EndOfArticle&pgtype=article.

18. S. Claessens, S. Djankov, and L. H. P. Lang, "The Separation of Ownership and Control in East Asian Corporations," *Journal of Financial Economics* 58, no. 1–2 (2000): 81–112.

19. J. P. H. Fan, and T. J. Wong, "Corporate Ownership Structure and The Informativeness of Accounting Earnings in East Asia," *Journal of Accounting and Economics* 33, 3 (2002): 401–425.

20. Z. Rezaee, *Volume 2: Corporate Governance in the Aftermath of Global Financial Crises: Functions and Sustainability* (Business Expert Press, 2018).

21. Much of the discussion on all seven function of corporate governance comes from Z. Rezaee, *Volume 2: Corporate Governance in the Aftermath of Global Financial Crises: Functions and Sustainability* (Business Expert Press, 2018).

22. The below list are not exclusive and come from Z.Rezaee. 2018

23. UK Corporate Governance Code, June 2010 (at s. A.3.1); and King III Code of Governance Principles for South Africa 2009 (at 2.16).

24. Securities and Exchange Commission (SEC), Proxy Disclosure Enhancements, Final Rule, adopted December 16, 2009.

25. http://www2.goldmansachs.com/our-firm/investors/corporate-governance/board-committees/comp-comm-charter.pdf.

26. Dodd-Frank Act of 2010.

27. J. Stein. "Engaging with Strategy after the Financial Crisis," Harvard Law School Forum on Corporate Governance and Financial Regulation, 2011, https://corpgov.law.harvard.edu/2011/09/11/engaging-with-strategy-after-the-financial-crisis/.

28. The Conference Board, "Sustainability in the Boardroom," June 2010, https://www.conference-board.org/publications/publicationdetail.cfm?publicationid=1812.

29. Dodd-Frank Act of 2010, HR 4173 Subtitle Section 951.

30. D. O. Edwards, "An Unfortunate 'Tail': Reconsidering Risk Manager Incentives After The Financial Crisis of 2007–2009," University of Colorado Law School, 2010.

31. Rezaee, 2018.

32. Rezaee, *Corporate Governance Post Sarbanes-Oxley*.

33. International Corporate Governance Network (ICGN), https://www.icgn.org/.

34. A. Brockett and Z. Rezaee, *Corporate Sustainability: Integrating Performance and Reporting* (Hoboken, NJ: John Wiley & Sons, Inc., 2012).

35. Organization for Economic Co-operation and Development (OECD), *China Country Study: Self-Assessment Against the OECD Principles of Corporate Governance*, 2011, oecd.org/China OECD study of CorpGov 01 06 2011.pdf.

36. T. J. Wong, "Corporate Governance Research on Listed Firms in China: Institutions, Governance and Accountability," *Foundations and Trends in Accounting*, 2016.

37. Institute of Directors (IoD), *The Handbook of International Corporate Governance: A Definitive Guide*, ed. IoD (Kogan Page, 2009).

38. D. Solomon, *China Economic Outlook: Q4 2017*, December 20, 2017, https://blog.euromonitor.com/2017/12/china-economic-outlook-q4-2017.html.

39. G. Ran, Q. Fang, S. Luo and K. Chan "Supervisory Board Characteristics and Accounting Information Quality: Evidence from China," *International Review of Economics & Finance* 37 (2015): 18.

40. Ibid.

41. Ibid.

42. Ibid.

43. Ibid.

44. J. Dahya, Y. Karbhari and J. Z.-Z. Xiao, "The supervisory board in Chinese listed companies: Problems, causes, consequences, and remedies," *Asia Pacific Business Review* 9 (2002): 118–137.

45. Ibid.

46. OECD, (2011), *Corporate Governance of Listed Companies in China: Self-assessment by the China Securities Regulatory Commission*, OECD.

47. J. D. Piotroski and T. J. Wong, "Institutions and Information Environment of Chinese Listed Firms" in *Capitalizing China* (University of Chicago Press, 2012), 201–242.

48. M. J. Conyon and L. He, "Executive Compensation and Corporate Fraud in China," *Journal of Business Ethics* 134, no. 4 (2016): 669–691.

49. M. J. Conyon and L. He, *Executive Compensation in China*, January 2012, https://www.researchgate.net/publication/267406508_Executive_Compensation_in_China

50. M. J. Conyon and L. He, "Executive Compensation and Corporate Governance in China," *Journal of Corporate Finance* 17 (2011) April 19: 1158–1175.

51. Deloitte China, *2014–2015 Executives Compensation Survey Report in A-share Market*, 2015.

52. C. Tanaka and A. Martin, "Average Chinese Executive Pay Reaches $150,000 Mark," *Nikkei Asian Review* (2017, June 28), https://asia.nikkei.com/Business/Trends/Average-Chinese-executive-pay-reaches-150-000-mark?page=2.

53. R. Sappideen, "Corporate Governance with Chinese Characteristics: The Case of State-Owned Enterprises," *Frontiers of Law in China* 12, no. 1 (2017): 90–113.

54. "Average Chinese Executive Pay Cheques Crossed 1 Million Yuan for The First Time in 2016," *South China Morning Post*, 27 June, 2017, https://www.scmp.com/business/china-business/article/2100250/average-chinese-executive-pay-cheques-crossed-1-million-yuan.

55. "Maximum US$1288 Monthly Salary for Senior Executive in SOE," Xinhua News Agency, July 12, 2015, http://en.people.cn/business/n/2015/0712/c90778-8919225.html.

56. Hong Kong Institute of Certified Public Accountants (HKICPA), *A Guide on Better Corporate Governance Disclosure*, 2014.

57. "Shanghai and Shenzhen Stock Exchanges Continue to Chip Away at Hong Kong's IPO Attractiveness," http://Www.Scmp.Com/Business/Companies/Article/2125869/Shanghai-And-Shenzhen-Stock-Exchanges-Continue-Chip-Away-Hong.

58. "Recent Developments in Corporate Governance in Hong Kong and PRC," https://Www.Charltonslaw.Com/Hong-Kong-Law/Recent-Developments-In-Corporate-Governance-In-Hong-Kong-And-Prc/6/.

59. http://Www.Oecd.Org/Corporate/2017-Oecd-Asian-Roundtable-On-Corporate-Governance.Htm.

60. OECD, *Corporate Governance in Asia: Asian Roundtable On Corporate Governance 2014*, https://Www.Oecd.Org/Daf/Ca/48806174.Pdf.

61. http://www.Hkiod.Com/Index.Html.

62. C. Wan, "Corporate Governance Score Card. Market Value Driver, New Market Entrants Urged to Up Their Game," HKIoD, 2017.

63. OECD, *Survey of Corporate Governance Frameworks in Asia 2017*.

64. PWC, *Up Close and Professional: The Family Factor Global Family Business Survey*, 2014, https://www.pwc.com/gx/en/pwc-family-business-survey/assets/family-business-survey-2014.pdf

65. "Hong Kong's Family Businesses Need to Enhance Governance to Succeed," *South China Morning Post*, May 13, 2017, http://www.scmp.com/business/companies/article/2094146/hong-kongs-family-businesses-need-enhance-governance-succeed.

66. T. Mok, "Should The Hong Kong Code On Corporate Governance Practices Be Given Statutory Backing?" *Hong Kong Lawyer; The Official Journal of Law Society of Hong Kong*, 2014, http://www.hk-lawyer.org/content/should-hong-kong-code-corporate-governance-practices-be-given-statutory-backing.

67. O. Goswami, *Corporate Governance in India* (Manila: ADB/OECD, 2002) 85–106.

68. R. Chakrabarti, W. Megginson, and P. K. Yadav, "Corporate Governance in India," *Journal of Applied Corporate Finance* 20, no. 1 (2008): 59–72.

69. O. Goswami, *Corporate Governance in India* (Manila: ADB/OECD, 2002) 85–106.

70. R. Chakrabarti, W. Megginson, and P. K. Yadav, "Corporate Governance in India," *Journal of Applied Corporate Finance* 20, no. 1 (2008): 59–72.

71. Oxford LibGuides, Indian Law: Legal system, https://ox.libguides.com/c.php?g=422964&p=2888488.

72. D. Gardner, and G. Ward, "India," in *The Handbook of International Corporate Governance: A Definitive Guide*, ed. A. Jolly and A. Burmajster (London and Philadelphia: Institute of Directors, 2009) 182–190.

73. Capital Market Services, "Listing Obligations and Disclosure Requirements," 2016, http://www.vivro.net/blog/Listing-Obligations-and-Disclosure-Requirements.

74. OECD, *OECD Corporate Governance Factbook 2017*, 2017, s. l.

75. S. Deb and I. Dube, "Corporate Governance Disclosure for Complex Ownership Structure in India," *Indian Journal of Corporate Governance*, December, 10, no. 2 (2017): 143–175.

76. Institute of Directors, *The Handbook of International Corporate Governance: A Definitive Guide*, 2005, s. l.

77. D. Gardner, and G. Ward, "India," in *The Handbook of International Corporate Governance: A Definitive Guide*, ed. A. Jolly and A. Burmajster (London and Philadelphia: Institute of Directors, 2009) 182–190.

78. Ibid.

79. Institute of Directors, *The Handbook of International Corporate Governance: A Definitive Guide*, Institute of Directors, 2005, s. l.

80. OECD, *Disclosure and Transparency in the State-Owned Enterprise Sector in Asia: Stocktaking of National Practices*, 2017, s. l.

81. R. Chakrabarti, W. Megginson, and P. K. Yadav, "Corporate Governance in India," *Journal of Applied Corporate Finance* 20, no. 1 (2008): 59–72.

82. D. Gardner, and G. Ward, "India," in *The Handbook of International Corporate Governance: A Definitive Guide*, ed. A. Jolly and A. Burmajster (London and Philadelphia: Institute of Directors, 2009) 182–190.

83. A. Melin, and W. Lu, "CEOs in U.S., India Earn the Most Compared With Average Workers," 2017, https://www.bloomberg.com/news/articles/2017-12-28/ceos-in-u-s-india-earn-the-most-compared-with-average-workers.

84. S. Mishra, *The Corporate Governance World in 2018: A Global Review*, 2018, https://corpgov.law.harvard.edu/2018/01/28/the-corporate-governance-world-in-2018-a-global-review/.

85. R. O'Kelley III, A. Goodman, and M. Martin, *Global and Regional Trends in Corporate Governance for 2018*, 2017, https://corpgov.law.harvard.edu/2017/12/29/global-and-regional-trends-in-corporate-governance-for-2018/.

86. D. Hartono and D. Hermann, "The Indonesian Economic Crisis and Its Impact On Educational Enrolment and Quality," *Institute of Southeast Asian Studies* 7, May 2001.

87. IFC Indonesia, *The Indonesia Corporate Governance Manual* (Jakarta: IFC, January 2014).

88. KPMG, *The KPMG Indonesia Board Governance Toolkit*, November 2015, https://home.kpmg.com/content/dam/kpmg/pdf/2016/07/id-kpmg-indonesia-board-governance-toolkit-nov15-hyperlink.pdf.

89. IFC Indonesia, *The Indonesia Corporate Governance Manual* (Jakarta: IFC, January 2014).

90. International Comparative Legal Guides, *Corporate Governance 2017—Indonesia*, 2017, https://iclg.com/practice-areas/corporate-governance/corporate-governance-2017/indonesia.

91. Clearstream, "Disclosure Requirements—Indonesia," June 6, 2017, http://www.clearstream.com/clearstream-en/products-and-services/market-coverage/asia-pacific/indonesia/disclosure-requirements—indonesia/7728.

92. International Comparative Legal Guides, *Corporate Governance 2017—Indonesia*, 2017, https://iclg.com/practice-areas/corporate-governance/corporate-governance-2017/indonesia.

93. IFC Indonesia, *The Indonesia Corporate Governance Manual* (Jakarta: IFC, January 2014).

94. International Comparative Legal Guides, *Corporate Governance 2017—Japan*, June 2017.

95. K. Van Wolferen, *The Enigma of Japanese Power: People and Politics in a Stateless Nation* (London: Macmillan, 1989) 163.

96. Y. Horie, "The Role of the Ie ($- House) in the Economic Modernization of Japan," 36 *Kyoto U. Econ. Rev.* 1 (1966); see also Y. Sakudo, "The Management Practices of Family Business," in *Tokugawa Japan: The Social and Economic Antecedents of Modern Japan*, ed. C. Nakane and S. Oishi (University of Tokyo Press, 1990) 147–166.

97. C. Nakane, *Japanese Society* (University of California Press, 1973) 3.

98. C. Pejovic, "Japanese Corporate Governance: Behind Legal Norms," *Penn State International Law Review* 29, no. 3 (2011): Article 7.

99. Ibid.

100. R. J. Gilson and M. J. Roe, "Understanding the Japanese Keiretsu: Overlaps Between Corporate Governance and Industrial Organization," 102 *Yale L.J.* (1993): 871.

101. C. Pejovic, "Japanese Corporate Governance: Behind Legal Norms."

102. J. C. Abegglen and G. Stalk Jr., *Kaisha—The Japanese Corporation* (Tokyo: Charles E. Tuttle Company, 1985) 183–88, 191–92, 194–206; R. Gilson and M. Roe, "Lifetime Employment: Labor Peace and the Evolution of Japanese Corporate Governance," *Colum. L. Rev.* 99 (1999): 508.

103. M. Aoki, *Information, Incentives, and Bargaining in The Japanese Economy* (Cambridge University Press, 1988) 116–119.

104. C. Pejovic, "Japanese Corporate Governance: Behind Legal Norms."

105. A. Jolly and A. Burmajster, *The Handbook of International Cooperate Governance: A Definitive Guide*, 2nd ed. (Institute of Directors in association with Kogan Page, 2009), ISBN 978 0 7494 5508 8.

106. Clifford Chance, "Companies Act Reform: Supervisory Function of the Board of Directors," 2014, https://www.cliffordchance.com/briefings/2014/07/companies_act_reformsupervisoryfunctiono.html.

107. T. Hiura and J. Ishikawa, *Corporate Governance in Japan: Board Membership and Beyond*, Bain report, February 2016.

108. International Comparative Legal Guides, *Corporate Governance 2017—Japan*, June 2017.

109. A. Jolly and A. Burmajster, *The Handbook of International Cooperate Governance: A Definitive Guide*, 2nd ed. (Institute of Directors in association with Kogan Page, 2009), ISBN 978 0 7494 5508 8.

110. H. Shibata, "Executive Compensation & Employee Benefits," Getting the Deal Through, July 2017, http://www.uubo.org/media/1347/getting-the-deal-through-executive-compensation-and-employee-benefits-nigeria.pdf.

111. SolAbility, *Corporate Sustainability, Governance, & ESG in Korea—State & Trends 2013, Korea*: s.n, 2013.

112. J. Solomon, A. Solomon, and C. Park, "A Conceptual Framework for Corporate Governance Reform in South Korea," *Corporate Governance: An International Review*, January, 10, no. 1 (2002): 29–46.

113. F. A. Gul, and B. T. Kealey, "Chaebol, Investment Opportunity Set and Corporate Debt and Dividend Policies of Korean Companies," *Review of Quantitative Finance and Accounting* 13 (1999): 401–416.

114. J. Tsui. and T. Shieh, "Corporate Governance in Emerging Markets: An Asian Perspective," in *International Finance and Accounting Handbook*, 3rd ed., ed. F. D. Choi (Hoboken, NJ: John Wiley & Sons, Inc, 2004).

115. J. Solomon, "Corporate Governance: South Korea," in *Governance, Risk, and Compliance Handbook: Technology, Finance, Environmental, and International Guidance and Best Practices*, ed. A. Tarantino (Hoboken, NJ: John Wiley & Sons, Inc., 2008), s. l.

116. Gul and Kealey, "Chaebol, Investment Opportunity Set and Corporate Debt and Dividend Policies of Korean Companies."

117. C. Tejada, "Money, Power, Family: Inside South Korea's Chaebol," 2017, https://www.nytimes.com/2017/02/17/business/south-korea-chaebol-samsung.html?action=click&contentCollection=DealBook&module=RelatedCoverage&region=EndOfArticle&pgtype=article.

118. E. H. Kim and W. Kim, "Changes in Korean Corporate Governance: A Response to Crisis," *Journal of Applied Corporate Finance* 20, no. 1 (2008): 47–58.

119. Gul and Kealey, "Chaebol, Investment Opportunity Set and Corporate Debt and Dividend Policies of Korean Companies."

120. C. Tejada, "Money, Power, Family: Inside South Korea's Chaebol," 2017, https://www.nytimes.com/2017/02/17/business/south-korea-chaebol-samsung.html?action=click&contentCollection=DealBook&module=RelatedCoverage&region=EndOfArticle&pgtype=article.

121. Kim and Kim, "Changes in Korean Corporate Governance: A Response to Crisis."

122. Ibid.

123. S.-J. Kim, *How to Boost Shareholder Activism in Asia: Lessons from the Korean Experiences*, 2007, http://www.csr-asia.com/summit07/presentations/shareholder_ppt_SJKim.pdf.

124. Kim and Kim, "Changes in Korean Corporate Governance: A Response to Crisis."

125. PSPD, *People's Solidarity for Participatory Democracy(PSPD) Non-Governmental Organization Seoul, South Korea*, 2017, http://www.peoplepower21.org/English/39340.

126. Solomon, Solomon, and Park, "A Conceptual Framework for Corporate Governance Reform in South Korea."

127. M. H. Cho, "President's Message," http://www.cgs.or.kr/ECGS_main.asp?MenuIndex=F.

128. Korea Fair Trade Commission, "About KFTC: Who we are," http://www.ftc.go.kr/eng/contents.do?key=493.

129. Kim and Kim, "Changes in Korean Corporate Governance: A Response to Crisis."

130. http://www.inhousecommunity.com/article/new-amendment-to-the-korean-commercial-code/.

131. O.-R. Song, "Improving Corporate Governance Through Litigation: Derivative Suits and Class Actions in Korea," in *Transforming Corporate Governance in East Asia*, ed. H. Kanda, K. Kim and C. J. Milhaupt (Abingdon, Oxon: Routledge, 2008).

132. Ibid.

133. Ibid.

134. Kim and Kim, "Changes in Korean Corporate Governance: A Response to Crisis."

135. Ibid.

136. Ibid.

137. OECD, *OECD Survey of Corporate Governance Frameworks in Asia 2017*, 2017, s. l.

138. Kim and Kim, "Changes in Korean Corporate Governance: A Response to Crisis."

139. Ibid.

140. B. S. Min, "Corporate Governance Reform: The Case of Korea," *Asian Journal of Political Science* 24, no. 1 (2016): 21–41.

141. Kim and Kim, "Changes in Korean Corporate Governance: A Response to Crisis."

142. Min, "Corporate Governance Reform: The Case of Korea."

143. Solomon, Solomon, and Park, "A Conceptual Framework for Corporate Governance Reform in South Korea."

144. Solomon, "Corporate Governance: South Korea,"

145. D. Oh and S. A. Ahn, "Improving South Korean corporate govenance," 2015, http://www.iflr.com/Article/3429769/Improving-South-Korean-corporate-governance.html.

146. Koreaboo, "This Is How Much More Korean CEOs Make Than Their Employees," 2017, https://www.koreaboo.com/buzz/much-korean-ceos-make-employees/.
147. J. Suk-yee, "Korean CEO Compensation: What is Annual Income of Korean Top CEOs?" 2016, http://www.businesskorea.co.kr/english/news/money/14277-korean-ceo-compensation-what-annual-income-korean-top-ceos.
148. http://www.dailyexpress.com.my/news.cfm?NewsID=112476.
149. "Malaysia Discloses Details of Bank Scandal," *New York Times*, https://www.nytimes.com/1985/01/08/business/malaysia-discloses-details-of-bank-scandal.html.
150. https://bibliotheca.limkitsiang.com/1986/05/30/malaysia-has-become-a-nation-of-scandals-with-corruption-and-abuse-of-power-at-high-political-places-becoming-a-central-issue-in-the-coming-general-elections/.
151. http://news.bbc.co.uk/2/hi/business/3475703.stm.
152. "Powering Business Sustainability (A Guide for Directors)," http://www.bursamalaysia.com/misc/sustainability_guide_for_directors.pdf.
153. *Journal of Corporate Governance in Asia 2010*, http://Www.Corporategovernanceasia.Info/Yahoo_Site_Admin1/Assets/Docs/Cga-August-October2010.16191135.Pdf.
154. World Economic Forum, *The Global Competitiveness Report 2011–2012*, http://www3.weforum.org/docs/GCR2011-12/CountryProfiles/Malaysia.pdf
155. F. A. Gul and J. S. L. Tsui, eds., *The Governance of East Asian Corporations: Post Asian Financial Crisis* (Basingstoke; New York: Palgrave Macmillan, 2004).
156. A. B. Che-Ahmad and A. S. Mustafa, "Ownership Patterns and Control of Top 100 Malaysian listed companies," The 17th Annual Conference of the Asian Academic Accounting Association (2016 FourA Conference), 2017, DOI: https://doi.org/10.1051/shsconf/20173401006.
157. A. Bin-Zulkafli, M. AdulSamad, and M. Ismail, "Corporate governance in Malaysia," *Malaysian Institute of Corporate Governance* 1, no. 1 (2007): 18.
158. *Malaysian Code on Corporate Governance 2017*, https://www.Sc.Com.My/Wp-Content/Uploads/Eng/Html/Cg/Mccg2017.Pdf.
159. "This Corporate Governance Guide ('Guide') Is Issued by Bursa Malaysia (2017)," http://Www.Bursamalaysia.Com/Misc/System/Assets/23005/Consolidated_Cg_Guide_3.Pdf
160. C. Chantanayingyong, "Regulatory Discipline—Fostering Enforcement Mechanisms: The Regulatory Challenge," 2006 Asian Roundtable on Corporate Governance Development in Thailand: The Three Disciplines, held at Bangkok, Thailand on September 13, 2006.
161. Z. Othman, "Ethics in Malaysian Corporate Governance Practices," *Journal of Business and Social Science*, 2010, http://ijbssnet.com/journals/_1_No._3_December_2010/10.pdf.
162. N. a., "Corporate Governance in a Philippine Setting," *International Financial Law Review*, Oct 10, 2002.
163. Philippine Stock Exchange, "Listing & Disclosure Rules," 2012, http://www.pse.com.ph/stockMarket/listedCompaniesRules.html?tab=0
164. C. G. Gañac, "The State of Corporate Governance in the Philippines. Shareholders Association of The Philippines," September 4, 2016.
165. Ibid.
166. Securities and Exchange Commission, *Philippine Corporate Governance Blueprint 2015*.
167. Ibid.
168. R. C. B. Gonzalez, *Recent Developments in Philippine Corporate Governance: The New Code of Corporate Governance for Publicly-Listed Companies* (International Finance Corporation, 2016).
169. R. S. Monzon, "Listing & Disclosure Rules. Philippines Stock Exchange. Inc.," 2013.
170. Securities and Exchange Commission, *Code of Corporate Governance for Publicly-listed Companies*, November 22, 2016.

171. J. Koh and A. Yip (n.d.), *The Evolution of Corporate Governance in Singapore* (Singapore Institute of Directors, Boardroom Matters Volume II).

172. ACCA, *Corporate Governance in Singapore*, 2011.

173. Ibid.

174. Institute of Singapore Chartered Accountants, *The Singapore Directorship Report*, 2014.

175. Institute of Singapore Chartered Accountants, *SID-ISCA Singapore Directorship Report 2016*, October 2016.

176. F. J. Aquila, *The Shareholder Rights and Activism Review. The Projects and Construction Review*, 7th ed., September 2017, ISBN 978-1-910813-84-3.

177. Singapore Academy of Corporate Management, *Corporate Governance: Disclosure and Transparency*, n.d.

178. P. Thompson and A. C. Hung, *Cracking the Singapore Code of Corporate Governance: A Step Toward World-Class Corporate Governance and Superior Performance* (Nottingham University Business School, University of Nottingham, 2002, No. 09/2002).

179. KPMG, *Review of Mainboard Companies' Code of Corporate Governance Disclosures*, Singapore Exchange, July 2016.

180. Corporate Governance Guides for Boards in Singapore, *eGuide to the Code of Corporate Governance*, Singapore Institute of Directors, n.d.

181. Taiwan Stock Exchange Corporation, *Regulatory Framework of Corporate Governance*, n.d.

182. W. J. L. Calkoen, ed. "Overview of Governance Regime" in *The Corporate Governance Review*, 7th ed. (The Law Reviews, 2017).

183. Taiwan Stock Exchange Corporation, *Regulatory Framework of Corporate Governance*, n.d.

184. Securities and Futures Institute, *Corporate Governance in Taiwan*, European Corporate Governance Institute, May 2017.

185. Calkoen, ed. "Overview of Governance Regime."

186. Ibid.

187. Taiwan Stock Exchange Corporation, *Information Disclosure and Transparency Ranking System Overview*, n.d.

188. Calkoen, ed. "Overview of Governance Regime."

189. Ibid.

190. World Bank, *The 2012 Corporate Governance ROSC for Thailand*, World Bank, 2013, s. l.

191. Ibid.

192. Securities and Exchange Commission, "About the SEC," 2016, http://www.sec.or.th/EN/AboutSEC/Pages/Introduction.aspx.

193. World Bank, *The 2012 Corporate Governance ROSC for Thailand*, World Bank, 2013, s. l.

194. Securities and Exchange Commission, "SEC Announces Three-Year Strategic Plan (2018–2020)," 2018, http://www.sec.or.th/EN/SECEvent/Pages/event61_150161.aspx.

195. World Bank, *The 2012 Corporate Governance ROSC for Thailand*, World Bank, 2013, s. l.

196. OECD, *Disclosure and Transparency in the State-Owned Enterprise Sector in Asia: Stocktaking of National Practices*, 2017, s. l.

197. Thai Institute of Directors Association, "About IOD," http://www.thai-iod.com/en/aboutIOD.asp.

198. World Bank, *The 2012 Corporate Governance ROSC for Thailand*, World Bank, 2013, s. l.

199. Ibid.

200. U. Detthamrong, N. Chancharata, and C. Vithessonthi, "Corporate Governance, Capital Structure and Firm Performance: Evidence from Thailand," *Research in International Business and Finance* 42 (2017): 689–709.

201. Ibid.
202. World Bank, *The 2012 Corporate Governance ROSC for Thailand*, World Bank, 2013, s. l.
203. OECD, *Disclosure and Transparency in the State-Owned Enterprise Sector in Asia: Stock-taking of National Practices*, 2017, s. l.
204. World Bank, *The 2012 Corporate Governance ROSC for Thailand*, World Bank, 2013, s. l.
205. S. Inlakorn, S. Lhaopadchan, and N. Sabsombat, *The Stock Exchange of Thailand*, n.d., https://www.set.or.th/dat/vdoArticle/attachFile/AttachFile_1495692812326.pdf.
206. International Finance Corporation, *Corporate Governance Manual* (Hanoi: World Bank Group, 2010).
207. Ibid.
208. BBC News, "Vietnam Profile—Timeline," 2018, http://www.bbc.com/news/world-asia-pacific-16568035.
209. International Finance Corporation, *Corporate Governance Manual* (Hanoi: World Bank Group, 2010).
210. OECD, *3rd Meeting of the OECD—Southeast Asia Corporate Governance Initiative*, 2016, s. l.
211. General Statistics Office of Vietnam, *Monthly Statistical Information: Social and Economic Situation in The First Quarter of 2018*, 2018, https://www.gso.gov.vn/default_en.aspx?tabid=622&ItemID=18799.
212. State Securities Commission, Development, "History: 1. The Coming into Being of the State Securities Commission (SSC)," n.d., http://www.ssc.gov.vn/ubck/faces/en/enmenu/enpages_engioithieu?_afrLoop=22809038324616794&_afrWindowMode=0&_afrWindowId=sl3xehs45_1#%40%3F_afrWindowId%3Dsl3xehs45_1%26_afrLoop%3D22809038324616794%26_afrWindowMode%3D0%26_adf.ctrl-state%3D1skanf6sq_4.
213. OECD, *OECD—Southeast Asia Corporate Governance Initiative*, 2015, s. l.
214. State Securities Commission, *ASEAN Green Bond Standards Roundtable Meeting toward ASEAN Green Asset Class*, 2018, http://www.ssc.gov.vn/ubck/faces/oracle/webcenter/portalapp/pages/en/newsdetail.jspx?dDocName=APPSSCGOVVN162118350&_afrLoop=22816746725813794&_afrWindowMode=0&#%40%3F_afrLoop%3D22816746725813794%26dDocName%3DAPPSSCGOVVN162118350%26_afrWindowMode%3D0%26_ad.
215. State Securities Commission, *28th ASEAN Capital Markets Forum Meeting to Enhance ASEAN Capital Market Integration*, 2018, http://www.ssc.gov.vn/ubck/faces/oracle/webcenter/portalapp/pages/en/newsdetail.jspx?dDocName=APPSSCGOVVN162118323&_afrLoop=22817426992906794&_afrWindowMode=0&#%40%3F_afrLoop%3D22817426992906794%26dDocName%3DAPPSSCGOVVN162118323%26_afrWindowMode%3D0%26_ad.
216. State Bank of Vietnam, "About SBV: The History," n.d., https://www.sbv.gov.vn/webcenter/portal/en/home/sbv/aboutsbv/history?_afrLoop=761215684780000#%40%3F_afrLoop%3D761215684780000%26centerWidth%3D80%2525%26leftWidth%3D20%2525%26rightWidth%3D0%2525%26showFooter%3Dfalse%26showHeader%3Dfalse%26_adf.ctrl-state%.
217. State Securities Commission, "Development History: 1. The Coming Into Being of the State Securities Commission (SSC)," n.d., http://www.ssc.gov.vn/ubck/faces/en/enmenu/enpages_engioithieu?_afrLoop=22809038324616794&_afrWindowMode=0&_afrWindowId=sl3xehs45_1#%40%3F_afrWindowId%3Dsl3xehs45_1%26_afrLoop%3D22809038324616794%26_afrWindowMode%3D0%26_adf.ctrl-state%3D1skanf6sq_4.

218. International Finance Corporation, *Corporate Governance Manual* (Hanoi: World Bank Group, 2010).
219. OECD, *OECD—Southeast Asia Corporate Governance Initiative*, 2015, s. l.
220. International Finance Corporation, *Corporate Governance Manual* (Hanoi: World Bank Group, 2010).
221. State Capital Investment Corporation, "Corporate Profile," n.d., http://www.scic.vn/english/index.php.
222. State Capital Investment Corporation, *The State Capital Investment Corporation (SCIC) holds its 2017 Business and Communist Party Review and 2018 Plan Expansion Workshop*, 2018, http://www.scic.vn/english/index.php/thong-tin-bao-chi/279-the-state-capital-investment-corporation-scic-holds-its-2017-business-and-communist-party-review-and-2018-plan-expansion-workshop.html.
223. OECD, *OECD—Southeast Asia Corporate Governance Initiative*, 2015, s. l.
224. International Finance Corporation, *Corporate Governance Manual* (Hanoi: World Bank Group, 2010).
225. LOE, Articles 104.2(d) & 111.1.
226. Circular 06/2010/TT-NHNN (Circular 06) of the SBV dated February 26, 2010.
227. International Finance Corporation, *Corporate Governance Manual* (Hanoi: World Bank Group, 2010).
228. OECD, *Disclosure and Transparency in The State-Owned Enterprise Sector*, South Korea, OECD, 2016.
229. S. Ganu, *Executive Remuneration Disclosures in Asia* (New York: Mercer LLC, 2014).
230. T. L. Minh and G. Walker, "Corporate Governance of Listed Companies in Vietnam," *Bond Law Review* 20, no. 2 (2008).
231. Ibid.
232. Ibid.
233. Council of Institutional Investors, *Corporate Governance Policies*, October 13, 2004, www.cii.org.
234. Deloitte & Touche, "Audit Committee Financial Expert Designation and Disclosure Practice Survey," 2003, www.deloitte.com/dtt/article/0,1002,sid%253D2006%2526cid%253D13514,00.html.
235. Commission of the European Communities, *Modernizing Company Law and Enhancing Corporate Governance in The European Union: A Plan to Move Forward*, COM 284 final, May 21, 2003.

CHAPTER 7

Social Dimension of Sustainability

1. EXECUTIVE SUMMARY

There has been growing international interest in business sustainability including corporate social responsibility (CSR), and environmental, ethical, and governance issues. Corporations have shifted their primary goals from profit-maximization to creating shared value for all stakeholders including shareholders while fulfilling their social and environmental responsibilities. Particularly, the CSR program is designed to minimize conflicts between corporations and society caused by the differences between private and social costs and benefits and to align corporate goals with those of society. CSR requires business organizations to take initiatives to advance some social good beyond their own interests and compliance with applicable regulations. This chapter presents the social dimension of sustainability performance, reporting, and assurance with a keen focus on CSR in Asia.

2. INTRODUCTION

CSR is an ethical or ideological issue that suggests that entities, regardless of types or size, have a responsibility to protect the society in which they operate and that such responsibility varies across countries and is influenced significantly by a culture's socio-economic attributes. Social performance reflects how well an entity has translated its social goals into practice and is measured through the principles, actions, and corrective initiatives implemented. Social performance, or the social bottom line, is about making an organization's social mission a reality and aligning it with the interests of society by including accepted social values and fulfilling social responsibility. A professional and socially-driven organizations providing regulations or standards for disclosures on social responsibility will enhance the transparency, accuracy and usefulness of such reports. This chapter presents the social dimension of sustainability performance reporting and assurance in general and its implications in Asia.

3. SOCIAL PERFORMANCE DIMENSION OF SUSTAINABILITY

CSR has emerged as an important area of challenges and opportunities for corporations worldwide. Corporations are facing challenges of how to respond to CSR issues and the perceived pressure of localization and globalization in determining their CSR policies and procedures. Employee-related CSR initiatives are intended to address social, political, and economic opportunities for existing and potential employees, contract workers, society, and other stakeholders. These initiatives range from empowering employee participation in making strategic decisions to improving employee benefits, wages and work conditions, giving a voice to customer satisfaction to being a good citizen. These initiatives include addressing specific issues of diversity in terms of female participation, ethnic makeup or linguistic capabilities among others. Product- and marketing-related CSR initiatives and activities are gaining considerable attention from customers, suppliers, manufacturers, government and society. Consumer-driven CSR includes producing products and delivering services that are not detrimental to society, product and process innovations, environmental issues, promotions, advertising and distribution policies and practices.

Social performance measures how well a company has translated its social goals into practice. Social performance is about making the company's social mission a reality and aligning it with the interests of society. Variables in the social area are associated with the existence of corporate policies that are mainly community service-related or geared toward improving social conditions. Social measure strengths include (1) charitable giving (2) innovative giving (3) support for housing (4) support for education (5) other community strengths (6) promotion of minorities (7) diversity of board of directors (8) work/life benefits (9) women and minority contracting (10) employment of the disabled (11) gay and lesbian policies and (12) other diversity strength. Concerns include (1) investment controversies (2) negative economic impact (3) tax disputes (4) other community concerns (5) diversity controversies (6) minority non-representation and (7) other diversity concerns.

Business organizations typically strive to promote social responsibility among all their stakeholders. They focus their efforts towards building and maintaining a diverse community of extremely engaged employees and establishing a good relationship with vendors and contractors. Businesses often offer global philanthropic activities in the US and in other countries, particularly in those communities where the company has affiliate operations. Business organizations can contribute to their communities by engaging in social and philanthropic activities, such as the World Food Program, which formed a school feeding program, and other community involvement.

International Organization for Standardization (ISO) 26000 covers a broad range of organizational activities from economic to social, governance, ethical and environmental issues.[1] ISO 26000 is a globally accepted guidance document for social responsibility that assists organizations worldwide in fulfilling their CSR goals (ISO, 2010). Social responsibility performance promoted in ISO 26000 is conceptually and practically associated with achieving sustainable performance because the fulfillment of social responsibility necessitates and ensures sustainability development. ISO 26000 goes beyond profit-maximization by presenting a framework for organizations to contribute to sustainable development and the welfare of society. The core subject areas of ISO 26000 take into account all aspects of the triple bottom line's (TBL) key financial and non-financial performance relevant to people, planet and profit. The following provisions of ISO 26000 are designed to help business organizations operate in a socially responsible manner by providing guidance on:

- Concepts, frameworks, terms and definitions pertaining to CSR.
- Background, trends, characteristics and best practices of socially responsible organizations.
- Principles, standards and best practices relevant to CSR.
- Policies, procedures and best practices for integrating, implementing and promoting CSR.

- Engagement of all stakeholders including shareholders in socially responsible activities.
- Disclosure of information and non-financial Key Performance Indicators (KPIs) related to social responsibility.

Social performance and responsibilities are obligations to respond effectively to societal and stakeholder concerns by integrating social considerations into business strategic decisions, activities and operations through voluntary initiatives that go above and beyond regulatory requirements and philanthropic activities. Many factors have encouraged companies to engage in CSR activities including consumer activism, corporate malfeasance and improper corporate behavior and actions (Enron, WorldCom, Parmalat) and socially responsible investing (SRI).

Social performance involves three components (1) the identification of the domains of an organization's social responsibility (2) the development of processes to evaluate stakeholder demands and (3) the implementation of programs to manage social issues.[2]

An organization's social responsibility can be classified into four categories namely economic, legal, ethical and discretionary responsibilities.[3]

- **Economic responsibilities**—Entities of all types and sizes must produce goods and services that society needs and wants which are safe and not detrimental to society. The business of corporations is to achieve economic performance in making reasonable profit for shareholders and unless businesses fulfill their economic function, they will neither have the resources to perform other roles nor will survive long enough to be an agent for any forms of societal change.
- **Legal responsibilities**—Society grants business entities the right to pursue their economic goals of creating shareholder value but explicitly requires companies to fulfill these goals within the framework of legal system and compliance with regulations and requirements.
- **Ethical responsibilities**—Society also has expectations for business entities over and above legal requirements. Ethical responsibilities require corporations to engage in ethical business practices in a manner consistent with societal values in such matters as fair employment ethical work place and the environmental impact of production.
- **Discretionary responsibilities**—Socially desirable actions taken by business entities that are beyond their economic, legal, and ethical obligations. Corporations have discretion over the type, timing and extent of their involvement in discretionary social performance, which may include activities such as responses to natural disasters philanthropy and community leadership.

Organizations can no longer isolate their operations from the wider society and the environment in which they operate and thus they should effectively measure their social and environmental impacts. Measuring social performance implies the evaluation of principles, actions, outputs, some elements of outcome, and corrective measures taken by companies in reflecting their social impacts.. Social activities include improving reputation, brand value, employee satisfaction, crisis management, environmental preservation, and philanthropic activities. Emphasizing the end results and their impact, social performance should include an analysis of the declared objectives of institutions, the effectiveness of their systems and services in meeting these objectives, related outputs (for example, reaching larger numbers of very poor households), and success in effecting positive changes in the lives of mankind.

Key Performance Indicators (KPIs) are quantifiable measurements that reflect the critical success factors and impacts of an organization and help them define and measure progress toward organizational goals. Appropriate KPIs must reflect the organization's goals, be recognized as key determinants of its success and be quantifiable (measurable). KPIs usually have long-term considerations. KPIs for social responsibility play a key role in evaluating short-term, medium and long-term social responsibility initiatives and achieving social impacts. Social activities can be measured through social contribution, strategic partners, community outreach and involvement and time spent volunteering. Proper measurement of the KPIs pertaining to social activities and responsibilities enables organizations to effectively report their social performance and fulfill their social responsibilities. Commonly used social KPIs include building responsible networks, reputation, employee, customer satisfaction diversity, supporting the community and social impact activities.

4. CORPORATE SOCIAL RESPONSIBILITY IN ASIA

4.1   Overview of CSR in Asia

CSR challenges vary based on how related parties are affected by CSR and how their interest is protected. Stakeholders in society expect businesses to act in a socially responsible manner and require businesses to respond and ensure that social needs are met. From proper reporting and disclosure to the enforcement of rules and regulations, responsibility for a large percentage of the achievement of the goals lies on the government and other independent bodies. CSR continues to be viewed as a cost item. Its benefits are difficult to quantify in the short term and local companies are reluctant to engage in CSR activities as they perceive them as costly practices. According to Debroux (2006), "Delivering price-competitive manufacturing while sharing also the costs of CSR is hard to swallow for most Asian suppliers and smacks easily of large companies' hypocrisy or PR postures in their minds."[4]

Moreover, Asian companies lack the technical and financial ability to practice CSR and adhere to its environmental management and labor rules. Many Asian companies are small to medium-sized enterprises (SMEs) and they make up a significant proportion of the business enterprises in the ASEAN region that provide a source of employment for its people. There are also some conflicting concepts of what CSR entails. Some companies view CSR as mere compliance with the laws while others may see it as corporate philanthropy. There is a need for CSR policies and disclosures to identify CSR practices and make provisions to assist SMEs from different economic landscapes and levels to improve and achieve proper compliance within their financial and technical capability.[5] According to Sharma (2013) "The challenge for Asian business is to envision and redefine the CSR debate and action to meet its local realities rather than respond to the West's articulation of the CSR space."[6] The remainder of this section presents CSR in 12 jurisdictions in Asia.

4.2   Mainland China

4.2.1   Development of CSR in Mainland China   There are many unique features of CSR sustainability in Mainland China. There are different socio-political factors arising from the central and regional government directives that affect the implementation of CSR sustainability. The Chinese central government has played and will continue to play a dominant role in promoting CSR sustainability practices in Mainland China.[7]

This high level of government initiatives and interventions is intended to align the nationwide CSR sustainability programs with the country's development policy. The influence of the Chinese government in promoting CSR sustainability is exerted in a number of ways. First, the two mainland stock exchanges in Shanghai and Shenzhen are controlled by the Chinese Securities Regulatory Commission (CSRC), which has issued a series of CSR guidelines for its listed companies. Second, the Chinese Academy of Social Science (CASS), a government-affiliated research institute, ranks Chinese firms' CSR sustainability performance annually. CASS monitors the CSR implementation of Chinese firms and the Academy encourages competition among Chinese firms in promoting CSR sustainability. Third, a survey conducted by CSR-Asia and the embassy of Sweden in Beijing in 2015 indicates that the majority of respondents report that the key driver of CSR development in Mainland China is the government (76 percent), and the major incentive for implementing CSR sustainability is compliance with central government's policy (55 percent).[8]

The rising domestic pressure for socially responsive companies, rising CSR standards in foreign markets (especially North America and Europe), and the commitment of Mainland China's government to achieve eco-friendly and sustainable goals continue to support CSR. Released in March 2015, the Vision and Actions on Jointly Building the Silk Road Economic Belt and 21st-Century Maritime Silk Road stressed that Chinese enterprises should pay attention to "developing local economy, increasing local employment opportunities, and improving local living conditions to fulfill CSR and protect local species diversity and ecological environment." In May 2017, to highlight the concept of ecological progress, promote green development, strengthen eco-environmental protection, and jointly build the green Silk Road, the Ministry of Environmental Protection (MEP) issued the Belt and Road Ecological and Environmental Cooperation Plan, which proposed to promote the achievement of environmental goals in the Agenda for Sustainable Development by 2030.[9]

Listed companies in Mainland China are encouraged to report their business sustainability, including CSR activities. In December 2008, the Shanghai and Shenzhen Stock Exchanges required a subset of Chinese listed firms to issue sustainability/CSR reports.[10] The Rankins Ratings (RKS) is an independent rating agency which has ranked and reported on the CSR activities of Chinese listed companies since 2009 in the three broad categories of "macrocosm, content, and techniques."[11] The agency reports that more firms in Mainland China will disclose, in addition to corporate governance, their overall sustainability strategies, activities and performance. The move toward sustainability performance reporting and assurance in Mainland China is expected to improve the content, depth, coverage, and consistency of sustainability reporting.

Several social issues also emerged in Mainland China in recent years. For example, the decrease in birth rates has accelerated the aging of the population with the ratio of the number of people above 60 to total population having increased to around 17 percent. This poses problems to a host of financial and social programs as well as the health care and pension systems. Other social issues include concerns about unfavorable labor rights and working conditions. Mainland China's recent urbanization policy, which aims to transition to a more productive service-based economy, resulted in a large wave of migration from rural to urban areas. This creates social issues such as inequality in access to public services, which is limited by *Hukou*, and potential mental health problems of new migrants and their families.

4.2.2   Consumer Rights   Food safety is one of the most common ethical concerns in Mainland China. In 2008, China's Ministry of Health reported that more than 300,000 children were affected by the San Lu milk formula, which was reported to contain melamine, a chemical that can cause renal failure. In 2015 alone, there were reports of fake rice made with plastic, fake duck blood, gutter oil and many food poisoning scandals that caused public concern over food safety. As a result, the government has been making efforts to protect consumers' rights. The Decision on Amending the PRC Law on the Protection of Consumer Rights and Interests was adopted at the 5th Session of the Standing Committee of the Twelfth National People's Congress (NPC) on October 25, 2013 and released to take effect on March 15, 2014. On April 24, 2015, the NPC passed significant revisions to the Food Safety Law that have the potential to strengthen the regulation of food production companies in Mainland China and enhance monitoring of their supply chain.

4.2.3   Labor Conditions   In Mainland China, protection of workers is regulated under the national labor law but the actual practice of labor protection is not always in line with international standards. There have been concerns over the treatment of migrant workers including issues like the minimum wage, overtime pay, working hours, and health and safety. In 2016, there were 218.7 million migrant workers, who make up around 35 percent of Mainland China's total workforce of about 807 million.[12] The number of short-distance migrants has increased by 3.4 percent in 2016 to reach 112 million while the number of long-distance migrants has increased only by 0.3 percent to reach 169 million.[13]

Migrant workers have played an important role in Mainland China's spectacular economic growth over the last 30 years. However, they have a weak educational background and their labor rights have not been well protected. Until 2016, most migrant workers are employed in low-paid jobs in the manufacturing, construction, and service industries. The average monthly wage in 2016 was 3,275 RMB (around US$458), which was increased by 6.6 percent from the previous year. A monthly salary of about 3,000 RMB (around US$420) is far below the normal living standard in Mainland China.[14]

Moreover, in 2016, about 85 percent of migrant workers were working in excess of 40 hours a week according to the China Labor Bulletin. Although the 2008 Labor Contract Law mandated that employers must sign formal employment contracts with employees, the law was not widely implemented. In 2016, only 35 percent of migrant workers had contracts that complied with the Labor Contract Law, which suggests that the enforcement of labor laws is not rigid, particularly in smaller cities. There were 2.37 million migrant workers suffering from wage arrears in 2016, a decrease of 14 percent (and an improvement) when compared with the previous year according to the National Bureau of Statistics of China (NBS) survey.[15] Since December 15, 2017, the Guangdong government in South China has initiated a three-month long action to crack down on unpaid wages. Local police in the Guangdong Province have helped migrant workers claim back over 61.92 million RMB (US$9.7 million) in unpaid wages over a 40-day period.[16]

4.3 Hong Kong

4.3.1 Development of CSR in Hong Kong In 2015, the Hong Kong Stock Exchange (HKSE) issued the Environmental, Social and Governance (ESG) Reporting Guide, which requires listed companies to disclose CSR on a comply-or-explain basis effective for financial years ending on or after December 31, 2015. The Guide identifies general disclosure and key performance indicators on four ESG sustainability areas: Workplace Quality, Environment Protection, Operating Practices and Community Involvement, in addition to Corporate Governance, which was covered by the Main Board Listing Rules in an earlier code issued in 2005. The Exchange allows the company to specify the subject areas, aspects, and indicators that are relevant and material in the context of its corporate strategy. In April 2014, the Hong Kong Institute of Certified Public Accountants (HKICPA) issued A Guide on Better Governance Disclosure.

The argument put forward against the upgrade of ESG reporting requirements in Hong Kong is that it would increase reporting costs and impose a greater administrative burden on the issuers, particularly SMEs. The advantages of ESG reporting for SMEs (for instance, cost savings) may not be as compelling, especially when weighed against the resources required to develop the data collection/analysis systems and to hire suitable personnel for the reporting process.[17] Furthermore, SMEs generally do not appeal to institutional investors in financing their projects and they do not find ESG reporting will enhance their share value and lead to higher levels of investment. Another concern is the limited pool of personnel who are qualified and capable of guiding companies through the ESG reporting process.[18] There are different beliefs that the drive for adoption is based on internal pressures from individuals who believe the institution should be held environmentally accountable, and those responsible for the corporate governance of institutions who see environmental disclosure as a process allowing their institutions to gain legitimacy.[19]

4.3.2 The Aging Society Hong Kong is facing a declining labor force, shrinking family size, and rising elderly dependency ratio. The *Hong Kong Population Projections 2015-2064*[20] estimates that the number of Hong Kong elderly (age 65 or above) will increase to 2.58 million by 2064, which is about 35.9 percent of the population. The labor force, those aged between 15 and 64, is projected to decline to 3.92 million, around 54.6 percent of the population. The average family size is forecast to decrease from 3.9 people in 1981 to 2.8 in 2024.[21]

Based on the latest government statistics, the number of elderly aged 80 or above rose by 67 percent to more than 340,000, representing a bigger proportion when compared with data from the last decade. A mid-2016 study from the Census and Statistics Department found that 15.9 percent of the Hong Kong population (7.4 million), were aged 65 or above, compared with 12.4 percent in 2006. The statistics indicate that the pace of the aging society has become faster in the past decade.[22]

4.3.3 Labor The labor force statistics revealed that from February to April 2018, the seasonally adjusted unemployment rate was around 2.8 percent, which was

0.1 percentage point lower than that from January to March 2018. Hong Kong's unemployment rate (February to April 2018) reached a 20-year record low since 1998.[23]

The statutory minimum wage (SMW) in Hong Kong came into effect on May 1, 2011. The first SMW rate was set by the Minimum Wage Ordinance at HK$28 (around US$3.64) an hour. The minimum wage would be reviewed every two years.[24] From May 1, 2017, the SMW rate has increased from HK$32.5 (around US$4.23) to HK$34.5 (around US$4.49) an hour, which is lower than the cost of a McDonald's meal. At the same time, the monetary cap on the total number of working hours has been adjusted from HK$13,300 (around US$1,729) a month to HK$14,100 (around US$1,833) per month.[25] The Hong Kong Federation of Trade Unions (HKFTU) was established in 1948. It has a total of 251 subsidiary unions and is the largest labor union in Hong Kong with more than 410,000 members as of December 2016. The HKFTU is committed to resolving labor, social, and political conflicts, fighting for labor rights, and safeguarding welfare services for its members and Hong Kong residents. The HKFTU protects the interests of grassroots workers as well as white-collar clerical staff by offering value-added continuing education courses and medical services.[26]

4.3.4 Discrimination   A recent research study showed that six out of 10 of the Chinese residents in Hong Kong discriminate against ethnic minorities. Discrimination is not uncommon in Hong Kong.[27] Apart from ethnic discrimination, there is gender inequality. In the Hong Kong Legislative Council, there are only 11 women out of 60 legislative members. The judiciary is also male-dominated with all 21 judges of the Court of Final Appeal being men. Within Hong Kong's top business firms, women hold only 8.9 percent of directorships. Based on Community Business research in 2009, women account for 7 percent of executive positions. Women also earn less than men on average according to recent government statistics.[28]

According to a Human Rights Watch report, 2018 would be the "year of the courts" for lesbian, gay, bisexual and transgender (LGBT) people's rights. Judges from all over the world with diverse legal traditions agree that LGBT people should be legally entitled to equal treatment, dignity, and fairness. Recently, the Hong Kong Immigration Department refused to grant a dependent visa to the same-sex spouse of a British and South African national who is working in Hong Kong on a work visa. In July 2018, the Court of Final Appeal of the HKSAR ruled that the government can turn down such a visa only if it could offer "particularly convincing and weighty reasons" to justify the difference in treatment between same-sex and different-sex spouses. The Hong Kong government did not meet this standard and the court ruled that the same-sex spouse was discriminated against because of her sexual orientation.[29]

4.4 India

India is home to 17.7 percent of the world's population. In 2017, the population of India was 1,353 million, spread across 3.3 million square kilometers of the country, ranking India as the second-most-populated nation in the world.[30] Since the 2000s, rapid economic growth, a rise in rural wages, greater rural–urban integration, and an increase in non-farm activity in India have lifted millions of residents out of poverty. Despite that, around 25 percent of the population continues to live under the poverty line.[31] Illiteracy is another major social problem with lack of access to quality education. About a fifth of the country's population, 266 million Indians aged 15 years and older, are illiterate according to the latest data from the United Nations Educational, Scientific and Cultural Organization (UNESCO).[32]

4.4.1 Development of CSR in India   India has a long tradition of paternalistic philanthropy. One of the major historical drivers of philanthropy were the charities who built temples, infrastructure and shelters for pilgrims or people in need. Businessmen also invested in education as well as providing dowries for poor girls.[33] During the pre-industrialized period, philanthropy, religion and charity were the main drivers of CSR in India. The newly-rich family-owned enterprises established endowments for temples, schools, colleges and public infrastructure such as museums, art galleries and hospitals.[34]

Awareness of business sustainable growth accompanied by social progress has initiated a progression from charitable philanthropy toward direct engagement by businesses in CSR initiatives.[35] In the late-nineteenth century, Mohandas Karamchand Gandhi introduced the concept of "trusteeship," whereby owners of capital willingly managed their wealth to benefit society. In the early-twentieth century, the Tata Group established social welfare provisions, labor compensation standards, and gratuity and pension funds for workers. Today, large Indian business industrialists like Ghanshyam Das Birla, Jamnalal Bajaj, Lala Shri Ram, and Ambalal Sarabhai have followed in the footsteps of Jamshedji Nusserwanji Tata (the founder of the Tata Group) by establishing educational institutions, supporting cultural developments as well as contributing to the freedom struggle and nationalist movement.[36] The 2013 Companies Act requires that Indian companies with an annual turnover of more than 1,000 Crore INR (around US $ 150 million), a net worth of more than 500 Crore INR (around US $ 75 million), or a net profit of more than five Crore INR (around US $ 0.75 million) in a financial year should spend 2 percent of their net profits on CSR programs. The Act also requires Indian companies to form CSR committees consisting of corporate board members with at least one independent director to handle CSR affairs.

4.4.2 Child Labor   Elimination of child labor is an area of high priority for the Indian government due to extreme poverty and illiteracy in India. Many families cannot afford to send their children to school and these children work to help their families. Companies exploit the social economic conditions of the unorganized, not well-educated, unskilled or semi-skilled workers and hire them at very low wages. Under-age children from poor families are employed under poor working environment in unfit and risky small-scale industries or factories.

The Child Labour Prohibition and Regulation Act and the Factories Act restrict working ages, hours, and conditions for workers in India. In 2012, the State of Rajasthan passed legislation establishing a legal minimum working age of 18 years. However, many children continued to be engaged in the workforce. According to the Census in 2011, 10.1 million (around four percent of the total child population) are working as a "main worker" or "marginal worker" in India. Although the number decreased by 2.6 million between 2001 and 2011, the number of child workers has increased in urban areas with a growing demand for child workers in menial jobs.[37] In 2014, there was a positive sign in the decrease in the number of child laborers by 65 percent between the Census of 2001 and 2011.[38]

4.4.3 Working Conditions   The total workforce in India increased from 459 million in 2010 to 472.9 million in 2012 with the increase mostly in urban areas.

As a labor surplus country, India does not have a uniform wage policy for all sectors or progressive labor laws. Most Indian employees earn a living in the growing informal sector, which does not have regulated working conditions and social security. More than 90 percent of Indian workers work in an unorganized sector. Those workers suffer from cycles of excessive seasonality of employment, and lack a formal employer–employee relationship and social security protection.[39]

An analysis of Business Responsibility Reports (BRR) of the top 100 companies for 2015–2016 shows that only five have reported that they have no contractual workers (State Bank of India, Yes Bank, Bajaj Finserv, DLF Limited and Shriram Transport and Finance) and 22 companies did not report any details. The BRR reports also revealed that only six companies have publicly stated their commitment to and detailed their systems of human rights related to freedom of association. The absence of bargaining power of workers is one factor that contributes to income disparity in India as well as inadequate accountability to workers by businesses.[40]

4.4.4 Gender Inequality   Discrimination affects minority groups such as indigenous peoples, migrants and members of scheduled castes in India. Gender discrimination is often found in male-dominated, lower-paid industries.[41] India's preference for sons over daughters has led to the birth of around 21 million girls who are "unwanted" according to the Economic Survey 2017–18 by the government. India has one of the most skewed sex ratios in the world. For every 107 males born in India, there are 100 females, while the natural sex ratio at birth is 105 males for every 100 females, according to the World Health Organization. In addition, India ranked in the bottom third for education of women and girls according to a 2017 World Economic Forum report.[42]

During the period from 2010 to 2012, male employment grew by 1.9 percent while female employment increased by only 0.3 percent. A sizable gender gap persists with the labor force participation rate of women decreasing from 42.7 percent in 2004–2005 to 31.2 in 2011–2012.[43] Based on Census 2011, the total number of female workers in India is 149.8 million. The participation rate of women in the workplace remains low, dropping from 35 percent in 1991 to 23.7 percent in 2015–2016. A study by Bombay Stock Exchange (BSE) shows that no company has more than 50 percent female workforce. While 57 percent of companies have employed women, they form less than 10 percent of the workforce.[44]

4.5   Indonesia

4.5.1 Development of CSR in Indonesia   CSR is a relatively new concept in Indonesia, although transnational corporations (TNCs) have existed for many years. In Indonesia's early business history, the prototype of TNC was the colonial trading company, who had negligible CSR practices. Power and wealth are concentrated in the large conglomerates, which operate similar to state-owned enterprises (SOEs). Throughout the years, many SOEs have been transformed to limited companies with a certain level of flexibility akin to private companies. Multinational companies (MNCs) and foreign direct investments (FDI) have strict requirements for local

Indonesian companies to practice CSR in line with global standards with respect to accountability and transparency.

4.5.2 Inequality   For the past 20 years, the gap between rich and poor has risen significantly in Indonesia. The Gini coefficient and the Palma index for consumption report that the scores in urban areas are higher than those in rural areas. In 2016, the richest 1 percent of the population had around 49 percent of the total wealth. The wealthiest 10 percent of the Indonesians in urban areas earn more than one-third of total income, which implies that inequality is highly associated with the growth of urbanization in Indonesia.[45]

Family relations in Indonesia are determined by religion as well as civil, informal customary, and Sharia (Islamic) law. Females within the Muslim religion are allowed to marry and divorce only under the Islamic law.[46] The Law of Child Protection[47] recommends that the legal age for marriage is 18 years. However, the legal marriage ages for females and males are 16 years and 19 years under the civil Marriage Law.[48] According to the World Economic Forum's Gender Gap Index, Indonesia ranked 88th out of 144 countries with a score of 0.682 (0 = imparity, 1 = parity).[49] The 2014 Organization of Economic Co-operation and Development's (OECD) Social Institutions and Gender Index marked Indonesia at "medium" level.[50] Indonesia ranks low on gender equality in economic participation and opportunity (107th out of 144).[51]

4.6   Japan

The Tokyo Foundation launched a CSR research project in 2013 to investigate the prospects of CSR in Japan by surveying around 2,000 Japanese companies. Based on the survey, the Tokyo Foundation classified the CSR issues to include human rights, poverty and hunger, child mortality, women's advancement and environmental sustainability, among others. Ninety-six percent of the surveyed companies have engaged in environmental initiatives such as efforts to protect biodiversity and to counter pollution and climate change. Other categories with high responses were cultural preservation, improvement of maternal health, human rights, and women's advancement. Over half of the responding companies had been undertaking initiatives to address the issues in these areas. Relatively few of the responding companies reported activities in the area of disease and illness prevention, accidents, suicides and other common causes of death for each age group. Despite the fact that the relative poverty rate has been on the rise in Japan, there is little attention to the areas of eliminating child poverty or eradicating poverty and hunger. The survey shows that overall, Japanese firms are well aware of CSR issues and have participated actively in CSR initiatives.

Initiatives from the government, the financial regulator, and the stock exchange in Japan have contributed to the increased adoption of Integrated Reporting in the country. In 2003, Keizai Doyukai, the Japan Association of Corporate Executives, published its 15th Corporate White Paper, titled *Market Evolution and Socially Responsible Management: Toward Building Integrity and Creating Stakeholder Value*. Keizai Doyukai regarded CSR and corporate governance as the most important elements for companies to build trust and create sustainable stakeholder value. In 2004, Nippon Keidanren revised the Charter of Corporate Behavior.

The revised charter put greater emphasis on CSR. Also, concepts like "human rights," "communication with the stakeholders," and "supply chain management" were introduced in the revised charter. In the same year, Keizai Doyukai published the findings of a survey on CSR and corporate governance in Japan. It concluded that Japanese companies need to build compliance systems with more effective control mechanisms to ensure sustained CSR and good corporate governance.[52]

In 2014, the Japanese Ministry of Economy, Trade and Industry (METI) produced a report on competitiveness and incentives for sustainable growth (known as the Ito Review). This report, among other recommendations, promoted two-way dialogue between companies and investors on the topic of sustainable growth. Integrated Reporting has become a useful tool for such dialogue. Also in 2014, the Japanese Financial Services Agency (FSA), the authority responsible for ensuring the stability of the Japanese financial system, published a Stewardship Code for institutional investors that reminds investors of their fiduciary duty and promotes sustainable growth within the Japanese economy. The code stipulates that investors should encourage their investee companies to practice Integrated Reporting. The following year, 2015, the Tokyo Stock Exchange published its Corporate Governance Code, which also encourages companies to adopt Integrated Reporting. Leading Japanese companies have set a trend for investing in assurance of corporate responsibility data in recent years and their example has encouraged others to follow.

4.7   South Korea

Although South Korea is a democratic country, the society has severe social issues in the areas of human rights, political liberties, discrimination and labor conditions. The South Korean government imposes restrictions on freedom of assembly, association, and expression. The National Security Law restricts residents' freedom on establishing and participating in political associations. Anyone who takes part (or induces others to) in an "anti-government organization" may face criminal penalties. However, the term "anti-government organization" is not precisely defined in law. The law also criminalizes any North Korean "propaganda" activities and positive comments.[53]

Discrimination is another social issue in South Korea. In February 2017, the Seoul Education Ministry officials announced that the nation's new sex education curriculum would exclude topics about homosexuality. The new policy was in line with a 2015 plan that the topic of sexual minorities be excluded from sex education guidelines for district education officials.[54] Therefore, discrimination against women remains a major problem. Recently, gender equality in South Korea was ranked 118th out of 144 countries by the World Economic Forum (2017). The #MeToo movement in 2017 involved South Korean women requesting government action on sexual harassment.[55] The glass ceiling is another discrimination issue in South Korea as evidenced by the fact that the number of female employees is far below the average of developed countries. In 2017, the Korea Economic Research Institute (KERI) reported that among the nation's top 600 companies, women accounted for only around 24 percent while the total workforce participation in business sector was 1.13 million.[56] According to an OECD report (2018), the gender wage gap in South Korea is the highest among OECD member countries.[57]

South Korean labor market conditions have become worse in recent years. Job growth has been decreasing since February 2018. The youth unemployment rate was 10.5 percent in May 2018, marking the highest May number since 1999. The statistics showed that 1,121,000 people were unemployed in May 2018, up 126,000 from 2017. The overall unemployment rate increased 0.4 percentage points over the year to 4 percent in May 2018, which is the highest number in about 18 years. The current president, Moon Jae-In, stated that job creation would be his top priority. The government had a supplementary budget plan of 3.9 trillion won (around US$3.7 billion) to create 50,000 jobs for youths in 2018, and to help laid-off workers in southern regions where shipbuilders and automakers are experiencing a restructuring process.[58] A recent OECD employment outlook (2018) finds that there is a large age gap between regular and non-regular workers in South Korea. The productivity gap between large firms and SMEs is also large.[59]

4.8 Malaysia

4.8.1 Human Rights The Malaysian government has attempted to suppress the voice of the people and limit freedom of speech, as reported by a Human Rights Watch report of 2018.[60] Malaysia's Communications and Multimedia Act (CMA 1998) gives the government authority to investigate and arrest those who criticize the government through social media. For example, a blogger who posted a picture of Prime Minister Najib Razak behind bars violated Section 233(1), which states that criminal penalties can be imposed including up to one year in prison for a communication that "is obscene, indecent, false, menacing, or offensive in character with intent to annoy, abuse, threaten, or harass another person."

4.8.2 Employment Work place discrimination is another social issue experienced by both local and foreign workers in Malaysia. The workers in Malaysia assembled in May 2018 to protest for better salaries, upward review of the minimum wage, better working benefits, affordable housing, and the application of goods and services tax (GST) on luxury goods only. They urged the authorities through the media to create awareness of the rights of workers and to enact policies such that the needs of workers are met.[61] In 2018, hundreds of local and foreign workers gathered in front of Wisma Malaysia Trades Union Congress (MTUC) where the MTUC Labor Day celebrations were held and called for better salaries and an end to labor force discrimination. These workers also participated in a short parade holding placards with slogans to urge authorities to meet their demands.[62]

Other social issues include inadequate laws to protect refugees and asylum seekers, who are harbored in poor living conditions without access to basic necessities, government restrictions on freedom of religion and freedom of speech, election fraud and lack of transparency.

4.9 The Philippines

The Philippines has been a fertile country for corporations and multinational companies seeking to outsource manufacturing and other business processes due to the large English-speaking work force. Recently, some foreign companies signed temporary contracts with employees to avoid providing them with full employment benefits. Likewise, the state regulatory and enforcement agencies do not have adequate safeguards for the mining industry and its workers.

The Human Rights Watch *World Report* (2018) claims that the Philippines has entered the worst human rights crisis since President Duterte took office in June 2016, as evidenced by several aspects including violation of children's rights.[63] A Philippines children's rights organization released information about 56 children being killed by the police since the "drug war" in July 2017. The children were killed while they were accompanied by adults who were the target of the shooting. Both President Duterte and Justice Secretary Vitaliano Aguirre II have dismissed the children's killings as "collateral damage." In August 2017, the government passed mandatory drug testing for high school and college students, which allows the police to extend the abusive anti-drug operations on campuses.[64]

In 2016, Human Rights Watch reported discrimination and abuses against lesbian, gay, bisexual and transgender (LGBT) students in secondary schools including bullying, harassment and discriminatory policies and practices. There is a lack of education on sexual orientation and harassment under international law that puts LGBT youth at risk. In September 2017, the House of Representatives passed House Bill 4982, a proposed law against discrimination based on sexual orientation and gender identity and expression (SOGIE).[65]

The Department of Labor and Employment (DOLE) is the primary administrative entity of the Executive Branch of the government, and is responsible for policy-making, programming, and coordinating labor and employment issues. The DOLE contributes to employment opportunities, the development of the nation's manpower resources, workers' welfare and protection of working conditions.[66] Health Justice Philippines is a non-governmental organization (NGO) which helps to bridge the gap between public health and law. In a celebration of World No Tobacco Day, Health Justice Philippines, cooperating with Millennials Philippines (Millennials PH), launched the "LSS: Let's Stop Smoking" and "Health and Tobacco Summit" projects at the University of Cordilleras. These projects raise awareness of the harm of tobacco, encourage students to adopt healthy habits and help local governments to enforce smoke-free ordinances.[67] Established by the Philippine Constitution, the Commission on Human Rights (CHR) is an independent National Human Rights Institution (NHRI). The CHR is responsible for investigating violations of human, civil, and political rights.[68]

4.10   Singapore

4.10.1   Development of CSR in Singapore   Although CSR is still a relatively new concept in Singapore, the spirit of CSR has been reflected in the practice of Singaporean companies for a long time. In the 19th and early-20th centuries, with the emergence of large numbers of Asian immigrants from Mainland China and India, and indigenous Malays, many SMEs had developed with close ties with its ethnic communities. Influenced by the Asian values that focus on family, business operators have been contributing to tribal associations and communities, including providing scholarships, grants, and other funds for community development projects.

In recent years, the government of Singapore has established organizations dedicated to the promotion of CSR and has encouraged increased media attention to CSR issues. Modernization of the implementation of CSR can be traced back to 2003, when the Consumer Protection (Fair Trade) Act was proposed as a platform for companies to explore and improve their CSR activities. In August 2003, the Faculty of Law of the National University of Singapore organized a seminar titled "Business Excellence: The Emerging Role of Corporate Social Responsibility," whereby a comprehensive concept of CSR for a fair-trade environment was introduced as a more advanced idea of social responsibility. The CSR Centre was established in April 2001 as the first NGO in Singapore to focus on CSR research and development. It adopts CSR as a holistic concept involving multiple stakeholders, issues, and approaches. With the growing attention to social responsibility in Singapore, the National Social Responsibility Tripartite Initiative was established in May 2004 involving representatives from industry, trade unions and government.[69]

In 2005, the CSR Compact was launched in Singapore. In June 2015, the Compact was renamed the Singapore Global Compact Network, as it became the official network of the United Nations Global Compact (UNGC), a global initiative that began 15 years ago to promote business practices based on the principles of sustainability, including safeguarding human and labor rights, protecting the environment and combating corruption. Since the inception of the initiative, much progress has been made in CSR in Singapore, with the support of many Tripartite leaders.[70]

4.10.2 Human Rights The Singaporean government imposes draconian constraints on the right of public gathering under the Public Order Act, which was amended in 2017 to tighten the restrictions. Police authorization is required if the assembly is held in a public area or if members of the general public are invited. Speakers' Corner at Hong Lim Park is the only place where citizens or permanent residents may join in assemblies without a police permit. According to the opinion of Human Rights Watch, those laws and regulations impose severe restrictions on the rights of freedom of speech in Singapore. Prime Minister Lee sued Roy Ngerng, an active blogger, for defamation. Ngerng criticized the Singaporean government and its policies and inequalities in relation to the government's handling of the Central Provident Fund (mandatory pension fund). Ngerng was fired from his job and had to pay the Prime Minister S$100,000 (around US$72,000) in general damages, S$50,000 (around US$36,000) in aggravated damages, and S$29,000 (around US$20,880) in legal costs.[71]

Lesbian, gay, bisexual, and transgender (LGBT) rights are also strictly restricted. There are no laws to protect gender identity and sexual orientation discrimination. Sexual relation between two male persons is unlawful and even positive depictions of LGBT programs are forbidden under the Media Development Authority. In June 2017, the Advertising Standards Agency required a shopping mall to remove a reference to "Supporting the Freedom to Love" from an advertisement at the annual Pink Dot festival. In November 2017, the "T Project," which supports the transgender community, was not allowed to be registered as a not-for-profit entity since the group allegedly stands against national security or interests.[72]

4.10.3 Employment and Labor The Employment Act and other labor laws do not protect foreign and domestic workers in relation to working hours limitations and minimum wages. The labor law prohibits foreign laborers from forming and registering a union or serving as union leaders. Migrant domestic workers in Singapore are permitted to work for a particular employer only, which makes them vulnerable to exploitation.[73] According to a 2018 CNN report, there is a large wage gap between migrant domestic workers (from India and Bangladesh) and Singapore residents' average salaries. The basic monthly wage for migrant domestic workers is US$400–465 while the average monthly wage of a Singaporean is around US$3,077.[74]

Singapore's construction industry is an important part of the economy and it relies on a large foreign labor force. According to the Ministry of Manpower (MOM) of Singapore,[75] Singapore had around 296,700 migrant construction laborers from Mainland China, Myanmar, India and Bangladesh as of June 2017. The Singapore MOM is dedicated to developing a great workforce and workplace by maintaining a manpower-lean and competitive economy. The MOM complements the local workforce with a skilled foreign workforce, enables job opportunities for migrant workers, and enhances working conditions for vulnerable workers.[76] In 2016, the MOM received about 9,000 wage claims including around 4,500 from local and migrant workers. Ninety-five percent of those claims were solved through mediation or the Labor Court. Around 158 employers had been prosecuted and convicted over the past three years for unsettled salaries.[77] In Singapore, Transient Workers Count Too (TWC2) is a non-profit organization operated by migrant rights organizations. TWC2 is committed to enhancing labor conditions for low-wage migrant workers. There are approximately 1 million migrant workers out a 5 million population in Singapore.[78] In TWC2's drop-in center, there are more than five hundred migrant workers every night who are seeking help to claim unpaid salaries or seeking jobs.[79]

4.11 Taiwan

4.11.1 Development of CSR in Taiwan
The prospects for CSR in Taiwan have been promising. The Taiwan government has been the main driving force for the development of CSR. The government has strengthened the refinement and implementation of relevant legislations, while business, non-governmental organizations, and industry associations have been cooperating with each other in all areas of CSR. International trade between major suppliers, large companies, and SMEs, as well as foreign companies, has played an important role in promoting CSR development. Environmental protection, labor rights, and consumer safety have been the most pressing issues facing Taiwanese businesses. Promoting corporate transparency, combating corruption, and enhancing business ethics were identified as key priorities on the CSR agenda. Companies have focused on assessing and implementing their CSR strategies and implementing CSR through better planning and action. In addition, support from the corporate board of directors and the distribution of CSR functions by senior managers can be seen as an important factor in achieving a long-term and effective CSR strategy.[80]

4.11.2 Human Rights
According to Taiwan's 2016–2017 human rights report, the most significant human rights concerns included official corruption and exploitation of foreign workers, forced labor and domestic violence. Other human rights issues were illegal canvassing, violation of statutory working hours, gender discrimination and an increase in child abuse.[81,82]

The Taiwan Association for Human Rights is a Taiwanese civil independent non-governmental organization established on International Human Rights Day,

December 10, 1984. It aims at publicizing and improving human rights in Taiwan in various ways.[83] The Taiwan government has also been supporting the promotion of human rights. The Ministry of the Interior is the governmental body which oversees human rights and social welfare issues. Some of its duties include the review and revision of regulations that are in conflict with the International Covenant on Civil and Political Rights and the International Covenant on Economic, Social, and Cultural Rights. The Ministry also promotes and implements the Refugee Act, which ensures the rights of refugees.[84]

4.11.3 Labor Conditions In 1984, the Taiwan government promulgated the Labor Standards Law, which provides basic legal definitions of specific employee/employer wage contracts, and outlines the rights and obligations between employees and employers, including protecting employees from unreasonable working hours and forced overwork. Despite these legal safeguards, there have been a growing number of allegations in recent years about Taiwan's "overwork culture". These allegations have been brought to the attention of Taiwan's Council of Labour Affairs. According to government data, Taiwanese employees work about 2,200 hours a year, which is 20 percent higher than the average in Japan and the United States, 30 percent more than in the United Kingdom and 50 percent more than in Germany. According to statistics, Taiwan is one of the regions with the longest working hours in the world.[85]

On January 1, 2016, to tackle the problem of excessive working hours, the government announced an amendment to the Labor Standards Law to limit the working week in Taiwan to 40 hours. The amendment reduces the previous maximum working time limit of 84 hours per fortnight to 40 hours per week and stipulates that employees should not work more than eight hours per day.[86] On January 31, 2018, the Labor Standards Law was once again refined and revised to better protect employees' physical and mental health.[87]

4.12 Thailand

4.12.1 Development of CSR in Thailand CSR in Thailand did not emerge until the late 1990s, when local companies had to adjust in response to global standards. Foreign Direct Investment (FDI) has brought foreign business standards to CSR practice in Thailand. In the 21st century, many multinational enterprises (MNEs) and their subsidiaries are required to implement CSR programs. However, a majority of local Thai companies have not adopted CSR in their business practices. In fact, many Thai companies claim that they host CSR programs, but they are not aware of the CSR concept and the related responsibilities.[88] CSR today in Thailand is implemented on different levels: from philanthropy to the development and practice of the UN sustainable development goals (SDG) in business strategy. SMEs represent around 90 percent of the businesses in Thailand; these perform well in traditional CSR contexts like philanthropy and charitable donations. Larger companies are increasingly aware that socially responsible investment (SRI) may strengthen companies' competitiveness in the long run. MNEs are contributing to the improvement in CSR standards in line with Western practice.[89]

4.12.2 Gender Inequality Gender inequality is a serious issue in Thailand which triggers other social vices such as violence, discrimination, and prostitution. Although the constitution of 1997 provides women with equal rights and protections, gender inequalities remain in society. Police and military schools do not accept female students. Sexual harassment in business organizations was made illegal in 1998. There is still a gap between the average wage of men and women and a significant number of women are working in lower-paying jobs.[90]

4.13 Vietnam

4.13.1 Development of CSR in Vietnam   In Vietnam, the World Bank's Strengthening Developing Country Governments CSR Program was introduced in 2003. In 2007, Vietnam became a member of the World Trade Organization (WTO), which was a milestone for globalization and implementation of CSR in Vietnam. Since then, CSR has been widely promoted by labor laws and union laws. In addition, the European Union and Vietnam Chamber of Commerce jointly supported the United Nations Industrial Development Organization's Adapt and Adopt CSR for Improved Linkages with Global Supply Chains in Sustainable Production to help SMEs in Vietnam.[91] In 2012, the Vietnamese government approved the Vietnam Sustainable Development Strategy for 2011–2020 in order to enhance environmental protection and economic growth.[92]

4.13.2 Human Rights   In Vietnam, independent human rights organizations or labor unions are not allowed. Public gathering or marching must be approved by the government. According to the Human Rights Watch 2017 report, the situation of human rights in Vietnam has become worse. In 2017, more than 20 people who engaged in speech critical of the government and in peaceful activism were charged with "national security" offenses.[93]

4.13.3 Working Conditions   In Vietnam, freedom of association, or collective bargaining, is not allowed. The state has strict labor restrictions. Working conditions have improved slightly in recent years, as Vietnam has a low percentage of poor labor conditions, with only 6.6 percent of labor in the garment sector paid less than the minimum wage. In the Vietnamese garment sector, 7.9 percent of women earned less than minimum wage, while the figure for men was only 2.2 percent, which indicates a gender inequality problem.

4.13.4 Gender Inequality   Vietnam's economic model neglects the gender equality problem in the country, causing extreme economic inequality. The economic model is focused on economic growth, which makes it difficult for women to get quality work opportunities with fair wages and labor protection compared to their male counterparts. Research studying 67 developing countries reported that on average 20 percent of men do not allow women to work outside the home. Women work more than 18 hours a day or even overnight in the garment factories in Vietnam with salaries that are not sufficient to meet their immediate and familial needs.[94]

5.   BEST PRACTICES OF CSR

Several models and best practices of CSR have been presented for holding business organizations accountable for fulfilling their CSR. Stehi (1975) suggests a three-level model for corporate social performance which reflects business organizations' behavior to society: (1) a social liability as demanded by regulatory constraints and market mechanisms (2) a social responsibility beyond the legal and market requirement to benefit society and (3) social accountability to all stakeholders, including shareholders, employees, customers, creditors, suppliers, government, the environment and society.[95] Carroll (1999) develops a CSR conceptual model that consists of the four dimensions of economic, legal, moral and philanthropic responsibilities.[96] The first dimension is economic responsibility, which includes a commitment to the desired return on investment for shareholders and creditors, job opportunities and proper compensation for employees, exploration of new resources, promotion of technology and innovation and the production and offering of high-quality and safe services and products. The legal dimension of CSR responsibility includes compliance with all applicable laws, rules, regulations, policies and standards. The moral dimension of CSR represents engagement in social activities above and beyond legal requirements and personal benefits by maximizing social benefits and minimizing costs to society. The philanthropic dimension of CSR suggests that involvement in activities and programs that provide financial and non-financial assistance to the community tend to be less strategic than other forms of CSR involvement in terms of adding social and business value.

CSR best practices enable organizations minimize conflicts between corporations and society and to align corporate goals with those of society. Conflicts are caused by differences between private and social costs and benefits, examples of which are related to environmental issues (pollution, acid rain, green house gas emission, global warming), and labor issues such as wages paid by multinational corporations in poor countries and child labor in developing countries. Corporate governance measures, which include rules, regulations and best practices of CSR programs, can raise companies' awareness of the social costs and benefits of their business activities. These CSR models and best practices assist business organizations to develop their own CSR program to achieve and enhance their social performance. The Organization of Economic Co-operation and Development (OECD) defines the purpose of a CSR program as "to encourage the positive contributions that multinational enterprises can make to economics, environmental, and social progress and to minimize the difficulties to which their various operations may give rise."[97] This definition focuses on two important aspects of a CSR program, namely the creation of social value through corporate activities (social value-added activities) and the avoidance of conflicts between corporate goals and societal goals (societal consensus).

The primary concepts of CSR programs are:

1. CSR programs are important ingredients of business sustainability and companies must strive to make a footprint on CSR.
2. One of the most important investments a company can make is in CSR programs, encompassing its employees, investors, customers and communities.
3. Philanthropic programs are important in aiding those who are less fortunate, a common theme among companies with a global reach.

These CSR programs are not without costs and they should be viewed as corporate investments in employees, community customers, the environment and society which should generate long-term and sustainable financial performance. However, there are two differing views regarding the relationship between investing in CSR programs and firm financial performance.[98] The first view suggests that socially responsible behavior is costly due to increases in expenses but no increase in benefits. This suggests that any investment on CSR is the money taken away from investors with no impacts on the bottom line earnings. The second view indicates a positive association exists between CSR and firm performance because CSR programs and activities enhance employee morale and productivity, attract and enable retention of high-quality employees, generate a positive corporate image and reputation, enhance product evaluation via overall evaluation of the firm, and improve a firm's access to sources of capital.

Business organizations worldwide are now recognizing the importance of quality as it relates to CSR and the link between profitability and social behavior. Justifications for CSR are: moral obligation, maintaining a good reputation, ensuring sustainability, license to operate, and creating shared value. In a shared value approach, corporations identify potential social issues of concern and integrate them into their strategic planning. There are many reasons why a company should follow CSR, such as: pressure from the labor movement, the development of moral values and social standards, the development of business education, and the change in public opinion about the role of business. Companies which are, or aspire to be, leaders in CSR are challenged by rising public expectations, increasing innovation, continuous quality improvement, and heightened social and environmental problems. Companies should fulfill their social responsibility for reasons of: public image, consumer movements, government requirements, investor education, tax benefits, better relations with stakeholders, employee satisfaction, a sense of pride, and an appropriate way to improve quality.

Globalization creates incentives and opportunities for multinational corporations (MNCs) and their stakeholders and executives to influence the CSR initiatives and strategies of headquarters as well as those of subsidiaries. MNCs can choose from a variety of CSR initiatives in terms of scope, extent, and type of strategy, focusing on different issues, functions, areas, and stakeholders that vary across their subsidiaries. Given that MNCs are also constrained by scarce resources, they must be selective when deciding on the scope, extent, and type of CSR initiative. Subsidiaries' CSR initiatives typically have distinct "home country" characteristics. Nonetheless, global/local CSR initiatives often vary depending on the type of initiative and the CSR strategies being pursued. International Organization for Standardization (ISO) 26000 covers a broad range of organizational activity from economic to social, governance, ethics and environmental issues.[99] ISO 26000 is a globally accepted guidance document for social responsibility that assists organizations worldwide in fulfilling their CSR goals (ISO 2010). Social responsibility performance promoted in ISO 26000 is conceptually and practically associated with achieving sustainable performance because the fulfillment of social responsibility necessitates and ensures sustainability development. ISO 26000 goes beyond profit-maximization by presenting a framework for organizations to contribute to sustainable development and the welfare of society. The core subject areas of ISO 26000 consider all aspects of the triple bottom line's (TBL) key financial and non-financial performance relevant to people, planet, and profit.

The ISO 26000 standards are voluntary and aspirational rather than prescriptive, providing a framework for incorporating CSR issues into business and investment decision-making and ownership practices. Compliance with ISO 26000 standards is expected to lead not only to a more sustainable financial return, but also to a close alignment of the interests of businesses and investors with those of global society at large. Management should develop and maintain proper CSR programs that provide a common framework for the integration of CSR issues and activities that consist of:

- Integration of CSR issues into the business and investment analysis and decision-making processes.
- Incorporation of CSR issues and activities into business and investment policies and practices.
- Promotion of appropriate disclosure on CSR issues and performance.
- Collaboration among all stakeholders to enhance the effectiveness of CSR programs.
- Promotion of product innovation and quality, customer retention and attraction, and employee satisfaction and productivity through CSR programs.
- Periodic disclosures of both financial and non-financial KPIs relevant to CSR activities to all stakeholders.

In summary, the social dimension of sustainability performance requires business organizations to take initiatives to advance some social good beyond their own interests and beyond compliance with applicable regulations. Simply put, CSR means enhancing corporations' positive impacts and minimizing their negative effects on society, as well as minimizing harm to society and the environment and creating positive impacts on the community, environment, employees, customers and suppliers.

6. CSR ISSUES

There is a significant debate on the degree to which CSR constitutes a legitimate activity for a corporation to be engaged in when the cost of CSR activities is immediate and tangible, and the related benefits may not materialize in the short term.[100] Some of the challenging issues are: competition (the use of advertising and the arrival of new types of CSR risk with new technology); environment (climate change and regulatory change for hazardous substances and waste); human rights (labor rights); product responsibility (access, safety, risk, disclosure labeling and packaging); bribery and corruption (financial reporting fraud, financial scandals, money laundering); respect for privacy; ensuring transparency and accountability; institutionalization of CSR; stakeholder engagement; battle for talent; community investment; supply chain and product safety; social enterprises; and poverty alleviation.[101]

6.1 Globalization-Related CSR

CSR has emerged as an important area of challenges and opportunities for the business community and the accounting profession worldwide. Particularly, multinational corporations are facing challenges on how to respond to CSR issues while balancing localization and globalization realities in determining CSR policies and procedures for their headquarters and more importantly for subsidiaries abroad with different political and cultural norms.

Conceptually, the long-term value and success of businesses are inextricably linked to the integration of economic, social, environmental, ethical and governance factors into corporate culture, business environment, management and operations. The main drivers of CSR strategies have been the measurement of social impacts environmental and ethical impacts and their proper disclosures. As correctly stated by the Global Head of KPMG Sustainability Services, Wim Bartels, "In a world of changing expectations, companies must account for the way they impact the communities and environments where they operate."[102] CSR is the key condition for a continued global market economy, and companies will need to accept and implement this condition if they want to be sustainable to keep their license to operate. If every business organization refused to pay bribes, implemented fair labor practices and adopted environmentally, economically, engage in fraudulent activities, earnings management, and socially responsible practices locally, then the world could be transformed to be more balanced, transparent, legitimate, more just and more sustainable.[103]

6.2 Employee-Related CSR

Employee-related CSR initiatives typically address work conditions, fairness and equality and are derived from and directed toward improving social impacts. These employee-related CSR initiatives include social, political and economic opportunities for existing and potential employees, contract workers, society and other stakeholders. These initiatives range from empowering employee other associates. participation in strategic decisions to improving employee fairness, mutual respect, benefits, wages, and work conditions and being a good citizen. These initiatives also address specific issues of diversity in terms of female participation, ethnic issues or linguistic capabilities.

6.3 Product and Marketing-Related CSR

Product and marketing-related CSR issues suggest companies take initiatives to maximize the positive impacts and minimize the negative impacts of their operations on society. These initiatives enable companies to produce products and perform services that are not detrimental to society. Consumer-driven CSR includes product and process innovations, safety, life cycle and footprint assessments, promotion, advertising and distribution policies and practices. Implementing product and marketing-related CSR initiatives will improve product quality, functionality, transparency branding and corporate philanthropy as well as offer the potential to build brand loyalty (for example, Timberland, Interface and Patagonia).

6.4 Supply Chain-Related CSR

Supply chain-related CSR initiative suggest the integration of CSR performance into supply chain management (SCM) through sustainability continuous improvement, and best practices. CSR supply chain covers the entire chain of input manufacturing, and output process, which includes buying raw materials from socially responsible suppliers, designing and producing products and performing services that are not detrimental to society or harmful to customers and marketing and selling products that benefit society minimize the use of scarce resources (e.g., smaller and environmentally conscientious packaging). CSR processing and production activities, including permits to operate (licenses for mine sites), are becoming integral components of sustainable supply chains. Organizations that undertake CSR programs not only integrate them into their own production process but also influence CSR initiatives for a variety of counter parts, peers and stakeholders in their supply chain process (suppliers, customers).

6.5 Stakeholder-Related CSR

Corporate governance has progressed from the shareholders only focus to the broader aspect of stakeholders. Corporations are no longer isolated from their stakeholders, who contribute to their success. They affect the welfare of their stakeholders and they are affected by their stakeholders' contributions in creating shared value. Social responsibility does not refer to responsibility *to* stakeholders but designates a responsibility *by* stakeholders. Socially responsible investing and ethical consideration, social and environmental impacts the 'green' consumer movement and the growth of 'vigilante consumerism' are examples of how such 'conscientious stake-holding' can influence the way business operates. A growing number of investors are now consider impact investing with a keen focus on financial return and social an environmental impacts relevant to ESG sustainability factors. Regulators mandate ESG sustainability performance disclosure and public companies prepare and disseminate sustainability reports. In this era of CSR sustainability-oriented investors, directors and executives, understand and consider that ESG sustainability factors of performance, risk and disclosure contribute to the bottom line earnings and long-term return.

6.6 CSR and Financial Performance

There are two views on the relationship between CSR performance and financial performance. One view is that any investment in CSR initiatives is an expense that reduces the bottom line earnings. The second view is that CSR investments produce returns on investment that contribute to the long-term earnings. Anecdotal evidence and empirical findings are mixed. However, companies worldwide have created their own CSR programs that aim to balance their financial impacts with social and environmental impacts as well as aligning their operations with the concerns of employees and external stakeholders such as customers, unions, local communities, NGOs and governments. Social and environmental consequences are weighed against economic gains. Although the field of CSR has grown exponentially, the debate still exists about the legitimacy, feasibility and value of corporate responses to CSR concerns. The relationship between CSR performance and financial performance is generally positive, varying between highly positive and moderately positive.[104] Socially responsible practices such as minority hiring and diversity, community involvements employee and customer satisfaction have a greater effect on financial performance than environmental responsibility. Social responsibility and financial performance affect each other in a "virtuous cycle": successful firms spend more because they can afford more, and such spending helps them to become more successful.

Corporate decision-makers and gatekeepers (directors and officers) must consider a range of social and environmental matters if they are to maximize medium and long-term financial returns rather than short-term profits. An initial challenge in determining the relationship between CSR and financial performance is identifying those companies/services that have adopted CSR and have issued a sustainability report. Improvements in CSR performance as reflected in a sustainability report provides information to external stakeholders about the conduct of a company, allowing consumers, employees, investors and others to make informed decisions when dealing with the company. Importantly, the preparation of a sustainability report also provides company management with information about social and environmental performance and impacts, facilitating improved decision-making.

In summary, there are two differing views regarding the relationship between CSR and firm financial performance:

1. Socially responsible behavior is costly due to increased expenses, but no increase in benefits. Thus, any investment in CSR is the money taken away form shareholders.
2. CSR investments create a positive association between CSR performance and firm financial performance that:
   a. Create customers loyalty and branding.
   b. Improves employee morale and productivity.
   c. Attracts and enables retention of high-quality employees and loyal customers.
   d. Generates a positive corporate image reputation.
   e. Enhances product improvement via overall evaluation of the firm.
   f. Improve a firm's access to sources of capital.
   g. Attract investors with socially responsible preferences.
   h. Enables new business opportunities.
   i. Provides a more secure and sustainable working environment.

7. CSR REPORTING AND ASSURANCE

Social responsibility is an ethical or ideological theory that suggests that entities, regardless of type or size, have a responsibility to protect the society in which they operate and that such responsibility varies across countries and is influenced significantly by a culture's socio-economic attributes. Social performance reflects how well an entity has translated its social goals into practice and is influenced the principles, actions, strategic decisions, and corrective measures implemented. Social performance or the social impacts is about making an organization's social mission a reality, aligned with the interests of the society by adding accepted social value contributing to society and fulfilling social responsibility.

Companies generally issue CSR/sustainability reports on an annual basis, which enables them to integrate CSR/sustainability reporting with the annual financial reporting process and/or report. CSR reporting on social performance is a key to building stakeholder buy-in and support for the goals and ongoing social achievements. External reporting of social performance in corporate annual reports is becoming widespread, largely because of public and regulatory pressures and companies' incentives to disclose their good CSR and social impacts. There are many ways to report on social performance, though there are no standard methods, and companies have to choose from among several generally accepted alternatives. In most cases, companies start with the basics—choose a theory of social performance disclosure, decide on the method of annual report presentation and the annual activities for disclosure, which can vary widely among companies. An important goal of CSR is to exhibit commitment to social performance and to embrace responsibility for the company's actions. Socially responsible companies have more incentives and desire to disclosure their good CSR performance and social impacts to differentiate themselves for less socially responsible companies.

8. CONCLUSIONS

In the aftermath of the 2007–2009 global financial crisis, the global business community and socially responsible investors has become more conscious than ever of the importance of sustainability and social responsibility as they relate to the environment, safe products human rights and the economy. Contemporaneously, attitudes and commitments toward the importance of sustainability and social responsibility have also progressed among individuals, organizations investors and businesses. Nonetheless, every organization has its own unique social performance impact on global sustainability, perspective on what it means to be socially responsible and the recognition of how important social responsibility is and how to measure and report the organization's social efforts to the public. CSR promotes a vision of business accountability and social impacts to a wide range of stakeholders besides shareholders and investors. Business is "socially responsible" only if it pursues some "socially responsible" objectives and performance beyond maximizing profit and complying with regulations. The way for a business to be ethical is by pursuing some social welfare, environmental or religious end in addition to profit.

Adequate CSR disclosure has important implications for the credibility of the capital markets in transition economies. The goal of CSR is to embrace responsibility for the company's actions and encourage, through its activities, a positive impact on the environment, consumers, employees, communities and stakeholders. Ideally, CSR reporting should be integrated into financial reporting. Integrated sustainability reporting provides an approach to CSR reporting for organizations worldwide.

9. CHAPTER TAKEAWAY

1. Pay attention to social impacts including product innovation and quality, customer retention and attraction, employee satisfaction and productivity, socially responsible citizenship and environmentally conscientious operation.
2. Prepare and disseminate a CSR report to all stakeholders that the organization is taking proper initiatives to further social good above and beyond its interests, compliance with requirements and legal obligations.
3. Disclose the organization's CSR activities and practices in responding to stakeholder expectations including minimizing negative impacts of the company's operations on society or the environment, while maximizing positive impacts on the community customers, employees, suppliers and society.
4. Obtain assurance reports on your CSR sustainability reports from the third-party assurance providers.

5. Advance some social good beyond the organization's own interests, beyond compliance and exceeding legal obligations by improving the organization's positive impacts and minimize negative effects on society.

ENDNOTES

1. International Organization for Standardization (ISO), ISO 26000, Social Responsibility, 2010, http://www.iso.org/iso/iso_catalogue/management_and_leadership_standards/social_responsibility/sr_iso26000_overview.htm#sr-1.
2. A. B. Carroll, "A Three-Dimensional Conceptual Model of Corporate Performance," *Academy of Management Review* 4, no.4 (1979): 497–505.
3. Ibid.
4. P. Debroux, "Corporate Social Responsibility in Asia: The Beginning of the Road," 2006, https://www.soka.ac.jp/files/ja/20170420_202931.pdf.
5. M. E. B. Herrera, *Corporate Social Responsibility in Southeast Asia: An Eight Country Analysis*, Ramon V. del Rosario, Sr., Center for Corporate Social Responsibility, Asian Institute of Management, 2015.
6. B. Sharma, *Contextualizing CSR in Asia: Corporate Social Responsibility in Asian Economies*, Singapore: Lien Centre for Social Innovation, 2013.
7. B. Vermander, *Corporate Social Responsibility in China: A Vision, an Assessment and a Blueprint* (Singapore: World Scientific Publishing Co. Pte. Ltd, 2014).
8. CSR-Asia, *A Study on Corporate Social Responsibility Development and Trends in China*, 2015, http://www.csr-asia.com/report/CSR-development-and-trends-in-China-FINAL-hires.pdf.
9. Sino-Swedish CSR, "'The Belt and Road' and Corporate Social Responsibility," Sino-Swedish Corporate Social Responsibility website, October 13, 2017, http://csr2.mofcom.gov.cn/article/Nocategory/201710/20171002657050.shtml.
10. X. Wang, F. Cao, and K. Ye, "Mandatory Corporate Social Responsibility (CSR) Reporting and Financial Reporting Quality: Evidence from a Quasi-Natural Experiment," *Journal of Business Ethics* (2016): 1–22.
11. Rankins CSR Ratings (RKS), http://www.rksratings.com.
12. National Bureau of Statistics, *2016 年农民工监测调查报告*, National Bureau of Statistics of the People's Republic of China, April 28, 2017, http://www.stats.gov.cn/tjsj/zxfb/201704/t20170428_1489334.html.
13. China Labour Bulletin, "Migrant Workers and Their Children," http://www.clb.org.hk/content/migrant-workers-and-their-children.
14. Ibid.
15. National Bureau of Statistics, *2016 年农民工监测调查报告*, National Bureau of Statistics of the People's Republic of China, April 28, 2017, http://www.stats.gov.cn/tjsj/zxfb/201704/t20170428_1489334.html.
16. "South China Police Recover Unpaid Migrant Worker Salaries," XinhuaNet, January 26, 2018, http://www.xinhuanet.com/english/2018-01/26/c_136926607.htm.
17. Deloitte, "Finding the Value in Environmental, Social, and Governance Performance," *Deloitte Review* 12 (2013): 101.
18. "Value of Sustainability Reporting" conducted by Boston College Center for Corporate Citizenship and Ernst & Young, 2013.
19. M. Lynn, "A Note On Corporate Social Disclosure in Hong Kong," *British Accounting Review* 24 (1992): 105–110.
20. Demographic Statistics Section (1) Census and Statistics Department, *Hong Kong Population Projections 2015–2064*, 2015, https://www.statistics.gov.hk/pub/B1120015062015XXXXB0100.pdf.

21. J. Mok, "Hong Kong Faces Challenge in How to Manage Its Ageing Population," 2018, https://www.scmp.com/news/hong-kong/education/article/2146677/hong-kong-faces-challenge-how-manage-its-ageing-population.

22. R. Yeung, "With More Elderly Households and People Aged Above 80, Can Hong Kong Cope With Its Greying Population?" 2018, https://www.scmp.com/news/hong-kong/community/article/2136598/more-elderly-households-and-people-aged-above-80-can-hong.

23. S. Xinqi, "Hong Kong Unemployment Hits 20-Year Record Low, But Experts Say Labour Market Is Still Under Pressure," 2018, https://www.scmp.com/news/hong-kong/hong-kong-economy/article/2146652/hong-kong-unemployment-hits-20-year-record-low.

24. Ibid.

25. Labour Department, *Public Services: Employees' Rights and Benefits-Statutory Minimum Wage*, n.d., https://www.labour.gov.hk/eng/news/mwo.htm.

26. Hong Kong Federation of Trade Unions (HKFTU), "About Us: Introduction," n.d., http://www.ftu.org.hk/en/about?id=12.

27. "Racial Discrimination Is Still a Problem in Hong Kong, But Attitudes Are Changing," *South China Morning Post (SCMP)*, 2018, https://yp.scmp.com/news/hong-kong/article/109138/racial-discrimination-still-problem-hong-kong-attitudes-are-changing.

28. B. Wassenerfeb, "Women Still Face Barriers in Hong Kong," *New York Times*, 2011, https://www.nytimes.com/2011/02/22/world/asia/22iht-women22.html.

29. B. Dittrich, "From the Americas to the Far East, Courts Are Advancing LGBT Rights," 2018, https://www.hrw.org/news/2018/07/30/americas-far-east-courts-are-advancing-lgbt-rights.

30. Population Reference Bureau, *2017 World Population Data Sheet*, Washington, DC: Population Reference Bureau, 2017.

31. Netherlands Enterprise Agency, *Corporate social responsibility in India*, Netherlands Enterprise Agency, 2016, s. l.

32. UNESCO, *India: Country Profile*, 2011, http://uis.unesco.org/en/country/IN.

33. B. Sharma, *Contextualizing CSR in Asia: Corporate Social Responsibility in Asian Economies*, Singapore: Lien Centre for Social Innovation, 2013.

34. J. Singh et al., *Corporate Social Responsibility in India*, India: Ernst & Young LLP, 2013.

35. Ibid.

36. B. Sharma, *Contextualizing CSR in Asia: Corporate Social Responsibility in Asian Economies*, Singapore: Lien Centre for Social Innovation, 2013.

37. International Labour Organization, *Child Labour in India*, New Delhi: International Labour Organization, 2017.

38. Save the Children, *Statistics of Child Labour in India State Wise*, 2016, https://www.savethechildren.in/articles/statistics-of-child-labour-in-india-state-wise

39. Ministry of Labour & Employment Government of India, *Annual Report 2016–17*, 2017, s. l.

40. Corporate Responsibility Watch, *Status of Corporate Responsibility in India, 2017*, Praxis, 2017, s. l.

41. International Labour Organization, *Child Labour in The Primary Production of Sugarcane*, Geneva: International Labour Organization, 2017.

42. E. McKirdy, "India's Gender Inequality Has Led to Millions of 'Unwanted' Girls," 2018, https://www.cnn.com/2018/01/30/health/india-unwanted-girls-intl/index.html.

43. International Labour Organization, *India Labour Market Update*, International Labour Organization, 2016, s. l.

44. Corporate Responsibility Watch, *Status of Corporate Responsibility in India, 2017*, Praxis, 2017, s. l.

45. L. Gibson, *Towards a More Equal Indonesia*, Oxford, Oxfam GB for Oxfam International, 2017.

46. OECD, *Social Institutions & Gender Index*, n.d., https://www.genderindex.org/country/indonesia/.

47. No. 23, year 2002.

48. Marriage Law No. 1 of 1974, Article 7.

49. World Economic Forum, *The Global Gender Gap Report 2016*, n.d., http://reports.weforum.org/global-gender-gap-report-2016/economies/#economy=IDN.

50. OECD, *Social Institutions & Gender Index*, n.d., https://www.genderindex.org/country/indonesia/.

51. L. Gibson, *Towards a More Equal Indonesia* (Oxford, Oxfam GB for Oxfam International, 2017).

52.

53. Human Rights Watch, *South Korea Events of 2017*, 2018, https://www.hrw.org/world-report/2018/country-chapters/south-korea.

54. Ibid.

55. H. Barr, "South Korean Women Are Fed Up with Inequality," 2018, https://www.hrw.org/news/2018/06/14/south-korean-women-are-fed-inequality.

56. Y. Ja-young, "Glass ceiling Still Thick in South Korea," 2018, https://www.scmp.com/news/asia/east-asia/article/2148095/glass-ceiling-still-thick-south-korea.

57. OECD, *OECD Employment Outlook 2018*, 2018, https://www.oecd.org/korea/Employment-Outlook-Korea-EN.pdf.

58. Xinhua, "S. Korea Faces Employment Shock as Job Increase Hits 8-Year Low," 2018, http://www.xinhuanet.com/english/2018-06/15/c_137256209.htm.

59. OECD, *OECD Employment Outlook 2018*, 2018, https://www.oecd.org/korea/Employment-Outlook-Korea-EN.pdf.

60. Human Rights Watch, "Malaysia," 2018, https://www.hrw.org/world-report/2018/country-chapters/malaysia.

61. A. Camoens, "Workers call for better wages and end to discrimination," 2018, https://www.thestar.com.my/news/nation/2018/05/01/workers-call-for-better-wages-and-end-to-discrimination/#5rXFfwRT3qfdVCtV.99.

62. Ibid.

63. https://www.hrw.org/world-report/2018/country-chapters/philippines.

64. Human Rights Watch, *Philippines Events of 2017*, 2017, https://www.hrw.org/world-report/2018/country-chapters/philippines.

65. Ibid.

66. Department of Labor and Employment (DOLE), "DOLE Profile—Vision, Mission, and Functions," n.d. https://www.dole.gov.ph/pages/view/7.

67. HealthJustice Philippines, "Millennials Say No to Smoking," 2018, http://www.healthjustice.ph/?p=2354.

68. Commission on Human Rights (CHR), About the Commission, n.d., http://chr.gov.ph/about-us/.

69. Asia-Pacific Economic Cooperation, *Corporate Social Responsibility in the APEC Region*, 2005.

70. J. Cheam, "The Evolution of CSR in Singapore," *Straits Times*, September 2015.

71. Human Rights Watch, *Singapore: End Broad Restrictions on Speech*, 2018, https://www.hrw.org/news/2018/06/14/singapore-end-broad-restrictions-speech.

72. Human Rights Watch, *Singapore Events of 2017*, 2018, https://www.hrw.org/world-report/2018/country-chapters/singapore.

73. Ibid.

74. https://edition.cnn.com/2018/02/24/asia/singapore-migrant-workers-intl/index.html.

75. http://www.mom.gov.sg/documents-and-publications/foreign-workforce-numbers.

76. Ministry of Manpower (MOM), "MOM's Vision, Mission and Values," 2017, http://www.mom.gov.sg/about-us/vision-mission-and-values.

77. K. Han, "Singapore's Migrant Workers Struggle to Get Paid," 2018, https://www.cnn.com/2018/02/24/asia/singapore-migrant-workers-intl/index.html.

78. Transient Workers Count Too (TWC2), "Who We Are," 2011, http://twc2.org.sg/who-we-are/.

79. K. Han, "Singapore's Migrant Workers Struggle to Get Paid," 2018, https://www.cnn.com/2018/02/24/asia/singapore-migrant-workers-intl/index.html.

80. V. L. Kane, *Corporate Social Responsibility Development and Trends in Taiwan (R.O.C.)*, Ministry of Foreign Affairs, Republic of China (Taiwan), August 1, 2016.

81. U.S. Department of State, *Diplomacy in Action*, Taiwan, 2016 Human Rights Report.

82. Ibid.

83. Taiwan Association for Human Rights, https://www.tahr.org.tw/.

84. B. Sharma, *Contextualizing CSR in Asia: Corporate Social Responsibility in Asian Economies*, Singapore: Lien Centre for Social Innovation, 2013.

85. V. L. Kane, *Corporate Social Responsibility Development and Trends in Taiwan (R.O.C.)*, Ministry of Foreign Affairs, Republic of China (Taiwan), August 1, 2016.

86. Ministry of Labor of Taiwan, *Labor Standards Act*, 2016, https://laws.mol.gov.tw/Eng/ChiContent.aspx?msgid=553.

87. Ministry of Labor of Taiwan, *Labor Standards Act*, 2018, https://laws.mol.gov.tw/Eng/EngContent.aspx?msgid=584.

88. APEC, *Corporate Social Responsibility in the APEC Region—Current Status and Implications: Economy Paper: Thailand*, n.d., Asia-Pacific Economic Cooperation, s. l.

89. Ibid.

90. Countries and Their Cultures, "Thailand," n.d., http://www.everyculture.com/Sa-Th/Thailand.html.

91. H. N. T. Trang and L. S.Yekini, "Investigating the Link Between CSR and Financial Performance—Evidence from Vietnamese Listed Companies," *British Journal of Arts and Social Sciences* 17, no. 1 (2014): 85–101.

92. Reporting Exchange, *An Overview of Sustainability and Corporate Reporting in Vietnam*, WBCSD, n.d., s. l.

93. Human Rights Watch, *World Report 2018*, 2018, https://www.hrw.org/world-report/2018/country-chapters/vietnam.

94. F. Rhodes, *An Economy that Works for Women*, Oxfam International, 2017, s. l.

95. S. P. Sethi, "Dimensions of Corporate Social Performance: An Analytical Framework," *California Management Review* Spring 17, no. 3 (1975): 58.

96. A. B. Carroll, "Corporate Social Responsibility: Evolution of a Definitional Construct," *Business and Society* 38, no. 3 (1999): 268–295.

97. OECD, *Guidelines for Multinational Enterprises*, 2003, www.oecd.org.

98. Z. Rezaee. (2016). Business sustainability research: A theoretical and integrated perspective. *Journal of Accounting Literature* 36, 48–64.

99. International Organization for Standardization (ISO), ISO 26000, Social Responsibility, 2010, http://www.iso.org/iso/iso_catalogue/management_and_leadership_standards/social_responsibility/sr_iso26000_overview.htm#sr-1.

100. Z. Rezaee. (2016). Business sustainability research: A theoretical and integrated perspective. *Journal of Accounting Literature* 36, 48–64.

101. Much of the discussion in this section comes from Z. Rezaee. 2015. Business sustainability: Performance, Compliance, Accountability and Integrated Reporting, Green Leaf publishing, October 2015.

102. KPMG International, *KPMG International Survey of Corporate Responsibility Reporting 2008*, Geneva.

103. J. Njoroge, Effects of the Global Financial Crisis On Corporate Social Responsibility in Multinational Companies in Kenya, Covalence Intern Analyst Papers, 2009.

104. L. McKnight, "Companies that Do Good Also Do Well," Market Watch, *Wall Street Journal (Digital Network)*, 2011, http://www.marketwatch.com/story/companies-that-do-good-also-dowell-2011-03-23.

CHAPTER 8

Ethical Dimension of Sustainability

1. EXECUTIVE SUMMARY

Ethics in the generic term, which is driven by a combination of individual and/or family values, moral principles, religious beliefs, cultural norms and best practices. Individual's values are derived from moral principles that define what is right or wrong, whereas an individual's choices are actions taken in doing what is right or wrong. The 2007–2009 global financial crisis was partially caused by a number of ethical lapses by both organizations and individuals involved in the mortgage markets, including mortgage originators, financial intermediaries, investment banks, and mortgage borrowers. These lapses collectively contributed to the 2007–2009 global financial crisis and resulted in the global economic meltdown, and have threatened the sustainability of individuals, businesses and governments. The crisis and related financial scandals have caused policymakers, regulators and ethics advocates to ask the question: To what extent do ethics and corporate culture affect the business process? Another question posed is whether ethics performance should be reflected in overall corporate reporting. This chapter addresses these and other ethics-related questions in the context of the ethical dimension of sustainability performance worldwide and particularly in Asia.

2. INTRODUCTION

Ethics are broadly described in the literature as (1) moral principles about right and wrong and (2) honorable behaviors reflecting values or standards of conduct.[1] Honesty, openness, responsiveness, accountability, due diligence and fairness are core ethical principles. Business ethics is a specialized study of moral righteousness. An appropriate code of ethics that sets the right tone at the top promoting ethical and professional conduct and establishing the moral structure for the entire organization is the backbone of effective corporate governance. Corporate culture and compliance rules should provide incentives and opportunities to maintain honesty. Attributes of an ethical corporate culture or an integrity-based culture refer to employee responsibility, freedom to raise concerns, managers modeling ethical behavior and expressing the importance of integrity. The company's directors and executives should demonstrate through their actions as well as their policies a firm commitment to ethical behavior throughout the company and a culture of trust within the company. Although the "right tone at the top" is very important in promoting an ethical culture, actions often speak louder than words. This chapter presents the ethical dimension of sustainability performance reporting and assurance worldwide and in Asia.

3.   BUSINESS ETHICS

Business ethics is a set of moral principles, organization culture and values, best practices and standards that guide business behaviors. Business ethics refers to the collective values of a business organization, which can be used to evaluate whether the behavior of the members of the organization is considered acceptable and appropriate, and whether the business is held accountable in terms of its openness, integrity and behaviors. Organizational ethics is a set of formal and informal standards of conduct that people use to guide their behaviors at work. These standards are partly based on core values such as honesty, mutual respect, openness, fairness, mutual respect and trust but they can also be learned directly from the actions of others including colleagues and superiors.

Ethics is a relatively broad concept that can be viewed from different aspects. The strongest form of defense against business failure comes from an organization's ethical culture and honorable behaviors. The effectiveness of ethics performance depends on employees' moral conscience and begins with the tone that management sets at the top and workplace integrity. The attributes of an ethical corporate culture include the existence of codes of conduct for senior executives and employees. Appropriate ethical policies and procedures in the workplace can affect the integrity and quality of financial reporting and thus the cost of capital.

Business sustainability in the ethical dimension provides information to investors about the relationship between the corporation and employees. Such information is beneficial to both debt-holders and stockholders when they are assessing the expected return on securities issued by the firm. However, the effect of the ethical dimension of business sustainability should be different for debt and equity holders. Bond holders should benefit more from this dimension of business sustainability as they can benefit from the improved employer–employee relationship between the firm and its workers, but do not need to bear the higher cost associated with the improved relationship such as higher salary or cash-profit sharing. Many factors affect an ethical workplace for employees including employee relations and human rights. Some of the good attributes for employees of an ethical workplace are (1) strong union relations (2) no-layoff policy (3) cash-profit sharing (4) employee involvement (5) retirement benefits (6) health and safety (7) other employee relationship strengths (8) indigenous people relationship strengths and (9) other human rights strengths. In relation to employees and the ethical workplace, bad attributes include (1) weak union relation (2) health and safety practices (3) workforce reductions (4) retirement benefits (5) other employee relations concerns (6) labor rights concerns (7) indigenous people relations concerns and (8) other human rights concerns.

Corporations should establish an ethical workplace culture of integrity and competency that encourages all employees to follow and exemplify. Some of the core cultural values that are intended to inspire a culture of integrity and competency in the workplace include:

- Upholding the highest ethical standards and integrity along with a culture of accountability in the workplace.
- Promoting the culture of good citizenship by adding value to the organization, protecting employee health and safety and managing and taking responsibility for natural resources.

- Avoiding conflicts of interest by considering what is best for the entire organization when making decisions.
- Focusing on producing safe and good quality products and services by achieving business results and customer success.
- Being fair and treating others with dignity and respect and promoting diversity.
- Promoting excellence by helping others reach their potential.
- Participating in developing objectives and embracing changes.

The growth of the field of business ethics globally is enhanced and accelerated by (1) the existence of an active global business ethics network which promotes business ethics through facilitating reciprocal learning and research (2) the societal demand to stop business scandals (3) regulatory pressure through corporate governance reform and corruption prevention.[2]

Business ethics is often interpreted as (1) complying with all applicable laws, rules, regulations and standards (2) refraining from breaking the criminal law relevant to all business activities (3) avoiding conflicts of interest that is detrimental to business success (4) avoiding any actions that may result in civil lawsuits against the company and (5) refraining from actions that are bad for the company image and reputation. Businesses are especially concerned with actual and perceived unethical business activities that may cause the loss of money, business damages and reputation. Public companies are required by the US SEC to have business codes of conduct that address these and other ethical issues and existence of such codes of business conduct should be disclosed publicly. Public companies also retain corporate attorneys and public relations experts to monitor employees in their daily activities in observing the established codes of conduct. The audit committee should oversee the establishment and implementation of business ethics programs and processes. Although being moral may prevent a company from some legal and public relations challenges, morality in business is not without cost. A morally responsible company should invest in employee satisfaction, product safety, environmental impact, truthful advertising and scrupulous marketing.

There is always an apparent conflict between the ethical interests of the money-minded business person and the ideal-minded philosopher. A business-oriented individual may argue that there is a symbiotic relationship between ethics and business. This means that ethics naturally emerges from a profit-oriented business. In this context, good ethics result in good business which simply implies that moral business practices are profitable and sustainable. For example, it is profitable to make safe products since this will reduce product liability lawsuits. Similarly, it may be in the best financial interests of businesses to respect employee privacy since this will improve morale and thus improve work efficiency. Some moral business practices may not be economically viable even in the long run. Retaining older workers who are inefficient as opposed to replacing them with younger and more efficient workers may be an example of this. It can also be argued that in a perfectly competitive and free market, an immoral company will be "priced" out in a morally proper environment in the long run. That is, when customers demand safe products or workers demand privacy, then they will buy from or work for only those businesses that meet their expectations. Businesses that do not meet these demands will not be sustainable as far as these employees are concerned.

Another approach to business ethics is that moral obligations require compliance with all applicable laws, rules, and regulations. Corporations that assume an obligation beyond mere compliance with law, and regulations, take on responsibilities that are normally considered optional and ethical. Strictly following this legal approach to business ethics may indeed prompt businesses to do the right thing as prescribed by law. However, there are overriding challenges with restricting morality solely to what the law requires. First, even in the best legal context, the appropriate law will lag behind moral condemnation of certain unscrupulous yet legal business practices. For example, drug companies could previously make exaggerated claims about the miraculous curative properties of their products. New government regulations may prohibit exaggerated claims. Prior to the enactment of a law, there will be a period when a business practice can be deemed immoral, yet the practice will still be legal. This will be a continuing problem since innovations in products, technology, and marketing strategies will present new questionable practices that cannot be addressed by existing legislation. A second problem with the law-based approach is that, at best, it applies only to countries whose business-related laws are morally conscientious. The environment may be different for developing countries that lack sophisticated laws and regulatory agencies.

4. PROFESSIONAL CODES OF CONDUCT

Organizations communicate their values, accepted standards for decision-making, and all other rules of behavior to their employees, clients, members and trading partners. Professional organizations such as the American Institute of Certified Public Accountants (AICPA), Institute of Management Accountants (IMA), Institute of Internal Auditors (IIA), American Certified Fraud Examiners (ACFE) and American Accounting Association (AAA) among others have their codes of ethical conduct. All of these organizations have standards of conduct explicitly or implicitly. Some publish some codes of conduct or ethics which help organizations deal with the underlying values, commitment to employees, standards for doing business, and relationship with wider society, while some do not.

These codes of conduct not only demand maximization of social welfare and transparency but also increased focus on ethics, corporate governance, and corporate responsibility. These codes may be required by laws and regulations in some countries. Some codes are prompted by market mechanisms such as movements in share price or a combination of market forces and regulations while some codes are published by psychological organizations or other organizations. Below are some examples of professional codes of conduct:

1. The American Psychological Association (APA) has the APA Ethical Principles of Psychologists and Code of Conduct.[3]
2. The Canadian Psychological Association (CPA) articulates ethical principles, values, and standards to guide all members of the CPA whether scientists, practitioners, or scientist practitioners or whether acting in the role of research, direct service, teaching, student, trainee, administration, management, employer, employee, supervisory, consultative, peer review, editorial, expert witness, social policy or any other role related to the discipline of psychology.[4]
3. The Society for Research in Child Development (SRCD) provides ethical standards for research with children.[5]

4. The Association for Computing Machinery (ACM) Code of Ethics and Professional Conduct is a professional code of conduct which is expected by every member (voting members, associate members and student members) of the ACM.[6]

By implementing codes of conduct effectively and consistently, organizational performance and control can be improved. This would result in fewer irregularities and corporate scandals. Trust would be built up gradually between organizations and their stakeholders.

5. WORKPLACE ETHICS

Workplace ethics is receiving a considerable amount of attention as the emerging corporate governance reforms require the setting of an appropriate tone at the top to promote ethical conduct throughout organizations. A review of reported financial scandals suggests that most ethical dilemmas have financial consequences. Establishment of formal ethics programs is becoming increasingly common in organizations across the non-profit, for-profit, and government sectors. The 2009 National Business Ethics Survey (NBES) provides valuable information about ethics in the workplace in the aftermath of the 2007–2009 Global Financial Crisis.[7] The 2009 NBES indicates that (1) employees reporting that they observed ethical misconduct in workplace went down to about 49 percent in 2009 compared to 56 percent in 2007 (2) whistle-blowing reporting was up to more than 63 percent in 2009 compared with 58 percent in 2007 (3) improvements in key measures (integrity, openness, responsibility and accountability) of ethical culture in the workplace reported by employees (62 percent in 2009 compared with 53 percent in 2007) and (4) perceived pressure to commit unethical actions, cut corners or violate ethical standards declined from 10 percent in 2007 to less than 8 percent in 2009.[8] Nonetheless, about 22 percent of surveyed employees agreed that the Financial Crisis and related economic meltdown had negatively affected the ethical culture in their company (with more than 10 percent reporting that their company had lowered its ethical standards in the post-2007 recession era) and that retaliations against employee whistleblowers had increased.[9] Furthermore, about 80 percent of surveyed employees believed that they work in a company that holds them accountable for their ethical conduct and more than 70 percent reported that their corporate leaders are transparent regarding their ethical decisions and wellbeing of employees.[10] The results suggest that many executives perceive value in actively promoting ethics within their organizations.

Organizations of all types and sizes can benefit significantly from the establishment and enforcement of effective workplace ethics standards. The list of potential benefits linked to an effective ethics program includes the following:[11]

- Demonstrating commitment to ethical principles and values throughout the organization.
- Ability to hire the most ethical senior executives including chief executive officer (CEO) and chief financial officer (CFO).
- Recruiting and retaining ethical and top-quality employees.
- Promoting a satisfying, rewarding and productive working environment.
- Establishing and maintaining a good reputation within the community.

- Securing the trust of all stakeholders to ensure continued self-regulation and prevent intervention by regulators.
- Reducing incidents of unethical behavior.
- Promoting fairness, mutual respect and integrity throughout the organization.
- Aligning the work efforts of employees with the organization's mission and vision and enabling employees to work toward the organization's goals.

Established workplace ethics programs are intended to guide and influence how employees tackle and resolve work-related ethical issues. Some actions toward the establishment and enforcement of effective workplace ethics standards include:[12]

- Encouraging moral principles, ethical values and integrity.
- Promoting an open and candid discussion of ethical issues.
- Presenting ethical guidance and resources for employees to make appropriate ethical decisions.
- Establishing incentives and opportunities for employees in the workplace to do the right thing and behave ethically.
- Providing fair mechanisms to promptly resolve potential internal conflicts of interest.

Ethics programs cannot prevent all misconducts from occurring but surely can reduce they incidences. Even in the most efficient and ethical organizations, there are always employees who willfully disregard the organization codes of conduct and the rules. In such cases, there is no substitute for clear procedures and sanctions. A good ethics program promotes employees to do the right thing. Employees need to be aware, sensitive and responsive to workplace ethical issues and willing to work within their organization to address them internally rather than resort externally to resolve them. External disposition and exposure of workplace unethical issues is generally neither in the best interest of the organization nor its employees.

Employees typically have high ethical expectations and expect their organizations to do what is right and fair, not just what is profitable. Most executives realize that the success of any ethics program requires a right tone at the top by directors and executives and the active support of and participation by employees. Employees who consider their workplace ethical as exemplified by their leaders and supervisors modeling ethical behavior and the promotion of honesty, mutual respect, fairness and trust generally report positive experiences regarding a range of outcomes. Some of these outcomes include more ethical workplace culture, fairness, integrity and mutual respect, less observed misconduct at work, less pressure on employees to compromise ethics standards, more incentives and opportunity to do the right thing, along with more reasons for "feeling valued" by the organization. These outcomes also include a greater willingness to report misconduct, greater satisfaction with the organization's response to reported misconduct, greater overall satisfaction with the workplace and greater loyalty to the organization.

Directors and executives should set an appropriate tone at the top promoting ethical culture of integrity, fairness, mutual respect and competency throughout the organization with a keen focus on ethics programs and adherence to ethical principles and codes of conduct by leaders, supervisors and employees. A good workplace reputation maintained by a company toward its employees, customers, suppliers and key stakeholders is an immeasurable asset that executives naturally should protect. Executives generally recognize that employees through hard work, dedication and ethical conduct can influence the company's reputation through their daily decisions and interactions but often fail to appreciate how an ethics program can give employees the tools to enhance that reputation.

Enron, in 2001, had gone from being considered one of the most innovative companies of the late-20th century to being considered the most corrupted and unethical workplace. Its investors lost billions of dollars, executives were indicted and subsequently convicted, employees lost their jobs and pension investments, and the auditor was derided. Enron is a classic example of a failure of ethics in the workplace. The primary failure of Enron's directors and executives was self-dealing and the violation of their fiduciary duty to protect the interests of its stakeholders (investors, employees, suppliers, creditors, customers, government and society). The main objective of Enron's directors and officers was to manage earnings and be leader in the industry rather than to do the right thing and conduct their business ethically. Enron was the seventh-largest public company in the US at the beginning of 2001 and in 2002 it was the largest company to declare bankruptcy in US history. The consequences of compromising ethical code and maintaining an unethical workplace can be the demise of the company and loss of reputation and investment by all stakeholders.

6. CORPORATE CULTURE

The delegation of authority, the assignment of responsibilities, and the process of accountability influence corporate culture. It is the responsibility of directors and executives to set a right tone at the top of promoting a corporate culture of integrity and competency. Proper communication of corporate culture such as codes of conduct and job descriptions throughout the company are essential in promoting and enforcing ethical behaviors. Corporate culture and compliance rules should provide incentives and opportunities for ethical individuals to be honest and to act with integrity, and provide measures for monitoring, penalizing and correcting unethical individuals, the minority, for such unethical behaviors. Companies should promote a spirit of integrity that goes beyond compliance with the established code of business ethics or compliance with the letter of the law by creating a business culture of doing what is right.[13]

Three factors may be the most important in affecting people's behaviors: incentives, opportunities, and choices.[14] Incentives pressure are perhaps the most essential factor of business ethics. Individuals within the company (managers and employees) tend to act according to incentives provided to them in terms of rewards arising from the performance evaluation process. Corporate culture and incentives can encourage individuals to behave in the desired ethical manner. However, individuals who have the incentives to do the wrong thing, if opportunities exist, wrongdoers will take advantage and behave in an opportunistic manner. Thus, effective corporate governance, internal controls and enterprise risk management can reduce the opportunities for unethical conduct.

In general, individuals are rational and often are given the freedom to make choices and usually choose those that will maximize their wellbeing. Managers and employees make decisions, take actions, and exercise their choices in compliance with the applicable codes of conduct.. on behalf of the company as agents of their company. A corporate culture promoting ethical and competent behaviors throughout the organization along with strengthening incentives for doing the right thing and reducing opportunities for unethical actions can improve the ethics performance in the workplace.

7. BUSINESS ETHICS IN ASIA

Modern business ethics was initiated in the Western region and spread through the discourse of the free market to other parts of the world. Each historical period had its norms about business ethics and as time evolved, acceptable behaviors became objective. For example, South Korea's racing authority has legitimized horse racing by promoting it as a leisure service. Business ethics in Asian countries has evolved from the Chinese Confucian virtues. Asian values place emphasis on hierarchical relationships and social harmony while European values emphasize freedom and human rights.[15] Although Koehn (2013) is of the opinion that business ethics can be drawn from different cultures, religions or thought processes, they still converge at a common practice without imposition of hegemony by either party especially in global business practices.[16]

There has been a growing interest in business ethics in Mainland China and in the other parts of Asia, because of the following three key factors:

- Increasing expectations from Western companies for organizations to operate in a more ethical manner in line with Western standards. This comes as a result of the need for Western firms to be consistent in meeting the expectations of government, media and other stakeholders in their home countries.
- The interest of Asian countries in deploying capital abroad by forming partnerships or purchasing European and American companies, which leads to pressure on Asian firms from business partners and governments to exhibit Western ethical practices.[17]
- Business ethics is also influenced by the religion of the people in a particular group as different religious teachings may promote or frown at some attitude or behavior of its people based on its values and norms, as moral content differs from one religion to another.

An academic study suggests that regions which practiced Christianity were found to have higher ethical standards while the traditional Chinese religion had more room for the acceptability of unethical behaviors.[18] This implies that as Mainland China and other transition economies reviewed in the study open up to the Western capitalist market, they are also exposed to the religious influences of Western countries (Christianity), which may instill more orderly and ethical development of their economies.[19] A 2017 academic study argues that business ethics has certainly become a universal concept in most jurisdictions including those in East Asia like Mainland China, Hong Kong, Taiwan, Singapore, South Korea and Japan. Even though capitalist business ethics now includes both socialist and traditional ethical values, there is significant transition from one particular mode to another.[20]

Japan was the first non-Western Asian country to adopt and practice the concept of Western business ethics, in the 1920s, which aided its rapid economic development and Westernization at that time.[21] The establishment of a Code of Ethics by Japanese companies started actively in 1993 as a result of the publication of the Charter of Corporate Behavior in 1991 by Nippon Keidanren (the Federation of Economic Organizations in Japan). Shortly afterwards, the Japan Society for Business Ethics Study (JABES) was established to promote the research and practice of business ethics.[22]

Mainland China, on the other hand, has been considered deficient in terms of the practice of business ethics. Until recently the practice of business ethics in Mainland China was influenced by respect for the chain of command, avoiding loss of face (*mianzi*) and a reluctance to whistle-blow on colleagues.[23] In combating corruption rooted in the culture of *mianzi*, the Central Commission for Discipline Inspection (CCDI), an internal control institution of the Communist Party of China (CPC), has further encouraged whistle-blowing by providing various channels including mail, email and hotlines after the anti-corruption campaign initiated by President Xi Jinping in 2012. Rossouw (2011) has classified global business ethics prevalence according to three categories where the West (North America and Europe) was placed at high level; Sub-Saharan Africa, South and South East Asia, East Asia and the Oceania region at medium; while Latin America and Central Asia are in the low category. Given that this is a general estimate, there exists some variability in individual countries. For example, there are differences in South and South East Asia, where India, Bangladesh, Sri Lanka, Thailand and Malaysia are leading the development of the field, while business ethics as a field of training is more prevalent in countries such as Singapore.[24]

The region still experiences a high level of corruption, which is the backbone that supports unethical behaviors at different levels of organizations in each country.[25] Transparency International, in its 2017 Corruption Perception Index, gave the Asia-Pacific Region an average score of 44 out of 100 marks with Singapore scoring the highest with 84 points and North Korea with the lowest at 17 points. Cases of corruption in the region are quite common in developmental infrastructure projects, with government officials taking part in land sale deals with large multinational and local companies while displacing local residents without a fair and equitably structured resettlement plan. To mitigate and combat corruption, companies and stakeholders must include business ethics codes and integrate the right perspectives on handling ethical issues in educating executives in the region.

Organizational and cultural challenges affect firms in the region, as seen in Japan where large firms such as Olympus, Toyota and Toshiba still battle with business ethics issues with respect to diversity and gender regardless of the fact that Japan was one of the pioneers of business ethics in the region.[26] Tackling business issues might work if addressed from the underlying factor of poor personal ethics because unethical conduct breeds from this aspect and then spreads rapidly in an organization.

The separation of business ethics and CSR as two distinct fields in some regions (like Europe and South and East Asia) also poses some challenges as business ethics are usually considered on an individual level while CSR is perceived as a managerial field involving the external responsibility of firms to their stakeholders and the community. However, the two concepts are intertwined and cannot be narrowed down to certain fields as both CSR and business ethics concepts involve duties within and outside an organization. They may be considered as tools allowing each other to succeed, that is, a firm can maximize the benefits of both practices.[27]

There is an opinion that what the Chinese consider to be ethical may differ from the thoughts of the West. There is said to exist some form of flexibility in the region when corruption involves relationships such as superiors, parents, husbands/wives, elders and friends, relationships which lie at the center of Confucianism. For example, in Mainland China tax evasion may not necessarily be perceived as unethical as it is very common. The justification for this is dependent on the distance of the relationship and the utility of the process.[28]

7.1 Mainland China

7.1.1 Culture and Its Impact Mainland Chinese society has been influenced by the effects of Confucianism on employees' behavior in the corporate setting. The Chinese term for business ethics is *Shang De*, *Ru Shang* or 'Confucianist Trader' and as such is traditionally thought to be a route to success.[29] In line with Confucian principles, Mainland Chinese business people rely less on formal contracts and prefer to rely on individual informal agreements and their personal assessment of business partners' trustworthiness.[30] The *guanxi* tradition puts close, reciprocal, trusting and interpersonal ties at the core of human interactions. However, commentators may have mistakenly questioned whether in Mainland Chinese business relations the *guanxi*-informed practice of gift-giving in fact amounts to bribery.[31] In Mainland China, *guanxi* is an essential practice in business since it may be the only way to gain access in a highly hierarchical system. In recent years procedures, laws and regulations have become more standardized and conform more closely to international norms.[32]

Geert Hofstede's five cultural dimensions provides a useful framework for understanding the characteristics of Chinese culture. Mainland China's concept of high-power distance demonstrates Mainland China's hierarchical structure, i.e., people should respect and honor those who have higher status. It also implies that individuals in this hierarchical society tend to accept formal authority and are less likely to challenge their superiors in the workplace. The low degree of individualism in Mainland China suggests that people are likely to look after themselves and their family or anyone to whom they have a *guanxi*-related obligation. Mainland China exhibits a high score on the masculinity dimension, indicating that many Mainland Chinese will sacrifice family and leisure priorities for work, i.e., working long hours to achieve higher pay and promotions. High examination scores are all important to Mainland Chinese people, as salaries and results are measures of success. Mainland China has a low score on uncertainty avoidance, indicating that Mainland Chinese people are risk takers. Finally, Mainland China is a highly long-term-oriented society in which employees are likely to work hard in pursuit of rewards in the long run. Mainland Chinese people are not so much about instant gratification. As a result, the concept of business ethics as originated in the West may not be suitable for application in Mainland China.

7.1.2 Historical Development Mainland China has experienced the transformation from a centrally planned economy (Communism) to a free market system in a very short period. As a result, Mainland China's business ethics evolved over time with the changes in the market infrastructure.[33] After the 1978 reform, Mainland Chinese businesses became receptive to the idea of a relationship between business economic activity and morality. In 1982, Mainland China revised its constitution and adopted a mixed market economy namely "Socialism with Chinese characteristics". During this period, business ethics, which covered many aspects of commerce, economics, sociology and management, was driven by the Communist Party's "strengthening the construction of socialist spiritual civilization". In 1994, there was another wave of reforms to establish a socialist market economy, which resulted in rapid decentralization and privatization. The government had privatized many SOEs, making them accountable for their business actions and performance. In this period of rapid change, Mainland Chinese media covered a wide range of ethics topics including pollution, product quality and safety at work.[34]

The rise of business ethics began in early 2002 when Mainland China joined the WTO. To comply with WTO regulations, Mainland China began to focus on ethical requirements to curb scandals like faulty products and human rights abuses. In 2002, former premier Zhu Rongji announced the slogan "Don't cook the books," which focused on the credibility crisis and was intended to stimulate public discussion about integrity in business. "*Cheng xin*" which means "credibility and integrity" became a goal for both corporations and government departments. On the macro level, many laws and rules were refined to link with international standards.

Since 2004, CSR through ethical action has become a prominent issue in Mainland China. The 2006 Chinese Company Law (Article 5) requires companies to "undertake social responsibility" in the course of business. The Sixth General Meeting of the Sixteenth Central Commission of the Communist Party of Chinese, which was held in 2006, made a declaration that "building a harmonious society" is the long-term goal of Chinese Socialism.[35]

7.1.3 Business Ethics Issues

7.1.3.1 Business Corruption Transparency International's (TI) Corruption Perception Index 2016 reported that Mainland China ranked 79th out of 176 countries. Mainland China improved by three points in the Index score but still remains low, with a poor score of 40 out of 100; the improvement can be explained by the recent anti-corruption campaign.[36] President Xi Jinping launched the campaign in December 2012, shortly after his assumption of the presidency. He vowed to target all party members regardless of their rank in the government ("tigers and flies").[37] President Xi has made fighting official corruption a cornerstone of his reign. The Chinese Communist Party (CCP) disciplined around 415,000 officials in 2016, almost a 25 percent increase compared to the previous year. Of the officials disciplined, about 11,000 officials were expelled from the CCP and handed over to the courts for prosecution.[38] In the CCDI's second plenary session, held in January 2017, the CCDI announced that 527,000 people were punished in 2017.[39] Although the anti-corruption campaign primarily aims at public officials, the campaign also had a profound effect on the upholding of business ethics by punishing private firms backed by government officials. For example, Anbang Insurance Group Co Ltd, one of Mainland China's most politically connected firms, was taken under government control in February 2018 because the firm was alleged to have violated related laws and regulations.[40] Wu Xiaohui, the chair and key shareholder of Anbang Insurance Group, was prosecuted for economic crimes. Another recent and notable case is Changchun Changsheng Bio-technology, a private company that produced around 0.5 million substandard vaccines for children and threatened numerous children's safety in Jilin Province. After the scandal was reported, the chair and several other key managers were investigated by the government. In August 2018, President Xi chaired the Party's Politburo Standing Committee and ordered the sacking of several senior officials, including the vice-governor of Jilin Province.[41]

To further combat corruption, several laws were amended. In August 2015, the National People's Congress amended several corruption-related provisions of Mainland China's Criminal Law. On March 20, 2018, Mainland China passed the National Supervision Law, which consolidated supervisory powers and "serve[d] as a fundamental and guiding law against corruption and for state supervision, aimed at enhancing the leadership of the Communist Party of China (CPC) on anti-corruption campaigns."[42]

7.2 Hong Kong

Conceptually, business ethics and corporate governance go together with one reinforcing the other. Some concepts embodied by corporate governance—such as transparency, accountability, fairness and integrity—are also principles embraced by business ethics.[43] To enhance corporate governance and business ethics, Hong Kong has introduced the Listing Rules or Code of Best Practice.

Hong Kong was going through a period of rapid change in the 1960s and the 1970s. The population was increasing at a very fast pace as was the development of the manufacturing industries. The government was unable to meet the insatiable needs of the growing population with the accelerated pace of social and economic development. This led to a sharp increase in corruption cases in Hong Kong. Offering bribes to public officials became the order of the day for business survival and access to public services. Law and order were under threat and corruption was weaved into the social–economic fabric of all walks of life. Corruption was common and yet, people in Hong Kong swallowed their anger.

In the early 70s, the government began its campaign to take decisive action against corruption. The then Governor, Sir Murray MacLehose, articulated for an independent anti-corruption organization that was entirely independent of and separate from any department of government, including the police, in hopes of regaining the confidence of the public. This developed into an effective anti-corruption regime and the Independent Commission Against Corruption (ICAC) in Hong Kong was formed in February 1974.[44]

It has been suggested that business ethics practices in Hong Kong are strongly influenced by Confucianism. One study reports that the CEOs of five Hong Kong companies displayed leadership approaches based on the Confucian principles of "benevolence, harmony, learning, loyalty, righteousness and humility" (p. 47).[45] Another study emphasizes the central importance of the Confucian moral principle of trustworthiness.[46] A recent survey highlights that 76 percent (38 companies) of the sample companies had a written corporate code of conduct or business ethics in place.[47] Most of these codes of behavior had similar contents and they were rated as satisfactory and often well-constructed, monitored and enforced.

7.2.1 Current Status and Future Opportunities   In April 2007, the Hong Kong Institute of Chartered Secretaries and the Enterprise and Social Development Research Centre of Hong Kong Shue Yan University jointly conducted a survey of the 1,150 Hong Kong listed companies and reported that business ethics codes were not widely adopted. They suggested that Hong Kong had ample room for improvement, and given its position as a global financial center, it must catch up with international practices in ethics.[57]

In view of the requirement on disclosure of anti-corruption policies by all listed companies in Hong Kong which became effective from the 2016 fiscal year, the Corruption Prevention Advisory Service (CPAS) of ICAC's Corruption Prevention Department (CPD) published the *Anti-Corruption Program—A Guide for Listed Companies* to assist listed companies in formulating, implementing and reviewing corporate anti-corruption policies and programs. Over the years, the CPAS has helped companies and private organizations to strengthen their systems and procedures for the prevention of corruption and related malpractice.[56]

7.3 India

In India, business ethics and compliance are at development stage since Indian firms face lower business ethics standards as compared to Western countries. Corruption is a great concern in India.[48]

7.3.1 Historical Development

Traditionally, Hinduism in India applied ethical standards to all aspects of life. In the old days, *Panchayati* was the major ethical ruling mechanism in India. The *Panchayati* system emphasized a high level of business ethics while maximizing wealth. Under British colonial rule, traditional business ethical principles were replaced with new systems of ethics based on Anglo-Saxon and Greco-Roman practices. Since British colonial rule, it has been observed that there has been a decline in ethical conduct in India as emphasis shifted to economic growth and away from ethical standards.[49]

In 1947, India became an independent nation. Between 1947 and 1990, the *License-Raj* was a government arm that helped to regulate business ethics activities in India and trained business ethics professionals through SOEs, government research and development (R&D) laboratories and universities. The *License-Raj* produced well-trained managerial staff. However, it failed to teach the underlying value of one's ethics and morality and the need to integrate this with business ethical settings. The over-reliance of Indian business infrastructures on government controlled sectors caused immorality, inefficiency and corruption by SOEs.[50]

The pursuit of *Artha* (accumulation of wealth) in the early development of international markets resulted in lower business ethical standards in India. *Jugaad* (finding a low-cost solution to any problem in an intelligent way) is a component of the *Karma* which means working with lower-cost resources. *Jugaad* is part of Indian business culture and allows the use of a flexible approach in business problem-solving taking into consideration the limited availability of resources and the utilization of innovation. Although India's economy is now in an expansion stage, the serious high poverty level and the lack of resources are largely due to the *Jugaad* culture.[51]

7.3.2 Current Status

The modern Indian business environment operates in an uncertain economy with the pressures of globalization, political instability and slow growth as an emerging market. Compliance policies and processes are not aligned with ethical conduct despite a growing number of firms in India having instilled these compliance elements into their corporate culture. The government of India has been making efforts in fighting corruption. Ernst & Young (EY)'s 2017 fraud survey reported that 70 percent of the respondents in India believe that government efforts against bribery had a significant impact on Indian firms.[52] However, only 52 percent of those surveyed believe that regulation has a positive impact on ethical behavior.[53]

Focusing on governance and ease of doing business in India, the Companies Amendment Bill 2016 is an important factor in improving ethical standards. The Bill introduced a whistle-blowing system for Indian listed firms. Whistle-blowing hotlines have become widely accepted with a 6 percent increase found by the EY (2017) fraud survey. Sixty-one percent of the respondents claimed that their firms have developed whistle-blowing initiatives. According to the survey, 47 percent of those surveyed feel it is stressful to hide information about misconduct and more than 50 percent worry about inadequate legal protection.[54]

Unethical behavior and high degrees of mistrust remain in Indian companies, particularly among young executives. EY fraud survey shows that 60 percent of respondents in India reported that their firms' ethical standards have improved in the last two years. Nevertheless, 78 percent claimed that fraud, bribery and corrupt practices are still common, with 48 percent reporting that bribery would win contracts in India.[55]

7.4 Indonesia

7.4.1 Culture and Its Impact
In Indonesian culture, the family exists in the form of a traditional structure and its members have clearly defined roles. Hierarchy is very important in the family and every member of the family will respect, emphasize and maintain the hierarchy. Indonesia is also a collectivist society. In this cultural context, Indonesians have always placed the interests of their families and communities above those of the individual. Therefore, the impact of relations on business is very important. Indonesians like to develop intimate relationships with their business partners before negotiating business. The resulting moral problems are highlighted by the corruption and unfair competition brought about by such intimate relationships.[56]

7.4.2 Enforcement Agencies
The government committed to stamping out bribery by establishing two government agencies and enacting related legislations.

7.4.2.1 **Komisi Pemberantasan Korupsi** In Indonesia, the main government agency for the implementation of anti-corruption laws is the Komisi Pemberantasan Korupsi (Corruption Eradication Commission, KPK). The KPK collaborates with other authorized agencies in connection with phishing, bribery and corruption, investigating and prosecuting bribery in suspicious enterprises. The KPK can act effectively to prevent bribery and oversee corporate governance and the management of national budgets.

7.4.2.2 **Pusat Pelaporan dan Analisis Transaksi Keuangan (PPATK)** Indonesia's PPATK (Indonesian Financial Transaction Reporting and Analysis Center) works with other countries to fight international organized crime including money laundering. Specifically, PPATK is primarily responsible for tracking the financial flows deriving from corruption and bribery offenses.[57]

7.4.3 Laws and Policies
7.4.3.1 **Anti-Money Laundering Laws** Under the Anti-Money Laundering Act, Indonesia's Financial Intelligence Unit (FIU) has comprehensive anti-money-laundering regulatory and supervisory powers, including sanctions powers. The Anti-Money Laundering Act also empowers the KPK (Corruption Eradication Commission), Customs Office, National Narcotics Bureau, and the General Directorate

of Taxation to investigate money-laundering cases in conjunction with the national police. The Anti-Money Laundering Act also strengthens the review powers of the PPATK (Indonesian Financial Transaction Reporting and Analysis Center), enabling it to temporarily freeze business transactions and to verify, analyze and disclose suspected money laundering. Under this Act, financial institutions are required to report to the PPATK any suspicious financial transactions whether it be one transaction or a series of transactions within a working day as well as any cross-border financial transactions.

Suspicious financial transactions subject to this disclosure obligation include any transaction that lacks a clear commercial and financial objective, transactions involving relatively large amounts of cash or unreasonably frequent transactions and any customer activity that goes beyond its usual practice.[58]

7.4.3.2 The Anti-Corruption Law The main anti-corruption legislation that makes corruption a substantive offense is Law No. 31 of 1999 on the Eradication of Crimes of Corruption, which is amended by Law No. 20 of 2001 (the Anti-Corruption Law). The main purpose of the Anti-Corruption Law is to regulate and prevent corruption by public officials. According to the Anti-Corruption Law, anyone who gives a gift to a public official must obtain the approval of the KPK (Corruption Eradication Commission). Any unauthorized gift is considered an offense under Articles 12B and 12C. However, this does not mean that all rewards and honorariums given to government officials are illegal. Self-dealing could be considered illegal only if the official's status, powers, or authority were taken into account and his or her obligations (i.e., given with a corrupt intent) were breached. In addition, there are no provisions in the Anti-Corruption Law that specifically deal with facilitating payment. However, on the basis of the law's broad scope, facilitating payment can be said to be included and is therefore also considered to be a bribe to a public official.[59]

7.5 Japan

7.5.1 Culture and Its Impact Like other Asian countries, Japanese business ethics is largely affected by the Confucian culture. Some common Confucian values are 1) filial piety 2) brotherhood, peer-ship and equality 3) loyalty and fidelity 4) trustworthiness 5) courtesy and politeness 6) righteousness, right conduct and courage 7) uprightness, honor, integrity and character and 8) humility and shamefulness. Employees in Japan believe that individuals who embrace and practice Confucian ethics would establish good relationships with each other. Similarly, more people would be encouraged to attain similar good virtues, and by continuing to do so, there would be less friction in relationships, which consequently creates positive energies in group dynamics and teams.[60,61,62]

7.5.2 Historical Development In the 1990s, two clear-cut trends in business ethics activities appeared in Japan. On the positive side, many corporations which were successful during the bubble economy have become more seriously involved in philanthropical activities than before. For the development of business ethics, however, the passive trend is much more important. Since the late 1980s, a series of scandals has come to light. There were also other important social changes that have also contributed to this passive trend. With these scandals and social changes, both mass media and academia have strongly insisted on the necessity of developing good business ethics.[63]

The process of managing ethics in companies was stimulated with the publication of the Charter of Corporate Behavior in 1991 by the Nippon Keidanren (the Federation of Economic Organizations in Japan). In response to the publication of this charter, many large companies have established a code of ethics or a code of conduct. In 1993, the Japan Society for Business Ethics Study (JABES) was established to promote the research and practice of business ethics.

7.5.3 Current Status and Future Challenges   Currently, Japan is in the middle of a major economic environmental shift. There is an urgent need for Japan to transform its business style and improve its business education in order to survive in the new business paradigm of the 21st century. Japan still maintains the old Japanese style management, which permits questionable business conduct such as (1) political donations (2) socializing with high-ranking bureaucrats, amounting to bribery (3) corrosive price-fixing exchange and (4) *Sokaiya* business gang relationships. If Japan wishes to regain the trust of other countries or be successful in the mega-competition that characterizes the global market, businesses must abide by the new rules of the global economy, which require fair and transparent business practice.

Japanese society also has its own idiosyncratic issues of business practice. For example, astonishingly long hours of work often leads to "death from overwork." Diligence and industriousness are not confined to the Protestant work ethics, but rather are universal virtues of the modern world. For this reason, the promotion of business ethics in Japan still has a long way to go.[64]

7.6   South Korea

The five main elements in Confucian ethics principles—loyalty, wisdom, morality, justice and benevolence—have great influence on South Korean business culture.[65] Although the South Korean business culture is deeply influenced by Confucianism, employees in organizations are not willing to disclose the corrupt practices among them. The South Korean government established the Korean Whistle-blower Protection System in 2002. This system encourages employees to disclose unethical behaviors and provides legal protection for the whistle-blowers.[66] The government agencies of South Korea also promote business ethics by establishing programs so that residents can monitor the ethical practices of the nation. The Korea Independent Commission Against Corruption (KICAC) launched the Business Ethics Team in 2003 and established the Business Ethics Centre in 2004. The KICAC has developed a website called the Digital Business Ethics Centre to allow more information to be shared in order to promote business ethics in enterprises.

In contemporary South Korean ethics, the role of Confucianism does not conflict with the religion and belief of the people. For example, Shamanism is the belief in gods, demons and the spirits of ancestors, and Shaman rituals are still popular in the opening ceremonies of new South Korean firms or buildings, with the hope of bringing a good future. However, there are criticisms that Shamanism has a culturally backward influence.[67]

Other examples of Korean laws that promote business ethics in South Korea include

- The Domestic Bribery Law governed by the Criminal Code
- The Pharmaceutical Affairs Act
- The Medical Devices Act
- The Framework Act on the Construction Industry
- The Foreign Bribery Prevention in International Business Transactions Act (the FBPA)
- The primary anti-money laundering laws which guide the Regulation of Punishment of Criminal Proceeds Concealment
- The Act on Reporting and Using Specified Financial Transaction Information (the Financial Transaction Reporting Act), which is intended to prohibit money laundering and financing of terrorism.

The Ethical Code of Conduct for government officials was enacted to ensure that government officials also perform their duties in an ethical manner. The code forbids public officials from receiving gifts valued at more than KRW 30,000 (approximately US$30) or cash gifts for family events (for example, weddings, funerals) in excess of KRW 50,000 (approximately US$50). Anyone who does not comply with this in South Korea violates this criminal code.

7.7 Malaysia

7.7.1 Historical Development Malaysia has been on a steady economic growth path. It aspires to become a developed country in 2020. However, the development of business ethics has been sacrificed at the expense of the country's growth. The Political and Economic Risk Consultancy (PERC) annual report on the perception of corruption in Asia in the latest survey, which was based on 1,802 responses, ranked Malaysia at 6.78 in 2018, which is low compared to other ASEAN countries and to its performance in prior years. (A perfect score in the survey is 0 while the worst score is 10.[68])

The poor score from the survey might lead to a decline in Malaysia's ability to attract foreign direct investments (FDI). As its performance appears to have deteriorated when compared to the previous year, the government need take steps to stop the downward trend, which may hinder Malaysia's growth in the long run.

Some actions taken by the government to enforce and enhance business ethics in the workplace and in the public sector include:

- The release of the Code of Ethics for Malaysian Businesses by Malaysia's Ministry of Domestic Trade and Consumer Affairs to create awareness of best practices of business ethics as well as to encourage ethical practices in Malaysia.[69]
- "Work Culture, Performance Now," a government initiative that was announced in 2009, aims to build a strong ethical culture in the public sector through programs, seminars and workshops targeted to achieve public sector efficiency.[70]
- Listed companies were also required to provide information on the organization's policies for ethical conduct and corporate responsibilities.

7.7.2 Culture and Its Impact Malaysia consists of three predominant ethnic groups, namely Malays, Chinese and Indians. Each of these ethnic groups has different ethnic cultures, identities, values, beliefs and norms which have contributed to the diversity of Malaysia's workforce. This variety in culture may result in tension or misunderstanding and different perceptions on the difference between right or wrong. This may have impacted on the ethical development of businesses in Malaysia.

7.7.3 Current Practice The revision of the Malaysian Code of Corporate Governance (MCCG) introduced new requirements by which public listed companies need to formalize ethical standards in a code and to ensure compliance. A disclosure index based on the MCCG requirements was developed to analyze disclosure. A study examined the level of ethics practices among Malaysian companies in their 2013 Annual Reports and revealed that almost half of the sample (47.8 percent) did not disclose whether the company has a formal code of ethics or not. The remaining companies (52.2 percent) clearly stated that they had a formal code of ethics or had formalized the code of ethics, with 33.5 percent providing additional information on the code. Having a code of ethics without a proper supporting mechanism will impair the effectiveness of the code. This support can include dedicated employees to monitor the implementation of the code and to provide resources in implementing the code.

The study concluded that although less than half of the sample surveyed did not have a company code of ethics, those which did have a formal code of ethics showed a lack of commitment and did not have any systematic way to promote, support and ensure compliance with the code. The results suggested that businesses in Malaysia may have not achieved good ethics practices in their day-to-day business activities.[71] This may be the underlying reason why the KPMG fraud survey reported that fraud, bribery and corruption are major business problems in Malaysia and a majority of Malaysians believe that business cannot be done without paying bribes (KPMG, 2013).[72] These findings question the effectiveness of the government in raising corporate governance awareness and reducing corporate scandals and managing other business ethics-related issues in Malaysia.

Tan Sri Yong Poh Kon, Managing Director of Royal Selangor International Sdn Bhd, mentioned in an interview that for the government to successfully enforce laws and policies to ensure proper ethical conduct, it must have qualified and resourceful enforcement officers who are backed up by competent prosecuting officers from the attorney general's chambers. Successful criminal convictions in major corruption cases may lead society to fall in line and ensure leaders are leading by example.[73]

7.8 The Philippines

7.8.1 Historical Development The Philippines has enjoyed a flow of new businesses due to an enabling business environment accompanied by the benefits of the natural resources and endowments of its location and diversity. There was sustained growth since its independence from the US in 1946 until the beginning of the Ferdinand Marcos regime in 1970. However, the poor economic policies, corruption and human rights issues associated with the Marcos regime gradually led to the decline of economic growth in the country. Government corruption is often signaled as the major problem that the country faces in its quest for economic growth. In 2011, for example, Gloria Macapagal, who was the president at that time, was charged with corruption and distorting an election, for which she faced several impeachments attempts. Even current President Rodrigo Duterte's death squads have not eliminated corruption, as it has cut deep into the roots of the country's system. The 2017 corruption index by Transparency International allocates a score of 34 out of 100 to the Philippines, which suggests that it struggles, along with other highly corrupted Asian countries like Pakistan, and is far below countries like Singapore and New Zealand that are almost corruption free.[74]

Although there have been improvements in recent years, many Philippine companies still need to ensure that their operations are not affected by corruption. Companies should pay special attention to contributions to local authorities, in particular donations to political parties, to avoid corrupt practices that are perceived by citizens as improper. Businesses can help minimize the risk of corruption by increasing the transparency of transactions and costs, in particular by using electronic transactions with back-office records.[75]

Corruption is one of the major concerns of investors (both local and international) when considering doing business in the Philippines.[76] The scope of corruption in the Philippines has reached the largest institutions, including the military, industrial groups and the government. Massive business scandals over the years as well as the detention and charging of several senior political leaders, including former presidents, have made the Philippines aware of the prevalence and seriousness of corruption across the country.

The 2012 Visayas earthquake not only caused huge human and material losses in the Philippines but also exposed the problem that many buildings in the country did not conform to the national building code. These preventable tragedies have not only deepened public awareness of corruption issues related to building codes, among others, but have also raised public concern that existing laws and regulations are insufficient to protect the public interest.

7.8.2 Policies

7.8.2.1 Anti-Money Laundering Act of 2011 The Philippines government enacted the Anti-Money Laundering Act in 2011. The Act defines the offense of money laundering and establishes corresponding penalties for this and other similar issues. The Act establishes policies in the Philippines to protect the integrity and confidentiality of bank accounts and to ensure that the Philippines are not used as a place for laundering the proceeds of illegal activities. In accordance with its foreign policy, the Philippines will cooperate in relevant transnational investigations and prosecutions of persons involved in anti-money-laundering activities.[77]

7.8.2.2 Code of Business Conduct and Ethics On September 22, 2016, the Securities and Exchange Commission of the Philippines issued a draft code of practice for listed companies and solicited public comments. The draft is intended to help businesses to develop and maintain a standard corporate culture of business ethics. One of the recommendations of the draft was to develop a Code of Business Conduct and Ethics that provides standards for various ethically related conduct and to clarify acceptable and unacceptable behaviors and practices to the public. The responsibility of the board of directors is to fully comply with the code and to ensure that management and employees comply with internal policies. The enforcement of the Code of Business Conduct and Ethics is a powerful safeguard for enterprises in the regulatory environment to promote ethical behaviors.[78]

7.9 Singapore

Business ethics in Singapore has been well developed. The Prevention of Corruption Act, which was enacted as early as June 17, 1960, is Singapore's main anti-corruption law. The Prevention of Corruption Act empowers the Commission on Criminal Justice and specifies the definition and punishment of corruption.[79] According to Lim's 1993 survey, Singaporeans are less likely to engage in unethical activities because there are strict laws governing the country's business practices. Among Asia-Pacific countries, Singapore has been the country with the lowest level of corruption. In almost all cases, Singapore imposes severe penalties on citizens who have committed corruption offenses. It is this punitive effect that ensures a very low crime rate in Singapore.[80] Despite the rapid changes in society, Singapore's moral standards remain strict. However, the country has been hit by a series of scandals over the past few years over the conduct of senior private sector officials and senior executives at home and abroad. Prime Minister Lee Hsien Loong announced on January 13, 2015 that the Prevention of Corruption Act will be reviewed and measures will be taken to severely punish corruption with a view to restore the tarnished image of Singapore, marred by scandals. Singapore will also set up a Corrupt Practices Investigation Bureau and a Central Corruption Reporting Centre to encourage citizens to report corruption. The move is aimed at curbing Singapore's decline in the Transparency International Corruption Awareness Index and restoring its leading reputation for non-corruption.[81]

7.10 Taiwan

7.10.1 Culture and Its Impact Taiwan, similar to most Asian cultures, is deeply influenced by *mianzi*. The concept of *mianzi* is related to "harmony but difference" and "conflict avoidance."[82] In addition, Taiwanese apply *guanzi* in their daily life and business.[83] *Guanxi* emphasizes social obligations and collective goals. It represents a variety of carefully managed networks of people in Taiwan. *Guanxi* sets out the obligation to exchange benefits with people who know each other in future business activities. Even within the bureaucracy, *guanxi* takes precedence over the law.[84]

As *mianzi* and *guanxi* are important components of Taiwanese culture, business ethics is adversely affected. Managers of enterprises provide privileges to members who are associated with them which in turn has a negative impact on fair competition. This cultural identity extends to and permeates the government and corporate sectors leading to corporate scandals, government corruption and misconduct.

7.10.2 Enforcement Agencies

7.10.2.1 The Agency Against Corruption Founded in 2011, the Agency Against Corruption (AAC) is the first government agency dedicated to fighting corruption. The main objectives of the AAC are to strengthen existing anti-corruption mechanisms, increase conviction rates in corruption cases and further protect human rights in Taiwan.

7.10.2.2 Special Investigation Division The Special Investigation Division was set up by the Supreme Court Prosecutors Office to investigate corruption involving senior officials including the president, the vice president, the head of the legislature, ministers, and high-ranking officers. It is also responsible for investigating acts of corruption involving elections. The Supreme Court Prosecutors Office also has the power to investigate other major types of corruption.[85] In 2008, the Special Investigation Division Prosecutors of the Supreme Prosecutors Office investigated and arrested former president Chen Shuibian for alleged embezzlement of government funds.

7.10.3 Policies

7.10.3.1 Anti-Money Laundering Laws The Money Laundering Control Act applies to financial institutions and currently defines 17 types of financial institution and gives the competent authority discretion to designate additional types of financial institutions in the future.[86] The Money Laundering Control Act obliges financial institutions to develop guidelines and specific measures to prevent money laundering and to submit them to the competent authorities and the Ministry of Finance for review.

7.10.3.2 The Anti-Corruption Informant Rewards and Protection Regulations The Anti-Corruption Informant Rewards and Protection Regulations were issued and implemented in July 2011. Section 10 of the regulations guarantee that the name, sex, date of birth, identity card number and address of a whistle-blower must be protected. Any statements, affidavits or other relevant information relating to the informant must remain confidential and be stored securely. Any violation in handling the information of a whistle-blower will be dealt with under the Criminal Code and other relevant laws.[87] Despite such law, business ethics is still not well inculcated in the ethical behavior of business executives. This is possibly due to Taiwan's culture.

7.11 Thailand

In Thailand, caring for others and quality of life are the main values in people's daily lives. Thai culture is more collectivist and less masculine. Such "feminine" culture drives a preference toward nurturing behavior and avoidance of uncertainty. In Thailand, the high-power distance characteristic indicates that social status, seniority, trust and loyalty govern relationships within business organizations. Thai people respect elders, seniors and persons with power. In recent years, most institutions, public schools and businesses in Thailand have provided mandatory lectures or training programs on business ethics. Additionally, most government agencies and companies have codes of conduct or codes of ethics.[88]

Empirical studies show that ethics education in Thailand is underdeveloped and not sufficient.[89] Srinivasan (2011) surveyed 14 schools in Thailand and found that only four offer courses related to business ethics: two provide lectures on Business Ethics, one on Sustainable Tourism, and one on CSR and Ethics.[90] Srinivasan (2011) suggests that more universities should offer business ethics courses at both undergraduate and post-graduate level.

The World Bank's Worldwide Governance Indicators (WGI) reported that Thailand had fair performance in control of corruption from 1996 to 2016 with slight improvement in recent years.[91] Thailand also received stable scores (around 36.67 from 2012 to 2015), which indicates that the nation is perceived as a highly corrupted country.[92] The Transparency International report reveals that in 2017, Thailand ranked 96th among 180 countries and jurisdictions, with a score of 37. According to the 2017 Global Corruption Barometer survey, the Thai people seem to have a positive view of the corruption level and toward their government's efforts to prevent corruption in their country. Only 14 percent of respondents in Thailand thought that the level of corruption had increased. People in Thailand were likely to think that police officers in their country were corrupt (78 percent). The bribery rate measures the percentage of people who had paid a bribe when accessing basic services. In 2017, Thailand scored 41 percent in the bribery rate with 34 percent of the richest and 46 percent of the poorest people having paid a bribe.[93]

7.12 Vietnam

Business ethics in Vietnam is still at the development stage. Vietnam is a highly centralized country and the Vietnamese believe that ethical behavior means obeying or complying with instructions from seniors or managers within companies (power distance).[94] After adopting a market-oriented economy, business ethics and CSR are becoming important topics in Vietnamese companies.

The 2017 Corruption Perception Index (CPI) reveals that corruption is a serious problem in Vietnam as the nation is trailing far behind other Asian countries.[95] The Vietnamese government's and the National Assembly's efforts to fight corruption and find solutions have been inefficient, with limited results. There is evidence of weak implementation and enforcement of Vietnamese laws. The 2005 Anti-Corruption Law provides protection for whistle-blowers and establishes the Asset Declaration to regulate the asset disclosure requirements for government employees,[96] and to monitor and charge people who commit corruption.

The government also adopted the National Anti-Corruption Strategy Toward 2020, in 2009. The strategy highlighted efforts to reduce corruption in five areas: (1) improving transparency of authorities and agencies (2) ensuring the economic management regime (3) establishing a fair and competitive business environment (4) enhancing monitoring, surveillance, investigation and prosecution of corruption cases (5) raising society's awareness of corruption issues.[97]

8. ETHICS REPORTING AND ASSURANCE

Ethics reporting is an emerging undertaking. It is about disclosure of an organization's ethics performance and related assurance. Section 406 of SOX requires public companies to disclose in their annual financial statements the establishment (or lack) of a corporate code of conduct and the SEC related implementation rules require disclosure of the corporate codes of conduct. Nevertheless, public companies may choose to disclose their business ethics performance as a separate report to their shareholders or as part of their regular filings with the SEC. Ethics reporting is usually a component of corporate reporting and thus, standalone ethics reporting and assurance has yet to receive common acceptance in corporate reporting. The process of external ethics reporting has to be standardized and guidelines need to be established for the reporting process. The existing ethics reporting guidance, such as the AA1000 Accountability Principles, can be adapted to determine the structure and content of ethics reporting.[98] The three Principles are the foundation principle of inclusivity, the principle of materiality and the principle of responsiveness.

The principle of inclusivity is the starting point for determining materiality. The materiality process determines the most relevant and significant issues for an organization and its stakeholders. Responsiveness refers to the decisions, actions and performance related to those material issues. All three principles can be used for guidance and reference in preparing ethics reporting.

The establishment and implementation of ethics key performance indicators (KPIs) enable an organization to measure its success in reaching its ethical goals or objectives.[99] The KPIs can be useful as a means of assessing an organization's compliance with its internal established codes of ethical conduct and with external applicable laws, rules, regulations and standards as well as best practices and norms. Proper use of KPIs enables an organization to define its ethical culture and goals, and to establish metrics to measure its ethical performance and to effectively report its ethics performance. The ethics KPIs are classified into corporate culture of integrity and competency and ethical values, ethics code of conduct and its enforcement, ethics performance and the process of promoting ethical behaviors.

In the absence of commonly accepted and standardized authoritative standards for ethics reporting, an ethics report can contain the following information:

1. Formation of ethics-related board committee or chief ethics executive position (chief ethics and compliance officer) to oversee the organization's code of ethical conduct and its effective implementation.
2. Establishment, maintenance and enforcement of the code of ethical conduct, including an ethics training program and ethics policies and procedures.
3. Establishment of positive incentives and right opportunities for ethical leadership and ethical behavior throughout the organization.
4. Communication, implementation and certification of compliance with the established codes of conduct and related ethics policies and procedures.
5. Adoption of internal mechanisms for resolution of ethical dilemmas to minimize their existence.
6. Integration of ethics management with other managerial functions.
7. Development of grievance policies and procedures to internally resolve disagreements and disputes with supervisors and staff including the integration of whistle-blowing policies into ethics programs and practices to institutionalize ethics in the workplace.
8. Establishment of an ethics hotline or anonymous suggestion box in which personnel are enabled to report internally suspected unethical activities.
9. Statement of policy for anti-discrimination based on race, color, ethnic, gender and religion.
10. Design and implementation of mechanisms for minimizing pressure, incentives and opportunities for employees to compromise their professional responsibilities and ethical standards.
11. Strengthening of customer relations to enhance the company's reputation.
12. Implementation of a control structure which eliminates opportunities for individuals to engage in unethical activities.

Ethics reporting should promote not only the practice of complying with applicable laws, rules and regulations but also committing to doing the right thing and observing ethical principles of professional conduct in avoiding potential conflicts of interest. More specifically, the ethics report should provide relevant, timely, useful, transparent and reliable information pertaining to all established, practiced and enforced ethics KPIs discussed above including the following:

- The existence of corporate codes of conduct.
- Policies and procedures for resolution of conflicts of interest.
- Contemporary issues in business ethics
- Stakeholders and corporate responsibility
- Corporate governance and compliance
- Ethics and the environment
- Healthcare ethics
- Ethics and information technology
- Strategic planning and corporate culture
- Ethics and financial reporting
- Establishing a code of ethics and ethical guidelines
- Evaluating corporate ethics
- Integrity
- Objectivity
- Professional competence and due care
- Confidentiality
- Fairness and mutual respect
- Promoting diversity.
- Professional behavior
- Ethics aspirations of trust, openness, mutual respect and accountability.

To improve reliability and strengthen the credibility of the ethics report, assurance should be obtained on the report. The assurance process should gather sufficient and appropriate evidence pertaining to the organization's code of ethics, implementation, enforcement and compliance with established ethics policies and procedures and other elements of reported ethics performance. The ethics assurance provider should gather evidence and provide assurance related to at least the following questions:

1. Does the company have an ethics committee at board level or Chief executive ethics and compliance position?
2. Does the company establish and maintain effective codes of conduct and ethics standards?
3. Does the company establish and maintain effective whistle-blowing policies and procedures?
4. Do employees' actions comply with the spirit and letter of all applicable laws, rules, regulations and standards?
5. Is personnel behavior and action consistent with the company's core values and ethical standards?
6. Are there mechanisms for providing incentives and opportunities to behave ethically and do the right thing?
7. Are there policies and procedures for hiring the most competent and ethical personnel?
8. Are there whistle blowing policies and procedures for anemones reporting of unethical behavior and actions.
9. Are there proper mechanisms for effective resolution of conflicts of interest?

9. CONCLUSIONS

Amid the wave of financial scandals and crises, demand for and interest in ethics and compliance training programs have been galvanized. Ethics is broadly described in the literature as moral principles ethical values about right and wrong, honorable behavior reflecting values or standards of conduct. Honesty, openness, responsiveness, accountability, due diligence mutual respect, diversity, inclusiveness and fairness are the core ethical principles. Business ethics is a specialized study of moral rights and wrongs, using appropriate professional judgement and being accountable for ethical decisions and actions. An appropriate code of ethics that sets the right tone at the top for promoting ethical integrity, competency, and professional conduct and establishing the moral structure for the entire organization is the backbone of effective corporate governance.

Corporate culture and compliance rules should provide incentives and opportunities for personnel to maintain their honesty and integrity and should provide mechanisms whereby unethical individuals may be monitored, punished and corrected for their unethical conduct. Attributes of an ethical corporate culture or an integrity-based culture refer to a sense of employee responsibility, freedom to raise concerns, managers modeling ethical behavior and expressing the importance of integrity. The company's directors and executives should demonstrate, through their actions as well as their policies, a firm commitment to ethical behaviors throughout the company and a culture of trust within the company. Although the "right tone at the top" is very important in promoting an ethical culture, actions often speak louder than words. Ethics reporting is the effective way to communicate the organization's ethics aspirations and values of trust, integrity, openness, fairness, mutual respect and professional responsibility and accountability.

The ethical dimension of sustainability performance in Asia is shaped by Asia's cultural, political, legal and business environments. In addition, business ethics in the region has been influenced by MNCs from the West which have invested in these countries. These expect companies they work with in the region to meet the expectations of governments and other stakeholders in the West. However, it will take time for this to influence and overcome the deep-rooted cultural and religious characteristics, and the "ways of doing business" that exist in different Asian jurisdictions. In general, corruption seems to still be prevalent in business enterprises in Asian jurisdictions although governments are trying hard to varying degrees to establish codes of ethical conduct to guide behavior.

10. CHAPTER TAKEAWAY

1. Encourage the organization to set a tone at the top encouraging "do the right thing".
2. Establish on a corporate culture of promoting ethical values, moral principles, integrity and competency.
3. Create a business culture of integrity and competency.
4. Inform stakeholders about dedication and commitment to ethical values and an ethical workplace.

5. Do not cross ethical boundaries.
6. Be aware of the influence of culture, politics and legal and business environments on ethical choices and actions.

ENDNOTES

1. Z. Rezaee. 2015. Business Sustainability Research: A Theoretical and Integrated Perspective. *Journal of Accounting Literature*, Volume 36, June 2016: 48–64. http://www.sciencedirect.com/science/journal/07374607/36/supp/C.
2. G. J. Rossouw, "A Global Comparative Analysis of The Global Survey of Business Ethics," *Journal of Business Ethics* 104, no. 1 (2011): 93–101.
3. http://www.apa.org/science/programs/research/codes.aspx.
4. https://www.cpa.ca/.
5. https://www.srcd.org/.
6. http://www.acm.org/.
7. Ethics Resource Center (ERC), *The 2009 National Business Ethics Survey (NBES)*, http://www.ethics.org/nbes/files/nbes-final.pdf.
8. Ibid.
9. Ibid.
10. Ibid.
11. J. Joseph and the Ethics Resource Center, *Ethics Resource Center's 2000 National Business Ethics Survey*, 2000, http://www.asaecenter.org/Resources/articledetail.cfm?ItemNumber=13073.
12. Z. Rezaee. 2015. Business sustainability: Performance, Compliance, Accountability and Integrated Reporting, Green Leaf publishing, October 2015.
13. Z. Rezaee, *Corporate Governance and Ethics* (Hoboken, NJ: John Wiley & Sons. Inc, 2009) 65.
14. Z. Rezaee. 2015. Business sustainability: Performance, Compliance, Accountability and Integrated Reporting, Green Leaf publishing, October 2015.
15. K. Y. Chung, J. W. Eichenseher, and T. Taniguchi, "Ethical Perceptions of Business Students: Differences Between East Asia and the USA and Among 'Confucian' Cultures," *Journal of Business Ethics* 79, no. 1–2 (2008): 121–132.
16. D. Koehn, "East Meets West: Toward a Universal Ethic of Virtue for Global Business," *Journal of Business Ethics* 116, no. 4 (2013): 703–715.
17. Kirk O. Hanson is executive director of the Markkula Center for Applied Ethics. He delivered these remarks at a seminar, "Worlds in Collision?" co-sponsored by the Ethics Center and Morrison & Foerster, Dec. 15, 2010.
18. K. C. Lam and G. Shi, "Factors Affecting Ethical Attitudes in Mainland China and Hong Kong," *Journal of Business Ethics* 77, no. 4 (2008): 463–479.
19. Ibid.
20. I. Oh, "Comparing State Economic Ideologies and Business Ethics in East Asia" in *The Political Economy of Business Ethics in East Asia* (Chandos Publishing, 2016), 1–14.
21. C. Rowley and I. Oh, "Relinquishing Business Ethics from a Theoretical Deadlock: The Requirement for Local Grounding and Historical Comparisons in the Asia Pacific Region," *Asia Pacific Business Review* 22, no. 3 (2016): 516–521.
22. N. Demise, "Business Ethics and Corporate Governance in Japan," *Business & Society* 44, no. 2 (2005): 211–217.
23. J. Irwin, *Doing Business in China: An Overview of Ethical Aspects* (UK: Institute of Business Ethics, 2012).
24. Rossouw, "A Global Comparative Analysis of The Global Survey of Business Ethics."

25. V. Srinivasan, "Business Ethics in the South and South East Asia," *Journal of Business Ethics* 104, no. 1 (2011): 73–81.
26. Rowley and Oh, "Relinquishing Business Ethics from a Theoretical Deadlock."
27. Rossouw, "A Global Comparative Analysis of The Global Survey of Business Ethics."
28. C. A. Rarick, "Historical Antecedents of Chinese Business Ethics," Working paper, 2008.
29. J. Irwin, *Doing Business in China: An Overview of Ethical Aspects* (London: Institute of Business Ethics, 2012).
30. A. Ardichvili, "Dimensions of Ethical Business Cultures: Comparing Data from 13 countries of Europe, Asia, and the Americas," *10th International Conference on Human Resource Development Research and Practice across Europe*, 2010.
31. A. Crane and D. Matten, *Business Ethics: Managing Corporate Citizenship and Sustainability in the Age of Globalization* (Oxford University Press, 2016).
32. J.-F. Arvis and R. E. Berenbeim, *Fighting Corruption in East Asia: Solutions from the Private Sector*, World Bank, 2003.
33. R. Berger and R. Herstein, "The Evolution of Chinese Business Ethics," *Management Research Review* 37, no. 9 (2014): 778–790.
34. Ibid.
35. Ibid.
36. Transparency International, *Corruption Perceptions Index 2016*, January 25, 2017, https://www.transparency.org/news/feature/corruption_perceptions_index_2016#regional.
37. K. Hanlon, *Asia Pacific: Fighting Corruption is Side-lined*, Transparency International, January 25, 2017, https://www.transparency.org/news/feature/asia_pacific_fighting_corruption_is_side_lined
38. Export Gov, *China-9-Corruption*, July 25, 2017, https://www.export.gov/article?id=China-Corruption.
39. "China's Anti-Graft Campaign: 527,000 People Punished in 2017," *Diplomat*, January 12, 2018, https://thediplomat.com/2018/01/chinas-anti-graft-campaign-527000-people-punished-in-2017/
40. "Chinese Government Takes Over Troubled Insurance Giant Anbang," *Guardian*, February 23, 2018, https://www.theguardian.com/world/2018/feb/23/chinese-government-anbang-insurance-giant.
41. "Top Officials Sacked over China's Vaccine Scandal," *South China Morning Post*, Aug 16, 2018, https://www.scmp.com/news/china/policies-politics/article/2160081/top-officials-sacked-over-chinas-vaccine-scandal.
42. "China Focus: Supervision law gives legal teeth to China's graft-busting agency," Xinhua News Agency, March 20, 2018, http://www.xinhuanet.com/english/2018–03/20/c_137053224.htm.
43. Hong Kong Institute of Chartered Secretaries and Hong Kong Shue Yan University, *Business Ethics*, April 2007.
44. http://www.icac.org.hk/new_icac/eng/abou/history/main_7.html.
45. C. Cheung and C. Chan, "Philosophical Foundations of Eminent Hong Kong Chinese CEOs' Leadership," *Journal of Business Ethics* 60 (2005): 47–62.
46. D. Koehn, "Confucian Trustworthiness and the Practice of Business in China," *Business Ethics Quarterly* 11, no. 3 (2001): 415–429.
47. Survey on the Hang Seng Index Constituents Environmental, Social and Governance, Oxfam, Hong Kong RepuTex, June 2016.
48. R. Berger and R. Herstein, "The Evolution of Business Ethics in India," *International Journal of Social Economics* 41, no. 11 (2014): 1073–1086.
49. Ibid.
50. Ibid.
51. Ibid.

52. EY, *Asia-Pacific Fraud Survey 2017*, EYGM Limited, 2017, s. l.

53. EY, *Europe, Middle East, India and Africa Fraud Survey 2017*, EYGM Limited, 2017, s. l.

54. EY, *Asia-Pacific Fraud Survey 2017*.

55. Ibid.

56. CVM Davidescu, "Culture and Ethics in Indonesian Business," Universitas Padjadjaran Bandung, 2012.

57. B. Bernarto, *Business Ethics and Anti-Corruption Laws: Indonesia*, Norton Rose Fulbright, June 2016.

58. Ibid.

59. Ibid.

60. K. C. P. Low and S. L. Ang, "The Value of Integrity, The Confucian Perspective," *i-manager's Journal on Management* 6, no. 4 (2012a).

61. K. C. P. Low and S. L. Ang, "The Theory and Practice of Confucian Value of Integrity," *International Journal of Business and Management* 7, no. 14 (2012b): 114–124.

62. K. C. P. Low and S. L. Ang, "Confucian Leadership and Corporate Social Responsibility (CSR), the Way Forward," *Asian Journal of Business Research* 2, no. 1 (2012): 85–108.

63. I. Taka. "Region and Country-Related Reports on Business Ethics," *Journal of Business Ethics* 16, no. 14 (Oct. 1997): 1499–1508.

64. M. Umezu, "Japanese Society for Business Ethics," *Information Bulletin of the Union of National Economic Associations in Japan* 30 (2010): 22–26.

65. S. Horak and I. Yang, "A Complementary Perspective On Business Ethics in South Korea: Civil Religion, Common Misconceptions, and Overlooked Social Structures," *Business Ethics: A European Review* 27 (2018): 1–14.

66. J. Irwin, *Doing Business in South Korea: An Overview of Ethical Aspects*, 2010, s. l. Institute of Business Ethics.

67. Horak and Yang, "A Complementary Perspective On Business Ethics in South Korea."

68. The Perception of Corruption in Asia, US, Australia in 2018, http://www.asiarisk.com.

69. Business Ethics Practiced in Malaysia, https://business.lovetoknow.com/wiki/Business_Ethics_Practiced_in_Malaysia

70. N. F. Takril, S. W. S. A. Sanusi, and T. S. Tajuddin, "Revisited Notes On The Professional Ethics in Malaysia Public Sector," Proceedings of the 2nd International Conference on Management and Muamalah, 2015.

71. A. S. A. P. Salin, and Z. Ismail, "Ethics Practices of Malaysian Public Listed Companies—Empirical Evidence," in *10th Annual London Business Research Conference*, August 2015, 10–11.

72. KPMG, *KPMG Malaysia Fraud, Bribery and Corruption Survey 2013*.

73. http://investvine.com/ethics-in-business-walking-the-ethical-track-in-malaysia-a-perspective/.

74. PanosMourdoukoutas, "Corruption Is Still a Big Problem in The Philippines," *Forbes*, February 21, 2018.

75. G. Unruh and F. Arreola, "Global Compliance: Philippines," Ethisphere Institute, June 4, 2013.

76. Ibid.

77. Philippines Stock Exchange, "Anti-Money Laundering Act, 2011," http://www.pse.com.ph/stockMarket/amla.html?tab=0.

78. PWC, "Integrating Ethics in the Workplace," October 28, 2016, https://www.pwc.com/ph/en/pwc-needles-in-a-haystack/integrating-ethics-in-the-workplace.html.

79. Corrupt Practices Investigation Bureau, Prevention of Corruption Act, Singapore Government, February 2018.

80. P. Lim, *Myths, Fantasies, and Realities of Entrepreneurship* (Singapore, 1993).

81. Norton Rose Fulbright, "Business Ethics and Anti-Corruption World," January 2016, http://www.nortonrosefulbright.com/files/beac-issue-4–137748.pdf.

82. D. K. Tse, J. Francis, and J. Walls, "Cultural Differences in Conducting Intra- and Inter-Cultural Negotiations," *Journal of International Business Studies* 3 (1994): 537–555.

83. J. M. Banthin and L. Stelzer, "Opening China: Negotiation Strategies when East Meets West," *MidAtlantic Journal of Business* 25 (1989): 2–3.

84. Y. Stedham, J. H. Yamamura and S. C.-C. Lai, "Business Ethics in Japan and Taiwan: Relativist and Utilitarian Perspectives," *Asia Pacific Business Review* 14, no. 4 (2008): 535–551.

85. J. Eastwood, *Business Ethics and Anti-Corruption Laws: Taiwan*, Norton Rose Fulbright, June 2016.

86. Ministry of Justice, Taiwan, Money Laundering Control Act, December 28, 2018, https://law.moj.gov.tw/Eng/LawClass/LawAll.aspx?PCode=G0380131.

87. Ibid.

88. B. G. Mujtaba, F. J. Cavico, and J. Sungkhawan, "Business Ethics of Government Employees and Future Lawyers in Thailand: A Study of Age, Gender, Management Experience, and Education," *International Business Research* 4, no. 1 (2011): 16–27.

89. K. Koonmee, A. Singhapakdi, B. Virakul, and D.-J. Lee, "Ethics Institutionalization, Quality of Work Life, and Employee Job-Related Outcomes," *Journal of Business Research* (2010) 20–26.

90. V. Srinivasan, "Business Ethics in the South and South East Asia," *Journal of Business Ethics* 104 (2011): 73–81.

91. World Bank, *Worldwide Governance Indicators*, http://databank.worldbank.org/data/reports.aspx?Report_Name=Eastern-Europe-World-Governance-Indicators&Id=71ec9e89.

92. Transparency International, *Corruption Perceptions Index 2017*, 2018, https://www.transparency.org/news/feature/corruption_perceptions_index_2017.

93. C. Pring, *People and Corruption: Asia Pacific-Global Corruption Barometer*, Berlin, Transparency International, 2017.

94. L. D. Nguyen, B. G. Mujtaba, and F. J. Cavico, "Business Ethics Development of Working Adults: A Study in Vietnam," *Journal of Asia Business Studies* 9, no. 1 (2015): 33–53.

95. Transparency International, *Corruption Perceptions Index 2017*, 2018.

96. M. Martini, *Overview of Corruption and Anti-Corruption in Vietnam*, U4 Anti-Corruption Resource Centre, 2012, s. l.

97. Ibid.

98. AccountAbility (AA), AA1000 Accountability Standard 2008, http://www.accountability.org/images/content/0/7/074/AA1000APS%202008.pdf.

99. Much of the discussion on ethics reporting and related KPIs comes from Z. Rezaee. 2015. Business sustainability: Performance, Compliance, Accountability and Integrated Reporting, Green Leaf publishing, October 2015.

CHAPTER 9

Environmental Dimension of Sustainability

1. EXECUTIVE SUMMARY

To maintain financial sustainability and to effectively compete in the global market, companies worldwide should integrate environmental sustainability into their business strategies and models. Many of the business disasters that have occurred over the past decade accentuate that corporate environmental responsibilities are vital to economic sustainability, the wellbeing of society and future generations. Companies should respond to environmental challenges and turn them into opportunities by strengthening their environmental management, adopting policies and practices that safeguard the global environment and improving their environmental performance. This chapter presents the environmental dimension of sustainability performance worldwide and particularly in Asia.

2. INTRODUCTION

The environmental dimension of sustainability performance enables business organizations to assess the impact of their operation on the environment. Many of the business disasters that occurred in the past decade underscore that corporate environmental policies are vital to economic sustainability and the wellbeing of society. Environmental sustainability is defined as a process of preserving the quality of the environment in the long term, assessing the environmental impact and creating a better environment for future generations while creating shareholder value. In 2010, the SEC released guidance reiterating the relevance and importance of adequate disclosure of material risk associated with climate change by public companies.[1] Current and future legislation coupled with society's increasing sensitivity to the environment (especially toward pollution, hazardous waste, human health, green house gas emission and other general environmental concerns) necessitate high-level management attention to companies' environmental practices and obligations.

The International Standardization Organization (ISO) has released ISO 14000, which requires executive management to conduct regular evaluations of the company's Environmental Management System (EMS) to ensure that the system is realizing the set goals and missions of the environmental policies.[2] The main goal for management's review of the EMS is to identify deficiencies and successes in order to improve environmental practices in the future. A company will benefit economically and socially through the implementation and continuous usage of an EMS that is relevant, accurate and sustainable in monitoring and developing environmental best practices, missions and goals. This chapter presents the environmental dimension of EGSEE sustainability performance with a keen focus on Asia including (1) environmental key performance indicators (KPIs) (2) global environmental initiatives (3) environmental management systems (4) environmental reporting (5) environmental assurance and auditing and (6) environmental best practices.

3.   GLOBAL ENVIRONMENTAL INITIATIVES

The environmental dimension of sustainability performance reflects the company's efforts in leaving a better environment for the next generations and includes reducing an organization's carbon footprint, creating a better work environment and improving the air and water quality of the company's property and the surrounding community. Many of the business disasters (e.g., the BP oil spill) that occurred in the past decade proved that corporate environmental responsibilities are vital to economic sustainability, the wellbeing of society and future generations. Sustainability disclosures with respect to the environmental dimension are mainly related to effects on natural resources and environment that could directly or indirectly affect the living conditions of human beings. Environmental strengths in the environmental areas include (1) beneficial products and services (2) anti-pollution policies (3) recycling (4) clean energy and (5) other environmental strengths. Concerns include (1) hazardous waste (2) regulatory problems (3) ozone-depleting chemicals (4) substantial emissions (5) agricultural chemicals (6) climate changes and (7) other environmental concerns.

Widening sensitivities to the environment (e.g., pollution, hazardous waste, human health and other general environmental concerns) along with ever-increasing environmental laws and regulations force corporations to pay attention to their environmental practices and obligations. Reporting environmental performance in the United States in a corporate setting has been built on regulations and societal demand for accurate environmental reporting. Corporations have developed environmental reporting tools through voluntary and enforced standards via various social and governmental initiatives. Environmental initiatives and regulations have far-reaching consequences for how corporations are viewed in society and held liable for inadequate environmental consideration. Environmental business sustainability created through best practices, regulations or accounting standards is forcing Corporate America to rethink how business is conducted. Moreover, corporations are developing or adapting voluntary reporting tools to be compliant with regulatory bodies and to enhance their social responsibility. The United States Congress has recognized that human activities have a dramatic impact on natural ecosystems through population growth, urbanization, industrialization, resource use and technological advancements.[3] It is critical that sustainable systems are put in place to maintain environmental, social and economic sustainability to ensure the success and livelihood of future generations. Furthermore, the US Congress stresses the cooperation of state and local governments as well as public and private organizations to facilitate the creation of solutions to environmental issues.

Developing an environmental strategy for a company is only the beginning. Companies which have large supplier relationships must ensure the integrity of the specific suppliers' environmental KPIs to ensure sustainability throughout the value chain. Implementing these practices is voluntary in the United States. However, the increase in environmental regulations has induced the Federal government to enforce the regulations through the Environmental Protection Agency (EPA). The EPA is responsible for identifying and enforcing environmental laws and regulations, and forcing companies to clean-up or seeking recovery of the cost of clean-up of a contaminated site. Companies that do not comply will be made liable for (1) clean-up costs (2) paying fines (3) reducing or eliminating future contamination (4) degradation of natural resources (5) societal litigation and (6) criminal charges. Effective compliance with environmental laws and regulations requires full commitment by companies to initiate environmental management systems, accounting and auditing practices.[4]

In general, corporations that are involved in resource intensive industries are required to follow environmental requirements, laws and regulations (e.g., the Clean Air Act and the Superfund Act). On a broad scale, the EPA issues and enforces health and environmental regulations relevant to the Clean Air Act, Clean Water Act, Solid Waste Act and Superfund Amendment and Reauthorization Act (SARA) as well as other regulations affecting environmental reporting. For specific industries such as construction, the EPA has developed a set of environmental KPIs for businesses to use as a guideline. The six basic guidelines are as follows: diesel emission reduction strategies, smart energy practices, green remediation, green building/construction practices, water management and environmentally preferable purchasing. The EPA uses a National Priorities List (NPL) to identify contaminated sites that need or potentially need to be cleaned up. An NPL site is defined as those having a release of hazardous materials, pollutants or contaminants that have negative effects on the environment and human health. At the end of 2009, the NPL concluded there were 1,111 seriously contaminated (non-federal sites).[5] In 2009, the EPA spent over US\$4 billion on clean-up efforts on sites that had severe human exposure or unknown exposure. From 2010 to 2014, the EPA expects to spend US\$335–681 million each year on contaminated sites. As of April 1, 2011, the EPA had identified 1,132 non-federal sites and 158 federal sites that are in immediate need of clean-up with no direct cost estimations.[6]

In June 2009, Ceres (a Boston-based non-profit sustainability organization) and the Environmental Defense Fund released a joint report on their analysis of climate risk disclosures of 100 companies in five sectors for the 2007 fiscal year and concluded that investors have not received adequate climate information from corporate filings with the SEC.[7] The SEC is currently addressing climate change and establishing guidelines for the proper disclosure if public companies responses to the challenges of climate change. The report, on climate change disclosures of about 6,400 10-K filings by S&P 500 companies from 1995 to 2009, reveals that there was "an alarming pattern of nondisclosure by corporations regarding climate risks."[8] A survey conducted by Ernst & Young in 2010 suggests the following five global themes regarding climate change:[9]

1. Appropriate tone at the top is crucial in dealing with emerging challenges of climate change.
2. Executive leadership is critical to effective governance and understanding and realizing the full potential of the business response to climate change. More than 90 percent of executives surveyed indicate that climate change governance should be addressed at board and top-management level.
3. Business drivers are dominated by top-line and bottom-line impacts of climate change initiatives with a keen focus on meeting changes in customer demand.

4. Business executives are committed to addressing the ever-increasing challenges of climate change.
5. Climate change investments have increased despite regulatory uncertainty.

In 2010, the SEC released guidance reiterating the relevance and importance of adequate disclosure of material risk associated with climate change by public companies.[10] Relevant items in SEC documents S-K or S-X that trigger climate-related disclosure are items 101, 103, 503(c) and 303. Item 101 pertains to any material capital expenditures on facilities and environmental controls and related risk assessment and management during the company's current fiscal year and previous periods where the company finds it material.[11] Item 103 requires a company or its subsidiaries to describe any material legal proceedings it may be involved in.[12] Item 503(c) gives guidance on what risk factors a company should review assess, manage, and disclose regarding existing or pending regulation on climate change.[13] Item 303 requires public companies to determine the effect any enacted climate change legislation or regulation will have on the company's financial position and operations.[14] For example, pending legislation or regulations on climate change can affect costs of purchasing supply chain management or improving facilities and demand for products and services.

In a survey, conducted by Ernst & Young in 2010, respondents reported that the top three factors driving their climate change initiatives were (1) energy costs (2) changes in customer demand and (3) new revenue opportunities.[15]

A list of EPA regulations relevant to environmental issues can be found on the EPA website.[16] The EPA has other programs which are voluntary and are helping to drive industry-wide adoption and awareness of environmental practices. The voluntary programs are: Green Lights, Climate Wise, Waste Wise and Energy Star. Corporations in the United States are not required to issue environmental reports or follow ISO 14000 environmental management, auditing and accounting standards. They are, however, liable for environmental degradation inflicted by them or their subsidiaries (e.g. the BP oil spill). Many large corporations like IBM, Pfizer, GE, GM, Google, and Apple have developed their own tools in developing environmental KPI-reporting items. The reports are produced annually and include tailored KPIs and goals which include energy conservation, waste reduction, green house gas emission reduction increased recycling and use of environmentally friendly materials.

The United Kingdom and the United States both have large corporations or conglomerates that operate worldwide. The UK has developed environmental laws that enforce environmental practices whereas the US has regulations that govern industries involved in the use of natural resources. Although both countries have laws and regulations to ensure public safety and reasonable use of natural resources now and neither has standards on how to disclose environmental practices. Furthermore, such disclosure is voluntary, but increasing in popularity as a result of societal demand. In the US, the SEC and the Financial Accounting Standards Board (FASB) have given corporations support in developing reporting standards. However, the major increase in reporting is mainly attributed to the increase in social awareness and governmental regulation.[17] The EPA has influenced the types of KPIs being established monitored and used throughout the business world. Moreover, systems have been developed to help report environmental information. The EPA has put through several environmental regulations to control and monitor environmental degradation, which enables them to enforce the regulations when companies fail to act accordingly.[18]

General guidelines for implementing ISO 14000 are as follows:[19]

ISO 14001—Environmental Management Systems—Specification with Guidance for Use

ISO 14004—Environmental Management Systems—General Guidelines on Principles Systems and Supporting Techniques

ISO 14010—Guidelines for Environmental Auditing—General Principles

ISO 14011—Guidelines for Environmental Auditing—Audit Procedures— Auditing of Environmental Management Systems

ISO 14012—Guidelines for Environmental Auditing—Qualification Criteria for Environmental Auditors

ISO 14020—Environmental Labeling— General Principles

ISO 14021—Environmental Labels and Declarations—Self-declaration Environmental Claims— Guidelines and Definition and Usage of Terms

ISO 14022—Environmental Labels and Declarations—Self-declaration Environmental Claims— Symbols

ISO 14024—Environmental Labels and Declarations—Environmental Labeling Type 1—Guiding Principles and Procedures

ISO 14031—Environmental Management—Environmental Performance Evaluation—Guidelines

ISO 14040—Environmental Management—Life Cycle Assessment—Principles and Framework

ISO 14041—Environmental Management—Life Cycle Assessment—Goal and Scope Definition and Inventory Analysis

ISO 14050—Environmental Management—Vocabulary

Environmental sustainability has become a strategic focus of corporations worldwide. The response to environmental challenges and the pursuit of opportunities has resulted in policies and practices that seek to safeguard the environment and improve the wellbeing of society. Global environmental calamities like the Union Carbide Bhopal chemical leak in 1984 and the 2010 British Petroleum oil spill in the Gulf of Mexico are examples of events that have forever changed the affected environments, ecosystems, corporations and communities.

Public awareness of both corporate and individual responsibilities has increased as has stakeholder input. Environmental risk mitigation is an integral part of economic sustainability, both present and future. Increased CO_2 levels from greenhouse gases (coal, oil and natural gas) are linked to atmospheric temperature, which will affect weather patterns. Volatility in climate patterns increases uncertainty about future demand, supply chains and the stability of infrastructure. Hence business policy will evolve as these patterns become better understood. Extreme weather conditions are well understood and responded to in most cases and this is generally part of an organization's business continuity plan. Both extreme weather and climate change impact sustainability. Energy and fuel supply uncertainties increase volatility in fossil fuel markets. Managing corporate reputation, customer expectations and efficiency drives interest to a greater extent than does legal compliance in most cases. Independent ranking agencies rate companies on emissions and goals. Carbon footprints are found in supply chains and are an efficiency and risk measure that is a liability demanding stakeholder management. Scarcity of material resources will increase in line with population growth and urbanization. Shareholders have become more educated about these challenges and recognize the corporate investment required to meet long-term sustainability. Several sustainability indices are being developed by agencies such as Bloomberg to provide valuation tools for the measurement and comparison of indices.

The stresses placed on the natural environment over the last century have increased strains and crises worldwide. In addition to the identification of ozone depletion in the late-20th century, the identification of climate change is a manifestation of this deterioration. Initiatives like the Kyoto Protocol, the European Union Emission Trading System (EU ETS), the Carbon Reduction Commitment (CRC), the Montreal Protocol and the Paris Agreement are all efforts to gain consensus on mechanisms by which to measure impacts to the environment and to set limits on activities deemed detrimental. Specifically, the Kyoto Protocol sets greenhouse gas emission limits and provides signature nations with three mechanisms by which to meet the necessary output level, namely emission trading, clean development mechanisms and joint implementation.

In addition to the numerous organizations, like the Alliance for Global Sustainability, which seek to improve the scientific understanding of global environmental challenges as well as the education of a new generation of leaders committed to sustainable development, the International Organization for Standardization (ISO) established global standards to assist firms in developing adequate environmental management systems.

The global success of the ISO 9000 quality assurance standards serves as the model for the ISO 14000 series standards. While not mandatory, many organizations are also required by their customers to be ISO 14000-certified prior to conducting business. Meeting ISO 14000 standards is increasingly becoming a prerequisite for competition in the global market. Further, the 14000 series standards can serve as the framework for environmentally sustainable business plans and mission statements, which, if well-built and adhered to, will likely limit a company's future liability and constrain the cost of enforcement. As energy dependence rises, further visibility and development of ISO standards which specifically address energy management throughout organizations is to be expected.

In total, there are numerous initiatives and organizations committed to creating sustainable business practices. Regardless of the mechanism by which any organization or nation decides to participate in and measure compliance with established protocols, the simple act of adopting and attempting adherence to any of the protocols makes members keenly aware of how their activities impact the environment. This awareness and understanding furthers advancements in technology which can negate or offset the harmful impacts of daily activities.

4.   ENVIRONMENTAL INITIATIVES IN ASIA

4.1   Mainland China

Mainland China faces increasing environmental challenges along with its economic growth, industrialization and urbanization over the last three decades. Since 1990, China's CO_2 emissions have increased, reaching 10,291,926.9 kt (thousand metric tons) in 2014 according to data from the World Bank. The increased emissions have resulted in health costs. A study by Nanjing University's School of the Environment provides the latest scientific estimates, establishing that in 2013, there were 3.03 million deaths in 74 cities in the Beijing-Tianjin-Hebei region and the Yangtze River Delta and Pearl River Delta of which 31.8 percent could be linked to PM 2.5 (particle) pollution—the tiny smog particles most hazardous to health.[20]

On June 5, 2017, the Ministry of Environmental Protection (MEP) released the 2016 *State of Environment* report, which showed that 45.4 percent of groundwater stations rated "bad" with 6,124 observations. Only 10.1 percent of groundwater stations rated "excellent". Between 2012 and 2015, the percentage of groundwater stations with "excellent" quality fell from 11.8 percent to 9.1 percent while the percentage of groundwater stations with "very bad" quality rose from 16.8 percent to 18.8 percent.[21]

Mainland China's rapid economic rise has come at the expense of its environment and hidden costs associated with health. Mainland China is the world's largest producer of carbon emissions and the pollution levels in many cities fail to comply with Organization for Economic Co-operation and Development (OECD) standards.[22] In 2015, air pollution killed more than 1.1 million people in Mainland China, the greatest number of any country in the world.[23] The Environment Ministry found that thousands of manufacturers in northern Mainland China have faked emissions data to avoid penalties.[24] The local government in Shijiazhuang Hebei province has encouraged the installation of environmentally unfriendly new coal furnaces. Official reports found that 20 percent of Mainland China's arable land and one-third of its surface water are polluted. In January 2016, the underground water reserves in Mainland China's major plains had decreased by approximately 8.24 billion tons since a year previously.[25]

The Mainland Chinese government is aware of the environmental problems and has been making efforts to enact stricter laws and regulations to raise expectations regarding business performance in environmental issues. Mainland China's air quality improved across the country in 2017. According to Greenpeace's analysis, the levels of toxic PM2.5 in Beijing, Tianjin and 26 nearby cities dropped by 33.1 percent year on year as the government shut down factories and dispatched inspectors to enforce environmental targets. The 13th Five-Year Plan (2016–2020) puts into effect the strictest possible water resources management system to ensure that over 80 percent of the major rivers and lakes meet water quality standards. The government also ensures that Mainland China's total water usage will stay below 670 billion cubic meters.[26]

4.2 Hong Kong

Hong Kong is struggling to meet the target of reducing CO_2 emissions from 2005 levels by 36 percent per capita by 2030. Local electricity generation by the two utility companies accounts for around 70 percent of CO_2 emissions. Hong Kong gets 48 percent of its energy from coal, 27 percent from natural gas and the remaining 25 percent from a mix of nuclear and renewable energy. By 2020, the supply of electricity generated from natural gas is anticipated to increase to 50 percent. Nuclear power is expected to account for 25 percent while "coal and renewable energy" would generate the remaining 25 percent. In 2014, CO_2 emission per capita was 6.2 tons. The goal of the Hong Kong government is to reduce the emission level to below 4.5 tons by 2020 and eventually to 3.3 tons.[27]

Hong Kong lacks a concerted effort to reduce waste at source by manufacturers and businesses without a mature recycling policy and facilities. In Hong Kong, 90 percent of rubbish is exported to Mainland China. Recently, Mainland China issued a ban on the import of 24 types of unprocessed rubbish, which meant that rubbish from Hong Kong has nowhere to go.[28] Large amounts of old newspapers, cardboard and office scrap have piled up on Hong Kong's docks over the past few months. Hong Kong people throw away an average of 1.4 kilograms of waste per day, which is higher than the rate in Tokyo, Seoul or Taipei. With a population of around seven million, Hong Kong deposits about 5.6 million tons, about two-thirds of its waste, into landfill per year. The amount of food waste in Hong Kong comprises 3,600 tons daily. The government is planning to establish a facility in 2018 that may transform food waste into energy and usable resources. Nevertheless, the total recycling amount is estimated at only 200 tons per day.[29]

4.3 India

4.3.1 Air Pollution India faces massive environmental problems from many aspects. The country relies heavily on coal for its power supply, which leads to serious smog problems. Many industrial companies do not follow the environmental protection guidelines. As its economy grows, India's air pollution has not improved over the past 25 years. Thick smog from vehicle exhaust fumes, dust and illegal burning of crops is causing serious problems in India. The gray air has caused road accidents and the toxic air leads to health problems. The World Health Organization ranked India's capital New Delhi the most polluted city in the world. Researchers estimated that 75 percent of deaths from air pollution in 2015 in India were in rural areas.[30] India is among the bottom five countries in the 2018 Environmental Performance Index (EPI) for the categories of environmental health, air quality, PM2.5 exposure and PM2.5 exceedance. The overall EPI ranks 177th out of 180 regarding air quality.[31]

4.3.2 Waste Management Indian cities generate a massive amount of untreated waste as a result of urbanization and industrialization. Large global corporations in India are still following the cheap-and-dirty practices that Western developed countries stopped tolerating over 10 years ago.[32] Mumbai is the world's fifth most wasteful city. India generates over 150,000 tons of municipal solid waste (MSW) per day, with 83 percent of the waste being collected and less than 30 percent treated. India's daily waste is estimated to reach 377,000 tons by 2025 according to the World Bank.[33] There is an urgent need for effective legislation and market strategies in India to promote product stewardship, producer responsibility and waste minimization for businesses.

4.4 Indonesia

Indonesia is home to the world's richest biodiversity, tropical forests and marine ecosystems. However, as a result of deforestation, overfishing and adverse weather changes, Indonesia is suffering from serious environmental threats.[34] Total economic losses due to inadequate safe water and sanitation were estimated to be 2 percent of GDP per year. The costs of air pollution to the Indonesian economy was approximately US$400 million annually.[35] Since the 1990s, both agricultural expansion and heavy mining contributed to large-scale deforestation. From 1990 to 2010, nearly

90 percent of oil palm plantations in Kalimantan were built on land once populated by tropical rain forests. In 2010, deforestation and peat fires accounted for 85 percent of total national greenhouse gas (GHG) emissions in Indonesia.[36]

To protect the domestic environment and improve its capacity to respond to extreme weather changes and natural disasters, the Indonesian government collaborated with environmental protection organizations around the world to formulate and implement environmental protection policies, laws and regulations. Meanwhile, the Indonesian government encourages businesses to develop economic strategies for sustainable resource management. Indonesia's marine biodiversity is threatened by overfishing, extreme weather changes, pollution and overexploitation. To address marine environmental issues, the government has strengthened the relevant technical and operational capacities of the Ministry of Ocean Affairs and Fisheries to improve sustainable fisheries management and enhance marine biodiversity conservation. Together with local communities, the government has succeeded in establishing 8 million hectares of Marine Protected Areas.

Indonesia also faces the challenge of greenhouse gas reduction. About 87 percent of Indonesia's targets to reduce greenhouse gas emissions comes from the natural resources sector. The government is improving land use planning, natural resources governance, forest management and adaptation to low emission development strategies for communities that are highly dependent on natural resources. Indonesia also made an international commitment to a 26 percent reduction in greenhouse gas emissions by 2020 with a further reduction of up to 41 percent with assistance worldwide. The target depends on the government's ambitious goal of achieving 23 percent of its energy from renewable sources by 2025, which is more than double current levels.[37]

4.5 Japan

Japan has become a cleaner and a more environmentally responsible nation in recent decades and the country's business, agricultural and industrial activities continue to contribute toward a broad range of environmental issues. One of the biggest environmental concerns in Japan is waste management. Modern Japanese society produces voluminous amounts of trash with little room to dispose of it. Japan had developed municipal facilities to incinerate high volumes of trash, which resulted in serious air pollution issues. The government has tried to adopt alternate recycling policies. A 2010 review by the Organization for Economic Co-operation and Development (OECD) concluded that Japan still needs to improve and refine its waste reduction programs.

The 2013 Fukushima Daiichi nuclear plant disaster has created immense environmental issues and the Japanese government is still handling its aftermath. The plant was disabled in March 2013, but problems associated with the disaster continue to plague the environment and Japanese society.[38] Moreover, the shutdown of all nuclear power plants after the accident led to a significant rise in fossil fuel use, increased fuel imports and a rise in carbon dioxide emissions. This brought electricity prices in Japan to unsustainable levels. Faced with these challenges, the government has revised its energy policy in recent years to focus on further diversification of its energy mix (less use of fossil fuels, more reliance on renewable energy, restarting nuclear plants when declared safe) and curbing carbon emissions. Building on these plans, Japan has outlined ambitious goals to cut greenhouse gas emissions by 26 percent between 2013 and 2030.[39]

4.6   South Korea

South Korea has been ranked as one of the most polluted countries in the world. Seoul (South Korea), Beijing (Mainland China), and New Delhi (India) are the three most polluted Asian capitals. Carbon dioxide emissions, industry operations, and power plants are the main causes of environmental concerns in South Korea.[40] The level of fine dust in South Korea was 149 parts per million in 2018. The duration of warnings rose from 16.3 hours in 2017 to 19.8 hours in 2018.[41]

Air quality in South Korea has been deteriorating. Although South Koreans tend to blame pollution drift over the border from Mainland China, experts claim that much of the pollution is produced locally.[42] According to World Bank data, global CO_2 emissions remained stable over this decade but the figure for South Korea was up to 11 metric tons per capita in 2014. Visibility in Seoul is significantly affected by increased pollution emissions from vehicles, power plants and industrial facilities. Polluted air can lead to asthma, lung cancer, a range of respiratory diseases, cardiovascular complaints, birth defects and premature death.[43]

The Seoul Metropolitan government and the Seoul Metropolitan Office of Education signed an amended law to mitigate the air pollution issue and its effect on students. The law was amended to ban elementary, middle and high schools from organizing outdoor classes whenever there is a PM2.5 (particulate matter with a diameter of 2.5 micrometers or less) reading with 76 micrograms per cubic meter sustained for over two hours.[44] The Seoul Banghak Elementary School in March 2018 disallowed all outdoor sports for students. A virtual e-sports classroom including a big screen and high-tech sensors replaced outdoor games. The South Korea Education Ministry is planning to invest approximately £4.25 million (around US$5.44 million) on new virtual e-sport facilities at 178 schools by 2018. The Ministry is committed to installing air purifiers in kindergarten and elementary school classrooms within the next three years.[45]

4.7   Malaysia

With the urbanization of Malaysia comes the issues of environmental degradation. Malaysians face great risks, from climate change to environmental pollution, which are the consequences of increased economic activities. The industrialization of Malaysia started in 1960. As industrialization has its benefits, it also imposes costs on society. The more prevalent environmental issues in Malaysia are water pollution and deforestation. With new commercial and residential buildings being constructed in recent years, urbanization issues have arisen with varying local intensity, issues such as industrial and household wastewater, air pollution from industrial activities, forest fires and vehicular emission from increased traffic intensity especially in urban areas. There are also environmental issues, such as sea pollution from oil spills and deforestation. A recent study shows that the Malaysian public are more concerned about environmental issues that involve water pollution and that people are taking active individual conservative measures and actions.[46] The three major contributors to water pollution in Malaysia are the palm oil, natural rubber and tin mining industries. The government organizes environmental programs and gives priority to sectors that reduce water pollution in the country.[47]

Malaysia experiences fewer natural environmental challenges from flood, landslide and forest fires than its neighboring country Indonesia. Most of the environmental issues in Malaysia are consequences of human activities. In 2011, as part of the economic reforms championed by the then prime minister Najib Razak, the government announced its plan to build a Green Economy to ensure that the country is more efficient in managing its resources and has lower carbon emissions by 2020. The government intends to turn Malaysia into a smart country, capitalizing on technological advancement to achieve its goal with the support of experts in different sectors, especially for the palm oil industry.

The 2018 Environmental Performance Index (EPI) collated for 180 countries ranks Malaysia 78th, with an EPI score of 59.22 out of 100 points. The EPI reports a country's performance based on 24 indicators which highlight countries' environmental health issues in meeting their environmental policy goals. Malaysia seems to perform well overall when compared to other Asian countries. However, it performed poorly in the forest indicator with a ranking of 135th and a score of 0 out of 100, which suggests that tree cover and deforestation are major concerns in Malaysia, as there are insufficient government policies to protect against deforestation in the country. On the other hand, Malaysia performed well in managing water resources with a score of 82.3 out of 100 points.[48] The government's initiatives on environmental issues have not transferred to business enterprises, which remain more focused on economic sustainability.

4.8 The Philippines

The Philippines lies within the active volcanic region, the "Pacific Ring of Fire". The region is geologically unstable between the Pacific and Eurasian tectonic plates. The Philippines is in the typhoon belt and it experiences 15 to 20 typhoons a year of which 5 to 6 cause serious destruction and death. Floods, landslides, volcanic eruptions, earthquakes and tsunamis are some of the many causes of natural disasters in the Philippines.[49] With one of the fastest-growing economies in Asia, the Philippines faces environmental challenges including lack of biodiversity resources, water and air pollution and increasing greenhouse gas emissions.[50] According to the World Bank, CO_2 emissions have been increasing since 1990 and reached 1.055 metric tons per capita in 2014.[51] The environmental deterioration is also a result of high population growth, loss of agricultural lands, deforestation, soil erosion, loss of coral reefs and overfishing.[52]

The Department of Environment and Natural Resources (DENR) is the primary government agency committed to the protection, monitoring, development, and usage of the nation's environment and natural resources especially forest and grazing lands, mineral resources including those in reservation and watershed areas, and lands of the public domain.[53] The DENR established a National Greening Program (NGP) for 2011 to 2016 and the Expanding the Coverage of the National Greening Program (ENGP) project, which contributes to rejuvenating 7.1 million hectares of unproductive, denuded and degraded forestlands nationwide.[54] Business enterprises are more concerned about economic sustainability than environmental concerns, which is seen as more of a government issue.

4.9 Singapore

4.9.1 Air Pollution   While Singapore's air quality is generally good compared with other major Asian cities, its levels of fine particulate matter such as sulfur dioxide and PM2.5 remain high. The main sources of air pollution in Singapore are cars, power stations, and refineries. Unfortunately, these are national infrastructures that Singapore cannot afford to abandon. In order to ensure good air quality, the Singaporean government has established emission standards and encouraged the gradual introduction of clean fuels in the industrial and transport sectors.[55]

4.9.2 Waste Waste has been a problem for the Singaporean government. In Singapore, non-biodegradable bags account for about one-third of household waste, more than half of which are packaging for food and beverages. Environmentally unfriendly packaging not only consumes resources but also increases waste generation. With population and economic growth, the amount of waste generated in Singapore has increased more than sixfold over the past 40 years. In 1970, Singapore produced about 1,200 tons of waste daily and by 2010 the number had risen to 7,600 tons. Since Singapore is geographically small, it does not have enough space for waste disposal. The government organized events such as "recycling week" to promote the importance of recycling and reducing waste. All families have access to recycling bins. In 2014, the government also encouraged family recycling through the introduction of a recycling incentive program.[56]

4.9.3 Energy The United Nations Framework Convention on Climate Change acknowledges that Singapore is a country with "scarce alternative energy." Because of its small land area, geographical location, and other related characteristics, Singapore had difficulty in adopting alternate energy sources to conventional fossil fuels. This resulted in significant emissions of carbon dioxide and other greenhouse gases. In this regard, the Energy Efficiency Programme Office (E2PO) in Singapore has been actively promoting energy conservation in various sectors. It encourages the public to consume energy efficiently and reduce carbon emissions. The Office adopts an energy pricing strategy to encourage informed production and consumption choices by the public.[57]

4.10 Taiwan

Taiwan has long been committed to environmental protection. Environmental action in Taiwan is driven in concert by different groups, from middle-class intellectuals and scholars educated overseas to victims of environmental pollution. They are all working to make Taiwanese citizens aware of the importance of the environment and they continuously cooperate to promote the protection of the environment. Their messages and actions are consistent with those of the international environment community.[58] On the government side, the Democratic Progressive Party (DPP), which was founded in 1987, chose environmental protection as one of the main principles of its political platform. In 2010, the DPP launched the Water Disclosure program, which aims to encourage investors to invest in sustainable water projects. The government of Taiwan established the Department of Environmental Protection on January 15, 1988. The department has enacted a series of environmental laws and regulations in the past years. The Vehicular Air Pollutant Emission Standards, published on December 27, 2016, aims to improve Taiwan's air quality and encourage citizens to use environmentally friendly vehicles.[59] The Waste Disposal Act, promulgated on January 18, 2017, focuses on the effective removal and disposal of waste to improve sanitation and maintain national health.[60]

Despite these efforts, according to a 2018 Central Intelligence Agency survey, Taiwan continues to face environmental problems such as air pollution, water pollution caused by industrial emissions, illegal trade in endangered species and radioactive waste disposal.[61] There remains a lot of work for Taiwan on matters relating to environmental protection. Business enterprises are more aware of environmental issues such as recycling because of government initiatives.

4.11 Thailand

As Thailand began its industrialization in the 1970s, its natural resources were over-consumed to maximize profit.[62] As a result, 80 percent of the country's original thick-growth forests have been destroyed.[63] Rapid urbanization exerts pressure on water resources and the management of water quality.[64] Factories discharge untreated polluted water directly into the Chao Phraya River, which serves millions of people downstream in Bangkok. The Map Ta Phut Industrial Estate is a large industrial park that has created a festering, toxic and poisonous environment on the Gulf of Thailand.[65]

Thailand is ranked the sixth biggest contributor of plastic waste to oceans among 192 countries in the world. It is estimated that its 23 coastal provinces produce 11.47 million tons of waste per day. Plastic waste will take about a century to decompose[66] and in the past 10 years, around two million tons of plastic waste were produced annually in Thailand with only half a ton being recycled or reused during each year. Thailand's Health Ministry reported that the country's air pollution came from vehicular emissions, smoke from the burning of waste and unusual weather patterns. Over the past decade, CO_2 emissions have been increasing slowly up to 4.6 in 2014. Thai officials are concerned about the smog and warns schools and people who are sensitive to pollution to reduce outdoor activities.[67]

4.12 Vietnam

Increasing industrial construction has led to serious environmental issues in Vietnam. Short-term development strategies have caused deforestation, water pollution and air pollution in many cities. In 2015, the Vietnamese government planned to cut down thousands of trees in Hanoito to establish a US$3.4 million sightseeing program.[68] Criticisms from residents, celebrities and social media mounted a strong reaction against the government plan after the trees were cut. There is a rising awareness of environmental protection in Vietnam.

Environmental issues continue to haunt Vietnam, particularly air pollution. There are about 1.5 million people suffering lung-related diseases annually due to the poor air quality. Ho Chi Minh City's air pollution problem has recently reached an alarming level. Traffic is a major reason for air pollution, with about 85 percent of emissions coming from cars. In Vietnam, the air pollution level in construction is higher than that in other places.[69] Again, business enterprises do not act on environmental issues and leave this to the government.

5. ENVIRONMENTAL KEY PERFORMANCE INDICATORS

To help reduce their environmental footprint, corporations are adopting formal eval-uation processes to measure their impact on the planet. Various environmental KPI measures are being developed and adopted. Best practices among the environmental KPIs adopted are:

- Production and delivery of environmentally safe products by the use of biodegradable, non-toxic and naturally derived materials in the production.
- Efficient and effective utilization of scarce natural resources like power, energy and scarce natural materials.
- Efficient and effective use of recycled materials.
- Low-carbon model towns.
- Leveraging technology to maximize utilization of scarce resources and replace-ment of non-renewable resources.
- Effective and efficient utilization of non-waste technologies.
- Minimization of the use of harmful and unsafe materials and products.
- Assessment and management of environmental risks including providing for appropriate insurance against risks and environmental remediation and disposal efforts.
- Environmental reporting that discloses environmental risk assessment and management, compliance with environmental requirements and measurement of environmental liabilities.
- Environmental external auditing and assurance on environmental reports.

6. ENVIRONMENTAL MANAGEMENT SYSTEMS

The Environmental Management Systems (EMS) within a corporation are programs established by the corporation to improve the environmental performance of the company. EMS programs allow companies to achieve environmental goals based on the company's control of its processes. EMS programs maintain themselves through mission statements and company policies. These policies and goals are available to all stakeholders. It is believed that when a company can control its environmental impact through goals, the company will improve its environmental performance. Most companies benefit from EMS programs through the saving of energy.

The management team is responsible for determining the policies and goals for EMS programs. Once goals and policies have been established, a plan is developed to attain the goals set. The company must then implement the plan and develop a monitoring system to determine the effectiveness and achievement of the goals and policies. This ultimately comes down to review by management to further develop goals and policies.

The documentation for EMS programs is specifically based on ISO 14000 stan-dards. ISO 14001 is the leading standard for EMS programs. It requires exten-sive documentation as well as regular review of the documentation by executive management.

The corporation establishes its EMS programs and applies for ISO 14000 certification. The company will then be audited regarding its goals and policies. Once the company gains certification, it will be subject to periodic reviews. Some benefits of becoming certified include new market customers, increased employee morale, increased efficiency, and a better public image. Some of the best practices and goals of an effective EMS are:

- Appropriate tone at the top set by the board of directors and senior executives to provide leadership and commit adequate resources necessary for responsible environmental management.
- The compliance board committee and/or compliance officers are assigned primary responsibility for the environmental performance of the operations within their control.
- Proper education of all employees regarding environmental laws, regulations and best practices.
- Development of environmental policies and procedures in compliance with environmental rules and regulations.
- Assignment of qualified officers and staff to be in charge of compliance with environmental policies in order to advance the corporation's knowledge of environmental protection.
- Assessment and management of environmental risks and evaluation of environmental performance in ongoing monitoring process.
- Certification of compliance with established environmental operating procedures to ensure maintenance of environmental regulatory compliance and responsible environmental management.
- Establishment of an environmental audit program to ensure periodic review of environmental KPIs in operation.
- Proper disclosure of environmental policies, procedures, reporting and auditing to all stakeholders.

7. ENVIRONMENTAL REPORTING AND DISCLOSURE

Environmental KPIs should be managed, measured, and reported in compliance with the GRI reporting framework. Environmental reporting is often referred to as "green accounting" or "green reporting."[70] Environmental information can be included in the corporate annual reports filed with the SEC and disseminated to shareholders, provided in Management Discussion and Analysis (MD&A), or presented in a standalone environmental report. Environmental information has traditionally been disclosed in both annual reports and MD&A. The GRI framework developed a set of principles to establish whether the type of information the company wants to report will be included in the sustainability report.[71] The basic principles are as follows:

Materiality—The organization should report information that has the greatest impact on short- and long-term operations, societal impacts, and environmental influences, fulfilling all dimensions of EGSEE. The materiality of reporting sustainability information should reflect the organization's overall mission, vision, strategies, stakeholder welfare, societal impacts, and environmental issues.

Stakeholders—The report should disclose all major stakeholder expectations and address any concerns or interests. A stakeholder is any entity (living or not) that can be affected by an organization's operations.

Sustainability context—The objective is to disseminate sustainability information across all areas of EGSEE performance, prepared in a format that best reflects all of these areas.

Completeness—The report should reflect all areas of EGSEE in order to properly and transparently reflect the organization's overall sustainability performance.

There are a growing number of companies worldwide that now issue separate environmental reports. For example: "2,500 organizations in some 60 countries around the world now measure and disclose their greenhouse gas emissions and climate change strategies through the climate disclosure project (CDP) and over 1,300 organizations published a GRI based report in 2009."[72] There are several reporting and certification processes and guidelines to help develop proper reporting tools for public companies and government agencies and other stakeholders. Industry-led initiatives such as ISO 14000, ISO 26000, and Leadership in Energy and Environmental Design (LEED) are certification processes in the United States and in other countries that can be used to track environmental compliance and other sustainable business developments. These initiatives require companies to develop environmental management systems as discussed in the previous section, but do not require mandatory environmental accounting, auditing, and reporting. A more convincing argument for encouraging the issuance of separate environmental reports is that the existing annual reports presenting financial statements are already very complex. Addition of environmental disclosures in the annual reports would further increase the complexity of financial statements. More importantly, by producing a separate environmental report, the organization can signal that it considers and values environmental disclosures as being as important as financial information.

The Statement of Financial Accounting Standards (SFAS No. 5) on contingent gains or contingent losses discusses how potential gains and losses are accounted for in financial statements. Financial Reporting Standard 12 (FRS-12) sets the principles for accounting provisions, contingent liabilities, and contingent assets. In most cases, organizations faced with transforming their environmental management activities will need to report environmental provisions, contingent liabilities, and contingent assets. FRS-12 guidelines will help organizations to accurately report in accordance with generally accepted accounting principles (GAAP) and to deal with difficult accounting situations when dealing with environmental reporting.

Moreover, it is imperative that an organization seek an EMS to develop the necessary tools to report and track environmental performance. Through scientific advancement, e.g., global climate modeling, modeling of ecosystems, and alternative energy sources, society's awareness regarding the impact of humans on the environment has increased. This has multiplied the costs and obligations organizations will have to bear. Environmental laws and regulations will increase as well and will force organizations to take a more hands-on approach to voluntary environmental challenges. Voluntary disclosures of environmental information can create diversity in the format, structure, and content of environmental reporting whereas mandatory standardized environmental reporting promotes comparability and uniformity in environmental disclosures.

8.   ENVIRONMENTAL ASSURANCE AND AUDITING

Environmental assurance and auditing is a broad term used to encompass environmental compliance, assessment of risks, and company environmental sustainability and audits. ISO 14010 is a systematic verification process that evaluates the effectiveness of the EMS. The audit will provide assurance that the company is complying with regulations, reducing insurance costs and appropriately assessing operational environmental liabilities. There is a growing trend toward having the sustainability report assured in part or as a whole as the value of these efforts becomes embedded in business strategy and stakeholder value. To ensure that the company is always improving its risk reduction efforts, a third-party independent assurance provider can be hired to provide assurance reports on compliance with applicable environmental rules, laws and regulations. The third-party assurance provider can examine chemical hazards and security vulnerabilities, facilitate and apply the appropriate risk-analysis technique for the risks identified, and recommend, prioritize and review options to manage risk to a level appropriate for each company's specific risk tolerance.

9.   ENVIRONMENTAL BEST PRACTICES

Best practices are standards set informally through methods or processes that have proven successful over time. Generally, common sense plays a role in developing best practices, and standards such as ISO 9000 and ISO 14000 are examples of voluntary best practices. Environmental best practices are standards such as ISO 14000 that establish an EMS in the organization to fully integrate environmental best practices, leading to an environmentally sustainable organization. Some organizations choose to report, based on KPIs on an annual or quarterly basis, on company-specific missions, goals and accomplishments. Some examples are CO_2 output, energy consumption, recycled material, raw material used, recycled material used, employee health in the workplace, etc. However, useful internal KPIs such as ISO 14000 can set global standards for management to use to become leaders in environmental sustainability.

9.1   ISO 14000

In 1996, the ISO created the ISO 14000 standards to help organizations globally to develop adequate environmental management systems.[73] The ISO was established in 1946 to encourage the development and execution of uniform standards through international trade. The ISO 9000 standards on Quality Assurance and Quality Management are the best-known standards, with over one million certified members.[74] Globalization is creating competitive pressures on all globally competitive companies and is a driving force behind the staggering number of companies being certified to ISO 9000.

ISO 14000 standards are voluntary compliance guidelines and thus not mandatory. However, they are essential tools and guidelines to help organizations assess, manage, monitor, and comply with external stakeholder demands on their environmental actions as well as government laws and regulations. This certification will ensure that organizations meet the emerging environmental challenges faced by businesses and societies worldwide by providing globally set standards for EMS. The ISO 14000 standards are viewed by organizations as a way to engage in environmental initiatives and to improve environmental performance while reducing their impact on the environment and as a tool for organizations to use instead of reacting to governmental laws and regulations. ISO 14000 certification can also help prevent future government litigation or the passage of laws and regulations, and minimize companies' exposure to environmental costs enforced by governing bodies such as the EPA. Since the ISO 14000 standards are not mandatory, environmental groups, governments, legal representatives, accountants, and other stakeholders should become aware of the ISO 14000 standards and their impact.

ISO 14000 standards have six specific guidance areas that help an organization deal with environmental resolution, as discussed in the previous section. ISO 14000 standards are becoming a necessity in competing in the global market and are helping organizations to develop environmentally sustainable business plans, missions, and goals. For example, Apple has eliminated toxic chemicals and substances from its products, such as arsenic, brominated flame retardants (BFRs), mercury, phthalates, and polyvinyl chloride (PVC); reduced the size of packaging for its computers by 40 percent; and offered complete recycling programs for old computers.[75] Many organizations are becoming more vocal about their environmental achievements and will continue to satisfy the growing concern regarding environmental sustainability. Globally, there are other standards that comply with or are compatible with ISO 14000 in developing an EMS. One such system is British Standard 7750, which helps describe an EMS in that particular region.

Studies have shown some benefits of compliance with ISO 14,000, but overall they find that certified organizations or facilities do not have better environmental performance than non-certified organizations or facilities.[76] A study conducted by Deepa Aravind and Petra Christmann shows that while there is little difference in average performance between facilities that have and have not been certified, facilities that have high-quality implementation with the full commitment of management do have higher post-certification environmental performance.[77] This suggests the need for a regular auditing of environmental system that eliminates conflicts of interest while implementing proper interim monitoring systems to ensure ISO 14000 compliance and commitment. Despite some technical drawbacks, ISO 14001 certification does help organizations to comply with government regulations and various waste reduction schemes, and to reduce overall emissions.[78]

9.2   LEED Certification

Leadership in Energy and Environmental Design or LEED was developed in 2000 by the United States Green Building Council (USGBC) to provide building construction projects (existing building transformation or new construction) with a framework and a quantification process for developing sustainable green design buildings and construction or maintenance projects. LEED certification is useful in assessing if the organization is following environmentally sustainable development projects which are audited and documented accurately. LEED measures:[79]

- Sustainable Sites—reduction in the site's impact on the local ecosystem
- Water Efficiency—water use reduction inside and outside of the complex
- Energy and Atmosphere—sustainable design and energy monitoring systems
- Materials and Resources—recycled materials, sustainable, grown and harvested
- Indoor Environmental Quality—improvement in indoor air quality
- Locations and Linkages—transportation efficiency to locations
- Awareness and Education—provision of necessary information about the use of green buildings
- Innovation in Design—improvement in buildings' efficiency beyond what is necessitated by LEED.

These categories will lower the costs of operating the building, reduce waste, conserve energy and water, improve indoor living quality and reduce or eliminate GHG emissions. The certification process can also qualify for tax incentives from the United States government.[80] It is based on a point system.[81] In general, the levels of certification are as follows: Certified (40–49), Silver (50–59), Gold (60–79) and Platinum (greater than 80 points) with platinum certification being the highest achievement. Such certification can help an organization document and achieve tangible sustainable development with monetary value. The certification can be a part of an organization's ISO 14000 standard system development to create a sustainable business.

The key environmental issues that impact our world today have become the challenges of our time—the increase in world population and climate change. The increased need to reduce greenhouse gases in the atmosphere and the lack of natural resources make corporations vulnerable. Natural resources include water, energy, metals, rare earth minerals and forest products. Best practices are evolving at this time and companies are becoming increasingly proud to share their efforts, meet regulations and proactively lead the way in these practices. Non-compliance can be very costly as was evidenced in the nearly US$20 billion BP oil spill in the Gulf of Mexico.

There are many opportunities and challenges pertaining to environmental performance, reporting and assurance. The 2014 revision of ISO 14001 addresses the following emerging changes in environmental management systems:[82]

1. Strategic environmental management—The Company's strategic plans and processes play an important role in the effective management of environmental performance. Proper environmental strategies can be mutually beneficial to the company and the environment. Effective strategies should identify and consider both opportunities and challenges facing the company in meeting its environmental responsibilities and ensuring sustainable environmental performance.
2. Leadership—Proper leadership and tone at the top demonstrating a commitment to sustainable environmental performance is the key to successful environmental management systems.

3. Protecting the environment—Business organizations are expected to protect the environment by maximizing their positive impacts and minimizing the negative effects of their activities on the environment. Examples are prevention of pollution, protection of biodiversity and ecosystems, sustainable resource use, greenhouse gas initiatives, and climate change mitigation and adaptation.

4. Environmental performance—Business organizations should strive to continuously improve their environmental performance by strengthening their environmental management systems and policy commitments to sustainable environmental performance.

5. Lifecycle thinking—Business organizations need not only to manage their environmental aspects but also to extend their environmental management systems and related controls on impacts to the environment.

6. Communication—Business organizations should utilize environmental reporting as a channel of communication with all internal and external constituencies about their commitment to the environmental aspects of their business, effective management of environmental activities, and fulfillment of environmental responsibilities.

7. Documentation—Technological advances enable business organizations to effectively and digitally document their environmental performance, reporting, and assurance.

10.   CONCLUSIONS

Stakeholder value creation can only be achieved when business organizations focus on all five EGSEE dimensions of sustainability. This chapter presents the non-financial environmental dimension of sustainability performance reporting and assurance. Given that a company is the property of its owners and not stakeholders, the owners have the right to decide how to handle their property as either for profit or for social good, or for both if they desire. However, there has been a move in recent years to a middle ground view of "doing well by doing good" by focusing on both financial and non-financial sustainability performance. Companies that are doing well financially have more slack resources to undertake social and environmental activities. By the same token, companies that are managed more effectively through robust corporate governance measures, that are run ethically, and that pay attention to their social and environmental initiatives are more sustainable in the long term.

Environmental sustainability is a process of preserving the quality of the environment in the long term and leaving a better environment for future generations while creating shareholder value for the current generation. Environmental sustainability has become a strategic focus of corporations worldwide and those in Asia. Responses to the global environmental challenges and the pursuit of opportunities have advanced policies and practices that seek to safeguard the environment and improve the wellbeing of society. Many organizations including the International Organization for Standardization (ISO) have established global standards to assist organizations in developing adequate environmental management systems, environmental auditing and reporting. Due to the fact that economic development in Asia is mainly at an emerging stage, environmental concerns have mostly been left for governments to take the lead. Many business enterprises have not advanced to the stage of "do[ing] well while doing good" in Asia.

11. CHAPTER TAKEAWAY

1. Various incentives and pressures driven by socially and environmentally responsible investors and activists have encouraged companies to focus on their non-financial governance, social, ethical, and environmental (GSEE) performance, reporting, and assurance.
2. Leave a better environment for future generations.
3. Integrate environmental initiatives and guidelines established by professional organizations into corporate culture, business environment, and strategic decisions.
4. Utilize ISO 14000 guidelines in developing environmental management systems, environmental risk assessment, and environmental auditing and reporting.
5. External and independent verification of environmental reports lend objectivity and credibility to environmental sustainability reports.

ENDNOTES

1. Securities and Exchange Commission (SEC), *Commission Guidance Regarding Climate Change*. Release No. 33-9106; 34-61469, 2010, https://www.sec.gov/rules/interp/2010/33-9106.pdf.
2. International Standardization Organization (ISO), ISO 14000 Family: Environmental Management, https://www.iso.org/iso-14001-environmental-management.html.
3. National Environmental Policy Act of 1969.
4. "Introduction: Environmental Enforcement and Compliance," http://www.epa.gov/region9/enforcement/intro.html.
5. "Superfund: EPA's Estimated Costs to Remediate Existing Sites Exceed Current Funding Levels, and More Sites Are Expected to Be Added to the National Priorities List," http://www.gao.gov/products/GAO-10-380.
6. "National Priorities List," http://www.epa.gov/superfund/sites/npl/.
7. CERES and Environmental Defense Fund, *Climate Risk Disclosure in SEC Filing*.
8. CERES, the Environmental Defense Fund, and the Centre for Energy and Environmental Security, *Reclaiming Transparency in a Changing Climate: Trends in Climate Risk Disclosure by the S&P 500 from 1995 to the Present*.
9. Ernst and Young, *Action and Uncertainty: The Business Response to Climate Change*, 2010, www.ey.com/ccass.
10. Securities and Exchange Commission (SEC) *Commission Guidance Regarding Disclosure Related to Climate Change; Final Rule*, Federal Register 75, no. 25, February 8, 2010, 17 CFR Parts 211, 231 and 241, www.sec.gov.
11. Ibid. 6295–6296.
12. Ibid. 6293.
13. Ibid. 6296.
14. Ibid. 6296.
15. Ernst & Young LLP *Action Amid Uncertainty: The Business Response to Climate Change*, (EYG No. DK0054), May 21, 2010, http://www.ey.com/Publication/vwLUAssets/Action_amid_uncertainty:_the_business_response_to_climate_change/$FILE/Action_amid_uncertainty.pdf.

16. Environmental Protection Agency (EPA), "Summaries of Environmental Laws and Regulations," http://www.epa.gov/lawsregs/laws/.

17. L. Holland and Y. B. Foo, *Differences in Environmental Reporting Practices in The UK and The US: The Legal and Regulatory Context*, Department of Accounting and Finance, De Montfort University, Leicester, April 15, 2003, 1–18.

18. Environmental Protection Agency (EPA), "Regulations," www.epa.gov/laws-regulations/regulations.

19. ISO 14000.

20. A. Yan, "Smog Linked to Third of Deaths in China, Study Finds," *South China Morning Post*, December 22, 2016, http://www.scmp.com/news/china/society/article/2056553/smog-linked-third-deaths-china-study-finds.

21. China Water Risk, *2016 State of Environment Report Review*, China Water Risk, June 14, 2017.

22. S. O. Idowu and W. L. Filho, *Global Practices of Corporate Social Responsibility* (Berlin, Heidelberg: Springer, 2009).

23. Health Effects Institute, *New Global Burden of Disease Study Finds Air Pollution the Leading Environmental Cause of Death Worldwide*, Health Effects Institute, 2017.

24. Y. Suwen, Z. Tailai, and L. Rongde, "Northern China Chokes on Fake Emissions Data," April 6, 2017, https://www.caixinglobal.com/2017-04-06/101075101.html.

25. C. Xia, "80% Underground Water Undrinkable in China," April 11, 2016, http://www.china.org.cn/environment/2016-04/11/content_38218704.htm.

26. Central Compilation & Translation Press, *The 13th Five-Year Plan*, National Development and Reform Commission (NDRC) People's Republic of China, December 7, 2016, http://en.ndrc.gov.cn/newsrelease/201612/P020161207645765233498.pdf.

27. N. Kang-chung, "With Hong Kong struggling to meet emission targets, village leaders are keen for solar energy. But they say the government needs to offer incentives first," 2018, https://www.scmp.com/news/hong-kong/health-environment/article/2133766/rural-leaders-seek-incentives-hong-kong-villagers.

28. S. Pradhan, "How Hong Kong's Trash Problem Became More Visible on January 1," 2018, https://www.hongkongfp.com/2018/02/19/hong-kongs-trash-problem-became-visible-january-1/.

29. F. Master, "Hong Kong Drowning in Waste as China Rubbish Ban Takes Toll," 2018, https://www.reuters.com/article/us-hongkong-rubbish/hong-kong-drowning-in-waste-as-china-rubbish-ban-takes-toll-idUSKBN1FK0J4.

30. H. Wu, "75% of India's Air Pollution-Related Deaths Are Rural," Study Finds, 2018, https://www.cnn.com/2018/01/15/health/india-air-pollution-study intl/index.html.

31. Environmental Performance Index, *India*, 2018, https://epi.envirocenter.yale.edu/epi-country-report/IND.

32. B. Sharma, 2013. *Contextualising CSR in Asia: Corporate Social Responsibility in Asian economies*, Singapore: Lien Centre for Social Innovation.

33. S. Park and R. Singh, "India's Waste Management Problem," 2018, http://www.livemint.com/Opinion/V2CgeiUq89kl1k2fDwJXML/Swachh-Bharats-waste-management-problem.html

34. USAID, *Environmental Security*, July 23, 2018, https://www.usaid.gov/indonesia/environment.

35. World Bank, *World Bank and Environment in Indonesia*, 2014, http://www.worldbank.org/en/country/indonesia/brief/world-bank-and-environment-in-indonesia.

36. "Indigenous Climate Change Solutions," 2014, https://ifnotusthenwho.me/films/indigenous-climate-change-solutions/.

37. P. Jacobson, "How Is Indonesian President Jokowi Doing On Environmental Issues?" June 12, 2016, https://news.mongabay.com/2016/06/how-is-indonesian-president-jokowi-doing-on-environmental-issues/.

38. M. Fitzpatrick, "Japan's Green Energy Evolution," September 2013, Fortune.com.
39. International Energy Agency, "Japan," 2016, http://www.iea.org/countries/member countries/japan/.
40. B. Harris and k. Buseong, "South Korea Joins Ranks of World's Most Polluted Countries," 2017, https://www.ft.com/content/b49a9878-141b-11e7-80f4-13e067d5072c.
41. "More Fine Dust Warnings Issued in 2018 Compared With Last Year Amid Rising Concerns: Data," Yonhap, 2018, http://english.yonhapnews.co.kr/news/2018/04/10/0200000000AEN20180410003700320.html.
42. B. Haas, "South Koreans More Worried About Air Pollution Than Kim's Nukes," 2018, https://www.theguardian.com/world/2018/may/16/south-koreans-more-worried-about-air-pollution-than-kims-nukes.
43. J. Ryall, "Smog Forces South Korean Pupils to Practise Virtual Sports Indoors," 2018, https://www.telegraph.co.uk/news/2018/04/10/smog-forces-south-korean-pupils-practise-virtual-sports-indoors/.
44. K. Dong-hwan, "Tougher Air Pollution Law in The South Korean Capital Bans Outdoor Classes," 2018, https://www.scmp.com/news/asia/east-asia/article/2139435/tougher-air-pollution-law-thesouth-korean-capital-bans-outdoor.
45. J. Ryall, "Smog Forces South Korean Pupils to Practise Virtual Sports Indoors," 2018, https://www.telegraph.co.uk/news/2018/04/10/smog-forces-south-korean-pupils-practise-virtual-sports-indoors/.
46. N. S. Mei, C. W. Wai, and R. Ahamad, "Environmental Awareness and Behaviour Index for Malaysia," *Procedia—Social and Behavioral Sciences* 222 (2016): 668–675.
47. Ministry of Environment, *Overview of Environmental Issues and Environmental Conservation Practices in Malaysia*, https://www.env.go.jp/earth/coop/oemjc/malay/e/malaye1.pdf.
48. Environmental Index Report, 2018, https://epi.envirocenter.yale.edu/sites/default/files/2018-mys.pdf.
49. Tagalog Lang, n.d., https://www.tagaloglang.com/climate-environment-natural-resouces/.
50. United States Agency for International Development (USAID), *Philippines Environment*, 2017, https://www.usaid.gov/philippines/energy-and-environment.
51. https://data.worldbank.org/indicator/EN.ATM.CO2E.PC?locations=PH.
52. Tagalog Lang, n.d., https://www.tagaloglang.com/climate-environment-natural-resouces/.
53. Department of Environment and Natural Resources (DENR), "DENR Mandate, Vision and Mission," n.d., https://www.denr.gov.ph/about-us/mission-vision.html.
54. Department of Environment and Natural Resources (DENR), "Enhanced National Greening Program," n.d., https://www.denr.gov.ph/priority-programs/national-greening-program.html.
55. Ministry of the Environment and Water Resources, *Keeping Our Air Clean*.
56. Ministry of the Environment and Water Resources, *Managing Our Waste*.
57. Ministry of the Environment and Water Resources, *Using Energy Responsibly*.
58. M. Ho, "A Conflict in Environmental Cultures: Tea-serving Volunteers and Conservationists in Taiwan," Conference paper presented at Rikkyo University, 2012.
59. Environmental Protection Administration Executive Yuan, R.O.C. (Taiwan), *Vehicular Air Pollutant Emission Standards*, 2016, https://oaout.epa.gov.tw/law/EngLawContent.aspx?lan=E&id=175.
60. Environmental Protection Administration Executive Yuan, R.O.C. (Taiwan), Waste Disposal Act, 2017, https://oaout.epa.gov.tw/law/EngLawContent.aspx?lan=E&id=174.
61. Central Intelligence Agency, *The World Factbook*, January 2018, https://www.cia.gov/library/publications/the-world-factbook/fields/2032.html.
62. APEC, *Corporate Social Responsibility in the APEC Region—Current Status and Implications: Economy Paper: Thailand*, Asia-Pacific Economic Cooperation, n.d., s. l.

63. A. P. Mavro, "Thailand" in *The World Guide to CSR: A Country-by-Country Analysis of Corporate Sustainability and Responsibility*, ed. N. Tolhurst (Greenleaf Publishing, 2010) s. l.

64. OECD, *Multi-Dimensional Review of Thailand: Volume 1 Initial Assessment*, Paris: OECD Publishing, 2018.

65. A. P. Mavro, "Thailand" in *The World Guide to CSR: A Country-by-Country Analysis of Corporate Sustainability and Responsibility*, ed. N. Tolhurst (Greenleaf Publishing, 2010) s. l.

66. R. Charoonsak, "Thai Industry Declares War On Plastic Pollution With 'Unprecedented' Public-Private Effort," 2018, http://www.nationmultimedia.com/detail/national/30347045.

67. N. Chuwiruch and S. Suwannakij, "There's a New Contender for Title of Asia's Most Polluted City," 2018, https://www.bloomberg.com/news/articles/2018-02-15/planning-a-vacation-in-bangkok-don-t-forget-your-pollution-mask.

68. N. Chapman, "Rising Environmental Awareness in Vietnam," 2017, https://kyotoreview.org/yav/rising-environmental-awareness-vietnam/#return-note-11052-2.

69. Xinhua News Agency, "Air Pollution At Alarming Level in Vietnam's Hcm City: Expert," 2018, http://www.xinhuanet.com/english/2018-01/03/c_136870022.htm.

70. A. Brockett, and Z. Rezaee. 2012. Corporate Sustainability: Integrating Performance and Reporting, *November 2012*, John Wiley & Sons, Inc.

71. Global Reporting Initiative (GRI), *GRI Sustainability Reporting Guide*lines, Version 3.0, 2010, http://www.globalreporting.org/reporting framework.

72. GRI and CDP *Linking up GRI and CDP: How Do The Global Reporting Initiative Reporting Guidelines Match With The Carbon Disclosure Project Questions*, 2010, www.globalreporting.org and www.cdproject.net.

73. ISO 14000, Revision of ISO 14001 Environmental Management Systems, updated July 2014, ISO/TC 207/SC 1, www.iso.org/iso/tc207sc1home.

74. "ISO 9001 Certifications Top One Million Mark, Food Safety and Information Security Continue Meteoric Increase," Oct. 25, 2010, https://www.iso.org/news_index.html.

75. "MacBook Pro and the Environment," http://www.apple.com/macbookpro/environment.html.

76. N. Damall, and S. Sides, "Assessing the Performance of Voluntary Environmental Programs: Does Certification Matter?" *Policy Studies Journal* 36 (2008): 95–117.

77. D. Aravind and P. Christmann, "Decoupling of Standard Implementation from Certification: Does Quality of ISO 14001 Implementation Affect Facilities' Environmental Performance?" *Business Ethics Quarterly* 21, no. 1 (January 2011), ISSN 1052-150X.

78. Ibid.

79. "What LEED Measures," http://www.usgbc.org/DisplayPage.aspx?CMSPageID=1989.

80. "What LEED Delivers," http://www.usgbc.org/DisplayPage.aspx?CMSPageID=1990.

81. http://www.usgbc.org/ShowFile.aspx?DocumentID=8868.

82. N.a., ISO 14000, Revision of ISO 14001 Environmental Management Systems, updated July 2014, ISO/TC 207/SC 1, www.iso.org/iso/tc207sc1home.

CHAPTER 10

Business Sustainability Performance Reporting and Assurance

1. EXECUTIVE SUMMARY

Business organizations play important roles in society by interacting with a variety of constituencies in creating value for all stakeholders. Proper communication of sustainability performance is important in disclosing commitment to creating stakeholder value as well. Corporate reporting is a process by which public companies disclose their mandatory financial economic performance and voluntary non-financial information on governance, social, ethical and environmental (GSEE) activities to all stakeholders. Corporations report their economic activities and performance in compliance with regulatory requirements and contractual covenants to satisfy financial information demands by investors. Corporations also voluntarily disclose their non-financial information on GSEE matters for a variety of reasons including demand from stakeholders, as a means of avoiding the attention of regulatory bodies where sanctions for non-compliance are imminent, and as a means of signaling compliance with industrial codes and best practices. This chapter presents corporate reporting consisting of both financial economic sustainability performance (ESP) and non-financial GSEE sustainability performance reporting and assurance.

2. INTRODUCTION

The past decade has witnessed wide attention to the accountability and social responsibilities of corporations, caused by a wave of global financial scandals at the turn of the 21st century which led to growing demand for corporate accountability on issues ranging from economic to all-embracing social responsibilities. The demand for more transparent corporate reporting reflecting economic, social, governance, ethical and environmentally sustainable performance is increasing in the context of sustainability reporting. Corporate sustainability reporting originally focused on environmental and corporate social responsibility (CSR) matters and evolved into presenting all multiple-bottom-line (MBL) issues.

Corporate reporting in this chapter is referred to as sustainability performance reporting, CSR, or MBL reporting, and reflects the role of corporations in society and disclosure of their accountability to all stakeholders. Corporate reporting focuses on both financial and non-financial key performance indicators (KPIs) to ensure corporations are held accountable to all stakeholders and fulfill their responsibility in managing their affairs in a fair and transparent fashion. In recent years, both mandatory and voluntary sustainability initiatives have been developed to promote business sustainability and to advance sustainability from greenwashing and branding to a business imperative, since investors demand, regulators require and companies report sustainability performance information. This chapter presents both mandatory and voluntary business sustainability performance reporting and assurance initiatives worldwide and in Asia.

3.   FINANCIAL AND NON-FINANCIAL KEY PERFORMANCE INDICATORS

Corporate success stories can be measured and disclosed through KPIs. KPIs can be prepared for both financial and non-financial activities to present a company's progress toward achieving its goals. KPIs should reflect a company's strategic mission and goals and how these goals are measured and achieved. KPIs should communicate key activities used by the board of directors and officers in managing an organization such as achieving desired return on investment for shareholders, maximizing customer satisfaction or attracting and retaining the best and most talented employees. The extent and types of both financial and non-financial KPIs can vary among companies, their peers, industries, and countries with one overriding determinant—that of being relevant to the company and its operations. For example, KPIs most relevant to a petroleum industry are exploration success rate, refinery capacity and utilization, reserve resources and related replacement costs, whereas for the banking industry the most common KPIs are deposits and assets under management, loans and loan loss provisions, capital adequacy and asset quality. The number of KPIs depends on the type and size of the business and its strategy, mission, goals and activities, with at least one KPI for each major activity and sometimes multiple KPIs for each of the five economic, governance, social, ethical and environmental (EGSEE) dimensions of sustainability performance.

The guiding principles for relevant KPIs are linkage to corporate strategies, precise definitions and measurements, intended purposes, benchmarks, sources, interpretations, assumptions and limitations. KPIs should be forward looking in order to identify, measure and disclose trends, drivers, and factors relevant to stakeholders, particularly investors' assessment of current and future EGSEE sustainability performance. Exhibit 10.1 lists a set of KPIs for all five EGSEE dimensions of sustainability performance. The Balanced Scorecard as a strategic management system can be used to relate financial KPIs to non-financial KPIs and their integrated link to business strategy using a multi-dimensional set of financial and non-financial performance metrics. Financial and non-financial KPIs relevant to environmental, ethical, social, and governance (EESG) dimensions of sustainability performance are summarized in Exhibit 10.1.

EXHIBIT 10.1 Financial and non-financial key performance indicators

Financial	Governance	Social	Ethics	Environmental
▪ Economic value generated	▪ Number of board committees	▪ Percent of employees who consider that their business acts responsibly	▪ Donations and other social expenses	▪ Continuous replacement of non-renewable scarce resources
▪ Revenues earned	▪ Percentage of board independence	▪ Number of full-time employees (FTE) dedicated to social investment projects	▪ Description of social and ethical activities and projects	▪ Disclosure of ecosystem changes
▪ Resources consumed	▪ Full independence of board committees	▪ Funds raised per FTE for non-profit and humanitarian organizations	▪ Diversity and equal opportunities	▪ Disclosure of gigajoules of total energy consumed
▪ Costs recognized	▪ Board diversity in terms of ethnicity, sex, expertise, minority	▪ Philanthropy as a percent of (pretax) profit	▪ Fair wages, contracts, and benefits for employees	▪ Disclosure of metric tons of total CO_2 emitted
▪ Resources obtained (assets)	▪ Staggered board	▪ Percentage of operating income dedicated to social contribution	▪ Training and internal continuing education	▪ Disclosure of risk exposure and opportunities regarding climate change
▪ Capital raised	▪ Separation of the position of chair of the board and chief executive officer (CEO)	▪ Percentage of suppliers who affirm business code of conduct	▪ Employee diversity based on age, specialization, gender, ethnicity, etc.	▪ Disclosure of toxic chemical use and disposal
▪ Liabilities assumed	▪ Board accountability and liability	▪ Social contributions spent per employee	▪ Number of employees, turnover, and hiring/firing procedures	▪ Efficient utilization of unconventional renewable and non-renewable natural resources
▪ Expenses incurred	▪ Number of board meetings		▪ Whistle-blowing policies, programs, and procedures	
▪ Earnings retained	▪ Number of members of board		▪ Employee productivity	
▪ Earnings distributed	▪ Percentage of insider directors on the board			
▪ Compensation paid				
▪ Financial risk assessed				
▪ Donations given				
▪ Market share secured				
▪ Taxes paid				
▪ Value-creating information, such as customers, employees, suppliers, innovative brands, and supply chain				

(continued)

EXHIBIT 10.1 (*Continued*)

Financial	Governance	Social	Ethics	Environmental
■ Information about management, such as track record, compensation plans, and incentive plans	■ Number of members in the audit committee	■ Percent of eligible employees who signed the code of conduct and ethics policy	■ Employee satisfaction, competence, and commitment	■ Efficient use of recycled materials
■ Financial assistance received	■ Number of audit committee meetings	■ Number of initiatives to promote greater environmental responsibility	■ Customer satisfaction, retention, loyalty	■ Environmental profitability analysis and assessment
■ Research and development invested	■ Number of audit committee financial experts	■ Total investment in the community	■ Fair competition	■ Maximum utilization efficiency of scarce natural resources
■ New products discovered	■ Value of stock options awarded to directors	■ Donations and other social expenses	■ Truthful advertising	■ Measurement of resource depletion
■ Forecast, projections, and other technical and quantitative market information		■ Description of social and ethical activities and projects	■ Fair suppliers, contractual relationships, and bargaining	■ Minimization of use of environmentally harmful materials and products
■ Financial statements (balance sheet, income statement, statement of cash flow, owners' equity)		■ Diversity and equal opportunities	■ Supplier satisfaction, retention, commitment	■ Prevention of negative impacts on ecosystems
■ Note disclosures		■ Fair wages, contracts and benefits for employees	■ Political activities	■ Production and use of environmentally safe products
■ Accounting policies		■ Training and internal continuing education	■ Business codes of conduct	■ Promotion of environmental performance
■ Segment information		■ Employee diversity and composition by age, specialization, minority and ethnicity	■ Uniform and fair enforcement of business codes of conduct	
■ Changes in business structure (business combination, discontinued operation)			■ Certification of compliance with business codes of conduct	

- Material and unusual items
- Post balance sheet events
- Stock prices
- Risk management
- Codes of conduct and ethics
- Executive compensation
- Stock-based compensation
- Dividend policy
- Budget and performance evaluation
- Earnings releases
- Non-GAAP financial measures
- Operational information
- Quantitative analysis
- Forward-looking data
- Market information

- Number of employees, turnover, and hiring/firing procedures
- Whistle-blowing policies, programs, and procedures
- Employee productivity
- Employee satisfaction, competence, and commitment
- Customer satisfaction, retention, loyalty
- Fair competition
- Access to appropriate health care
- Access to education
- Access to information exchange
- Improved purchasing power
- Payroll for the entire company

- Resolution of conflicts of interest
- Compliance with applicable laws, rules, regulations, and standards
- Compliance with best practices and norms
- Promotion of core values of mutual respect, fairness, openness, honesty, and trust
- Enforcement of responsibility and accountability
- Promotion of tolerance, acceptance, caring, and compassion

(continued)

EXHIBIT 10.1 (*Continued*)

Financial	Governance	Social	Ethics	Environmental
		▪ Political freedom and well-protected human rights		
		▪ Preservation of cultural heritage		
		▪ Truthful advertising		
		▪ Productivity (volumes/sales/value added by employee)		
		▪ Protected consumer rights		
		▪ Wages, contracts, and benefits other than stock options		
		▪ Well-maintained national security		

Source: Adopted from Z. Rezaee. 2015. Business Sustainability Research: A Theoretical and Integrated Perspective. *Journal of Accounting Literature*, Volume 36, June 2016: 48–64. http://www.sciencedirect.com/science/journal/07374607/36/supp/C.

4. SUSTAINABILITY REPORTING

The role of corporations in our society has evolved from profit maximization to creating shareholder value and, in recent years, to protecting the interests of all stakeholders. In today's economic environment, global businesses face scrutiny and profound pressure from lawmakers, regulators, the investment community and their various stakeholders to focus on sustainability performance. Corporate disclosures, either mandatory or voluntary, are the backbone of financial markets worldwide. Public companies are required to disclose a set of financial information as long as their securities are held by the public. The primary purpose of corporate disclosures is to provide economic agents (e.g. shareholders, creditors) with adequate information to make appropriate decisions. Mandatory corporate reporting (including financial reports disseminated to investors and filed with regulators) is designed to provide investors with relevant, useful and reliable information in making sound investment decisions. Moral hazard occurs in the presence of information asymmetry when management knows more about the company's actions and effects than is disclosed in the financial reports and chooses to withhold proper financial information from investors.

Voluntary sustainability reports usually include any disclosures outside of financial statements that are not mandated by regulators and standard-setters. Until the late 1990s, sustainability reports have been largely voluntary as part of the firm's supplementary disclosures. In recent years, many jurisdictions have adopted sustainability reports including Australia, Austria, Canada, Denmark, France, Germany, Hong Kong, Malaysia, the Netherlands, Sweden, and the United Kingdom. Regulators in other countries are expected to follow suit. Many global regulators, standard-setters and other organizations including the Sustainability Accounting Standards Board (SASB), the Global Reporting Initiative (GRI) and the International Integrated Reporting Council (IIRC) now promote and suggest guidelines for integrated/sustainability reporting and assurance. Business sustainability requires organizations to focus on achieving all five EGSEE dimensions of sustainability performance by taking initiatives to advance some social good beyond their own interests (e.g., compliance with applicable regulations and enhancement of shareholder wealth).

The true measure of success for corporations should be determined not only by their reported earnings but also by their governance, social responsibility, ethical behavior and environmental performance. Business sustainability has received considerable attention from policymakers, regulators and the business and investment community over the past decade and is expected to remain the main theme for decades to come. Sustainability theories, standards, policies, programs, activities, risk management and best practices presented in the previous chapters of this book should assist business organizations worldwide with the integration of the five EGSEE dimensions of sustainability performance into their management processes in order to improve their KPIs as well as the quality of financial and non-financial sustainability information disseminated to their stakeholders.

The concept of sustainability performance suggests that management must extend its focus beyond maximizing short-term shareholder profit by considering the impact of the company's operation and entire value chain on all stakeholders including the community, society and the environment. Disclosure of EGSEE dimensions of sustainability performance while signaling management's commitment to sustainability and establishing legitimacy with all constituencies poses a cost-benefit trade-off with implications for investors and business organizations. In creating stakeholder value, management should identify potential social, environmental, governance and ethical issues of concern and integrate them into their strategic planning and managerial processes. There are many reasons and justifications why management should integrate sustainability performance into its processes and practices including pressure from the labor movement, the development of moral values and social standards and the change in public opinion about the role of businesses in environmental matters, governance and ethical scandals. Companies which are or aspire to be leaders in sustainability are challenged by rising public expectations, ever-increasing innovation, continuous quality improvement, effective governance measures, high standards of ethics and integrity and heightened social and environmental problems. Thus, management should develop and maintain proper sustainability programs that provide a common framework for the integration of all five EGSEE dimensions of sustainability into their management processes consisting of:

- Establishment of financial and non-financial KPIs relevant to all five EGSEE dimensions of sustainability performance that support management's strategic decisions and actions.
- Integration of financial and non-financial sustainability KPIs into business and investment analysis, supply chain management and the decision-making process.
- Communication of the company's management sustainability strategies, practices and expectations to major stakeholders including suppliers and customers to mitigate risks and foster corporate values and culture.
- Continuous assessment of the company's sustainability initiatives and related managerial processes to monitor and improve sustainability performance and identify challenging areas and risks that need further improvement.
- Promotion of product innovation and quality, customer retention and attraction, employee satisfaction and talent attraction and productivity through management sustainability processes.
- Development of environmental, social, ethical and governance initiatives that will impact the company's ability to generate sustainable financial performance for shareholders and create value for all stakeholders.
- Development of integrated sustainability reports to ensure that relevant financial and non-financial sustainability performance information is disclosed to all stakeholders.
- Periodic certification of both financial and non-financial sustainability KPIs, issuance of integrated sustainability reports and securing of external assurance reports on all five EGSEE dimensions of sustainability performance.

The global trend toward business sustainability performance, reporting and assurance encourages and rewards companies that focus on financial ESP and non-financial GSEE dimensions of sustainability performance and disclose their sustainability performance in sustainability reports with assurance. Taken together, the persistent challenges of maintaining sustainability have been the proper identification, measurement, recognition, reporting, and assurance of financial and non-financial KPIs. Examples of these challenges according to a 2015 report by the Corporate Economic Forum are:[1]

1. Operational resources: The integration of business sustainability into the company's supply chain management is challenging when dealing with price volatility and the availability of scarce resources.
2. Government regulation: Management faces the challenge of effective compliance with all sustainability regulations, rules and standards, all of which have increased the cost of compliance.
3. Mergers and acquisitions: Business sustainability generates and promotes merger and acquisition activities and can cause companies to add or divest assets. Management should recognize the sustainability impact of these changes and make proper decisions.
4. Major investors: Institutional and socially responsible investors have recently shown much interest in business sustainability. One can witness such developments in Asian jurisdictions such as Hong Kong, which has started to make impact investment products available in global private banks. Thus, management should recognize this continuing interest in sustainability and its possible impact on the cost of capital.
5. Activist shareholders: Shareholders are more actively involved with sustainability activities and many shareholder resolutions in recent years are related to the environment and society. Management should address these resolutions to avoid reputational or financial damages.
6. Reporting requirements: Financial and non-financial sustainability information is more popular and is demanded by external stakeholders. Management should recognize such continuous interest in sustainability information and integrate it into corporate reporting.
7. Talent acquisition: Employees are interested in business sustainability as shown by their desire to work in environmentally friendly, diverse and socially responsible companies. Thus, management should demonstrate commitment to sustainability to attract and retain talented employees.

5. SUSTAINABILITY ASSURANCE

Assurance providers play an important role in providing assurance on sustainability reports reflecting all five EGSEE dimensions of sustainability performance. Objectivity, reliability, transparency, credibility and usefulness of sustainability reports are important to both internal and external users of the reports and can be enhanced by the provision of assurance on reports. Sustainability assurance can be provided by internal auditors or external assurance providers. While internal auditors are well qualified to assist management in the preparation and assurance of sustainability reports, external users of sustainability reports may demand more independent and objective assurance on reports. This type of assurance can be provided by certified public accountants (CPAs), professional assurance providers or equivalent accredited individuals, groups or institutes. Current auditing standards are intended to provide reasonable assurance on financial and internal control reports prepared by management. However, the degree of reliance placed on non-financial information such as sustainability reporting is not clear. Assurance standards on different dimensions of sustainability performance reports vary in terms of rigorousness and general acceptability. For example, auditing standards governing reporting and assurance on economic activities presented in the financial statements are well established, and widely accepted and practiced. Assurance standards on other dimensions of sustainability including governance, ethics, social and environmental standards are yet to be fully developed and globally accepted.

An integrated model for assurance on all five EGSEE dimensions of sustainability performance reporting is desirable. Auditing standards published by the Public Company Accounting Oversight Board (PCAOB) are relevant to the economic dimension of sustainability in auditing financial statements and internal controls over financial reporting. Two recent standards released by the International Auditing and Assurance Standards Board (IAASB), namely the International Standard on Assurance Engagements "Other Than Audits or Reviews of Historical Financial Information" 3000 (ISAE 3000) and ISAE 3410 (Assurance Engagements on Greenhouse Gas Statements) can be used for each dimension of EGSEE sustainability.[2] This integrated model provides policy guidelines with practical and educational implications for employing EGSEE reporting and auditing. The growth of sustainability reporting use and its potential to raise important assurance issues will be very important in the future.

Recognition of the growing number of assurance services seems apparent from the issuance of assurance practice guidance statements by influential bodies such as AccountAbility,[3] the Global Reporting Initiative (GRI)[4] and the European Federation of Accountants (FEE).[5] Two important sources of guidance on the assurance of sustainability reporting, each released in 2003, are provided by AccountAbility's (AA) AA1000 and the IAASB's International Standard on Assurance Engagement (ISAE) 3000. The AA1000 assurance standard provides guidance for an assurance engagement for assurance providers from outside the accounting profession while ISAE 3000 provides guidance for an assurance engagement for members of the accounting profession. The ISAE 3000 (issued by the IAAS Board in 2004), the AICPA's Attestation Standards (AT section 101), CICA section 5025 and the AA1000 Assurance Standards (AS) (issued in 2008 by AccountAbility) all provide guidance for assurance on the non-financial dimensions of sustainability.[6]

External assurance is an important part of integrated reporting as assurance providers verify the information contained in the reports and publish those conclusions so that others, generally less experienced in the particular areas in which the assurance providers have expertise, may be assured that the practices faithfully confirm the statements made by management. The *G4 Guidelines* state that assurance providers must:

- Be independent from the organization and therefore able to reach and publish an objective and impartial opinion or conclusions on the report.
- Be demonstrably competent in both the subject matter and assurance practices.
- Apply quality control procedures to the assurance engagement.
- Conduct the engagement in a manner that is systematic, documented, evidence based and characterized by defined procedures.
- Assess whether the report provides a reasonable and balanced presentation of performance, taking into consideration the veracity of the data in the report as well as the overall selection of content.

- Assess the extent to which the report preparer has applied the *Guidelines* in the course of reaching his or her conclusions.
- Issue a written report that is publicly available and that includes an opinion or set of conclusions, a description of the responsibilities of the report preparer and the assurance provider, and a summary of the work performed to explain the nature of the assurance conveyed by the assurance report.[7]

Numerous bodies have developed methodologies and standards for external assurance for global, regional and country-specific audiences. Many of these bodies come in the form of trade associations of accountants, engineers and other professionals who come together to write standards that will raise the quality of their respective industries as a whole.[8] As reporting becomes more nuanced, there will be somewhat of a reckoning for companies. Those that have not been disclosing issues well may see a downtick in their equity capital as investors realize there are more liabilities than previously thought. Conversely, those that receive good marks from external assurance providers may see an uptick in their value as investors find that there is less risk than previously perceived. One of the benefits of having external assurance is that companies will be forced to deal with issues previously unforeseen (perhaps even by the companies themselves) and improve their procedures accordingly. Those that use this as an opportunity to grow will be rewarded accordingly in general while those that do not will suffer. From an overall market perspective, this will help the product and security markets to become more efficient and, all else being equal, more profitable for those with the best practices.

Business sustainability promotes long-term profitability and competitive advantage; helps maintain the wellbeing of society, the planet and people; and creates value for all stakeholders. It is expected that integrated reporting will play an important role in future corporate reporting and in rebuilding investor trust and confidence in public financial information. Trust in public companies' financial reporting has been eroded in recent years and there is concern about the short-term focus on only financial information and the lack of attention given to non-financial GSEE performance information. Integrated reporting enables organizations to integrate EGSEE sustainability performance reporting into the mainstream corporate reporting process.

The important principles of integrated reporting are:

1. Ensuring that corporate strategy is articulated well as a core part of the report
2. Connecting all parts of the business as a whole
3. Making information concise and easily readable
4. Being future oriented and inclusive of multiple stakeholders
5. Taking care to provide materiality, value, and assurance to the audience of the report.[9]

6. GLOBAL STATUS OF SUSTAINABILITY PERFORMANCE REPORTING AND ASSURANCE

Many countries have and are adopting laws and regulations that make sustainability reporting mandatory for large companies. According to the GRI, the number of organizations releasing standalone sustainability reports grew from 44 firms in 2000 to

1,973 in 2013.[10] This number is expected to rise as more and more companies realize the potential of reporting their practices. Sustainability reporting can be promoted in three ways:[11]

1. Through market forces including the demand for and interest in EGSEE performance reporting by investors and financial markets.
2. Through mandatory sustainability reporting requirements of regulators and listing standards of stock exchanges;[12] a successful case is that Directives of the European Parliament require large public companies in Europe to report on their social, governance, environmental and diversity initiatives.
3. Through a combination of mandatory and voluntary initiatives.

Over the last couple of years, companies have begun to stray away from the mindset of "profit only" to one that recognizes that building and maintaining sustainable business practices is a good strategy for their companies. The 2013 *Global Corporate Sustainability Report* released by the United Nations Global Compact presents the current state of business sustainability by reviewing the actions taken by companies worldwide in advancing their business sustainability.[13] The report uses 10 principles of sustainability and processes in its suggested model as benchmarks in assessing corporate sustainability actions and performance. The report presents the responses of 2,000 companies in 113 countries regarding their sustainability progresses and challenges. The key findings of the 2013 sustainability report are:

1. Companies are taking proper actions to achieve sustainability performance as evidenced by 65 percent of signatories committing to sustainability at CEO level, with about 35 percent training their managers to integrate sustainability into their strategies and operations.
2. Large companies are leading the way toward sustainability performance and integrated reporting while small and medium-sized enterprises (SMEs) still face challenges to achieve sustainability.
3. Supply chains are a roadblock to the achievement of improved sustainability performance.
4. Companies are moving forward with a focus on the achievement of all dimensions of sustainability performance from education to poverty eradication, employment growth and climate change.[14]

There is no mandatory guidance at this time for sustainability reporting. However, there are several voluntary guidelines for sustainability reporting, including the reporting frameworks released by the GRI, the Connected Reporting Framework and the reporting publications of AccountAbility. An alternative to mandatory sustainability reporting should be considered, taking account of the following issues:[15]

- Standardization of the diverse sustainability reports that are currently issued.
- Establishment of a globally accepted reporting framework for sustainability information.
- Creation of uniformity in objectively reporting all five dimensions of EGSEE performance.

- Action to ensure that a wide range of users including investors have access to uniform and comparable sustainability reports.
- Facilitation of uniform sustainability assurance.
- Unlike audit reports on financial statements, assurance reports on sustainability information are not standardized, regulated or licensed.
- As mentioned earlier, IFAC's ISAE 3000[16] and ISAE 3410 on reporting greenhouse gas (GHG) statements.
- GRI also recommends that assurance be provided on sustainability reports by external assurance providers, which can be designated with a "+" added to the application level declared by firms regarding their sustainability reporting and assurance. Alternatively, GRI can examine the content of sustainability reports and express an opinion on the extent of compliance with the GRI *Guidelines* but not comment on the quality and/or reliability of disclosed sustainability information.[17]

Currently, sustainability reports are voluntary and (normally) not audited by external auditors. Existing sustainability reports bearing different names (green reporting, CSR reporting) serve different stakeholders in achieving a variety of purposes and vary in terms of content, structure, format, accuracy and assurance. A more standardized, integrated and audited process is required to make sustainability reports on EGSEE performance comparable, commonly acceptable and relevant to all corporate stakeholders.

7. SUSTAINABILITY REPORTING AND ASSURANCE IN ASIA

Like the global trend, sustainability performance reports in many Asian countries are voluntary and generally not audited by external assurance providers. There is a substantial steady increase in the amount of sustainability reporting and the number of reports with assurance statements issued in all 12 examined Asian economies. The GRI database provides a snapshot of the current trends in sustainability reporting and assurance practices for a sample of 10,377 companies across the 12 Asian jurisdictions over the 2005–2016 period. Exhibit 10.2 presents the number of sustainability reports in these jurisdictions from 2005 to 2016. The majority (71 percent) of sustainability reports were issued in the past five years and sustainability assurance reporting made steady progress in Asia in the five years from 2010 to 2016. The top three countries/jurisdictions in Asia for sustainability reporting, represented by more than 10 years (2005–2016) of reporting, are Japan with 2,989 reports (28 percent of a total 10,610 reports), followed by Mainland China with 2,289 reports (22 percent) and Taiwan with 1,457 reports (13 percent). Mainland China has shown significant increases in sustainability reports from zero in 2005 to 632 sustainability reports in 2016.

With the development of CSR and CSR reporting practices, more Asian firms provide CSR reporting assurance to increase the credibility of their CSR reports. This provides an answer to critics who have concerns about the verification and viability of sustainability reporting. Simnett et al. (2009) used a sample of 31 countries to show that Japanese firms ranked top in Asia in terms of the number of firms providing

EXHIBIT 10.2 Trend in the number of sustainability reports in the 12 Asian economies 2005–2016

Jurisdiction	2016	2015	2014	2013	2012	2011	2010	2009	2008	2007	2006	2005	Total
Mainland China	632	325	336	328	279	195	93	60	25	11	5	0	2289
Hong Kong	98	68	60	56	41	38	25	22	8	5	2	2	425
India	158	96	79	70	56	55	30	26	24	6	7	7	614
Indonesia	55	63	48	46	35	26	15	10	11	7	1	0	317
Japan	341	365	375	354	324	332	245	208	183	134	96	32	2989
South Korea	83	82	114	117	113	99	95	80	82	49	29	18	961
Malaysia	39	37	31	28	31	17	15	9	7	4	3	1	222
The Philippines	22	20	21	23	17	13	12	9	5	2	1	1	146
Singapore	44	38	35	29	30	22	14	11	6	3	1	0	233
Taiwan	453	418	211	155	76	56	35	30	13	8	2	0	1457
Thailand	102	39	39	44	74	24	14	6	4	0	0	0	348
Vietnam	28	7	3	6	5	4	0	0	0	0	0	0	53
Total	2166	1651	1449	1332	1142	930	632	485	378	235	148	62	10610

CSR assurance followed by a handful of firms from Hong Kong, South Korea, India and Malaysia. However, there was no evidence of assurance of CSR reports in other Asia jurisdictions such as Singapore, the Philippines, Taiwan and Thailand. Their study suggests that Asia lagged behind the world average in terms of CSR assurance as of the end of 2004.[18]

Rao (2017) surveyed 1,100 international firms who assured sustainability reports in 2009, 2010 and 2011. The study reveals that Europe has the highest number of sustainability reports assured during the period (with 54 percent compared to Asia with 25 percent, South America at 9 percent followed by a tie between Australia and North America). Only 2 percent of reports came from Africa. More recently, the GRI dataset (Exhibit 10.3) presented the numbers for sustainability assurance in the 12 economies in Asia, with the top five economies for sustainability assurance over five years showing Taiwan with 589 statements (29 percent), South Korea with 378 statements (18 percent), Japan with 296 statements (14 percent), India with 205 statements (10 percent) and Mainland China with 151 statements (7%). The overall quality of both sustainability reports and assurance has substantially improved during the last five years in Asia. Exhibit 10.4 presents the status of sustainability reporting and assurance in Asia. A combination of mandatory and voluntary sustainability reporting and assurance is developed and practiced in the different jurisdictions, as further explained in the following subsections.

7.1   Mainland China

During the past 15 years, CSR reporting and assurance in Mainland China have gained momentum following the first CSR report by a state-owned giant, the China National Petroleum Corporation, in 2001, and the first CSR assurance report by another large SOE, the China Ocean Shipping Company, in 2006.[20] The majority of participants in the CSR assurance market including CSR report preparers and

EXHIBIT 10.3   Trend in the number of sustainability assurances in the 12 Asian economies 2012–2016

Jurisdiction	2016	2015	2014	2013	2012	Total
Mainland China	15	29	35	22	50	151
Hong Kong	30	29	28	25	8	120
India	58	51	45	41	10	205
Indonesia	11	10	8	14	11	54
Japan	71	49	46	36	94	296
South Korea	72	73	97	99	37	378
Malaysia	12	11	13	9	12	57
The Philippines	11	10	8	10	4	43
Singapore	8	5	6	7	8	34
Taiwan	219	195	87	65	23	589
Thailand	19	14	11	6	27	77
Vietnam	11	9	9	7	4	40
Total	2553	2500	2407	2354	2300	2044

EXHIBIT 10.4 Summary of sustainability reporting in Asia: state of progress

Jurisdiction	Sustainability Reporting Enforcement Level	Sustainability Reporting Written Guidance
Mainland China	Mandatory	GB/T 36001-2015 Guidance on Social Responsibility Reporting
Hong Kong SAR (China)	Mandatory	Hong Kong Exchanges and Clearing Limited (HKEX) Environmental, Social and Governance Reporting Guide (ESG Reporting Guide)
India	Mandatory	CSR Voluntary Guidelines 2009; Guidelines on CSR & Sustainability for Central Public Sector Enterprises
Indonesia	Mandatory	Not available
Japan	Mandatory	Environmental Reporting Guidelines
South Korea	Voluntary[19]	BSR Guidelines (Korea's sustainable management index developed specifically for Korea based on the GRI Guidelines)
Malaysia	Mandatory	BURSA's Sustainability Reporting Guide
The Philippines	Mandatory	Corporate Governance Guidelines for Listed Companies (PSE CG Guidelines)
Singapore	Mandatory	SGX's Guide to Sustainability Reporting for Listed Companies
Taiwan	Mandatory	CSRI's Guidance for Sustainability Reporting
Thailand	Voluntary	CSR Institute's (CSRI) Guidelines for Sustainability Reporting
Vietnam	Voluntary	Sustainability Reporting Hand Book for Vietnamese Companies (Circular No. 155/2015/TT-BTC on Public Disclosure)

CSR assurance providers have a governmental or quasi-governmental background. The Chinese government and its agencies have been intensively promoting CSR reporting since the early 2000s.

The two stock exchanges in Mainland China started to promote sustainability reporting in 2006 by setting and enforcing reporting standards for listed companies. Shenzhen Stock Exchange (SZSE) and Shanghai Stock Exchange (SHSE) promulgated CSR reporting guidelines from 2006 and 2008, respectively. Meanwhile, these two stock exchanges also mandated ESG reporting for certain listed companies such as the SHSE Corporate Governance Index firms, overseas listed firms listed on SHSE, financial firms listed on SHSE, and Shenzhen 100 Index firms. Shen et al. (2017) report that, as a result, before 2006 very few firms had CSR reports and from then on there was a dramatic growth with the number of firms that issue CSR with certification increasing from 78 in 2010 to 130 in 2013. More Mainland Chinese firms started to recognize the benefits of improving the credibility of CSR reporting by introducing certification. A more recent report released by GoldenBee shows that the overall level of CSR reports shows stepwise improvement from about 100 reports in 2011 to more than 450 reports in 2017.[21] According to data shown by an academic study, auditors and non-auditor institutions have almost equal market share in CSR assurance reports for Chinese listed companies.[22] Among the Big 4 auditors, PwC and KPMG provide the largest number of CSR assurance reports while non-Big 4 auditors provide assurance reports for listed Chinese companies. However, the market share of non-Big 4 auditors is significantly lower than their Big 4 counterparts.

7.2 Hong Kong

In Hong Kong, the first CSR report covering environmental, health and safety (EHS) performance was produced and issued by CLP Holdings (CLP) in 1997 (ACCA, 2002).[23] Then, a number of large Hong Kong corporations, mostly in the transportation, property management and electronics sectors, followed suit and issued environmental reports in full documents or summary pamphlets. To encourage sustainable disclosure, the Chief Executive of Hong Kong introduced an environmental reporting initiative in his 1998 Policy Address. From 1998 onwards, all government departments, bureaus and government-owned organizations were mandated to produce annual reports disclosing their environmental performance. A total of 87 departments, bureaus and semi-governmental organizations subsequently produced environmental reports. Issuance of sustainability reports was not common in Hong Kong then.[24] As of 2002, development of sustainability reporting was comparatively slow when compared with other developed economies such as Japan, the US, and the UK. The ACCA 2002 survey showed that only 17 private sector Hong Kong organizations had reported their environmental performance. In addition, the Companies Bill of 2011 proposed a clause that requires a business review to include ESG matters. However, no mandatory reporting guidelines or requirements for the private sector on sustainability reports were enacted.

The Hong Kong Stock Exchange (HKSE) has issued a mandate to require listed companies on the main board to disclose CSR on a comply-or-explain basis effective for financial years ending on or after December 31, 2015.[25] It mandates all Hong Kong incorporated companies (unless exempted) to include:

1. A discussion of their environmental policies and performance.
2. A discussion of their compliance with relevant laws and regulations that have a significant impact on them.
3. An account of their key relationships with employees, customers, and suppliers and others that have a significant impact on them and on which their success depends. In order to achieve sustainable growth, investors urged corporations to disclose information concerning the three main ethical considerations involved in CSR, namely environmental, social and governance (ESG).[26]

CSR assurance is not required by the HKSE. However, several companies especially multinational companies (MNCs) domiciled in Hong Kong engage Big 4 auditors to assure their CSR reports to enhance their credibility.

7.3 India

The government of India has been working on policies and framework to regulate and enhance CSR/ESG reporting. The CSR Voluntary Guidelines 2009 require companies to disclose information on CSR policies, activities and progress in a structured manner to the public on official websites and in annual reports and other communication media.[27] The National Voluntary Guidelines for Social, Environmental and Economic Responsibilities of Business (NVGs) were released by the Indian government in August 2011 and provided the Business Responsibility Reporting (BRR) Framework to guide businesses in CSR/ESG reporting.[28] The Securities and Exchange Board of India (SEBI) also provides a reporting template following the BRR Framework for companies to report their ESG performance. In 2013, the Indian government released Guidelines on CSR & Sustainability for Central Public Sector Enterprises and encouraged public sector firms to embrace sustainability reporting. The 2013 Companies Act requires the board of every company in India to publish their CSR report and disclose the details on the company's official website after incorporating the suggestions made by the CSR Committee.[29]

According to a KPMG Report, the Indian national rate of CSR reporting reached 99 percent in 2017, which is much greater than the global average rate.[30] Although the numbers for reporting in India is at the top of CSR disclosure performance, the quality of CSR disclosure needs to be improved. For example, there is little consistency among Indian companies' CSR reports because almost all companies adopt a self-regulatory approach.[31]

Many Indian companies engage third-party assurers to assure their CSR reports. Among various assurers, accounting firms and certification bodies are major players.[32] It is observed that the majority of assurers adopt the ISAE 3000 and the AA1000 Assurance Standards in their assurance practices.

7.4 Indonesia

In 2010, the Indonesia government enacted a law that mandates listed companies to disclose the consequences of their societal and environmental activities and requires companies to explain the reasons for failure to disclose the required information. Despite the regulatory effort, Indonesian firms' CSR reporting practices lag behind those of other Asian countries. Ernst and Young (EY) investigated the sustainable disclosures of the 100 Indonesian Stock Exchange (IDX) listed firms with the highest market capitalization in 2016,[33] and reported that only 32 firms had issued sustainability reports, with varying reporting methodologies. Among the 32 reports, 28 firms provided standalone CSR reports and the rest reported their CSR activities in the annual reports. There are large differences in the details of the CSR reports with a varying balance of views on the reports. Only 34 percent of the reporting firms provided fairly balanced reports and 16 percent of reports are regarded as truly balanced. In line with global trends, the report shows that Indonesian stakeholders increasingly expect materiality assessment of companies' sustainability activities, consistent with the GRI framework.

The percentage of firms adopting external assurance for their sustainability reports in Indonesia is still small. The ASEAN CSR network and the Center for Governance, Institutions and Organizations of the National Singapore University

Business School jointly conducted a study which examines CSR reporting in four Asian countries including Indonesia, Malaysia, Singapore and Thailand.[34] Based on analyzing the top 100 main board listed firms in terms of capitalization as of June 2015 from these four Asian countries, they find that only 4 out of 32 Indonesian CSR reporters assured their CSR reports, which is much lower than the figures for Malaysia and Thailand. The study suggests that Indonesian firms have room to improve the credibility of their CSR disclosures by providing assurance on the reports.

7.5 Japan

Japan has been leading in the level of CSR reporting not only in Asia but around the world.[35] Although CSR assurance is not mandatory in Japan, several CSR assurance-related regulations have been promulgated. In 2004, the Ministry of Environment (MOE) enacted the Law Concerning the Promotion of Business Activities with Environmental Consideration by Specified Corporations, etc., by Facilitating Access to Environmental Information, and Other Measures. The Environmental Consideration Promotion Law requires specified entities to maintain the reliability of environmental reports, to perform self-assessment, and have third-party assurance, among others (Article 9, Paragraph 2). The law also requires that the entities performing such assurance must maintain independence, have an established assurance system, and retain high-quality assurance staff (Article 10). In April 2006, the third Basic Environment Plan proposed the integration of improvements in environmental, financial, and social aspects as the direction of future environmental policy. To assure the reliability of information disclosed by companies, the MOE and the Japanese Institute of Certified Public Accountants (JICPA) set up a CSR Information Assurance Study Group to establish the basis for the assurance of CSR information in Japan.[36]

Although Japan is one of the leaders in CSR reporting, the engagement of assurance in CSR reporting is lower when compared to the practices in European countries. In 2011, while 99 percent of leading Japanese companies issued CSR reporting, only 23 percent of these firms engaged assurance services.[37] On the other hand, more than 60 percent of companies in Denmark, Spain, Italy and France adopted assurance in 2011.

7.6 South Korea

In the 1990s, the South Korean government required that environmental information must be disclosed in companies' financial reports to comply with the South Korean Accounting Standards.[38] The South Korean Ministry of the Environment (MOE) had been promoting disclosure guidelines for corporate environmental reporting.[39] The Ministry of Knowledge Economy's 2006 BEST Sustainable Management Guidelines and the MOE's 2007 Environmental Reporting Guidelines were both based on the GRI's *G3 Guidelines*. The South Korean Power Exchange introduced the Korean Socially Responsible Investment (SRI) Index in 2009 to engage companies in ESG reporting. In 2012, the Green Posting System required South Korean listed companies to disclose their greenhouse gas (GHG) emissions and energy usage in annual reports.[40] With the efforts of different parties, the number of CSR reports has increased from 49 CSR reports in 2009 to 77 in 2013.[41] A more recent survey conducted in 2017 by KPMG shows that the CSR reporting rate in South Korea was 74 percent and 73 percent in 2015 and 2017 respectively, rates which are lower than those of other Asian jurisdictions like Taiwan with 88 percent and Singapore with 84 percent.

Another study shows that South Korea engaged in a higher level of CSR assurance and reporting when compared with other countries.[42] Among the 115 CSR reports issued with CorporateRegister.com in 2013, 96 South Korean firms engaged external independent assurers to assure the CSR reports. The majority of CSR assurance services were provided by specialized assurance organizations with 25 percent engaging engineering firms and certification companies to assure their CSR reports and 14.6 percent employing accounting firms to provide CSR assurance reports.

7.7 Malaysia

CSR reporting among Malaysian firms has been increasing steadily from 1999.[43] To recognize Malaysian companies that have outstanding CSR reporting practices and to promote CSR reporting in Malaysia, ACCA Malaysia launched the Environmental and Social Reporting Awards (MESRA) in 2002. In September 2006, Bursa Malaysia amended its listing requirement and mandated listed companies to provide a description of their CSR activities, if any, in annual reports. Bursa Malaysia introduced a new Corporate Sustainability Framework in 2015, which took effect from 2016. With the initiatives from various parties, Malaysia ranked among the highest corporate social reporting rates in Asia (KPMG, 2017).[44]

Although the mandatory disclosure of CSR activities in annual reports motivates an increase in CSR assurance in Malaysia, only a small proportion of companies opts to assure their CSR reports. One explanation is that companies are reluctant to subject their CSR activities to public scrutiny due to reputational concern.[45] The lack of an agreed set of standards for CSR reporting and CSR assurance processes also contributed to the low level of CSR assurance in Malaysia.[46] However, the Malaysian Green Technology Policy in 2009 that focuses on "Green Economics", Sukuk green bonds and Socially Responsible Investment (SRI) provided motivation for businesses and publicly listed companies to engage more CSR assurance practices to access possible benefits from these green financing sources.

7.8 The Philippines

The Philippine government plays an important role in promoting CSR reporting. In August 2009, Philippine House of Representatives member and son of the President, Rep. Diosdado "Dato" M. Arroyo, submitted House Bill 6414, also known as the Corporate Social Responsibility Act of 2009. The Act requires companies to fulfill basic corporate social responsibilities or obligations. Specifically, enterprises should take into account the interests of society and take responsibility for their customers, employees, shareholders, communities and the environment in the course of their business development.[47] In addition, the Philippine Securities and Exchange Commission requires listed companies to include in their annual reports information on their compliance with environmental laws and regulations.

In 2010, the Philippine Institute of Certified Public Accountants (PICPA) established a Sustainability Reporting and Assurance special committee to provide training on CSR reporting. In addition, the Management Association of the Philippines gives an award for "Best Annual Report" every year, emphasizing transparency in both financial and non-financial information reporting.[48]

However, the progress of CSR assurance is relatively slow in the Philippines. According to the ACCA CSR reporting survey in 2010, there were no major companies in the Philippines engaging assurance on their CSR reporting process. The results of the survey were staggering, coming despite the efforts of the Philippine government and professional bodies to promote CSR assurance. The PICPA has put together a specific Committee on Sustainable Development Reporting and Assurance with reference to GRI, which "plays a key role in promoting sustainable development reporting and assurance practice in the Philippines." There is no doubt that the Philippines has a long way to go in terms of CSR assurance.[49]

7.9 Singapore

Singaporean firms have made great improvements in CSR reporting. However, they still lag behind other developed economies in Asia. According to the 2009 Asian sustainability ratings on the level of sustainability disclosure, Singapore ranked second last in the region, after only Pakistan.[50] In the KPMG 2015 Corporate Responsibility Report, Singapore had improved its rating, but was still behind Japan, India and other developed economies.[51] Neither the public nor regulators have put pressure on businesses to disclose detailed social responsibility information. There is a lack of formal regulatory provisions, both broad and specific, on CSR disclosure. The existing IFRS-based accounting standards in Singapore, while encouraging, do not require mandatory environmental reporting. It was not until recently that the Singapore government recognized the importance of CSR reporting and began work toward that end. In 2016, the Singapore Exchange Limited (SGX) issued sustainability reporting guidelines which require listed companies to provide CSR reports based on the "compliance or interpretation" approach effective from December 31, 2017.[52] In accordance with the guidelines, CSR reports must include a broad statement describing corporate sustainability actions; identifying environmental, social and governance factors that affect business strategies; explaining their practices and performance; and setting targets.[53]

The KPMG 2011 and 2013 surveys show that the rate of CSR assurance in Singapore is lower than that in other countries.[54] Although the SGX Sustainability Reporting Guide and Rule (2016) does not require listed companies to provide CSR assurance reports, companies that have been publishing CSR reports realize that external assurance could increase the credibility of their reports. Factors such as investor-driven indices, CSR rankings and procurement processes are creating demands for external assurance to ensure the credibility of the CSR information.

7.10 Taiwan

Both the Taiwanese government and the Taiwan Stock Exchange (TWSE) have been working to promote CSR, which has had a clear impact on reporting by listed companies in Taiwan. The TWSE issued mandatory reporting requirements and investment guidelines in 2014. Listed companies in the chemical, food, financial and insurance industries, as well as all companies with NT$10 billion (around US$330 million) in paid-in capital, are required to file CSR reports. By the end of 2015, the designation of companies required to file CSR reports was expanded to include those with NT$5 billion (around US$165 million) in paid-in capital. As a result, the TWSE became the first market in Asia and the Pacific to implement mandatory CSR reports and to enforce strict compliance with the G4 principles of the GRI. In 2016, Taiwanese companies were also named model companies by Bloomberg in CSR/ESG disclosure and performance evaluation in the Asia-Pacific region.[55] The TWSE expects its CSR reporting measures to attract more investors seeking sustainable investment opportunities in Taiwan's capital markets. The KPMG 2017 Corporate Social Responsibility Report survey reveals that Taiwan has made significant annual improvements in its global ranking in CSR reporting from 2015.[56]

Taiwan also made considerable efforts to promote CSR assurance. In June 2015, the GRI organized a series of events with the support of TWSE and the Business Council for Sustainable Development of Taiwan (BCSD) on how to improve the credibility of sustainable development reports published by enterprises in the most effective way. To support this activity, the TWSE announced a number of new rules that emphasize the role and importance of external assurance in non-financial reporting. Under the new regulations, listed companies in the food industry and those with at least 50 percent of their revenues coming from the food and beverage industry must obtain a written opinion from a certified public accountant. This submission represents the beginning of external assurance.[57]The Financial Supervisory Commission (FSC) encourages companies to monitor corporate governance by reporting CSR indicators and information verified by third parties.[58] Taiwan's efforts to promote CSR assurance have been rewarded by wide international recognition. The 2017 KPMG survey of CSR reporting shows that, between 2015 and 2017, the rate of external assurance of CSR reporting in Taiwan has increased by 14 percentage and was ranked top among Asian economies.[59]

7.11   Thailand

The Stock Exchange of Thailand (SET) have realized the importance of CSR and sustainability reporting of listed companies recently. To promote CSR and sustainability performance disclosure, the SET organizes workshops and seminars on the reporting format of CSR and sustainability. The training program is designed for listed Thai firms to learn about CSR reporting in line with the 56-1 Form of the Securities and Exchange Commission (SEC) as well as sustainability reporting following the GRI's G4 framework.[60] The 2017 KPMG survey shows that around 67 percent of Thai firms disclosed CSR information, which is lower than the global average of 72 percent.[61]

Despite low CSR reporting in Thailand, the percentage of firms that provide assurance on CSR reports is fairly high, especially in large companies. A study jointly conducted by the ASEAN CSR network and the Center for Governance, Institutions and Organizations of the National Singapore University Business School showed that 13 out of 38 (34 percent) of Thai CSR reporters assure their CSR reports as of 30 June 2015, which is higher than the figure for Indonesia.[62]

7.12   Vietnam

As an emerging market, Vietnam's stable political environment and growing economy attract substantial foreign direct investments (FDI), which introduce and promote global ESG reporting and disclosure standards.[63] Recently, the State Securities Commission (SSC) cooperated with the International Finance Corporation (IFC) to publish the Sustainability Reporting Handbook for Vietnamese Companies in order to provide ESG disclosure guidelines for listed firms in Vietnam.[64]

The Reporting Exchange reported that ESG reporting information and requirements were present after 2010.[65] In 2015, Vietnam introduced Circular No. 155/2015/TT-BTC on Public Disclosure for listed firms. The circular requires listed companies to disclose information related to the environment and society following the guidance of the SSC. Information including management of raw materials, energy consumption, water consumption, compliance with the law, policies related to employees, responsibility for local community and green capital market activities must be reported.[66]

The development level of CSR assurance falls far behind other Asian economies. In 2015, Bao Viet Holdings, the largest insurance company in Vietnam, appointed PwC Vietnam to assure its CSR reports, the first time that a Vietnamese company sought to hire external assurors to assure its CSR report.[67]

8.   BEST PRACTICES OF SUSTAINABILITY REPORTING AND ASSURANCE

In recent years, corporations have been under more pressure from a variety of stakeholders including regulators and socially responsible investors to disclose both financial and non-financial information pertaining to their ESP and GSEE sustainability performance. Corporations worldwide are now searching for an effective and efficient way to improve the quality of their financial reporting while ensuring compliance with all applicable rules, laws, regulations and standards through integrated sustainability reporting. Sustainability reports cover all areas of economic viability, ethical culture, corporate governance, social responsibility and environmental awareness. Sustainability reporting and assurance evolves as investors demand more relevant sustainability disclosures, regulators require more extensive sustainability reports and business organizations integrate sustainability into their strategic decisions, actions and performance. Best practices of sustainability performance, reporting and assurance have also been developed. According to greenbiz.com and United Parcel Service (UPS), there are five ways to convey the vital importance of sustainability to senior executives:[68]

1. It enables cost reduction and efficiency improvement.
2. It incentivizes organizations to focus on risk assessment, management and mitigation (financial, operational, compliance, strategic and reputational risks).

3. It creates new competitive and revenue-generating opportunities.
4. It encourages innovation.
5. It promotes talented employee recruitment, development and retention.

Best practices of sustainability performance, reporting and assurance (presented in Exhibit 10.5) suggest that:

1. Sustainability strategies should be integrated into corporate decision-making processes in promoting the achievement of all five EGSEE dimensions of sustainability performance.
2. Companies should use a principles-based approach in integrating both financial and non-financial sustainability information into their corporate reporting.
3. Companies should assess sustainability risks in all aspects of strategy, operations, compliance, finance, and reputation and minimize their impacts on EGSEE sustainability performance.
4. Companies should provide assurance on their sustainability reports to gain credibility, investor confidence and public trust.

Corporate sustainability in action for a small sample of global companies can set a benchmark for other companies to follow. Best practices of sustainability for a small sample of international companies, as presented in Exhibit 10.4, suggest that management should develop and maintain proper sustainability programs that provide a common framework for the integration of sustainability issues and activities into the business model that consists of:

- Integration of sustainability issues, programs and activities into the business and investment analysis and decision-making process.
- Incorporation of sustainability issues and activities into business and investment policies and practices to improve overall performance in both financial ESP and non-financial GSEE sustainability performance.
- Promotion of appropriate disclosure on sustainability ESP and GSEE performance in an integrated sustainability report.
- Collaboration among all stakeholders to enhance the effectiveness of sustainability programs.
- Promotion of product innovation and quality, customer retention and attraction, employee satisfaction and productivity through sustainability programs.
- Periodic disclosure of both financial and non-financial KPIs relevant to ESP and GSEE sustainability activities and performance to all stakeholders.

These best practices of sustainability reporting and assurance are gaining global acceptance. A 2014 survey of investors conducted by PwC finds that about 80 percent of responding investors stated that they considered GSEE sustainability issues in their investment decisions, when acting as voting proxies and when making investment portfolio decisions in the past year.[69] Among the top sustainability issues considered by investors are climate change, resource scarcity, CSR and good citizenship. Investors' primary drivers for considering sustainability issues, in order of performance, are risk reduction (73 percent), avoiding firms with unethical conduct (55 percent), performance enhancement (52 percent), cost reduction (36 percent),

EXHIBIT 10.5 Sample of sustainability programs and best practices

Apple	Apple requires its suppliers worldwide to provide safe working conditions, equitable treatment for employees and manufacturing practices that are not harmful to the environment.	https://www.apple.com/supplier-responsibility
BMW	BMW seeks to foster the South Carolina community where the company is headquartered, giving over US$30 million as of 2012 to education, the arts, and the community at large.	https://www.bmwusfactory.com/sustainability/social-responsibility/
Coca-Cola	Coca-Cola initiated the RAIN (Replenish Africa Initiative) program in 2009 to increase access to clean water for two million people in Africa.	http://www.coca-colacompany.com/rain-the-replenish-africa-initiative
CVS	CVS decided to forgo the sale of tobacco products at its store in order to promote healthier lifestyles among its customers and ensure that they can trust that the company has their health interests in mind.	http://www.cvshealth.com/research-insights/health-topics/this-is-the-right-thing-to-do
Colgate-Palmolive	The Colgate-Palmolive "Bright Smiles, Bright Futures" program has helped over 700 million children worldwide improve their oral health.	http://www.colgate.com/app/BrightSmilesBrightFutures/US/EN/HomePage.cvsp
Disney	Disney runs a number of domestic and international programs to improve the safety of their products and workplaces and seeks to improve the environment to ensure a positive environmental legacy for future generations.	http://thewaltdisneycompany.com/citizenship
Google	Google Green is an initiative that strives to support renewable energy projects, and to reduce its own environmental impact and aid other companies in doing the same.	https://www.google.com/green/
Honda Motors	Honda has a variety of programs to aid people in its communities in a variety of ways, from education to community development to making their factories more environmentally friendly.	http://csr.honda.com/

(continued)

EXHIBIT 10.5   (*Continued*)

IKEA	IKEA plans to utilize 100 percent renewable energy resources to power its stores by 2020, as well as encourage its customers to conserve energy and utilize renewable energy.	http://www.ikea.com/ms/en_US/this-is-ikea/people-and-planet/energy-and-resources/
Kellogg Company	The Kellogg Company donates food to areas suffering from disasters, specializing in non-perishable, ready-to-eat foods.	http://www.kellogg company.com/en_US/corporate-responsibility.html
Microsoft	Microsoft launched its YouthSpark program in 2012. The program helps youth around the world with opportunities to better their education, entrepreneurship and employment situations.	http://www.microsoft.com/about/corporatecitizenship/en-us/youthspark/
Sony	Sony started the Sony Science Program whereby the company operates science museums, runs workshops, educates youth on career opportunities and promotes programs focused on teaching science to youth around the world.	http://www.sony.net/SonyInfo/csr/ForThe NextGeneration/ssp/
Starbucks	Starbucks has CSR initiatives to create value for all of its stakeholders, including shareholders, customers and communities by promoting social responsibility, ethical sourcing goals and environmental stewardship.	https://www.starbucks.com/responsibility
Volkswagen	Volkswagen, unlike many other foreign car companies that locate themselves in areas with strong Right-to-Work laws to avoid unions, pushed to have a union for its workers in its Chattanooga, TN, plant, in line with the company's desire that all of its plants be unionized.	https://www.volkswagenag.com/en/Investor Relations/corporate-governance.html
Wal-Mart	Wal-Mart has initiated programs to reduce greenhouse emissions by 20 million metric tons by the end of 2015.	https://corporate.walmart.com/global-responsibility/sustainability/

attracting new capital (30 percent), improving capability to create value (30 percent) and being responsive to interest groups (21 percent).[70] Investors are typically more dissatisfied than satisfied with sustainability information provided by firms relevant to sustainability risk, challenges, opportunities and sustainability performance dimensions.

Assurance on sustainability reports is voluntary. The reports can be audited or reported on by an independent auditor. Auditors may perform assurance on sustainability reports for the intended parties or at the request of third parties or professional organizations. In these situations, auditors of public companies can consider the

EXHIBIT 10.6(a) Assurance reports on sustainability information: Example Examination Report on Sustainability Information

Example Examination Report on Sustainability Information

Report of Independent Auditor

Addressee:

The Identified Third Parties or Organizations

We have examined the sustainability report accompanying the financial statements of XYZ Company as of December 31, 20XX. Such sustainability reports are management's responsibility. Our responsibility is to express an opinion on such sustainability reports based on our examination.

Our examination was conducted in accordance with the attestation standards and procedures deemed necessary in the circumstances. We believe our examination provides a reasonable basis for our opinion.

The objective of sustainability reports is to present relevant information about sustainability performance in areas of social, environmental, and governance performance in addition to financial information relevant to economic performance as reflected in the audited financial statements.

[Additional paragraph(s) may be added to emphasize certain matters pertaining to sustainability reports and the attest engagement or the subject matter.]

In our opinion, management's assertions presented in the sustainability report accompanying the audited financial statements are fairly presented and are consistent with financial information reflected in the audited financial statements.

Name of Accounting Firm

City, State (or Country)

Date

EXHIBIT 10.6(b)   Assurance reports on sustainability information: Example Review Report
on Sustainability Information

Example Review Report on Sustainability Information

Report of Independent Auditor

Addressee:

The Identified Third Parties or Organizations

We have reviewed the sustainability report accompanying the financial statements of
XYZ Company as of December 31, 20XX. Such sustainability reports are management's responsibility. Our responsibility is to express an opinion on such sustainability reports based on our review.

Our review was conducted in accordance with the review standards and procedures
deemed necessary in the circumstances. A review is substantially less extensive in
scope than an examination of sustainability reports.

The objective of sustainability reports is to present relevant information about sustainability performance in areas of social, environmental, and governance performance in addition to financial information relevant to economic performance as
reflected in the audited financial statements.

[Additional paragraph(s) may be added to emphasize certain matters pertaining to
sustainability reports and the attest engagement or the subject matter.]

Based on our review, nothing came to our attention that caused us to believe that
management's assertions presented in the sustainability report accompanying the
audited financial statements are not fairly presented or are inconsistent with financial
information reflected in the audited financial statements.

Name of Accounting Firm

City, State (or Country)

Date

guidance in PCAOB AS 2710, Other Information in Documents Containing Audited
Financial Statements. In compliance with this guidance, the auditor should read sustainability information, consider whether such information or the manner of its presentation is inconsistent with the audited financial statements and ask management
to eliminate any discovered inconsistencies. The auditor's report on sustainability
information is an attestation engagement covered by attestation standards and is
limited to either assurance based on an examination or negative assurance based on
a review. The auditor's assurances pertain to the sustainability information presented

by management. Two types of assurance reports can be issued by auditors on sustainability reports: (1) Examination Report on Sustainability Information and (2) Review Report on Sustainability Information. Exhibit 10.6 presents samples of both types of assurance reports.

9. RELEVANCE OF SUSTAINABILITY INFORMATION

A report by the Conference Board presents many cases in which non-financial GSEE sustainability actions and performance have a positive impact on financial performance.[71] The report also highlights the importance of establishing the link between financial and non-financial EESG sustainability KPIs. Sustainability information on GSEE is typically considered an externality beyond disclosure of economic performance, which can be viewed positively or negatively by market participants.

A 2013 joint study by the Investor Responsibility Research Center Institute (IRRCI) and the Sustainable Investments Institute (Si2) reports that only 1.4 percent of the S&P companies (seven firms) issued a standalone sustainability report by mentioning sustainability reporting in their regulatory filing of 10-K reports whereas almost all S&P companies (499) disclosed at least one piece of sustainability information, 74 percent placed monetary value on their sustainability-related disclosures and about 44 percent linked their executive compensation to some type of sustainability criteria.[72]

Although business sustainability is a relatively new concept, research conducted by academic and professional bodies has highlighted the importance of sustainability performance as well as disclosure. Indeed, financial gains generated by sustainability performance in 2013 is up to 37 percent compared to 23 percent in 2010 and about 50 percent of companies adapted their business models in response to sustainability initiatives.[73] In its *G4 Guidelines* released in May 2013, the GRI promotes sustainability reporting as a standard practice of disclosing sustainability-related issues that are relevant to a company's business and stakeholders.[74] The *G4 Guidelines* present Reporting Principles, Standard Disclosures and an Implementation Manual for sustainability reporting on both ESP and ESG sustainability performance by all organizations regardless of their type, size, sector or location. Global investors consider various dimensions of sustainability performance in their investment analysis as socially responsible investing (SRI) increased by more than 22 percent to US$3.74 trillion in managed assets during the 2010–2012 period (Social Investment Forum).[75] At the same time, stock exchanges worldwide either require or recommend that their listed companies report sustainability information (e.g., Singapore Stock Exchange, 2011; Toronto Stock Exchange, 2014; Hong Kong Stock Exchange, 2015) and more than 6,000 European companies will be required to disclose their non-financial ESG sustainability performance and diversity information for their financial year 2017.[76]

The KPMG 2013 *Audit Committee Roundtable Report* highlights the importance of long-term sustainable performance by suggesting that focusing on quarterly earnings can undermine a firm's long-term sustainable performance.[77] The KPMG report suggests the use of additional financial and non-financial KPIs and drivers of sustainable performance like operational efficiency, customer satisfaction, talent management, and innovation to measure sustainability performance. Although the conventional measures of cash flows, earnings, and return on investment are essential in evaluating financial performance, they cannot reflect sustainable performance and future growth. To obtain a complete picture of business profitability and sustainability, the 2013 KPMG report identifies a number of key measures of performance that are essential for understanding business sustainability. These measures include operational efficiency, customer satisfaction, talent management and innovation, which could be derived from internal factors related to strategy, risk profile, strengths and weaknesses, and corporate culture as well as external factors related to reputation, technology, completion, globalization and utilization of natural resources.[78]

A 2013 United Nations study suggests that non-financial GSEE dimensions of sustainability performance are value relevant to investors by presenting new risks and opportunities that are fundamental in performance analyses and portfolio investment valuation.[79] The study argues that GSEE performance information enables investors to conduct economic and industry analyses of GSEE non-financial information including trends, externalities and industry competitiveness effects that may affect shareholder value creation as well as assessment of the company's sustainability strategies and practices that may change the traditional investment valuation parameters and assumptions.[80] Proper understanding of sustainability theories, standards, risk assessment and performance has been a major challenge for companies in measuring, recognizing and disclosing the five EGSEE dimensions of their sustainability performance, and for corporate stakeholders including shareholders in effectively using sustainability performance information in their investment valuations and portfolio analyses.

Companies have found that emphasizing sustainability improves their profitability, generates greater loyalty and commitment from employees, and cements relationships with customers and suppliers. The 10 key elements to sustainable business practices in SMEs include (1) taking a broad view of sustainability (2) defining in detail what sustainability means to your company (3) engaging all stakeholders (4) remembering that you are not alone (5) establishing responsibility and communicating widely (6) taking it step by step (7) walking the talk (8) tying sustainability to profit (9) measuring, monitoring and reviewing (10) investing in the future.[81] Integrated reporting in a broader context is far more common in the United States, as 499 out of 500 companies made at least one sustainability-related disclosure. In addition, nearly three-quarters of companies place a dollar figure on at least one sustainability-related initiative and 43.4 percent of companies link executive compensation to some type of sustainability criteria.[82]

10. CONCLUSIONS

Conventional corporate reports do not effectively reflect corporate accountability to all stakeholders. Future corporate reporting should disseminate high-quality financial and non-financial information regarding all five EGSEE dimensions of sustainability performance to enable all corporate stakeholders to make sound decisions. All relevant information pertaining to the five EGSEE dimensions of sustainability performance can be incorporated into one report commonly known as the "integrated report". This integrated report can be prepared in compliance with the *G4 Guidelines* of the GRI, be forward looking, and present both financial and non-financial KPIs discussed in this chapter. Integrated sustainability reporting and assurance has made steady progress in the 12 economies of Asia during the past decade. The most noticeable improvement is in Hong Kong and Taiwan regarding mandatory sustainability reporting on environmental, social and governance performance information. The development in Asia can be used as a benchmark for standard-setters (GRI, IIRC, and SASB), business organizations and researchers in other countries in promoting sustainability performance, reporting and assurance.

11. CHAPTER TAKEAWAY

1. Make sure corporate reports are comprehensive and relevant in portraying both financial and non-financial information on all five EGSEE dimensions of sustainability performance to all stakeholders.
2. Align corporate reporting and communication strategy.
3. Improve relationships with all key stakeholders.
4. Sustainability managers have more incentive to focus on financial sustainability performance that can create tangible shareholder value (return on investment) than social investment with less tangible outcomes.
5. Sustainability managers should use the balanced scorecard to link non-financial KPIs to financial KPIs and their integrated impacts on achieving the organization's objectives in creating sustainable value for all stakeholders.
6. Ensure incorporation of sustainability development into decision-making, planning, implementation and evaluation processes.
7. Expand and redesign corporate reporting on sustainability and accountability with a keen focus on supporting the information needs of long-term investors regarding sustainable performance as well as performance in the environmental, social, governance and ethical dimensions.

ENDNOTES

1. R. Nidumolu, P. J. Simmons, and T. F. Yosle. *Sustainability and the CFO: Challenges, Opportunities and Next Practices*, Corporate Eco Forum, April 2015, http://www .corporateecoforum.com/wp-content/uploads/2015/04/CFO_and_Sustainability_Apr-2015.pdf.
2. International Federation of Accountants (IFAC), "Revised International Standard on Assurance Engagements Other Than Audits or Reviews of Historical Financial Information 3000 (ISAE 3000)," 2011, http://www.ifac.org/auditing-assurance/.
3. AccountAbility, *AA1000 Assurance Standard Practitioners Note*. London: AccountAbility, 2003.
4. Global Reporting Initiative, *Sustainability Reporting Guidelines On Economic, Environmental and Social Performance*, Amsterdam: Global Reporting Initiative, 2002.
5. Fedération des Experts Comptables Européens (FEE), *Providing Assurance on Sustainability Reports. Discussion Paper*, Brussels: Fedération des Experts Comptables Européens, 2002.
6. A. Brockett and Z. Rezaee, *Corporate Sustainability: Integrating Performance and Reporting* (New York: John Wiley & Sons, Inc., 2012).

7. Global Reporting Initiative, *The External Assurance of Sustainability Reporting*, 2013, www.globalreporting.org.

8. "Carrots and Sticks," UNEP, GRI, KPMG, and the Centre for Corporate Governance in Africa, 2013, www.globalreporting.org.

9. C. Adams, "Integrated Reporting – What It Is – And Is Not: An Interview with Paul Druckman," 2013, http://drcaroladams.net/integrated-reporting-what-it-is-and-is-not-an-interview-with-paul-druckman/.

10. Global Reporting Initiative, G4 Exposure Draft, 2013, Frequently Asked Questions About The G4 Exposure Draft and The Second G4 Public Comment Period, 2013, https://www.globalreporting.org/resourcelibrary/G4-ED-PCP2-FAQs.pdf

11. Z. Rezaee. 2015. Business Sustainability Research: A Theoretical and Integrated Perspective. *Journal of Accounting Literature*, Volume 36, June 2016: 48–64. http://www.sciencedirect.com/science/journal/07374607/36/supp/C.

12. Singapore Exchange (SGX), "SGX Introduces Sustainability Reporting Guide to Support Listed Companies," Singapore Exchange Limited, 2011, http://rulebook.sgx.com/net_file_store/new_rulebooks/s/g/SGX_Sustainability_Reporting_Guide_and_Policy_Statement_2011.pdf.

13. Ibid.

14. Ibid.

15. Z. Rezaee. 2015.

16. International Federation of Accountants (IFAC), "Revised International Standard on Assurance Engagements Other Than Audits or Reviews of Historical Financial Information 3000 (ISAE 3000)," 2011, http://www.ifac.org/auditing-assurance/.

17. GRI 2013.

18. R. Simnett, A. Vanstraelen, and W. F. Chua, "Assurance On Sustainability Reports: An International Comparison," *Accounting Review* 84, no. 3 (2009): 937–967.

19. C. Cho, *Corporate Transparency and Sustainability Reporting: The South Korean Case*, 2014, http://knowledge.essec.edu/en/economy-finance/corporate-transparency-and-sustainability-reportin.html.

20. H. Shen, H. Wu, and P. Chand, "The Impact of Corporate Social Responsibility Assurance On Investor Decisions: Chinese Evidence," *Int J Audit* (February 5, 2017).

21. GoldenBee, "GoldenBee Research on CSR Reporting in China 2017 Released," December 19, 2017, GoldenBee Corporate Social Responsibility Consulting, http://en.goldenbeechina.com/index.php/Home/Insights/show/id/68.

22. L. Liao, T. P. Lin, and Y. Zhang, "Corporate Board and Corporate Social Responsibility Assurance: Evidence from China," *Journal of Business Ethics* (2016): 1–15.

23. ACCA, *The State of Environmental, Social and Sustainability Reporting in Hong Kong*, 2002.

24. Ibid.

25. Appendix 16 of the Main Board Listing Rules, paragraph 28(2)(d) (GEM Listing Rule 18.07A(2)(d)).

26. "Investors Want Mandatory Board Oversight, But Hong Kong Leadership Not CSR Savvy," December 20, 2017, http://csr-asia.com/newsletter-investors-want-mandatory-board-oversight-but-hong-kong-leadership-not-csr-savvy.

27. Ministry of Corporate Affairs, *Corporate Social Responsibility Voluntary Guidelines 2009*, New Delhi: Ministry of Corporate Affairs, Government of India, 2009.

28. Ministry of Corporate Affairs, *National Voluntary Guidelines for Social, Environmental and Economic Responsibilities of Business*, New Delhi: Ministry of Corporate Affairs, Government of India, 2011.

29. PwC, *Handbook on Corporate Social Responsibility in India*, Haryana: Pricewaterhouse-Coopers Private Limited, 2013.

30. KPMG, *The KPMG Survey of Corporate Responsibility Reporting 2017*, KPMG International Cooperative, 2017, s. 1.
31. R. Jain and L. H. Winner, "CSR and Sustainability Reporting Practices of Top Companies in India," *Corporate Communications: An International Journal* 21, no.1 (2016): 36–55.
32. A. Sharma, "Sustainability Reporting Trends in India," n.d., http://www.iodonline.com/Articles/Arvind% 20Sharma%20-%20Sustainability.
33. Ernst & Young, *Sustainability Reporting: Key Insights from the Indonesia Stock Exchange Top 100*, PT. Ernst & Young Indonesia, 2016, s. 1.
34. ASEAN CSR Network and Centre for Governance, Institutions and Organisations of NUS Business School, *Sustainability Reporting in ASEAN: State of Progress in Indonesia, Malaysia, Singapore and Thailand*, 2015, https://bschool.nus.edu.sg/Portals/0/docs/CGIO/susatainability-reporting-asean-cgio-acn-oct2016.pdf.
35. KPMG, *The KPMG Survey of Corporate Responsibility Reporting 2015*, 2015.
36. Ministry of the Environment, *Report on CSR Information Assurance Research*, Japanese Institute of Certified Public Accountants, May 2007.
37. KPMG, *International Survey of Corporate Responsibility Reporting 2011*, Amsterdam, 2011.
38. J.-S. Choi, J.-K. Jang, and I.-Y. Chang, *The Relations among Corporate Environmental Disclosures, Public Initiatives, and Corporate Characteristics: Korean Evidence*, 2007, https://www.researchgate.net/publication/233195183_An_evaluation_of_the_voluntary_corporate_environmental_disclosures_A_Korean_Evidence.
39. C. Cho, *Corporate Transparancy and Sustainability Reporting: The South Korean Case*, 2014, http://knowledge.essec.edu/en/economy-finance/corporate-transparency-and-sustainability-reportin.html.
40. Business Environment Council Limited, *ESG Reporting Requrements & Trends in Major Asian Markets*, Hong Kong: Business Environment Council Limited, 2015.
41. D. Oh, and S. A. Ahn, *Improving South Korean Corporate Govenance*, 2015, http://www.iflr.com/Article/3429769/Improving-South-Korean-corporate-governance.html.
42. S. Jin-Young, "Sustainability Reporting Trend in Korea," in *Corporate Social Responsibility in Korea: State and Perspectives*, ed. Konrad-Adenauer-Stiftung and J. McDonald (Seoul: Konrad-Adenauer-Stiftung, 2014), s. 1, 27–50.
43. Companies Commission of Malaysia, *Best Business Practice Circular 5/2013 Corporate Responsibility: Guidance to Disclosure and Reporting*, 2013, https://www.ssm.com.my/sites/default/files/cr_agenda/BBPC%205-2013%20-%20low%20res.pdf.
44. KPMG, *The KPMG Survey of Corporate Responsibility Reporting 2017*, KPMG International Cooperative, 2017, s. 1, https://Home.Kpmg.Com/Xx/En/Home/Insights/2017/10/The-Kpmg-Survey-Of-Corporate-Responsibility-Reporting-2017.Html.
45. F. Darus, Y. Sawani, M. M. Zain, and T. Janggu, "Impediments to CSR Assurance in an Emerging Economy," *Managerial Auditing Journal* 29, no. 3 (2014): 253–267, https://doi-org.lib-ezproxy.hkbu.edu.hk/10.1108/MAJ-04-2013-0846.
46. Ibid.
47. ACCA, *The Rise of the Report and the Regulator*, Corporate Sustainability Reporting, 2010.
48. C. T. Mangangey and K. Sadashiv, "The Rise of Sustainability Reporting," Business World, SGV, May 31, 2010.
49. ACCA, *The Rise of the Report and the Regulator*, Corporate Sustainability Reporting, 2010.
50. Singapore Institute of Directors, "Doing Great Business ... The Power of Corporate Social Responsibility," *Directors' Bulletin* 3 (2010), MICA (P) 093/05/2010.
51. KPMG, *Currents of Change*, 2015, https://assets.kpmg.com/content/dam/kpmg/pdf/2016/02/kpmg-international-survey-of-corporate-responsibility-reporting-2015.pdf.

52. PwC, *SGX Sustainability Reporting Guide*, PwC Singapore, 2017.

53. Global Compact Network Singapore, *Sustainability Reporting for All Listed Companies Mandatory from FY2017*, 2017.

54. KPMG, *The KPMG Survey of Corporate Responsibility Reporting 2013*, KPMG International Cooperative, 2013, s. 1.

55. Taiwan Institute for Sustainable Energy, *The 2017 Taiwan CSR Reporting Overview and Trends: Great Improvement on CSR Performance*, March 24, 2017.

56. KPMG, *The Road Ahead—The KPMG Survey of Corporate Responsibility Reporting 2017*, 2017.

57. GRI, "Going The Extra Mile: External Assurance in Taiwan," September 9, 2015.

58. KPMG, *Currents of Change—The KPMG Survey of Corporate Responsibility Reporting 2015*, 2015.

59. KPMG, *The Road Ahead—The KPMG Survey of Corporate Responsibility Reporting 2017*, 2017.

60. Stock Exchange of Thailand, *Development of Sustainability Reporting*, n.d., https://www.set.or.th/sustainable_dev/en/sr/sd/report_p1.html.

61. KPMG, *The Road Ahead—The KPMG Survey of Corporate Responsibility Reporting 2017*, 2017, s. 1.

62. ASEAN CSR Network and Centre for Governance, Institutions and Organisations of NUS Business School, *Sustainability Reporting in ASEAN: State of Progress in Indonesia, Malaysia, Singapore and Thailand*, 2015, https://bschool.nus.edu.sg/Portals/0/docs/CGIO/susatainability-reporting-asean-cgio-acn-oct2016.pdf.

63. Reporting Exchange, *An Overview of Sustainability and Corporate Reporting in Vietnam*, n.d., WBCSD, s. 1.

64. Business Environment Council Limited, *ESG Reporting Requirements & Trends in Major Asian Markets*, Business Environment Council Limited, 2015, s. 1.

65. Reporting Exchange, *An Overview of Sustainability and Corporate Reporting in Vietnam*, n.d., WBCSD, s. 1.

66. CSR Asia, *Sustainability Disclosure in ASEAN: The ASEAN Extractive Sector*, CSR Asia, s. 1, http://www.csr-asia.com/report/GRI_ExtractiveReport.pdf.

67. "First Independent Assurance for Vietnamese Sustainability Report," *Vietnam Investment Review*, Nov 27, 2015, http://www.vir.com.vn/first-independent-assurance-for-vietnamese-sustainability-report-38695.html.

68. K. Kuehn, "Five Ways to Convince Your CFO that Sustainability Pays," 2010, www.greenbiz.com.

69. PwC, *Sustainability Goes Mainstream: Insights into Investor Views*, May 2014, http://www.pwc.com/us/en/pwc-investor-resource-institute/index.jhtml.

70. Ibid.

71. M. Bertoneche and C.V. Lungt, *Director Notes, The Sustainability Business Case: A Model for Incorporating Financial Value Drivers*, The Conference Board, June 2013, www.conference board.org.

72. Investor Responsibility Research Center Institute (IRRCI) and Sustainable Investments Institute (Si2), 2013, *Integrated Financial and Sustainability Reporting in the United States*, April 2013, www.irrcinstitute.org.

73. D. Kiron, N. Kruschwitz, K. Haanaes, M. Reeves, and E. Goh, *The Innovation Bottom Line: The Benefit of Sustainability-Driven Innovation*, MIT Sloan Management Review and the Boston Consulting Group, Research Paper 54, no. 2 (Winter 2013): 69–73, http://sloanreview.mit.edu/sustainability.

74. Global Reporting Initiative, G4 Sustainability Reporting Guidelines, 2013, https://www.globalreporting.org/resourcelibrary/GRIG4-Part1-Reporting-Principles-and-Standard-Disclosures.pdf.

75. Social Investment Forum (SIF), *Report On Sustainable and Responsible Investing Trends in The United States*. US SIF foundation: The forum for sustainable and responsible investment, November 2012.

76. European Commission, *Disclosure of Non-Financial Information: Europe Information: Europe Council, The European Economic and Social, Environmental Issues*, September 29, 2014, http://ec.europa.eu/internal_market/accounting/non-financial_reporting/index_en.htm.

77. KPMG, *Beyond Quarterly Earnings: Is the Company on Track for Long-Term Success?* Audit Committee Roundtable Report, Spring 2013, auditcommittee@kpmg.com.

78. Ibid.

79. United Nations (UN), *How Investors are Addressing Environmental, Social and Governance Factors in Fundamental Equity Valuation*, United Nations-supported Principles for Responsible Investment (PRI), February 2013, http://www.unpri.org/viewer/?file=wp-content/uploads/Integrated_Analysis_2013.pdf.

80. Ibid.

81. Chartered Global Management Accountant (CGMA), "Ten Key Elements to Sustainable Business Practices in SMEs," *CGMA Tools*, 2013.

82. Investor Responsibility Research Center Institute (IRRCI) and Sustainable Investments Institute (Si2), *Integrated Financial and Sustainability Reporting in the United States*, April 2013, www.irrcinstitute.org and www.siinstitute.org.

CHAPTER 11

Emerging Issues in Sustainability Performance, Reporting and Assurance

1. EXECUTIVE SUMMARY

Business sustainability is gaining considerable attention as socially responsible investors prefer to invest in sustainable and socially responsible corporations while regulators worldwide recommend and/or demand that public companies disclose the non-financial dimensions of their sustainability performance in areas of governance, social, ethical and environmental (GSEE), and diversity activities. Business sustainability with a keen focus on the achievement of long-term stakeholder value creation is gaining momentum with investors with long-term investment horizons and business organizations that value their customers' satisfaction, employees' welfare and social and environmental responsibilities. Business organizations worldwide and those in Asia will be encouraged and/or required to disclose their non-financial GSEE performance along with financial economic sustainability performance. This chapter presents future trends in sustainability performance, reporting and assurance worldwide and particularly in Asia by exploring the best practices of sustainability in moving toward the achievement of profit-with-purpose companies, the use of the Extensible Business Reporting Language (XBRL) in sustainability reporting and the use of continuous auditing for sustainability assurance.

2. INTRODUCTION

Starting in 2017, more than 6,000 public companies in Europe are required to disclose their sustainability performance information regarding governance, social, environmental and diversity activities.[1] Delaware-governed entities are recommended to disclose their commitments to corporate social responsibility (CSR) and sustainability beginning October 2018 by voluntarily certifying their compliance with sustainability standards in Delaware.[2] Other countries are expected to follow suit. The global move toward the adoption of benefit corporations and profit-with-purpose companies and toward sustainability performance, reporting and assurance is inevitable as sustainability initiatives are being integrated into corporate strategies, supply chain, decisions, actions and performance. Countries in Asia have also started integrating sustainability performance reporting into their corporate reporting.

The content and format of sustainability reporting is also evolving toward online real-time reporting. The Extensible Business Reporting Language (XBRL) format is being used in financial, tax and statutory reporting and its relevance to sustainability reporting is being explored by researchers. Continuous auditing techniques are being applied to audit the automated financial reporting process and their application in providing continuous assurance on sustainability reporting is examined in this chapter. The XBRL platform for sustainability reporting and the outline of the implementation methods for using XBRL-based architectures for sustainability reporting are viewed by many as the future for corporate reporting and assurance services. Several stock exchanges worldwide require their listed companies to disclose sustainability performance information. Best practices of business sustainability development, programs, and performance are being initiated, and reporting and assurance established. This chapter discusses the best practices of sustainability performance, reporting, and assurance in action as well as the future of business sustainability worldwide and in Asia.

3. SUSTAINABILITY REPORTING GUIDELINES

The terms "sustainability reporting," "integrated reporting," "environmental, social and governance (ESG) reporting," "corporate social responsibility (CSR) reporting," and "risk compliance and governance (RCG)," have been used interchangeably in business literature to describe reports with a wide range of coverage and different degrees of focus on risk and performance in relation to environmental, social, or governance issues.[3] Sustainability reporting is a complex and not easily understood process. As such, many companies do not, or have not yet begun to, report on their sustainability practices. It is, however, not an insurmountable task, as Nick Topazio states in his article titled, "6 Tips for Integrated Thinking," and he lists a few ways by which companies can more easily prepare integrated sustainability reports:[4]

1. Value Creation: A business organization must understand what makes it tick, what makes it stand above others and what inputs and outputs come into and out of the organization. This is more all-encompassing than a simple production line, as all organizations have multiple relationships that are important for many reasons, and these are all interconnected. The main objective of integrated reporting is to reflect the company's stakeholder value creation.
2. Current and Future Trends: An organization should be familiar not only with the current environment in which it operates, but also with the environment in which it will operate in the future. This includes not only the positive externalities, such as sales/profit growth, new markets and trends, but also the negative externalities, such as new competition, falling prices/sales and agency issues. An organization should be able to explain why these are happening, how they affect the organization, and what will be done to increase or decrease their effects.
3. Non-Financial Metrics: Determine what non-financial measures may be in play for the organization, study them and report them to the stakeholders as a main point, not just an annex to the financial statements. If it is evident that the organization is not giving prominence to the ways in which it is promoting sustainability, then stakeholders cannot know to what extent their demands are

being met. Typical non-financial dimensions of sustainability performance are
environmental, social and governance (ESG).
4. Link between Non-Financial Measures and Long-Term Financial Success: Show
   stakeholders the importance of the above non-financial measures to the long-
   term financial stability of the organization. An investment in low-energy light
   bulbs, for instance, may be expensive in the short term, but the cost savings may
   be great over their lifespan as they last longer and utilize less electricity than do
   regular light bulbs.
5. Tone at the Top Commitment to Sustainability Performance Reporting: Give
   evidence to the entire board that all parts of the organization are linked to each
   other through the financial and non-financial information. The executive members should already be knowledgeable on the practice and theory behind these
   interactions, but that is not necessarily the case for all members. All members
   should be able to see, if only at a limited level, how each of these measures
   affects the others, and have any questions they may have answered. The ways in
   which new ventures are helping and will help the bottom line in the end should be
   explained in an easy-to-understand manner, not limited to those with advanced
   prior knowledge.
6. Holistic and Integrated Sustainability Reporting: Be extensive when it comes to
   reporting. While few would read a report with every single piece of sustainability
   information that an organization has made available, readers should be able
   to get a good overview of the measures that the organization is putting forth
   to create sustainable value. An important aspect of this is that the information
   should be easy to read and follow, as well as interconnected. This should help
   the organization to make decisions in a better manner.

The Global Reporting Initiative (GRI) releases guidelines to aid companies in
their pursuit of sustainable reporting. The latest version, known as G4, was released
in May 2013 and seeks to be the most comprehensive detailing of the steps companies
should take to ensure compliance with the best practices of sustainability reporting.
The guidelines are divided into two categories: (1) Principles and disclosures and (2)
Implementation. The first category aids the business in preparing its sustainability
report(s). The second category gives guidance on how to implement the use of data
in a proper and efficient manner. The suggested methodology for generating a proper
sustainability report is as follows:[5]

1. Obtain an overview of the G4 reporting guidelines.
2. Choose whether to make the report comprehensive or focused solely on core
   issues.
3. Prepare to disclose general standard disclosures used by all companies.
   a. Identify the General Standard Disclosures to use for the appropriate choice
      made in Step 2 and check if any apply to the industry.
   b. Plan out the process to disclose these General Standard Disclosures in line
      with standards of quality.
4. Prepare to disclose specific standard disclosures material to the company.
5. Prepare the sustainability report.

As these guidelines are followed and enacted, companies that comply with them
should be well on the road to having a sustainable practice. The GRI requests that

companies that release sustainability reports send these reports to the GRI to ensure that their guidelines are being followed in a proper manner. The GRI Reporting Principles are used to define the content and the quality of the sustainability reports and address stakeholder inclusiveness, sustainability context, materiality, completeness, comparability, accuracy, timeliness, reliability, clarity and transparency.[6]

4.   EFFECTIVE IMPLEMENTATION OF SUSTAINABILITY

Identifying and prioritizing key stakeholders to support the sustainable development of a multiple-bottom-line (MBL) will focus on the development of economic, governance, social, ethical and environmental (EGSEE) aspects of the business. The primary objective of business sustainability should be the promotion of sustainable shared value creation for all stakeholders. To effectively achieve this objective, business organizations worldwide should focus on enhancing shareholder wealth and customer satisfaction, retaining talented employees, operational efficiency, innovation, long-term growth and engagement in social and environmental responsibility as well as the ethical conduct of the business.

Collaborative efforts by the board of directors, management and auditors are very important in sustaining sustainability by setting a tone at the top in promoting business sustainability and committing to sustain sustainability performance, reporting, and assurance. New research by the MIT Sloan Management Review, the Boston Consulting Group, and the UN Global Compact shows that a growing number of companies are turning to collaborations—with suppliers, NGOs, industry alliances, governments and even competitors—to become more sustainable.[7] The study also looked at board engagement as a driver of sustainability success. Overall, 86 percent of respondents believe that the board of directors should play a strong role in driving their company's sustainability efforts, but only 42 percent of respondents see their boards as moderately or more engaged with the company's sustainability agenda. This disconnect affects performance, since, in companies whose boards are perceived as active supporters, 67 percent of respondents rate collaborations as very or quite successful. In companies whose boards are not engaged, the reported rate of success is less than half of that.

Corporate executives should refocus their efforts from short-term performance and earnings management to long-term growth and performance in creating value for all stakeholders. Management should utilize integrated reporting that provides all stakeholders with a long-term and broad perspective on stakeholder value creation. The integrated reporting framework developed by the International Integrated Reporting Council (IIRC) enables business organizations to articulate their stakeholder value creation and related investment value prospects; establish business strategies, EGSEE sustainability performance and prospects; and engage with all stakeholders to make business sustainability a reality and priority. Integrated reporting should build on conventional financial reporting and expand to include non-financial information on all five EGSEE dimensions of sustainability performance. Management should identify and fully utilize all financial and non-financial drivers of the five EGSEE dimensions of sustainability performance. Management should also use appropriate key performance indicators (KPIs) and their related metrics to assess and manage the risks associated with sustainability performance as discussed in the next section. Auditors provide assurance on sustainability reports, which lends credibility to the reports and makes them objective and reliable.

5. SUSTAINABILITY RISK ASSESSMENT AND MANAGEMENT

Global business is constantly changing and becoming more volatile, unpredictable, and complex. In this challenging business environment, the use of Enterprise Risk Management (ERM) is instrumental in turning challenges into opportunities. The global Financial Crisis of 2007–2009 can be attributed to many factors, including inadequate risk assessment of business transactions. Risk management has become an integral component of managerial functions affecting all transactions and economic activities. The move toward sustainability reporting underscores the importance of an adequate ERM in improving the effectiveness of all five EGSEE dimensions of sustainability performance. ERM is a risk-based approach to managing an enterprise, integrating concepts of strategic planning, operations management, sustainability and internal controls. The goal of implementing ERM is to maximize the value of the firm by managing its overall risks through identifying and reducing the possibility of events which create operational surprises and losses.[8] Managers have to identify challenges and opportunities and use methods and processes to enable them to take advantage of opportunities in managing related risks. The 2015 ERM survey conducted by the Enterprise Risk Management Initiative at North Carolina State University reveals that a majority of surveyed executives say that risk management is not an important strategic tool at their organizations, most have not managed their risk appetite in pursuit of objectives, and only 25 percent of companies have a formal ERM process in place.[9]

The International Organization for Standardization (ISO) published its new standard, ISO 31000: Risk Management—Principles and Guidelines, in 2009, which provides principles and guidelines on risk management.[10] These ISO 31000 risk guidelines assist business organizations in developing, implementing, maintaining, assessing, monitoring and continuously improving their risk management system in minimizing the negative effects of strategic, operational, financial, compliance and reputational risks.[11] These risks are interrelated and thus should be properly assessed and managed. For example, an excessive strategic risk can also cause operational, financial, compliance and reputational risks. The compliance risks directly or indirectly associated with business sustainability—including regulatory reforms; health and safety, human rights and labor laws; corporate governance measures; anti-bribery and environmental rules—can vary among organizations and across countries. For example, environmental risks can include direct effects (e.g., emissions trading cost exposures) and indirect consequences (e.g., energy price increases and accompanying reporting and compliance costs) of non-compliance with environmental laws, rules, and regulations. Business organizations should assess and manage the financial risk of producing and disclosing materially misstated financial reports. Minimization of reputational risk is vital to the success of sustainability programs and related performance, as stakeholder satisfaction is essential to sustainable business.

The development of sustainable programs moves the company from being reactive to social and government pressures to being proactive, moving beyond economic performance and toward EGSEE performance and risk management. Business sustainability enables management accountants to establish synergy and congruence between the two managerial concepts of cost management and performance management and to integrate sustainability into the business environment, corporate culture and supply chain processes. The concept of cost management suggests that management maximizes the utilization of scarce resources in generating revenue and delivers high-quality value to customers in improving performance. The concept of performance management suggests that management strikes a proper balance between short-term and long-term ESP as well as a trade-off between financial/quantitative ESP and non-financial/qualitative GSEE sustainability performance. The integrated cost management and performance management concepts under business sustainability suggest that a firm must extend its focus beyond maximizing short-term shareholder profit by considering the impact of its operations on the long-term interests of all stakeholders, including shareholders, creditors, customers, employees, the community, society, and the environment.

5.1 Sustainability Risk Identification and Assessment

A 2014 survey of institutional investors reveals that the primary driver for investors in considering GSEE sustainability issues is to mitigate risk. About three-quarters of responding investors believe that consideration of GSEE sustainability issues reduces investment risk, with other drivers for investors being enhancing performance and avoiding firms associated with unethical conduct.[12] The 2015 top 10 business risks, in order of ranking, are:

1. regulatory concerns regarding risk associated with compliance with laws, rules and regulations affecting the company's operations, governance and financial reporting
2. economic conditions that may affect the company's growth opportunities and market conditions
3. cyber-threat risks of failure to install adequate and effective security measures to prevent and mitigate the effects of cyberattacks
4. succession/recruitment planning—the risk of challenges associated with attracting and maintaining top executives and talented employees
5. cultural response to risk—that corporate culture is not sufficiently and promptly responding to challenges affecting the company's operations and achievement of its strategic goals
6. aversion to change—the risk of resistance to change that may have detrimental effects on business model and core operations
7. information technology (IT) security and privacy costs including the risk of not adequately investing in IT and privacy initiatives
8. reputational risk of not being able to respond to events and crises that affect the company's reputation
9. changes in customer preferences—not being able to satisfy customer demands and changes in their preferences and the associated risks of not sustaining customer loyalty and
10. not meeting performance expectation as related to quality, innovation, delivery and competition.[13]

EXHIBIT 11.1　Sustainability risks

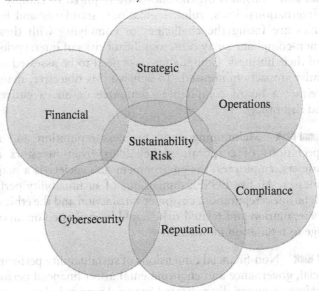

Brockett and Rezaee (2012) present five risks (strategic, operations, compliance, financial and reputation) relevant to sustainability performance.[14] An emerging risk that is currently threatening the sustainability of all types and sizes of organizations is the risk of potential cyberattacks and security breaches. Consideration and proper assessment and management of those six risks are becoming increasingly important and play an effective role in achieving EGSEE sustainability performance. Exhibit 11.1 presents these six risks and their interactions, and the following subsections briefly describe these risks individually.

5.1.1　Strategic Risk　There are several strategic risks triggered by business sustainability performance, reporting, and assurance including threats to survival and achievement of long-term performance, uncertainty regarding marketing position and volatility in security prices, abnormal changes in consumer demand, risks associated with strategic investments, stakeholder communications and investor relations. Of course, these strategic risks also create opportunities for possible improvements in operating, investing, financing activities, and proper communication with all stakeholders. Strategic risks should be identified, assessed, and managed with a keen focus on minimizing their negative effects and building on the opportunities provided by addressing these risks.

5.1.2　Operational Risk　Operations risks are associated with all five EGSEE dimensions of sustainability performance, the integration of all sustainability performance dimensions into operating activities across operational units, operations technology, supply chain, information technology and other functional areas. One of the greatest challenges for companies in implementing their sustainability strategy revolves around collaboration and integration across operational business units and key functional areas. Operating risks associated with both conventional financial key performance indicators (KPIs) such as earnings and return on investment and conceptualization KPIs such as social and natural performance need to be assessed and managed, and their negative impacts minimized.

5.1.3 Compliance Risk Business organizations are required to comply with a set of national and international laws, rules, regulations, standards and best practices. Many companies are facing the challenges of complying with these regulatory measures and non-compliance may cause significant risks of interruption and/or discontinuation of their business. Compliance risks need to be assessed and managed, and their negative impacts minimized. To achieve this objective, many companies have created either a board compliance committee or an executive position of compliance and risk officer.

5.1.4 Reputational Risk Maintaining good business reputation and meeting and exceeding expectations of corporate stakeholders from investors to creditors, suppliers, customers, employees, the environment and society is a major challenge for many businesses. All five EGSEE dimensions of sustainability performance are associated with business reputation, customer satisfaction and the ethical workplace. The company's reputation and related risk should be evaluated on an ongoing basis and any damage to reputation minimized.

5.1.5 Financial Risk Non-financial dimensions of sustainability performance including ethical, social, governance and environmental affect financial performance. The financial risk of issuing materially misstated financial reports is detrimental to the sustainability of corporations. Sustainability reports are expected to be value-relevant to both external and internal users of such reports. Investors and other stakeholders including suppliers, customers, government and society can obtain more transparent information about EGSEE performance, which enables them to make more informed decisions. Sustainability reporting improves internal management practices by enabling companies to establish better relationships with all stakeholders. Sustainability reporting creates more incentives and opportunity for management to refocus its goals, strategic decisions, and actions from a short-term to a long-term prospect.

Sustainability reporting can be used as a tool for more effective risk assessment and management in relation to identifying both opportunities and risks associated with operations. Thus, more transparent complete, accurate and reliable sustainability disclosure on EGSEE performance creates opportunities to identify and correct operational inefficiencies and reputational and financial risks in order to improve economic performance. Best practices of sustainability practices and reporting suggest that companies that ignore their social, governance, ethics and environmental issues and responsibilities would: (1) not be sustainable in the long term (2) be subject to higher risk of regulatory actions (3) lose their license to operate (4) lose customer reputation and confidence in their products and services (5) not be able to attract the most qualified and talented human capital and workforce (6) incur a higher cost of capital, both debt and equity (7) have less analyst following which may affect their market valuation (8) not attract investors with long-term horizons (9) encourage managerial practices of not being sensitive to or accountable for multi-dimensional EGSEE performance and (10) not set an appropriate tone at the top by directors, officers and corporate leaders in promoting ethical, accountable, socially and environmentally responsible behavior and practices throughout the organization.[15]

5.1.6 Cybersecurity Risk Destructive cyberattack such as the Sony Pictures incident is considered the most damaging cyberattack outside the norms of cyber practices and can be detrimental to the sustainability of public companies. Cybersecurity is becoming the top agenda of boards of directors and executives. While the United States has accused the government of North Korea of the Sony cyberattack, a group that identifies itself as the Guardians of Peace has claimed responsibility for the attack. The US government is considering a "proportional response" against those responsible for the Sony Cyberattack.[16] Cyber hacking and cybersecurity breaches of information systems are becoming a reality for many businesses (e.g., Sony, Target, Morgan Chase, ZTE) and risk assessment and control demand significant IT investment and commitment by directors and offices to prevent occurrences. The purpose of ISO 27001 is to offer organizations guidance on keeping information assets secure by providing requirements for an information security management system (ISMS). Use of this family of standards will help organizations to manage the security of assets such as financial information, intellectual property, employee details or information entrusted to the entities by third parties.[17] ISMS is a systematic approach to managing sensitive company information so that it remains protected. Furthermore, it helps identify risks to important information and puts appropriate controls in place to reduce the risk. It includes people, processes and IT systems by applying a risk management process. This standard is available to help any size organization in any sector.

The 2013 Global Information Security Survey conducted by Ernst & Young (EY) (2014) indicates four reasons for the increase in cyberattacks, and these are further explained in the following sections.[18]

5.1.6.1 Centralization of Operations and Information Systems Centralization of operations and information system internet-based technologies to improve cost efficiency and effectiveness across the supply chain creates security risks, high exposure, and dependency on the internet, which provides opportunities for cyber hackers to engage in rewarding cyberattacks. Centralization across organization functions requires the use of sophisticated operations technology (OT) and information technology (IT) with related network infrastructure to connect geographically and operationally diverse functions. Thus, both OT and IT security and controls are becoming increasingly important for centralized systems to prevent hackers from penetrating the system and engaging in costly cyberattacks.

5.1.6.2 Government-Led/State-Sponsored Cyberattacks The ever-increasing cyberwarfare activities of intelligence agencies and the military of sovereign states have made the practice of cyberwarfare a fair game at international level, as illustrated by the Stuxnet attack on the Iranian nuclear facilities. The alleged cyberattack on Sony Pictures by the government of North Korea is another example of government-led cyberattack. Many countries have developed sophisticated capabilities in launching major cyberattacks on IT infrastructures of other countries causing significant economic, social and political damage. Thus, there should be a treaty or protocol for all countries to mitigate any engagement in cyberwarfare detrimental to global society.

5.1.6.3 The Rise of Informal Activists Activists with social, political and economic agendas find it justifiable to engage in cyberattacks to advance their own agendas at the cost of businesses and society.

5.1.6.4 Outdated Security Programs Many OT and IT security programs are old, underdeveloped and obsolete, providing incentives and opportunities for cyber attackers to penetrate these programs and engage in costly cyber hacking activities. Security programs are designed to identify emerging cyber hacking or information security threats, but have no risk assessment or internal control procedures to immediately identify and respond to hacking or security breaches.

The risk associated with cyberattacks should be assessed and information security strategies developed to combat them. Management strategic cyber policies and procedures should include the following as a minimum to prevent, detect and deter cyberattacks:[19]

- Establishing a tone at the top making information security a board-level and senior management priority.
- Developing an integrated strategy to immediately respond to potential and real security threats.
- Assessing the risk of cyberattacks and security breaches.
- Establishing effective internal control activities relevant to the assessed threat risks to prevent and detect cyberattacks and security breaches.
- Using artificial intelligence, big data, data analytics and available advanced technologies to identify security breaches and cyberattacks and test the readiness of OT and IT programs to respond to threats.
- Assessing the current OT and IT systems and understanding their vulnerabilities and where a breach could likely occur.
- Understanding the applicable laws, rules, and regulations pertaining to cyberattacks and security breaches and how they are intended to protect organizations from cyberattacks and security breaches.
- Integrating control activities and response protocols for cyberattacks and security breaches to sustainable supply chain management.
- Establishing a committee consisting of the risk and compliance director/office, senior management, risk advisors, internal auditors and information system technicians to assess the existing OT and IT programs and their readiness and effectiveness in responding to potential cyberattacks and security beaches.
- Using artificial intelligence, big data and data analytics to identify and assess the threats and patterns of attacks.
- Conducting attack and penetration tests on an ongoing and continuous basis.

6.   FUTURE TRENDS IN SUSTAINABILITY PERFORMANCE

Anecdotal evidence suggests that sustainability is paying off and that companies continue to gain from sustainability initiatives focusing on the achievement of long-term financial and non-financial key performance indicators.[20] The 2014 survey of investors conducted by PricewaterhouseCoopers (PwC) finds that about 80 percent of responding investors said they had considered GSEE sustainability issues in their investment decisions, when acting as voting proxies, and when making investment portfolio decisions in the past year. Among the top sustainability issues that were considered by investors are climate change, resource scarcity, CSR and good citizenship. Investors' primary concerns for considering sustainability issues, in order of importance, are risk reduction (73 percent), avoiding firms engaged in unethical conduct (55 percent), performance enhancement (52 percent), cost reduction (36 percent), attracting new capital (30 percent), improving capability to create value (30 percent), being responsive to interest groups (21 percent).[21]

Novartis has published annual Corporate Responsibility (CR) Performance reports since 2000 to demonstrate its commitment to being a leader in CSR. The 2013 Novartis CR performance report discloses that its CR emphasizes two key areas: a) expanding access to healthcare for a large population of people worldwide and b) doing business responsively. CSR at Novartis focuses on developing innovative products for underserved patients, employing CSR approaches to better serve low- and middle-income communities, operating to the best ethical standards and promoting environmental sustainability.[22] The Novartis 2013 CR performance report highlights: (1) expanding access to healthcare (expanding social venture programs, serving billions of patients) and (2) doing business responsibly (responsible procurement, being included in the Dow Jones Sustainability World Index, being considered in the top 25 best places to work, reducing greenhouse gas emissions, being in the new UN 100 Index).[23] The 2013 CR report is prepared in compliance with the GRI *G4 Guidelines* with disclosure at the "Core" application level, and reflects the fact that the company complies with the GRI G4. The 2013 CR report also includes three other sustainability reports pertaining to the Carbon Disclosure Project (CDP): Investor Request Response, the CDP Water Information Request Response, and the Conflict Minerals Report.[24] Exhibit 11.2 shows the Novartis CR report prepared in compliance with the *G4 Guidelines*.

City Development Limited (CDL) has issued standalone sustainability reports for several years, and its 2013 sustainability report details its commitment to long-term viability beyond an opportunity to make a positive impact on the environment and society, which reflects its principles of sustainability in creating enduring value for all stakeholders.[25] CDL's 2013 sustainability report provides detailed information related to financial, governance, social and environmental performance in Singapore in 2013, prepared in compliance with the GRI guidelines.[26] This 2013 sustainability report enables CDL to take the lead in disclosing both financial and non-financial opportunities, challenges and risks and to integrate CSR strategies across all business operations to achieve balanced triple-bottom-line performance in all activities pertaining to people, planet and profit.[27] Exhibit 11.3 presents a sample of public companies worldwide with high sustainability ranking.

7. FUTURE TRENDS IN SUSTAINABILITY REPORTING

Sustainability reporting has evolved from voluntarily disclosing some aspects of sustainability performance such as CSR in annual reports, to issuing standalone voluntary sustainability reports on the GSEE dimensions of sustainability performance, to integrating both financial and non-financial dimensions of sustainability performance into corporate reporting. The future of sustainability reporting will be either a mandatory standalone or an integrated report on all five EGSEE dimensions of sustainability performance along with the use of Extensible Business Reporting Language (XBRL) in sustainability reporting. The use of XBRL-formatted reporting is an important step in applying XBRL to all dimensions of sustainability performance reporting. Several professional organizations are now developing sustainability taxonomies and related instances that can be effectively adopted by both providers

EXHIBIT 11.2   Novartis Corporate Responsibility Performance Report

Action	General Standard Disclosure	Specific Standard Disclosure
Core business contribution to UN goals and issues	Strategy and analysis	Economic performance
Strategic social investments and philanthropy	Organizational profile	Market presence
Advocacy and public policy engagement	Identified material aspects and boundaries	Indirect economic impacts
Partnerships and collective action	Stakeholder engagement	Procurement practices
Local networks and subsidiary engagements	Report profile	Materials
Global and local working groups	Governance	Energy
Issue-based and sector initiatives	Ethics and integrity	Water
Promotion and support of the UNGC		Emissions
		Supplier environmental assessment
		Labor/management relations
		Occupational health and safety
		Training and education
		Diversity and equal opportunity
		Human rights grievance mechanisms
		Local communities
		Anti-corruption

and users of sustainability performance and assurance reports. Future sustainability reporting will be market-driven and/or regulatory-mandated integrated reports using XBRL on all dimensions of sustainability performance reporting by the application of several existing taxonomies for financial and non-financial information relevant to the dimensions of sustainable performance. Many professional organizations including GRI, IIRC and the Sustainability Accounting Standards Board (SASB) are in the process of developing of business sustainability information systems that capture and consolidate the details necessary to prepare reports externally as well as monitor and control internally, by using XBRL to facilitate the integration, consolidation and audit trail of both conventional financial and emerging non-financial information.

EXHIBIT 11.3 Selected Top-15 Sustainable Companies[28]

Company	Link	Country	Industry	Example of sustainability initiative.
Westpac Banking Corporation	westpac.com.au	Australia	Banks	First bank in Australia to publish an environmental policy, 1992.
Biogen Idec, Inc.	biogenidec.com	United States	Pharmaceuticals & Biotechnology	Has created a series of initiatives to encourage science, technology, engineering and mathematics (STEM) research among youth.
Outotec OYJ	outec.com	Finland	Capital Goods	Promotes and undertakes worldwide seminars and initiatives to educate and help customers and locals.
Statoil ASA	statoil.com	Norway	Energy	Discloses all revenues and payments in the countries in which they operate.
Dassault Sytemes SA	3ds.com	France	Software & Services	Introduced SolidWorks Sustainability software to gage the environmental impact of customers' designs.
Neste Oil OYJ	nesteoil.com	Finland	Energy	Committed to responsible sourcing of fuel stock and non-deforestation.
Novo Nordisk A/S	novonordisk.com	Denmark	Pharmaceuticals & Biotechnology	Creates Blueprints for Change to measure the linkage between the company's triple-bottom-line and value created for the company and society.
Adidas AG	adidas-group.com	Germany	Consumer Durables & Apparel	Adopts so-called "Fair Play" pillars of sustainability vis-à-vis People, Product, Planet and Partnership.
Umicore SA	umicore.com	Belgium	Materials	Has created an interactive report wherein stakeholders can tailor the data received to their particular interests.

(continued)

EXHIBIT 11.3 (*Continued*)

Company	Link	Country	Industry	Example of sustainability initiative.
Schneider Electric SA	schneider-electric.com	France	Capital Goods	Develops solutions to give off-the-grid communities access to mobile electricity producers.
Cisco Systems, Inc.	cisco.com	United States	Technology Hardware & Equipment	Runs a product trade-in program wherein Cisco reuses old products to create new ones, saving on environmental costs of new production and of disposal.
BASF SE	basf.com	Germany	Materials	Has created AgBalance to evaluate sustainable practices across the entire value chain.
BMW	bmw.com	Germany	Automobiles & Components	Perform analyses to determine the matrix of sustainability matters most important to stakeholders and to the company at large.
Aeroports de Paris	aeroportsdeparis.fr	France	Transportation	Exceeds federal guidelines on environmental protection of all land the group owns.
ASML Holding IV	asml.com	Netherlands	Semiconductors & Semiconductor Equipment	Despite using much less water than most competitors, still strives to reduce water consumption significantly.

The SASB establishes and creates sustainability accounting standards which can be adapted to disclose material sustainability issues across 88 industries in 10 sectors, launching the process for mandatory filings to the Securities and Exchange Commission (SEC), such as Forms 10-K and 20-F, through the first quarter of 2015.[29] The goal of the SASB is to create standards that enable peer-to-peer comparison between companies, which can be useful for investment decisions and capital allocation. In June 2011, the Global Initiative for Sustainability Ratings (GISR) developed an ESG ratings standard toward maximum harmonization with leading complementary standard-setters, most notably the Global Reporting Initiative, the International Integrated Reporting Committee, the Carbon Disclosure Project and the SASB.[30] Harmonizing SASB standards with existing disclosure standards avoids additional reporting costs for companies and aligns SASB's work with global corporate transparency efforts. The products of the SASB, GRI and IIRC can be used in complementary ways for the development of sustainability reports for investors and all stakeholders. The SASB provides standards for mandatory filings, whereas GRI and IIRC provide frameworks for voluntary reporting.

7.1 Integrated Reporting

Both mandatory and voluntary corporate disclosure provides investors and stakeholders with reliable, relevant, useful and transparent financial and non-financial information for making sound decisions. Global public companies generally are required to disclose a set of financial statements under the corporate mandatory disclosures regime and they disclose other financial and non-financial information through corporate voluntary disclosures. Business sustainability disclosure is the communication of organizational performance on material matters relating to financial, environmental, social and governance activities. Information regarding an organization's sustainability has been disclosed through various channels, including external websites, social media channels, intranet sites, marketing materials, internal signage and postings, presentations and newsletters.

In 2013, the IIRC developed the International Integrated Reporting Framework, which provides guidelines for companies to integrate financial and non-financial performance information for all stakeholders.[31] The integrated reporting guidelines satisfy the information needs of long-term stakeholders including investors by reflecting the broader and longer-term consequences of decision-making. Integrated reporting provides the framework for disclosing the interactions between environmental, social, governance, ethical and financial performance. Existing sustainability reports may show some of the five EGSEE dimensions but often fall short of providing detailed information on all five EGSEE dimensions of sustainability performance. It is expected that the implementation of a set of fully integrated sustainability reporting guidelines will encourage and enable business organizations to integrate all dimensions including biodiversity and ecosystem performance in corporate reporting. The integrated reporting should provide standardized sustainability disclosures for all five EGSEE dimensions of sustainability performance. Integrated reports should be much more than the compilation of financial statements and sustainability financial KPIs within the same report.

Integrated reporting should disclose both financial and non-financial KPIs to enable stakeholders to access relevant sustainability information. However, investors have often and significantly been more dissatisfied than satisfied with sustainability information currently provided by firms regarding the following topics (in order of level of dissatisfaction): identification and disclosure of material sustainability risk and opportunities (82 percent); comparability of sustainability reporting between firms in the same industry (79 percent); relevance and implications of sustainability risks (74 percent); impacts of social and environmental issues on supply chain (69 percent); sustainability KPIs (68 percent); sustainability strategy that is linked to business strategy (68 percent); internal governance of sustainability issues (62); and processes used to identify material sustainability issues (57 percent).[32]

7.2 Electronic Sustainability Reports Using XBRL

The Extensible Business Reporting Language (XBRL) format, a derivative language of the Extensible Markup Language (XML), has recently gained considerable attention and is becoming an integral component of corporate reporting.[33] XBRL is a consortium consisting of a series of technical specifications intended to make business information more accessible and more easily communicated electronically. XBRL also facilitates the timely and accurate analysis of both internal and external business information. Companies and users of business reports can electronically search, download and analyze information that is "tagged" electronically. XBRL also facilitates the timely and accurate analysis of both internal and external business information. The primary benefits of XBRL are the ability to retrieve and analyze data and to facilitate interparty interactions without human interference, as well as the formalization of labels, definitions, and interpretations. XBRL defines and tags data using standard definitions which provide a mechanism for consistent structure and the use of the XBRL US GAAP Financial Reporting Taxonomy and/or other taxonomies (such as the IFRS Taxonomy) or extended (customized) tags based on either national or international accounting standards. The SEC has encouraged public companies to tag financial statement information on the EDGAR reporting system using XBRL since 2005, with approximately 9,600 public companies filing XBRL-formatted information with the SEC.[34] Since 2009, the SEC has required that public companies that use US GAAP file their financial statements in XBRL format.

XBRL can provide the technological foundation for the communication of both financial and non-financial information to stakeholders. The five EGSEE dimensions can be integrated into XBRL Global Ledger (GL) instance documents that contain tagged KPIs on both financial and non-financial information. However, no single taxonomy exists at present that can cover the world's diverse need for financial and non-financial sustainability reporting, but XBRL enables companies to define proper taxonomies and to incorporate them into corporate reporting.

7.2.1 Sustainability Taxonomies The development of taxonomies for sustainability performance encourages corporations to disclose both material ESP and GSEE sustainability to reflect the true value of corporate performance. Management has more latitude to choose the type, content, and timing of such disclosures in reflecting both their ESP and GSEE sustainability performance. The establishment of taxonomies for the five dimensions of sustainability performance provides material indicator taxonomies for both the financial ESP and non-financial GSEE dimensions of sustainability performance and disclosure, helping companies, directors and officers to make sound decisions in enhancing shared value for all stakeholders.

The format and content of integrated sustainability performance reporting is evolving rapidly. Although guidelines for sustainability reporting (e.g., GRI, IIRC, SASB) are helpful, currently there are no single taxonomy that can address the ESP and ESG dimensions of sustainability performance. Following the standards and guidelines of these professional and other organizations, we develop our material indicator taxonomies. Exhibit 11.4 presents taxonomies for financial ESP and non-financial ESG dimensions of sustainability performance.

The development of the XBRL taxonomy for EGSEE sustainability reports represents an important milestone in implementing the concept of EGSEE sustainability reporting. While the use of XBRL facilitates the standardization of EGSEE sustainability reporting, there are many challenges that must be addressed as the financial reporting paradigm shifts from a paper-based to an information-based model. A variety of XBRL taxonomies have been proposed for use in EGSEE reporting in order to harmonize the document structure for online communication by organizations. The EGSEE taxonomy will enable organizations to communicate sustainability information in the XBRL format in a much faster and more efficient manner.

The mandatory use of XBRL-formatted financial reporting is an important step in applying XBRL to the five EGSEE dimensions of sustainability performance as well as in enabling effective and efficient analysis by all participants (board of directors, management, auditors, legal counsel, financial analysts, regulators and investors) in the corporate reporting process. The tags for EGSEE sustainability taxonomies describe each of the five EGSEE dimensions of sustainability performance via labels that are both human- and machine-readable showing their relation to other sustainability data elements and applying sustainability frameworks (e.g., GRI G4). XBRL-tagged sustainability reports, when made publicly available, can be used by all stakeholders interested in sustainability information. The global acceptance of XBRL-formatted sustainability reports requires the proper development of taxonomies for each of the five EGSEE dimensions. Several organizations and interest groups are currently developing XBRL taxonomies, namely: GRI; Governance, Risk Management and Compliance (GRC); the Central Scoreboard for Corporate Social Responsibility (CSC); the Carbon Disclosure Project (CDP); the Climate Disclosure Standards Board (CDSB); the Climate Change Reporting Taxonomy (CCRT); the Integrated Scoreboard—Financial, Environmental, Social and Corporate Governance (IS-FESG); and the IIRC. CCRT is a joint project of the CDP and the CDSB and is currently working to provide a single CCRT in the XBRL format.[35]

The essence of EGSEE reporting using XBRL is the integrated presentation of non-financial information and the relationships among the different sustainability performance dimensions. A single EGSEE report can provide financial and non-financial sustainability information of interest to various stakeholders, and XBRL makes it possible to provide users with tools that enable them to analyze and compare performance dimensions. A single EGSEE report can provide all relevant information for a mutual conversation and ongoing dialogue between a company and all of its stakeholders, thereby adding a much greater dimension to the idea of EGSEE reporting using XBRL.

EXHIBIT 11.4 Summary of financial and non-financial reporting taxonomies and related standards

Description	Location	Name of Organization	Version	Sustainability Performance Dimension
IFRS Taxonomy 2015 files and support materials	http://www.ifrs.org/XBRL/IFRS-Taxonomy/2015/Pages/default.aspx	IFRS Foundation/IASB	March 2015	Financial Economic
2015 US GAAP Financial Reporting Taxonomy	http://www.fasb.org/jsp/FASB/Page/SectionPage&cid=1176164649716	FASB	2015	Financial Economic
Management's Discussion and Analysis Taxonomy	https://xbrl.us/sec-reporting/taxonomies/	US GAAP	2015	Financial Economic
GRI Taxonomy Architecture & Style Guide	https://www.globalreporting.org/resourcelibrary/GRI-Taxonomy-2014-Implementation-Guide.pdf	GRI and Deloitte Netherlands	2014	Non-Financial (Governance, Social, Environmental)
Central Scoreboard for Corporate Social Responsibility (CCI)	http://www.aeca.es/es/gaap/rsc/2010-05-31/CCI-XBRL-Description.doc	AECA	2010-05-31	Non-Financial (Environmental and Social)
World Intellectual Capital Initiative (WICI)	http://www.wici-global.com/taxonomy	WICI	V1.0 2010	Non-Financial (Environmental, Social and Governance)
Governance, Risk, and Compliance (GRC)	https://www.xbrl.org/TaxonomyRecognition/GRC%20Summary.htm	Open Compliance & Ethics Group	2009	Non-Financial (Governance and Ethics)
Carbon Disclosure Project (CDP)	https://www.cdproject.net/Documents/xbrl/CCRT-taxonomy-architecture-and-style-guide-v1-0.pdf	CDP/CDSB	V1.0 2012-11-06	Non-Financial (Environmental)
Climate Change Reporting Taxonomy (CCRT)	https://www.cdproject.net/Documents/xbrl/CCRT-taxonomy-architecture-and-style-guide-v1-0.pdf	CDP/CDSB	V1.0 2012-11-06	Non-Financial (Environmental)
Integrated Scoreboard of Financial, Environmental, Social and Corporate Governance (IS-FESG)	http://www.aeca.es/es/fr/gaap/csr/2012/IS-FESG-XBRL-Summary.pdf	AECA	V2.1 2012-01-25	Financial and Non-Financial (Financial, Environmental, Social, and Governance)

8.   FUTURE TRENDS IN SUSTAINABILITY ASSURANCE

Sustainability reporting is mandatory in Europe and other jurisdictions. The reliability, objectivity, transparency and credibility of sustainability reports can be improved by providing assurance on these reports. Unlike audit reports on the economic dimension of sustainability performance in the context of audit reports on financial statements and internal control over financial reporting, assurance opinions on non-financial GSEE dimensions of sustainability information are neither standardized, regulated or licensed. Several professionals, including internal auditors, external auditors and other service providers, can offer assurance on non-financial sustainability information. International accounting firms have developed expertise in sustainability reporting and assurance, and they are well-equipped, and trained to provide sustainability assurance services on financial and non-financial dimensions of sustainability performance reports. A more standardized, integrated, and audited process is required to make sustainability reports on EGSEE performance comparable, commonly acceptable and relevant to all corporate stakeholders.

Accounting and auditing standards have long been established for financial reporting and auditing.[36] Standards also exist for measuring, recognizing, reporting and auditing GSEE sustainability performance, but these are new and few by comparison. These standards include GRI and the AA1000 standard issued in 2008 by AccountAbility (AA). There is an AA1000 assurance standard, as well as ISO standards and accounting profession standards for auditing sustainability metrics. The AICPA Assurance Executive Committee (ASEC) Sustainability Assurance and Advisory Task Force developed application guidance assurance services.[37] The AICPA issued Statement of Position (SOP) No. 13-1, which supersedes SOP No. 03-2, Attest Engagements on Greenhouse Gas Emissions Information, specifying how to apply the attestation standards for a review engagement to the specific subject matter of Greenhouse Gas Protocol (GHG) emissions information.[38] The Statement of Position (SOP 03-2) is an essential resource for examinations or reviews, and provides guidance on performing and reporting relating to a GHG emissions inventory or a baseline GHG inventory as well as a schedule or an assertion relating to information about a GHG emission reduction in connection with the recording of the reduction with a registry or a trade of that reduction or credit.[39] Statement of Position SOP 13-1 provides guidance on the types of analytics and inquiries that might be performed in a review engagement on Greenhouse Gas Emissions Information. Consequently, performing analytics and inquiries alone with respect to GHG emissions information might not yield sufficient evidence for the limited assurance conclusion to be formed (otherwise known as "negative assurance" in the United States).

Several existing assurance standards have been developed for both the financial and non-financial dimensions of sustainability preformation information. Sustainability assurance reports prepared based on the AICPA Assurance Framework and Statement of Position SOP 13-2 can be used to address the completeness, mapping, consistency or structure of EESG sustainability information and include planning, performing evidence-gathering procedures and reporting audit findings on all five EGSEE dimensions of sustainability performance in an integrated audit report or a separate audit report on individual EGSEE dimensions. The end-product of sustainability assurance engagement is the sustainability report reflecting the auditor's either positive or negative opinion in the context of either reasonable or limited assurance on sustainability performance reports.

In general, the extent of test procedures performed differs between levels of assurance. Depending on the standards applied, these levels of assurance may have been described differently but their implications are essentially similar. The highest level of assurance is described as a reasonable assurance (ISAE 3000), examination (AT 101) or audit (CICA 5025) of sustainability reports. The lower level of assurance can be described as limited (ISAE 3000), moderate (AT 101) or review (CICA 5025) level assurance.[40] A reasonable assurance engagement provides a positive opinion on whether the subject matter is, in all material respects, appropriately stated. A limited assurance engagement provides what is called a negative opinion—"nothing has come to our attention to cause us to believe or we are not aware of any modifications that are needed to be made that the subject matter is not, in all material aspects, appropriately stated." A limited assurance engagement requires a lower level of work and consists primarily of enquiry and analytical procedures.

The content and format of the sustainability assurance report to be addressed to the entity's board of directors or management or intended user may vary and in general should include the following:[41]

1. Reference to sustainability information presented by management in the sustainability report and the year of reporting.
2. The assurance provider should use the criteria as a benchmark in assessing the effectiveness, efficiency, completeness, reliability and transparency of sustainability reports on all five dimensions of EGSEE performance.
3. Responsibilities of management and assurance providers: management is primarily responsible for the preparation, content, completeness and reliability of information in sustainability reports. The assurance provider is responsible for opinion or the assurance conclusion provided on the reports.
4. The scope of work done by the assurance provider should include the criteria used, tests of controls analytical procedures, inquiries and other evidence-gathering procedures performed to assess the risk of material misstatements in sustainability reports.
5. A statement that evidence gathered is used as a basis for reaching sustainability conclusions.

Assurance service providers should take the following steps:[42]

1. Obtain an understanding of the organization's five EGSEE sustainability performance measures.
2. Obtain an understanding of the organization's current and prospective sustainability initiatives.
3. Documentation of discussion with management regarding all five EGSEE dimensions of sustainability performance.
4. Management certification reports on all five EGSEE dimensions of sustainability reports.
5. Consideration of sustainability factors of performance, disclosure and risk.
6. Perform analytical procedures designed to enhance the understanding of the relations among different components of EGSEE sustainability performance and identify areas of high risk that might affect the reliability of financial statements.

7. Conduct assessment of sustainability risk financial, strategic, reputation, operation and compliance risks.

8. Encourage communication among the audit engagement team members regarding the EGSEE sustainability dimensions that might affect the risks of material misstatement of financial statements.

9. Test the effectiveness of the internal control system used to collect, compile, process and disclose EGSEE sustainability performance.

10. Perform audit procedures to gather sufficient and appropriate evidence on reported sustainability information.

11. Interview the board of directors, management and other personnel charged with the preparation of EGSEE sustainability reports.

12. Confirm certain sustainability information with outside parties where applicable (donations, environmental initiatives).

13. Review important documents relevant to business sustainability mission, objectives, strategies, policies and procedures.

14. Decide on the type and level of assurance either limited or reasonable that can be given on each dimension of EGSEE sustainability performance.

Business organizations that produce a standalone sustainability report may have their report audited/reviewed by external assurance providers, in many cases an independent auditor. In 2014, CDL engaged Ernst & Young (EY) as its auditor to provide independent limited assurance on its 2013 sustainability report.[43] The CDL 2013 assurance covers information in its sustainability report that is related to the Subject Matter agreed upon as per the Assurance Statement. EY deemed the company to follow ISAE 3000 Assurance Engagement Other than Audits and Reviews of Historical Financial Information after reviewing the underlying systems and processes that support the Subject Matters in the Sustainability Report and presenting the scope of the work and conclusions.[44] Exhibit 11.5 presents the 2014 CDL Assurance Statement.

9. EMERGENCE OF BENEFIT CORPORATIONS IN THE UNITED STATES

Under corporate law and in accordance with the shareholder theory, it has been well-defined and commonly accepted that shareholders are the owners of the firm and that the board of directors and management have a fiduciary duty to act in their best interests.[45] The primary goal of corporations has been to maximize profit and to increase shareholder wealth. In the past decade, firms (over 15,000 globally) that voluntarily focus on profit-seeking and social mission have emerged as social enterprises or hybrid-corporations (HCs) in pursuing the five EGSEE dimensions of sustainability performance. Recently, "benefit corporations" (BCs) have been formed as legal entities by legislation in 21 states, including under the Delaware General Corporation Law, which, since August 1, 2013, has authorized the formation of public BCs.[46]

Benefit corporations are legally for-profit entities incorporated as conventional corporations (CCs) under state law that have also chosen to adopt other ESG missions in their articles of incorporation. BCs are intended to minimize conflicts between corporations and society caused by differences between private and social costs and benefits as well as to align corporate goals with those of society under both

EXHIBIT 11.5   Independent Limited Assurance on Sustainability Report

Assurance Statement on the Management of City Development Limited (CDL)

Introductory Paragraph

We have performed limited assurance procedures in relation to CDL's Sustainability Report 2014 ('the Report').

Management Responsibility

CDL's Sustainability Report 2014 has been prepared by the Management of City Developments Limited, which is responsible for the collection and presentation of the information it contains and for maintaining adequate records and internal controls that are designed to support the sustainability reporting process.

Auditor Responsibility

Our responsibility in performing our limited assurance activities is to the Management of CDL only and in accordance with the terms of reference agreed with them. We do not accept or assume any responsibility for any other purpose or to any other person or organization.

Reporting criteria

As a basis for the assurance engagement, we have used relevant criteria in the sustainability reporting guidelines of the Global Reporting Initiative (GRI G3.1)

Assurance standard used and level of Assurance

Our limited assurance engagement has been planned and performed in accordance with the ISAE 300030 Assurance Engagement Other Than Audits or Reviews of Historical Financial Information. A limited assurance engagement consists of making enquiries and applying analytical and other limited assurance procedures.

Scope of work

We have been engaged by the Management of CDL to perform limited assurance on selected indicators of the Report as set out in Subject Matter environmental, labor practices and decent work, human rights, society, product responsibility, economic, construction and real estate sector supplement.

What we did to form our conclusions

The procedures performed aim to verify the plausibility of information. We designed our procedures in order to state whether anything has come to our attention to suggest that the Subject Matter detailed above has not been reported in accordance with the reporting criteria cited earlier.

(continued)

EXHIBIT 11.5 (*Continued*)

Our independence

EY has provided independent assurance services in relation to CDL's Sustainability Report 2014. In conducting our assurance engagement, we have met the independence requirements of the Institute of Singapore Chartered Accountants, Code of Professional Conduct and Ethics. Our

EY independence policies prohibit any financial interests in our clients that would or might be seen to impair independence. Each year, partners and staff are required to confirm their compliance with the firm's policies.

Observations and Areas for Improvement

Our observations and areas for improvement will be raised in an internal report to CDL's Management. These observations do not affect our conclusions on the Report set out below.

Conclusion

Based on the procedures performed and evidence obtained, nothing has come to our attention that causes us to believe that the information in the Report was not presented fairly, and calculated in all material respects in accordance with the reporting criteria detailed above.

Signed for Ernst & Young LLP by

Singapore, 29 April 2014

Source: adapted from 2014 City Developments Limited Sustainability Report. Available at: http://www .cdl.com.sg/sustainabilityreport2014/

the state corporate model and the benefit statute. Examples of conflicts between corporations and society relate to environmental issues (pollution, acid rain, global warming), wages paid by multinational corporations (MNCs) in poor countries, and child labor in developing countries. In pursuing their mission of protecting the interests of all stakeholders, BCs can raise companies' awareness of the social costs and benefits of their business activities. The major characteristics of BCs are: (1) a requirement that a BC must have a corporate purpose to create a material positive impact on society and the environment (2) an expansion of the duties of directors to require consideration of non-financial stakeholders as well as the financial interests of shareholders and (3) an obligation to report on their overall social and environmental performance using a comprehensive, credible, independent and transparent third-party standard.

Several benefits of BCs are the ability to: (1) gain the attention and market share of socially conscious investors (2) use the power of business and resources to solve social and environmental challenges (3) spur more trust in businesses by the public, shareholders, and potential employees and attract more customers to the company's brands and products (4) improve business, operational and investment efficacy and (5) assess, manage and minimize their strategic, operational, financial, reputational and compliance risks. These benefits can improve the financial and non-financial performance of BCs, which is reflected in their financial reporting quality, cost of capital, and firm value.

The BC structure is administered on a state-by-state basis by allowing the state's benefit corporation statutes to be placed within existing state corporation codes. The justification for BCs is that existing law does not hold boards of directors fiduciarily responsible to non-shareowner stakeholders by considering the impact of corporate decisions on other stakeholders, the environment or society at large. Thus, boards of directors of BCs are required to consider the impact of their decisions on specific corporate constituencies, including shareholders, employees, suppliers, the community, as well as on the local and global environment. In the past several years, 35 states, including New York, New Jersey, California, Louisiana, Maryland, Vermont, Virginia, South Carolina and Hawaii have enacted laws allowing the creation of BCs for businesses that wish to simultaneously pursue profit and benefit society (Hiller, 2013). Since August 1, 2013, the Delaware General Corporation Law has authorized the formation of public benefit corporations. This law: (1) allows entrepreneurs and investors to create for-profit Delaware corporations that are charged with promoting public benefits (2) modifies the fiduciary duties of directors of BCs by requiring them to balance public benefits with the economic interests of shareholders and (3) requires BCs to report to their shareholders with respect to the advancement of public benefits and/or other benefits to non-shareholders.

Other requirements are: (1) the certificate of incorporation of a BC must identify one or more specific public benefits to be promoted (2) the board of directors of a BC has a fiduciary duty to establish a right balance between shareholders' economic interests, the specific public benefits listed in the company's certificate of incorporation, and the best interests of those materially affected by the corporation's conduct (3) BCs must provide a biennial report to their shareholders disclosing the promotion of their specific public benefits and the best interests of those materially affected by their conduct (4) the board of directors of a BC does not have a fiduciary duty to any non-stockholder and (5) CCs can opt into BC status by merger or charter amendment with approval of 90 percent of the outstanding shares of each class of stock.

In summary, BCs are established to take initiatives to advance social good beyond their own interests in compliance with applicable regulations. BCs are intended to maximize positive impacts, minimize negative effects on and harm to society and environment and create positive impacts on the community, environment, employees, customers and suppliers. The true measure of success for BCs should be determined not only by reported earnings, but also by their governance, social responsibility, ethical behavior and environmental initiatives. BCs have received considerable attention from policymakers, regulators and the business investment community during the past decade and are expected to remain the main theme of the 21st century. Formation of BCs is an appropriate mechanism for public companies to move toward sustainability by creating value for shareholders while protecting interests of other stakeholders.

10. EMERGENCE OF PROFIT-WITH-PURPOSE COMPANIES AND THE SHARED VALUE CONCEPT

Public companies are being criticized for primarily focusing on profit maximization and thus shareholder value creation with minimal attention to the impacts of their operations on society and the environment.[47] As corporate sustainability is gaining more attention and being integrated into the business culture and model, there has been a shift from the creation of shareholder value to the development of "sustainable shared value creation" to protect interests of all stakeholders.[48] The concept of shared value is defined as "policies and practices that enhance the competitiveness of a company while simultaneously advancing the economic and social conditions in the communities in which it operates."[49] Under the shared value creation concept, management focuses on the continuous performance improvement of business operations in generating long-term value while maximizing the positive impacts of operations on society and the environment by measuring sustainable performance in terms of both ESP and GSEE. Thus, corporate objectives have advanced from profit maximization to increasing shareholder wealth and now to creating shared value for all stakeholders.

Business sustainability requires business organizations to expand their mission to not only generate profit and create shareholder value but also ensure shared value for all stakeholders. The concept of shared value challenges the way we think about profits, philanthropy, sustainability and development. Sustainable shared value creation enables business organizations to integrate financial ESP with non-financial ESG into business culture and corporate environment. Porter and Kramer (2011, p. 2) define the concept of shared value as "policies and operating practices that enhance the competitiveness of a company while simultaneously advancing the economic and social conditions in the communities in which it operates." This definition suggests that shared value initiatives can be created in three ways:

1. producing products and services that increase shareholder wealth and meet societal needs including improved nutrition, education, health and general wellbeing;
2. redefining productivity in the supply chain by investing in training and resources to create high-quality suppliers and improve ESP and GSEE sustainability performance; and
3. developing material indicator taxonomies to effectively measure revenue, costs and value of organizations.

Following GRI G4 performance indicators, corporations frequently discuss goals around ESG performance; the sourcing of raw materials and inputs for production; product innovations that lead to positive environmental, health or society impacts; employee safety, training and diversity; compliance with ethical principles and human rights standards; and community initiatives in the areas of health and wellbeing, education, employment and economic empowerment.

11. CHALLENGES AND OPPORTUNITIES IN BUSINESS SUSTAINABILITY IN ASIA

Countries in Asia have their own sustainability programs and initiatives that are shaped by their individual cultural, political, economic and legal infrastructures. Business sustainability has made steady progress in Asia. The corporate environment, including business sustainability in Asia, has evolved in the past several decades through the transformation of the socialist system into a market economy and legal system. To promote market-based corporate financing, many countries in Asia have established stock exchange markets. Exhibit 11.6 presents best practices of

EXHIBIT 11.6 Best practices of sustainability in Asia

Name	Organization Type	Sector	Country/ Jurisdiction	Title	Type	Adherence Level
Mitsubishi Materials	Private Company	Conglomerates	Japan	CSR Report 2015	GRI–G3	A+
China Cosco Holdings	State-Owned Company	Logistics	Mainland China	China Cosco Sustainability Report 2014	GRI–G3.1	A
Reiju Construction	Private Company	Construction	Taiwan	2014 Corporate Social Responsibility Report (Chinese Version)	GRI–G3.1	A+
Kyobo Life Insurance	Private Company	Financial Services	Korea, Republic of	Humanity and the Future	GRI–G3.1	A+
Jsw Steel Ltd.	Private Company	Metal Products	India	More Smiles per Ton of Steel (FY 2014–15)	GRI–G3.1	A+
Hang Seng Bank	Private Company	Financial Services	Hong Kong SAR	CSR Report 2014	GRI–G3.1	A+
Exat (Expressway Authority of Thailand)	State-Owned Company	Public Agency	Thailand	Corporate Social Responsibility Report 2014	GRI–G3.1	A
Isbank	Private Company	Financial Services	Turkey	Türkiye İş Bankasi 2014 Sustainability Report	GRI–G3.1	A
Asia Pulp & Paper Indonesia (APP Indonesia)	Private Company	Forest and Paper Products	Indonesia	APP Sustainability Report 2014	GRI–G3.1	A+
Keppel Corporation	Private Company	Conglomerates	Singapore	Aspire Sustainability Report 2014	GRI–G3.1	B+
Nestlé Malaysia	Private Company	Food and Beverage Products	Malaysia	Nestlé Society Report 2014	GRI–G3.1	A+
Abu Dhabi Company for Onshore Oil Operations (ADCO)	Subsidiary	Energy	United Arab Emirates	Sustainability Report 2014	GRI–G3.1	B
Delta Galil	Private Company	Textiles and Apparel	Israel	Corporate Social Responsibility Report 2013–2014	GRI–G3.1	A

sustainability in Asia. These best practices indicate the challenges and opportunities in business sustainability in the region.

The corporate governance system including sustainability programs of a country and its internal and external mechanisms are determined by a number of interrelated factors, including political infrastructure, cultural norms, legal system, ownership structures, market environments, level of economic development, CSR activities and ethical standards. CSR in Southeast Asia is undergoing a period of dynamic evolution. Many ambitious companies strive to become international players in the globalized world. This means adhering to global standards in all aspects of operations while maintaining loyal to traditions and unique cultures. Asian values including reciprocity, harmony with nature and surroundings and respect for others are a cultural framework that is highly relevant to sustainability.

12.   PLANNING FOR BUSINESS SUSTAINABILITY

To maintain sustainability in this global competitive business environment, companies should employ integrated thinking, decisions, actions and performance by focusing on the consequences of their integrated sustainability performance to create value for all stakeholders. Business organizations must move toward an integrated reporting model that presents forward-looking financial and non-financial information about all five EGSEE dimensions of sustainability performance. The following subsections present where we go from here in improving, advancing and promoting business sustainability that creates shared value for all stakeholders.

12.1   Total Impact Measurement and Management (TIMM)

The TIMM is developed by PwC as a framework to focus on the impact of a company's strategies, decisions, and actions on all stakeholders, particularly the economy, environment and society, which enables the company to think, act, and report on an integrated basis of creating sustainable value. The word "total" means an integrated and holistic consideration of all five EGSEE dimensions of sustainability performance, in particular the economic, social and environmental performance. The word "impact" signifies the ultimate consequences of EGSEE sustainability performance on sustainable value creation for all stakeholders. Measurement reflects the process of qualifying and monetizing the impacts, and management is the process of assessing options, optimizing and making the best decisions. Business sustainability promotes the achievement of long-term financial performance that generates enduring future cash flows for investors to maximize their long-term share value and thus maximizing overall societal welfare.

12.2   Sustainability Impact Investing

Impact investing is an emerging form of investment with a keen focus on the achievement of financial returns as well as the non-financial social and environmental return. Impact investing is defined as "Investments intended to create positive impact beyond financial return ... [that] require the management of social and environmental performance in addition to financial risk and return."[50] The Global Impact Investing

Network (GIIN) defines impact investing as investments that "aim to solve social or environmental challenges while generating financial profit. Impact investing includes investments that range from producing a return of principal capital (capital preservation) to offering market-rate or even market-beating financial returns."[51] Furthermore, the GIIN states "Impact investments are investments made into companies, organizations and funds with the intention to generate social and environmental impact alongside financial returns."[52] Proper measurement of impact investing is a complex process that evaluates the expected social and environmental impacts of investments. The GIIN suggests consideration of the following factors in measuring impact investing:[53]

1. Establishing social and environmental objectives and communicating them to relevant stakeholders.
2. Developing key performance indicators for social and environmental objectives using standardized metrics.
3. Assessing and managing the performance of investees against these KPIs.
4. Communicating and reporting on social and environmental performance to relevant stakeholders.

The two recent initiatives by the Delaware legislature have transformed business sustainability from a greenwashing and branding status to a business imperative strategy for public companies and their investors, as discussed in the previous chapters. First, there are the amendments to the Delaware General Corporation Law, effective as of August 1, 2013, which allow entities to incorporate as public benefit corporations.[54] The board of directors and executive of public benefit corporations are required to produce public benefit by balancing financial interests of shareholders with the best interests of stakeholders materially affected by the activities and conduct of their companies. Most recently, the Delaware Certification of Adoption of Transparency and Sustainability Standards Act (the Act) was signed into law on June 27, 2018.[55] The Act becomes effective on October 1, 2018 and represents Delaware's initiative to support sustainability practices by enabling Delaware-governed entities to disclose their commitment to CSR and sustainability. The Act is intended to demonstrate a firm commitment to sustainability and a proper response to the increasing calls from investors, customers and clients for greater transparency in sustainability practices. These initiatives in the United States along with the 2017 requirement for more than 6,000 European companies to disclose environmental, social and governance sustainability information have been instrumental in promoting business sustainability as a mainstream governance issue.

Sustainability enables investors to pursue their overall investment plan consisting of financial return and social and environmental goals. A growing number of investors consider impact investing with a keen focus on financial return and ESG sustainability factors; regulators mandate ESG sustainability performance disclosure; and public companies prepare and disseminate sustainability reports. In this era of sustainability-oriented investors, directors and executives, a major challenge is to show that non-financial GSEE sustainability factors contribute to bottom line earnings and long-term return. Non-financial GSEE information can be transmitted to the equity market through the impact investing mechanism.

12.3   Value-Adding Sustainability Development

Conventional performance measurements often focus on one-dimensional and short-term performance of total return to shareholders (TRS). This measurement of TRS is influenced by many financial attributes (e.g., return on investment, profit and cash flows) and non-financial variables. The proper measurement of sustainability performance should address: (1) the time horizon of balancing short-term and long-term performance with a keen focus on long-term performance; and (2) the multidimensional nature of sustainability performance in all EGSEE areas. The selection of an appropriate time horizon (period) to measure sustainability performance is important and should be linked to the factors that drive sustainability performance. The overriding factors that drive sustainability performance are: reaching the maturity stage of competitive positioning, efficient utilization of resources, and completing at least one business cycle. Achievement of this level of sustainable performance can take 10 or more years.

The EGSEE sustainability performance dimensions are interrelated. The relative importance of the dimensions with respect to each other and their contribution to the firm's overall long-term value maximization are affected by whether these EGSEE dimensions are viewed as competing, conflicting or complementary. We argue that these EGSEE dimensions are complementary because a firm that is governed effectively, adheres to ethical principles, is committed to CSR and environmental obligations is capable of being sustainable in generating long-term financial performance. Furthermore, firms must "do well" financially in the long-term to be able to "do good" in terms of CSR and environmental activities. Firms that engage in business sustainability can develop a long-term focus on sustainable economic performance as well as establishing other capabilities, resources and competencies to build up better customer/supplier relationships, workplaces for employee and environmental and CSR initiatives.

The main goal of sustainability is to maximize firm value by improving sustainable economic performance. The debate over the merit of all other sustainability performance GSEE revolves around whether GSEE investments and managerial efforts are viewed by shareholders as value-enhancing or value-destroying activities. Investments in achieving sustainable (GSEE) performance can be considered from a risk management perspective that management should use sustainability as a tool to manage risk. Business sustainability can enable management to develop better long-term focus, skills and processes to manage risks associated with financial, compliance, strategic, operating and reputational (Brockett and Rezaee, 2012).

12.4   Integrated Thinking

The ultimate success of business sustainability development, performance and reporting depends on the corporate culture of integrated thinking and tone at the top commitments to the promotion of all five EGSEE dimensions of sustainability performance and reporting of both financial and non-financial sustainability performance information in reflecting sustainability value creation for all stakeholders. Integrated thinking and reporting require focus on sustainable and forward-looking financial and non-financial information. Topazio (2014), the head of corporate reporting research at the Chartered Institute of Management Accountants (CIMA), proposes the following six suggestions for the proper and effective adoption of integrated thinking and integrated reporting on the five EGSEE dimensions of sustainability performance.[56]

1. Sustainability Value Creation—Define sustainability value creation in your organization and what this value means in the context of the organization, strategic decisions and performance and how your business model creates value. Sustainability value creation business models should identify and assess inputs, processes and outputs for all five EGSEE dimensions of sustainability performance and their integrated effects on creating sustainable value for all stakeholders.
2. Strengths and Concerns of Sustainability Performance—Identify and assess the positive and negative impacts of trends shaping your organization's five EGSEE dimensions of sustainability performance as suggested by the International Integrated Reporting Council relating to financial, social and relational, intellectual, natural and human aspects.
3. Identify non-financial metrics on non-financial dimensions of sustainability performance (governance, social, ethical and environmental) that are important in creating sustainable value and use them along with financial sustainability performance metrics in making decisions.
4. Link non-financial sustainability performance metrics to the sustainable financial success of the business. Integrated financial and non-financial sustainability performance is the key to the goal of achieving sustainable value creation.
5. Integrate strategy, strategic objectives, performance, risk and incentives across financial and non-financial information dimensions of sustainability activities and promote this linkage throughout the organization.
6. Use holistic and integrated internal and external reports in effectively communicating your business sustainability strategic decisions, actions and performance to both internal and external users of sustainability reports.

12.5   Shareholder Value Creation

The primary objective of business sustainability is to create stakeholder value, particularly enabling investors in making sound investment decisions. State Street Global Advisors (SSgA), an Australian financial services provider, considers sustainability disclosures, particularly environmental, social and governance matters in assessing and engaging with investee companies.[57] SSgA believes that while sustainability performance disclosures (ESG) can significantly impact the reputation of companies, they can also induce operational risks and costs for businesses.[58] Nonetheless, well-developed, and effective sustainability programs can promote efficiencies, improve productivity and mitigate risks, and thus contribute to shareholder value creation. SSgA engages with investee companies throughout the year, especially during the proxy season, on sustainability issues affecting investors' investment decisions by developing proprietary in-house screening tools to assist companies to focus on all dimensions of sustainability performance. In turn, this enables investors to assess and manage both the opportunities and challenges associated with sustainability performance reporting and assurance, as discussed throughout this chapter. Particularly, the broad framework suggested by SSgA in evaluating business sustainability consists of analyzing the following factors:[59]

1. The quality of a company's sustainability performance, reporting and assurance.
2. Consideration of key sustainability opportunities, challenges and risks by the company and their relation to its overall core business.
3. The relative quality of a company's sustainability performance compared to that of its peers.
4. The underlying economics of the company's sustainability development and programs.
5. The importance of tone at the top and the level of commitment by the company's board of directors and executives to its sustainability initiatives, programs and practices.
6. The importance of shareholder proposals on sustainability-related issues and their impacts on voting decisions.
7. Consideration of sustainability-related risks (reputational, financial, strategic, compliance) in overall risk assessment and management and thus sustainable shareholder value creation.

12.6   Measuring Sustainability Value Creation

The primary goal of business sustainability is to create sustainable value for all stakeholders including shareholders. The accounting and finance literature has suggested many models for measuring sustainable value creation for shareholders including market-based: capital market performance metrics such as market capitalization, market liquidity and stock returns, and financial-based: operating performance metrics such as return on assets (ROA), return on equity (ROE) and earnings growth. The most commonly used measures of capital market performance are total shareholder return (TSR) and relative TSR.[60] TSR is defined as the percentage gain or loss to shareholders measured in terms of share price end of period minus share price beginning of period, plus dividends, divided by share price beginning of period, whereas relative TSR is defined as the company's TSR as compared with peers. TSR does not directly measure business strategy success and management performance as they have been substantially affected by market and industry factors. Relative TSR, while better reflecting the company's performance in comparison to its peers, does not provide much relevant performance information about sustainable value creation. Financial-based performance measures such as reported earnings, earnings per share (EPS), ROA and ROE, while directly measuring accounting performance, fail to capture the level of invested capital and cost of capital in creating sustainable value. Thus, the economic profit as constructed below is a better measure of shareholder sustainable value creation because it measures sustainable profit after accounting for the desired cost of both equity and debt capital.[61]

1. Economic Profit = Net Operating Profit After Tax (NOPAT) *minus* Capital Charge
2. Net Operating Profit After Tax = EBIT *minus* Cash Taxes Paid
3. Capital Charge in dollars = Invested Capital *times* Weighted Average Cost of Capital.

The above calculated economic profit is a good proxy for measuring sustainable value creation for only one group of stakeholders, namely shareholders, by focusing on both current and future economic sustainability performance. To fully and comprehensively measure stakeholder sustainability value creation, the other four dimensions of sustainability performance, namely governance, social, ethical and environmental (GSEE), should also be incorporated into the measure. These GSEE dimensions are typically non-financial and difficult to measure analytically. Thus, global business organizations should view economic sustainability performance and its financial measures (economic profit, market-based or financial-based) as the main objective in achieving shareholder value creation and use non-financial KPIs for GSEE sustainability performance in measuring the achievement of sustainable value creation for stakeholders other than shareholders.

12.7   Business Sustainability for New Ventures and IPOs

Business sustainability performance and reporting is as important to new ventures and Initial Public Offerings (IPOs) as well-established and mature business organizations. New business ventures and IPOs often have more challenges in attracting new investors for their business. One pool of potential investors is the socially responsible investment funds (SRI). The United Nations Principles of Responsible Investing (UN PRI) was initiated in 2005 to encourage global investors to integrate ESG in their investment decisions.[62] The UN PRI covers many jurisdictions including the United States, the United Kingdom and Canada, and has over 1,100 signatories representing more than US$32 trillion in assets under management. Investors consider various sustainability issues on both financial economic sustainability and non-financial ESG sustainability in their investment analysis. SRI increased by more than 22 percent to $3.74 trillion in managed assets during the 2010–2012 period.[63] Particularly, IPOs that desire to go public must comply with the listing standards of stock exchanges. A report issued by the Toronto Stock Exchange (TSX) in March 2014 discusses mandatory and voluntary corporate reporting on ESG and suggests several investment implications of ESG disclosures including the opportunity and competitive advantages of social and environmental issues and their investment risk management.[64] Academic research in general finds a positive relation between firm value and the stakeholder welfare scores constructed to measure the extent to which firms meet the expectation of their stakeholders, including the SRI funds.[65] Non-financial ESG sustainability performance is more relevant to entrepreneurs and joint ventures that have reached the maturity and survival stage. Business sustainability makes it easier for emerging growth companies (EGCs) to make it to their IPO thus providing these companies with access to the significant funding opportunities related to public capital markets.

13.   MANAGEMENT ACCOUNTANTS' ROLE IN SUSTAINABILITY

Corporations worldwide are now recognizing the importance of both financial and non-financial performance and their link to profitability and social goals. Justifications for improved sustainability are: enhancing financial sustainability, moral obligation, maintaining a good reputation, ensuring CSR, license to operate and creating value for all stakeholders. In a shared value approach, corporations identify potential sustainability concerns and integrate them into their strategic planning. There are many reasons why a company should focus on sustainability such as: pressure from the labor movement, development of moral values and social standards, development of business education and change in public opinion about the role of business. Companies which are, or aspire to be, leaders in sustainability are challenged by rising public expectations, increasing innovation, continuous quality improvement and heightened social and environmental problems.

Cost management and performance management practices have continued to receive considerable attention in management and financial accounting and the business community. Cost management is defined in the context of enterprise sustainability as a process of planning and controlling the costs of products and services to promote maximum utilization of scarce resources in generating revenue and delivering high-quality and environmentally safe products and services to customers. Performance management, in the context of sustainability, consists of all business activities that generate financial ESP and non-financial ESG sustainability performance to maximize firm value and create shared value for all stakeholders.

Globalization created incentives and opportunities for MNCs and their stakeholders and executives to influence the sustainability initiatives and strategies of headquarters as well as their global subsidiaries. MNCs can choose from a variety of sustainability initiatives in relation to scope, extent, and type of strategy, with focus on different issues, functions, areas and stakeholders. Management should develop and maintain proper sustainability programs that provide a common framework for the integration of sustainability to their strategies and operations in accordance with the following:

- Integration of sustainability development and programs into the business and investment analysis and decision-making process.
- Incorporation of all five EGSEE dimensions of sustainability performance into business and investment policies, activities and practices.
- Promotion of appropriate reporting of sustainability performance.
- Collaboration among all stakeholders to enhance the effectiveness of implementing sustainability programs.
- Promotion of product innovation and quality, customer retention and attraction, employee satisfaction and productivity through sustainability programs.

Several recent reports released by Chartered Global Management Accountants (CGMA) suggest that companies underutilized the knowledge and skills of their management accountants in advancing sustainability programs and developments and in reporting the impacts of environmental, social, ethical and governance factors on financial performance. These reports suggest the following ways in which management accountants can assist their organizations in achieving sustainability performance and success:

1. Identify non-financial sustainability initiatives including the environmental and social trends that will affect the company's ability to create stakeholder value over time.
2. Link business sustainability challenges to the company's strategy, business model, operations and performance.

3. Assess and explain the impact of these sustainability issues, including challenges and concerns.

4. Develop both financial and non-financial KPIs that support achievement of sustainability strategic goals.

5. Apply management accounting tools and techniques including balanced scorecards, scenario planning of natural resource availability, data analytics, lifecycle costing and carbon foot-printing to integrate sustainability into the decision-making process.

6. Produce integrated/sustainability reports that include data on sustainability impacts in all business decisions including supply chains, budgeting and pricing decisions, cost analysis, investment appraisals and strategic planning.

7. Develop a sustainability reporting strategy that integrates all five dimensions of sustainability performance into strategic planning, decisions and operations.[66]

A business organization's success in effective achievement of all five EGSEE dimensions of sustainability performance demands commitment by the board of directors and top executives in effectively coordinating all sustainability strategies and activities and successfully implementing these strategies. There is an urgent need for the establishment of the position of chief sustainability officer (CSO) in the C-suite executives of business organizations.

14. GLOBAL COLLABORATION AND LEADERSHIP FOR SUSTAINABILITY

The 2015 research conducted by MIT Sloan Management Review, the Boston Consulting Group and the United Nations Global Compact indicates that an increasing number of companies are collaborating with their suppliers, industry alliances, peers and even competitors and government and non-government entities to become more sustainable.[67] This suggests that there is a need for integrated efforts by all stakeholders focused on achieving the five EGSEE dimensions of sustainability performance, addressing sustainability challenges and creating new product and market opportunities. The report suggests that sustainability has and will continue to march to the center of business as evidenced by the following:

1. 39 percent of responding companies are publicly reporting their sustainability efforts and this is expected to increase by 15 percent in the next four years;

2. the number of companies that utilize financial and non-financial sustainability KPIs and effective governance structures toward sustainability has increased by 6 percent in the past four years;

3. the number of companies that consider sustainability as a top management agenda item has increased substantially to 65 percent in 2014 compared to 46 percent in 2010; and

4. the number of companies with no focus on sustainability has significantly decreased in the past four years.[68]

The study also looked at board engagement as a driver of sustainability success. Overall, 86 percent of respondents believe that the board of directors should play a strong role in driving their company's sustainability efforts. But only 42 percent of respondents see their boards as "moderately or more" engaged with the company's sustainability agenda. These disconnects affect performance, which is illustrated by the fact that in companies whose boards are perceived as active supporters, 67 percent of respondents rate collaborations as very or quite successful. In companies whose boards are not engaged, the reported rate of success is less than half that. The report also suggests that the type and extent of collaboration may vary among companies, but at the minimum can include:[69]

1. Developing sustainability standards and promoting best practices of business sustainability.
2. Sharing information about best practices of sustainability to foster discoveries or communicate externally about sustainability performance.
3. Empowering all stakeholders to engage in business sustainability to create value.
4. Sharing in investments to save costs or reduce risks and create value.

15. CONCLUSIONS

In the past two decade, investors and creditors have shown increasing interest in non-financial sustainability information that impacts long-term viability and the wellbeing of the company in creating shareholder value. With the advent of social media and new technological developments, investors and creditors can easily obtain the necessary information they need from different sources beyond the traditional financial reporting. The number of business organizations providing sustainability information regarding their financial and non-financial EGSEE performance is on the rise and might be an indication that the traditional financial reporting model should be more inclusive of relevant non-financial sustainability information disclosures. Business sustainability performance reporting in terms of integrated reporting has extended the type and amount of financial and non-financial information that business organizations provide to their stakeholders regarding their EGSEE sustainability.

Integrated reporting provides the foundation for the communication of both financial and non-financial information to stakeholders. The content, format and method of disseminating sustainability reporting have been evolving and the optimal disclosure of sustainability information varies across countries and companies. However, a balance between economic sustainability performance and other GSEE dimensions of sustainability performance can lead to competitive advantage, as stakeholders value sustainability disclosures. Reliable and useful sustainability information on all five EGSEE dimensions of sustainability performance enables all stakeholders to make sound decisions regarding operating, financing, and investment activities. The use of the XBRL platform and continuous auditing improves the relevance and credibility of sustainability reports. It is expected that sustainability performance reporting and assurance will continue to make progress in Asia.

16. CHAPTER TAKEAWAY

1. Sustainability should be integrated into day-to-day management decision processes and particularly into operational, financing and capital investment decisions as well as supply chain management.

2. Identify all stakeholders who are affected and who will affect your business sustainability and its success.
3. There are primary stakeholders and secondary stakeholders. Primary stakeholders are visible and are able to influence corporate decisions whereas secondary stakeholders are disconnected from the company due to lack of interest and remoteness. Typical stakeholders include shareholders, creditors, customers, suppliers, employees, regulators, the environment and the community.
4. Achievement of successful business sustainability performance requires the firm commitment of the board of directors and executives to an integrated and comprehensive approach in promoting sustainability.
5. Make business sustainability, integrated thinking and integrated reporting key components of your business strategy and strategic decisions.
6. Director and executive commitment to integrated thinking, performance and reporting is vital in creating sustainable value for all stakeholders.
7. A balance between the five dimensions of sustainability performance can lead to competitive advantage and long-term and enduring value creation for all stakeholders.
8. Sustainability reporting should reflect business organizations' sustainability performance in all five dimensions of economic, governance, social, ethical and environmental (EGSEE) activities.
9. External assurance on sustainability reports improves their reliability, credibility and effectiveness in achieving the organizational objectives of creating value for all stakeholders.
10. Tone-at-the-top commitment to sustainability leadership requires organizations to define their sustainability mission, strategic objectives and actions, and integrate their processes to promote sustainability throughout the organization and its link to sustainable financial performance.
11. Sustainability performance in all five EGSEE dimensions is an important driver for building a corporate citizenship of trust, and retaining talented employees, satisfied customers and rewarded shareholders.
12. Business sustainability development enables organizations to integrate sustainability principles with everyday business operations, processes and performance.
13. The success and effectiveness of business sustainability is determined by integrating sustainability into all facets of business operations, measurements, performance reporting and assurance.

ENDNOTES

1. European Commission, *Disclosure of Non-Financial Information*, September 29, 2014, http://ec.europa.eu/internal_market/accounting/non-financial_reporting/index_en.htm.
2. Delaware General Assembly, House Bill 310: An Act to Amend Title 6 of the Delaware Code Relating to The Certification of Adoption of Sustainability and Transparency Standards by Delaware Entities, June 27, 2018, https://legis.delaware.gov/BillDetail/26304.
3. Z. Rezaee. 2015. Business sustainability: Performance, Compliance, Accountability and Integrated Reporting, Green Leaf publishing, October 2015.
4. N. Topazio, "Six Tips for Integrated Thinking," *CGMA Magazine*, October 6, 2014, http://www.cgma.org/magazine/features/pages/201410895.aspx.

5. Global Reporting Initiative, *Integrated Reporting: International Framework (IR)*, 2013, globalreporting.org/ COUNCIL-20131205-ITEM 3b-DRAFT-FRAMEWORK.docx.

6. Ibid.

7. D. Kiron, N. Kruschwitz, K. Haanes, M. Reeves, S. Fuisz-Kehrbach, and G. Kell, "Joining Forces: Collaboration and Leadership for Sustainability," MIT Sloan Management Review, Boston Consulting Group, and the United Nations Global Compact (UNGC), January 12, 2015, http://marketing.mitsmr.com/PDF/56380-MITSMR-BGC-UNGC-Sustainability2015.pdf?cid=1.

8. Committee of Sponsoring Organizations of the Treadway Commission (COSO), *Enterprise Risk Management – Integrated Framework*, September 2004, New York.

9. M. Beasley, B. Branson and B. Hancock, *Report on the Current State of Enterprise Risk Oversight: Update on Trends and Opportunities*, February 2015, http://www.aicpa.org/InterestAreas/BusinessIndustryAndGovernment/Resources/ERM/DownloadableDocuments/AICPA_ERM_Research_Study_2015.pdf.

10. International Organization for Standardization (ISO) (2009), *ISO 31000: Risk Management–Principles and Guidelines, 2009*, www.iso.org.

11. Ibid.

12. PwC, *Sustainability Goes Mainstream: Insights into Investor Views*, May 2014, http://www.pwc.com/us/en/pwc-investor-resource-institute/index.jhtml.

13. Ibid.

14. A. Brockett and Z. Rezaee, "Sustainability Reporting's Role in Managing Climate Change Risks and Opportunities," in *Managing Climate Change Business Risks and Consequences: Leadership for Global Sustainability* (Palgrave Macmillan, 2012) 143–158.

15. Z. Rezaee. 2015. Business sustainability: Performance, Compliance, Accountability and Integrated Reporting, Green Leaf publishing, October 2015.

16. P. Banker, "U.S. Weights Response to Sony Cyberattack, with North Korea Confrontation Possible," *New York Times*, December 18, 2014, http://www.nytimes.com/2014/12/19/world/asia/north-korea-confrontation-possible-in-response-to-sony-cyberattack.html?_r=0.

17. ISO 27001 – Information Security Management, http://www.iso.org/iso/home/standards/management-standards/iso27001.htm.

18. Ernst and Young (EY), "Cyber Hacking and Information Security: Mining and Metals," 2014, ey.com/mining metals.

19. Ibid.

20. D. Kiron, N. Kruschwitz, K. Haanas, M. Reeves and E. Goh, "The Innovation Bottom Line: The Benefit of Sustainability-Driven Innovation," MIT Sloan Management Review and the Boston Consulting Group, Research Paper 54, no. 2 (Winter 2013): 69–73, http://sloanreview.mit.edu/sustainability.

21. PwC, *Sustainability Goes Mainstream: Insights into Investor Views*, May 2014, http://www.pwc.com/us/en/pwc-investor-resource-institute/index.jhtml.

22. Novartis, *2013 Novartis Corporate Responsibility Performance Report*, July 2014, www.novartis.com/corporate-responsibility.

23. Ibid.

24. Ibid.

25. City Development Limited (CDL), *2013 Sustainability Report*, February 2014, www.cdl.com.sg/sustainabilityreport2014.

26. Ibid.

27. Ibid.

28. SASB, *A Conceptual Framework of Sustainability*, October 2013, https://www.sasb.org/wp-content/uploads/2013/10/SASB-Conceptual-Framework-Final-Formatted-10-22-13.pdf.

29. Sustainability Accounting Standards Board (SASB), *Conceptual Framework of Sustainability Accounting Standard Board*, October 2013, http://www.sasb.org/wp-content/uploads/2013/10/SASB-Conceptual-Framework.pdf.

30. International Integrated Reporting Committee, "Welcome to the IIRC," 2012, http://www.theiirc.org/wp-content/uploads/2011/02/IIRC-GOVERNANCE-2012-04.pdf.

31. International Integrated Reporting Council, *International Integrated Reporting Framework*, December 5, 2013, iirc.org. COUNCIL-20131205-ITEM 3b-DRAFT-FRAMEWORK.docx.

32. PwC, *Sustainability Goes Mainstream: Insights into Investor Views*, May 2014, http://www.pwc.com/us/en/pwc-investor-resource-institute/index.jhtml.

33. XBRL, *Corporate Reporting Evolved: Integrated Reporting and the Role of XBRL*, An Issues Brief of the XBRL International Best Practices Board, 2013, http://xbrl.org/sites/xbrl.org/files/imce/issues_brief_intgrpt2013.pdf.

34. Securities and Exchange Commission (SEC), "Remarks to The IFRS Taxonomy Annual Convention" (from April 25, 2010), 2012, http://www.sec.gov/news/speech/2012/spch042512ms.htm.

35. Climate Change Reporting Taxonomy, *Climate Change Reporting Taxonomy (CCRT) Due Process*, 2013, https://www.cdproject.net/en-us/news/pages/xbrl-due-process.aspx.

36. Brockett and Rezaee, "Sustainability Reporting's Role in Managing Climate Change Risks and Opportunities."

37. American Institute of Certified Public Accountants (AICPA), *Attest Engagements on Greenhouse Gas Emissions Information, Statement of Position 03-2*, New York, NY: AICPA, 2003.

38. Ibid.

39. Ibid.

40. Brockett and Rezaee, "Sustainability Reporting's Role in Managing Climate Change Risks and Opportunities."

41. Ibid.

42. Ibid.

43. City Developments Limited, *2014 City Developments Limited Sustainability Report*, www.cdl.com.sg.

44. Ibid.

45. M. Jensen, and W. Meckling, "Theory of the Firm: Managerial Behavior, Agency Costs and Ownership Structure," *Journal of Financial Economics* 3 (1976): 305–360.

46. Delaware Law Series, "DGCL Amended to Authorize Public Benefit Corporations," August 14, 2013, http://blogs.law.harvard.edu/corpgov/tag/delaware-law/.

47. M. E. Porter and M. R. Kramer, "Creating Shared Value," *Harvard Business Review*, January–February 2011: 62–77.

48. Ibid.

49. Ibid., page 65.

50. N. O'Donohoe, C. Leijonhufvud, Y. Saltuk, A. Bugg-Levine, and M. Brandenburg, *Impact Investments: An Emerging Asset Class*, JP Morgan, 2010.

51. Global Impact Investing Network (GIIN), "Impact Investments," 2018, https://thegiin.org/impact-investing/need-to-know/#what-is-impact-investing

52. Ibid.

53. Ibid.

54. Delaware Law Series, "DGCL Amended to Authorize Public Benefit Corporations," August 14, 2013, http://blogs.law.harvard.edu/corpgov/tag/delaware-law/.

55. Delaware General Assembly, House Bill 310: An Act to Amend Title 6 of the Delaware Code Relating to The Certification of Adoption of Sustainability and Transparency Standards by Delaware Entities, June 27, 2018, https://legis.delaware.gov/BillDetail/26304.

56. N. Topazio, "Six Tips for Integrated Thinking," *CGMA Magazine*, October 6, 2014.

57. R. Kumar and D. Honick, *IQ Insights: SSgA's Active Ownership Process on ESG Risks and Opportunities Facing Investee Companies*, State Street Global Advisors, 2014, http://statestreetfrance.org/library/povw/835433_SSgAs_Active_Ownership_Process_on_ESG_Risks_Opps..OverviewCCRI1413358102.pdf.

58. Ibid.

59. Ibid.

60. Investor Responsibility Research Center Institute (IRRCi), *IRRCi Research Report: The Alignment Gap between Creating Value, Performance Measurement, and Long-Term Incentive Design*, 2014, www.irrcistitute.org.

61. Ibid.

62. United Nations Principles of Responsible Investing (UN PRI), *The Freshfields Report*, 2005, www.unepfi.org/fileadmin/documents/freshfields_legal_resp_20051123.pdf.

63. Social Investment Forum (SIF), *2012 Report on Sustainable and Responsible Investing Trends in the United States*, US SIF foundation: The forum for sustainable and responsible investment, November 2012.

64. Toronto Stock Exchange (TSX), *A Primer for Environmental and Social Disclosure*, 2014, http:/www.tmx.com.

65. Y. Jiao, "Stakeholder Welfare and Firm Value," *Journal of Banking and Finance* 34, no. 10 (2010): 2549–2561.

66. S. White, "How Management Accountants Can Lead Their Organizations Toward Sustainability Success," January 6, 2015, http://www.cgma.org/Learn/Publications/Pages/Publications.aspx.

67. MIT Sloan Management Review, *Joining Forces: Collaboration and Leadership for Sustainability*, January 12, 2015, http://sloanreview.mit.edu/projects/joining-forces/?utm_source=SUEnews%201/13/15%20B&utm_medium=email&utm_campaign=susrpt15.

68. Ibid.

69. Ibid.

Index